Business Studies 1
Volume 1

A Pearson Custom Publication

Business Studies 1

Volume 1

Compiled from:

Strategic Management and Business Policy
9th Edition
by Thomas L. Wheelen and J. David Hunger

Corporate Financial Management
2nd Edition
by Glen Arnold

Operations Management
4th Edition
by Nigel Slack, Stuart Chambers and Robert Johnston

PEARSON
Custom
Publishing

Pearson Education Limited
Edinburgh Gate
Harlow
Essex CM20 2JE

And associated companies throughout the world

Visit us on the World Wide Web at:
www.pearsoned.co.uk

First published 2005
This Custom Book Edition © 2005 Published by Pearson Education Limited

Taken from:

Strategic Management and Business Policy 9th Edition
by Thomas J. Wheelen and J. David Hunger
ISBN 0 13 142179 4
Copyright © 2004, 2002, and 2000 by Pearson Education Inc., Upper Saddle
River, New Jersey 07458

Corporate Financial Management 2nd Edition
by Glen Arnold
ISBN 0 273 65148 X
Copyright © Financial Times Professional Limited 1998
Copyright © Pearson Education Limited 2002

Operations Management 4th Edition
by Nigel Slack, Stuart Chambers and Robert Johnston
ISBN 0 273 67906 6
Copyright © Nigel Slack, Stuart Chambers, Christine Harland, Alan Harrison and
Robert Johnston 1995, 1998
Copyright © Nigel Slack, Stuart Chambers and Robert Johnston 2001, 2004

ISBN 1 84479 104 1

Printed and bound by Antony Rowe

Contents

Introduction

Welcome to Business Studies 1.

I have pleasure in introducing you to these two volumes of our new customised text that have been designed exclusively for this course, in collaboration with Pearson Education UK. The readings and teaching materials contained herein bring together in one text essential reading tailored specifically to the goals, design and content of the course.

The modular design of Business Studies 1 covers the chief functional areas of the discipline, with the aim of providing a basic grounding in all aspects of business, including the key management specialisms. This will provide you with an informed basis from which to select options for more specialist study in subsequent years, in line with your own specific interests, aptitudes and career intentions. One problem with a course so designed is that no single textbook can simultaneously attain the required breadth of content, and the depth of treatment demanded by the individual specialist modules. Until now, we have recommended a key textbook for each module, an approach that has proved costly and inconvenient for students. This initiative will considerably ease these pressures by integrating into one affordable text, key readings from different specialist textbooks, as well as allowing incorporation of teaching and lecturing material from individual course contributors. The separate course booklet (the "Yellow Book") provides guidance on how the contents of this customised text relate to the individual modules and lectures.

Please note that the chapters we have selected for inclusion will contain references to other relevant chapters from the underlying works that have not been included in this custom edition. The Main Library stocks copies of all the underlying works, so that such cross-referencing provides a pathway for further reading. The yellow course-booklet also specifies some additional reading for specific topics. Moreover, there are web resources for each of the chapters from the underlying works. Students can access the link to these via WebCT.

As a means of directing students efficiently to relevant literature I am confident that this initiative represents a considerable advance in terms of costs and convenience, especially in courses such as this which seek to create a learning experience that combines breadth and depth of study.

Professor Irvine Lapsley

Head of School

The Management School and Economics

Business Policy and Strategy

Chapters from:
Strategic Management and Business Policy
9th *Edition*

Thomas L. Wheelen and J. David Hunger

Basic Concepts of Strategic Management

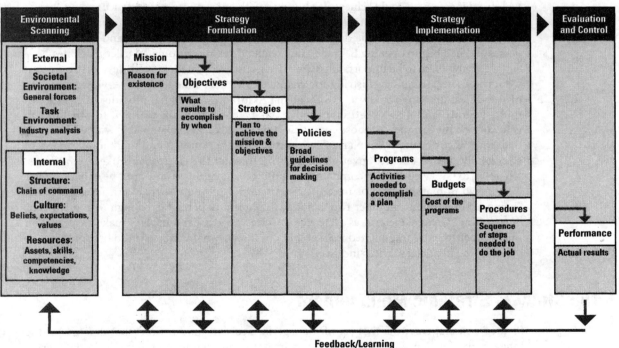

How does a company become successful and stay successful? Certainly not by playing it safe and following the traditional ways of doing business! Even a company like General Electric, an established, old-line *Fortune* 500 company with operations throughout the world, must constantly renew itself or else be outmaneuvered by aggressive newcomers. Realizing the potential impact of the Internet on all industries, Jack Welch, Chairman of the Board, issued a challenge at a March 1999 meeting to managers of the firm's business units to, in effect, replace their own product lines before competitors could do so. They also needed to learn how to conduct their business on the Internet. Welch had witnessed his own family and colleagues complete most or all of their Christmas shopping online and decided that the company had to

1

enter the Internet age with a vengeance. Welch directed the top 600 managers to find an internal "Internet mentor" who would tutor them in the World Wide Web. According to Welch, "There's no such thing as an 'old economy.' Commerce is the same as it was 500 years ago. People sell and people buy—whether it's from a wagon or the Internet."[1]

In early February 2000, General Electric quietly launched the General Electric Financial Network (gefn.com), its first financial Web site for consumers. After having already invested over $10 million in developing the new business, GE heavily advertised its Web site in the televised summer Olympics. Gefn.com was marketed as the Web site where consumers could go to simplify their investment lives and find everything from a bank account to life insurance and GE mutual funds. According to Michael Frazier, head of the GE Capital consumer unit in charge of creating gefn.com, "Make no mistake, we want to be as well known to consumers for financial security as we are for light bulbs and appliances."[2] Knowing that many of the 50+ "baby boomers" were in the market for financial services as a way to save for their retirement, gefn.com entered a market already crowded with strong competitors.

Acknowledging GE's thrust as a bold strategic move, a number of industry analysts questioned if gefn.com had what was needed to be a major competitor in this business. For example, even though the Web site allowed customers to do online banking and obtain GE insurance and loans, it did not provide the ability to trade stocks or buy non-GE mutual funds. They also wondered if gefn.com could achieve its objectives with only an Internet presence and no "bricks and mortar" branch offices in which customers and loan officers could interact. E*Trade, in contrast, had realized the limited growth potential of its online brokerage and banking businesses and had begun opening E*Trade Zone retail offices and automated teller machines.[3]

Realizing these to be important issues, GE executives claimed, nevertheless, that gefn.com would be an important new distribution channel for GE's existing financial services units. One of the fastest growing units was GE Financial Assurance (GEFA), a provider of insurance, mutual funds, and 401(k) retirement plans in 17 countries. GE planned to put links to gefn.com on the intranets of those companies that already had a relationship with GE through their insurance or retirement plans. GE executives were seriously examining the alternative of a "carefully crafted alliance" over an acquisition to enter the electronic brokerage business. Referring to GE's well-known companywide policy that a business unit must be either number one or two in market share or have the potential to achieve it, Michael Frazier argued that "being number one or number two is not as important as being big enough to control your own destiny." General Electric, as a late entrant, clearly had the resources to make an impact on this competitive and fragmented market, but did it have what was needed to become a major player in the financial services industry?

1.1 The Study of Strategic Management

Strategic management is that set of managerial decisions and actions that determines the long-run performance of a corporation. It includes environmental scanning (both external and internal), strategy formulation (strategic or long-range planning), strategy implementation, and evaluation and control. The study of strategic management, therefore, emphasizes the monitoring and evaluating of external opportunities and threats in light of a corporation's strengths and weaknesses. Originally called business policy, strategic management incorporates such topics as long-range planning and strategy. **Business policy**, in contrast, has a general management orientation and tends primarily to look inward with its concern for properly integrating the corporation's many functional activities. Strategic management, as a field of study, incorporates the integrative concerns of business policy with a heavier environmental and strategic emphasis. Therefore, strategic management has tended to replace business policy as the preferred name of the field.[4]

PHASES OF STRATEGIC MANAGEMENT

Many of the concepts and techniques dealing with strategic management have been developed and used successfully by business corporations such as General Electric and the Boston Consulting Group. Over time, business practitioners and academic researchers have expanded and refined these concepts. Initially strategic management was of most use to large corporations operating in multiple industries. Increasing risks of error, costly mistakes, and even economic ruin are causing today's professional managers in all organizations to take strategic management seriously in order to keep their company competitive in an increasingly volatile environment.

As managers attempt to better deal with their changing world, a firm generally evolves through the following four **phases of strategic management:**[5]

Phase 1. *Basic financial planning:* Managers initiate serious planning when they are requested to propose next year's budget. Projects are proposed on the basis of very little analysis, with most information coming from within the firm. The sales force usually provides the small amount of environmental information. Such simplistic operational planning only pretends to be strategic management, yet it is quite time consuming. Normal company activities are often suspended for weeks while managers try to cram ideas into the proposed budget. The time horizon is usually one year.

Phase 2. *Forecast-based planning:* As annual budgets become less useful at stimulating long-term planning, managers attempt to propose five-year plans. They now consider projects that may take more than one year. In addition to internal information, managers gather any available environmental data—usually on an ad hoc basis—and extrapolate current trends five years into the future. This phase is also time consuming, often involving a full month of managerial activity to make sure all the proposed budgets fit together. The process gets very political as managers compete for larger shares of funds. Endless meetings take place to evaluate proposals and justify assumptions. The time horizon is usually three to five years.

Phase 3. *Externally oriented planning (strategic planning):* Frustrated with highly political, yet ineffectual five-year plans, top management takes control of the planning process by initiating strategic planning. The company seeks to increase its responsiveness to changing markets and competition by thinking strategically. Planning is taken out of the hands of lower level managers and concentrated in a planning staff whose task is to develop strategic plans for the corporation. Consultants often provide the sophisticated and innovative techniques that the planning staff uses to gather information and forecast future trends. Ex-military experts develop competitive intelligence units. Upper level managers meet once a year at a resort "retreat" led by key members of the planning staff to evaluate and update the current strategic plan. Such top-down planning emphasizes formal strategy formulation and leaves the implementation issues to lower management levels. Top management typically develops five-year plans with help from consultants but minimal input from lower levels.

Phase 4. *Strategic management:* Realizing that even the best strategic plans are worthless without the input and commitment of lower level managers, top management forms planning groups of managers and key employees at many levels from various departments and work groups. They develop and integrate a series of strategic plans aimed at achieving the company's primary objectives. Strategic plans now detail the implementation, evaluation, and control issues. Rather than attempting to perfectly forecast the future, the plans emphasize probable scenarios and contingency strategies. The sophisticated annual five-year strategic plan is replaced with strategic thinking at all levels of the organization throughout the year. Strategic information, previously available only centrally to top management, is available via local area networks and intranets to people throughout the organization. Instead of a large centralized planning staff, internal and external planning consultants are available to help guide group strategy discussions. Although top management may still initiate the strategic planning process, the resulting strategies may come from anywhere in the organization. Planning is typically interactive across levels and is no longer top down. People at all levels are now involved.

General Electric, one of the pioneers of strategic planning, led the transition from strategic planning to strategic management during the 1980s.[6] By the 1990s, most corporations around the world had also begun the conversion to strategic management.

Until 1978, Maytag Corporation, the major home appliance manufacturer, could be characterized as being in Phase one of strategic management. Maytag's CEO, Daniel Krum, formed a strategic planning task force to answer the question: "If we keep doing what we're doing now, what will the Maytag Corporation look like in five years?" The answer to this question served as the impetus for the firm's subsequent expansion into a full line of major home appliances and its entry into the world market through the purchase of Hoover.

BENEFITS OF STRATEGIC MANAGEMENT

Research has revealed that organizations that engage in strategic management generally outperform those that do not.[7] The attainment of an appropriate match or "fit" between an organization's environment and its strategy, structure, and processes has positive effects on the organization's performance.[8] For example, a study of the impact of deregulation on U.S. railroads found that those railroads that changed their strategy as their environment changed outperformed those railroads that did not change their strategy.[9]

A survey of nearly 50 corporations in a variety of countries and industries found the three most highly rated benefits of strategic management to be:

- Clearer sense of strategic vision for the firm
- Sharper focus on what is strategically important
- Improved understanding of a rapidly changing environment[10]

To be effective, however, strategic management need not always be a formal process. As occurred at Maytag, it can begin with a few simple questions:

1. **Where is the organization now? (Not where do we hope it is!)**
2. **If no changes are made, where will the organization be in 1 year? 2 years? 5 years? 10 years? Are the answers acceptable?**
3. **If the answers are not acceptable, what specific actions should management undertake? What are the risks and payoffs involved?**

A survey by Bain & Company revealed the most popular management tools to be strategic planning and developing mission and vision statements—essential parts of strategic management.[11] Studies of the planning practices of actual organizations suggest that the real value of strategic planning may be more in the future orientation of the planning process itself than in any written strategic plan. Small companies, in particular, may plan informally and irregularly. Nevertheless, studies of small businesses reveal that even though the degree of formality in strategic planning may have only a small to moderate impact on a firm's profitability, formal planners have significantly greater growth in sales than do informal planners.[12]

Planning the strategy of large, multidivisional corporations can become complex and time consuming. It often takes slightly more than a year for a large company to move from situation assessment to a final decision agreement. Because of the relatively large number of people affected by a strategic decision in such a firm, a formalized, more sophisticated system is needed to ensure that strategic planning leads to successful performance. Otherwise, top management becomes isolated from developments in the business units, and lower level managers lose sight of the corporate mission and objectives.

1.2 Globalization and Electronic Commerce: Challenges to Strategic Management

Not too long ago, a business corporation could be successful by focusing only on making and selling goods and services within its national boundaries. International considerations were minimal. Profits earned from exporting products to foreign lands were considered frosting on the cake but not really essential to corporate success. During the 1960s, for example, most U.S. companies organized themselves around a number of product divisions that made and sold goods only in the United States. All manufacturing and sales outside the United States were typically managed through one international division. An international assignment was usually considered a message that the person was no longer promotable and should be looking for another job.

Similarly, until the mid-1990s, a business firm could be very successful without using the Internet for anything more than a public relations Web site. Most business was done through a sales force and a network of distributors with the eventual sale to the consumer being made through retail outlets. Few executives used a personal computer, let alone "surfed" the World Wide Web. The Internet may have been useful for research, but until recently it was not seriously viewed as a means to actually conduct normal business transactions.

IMPACT OF GLOBALIZATION

Today, everything has changed. **Globalization**, the internationalization of markets and corporations, has changed the way modern corporations do business. To reach the economies of scale necessary to achieve the low costs, and thus the low prices, needed to be competitive, companies are now thinking of a global (worldwide) market instead of a national market. Nike and Reebok, for example, manufacture their athletic shoes in various countries throughout Asia for sale on every continent. Instead of using one international division to manage everything outside the home country, large corporations are now using matrix structures in which product units are interwoven with country or regional units. International assignments are now considered key for anyone interested in reaching top management.

As more industries become global, strategic management is becoming an increasingly important way to keep track of international developments and position the company for long-term competitive advantage. For example, Maytag Corporation purchased Hoover not so much for its vacuum cleaner business, but for its European laundry, cooking, and refrigeration business. Maytag's management realized that a company without a manufacturing presence in the European Union (EU) would be at a competitive disadvantage in the changing major home appliance industry. See the 🖥 **Global Issue** feature to learn how regional trade associations are changing how international business is conducted. Similar international considerations have led to the strategic alliance between British Airways and American Airlines and to the merger between Daimler-Benz and Chrysler Corporation.

IMPACT OF ELECTRONIC COMMERCE

Electronic commerce refers to the use of the Internet to conduct business transactions. A 1999 survey conducted by Booz-Allen & Hamilton and the Economist Intelligence Unit of more than 525 top executives from a wide range of industries revealed that the Internet is reshaping the global marketplace and that it will continue to do so for many years. More than 90% of the executives believed that the Internet would transform or have a major impact on their corporate strategy within two years. According to Matthew Barrett, Chairman and CEO of the Bank of Montreal, "We are only standing at the threshold of a New World. It is as if we had just invented printing or the steam engine."[13] Not only is the Internet changing the way customers, suppliers, and companies interact, it is changing the way companies work internally.

Global Issue

Regional Trade Associations Replace National Trade Barriers

Previously known as the Common Market and the European Community, the **European Union (EU)** is the most significant trade association in the world. The goal of the EU is the complete economic integration of its 15 member countries—Austria, Belgium, Denmark, Finland, France, Germany, Greece, Ireland, Italy, Luxembourg, the Netherlands, Portugal, Spain, Sweden, and the United Kingdom—so that goods made in one part of Western Europe can move freely without ever stopping for a customs inspection. One currency, the euro, is being used throughout the region as members integrate their monetary systems. The steady elimination of barriers to free trade is providing the impetus for a series of mergers, acquisitions, and joint ventures among business corporations. The requirement of at least 60% local content to avoid tariffs has forced many American and Asian companies to abandon exporting in favor of a strong local presence in Europe. The EU has agreed to expand its membership to include the Czech Republic, Hungary, Estonia, Poland, Malta, Cyprus, and Slovenia by 2004; Latvia, Lithuania, and Slovakia by 2006; and Bulgaria and Romania by 2010. Turkey is being considered for admission in 2011.

Canada, the United States, and Mexico are affiliated economically under the **North American Free Trade Agreement (NAFTA)**. The goal of NAFTA is improved trade among the three member countries rather than complete economic integration. Launched in 1994, the agreement requires all three members to remove all tariffs among themselves over 15 years, but they are allowed to have their own tariff arrangements with non-member countries. Cars and trucks must have 62.5% North American content to qualify for duty-free status.

Transportation restrictions and other regulations are being significantly reduced. Some Asian and European corporations are locating operations in one of the countries to obtain access to the entire North American region. Vicente Fox, President of Mexico, is proposing that NAFTA become more like the European Union in that both people and goods would have unlimited access across borders from Mexico to Canada. In addition, there have been some discussions of extending NAFTA southward to include Chile, but thus far nothing formal has been proposed.

South American countries are also working to harmonize their trading relationships with each other and to form trade associations. The establishment of the **Mercosur** (**Mercosul** in Portuguese) free-trade area among Argentina, Brazil, Uruguay, and Paraguay means that a manufacturing presence within these countries is becoming essential to avoid tariffs for nonmember countries. Claiming to be NAFTA's southern counterpart, Mercosur has extended free-trade agreements to Bolivia and Venezuela. With Chile and Argentina cooperating to build a tunnel through the Andes to connect both countries, it is likely that Chile may soon form some economic relationship with Mercosur.

Asia has yet no comparable regional trade association to match the potential economic power of either NAFTA or the EU. Japan, South Korea, China, and India generally operate as independent economic powers. Nevertheless, the **Association of South East Asian Nations (ASEAN)**—composed of Brunei, Indonesia, Malaysia, the Philippines, Singapore, Thailand, and Vietnam—is attempting to link its members into a borderless economic zone. Increasingly referred to as ASEAN+3, it is already including China, Japan, and South Korea in its annual summit meetings. The ASEAN nations are negotiating the linkage of the ASEAN Free-Trade Area (AFTA) with the existing FTA of Australia and New Zealand. With the EU extending eastward and NAFTA extending southward to someday connect with Mercosur, pressure is already building on the independent Asian nations to soon form an expanded version of ASEAN.

In just the few years since its introduction, it has profoundly affected the basis of competition in many industries. Instead of the traditional focus on product features and costs, the Internet is shifting the basis for competition to a more strategic level in which the traditional value chain of an industry is drastically altered. A 1999 report by AMR Research indicated that industry leaders are in the process of moving 60 to 100% of their business to business (B2B) transactions to the Internet. The net B2B marketplace includes (a) Trading Exchange Platforms like VerticalNet and i2 Technologies's TradeMatrix, which support trading communities in multiple markets; (b) Industry-Sponsored Exchanges, such as the one being built by major automakers; and (c) Net Market Makers, like e-Steel, NECX, and BuildPoint, which focus on a specific industry's value chain or business processes to mediate multiple transactions among businesses. The Garner Group predicts that the worldwide B2B market will grow from $145 billion in 1999 to $7.29 trillion in 2004, at which time it will represent 7% of the total global sales transactions.[14]

The previously mentioned survey of top executives identified the following seven trends, due at least in part, to the rise of the Internet:[15]

1. The Internet is forcing companies to transform themselves. The concept of electronically networking customers, suppliers, and partners is now a reality.

2. New channels are changing market access and branding, causing the *disintermediation* (breaking down) of traditional distribution channels. By working directly with the customers, companies are able to avoid the usual distributors, thus forming closer relationships with the end users, improving service, and reducing costs.

3. The balance of power is shifting to the consumer. Now having unlimited access to information on the Internet, customers are much more demanding than their "nonwired" predecessors.

4. Competition is changing. New technology-driven firms plus older traditional competitors are exploiting the Internet to become more innovative and efficient.

5. The pace of business is increasing drastically. Planning horizons, information needs, and customer/supplier expectations are reflecting the immediacy of the Internet. Because of this turbulent environment, time is compressed into "dog years" in which one year feels like seven years.

6. The Internet is pushing corporations out of their traditional boundaries. The traditional separation between suppliers, manufacturers, and customers is becoming blurred with the development and expansion of extranets, in which cooperating firms have access to each other's internal operating plans and processes. For example, Lockheed Martin, the aerospace company, has an extranet linking Lockheed to Boeing, a project partner, and to the U.S. Defense Department, a key customer.

7. Knowledge is becoming a key asset and a source of competitive advantage. For example, physical assets accounted for 62.8% of the total market value of U.S. manufacturing firms in 1980 but only 37.9% in 1991. The remainder of the market value is composed of intangible assets, primarily intellectual capital.[16]

1.3 Theories of Organizational Adaptation

Globalization and electronic commerce present real challenges to the strategic management of business corporations. How can any one company keep track of all the changing technological, economic, political-legal, and sociocultural trends around the world and make the necessary adjustments? This is not an easy task. Various theories have been proposed to account for how organizations obtain fit with their environment. The theory of **population ecology**, for example, proposes that once an organization is successfully established in a particular environmental niche, it is unable to adapt to changing conditions. Too much inertia prevents the organization from changing. The company is thus replaced (bought out or goes bankrupt) by other organizations more suited to the new environment. Although popular in sociology, research fails to support the arguments of population ecology.[17] **Institution theory**, in contrast, proposes that organizations can and do adapt to changing conditions by imitating other successful organizations. To its credit, many examples can be found of companies that have adapted to changing circumstances by imitating another firm's strategies. The theory does not, however, explain how or by whom successful new strategies are developed in the first place. The **strategic choice perspective** goes one step further by proposing that not only do organizations adapt to a changing environment, but that they also have the opportunity and power to reshape their environment. Because of its emphasis on managers making rational strategic decisions, the strategic choice perspective is the dominant one taken in strategic management. Its argument that adaptation is a dynamic process fits with the view of **organizational learning theory** that organizations adjust defensively to a changing environment and use knowledge offensively to improve the fit between the organization and its environment. This perspective expands the strategic choice perspective to include people at all levels becoming involved in providing input into strategic decisions.[18]

In agreement with the concepts of organizational learning theory, an increasing number of companies are realizing that they must shift from a vertically organized, top-down type of organization to a more horizontally managed, interactive organization. They are attempting to adapt more quickly to changing conditions by becoming "learning organizations."

1.4 Creating a Learning Organization

Strategic management has now evolved to the point that its primary value is in helping the organization operate successfully in a dynamic, complex environment. Inland Steel Company, for example, uses strategic planning as a tool to drive organizational change. Managers at all levels are expected to continually analyze the changing steel industry in order to create or modify strategic plans throughout the year.[19] To be competitive in dynamic environments, corporations are having to become less bureaucratic and more flexible. In stable environments such as have existed in years past, a competitive strategy simply involved defining a competitive position and then defending it. As it takes less and less time for one product or technology to replace another, companies are finding that there is no such thing as a permanent competitive advantage. Many agree with Richard D'Aveni (in his book *Hypercompetition*) that any sustainable competitive advantage lies not in doggedly following a centrally managed five-year plan, but in stringing together a series of strategic short-term thrusts (as Intel does by cutting into the sales of its own offerings with periodic introductions of new products).[20] This means that corporations must develop strategic flexibility—the ability to shift from one dominant strategy to another.[21]

Strategic flexibility demands a long-term commitment to the development and nurturing of critical resources. It also demands that the company become a **learning organization**—an organization skilled at creating, acquiring, and transferring knowledge, and at modifying its behavior to reflect new knowledge and insights. Organizational learning is a critical component of competitiveness in a dynamic environment. It is particularly important to innovation and new product development.[22] For example, Hewlett-Packard uses an extensive network of informal committees to transfer knowledge among its cross-functional teams and to help spread new sources of knowledge quickly.[23] Learning organizations are skilled at 4 main activities:

- Solving problems systematically
- Experimenting with new approaches
- Learning from their own experiences and past history as well as from the experiences of others
- Transferring knowledge quickly and efficiently throughout the organization[24]

Learning organizations avoid stability through continuous self-examination and experimentation. People at all levels, not just top management, need to be involved in strategic management—helping to scan the environment for critical information; suggesting changes to strategies and programs to take advantage of environmental shifts; and working with others to continuously improve work methods, procedures, and evaluation techniques. Motorola, for example, developed an action learning format in which people from marketing, product development, and manufacturing meet to argue and reach agreement about the needs of the market, the best new product, and the schedules of each group producing it. This action learning approach overcame the problems that arose previously when the three departments met and formally agreed on plans but continued with their work as if nothing had happened.[25]

Organizations that are willing to experiment and are able to learn from their experiences are more successful than those that do not. For example, in a study of U.S. manufacturers of diagnostic imaging equipment, the most successful firms were those that improved products sold in the United States by incorporating some of what they had learned from their manufacturing and sales experiences in other nations. The less successful firms used the foreign operations primarily as sales outlets, not as important sources of technical knowledge.[26]

1.5 Basic Model of Strategic Management

Strategic management consists of four basic elements:

- **Environmental scanning**
- **Strategy formulation**
- **Strategy implementation**
- **Evaluation and control**

Figure 1–1 shows simply how these elements interact; **Figure 1–2** expands each of these elements and serves as the model for this book.[27] The terms used in **Figure 1–2** are explained in the following pages.

ENVIRONMENTAL SCANNING

Environmental scanning is the monitoring, evaluating, and disseminating of information from the external and internal environments to key people within the corporation. Its purpose is to identify **strategic factors**—those external and internal elements that will determine the future of the corporation. The simplest way to conduct environmental scanning is through **SWOT analysis**. SWOT is an acronym used to describe those particular **S**trengths, **W**eaknesses, **O**pportunities, and **T**hreats that are strategic factors for a specific company. The **external environment** consists of variables (**O**pportunities and **T**hreats) that are outside the organization and not typically within the short-run control of top management. These

Figure 1–1

Basic Elements of the Strategic Management Process

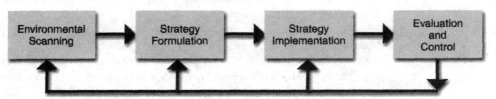

Figure 1–2
Strategic Management Model

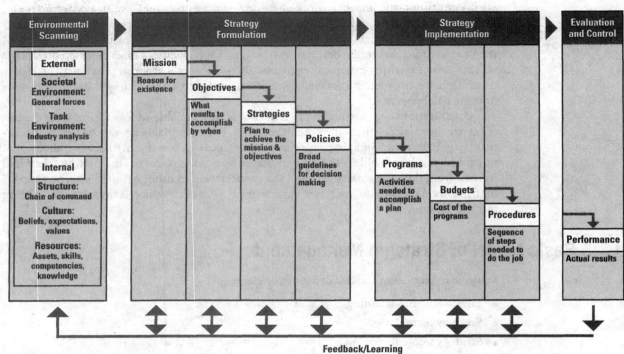

variables form the context within which the corporation exists. **Figure 1–3** depicts key environmental variables. They may be general forces and trends within the overall societal environment or specific factors that operate within an organization's specific task environment—often called its industry. (These external variables are defined and discussed in more detail in **Chapter 3**.)

The **internal environment** of a corporation consists of variables (Strengths and Weaknesses) that are within the organization itself and are not usually within the short-run control of top management. These variables form the context in which work is done. They include the corporation's structure, culture, and resources. Key strengths form a set of core competencies that the corporation can use to gain competitive advantage. (These internal variables and core competencies are defined and discussed in more detail in **Chapter 4**.)

STRATEGY FORMULATION

Strategy formulation is the development of long-range plans for the effective management of environmental opportunities and threats, in light of corporate strengths and weaknesses. It includes defining the corporate mission, specifying achievable objectives, developing strategies, and setting policy guidelines.

Mission

An organization's **mission** is the purpose or reason for the organization's existence. It tells what the company is providing to society, either a service like housecleaning or a product like automobiles. A well-conceived mission statement defines the fundamental, unique purpose

Figure 1–3
Environmental Variables

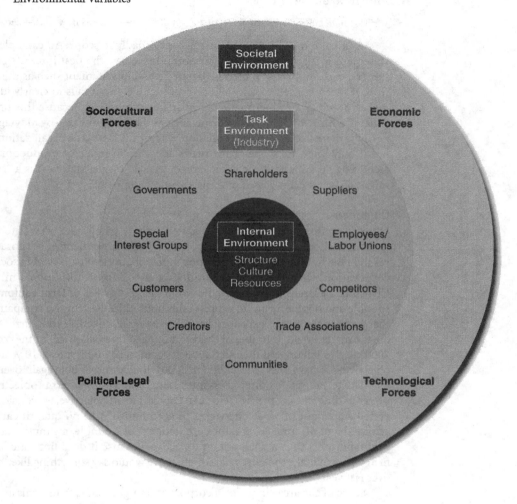

that sets a company apart from other firms of its type and identifies the scope of the company's operations in terms of products (including services) offered and markets served. It may also include the firm's philosophy about how it does business and treats its employees. It puts into words not only what the company is now, but also what it wants to become—management's strategic vision of the firm's future. (Some people like to consider vision and mission as two different concepts: A mission statement describes what the organization is now; a vision statement describes what the organization would like to become. We prefer to combine these ideas into a single mission statement.)[28] The mission statement promotes a sense of shared expectations in employees and communicates a public image to important stakeholder groups in the company's task environment. *It tells who we are and what we do as well as what we'd like to become.*

One example of a mission statement is that of Maytag Corporation:

To improve the quality of home life by designing, building, marketing, and servicing the best appliances in the world.

Another classic example is that etched in bronze at Newport News Shipbuilding, unchanged since its founding in 1886:

> *We shall build good ships here—at a profit if we can—at a loss if we must—but always good ships.*[29]

A mission may be defined narrowly or broadly in scope. An example of a **broad** mission statement is that used by many corporations: Serve the best interests of shareowners, customers, and employees. A broadly defined mission statement such as this keeps the company from restricting itself to one field or product line, but it fails to clearly identify either what it makes or which product/markets it plans to emphasize. Because this broad statement is so general, a **narrow** mission statement, such as the preceding one by Maytag emphasizing appliances, is more useful. A narrow mission very clearly states the organization's primary business, but it may limit the scope of the firm's activities in terms of product or service offered, the technology used, and the market served. Instead of just stating it is a "railroad," a company might be better calling itself a "transportation company."

Objectives

Objectives are the end results of planned activity. They state what is to be accomplished by when and should be quantified if possible. The achievement of corporate objectives should result in the fulfillment of a corporation's mission. In effect, this is what society gives back to the corporation when the corporation does a good job of fulfilling its mission. Robert Lane, Chairman of Deere & Company, the world's largest maker of farm equipment, uses the phrase "double and double again" to express ambitious objectives for the company. "It gives us a sense that we're on the move," explained Lane. For example, one of Deere's current objectives is to double the market value (number of shares multiplied by stock price) of the company ($8 billion in 2000) to $16 billion and then to double it again to $32 billion over 10 years. Similarly, the sales objective is to have sales ($13 billion in 2000) double and double again over the next 10 years.[30]

The term "goal" is often used interchangeably with the term "objective." In this book, we prefer to differentiate the two terms. In contrast to an objective, we consider a **goal** as an open-ended statement of what one wants to accomplish with no quantification of what is to be achieved and no time criteria for completion. For example, a simple statement of "increased profitability" is thus a goal, not an objective, because it does not state how much profit the firm wants to make the next year. An objective would say something like, "increase profits 10% over last year."

Some of the areas in which a corporation might establish its goals and objectives are:

- Profitability (net profits)
- Efficiency (low costs, etc.)
- Growth (increase in total assets, sales, etc.)
- Shareholder wealth (dividends plus stock price appreciation)
- Utilization of resources (return on investment or equity)
- Reputation (being considered a "top" firm)
- Contributions to employees (employment security, wages, diversity)
- Contributions to society (taxes paid, participation in charities, providing a needed product or service)
- Market leadership (market share)
- Technological leadership (innovations, creativity)
- Survival (avoiding bankruptcy)
- Personal needs of top management (using the firm for personal purposes, such as providing jobs for relatives)

Strategies

A **strategy** of a corporation forms a comprehensive master plan stating how the corporation will achieve its mission and objectives. It maximizes competitive advantage and minimizes competitive disadvantage. For example, after Rockwell International Corporation realized that it could no longer achieve its objectives by continuing with its strategy of diversification into multiple lines of businesses, it sold its aerospace and defense units to Boeing. Rockwell instead chose to concentrate on commercial electronics, an area that management felt had greater opportunities for growth.

The typical business firm usually considers three types of strategy: corporate, business, and functional.

1. **Corporate strategy** describes a company's overall direction in terms of its general attitude toward growth and the management of its various businesses and product lines. Corporate strategies typically fit within the three main categories of stability, growth, and retrenchment. For example, Maytag Corporation followed a corporate growth strategy by acquiring other appliance companies in order to have a full line of major home appliances.

2. **Business strategy** usually occurs at the business unit or product level, and it emphasizes improvement of the competitive position of a corporation's products or services in the specific industry or market segment served by that business unit. Business strategies may fit within the two overall categories of *competitive* or *cooperative* strategies. For example, Apple Computer uses a differentiation competitive strategy that emphasizes innovative products with creative design. The distinctive design and colors of its iMac line of personal computers (when contrasted with the usual beige of the competitor's products) has successfully boosted the company's market share and profits. In contrast, British Airways followed a cooperative strategy by forming an alliance with American Airlines in order to provide global service.

3. **Functional strategy** is the approach taken by a functional area to achieve corporate and business unit objectives and strategies by maximizing resource productivity. It is concerned with developing and nurturing a *distinctive competence* (see **Chapter 4**) to provide a company or business unit with a competitive advantage. Examples of R&D functional strategies are technological followership (imitate the products of other companies) and technological leadership (pioneer an innovation). For years, Magic Chef had been a successful appliance maker by spending little on R&D but by quickly imitating the innovations of other competitors. This helped the company to keep its costs lower than its competitors and consequently to compete with lower prices. In terms of marketing functional strategies, Procter & Gamble is a master of marketing "pull"—the process of spending huge amounts on advertising in order to create customer demand. This supports P&G's competitive strategy of differentiating its products from its competitors.

Business firms use all three types of strategy simultaneously. A **hierarchy of strategy** is the grouping of strategy types by level in the organization. This hierarchy of strategy is a nesting of one strategy within another so that they complement and support one another. (See **Figure 1–4**.) Functional strategies support business strategies, which, in turn, support the corporate strategy(ies).

Just as many firms often have no formally stated objectives, many firms have unstated, incremental, or intuitive strategies that have never been articulated or analyzed. Often the only way to spot a corporation's implicit strategies is to look not at what management says, but at what it does. Implicit strategies can be derived from corporate policies, programs approved

Figure 1–4
Hierarchy of Strategy

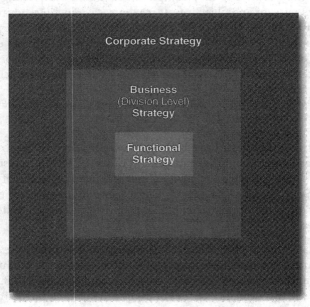

(and disapproved), and authorized budgets. Programs and divisions favored by budget increases and staffed by managers who are considered to be on the fast promotion track reveal where the corporation is putting its money and its energy.

Policies

A **policy** is a broad guideline for decision making that links the formulation of strategy with its implementation. Companies use policies to make sure that employees throughout the firm make decisions and take actions that support the corporation's mission, objectives, and strategies. For example, consider the following company policies:

- **Maytag Company:** Maytag will not approve any cost reduction proposal if it reduces product quality in any way. (This policy supports Maytag's strategy for Maytag brands to compete on quality rather than on price.)

- **3M:** Researchers should spend 15% of their time working on something other than their primary project. (This supports 3M's strong product development strategy.)

- **Intel:** Cannibalize your product line (undercut the sales of your current products) with better products before a competitor does it to you. (This supports Intel's objective of market leadership.)

- **General Electric:** GE must be number one or two wherever it competes. (This supports GE's objective to be number one in market capitalization.)

- **Nordstrom:** A "no questions asked" merchandise return policy, because the customer is always right. (This supports Nordstrom's competitive strategy of differentiation through excellent service.)

Policies like these provide clear guidance to managers throughout the organization. (Strategy formulation is discussed in greater detail in **Chapters 5, 6,** and **7.**)

STRATEGY IMPLEMENTATION

Strategy implementation is the process by which strategies and policies are put into action through the development of programs, budgets, and procedures. This process might involve changes within the overall culture, structure, and/or management system of the entire organization. Except when such drastic corporate-wide changes are needed, however, the implementation of strategy is typically conducted by middle and lower level managers with review by top management. Sometimes referred to as operational planning, strategy implementation often involves day-to-day decisions in resource allocation.

Programs

A **program** is a statement of the activities or steps needed to accomplish a single-use plan. It makes the strategy action oriented. It may involve restructuring the corporation, changing the company's internal culture, or beginning a new research effort. For example, consider Intel Corporation, the microprocessor manufacturer. Realizing that Intel would not be able to continue its corporate growth strategy without the continuous development of new generations of microprocessors, management decided to implement a series of programs:

- They formed an alliance with Hewlett-Packard to develop the successor to the Pentium Pro chip.
- They assembled an elite team of engineers and scientists to do long-term, original research into computer chip design.

Another example is FedEx Corporation's program to install a sophisticated information system to enable its customers to track their shipments at any point in time. FedEx thus installed computer terminals at 100,000 customers and gave proprietary software to another 650,000 so shippers could label much of their own packages.[31]

Budgets

A **budget** is a statement of a corporation's programs in terms of dollars. Used in planning and control, a budget lists the detailed cost of each program. Many corporations demand a certain percentage return on investment, often called a "hurdle rate," before management will approve a new program. This ensures that the new program will significantly add to the corporation's profit performance and thus build shareholder value. The budget thus not only serves as a detailed plan of the new strategy in action, but also specifies through pro forma financial statements the expected impact on the firm's financial future.

For example, General Motors budgeted $4.3 billion during 2000 through 2004 to update and expand its Cadillac line of automobiles. With this money, the company is increasing the number of models from five to nine, and offering more powerful engines, sportier handling, and edgier styling. The company hopes to reverse its declining market share by appealing to a younger market. (The average Cadillac buyer was 67 years old in 2000.)[32]

Procedures

Procedures, sometimes termed *Standard Operating Procedures* (*SOP*), are a system of sequential steps or techniques that describe in detail how a particular task or job is to be done. They typically detail the various activities that must be carried out in order to complete the corporation's programs. For example, Delta Airlines used various procedures to cut costs. To reduce the number of employees, Delta asked technical experts in hydraulics, metal working, avionics, and other trades to design cross-functional work teams. To cut marketing expenses, Delta instituted a cap on travel agent commissions and emphasized sales to bigger accounts. Delta also changed its purchasing and food service procedures. (Strategy implementation is discussed in more detail in **Chapters 8** and **9**.)

EVALUATION AND CONTROL

Evaluation and control is the process in which corporate activities and performance results are monitored so that actual performance can be compared with desired performance. Managers at all levels use the resulting information to take corrective action and resolve problems. Although evaluation and control is the final major element of strategic management, it also can pinpoint weaknesses in previously implemented strategic plans and thus stimulate the entire process to begin again.

Performance is the end result of activities.[33] It includes the actual outcomes of the strategic management process. The practice of strategic management is justified in terms of its ability to improve an organization's performance, typically measured in terms of profits and return on investment. For evaluation and control to be effective, managers must obtain clear, prompt, and unbiased information from the people below them in the corporation's hierarchy. Using this information, managers compare what is actually happening with what was originally planned in the formulation stage. For example, the success of Delta Airline's turnaround strategy was evaluated in terms of the amount spent on each airplane seat per mile of flight. Before the "Leadership 7.5" program was instituted, the cost per seat was 9.76¢. The program needed to reach 7.5¢ to achieve the company's objective of reducing annual expenses by $2.1 billion.

The evaluation and control of performance completes the strategic management model. Based on performance results, management may need to make adjustments in its strategy formulation, in implementation, or in both. (Evaluation and control is discussed in more detail in **Chapter 10**.)

FEEDBACK/LEARNING PROCESS

Note that the strategic management model depicted in **Figure 1–2** includes a feedback/learning process. Arrows are drawn coming out of each part of the model and taking information to each of the previous parts of the model. As a firm or business unit develops strategies, programs, and the like, it often must go back to revise or correct decisions made earlier in the model. For example, poor performance (as measured in evaluation and control) usually indicates that something has gone wrong with either strategy formulation or implementation. It could also mean that a key variable, such as a new competitor, was ignored during environmental scanning and assessment.

1.6 Initiation of Strategy: Triggering Events

After much research, Henry Mintzberg discovered that strategy formulation is typically not a regular, continuous process: "It is most often an irregular, discontinuous process, proceeding in fits and starts. There are periods of stability in strategy development, but also there are periods of flux, of groping, of piecemeal change, and of global change."[34] This view of strategy formulation as an irregular process can be explained by the very human tendency to continue on a particular course of action until something goes wrong or a person is forced to question his or her actions. This period of "strategic drift" may simply result from inertia on the part of the organization or may simply reflect management's belief that the current strategy is still appropriate and needs only some "fine-tuning." Most large organizations tend to follow a particular strategic orientation for about 15 to 20 years before making a significant change in direction.[35] After this rather long period of fine-tuning an existing strategy, some sort of shock to the system is needed to motivate management to seriously reassess the corporation's situation.

A **triggering event** is something that acts as a stimulus for a change in strategy. Some possible triggering events are:

- **New CEO:** By asking a series of embarrassing questions, the new CEO cuts through the veil of complacency and forces people to question the very reason for the corporation's existence.

- **External Intervention:** The firm's bank refuses to approve a new loan or suddenly demands payment in full on an old one. A customer complains about a serious product defect.

- **Threat of a Change in Ownership:** Another firm may initiate a takeover by buying the company's common stock.

- **Performance Gap:** A performance gap exists when performance does not meet expectations. Sales and profits either are no longer increasing or may even be falling.

- **Strategic Inflection Point:** Coined by Andy Grove, Chairman of the Board of Intel Corporation, this represents what happens to a business when a major change takes place due to the introduction of new technologies, a different regulatory environment, a change in customer's values, or a change in what customers prefer.[36]

Sun Microsystems is an example of one company in which a triggering event forced its management to radically rethink what it was doing. See the **Internet Issue** feature to learn how one phone call to Sun's president stimulated a change in strategy at Sun.

Internet Issue

TRIGGERING EVENT AT SUN MICROSYSTEMS

Sun Microsystems President Edward Zander received a personal phone call in June 2000 directly from Margaret Whitman, CEO of eBay, Inc., the Internet auction firm. After a string of small computer crashes, eBay had just suffered a 22-hour outage of its Web site. Whitman called Zander to report that there was a bug in Sun's top-of-the-line server and that Sun had better fix it immediately or else lose eBay's business. A series of around-the-clock meetings at Sun revealed that the problem was that Sun's customers had no idea of how to maintain a $1 million+ computer. eBay had failed to provide sufficient air conditioning to keep the machine cool. Even though Sun had issued a software patch to fix a problem many months earlier, eBay had neglected to install it. The list went on and on. Sun soon realized that the problem was bigger than just eBay. Over 40% of the servers that manage most Web sites were made by Sun.

As more firms were expanding their business to include the Internet, this market for Sun's servers was expected to boom. Nevertheless, many of these firms were too new and small to have the proper technology infrastructure. "It suddenly hit me," said Zander. "How many future eBays are buying their first computer from us this very minute?" According to Scott McNealy, CEO of Sun, "That's when we realized that it wasn't eBay's fault. It was our fault."

Since that realization, Sun's management team has been rebuilding the company to make its servers as reliable as the telephone system. In a drastic strategic change, management decided to expand beyond simply selling servers to providing many of the technologies required to make Web servers completely reliable. It now provides storage products, e-business software, and consultants who not only supply the hardware, but also work directly with the customers to ensure that the servers are operated properly. Just as high-tech mainframe managers used to say that "No one gets fired for choosing IBM," Zander aims to have the same said of Sun Microsystems. "I want to be the sage bet for companies that need the most innovative technology," added Sun's president.

Source: P. Burrows, "Sun's Bid to Rule the Web," *Business Week E.Biz* (July 24, 2000), pp. EB 31–42.

1.7 Strategic Decision Making

The distinguishing characteristic of strategic management is its emphasis on strategic decision making. As organizations grow larger and more complex with more uncertain environments, decisions become increasingly complicated and difficult to make. In agreement with the strategic choice perspective mentioned earlier, this book proposes a strategic decision-making framework that can help people make these decisions regardless of their level and function in the corporation.

WHAT MAKES A DECISION STRATEGIC

Unlike many other decisions, **strategic decisions** deal with the long-run future of the entire organization and have three characteristics:

1. **Rare:** Strategic decisions are unusual and typically have no precedent to follow.

2. **Consequential:** Strategic decisions commit substantial resources and demand a great deal of commitment from people at all levels.

3. **Directive:** Strategic decisions set precedents for lesser decisions and future actions throughout the organization.[37]

One example of a strategic decision was that made by Monsanto to move away from being a chemical company emphasizing fertilizers and herbicides to becoming a "life sciences" enterprise, devoted to improving human health by seeking synergies in biotech, pharmaceutical research, and food products. Management decided to sell its slow-growing chemical business and invest $4 billion into R&D and a series of acquisitions. Realizing that the planet couldn't survive an expected doubling of its population without serious environmental degradation, Monsanto decided to develop genetically engineered seeds to double crop yields using less fertilizer and poisons.[38]

MINTZBERG'S MODES OF STRATEGIC DECISION MAKING

Some strategic decisions are made in a flash by one person (often an entrepreneur or a powerful chief executive officer) who has a brilliant insight and is quickly able to convince others to adopt his or her idea. Other strategic decisions seem to develop out of a series of small incremental choices that over time push the organization more in one direction than another. According to Henry Mintzberg, the three most typical approaches, or modes, of strategic decision making are entrepreneurial, adaptive, and planning.[39] A fourth mode, logical incrementalism, was added later by Quinn.

■ **Entrepreneurial Mode:** Strategy is made by one powerful individual. The focus is on opportunities; problems are secondary. Strategy is guided by the founder's own vision of direction and is exemplified by large, bold decisions. The dominant goal is growth of the corporation. America Online, founded by Steve Case, is an example of this mode of strategic decision making. The company reflects his vision of the Internet provider industry. Although AOL's clear growth strategy is certainly an advantage of the entrepreneurial mode, its tendency to market its products before the company is able to support them is a significant disadvantage.

■ **Adaptive Mode:** Sometimes referred to as "muddling through," this decision-making mode is characterized by reactive solutions to existing problems, rather than a proactive search for new opportunities. Much bargaining goes on concerning priorities of objectives. Strategy is fragmented and is developed to move the corporation forward incrementally. This mode is typical of most universities, many large hospitals, a large number of governmental agencies, and a surprising number of large corporations. Encyclopaedia Britannica, Inc., operated successfully for many years in this mode. It continued to rely on the door-to-door selling of its prestigious books long after dual career couples made this marketing approach obsolete. Only after it was acquired in 1996 did the company change its marketing strategy to television advertising and Internet marketing. (See ⟨www.eb.com⟩.) It now offers an online version of the encyclopedia in addition to the printed volumes.

- **Planning Mode:** This decision-making mode involves the systematic gathering of appropriate information for situation analysis, the generation of feasible alternative strategies, and the rational selection of the most appropriate strategy. It includes both the proactive search for new opportunities and the reactive solution of existing problems. Hewlett-Packard (HP) is an example of the planning mode. After a careful study of trends in the computer and communications industries, management noted that the company needed to stop thinking of itself as a collection of stand-alone products with a primary focus on instrumentation and computer hardware. Led by its new CEO, Carly Fiorina, top management felt that the company needed to become a customer-focused and integrated provider of information appliances, highly reliable information technology infrastructure, and electronic commerce services. Consequently, products were merged into packages for electronic services solutions, such as software for building internal company portals and "e-speak," a software platform that can quickly create and combine different kinds of online services. HP also sold its venerable test and measurement unit—the business in which the company had begun. HP's research labs also received significant support and were encouraged to quit focusing on incremental improvements so that they could develop "disruptive technologies," such as molecular computing, a technology to build integrated circuits using molecules.[40]

- **Logical Incrementalism:** A fourth decision-making mode, which can be viewed as a synthesis of the planning, adaptive, and, to a lesser extent, the entrepreneurial modes, was proposed by Quinn. In this mode, top management has a reasonably clear idea of the corporation's mission and objectives, but, in its development of strategies, it chooses to use "an interactive process in which the organization probes the future, experiments and learns from a series of partial (incremental) commitments rather than through global formulations of total strategies."[41] Thus, although the mission and objectives are set, the strategy is allowed to emerge out of debate, discussion, and experimentation. This approach appears to be useful when the environment is changing rapidly and when it is important to build consensus and develop needed resources before committing the entire corporation to a specific strategy.

STRATEGIC DECISION-MAKING PROCESS: AID TO BETTER DECISIONS

Good arguments can be made for using either the entrepreneurial or adaptive modes (or logical incrementalism) in certain situations. This book proposes, however, that in most situations the planning mode, which includes the basic elements of the strategic management process, is a more rational and thus better way of making strategic decisions. Research indicates that the planning mode is not only more analytical and less political than are the other modes, but it is also more appropriate for dealing with complex, changing environments.[42]

Figure 1–5
Strategic Decision-Making Process

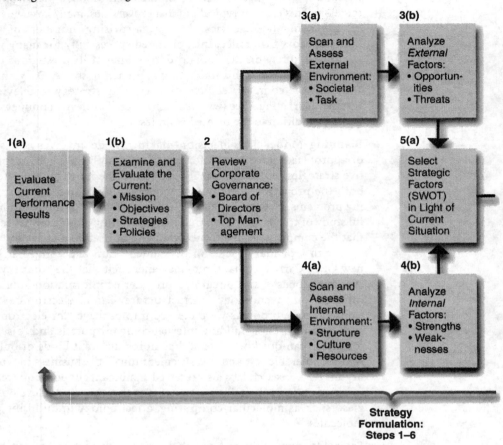

Source: T. L. Wheelen and J. D. Hunger, "Strategic Decision-Making Process," Copyright © 1994 and 1997 by Wheelen and Hunger Associates. Reprinted by permission.

We therefore propose the following eight-step **strategic decision-making process** to improve the making of strategic decisions (see **Figure 1–5**):

1. **Evaluate current performance results** in terms of (a) return on investment, profitability, and so forth, and (b) the current mission, objectives, strategies, and policies.

2. **Review corporate governance**, that is, the performance of the firm's board of directors and top management.

3. **Scan and assess the external environment** to determine the strategic factors that pose Opportunities and Threats.

4. **Scan and assess the internal corporate environment** to determine the strategic factors that are Strengths (especially core competencies) and Weaknesses.

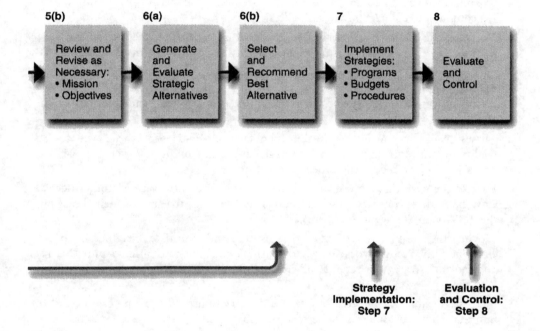

5. **Analyze strategic (SWOT) factors** to (a) pinpoint problem areas, and (b) review and revise the corporate mission and objectives as necessary.

6. **Generate, evaluate, and select the best alternative strategy** in light of the analysis conducted in Step 5.

7. **Implement selected strategies** via programs, budgets, and procedures.

8. **Evaluate implemented strategies** via feedback systems and the control of activities to ensure their minimum deviation from plans.

This rational approach to strategic decision making has been used successfully by corporations like Warner-Lambert, Dayton Hudson, General Electric, Avon Products, Bechtel Group, Inc., and Taisei Corporation. **It is also the basis for the Strategic Audit found in Chapter 10.**

1.8 Impact of the Internet on Strategic Management

Few innovations in history provide as many potential benefits to the strategic management of a corporation as does electronic commerce (e-commerce) via the Internet. The global nature of the technology, low cost, opportunity to reach millions of people, interactive nature, and variety of possibilities result in many potential benefits to strategic managers. E-commerce provides the following benefits to the strategic management of corporations.

- Expands the marketplace to national and international markets. All anyone now needs is a computer to connect buyers and sellers.

- Decreases the cost of creating, processing, distributing, storing, and retrieving information. The cost of electronic payment is $.02, whereas the cost of a paper check is $.43.

- Enables people to create new, highly specialized business ventures. Very narrow market niches can now be reached via special interest chat rooms and Internet search engines.

- Allows smaller inventories, just-in-time manufacturing, and less overhead expenses by facilitating pull-type supply chain management. Dell Computer orders the parts it needs as soon as it receives an order from a customer.

- Enables the customization of products and services to better suit customer needs. Customers are encouraged to select options and styles for the auto of their choice on the BMW Web site ⟨www.bmw.com⟩.

- Provides the stimulus to rethink a firm's strategy and to initiate reengineering projects. The arrival of Amazon.com forced Barnes and Noble to rethink its pure "bricks and mortar" strategy of retail book stores and to begin selling books over its own Web site.

- Increases flexibility, compresses cycle and delivery time, and provides easy access to information on customers, suppliers, and competitors.[43]

Projections for the 21st Century

- From 1994 to 2010, the world economy will grow from $26 trillion to $48 trillion.
- From 1994 to 2010, world trade will increase from $4 trillion to $16.6 trillion.[44]

Discussion Questions

1. Why has strategic management become so important to today's corporations?

2. How does strategic management typically evolve in a corporation?

3. What is a learning organization? Is this approach to strategic management better than the more traditional top-down approach?

4. Why are strategic decisions different from other kinds of decisions?

5. When is the planning mode of strategic decision making superior to the entrepreneurial and adaptive modes?

Strategic Practice Exercise

Mission statements vary widely from one company to another. Why is one mission statement better than another? Develop some criteria for evaluating a mission statement. Then, do one or both of the following exercises:

1. Evaluate the following mission statement of Celestial Seasonings:

> Our mission is to grow and dominate the U.S. specialty tea market by exceeding consumer expectations with the best tasting, 100% natural hot and iced teas, packaged with Celestial art and philosophy, creating the most valued tea experience. Through leadership, inno-

vation, focus, and teamwork, we are dedicated to continuously improving value to our consumers, customers, employees, and stakeholders with a quality-first organization.[45]

2. Using the Internet, find the mission statements of three different organizations, which can be business or not-for-profit. (*Hint*: Check annual reports and 10k forms. They can often be found via a link on a company's Web page or through Hoovers.com.) Which mission statement is best? Why?

Key Terms

adaptive mode (pp. 18–19)
Association of South East Asian
   Nations (ASEAN) (p. 6)
budget (p. 15)
business policy (p. 2)
business strategy (p. 13)
corporate strategy (p. 13)
electronic commerce (p. 15)
entrepreneurial mode (p. 18)
environmental scanning (p. 9)
European Union (EU) (p. 6)
evaluation and control (p. 16)
external environment (pp. 9–10)
functional strategy (p. 13)
globalization (p. 5)
goal (p. 12)

hierarchy of strategy (p. 13)
institution theory (p. 7)
internal environment (p. 10)
learning organization (p. 8)
logical incrementalism (p. 19)
mission (p. 10)
Mercosur/Mercosul (p. 6)
North American Free Trade
   Agreement (NAFTA) (p. 6)
objectives (p. 12)
organizational learning theory (p. 8)
performance (p. 16)
performance gap (p. 17)
phases of strategic management
   (p. 3)
planning mode (p. 19)

policy (p. 14)
population ecology (p. 7)
procedures (p. 15)
program (p. 15)
strategic choice perspective (p. 8)
strategic decision-making process
   (p. 20)
strategic decisions (p. 18)
strategic factors (p. 9)
strategic inflection point (p. 17)
strategic management (p. 2)
strategy (p. 13)
strategy formulation (p. 10)
strategy implementation (p. 15)
SWOT analysis (p. 9)
triggering event (p. 17)

Notes

1. E. Corcoran, "The E Gang," *Fortune* (July 24, 2000), p. 146.
2. P. L. Moore and G. Smith, "GE Catches Online Fever," *Business Week* (August 14, 2000), pp. 122–123.
3. L. Lee, "Not Just Clicks Anymore," *Business Week* (August 28, 2000), pp. 226–227.
4. For an excellent description of the evolution of business policy into strategic management, see R. E. Hoskisson, M. A. Hitt, W. P. Wan, and D. Yiu, "Theory and Research in Strategic Management: Swings of the Pendulum," *Journal of Management*, Vol. 25, No. 3 (1999), pp. 417–456.
5. F. W. Gluck, S. P. Kaufman, and A. S. Walleck, "The Four Phases of Strategic Management," *Journal of Business Strategy* (Winter 1982), pp. 9–21.
6. M. R. Vaghefi and A. B. Huellmantel, "Strategic Leadership at General Electric," *Long Range Planning* (April 1998), pp. 280–294.
7. T. J. Andersen, "Strategic Planning, Autonomous Actions and Corporate Performance," *Long Range Planning* (April 2000), pp. 184–200; C. C. Miller and L. B. Cardinal, "Strategic Planning and

Firm Performance: A Synthesis of More Than Two Decades of Research," *Academy of Management Journal* (December 1994), pp. 1649–1665; P. Pekar, Jr., and S. Abraham, "Is Strategic Management Living Up to Its Promise?" *Long Range Planning* (October 1995), pp. 32–44.
8. E. J. Zajac, M. S. Kraatz, and R. F. Bresser, "Modeling the Dynamics of Strategic Fit: A Normative Approach to Strategic Change," *Strategic Management Journal* (April 2000), pp. 429–453.
9. K. G. Smith and C. M. Grimm, "Environmental Variation, Strategic Change and Firm Performance: A Study of Railroad Deregulation," *Strategic Management Journal* (July–August 1987), pp. 363–376.
10. I. Wilson, "Strategic Planning Isn't Dead—It Changed," *Long Range Planning* (August 1994), p. 20.
11. R. M. Grant, "Transforming Uncertainty Into Success: Strategic Leadership Forum 1999," *Strategy & Leadership* (July/August/September, 1999), p. 33.

12. L. W. Rue and N. A. Ibrahim, "The Relationship Between Planning Sophistication and Performance in Small Businesses," *Journal of Small Business Management* (October 1998), pp. 24–32; M. A. Lyles, I. S. Baird, J. B. Orris, and D. F. Kuratko, "Formalized Planning in Small Business: Increasing Strategic Choices," *Journal of Small Business Management* (April 1993), pp. 38–50.

13. C. V. Callahan and B. A. Pasternack, "Corporate Strategy in the Digital Age," *Strategy and Business*, Issue 15 (2nd Quarter 1999), pp. 2–6.

14. J. Bowles, "How Digital Marketplaces Are Shaping the Future of B2B Commerce," Special Advertising Section on e Marketmakers, *Forbes* (July 23, 2000).

15. C. V. Callahan and B. A. Pasternack, "Corporate Strategy in the Digital Age," *Strategy & Business*, Issue 15 (2nd Quarter 1999), p. 3.

16. R. M. Kanter, "Managing the Extended Enterprise in a Globally Connected World," *Organizational Dynamics* (Summer 1999), pp. 7–23; C. Havens and E. Knapp, "Easing into Knowledge Management," *Strategy & Leadership* (March/April 1999), pp. 4–9.

17. J. A. C. Baum, "Organizational Ecology," in *Handbook of Organization Studies*, edited by S. R. Clegg, C. Handy, and W. Nord (London: Sage, 1996), pp. 77–114.

18. For more information on these theories, see A. Y. Lewin and H. W. Voloberda, "Prolegomena on Coevolution: A Framework for Research on Strategy and New Organizational Forms," *Organization Science* (October 1999), pp. 519–534, and H. Aldrich, *Organizations Evolving* (London: Sage, 1999), pp. 43–74.

19. C. Gebelein, "Strategic Planning: The Engine of Change," *Planning Review* (September/October 1993), pp. 17–19.

20. R. A. D'Aveni, *Hypercompetition* (New York: Free Press, 1994). Hypercompetition is discussed in more detail in Chapter 3.

21. R. S. M. Lau, "Strategic Flexibility: A New Reality for World-Class Manufacturing," *SAM Advanced Management Journal* (Spring 1996), pp. 11–15.

22. M. A. Hitt, B. W. Keats, and S. M. DeMarie, "Navigating in the New Competitive Landscape: Building Strategic Flexibility and Competitive Advantage in the 21st Century," *Academy of Management Executive* (November 1998), pp. 22–42.

23. D. Lei, J. W. Slocum, and R. A. Pitts, "Designing Organizations for Competitive Advantage: The Power of Unlearning and Learning," *Organizational Dynamics* (Winter 1999), pp. 24–38.

24. D. A. Garvin, "Building a Learning Organization," *Harvard Business Review* (July/August 1993), p. 80. See also P. M. Senge, *The Fifth Discipline: The Art and Practice of the Learning Organization* (New York: Doubleday, 1990).

25. T. T. Baldwin, C. Danielson, and W. Wiggenhorn, "The Evolution of Learning Strategies in Organizations: From Employee Development to Business Redefinition," *Academy of Management Executive* (November 1997), pp. 47–58.

26. W. Mitchell, J. M. Shaver, and B. Yeung, "Getting There in a Global Industry: Impacts on Performance of Changing International Presence," *Strategic Management Journal* (September 1992), pp. 419–432.

27. Research supports the use of this model in examining firm strategies. See J. A. Smith, "Strategies for Start-Ups," *Long Range Planning* (December 1998), pp. 857–872.

28. See A. Campbell and S. Yeung, "Brief Case: Mission, Vision, and Strategic Intent," *Long Range Planning* (August 1991), pp. 145–147; S. Cummings and J. Davies, "Mission, Vision, Fusion," *Long Range Planning* (December 1994), pp. 147–150.

29. J. Cosco, "Down to the Sea in Ships," *Journal of Business Strategy* (November/December 1995), p. 48.

30. W. Ryberg, "Deere Chief Takes 'Double' Aim," *Des Moines Register* (September 9, 2000), p. D1.

31. L. Grant, "Why FedEx Is Flying High," *Fortune* (November 10, 1997), pp. 156–160.

32. D. Welch, "Cadillac Hits the Gas," *Business Week* (September 4, 2000), p. 50.

33. H. A. Simon, *Administrative Behavior*, 2nd edition (NY: Free Press, 1957), p. 231.

34. H. Mintzberg, "Planning on the Left Side and Managing on the Right," *Harvard Business Review* (July–August 1976), p. 56.

35. This phenomenon of "punctuated equilibrium" describes corporations as evolving through relatively long periods of stability (equilibrium periods) punctuated by relatively short bursts of fundamental change (revolutionary periods). See E. Romanelli and M. L. Tushman, "Organizational Transformation as Punctuated Equilibrium: An Empirical Test," *Academy of Management Journal* (October 1994), pp. 1141–1166.

36. Speech to the 1998 Academy of Management. Reported by S. M. Puffer, "Global Executive: Intel's Andrew Grove on Competitiveness," *Academy of Management Executive* (February 1999), pp. 15–24.

37. D. J. Hickson, R. J. Butler, D. Cray, G. R. Mallory, and D. C. Wilson, *Top Decisions: Strategic Decision-Making in Organizations* (San Francisco: Jossey-Bass, 1986), pp. 26–42.

38. L. Grant, "Monsanto's Bet: There's Gold in Going Green," *Fortune* (April 14, 1997), pp. 116–118.

39. H. Mintzberg, "Strategy-Making in Three Modes," *California Management Review* (Winter 1973), pp. 44–53.

40. "Rebuilding the Garage," *Economist* (July 15, 2000), pp. 59–61.

41. J. B. Quinn, *Strategies for Change: Logical Incrementalism* (Homewood, Ill.: Irwin, 1980), p. 58.

42. I. Gold and A. M. A. Rasheed, "Rational Decision-Making and Firm Performance: The Moderating Role of the Environment," *Strategic Management Journal* (August 1997), pp. 583–591; R. L. Priem, A. M. A. Rasheed, and A. G. Kotulic, "Rationality in Strategic Decision Processes, Environmental Dynamism and Firm Performance," *Journal of Management*, Vol. 21, No. 5 (1995), pp. 913–929; J. W. Dean, Jr., and M. P. Sharfman, "Does Decision Process Matter? A Study of Strategic Decision-Making Effectiveness," *Academy of Management Journal* (April 1996), pp. 368–396.

43. E. Turban, J. Lee, D. King, and H. M. Chung, *Electronic Commerce: A Managerial Perspective* (Upper Saddle River, NJ: Prentice Hall, 2000), p. 15. See also M. J. Shaw, "Electronic Commerce: State of the Art," in M. J. Shaw, R. Blanning, T. Strader, and A. Whinston (eds.), *Handbook on Electronic Commerce* (Berlin: Springer, 2000), pp. 3–24.

44. J. Warner, "21st Century Capitalism: Snapshot of the Next Century," *Business Week* (November 18, 1994), p. 194.

45. P. Jones and L. Kahaner, *Say It & Live It: 50 Corporate Mission Statements That Hit the Mark* (New York: Currency Doubleday, 1995), p. 53.

chapter 3

Environmental Scanning and Industry Analysis

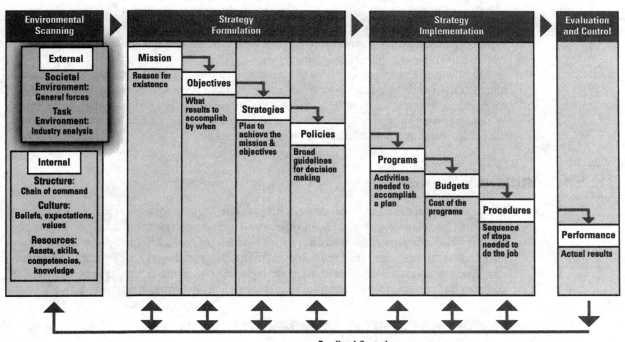

C hefs Unlimited was founded by Dodd and Michelle Aldred of Raleigh, North Carolina. As husband and wife veterans of the restaurant industry, they knew how difficult it was to work long hours and still allow time to prepare home-cooked meals. That was one reason why people were spending more at restaurants. (The percentage of food dollars spent away from home had increased from 36% in 1980 to 44% by the mid-1990s.) The Aldreds felt that many people were beginning to tire of eating out and would be willing to pay for a quality meal eaten in their own home. They offered people the opportunity to order entrees for either a one- or two-week period. Doing their own cooking in a 3,000 square foot commercial kitchen, the Aldreds delivered meals to customers for subsequent reheating. Although more

51

expensive, these meals were of higher quality than the typical frozen dinner. In just four years Chefs Unlimited was so successful catering to modern families that the Aldreds were planning to air express their meals to a nationwide audience the next year. Meanwhile, the U.S. Personal Chef Association was predicting a five-fold increase in the number of personal chef entrepreneurs in the United States and Canada.[1]

Pioneering companies have gone out of business because of their failure to adapt to environmental change or, even worse, by failing to create change. For example, Baldwin Locomotive, the major manufacturer of steam locomotives, was very slow in making the switch to diesel locomotives. General Electric and General Motors soon dominated the diesel locomotive business. The dominant manufacturers of vacuum tubes failed to make the change to transistors and consequently lost this market. Failure to adapt is, however, only one side of the coin. The aforementioned Chefs Unlimited example shows how a changing environment can create new opportunities at the same time it destroys old ones. The lesson is simple: To be successful over time, an organization needs to be in tune with its external environment. There must be a strategic fit between what the environment wants and what the corporation has to offer, as well as between what the corporation needs and what the environment can provide.

Current predictions are that the environment for all organizations will become even more uncertain with every passing year. What is **environmental uncertainty**? It is the *degree of complexity* plus the *degree of change* existing in an organization's external environment. As more and more markets become global, the number of factors a company must consider in any decision become huge—more complex. With new technologies being discovered every year, markets change and products must change with them.

On the one hand, environmental uncertainty is a threat to strategic managers because it hampers their ability to develop long-range plans and to make strategic decisions to keep the corporation in equilibrium with its external environment. On the other hand, environmental uncertainty is an opportunity because it creates a new playing field in which creativity and innovation can have a major part in strategic decisions.

3.1 Environmental Scanning

Before an organization can begin strategy formulation, it must scan the external environment to identify possible opportunities and threats and its internal environment for strengths and weaknesses. **Environmental scanning** is the monitoring, evaluating, and disseminating of information from the external and internal environments to key people within the corporation. A corporation uses this tool to avoid strategic surprise and to ensure its long-term health. Research has found a positive relationship between environmental scanning and profits.[2]

IDENTIFYING EXTERNAL ENVIRONMENTAL VARIABLES

In undertaking environmental scanning, strategic managers must first be aware of the many variables within a corporation's societal and task environments. The **societal environment** includes general forces that do not directly touch on the short-run activities of the organization but that can, and often do, influence its long-run decisions. These, shown in **Figure 1–3**, are as follows:

- **Economic** forces that regulate the exchange of materials, money, energy, and information
- **Technological** forces that generate problem-solving inventions
- **Political-legal** forces that allocate power and provide constraining and protecting laws and regulations
- **Sociocultural** forces that regulate the values, mores, and customs of society

The **task environment** includes those elements or groups that directly affect the corporation and, in turn, are affected by it. These are governments, local communities, suppliers, competitors, customers, creditors, employees/labor unions, special-interest groups, and trade associations. A corporation's task environment is typically the industry within which that firm operates. **Industry analysis** refers to an in-depth examination of key factors within a corporation's task environment. Both the societal and task environments must be monitored to detect the strategic factors that are likely to have a strong impact on corporate success or failure.

Scanning the Societal Environment

The number of possible strategic factors in the societal environment is very high. The number becomes enormous when we realize that, generally speaking, each country in the world can be represented by its own unique set of societal forces—some of which are very similar to neighboring countries and some of which are very different.

For example, even though Korea and China share Asia's Pacific Rim area with Thailand, Taiwan, and Hong Kong (sharing many similar cultural values), they have very different views about the role of business in society. It is generally believed in Korea and China (and to a lesser extent in Japan) that the role of business is primarily to contribute to national development; whereas in Hong Kong, Taiwan, and Thailand (and to a lesser extent in the Philippines, Indonesia, Singapore, and Malaysia), the role of business is primarily to make profits for the shareholders.[3] Such differences may translate into different trade regulations and varying difficulty in the **repatriation of profits** (transferring profits from a foreign subsidiary to a corporation's headquarters) from one group of Pacific Rim countries to another.

Monitoring Societal Trends   As noted in **Table 3–1**, large corporations categorize the societal environment in any one geographic region into four areas and focus their scanning in each area on trends with corporatewide relevance. Obviously trends in any 1 area may be very important to the firms in one industry but of lesser importance to firms in other industries.

Table 3–1   Some Important Variables in the Societal Environment

Economic	Technological	Political-Legal	Sociocultural
GDP trends	Total government spending for R&D	Antitrust regulations	Lifestyle changes
Interest rates		Environmental protection laws	Career expectations
Money supply	Total industry spending for R&D		Consumer activism
Inflation rates		Tax laws	Rate of family formation
Unemployment levels	Focus of technological efforts	Special incentives	Growth rate of population
Wage/price controls	Patent protection	Foreign trade regulations	Age distribution of population
Devaluation/revaluation	New products	Attitudes toward foreign companies	Regional shifts in population
Energy availability and cost	New developments in technology transfer from lab to marketplace	Laws on hiring and promotion	Life expectancies
Disposable and discretionary income		Stability of government	Birth rates
	Productivity improvements through automation		
	Internet availability		
	Telecommunication infrastructure		

Trends in the *economic* part of the societal environment can have an obvious impact on business activity. For example, an increase in interest rates means fewer sales of major home appliances. Why? A rising interest rate tends to be reflected in higher mortgage rates. Because higher mortgage rates increase the cost of buying a house, the demand for new and used houses tends to fall. Because most major home appliances are sold when people change houses, a reduction in house sales soon translates into a decline in sales of refrigerators, stoves, and dishwashers and reduced profits for everyone in that industry.

Changes in the *technological* part of the societal environment can also have a great impact on multiple industries. For example, improvements in computer microprocessors have not only led to the widespread use of home computers, but also to better automobile engine performance in terms of power and fuel economy through the use of microprocessors to monitor fuel injection. Researchers at George Washington University have identified a number of breakthrough developments in technology, which they forecast will have a significant impact during the decade from 2000 to 2010:

- **Portable Information Devices and Electronic Networking:** Combining the computing power of the personal computer, the networking of the Internet, the images of the television, and the convenience of the telephone, these appliances will soon be used by over 30% of the population of industrialized nations to make phone calls, send e-mail, and transmit data and documents. Even now, homes, autos, and offices are being connected (via wires and wireless) into intelligent networks that interact with one another. The traditional stand-alone desktop computer may soon join the manual typewriter as a historical curiosity.

- **Fuel Cells and Alternative Energy Sources:** The use of wind, geothermal, hydroelectric, solar, biomass, and other alternative energy sources should increase from their present level of 10% to about 30% by the end of the decade. Once used exclusively to power spacecraft, fuel cells offer the prospect of pollution-free electrical power. Fuel cells chemically combine hydrogen and oxygen to produce electricity with water as a byproduct. Although it will take a number of years before fuel cells replace gas-powered engines or vast power generation plants, this technology is already providing an alternate source of power for large buildings.

- **Precision Farming:** The computerized management of crops to suit variations in land characteristics will make farming more efficient. Farm equipment dealers, such as Case and Deere, add this equipment to tractors for an additional $6,000. It enables farmers to reduce costs, increase yields, and decrease environmental impact. The old system of small, low-tech farming will become less viable as large corporate farms are able to increase crop yields on limited farmland for a growing population.

- **Virtual Personal Assistants:** Very smart computer programs that monitor e-mail, faxes, and phone calls will be able to take over routine tasks, such as writing a letter, retrieving a file, making a phone call, or screening requests. Acting like a secretary, a person's virtual assistant (VA) could substitute for a person at meetings or in dealing with routine actions.

- **Genetically Altered Organisms:** A convergence of biotechnology and agriculture is creating a new field of life sciences. Plant seeds can be genetically modified to produce more needed vitamins or to be less attractive to pests and more able to survive. Animals (and people) could be similarly modified for desirable characteristics and to eliminate genetic disabilities and diseases.

- **Smart, Mobile Robots:** Robot development has been limited by a lack of sensory devices and sophisticated artificial intelligence systems. Improvements in these areas mean that robots will be performing more sophisticated factory work, run errands, do household chores, and assist the handicapped.[4]

Trends in the *political-legal* part of the societal environment have a significant impact not only on the level of competition within an industry, but also on which strategies might be successful.[5] For example, periods of strict enforcement of U.S. antitrust laws directly affect corporate growth strategy. As large companies find it more difficult to acquire another firm in the same or in a related industry, they are typically driven to diversify into unrelated industries.[6] In Europe, the formation of the European Union has led to an increase in merger activity across national boundaries.

Demographic trends are part of the *sociocultural* aspect of the societal environment. The demographic bulge in the U.S. population caused by the "baby boom" in the 1950s strongly affects market demand in many industries. For example, between 1995 and 2005, an average of 4,400 Americans turns 50 every day. This over-50 age group has become the fastest growing age group in all developed countries. Companies with an eye on the future can find many opportunities offering products and services to the growing number of "woofies" (well-off old folks)—defined as people over 50 with money to spend.[7] These people are very likely to purchase recreational vehicles, take ocean cruises, and enjoy leisure sports such as boating, fishing, and bowling, in addition to needing financial services and health care.

This trend can mean increasing sales for firms like Winnebago (RVs), Carnival Cruise Lines, and Brunswick (sports equipment), among others. To attract older customers, retailers will need to place seats in their larger stores so aging shoppers can rest. Washrooms need to be more accessible. Signs need to be larger. Restaurants need to raise the level of lighting so people can read their menus. Home appliances need simpler and larger controls. Already, the market for road bikes is declining as sales for tread mills and massagers for aching muscles increase.

Seven sociocultural trends in the United States that are helping to define what North America and the world will soon look like are:

1. **Increasing environmental awareness:** Recycling and conservation are becoming more than slogans. Busch Gardens, for example, eliminated the use of disposable styrofoam trays in favor of washing and reusing plastic trays.

2. **Growth of the seniors market:** As their numbers increase, people over age 55 will become an even more important market. Already some companies are segmenting the senior population into Young Matures, Older Matures, and the Elderly—each having a different set of attitudes and interests.

3. **Impact of Generation Y boomlet:** Born after 1980 to the boomer and X generations, this cohort may end up being as large as the boomer generation. In 1957, the peak year of the postwar boom, 4.3 million babies were born. In 1990, there were 4.2 million births. By the mid-1990s, elementary schools were becoming overcrowded.[8] As a result, both Republican and Democratic candidates in the 2000 presidential election made "education" a primary issue. The U.S. census bureau projects Generation Y to crest at 30.8 million births by 2005. Expect this cohort to have a strong impact on future products and services.

4. **Decline of the mass market:** Niche markets are beginning to define the marketers' environment. People want products and services that are adapted more to their personal needs. For example, Estee Lauder's "All Skin" and Maybelline's "Shades of You" lines of cosmetic products are specifically made for African American women. "Mass customization"—the making and marketing of products tailored to a person's requirements (e.g., Dell and Gateway Computers)—is replacing the mass production and marketing of the same product in some markets.

5. **Changing pace and location of life:** Instant communication via fax machines, cell phones, and overnight mail enhances efficiency, but it also puts more pressure on people.

Merging the personal computer with the communication and entertainment industry through telephone lines, satellite dishes, and cable television increases consumers' choices and allows workers to leave overcrowded urban areas for small towns and "telecommute" via personal computers and modems.

6. **Changing household composition:** Single-person households could become the most common household type in the United States after the year 2005. By 2005, only households composed of married couples with no children will be larger.[9] Although the Y generation baby boomlet may alter this estimate, a household clearly is no longer the same as it was once portrayed in *The Brady Bunch* in the 1970s or even *The Cosby Show* in the 1980s.

7. **Increasing diversity of workforce and markets:** Minority groups are increasing as a percentage of the total U.S. population. From 1996 to 2050, group percentages are expected by the U.S. Census Bureau to change as follows: whites—from 83% to 75%; African Americans—from 13% to 15%; Asian—from 4% to 9%; American Indian—slight increase. Hispanics, who can be of any race, are projected to grow from 10% to 25% during this time period.[10] Traditional minority groups are increasing their numbers in the workforce and are being identified as desirable target markets. For example, the South Dekalb Mall in Atlanta, Georgia, restyled itself as an "Afrocentric retail center" in response to the rapid growth of the African American 18-to-34 age group.[11]

International Societal Considerations

Each country or group of countries in which a company operates presents a whole new societal environment with a different set of economic, technological, political-legal, and sociocultural variables for the company to face. International societal environments vary so widely that a corporation's internal environment and strategic management process must be very flexible. Cultural trends in Germany, for example, have resulted in the inclusion of worker representatives in corporate strategic planning. Differences in societal environments strongly affect the ways in which a **multinational corporation (MNC)**, a company with significant assets and activities in multiple countries, conducts its marketing, financial, manufacturing, and other functional activities. For example, the existence of regional associations like the European Union, the North American Free Trade Zone, and Mercosur in South America has a significant impact on the competitive "rules of the game" both for those MNCs operating within and for those MNCs wanting to enter these areas.

To account for the many differences among societal environments from one country to another, consider **Table 3–2**. It includes a list of economic, technological, political-legal, and sociocultural variables for any particular country or region. For example, an important economic variable for any firm investing in a foreign country is currency convertibility. Without convertibility, a company operating in Russia cannot convert its profits from rubles to dollars. In terms of sociocultural variables, many Asian cultures (especially China) are less concerned with the value of human rights than are European and North American cultures. Some Asians actually contend that American companies are trying to impose Western human rights requirements on them in an attempt to make Asian products less competitive by raising their costs.[12]

Before planning its strategy for a particular international location, a company must scan the particular country environment(s) in question for opportunities and threats, and compare these with its own organizational strengths and weaknesses. For example, to operate successfully in a global industry such as automobiles, tires, electronics, or watches, a company must be prepared to establish a significant presence in the three developed areas of the world known collectively as the **Triad**. This term was coined by the Japanese management expert, Kenichi Ohmae, and it refers to the three developed markets of Japan, North America, and Western Europe, which now form a single market with common needs.[13] Focusing on the Triad is

Table 3–2   Some Important Variables in *International* Societal Environments

Economic	Technological	Political-Legal	Sociocultural
Economic development	Regulations on technology transfer	Form of government	Customs, norms, values
Per capita income	Energy availability/cost	Political ideology	Language
Climate	Natural resource availability	Tax laws	Demographics
GDP trends	Transportation network	Stability of government	Life expectancies
Monetary and fiscal policies	Skill level of work force	Government attitude toward foreign companies	Social institutions
Unemployment level	Patent-trademark protection	Regulations on foreign ownership of assets	Status symbols
Currency convertibility	Internet availability	Strength of opposition groups	Lifestyle
Wage levels	Telecommunication infrastructure	Trade regulations	Religious beliefs
Nature of competition		Protectionist sentiment	Attitudes toward foreigners
Membership in regional economic associations		Foreign policies	Literacy level
		Terrorist activity	Human rights
		Legal system	Environmentalism

essential for an MNC pursuing success in a global industry, according to Ohmae, because close to 90% of all high–value-added, high-technology manufactured goods are produced and consumed in North America, Western Europe, and Japan. Ideally a company should have a significant presence in each of these regions so that it can develop, produce, and market its products simultaneously in all three areas. Otherwise, it will lose competitive advantage to Triad-oriented MNCs. No longer can an MNC develop and market a new product in one part of the world before it exports it to other developed countries.

Focusing only on the developed nations, however, causes a corporation to miss important market opportunities in the developing nations of the world. Although these nations may not have developed to the point that they have significant demand for a broad spectrum of products, they may very likely be on the threshold of rapid growth in the demand for specific products. This would be the ideal time for a company to enter this market—before competition is established. The key is to be able to identify the "trigger point" when demand for a particular product or service is ready to boom. See the 🌐 **Global Issue** feature for an in-depth explanation of a technique to identify the optimum time to enter a particular market in a developing nation.

Scanning the Task Environment

As shown in **Figure 3–1**, a corporation's scanning of the environment will include analyses of all the relevant elements in the task environment. These analyses take the form of individual reports written by various people in different parts of the firm. At Procter & Gamble (P&G), for example, people from each of the brand management teams work with key people from the sales and market research departments to research and write a "competitive activity report" each quarter on each of the product categories in which P&G competes. People in purchasing also write similar reports concerning new developments in the industries that supply P&G. These and other reports are then summarized and transmitted up the corporate hierarchy for top management to use in strategic decision making. If a new development is reported regarding a particular product category, top management may then send memos asking peo-

Global Issue 🌐

Identifying Potential Markets in Developing Nations

Research by the Deloitte & Touche Consulting Group reveals that the demand for a specific product increases exponentially at certain points in a country's development. Identifying this trigger point of demand is thus critical to entering emerging markets at the best time. A **trigger point** is the time when enough people have enough money to buy what a company has to sell, but before competition is established. This can be done by using the concept of **purchasing power parity (PPP)**, which measures the cost in dollars of the U.S.–produced equivalent volume of goods that an economy produces.

PPP offers an estimate of the material wealth a nation can purchase, rather than the financial wealth it creates as typically measured by Gross Domestic Product (GDP). As a result, restating a nation's GDP in PPP terms reveals much greater spending power than market exchange rates would suggest. For example, a shoe shine costing $5 to $10 in New York City can be purchased for 50¢ in Mexico City. Consequently the people of Mexico City can enjoy the same standard of living (with respect to shoe shines) as people in New York City with only 5% to 10% of the money. Correcting for PPP restates all Mexican shoe shines at their U.S. purchase value of $5. If one million shoe shines were purchased in Mexico last year, using the PPP model would effectively increase Mexican GDP by $5 million to $10 million. Using PPP, China becomes the world's second largest economy after the United States, with Brazil, Mexico, and India moving ahead of Canada into the top 10 world markets.

Trigger points identify when demand for a particular product is about to rapidly increase in a country. This can be a very useful technique to identify when to enter a new market in a developing nation. Trigger points vary for different products. For example, an apparent trigger point for long-distance telephone services is at $7,500 in GDP per capita—a point when demand for telecommunications services increases rapidly. Once national wealth surpasses $15,000 per capita, demand increases at a much slower rate with further increases in wealth. The trigger point for life insurance is around $8,000 in GDP per capita. At this point, the demand for life insurance increases between 200% and 300% above those countries with GDP per capita below the trigger point.

Source: Summarized from D. Fraser and M. Raynor, "The Power of Parity," *Forecast* (May/June, 1996), pp. 8–12.

Figure 3–1
Scanning the External Environment

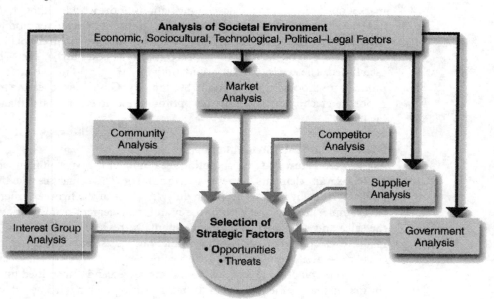

ple throughout the organization to watch for and report on developments in related product areas. The many reports resulting from these scanning efforts, when boiled down to their essentials, act as a detailed list of external strategic factors.

IDENTIFYING EXTERNAL STRATEGIC FACTORS

Why do companies often respond differently to the same environmental changes? One reason is because of differences in the ability of managers to recognize and understand external strategic issues and factors. No firm can successfully monitor all external factors. Choices must be made regarding which factors are important and which are not. Even though managers agree that strategic importance determines what variables are consistently tracked, they sometimes miss or choose to ignore crucial new developments.[14] Personal values and functional experiences of a corporation's managers as well as the success of current strategies are likely to bias both their perception of what is important to monitor in the external environment and their interpretations of what they perceive.[15]

This willingness to reject unfamiliar as well as negative information is called **strategic myopia**.[16] If a firm needs to change its strategy, it might not be gathering the appropriate external information to change strategies successfully.

One way to identify and analyze developments in the external environment is to use the **issues priority matrix (Figure 3–2)** as follows:

1. Identify a number of likely trends emerging in the societal and task environments. These are strategic environmental issues—those important trends that, if they occur, determine what the industry or the world will look like in the near future.

2. Assess the probability of these trends actually occurring from low to high.

3. Attempt to ascertain the likely impact (from low to high) of each of these trends on the corporation being examined.

Figure 3–2
Issues Priority Matrix

Probable Impact on Corporation

	High	Medium	Low
High	High Priority	High Priority	Medium Priority
Medium	High Priority	Medium Priority	Low Priority
Low	Medium Priority	Low Priority	Low Priority

(Vertical axis label: **Probability of Occurrence**)

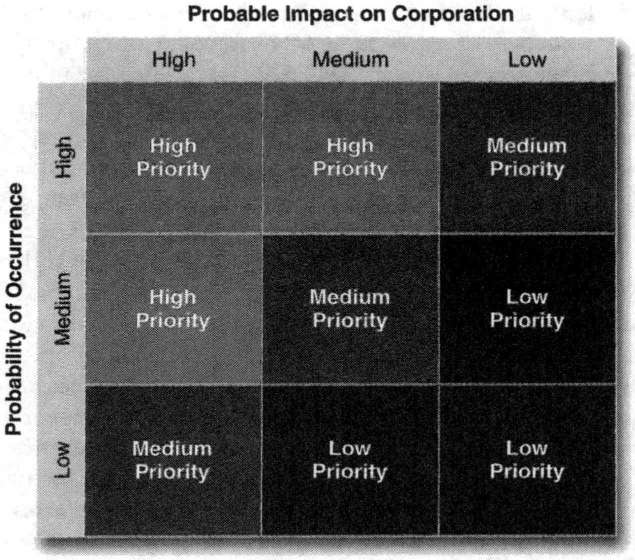

Source: Reprinted from L. L. Lederman, "Foresight Activities in the U.S.A.: Time for a Re-Assessment?" *Long-Range Planning* (June 1984), p. 46. Copyright © 1984. Reprinted with permission from Elsevier Science.

A corporation's **external strategic factors** are those key environmental trends that are judged to have both a medium to high probability of occurrence and a medium to high probability of impact on the corporation. The issues priority matrix can then be used to help managers decide which environmental trends should be merely scanned (low priority) and which should be monitored as strategic factors (high priority). Those environmental trends judged to be a corporation's strategic factors are then categorized as opportunities and threats and are included in strategy formulation.

3.2 Industry Analysis: Analyzing the Task Environment

An **industry** is a group of firms producing a similar product or service, such as soft drinks or financial services. An examination of the important stakeholder groups, such as suppliers and customers, in a particular corporation's task environment is a part of industry analysis.

PORTER'S APPROACH TO INDUSTRY ANALYSIS

Michael Porter, an authority on competitive strategy, contends that a corporation is most concerned with the intensity of competition within its industry. The level of this intensity is determined by basic competitive forces, which are depicted in **Figure 3–3**. "The collective strength of these forces," he contends, "determines the ultimate profit potential in the industry, where profit potential is measured in terms of long-run return on invested capital."[17] In carefully scanning its industry, the corporation must assess the importance to its success of each of the six forces: threat of new entrants, rivalry among existing firms, threat of substitute products or services, bargaining power of buyers, bargaining power of suppliers, and relative power of other stakeholders.[18] The stronger each of these forces, the more limited companies are in their ability to raise prices and earn greater profits. Although Porter mentions only five forces, a sixth—other stakeholders—is added here to reflect the power that governments, local communities, and other groups from the task environment wield over industry activities.

Using the model in **Figure 3–3**, a high force can be regarded as a threat because it is likely to reduce profits. A low force, in contrast, can be viewed as an opportunity because it may allow the company to earn greater profits. In the short run, these forces act as constraints on a company's activities. In the long run, however, it may be possible for a company, through its choice of strategy, to change the strength of one or more of the forces to the company's advantage. For example, in order to pressure its customers (PC makers) to purchase more of Intel's latest microprocessors for use in their PCs, Intel supported the development of sophisticated software needing increasingly larger amounts of processing power. In the mid-1990s Intel began selling 3D graphics chips—not because it wanted to be in that business, but because 3D chips needed large amounts of processing power (provided of course by Intel). Intel also introduced software that made it easier for network administrators to manage PCs on their networks, which Intel believed would help sell more PCs and neutralize a threat from network computers.[19]

A strategist can analyze any industry by rating each competitive force as **high**, **medium**, or **low** in strength. For example, the athletic shoe industry could be currently rated as follows: rivalry is high (Nike, Reebok, Adidas, and Converse are strong competitors worldwide); threat of potential entrants is low (industry has reached maturity; sales growth rate has slowed); threat of substitutes is low (other shoes don't provide support for sports activities); bargaining power of suppliers is medium but rising (suppliers in Asian countries are increasing in size and ability); bargaining power of buyers is medium, but increasing (athletic shoes are dropping in popularity as brown shoes gain); threat of other stakeholders is medium to high (government regulations and human rights concerns are growing). Based on current trends in each of these competitive forces, the industry appears to be increasing in its level of competitive intensity, meaning profit margins will be falling for the industry as a whole.

Figure 3–3
Forces Driving Industry Competition

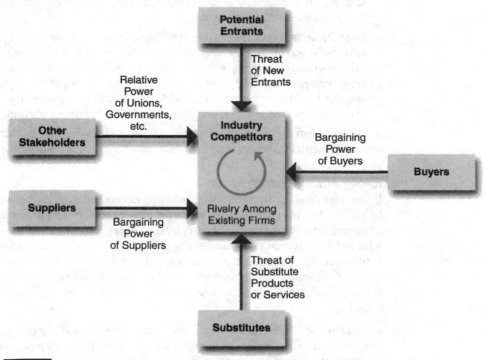

Source: Adapted with permission of The Free Press, a Division of Simon & Schuster, from *Competitive Strategy: Techniques for Analyzing Industries and Competitors* by Michael E. Porter. Copyright © 1980, 1988 by The Free Press.

Threat of New Entrants

New entrants to an industry typically bring to it new capacity, a desire to gain market share, and substantial resources. They are, therefore, threats to an established corporation. The threat of entry depends on the presence of entry barriers and the reaction that can be expected from existing competitors. An **entry barrier** is an obstruction that makes it difficult for a company to enter an industry. For example, no new domestic automobile companies have been successfully established in the United States since the 1930s because of the high capital requirements to build production facilities and to develop a dealer distribution network. Some of the possible barriers to entry are:

- **Economies of Scale:** Scale economies in the production and sale of microprocessors, for example, gave Intel a significant cost advantage over any new rival.

- **Product Differentiation:** Corporations like Procter & Gamble and General Mills, which manufacture products like Tide and Cheerios, create high entry barriers through their high levels of advertising and promotion.

- **Capital Requirements:** The need to invest huge financial resources in manufacturing facilities in order to produce large commercial airplanes creates a significant barrier to entry to any competitor for Boeing and Airbus.

- **Switching Costs:** Once a software program like Excel or Word becomes established in an office, office managers are very reluctant to switch to a new program because of the high training costs.

- **Access to Distribution Channels:** Small entrepreneurs often have difficulty obtaining supermarket shelf space for their goods because large retailers charge for space on their shelves and give priority to the established firms who can pay for the advertising needed to generate high customer demand.

- **Cost Disadvantages Independent of Size:** Once a new product earns sufficient market share to be accepted as the *standard* for that type of product, the maker has a key advantage. Microsoft's development of the first widely adopted operating system (MS-DOS) for the IBM-type personal computer gave it a significant competitive advantage over potential competitors. Its introduction of Windows helped to cement that advantage so that the Microsoft operating system is now on over 90% of personal computers worldwide.

- **Government Policy:** Governments can limit entry into an industry through licensing requirements by restricting access to raw materials, such as oil-drilling sites in protected areas.

Rivalry Among Existing Firms

In most industries, corporations are mutually dependent. A competitive move by one firm can be expected to have a noticeable effect on its competitors and thus may cause retaliation or counterefforts. For example, the entry by mail order companies such as Dell and Gateway into a PC industry previously dominated by IBM, Apple, and Compaq increased the level of competitive activity to such an extent that any price reduction or new product introduction is now quickly followed by similar moves from other PC makers. The same is true of prices in the U.S. airline industry. According to Porter, intense rivalry is related to the presence of several factors, including:

- **Number of Competitors:** When competitors are few and roughly equal in size, such as in the U.S. auto and major home appliance industries, they watch each other carefully to make sure that any move by another firm is matched by an equal countermove.

- **Rate of Industry Growth:** Any slowing in passenger traffic tends to set off price wars in the airline industry because the only path to growth is to take sales away from a competitor.

- **Product or Service Characteristics:** Many people choose a videotape rental store based on location, variety of selection, and pricing because they view videotapes as a commodity—a product whose characteristics are the same regardless of who sells it.

- **Amount of Fixed Costs:** Because airlines must fly their planes on a schedule regardless of the number of paying passengers for any one flight, they offer cheap standby fares whenever a plane has empty seats.

- **Capacity:** If the only way a manufacturer can increase capacity is in a large increment by building a new plant (as in the paper industry), it will run that new plant at full capacity to keep its unit costs as low as possible—thus producing so much that the selling price falls throughout the industry.

- **Height of Exit Barriers: Exit barriers** keep a company from leaving an industry. The brewing industry, for example, has a low percentage of companies that voluntarily leave the industry because breweries are specialized assets with few uses except for making beer.

- **Diversity of Rivals:** Rivals that have very different ideas of how to compete are likely to cross paths often and unknowingly challenge each other's position. This happens often in the retail clothing industry when a number of retailers open outlets in the same location—thus taking sales away from each other.

Threat of Substitute Products or Services

Substitute products are those products that appear to be different but can satisfy the same need as another product. For example, fax machines are a substitute for FedEx, Nutrasweet is a substitute for sugar, and bottled water is a substitute for a cola. According to Porter,

"Substitutes limit the potential returns of an industry by placing a ceiling on the prices firms in the industry can profitably charge."[20] To the extent that switching costs are low, substitutes may have a strong effect on an industry. Tea can be considered a substitute for coffee. If the price of coffee goes up high enough, coffee drinkers will slowly begin switching to tea. The price of tea thus puts a price ceiling on the price of coffee. Identifying possible substitute products or services is sometimes a difficult task. It means searching for products or services that can perform the same function, even though they have a different appearance and may not appear to be easily substitutable.

Bargaining Power of Buyers

Buyers affect an industry through their ability to force down prices, bargain for higher quality or more services, and play competitors against each other. A buyer or a group of buyers is powerful if some of the following factors hold true:

- A buyer purchases a large proportion of the seller's product or service (for example, oil filters purchased by a major auto maker).

- A buyer has the potential to integrate backward by producing the product itself (for example, a newspaper chain could make its own paper).

- Alternative suppliers are plentiful because the product is standard or undifferentiated (for example, motorists can choose among many gas stations).

- Changing suppliers costs very little (for example, office supplies are easy to find).

- The purchased product represents a high percentage of a buyer's costs, thus providing an incentive to shop around for a lower price (for example, gasoline purchased for resale by convenience stores makes up half their total costs).

- A buyer earns low profits and is thus very sensitive to costs and service differences (for example, grocery stores have very small margins).

- The purchased product is unimportant to the final quality or price of a buyer's products or services and thus can be easily substituted without affecting the final product adversely (for example, electric wire bought for use in lamps).

Bargaining Power of Suppliers

Suppliers can affect an industry through their ability to raise prices or reduce the quality of purchased goods and services. A supplier or supplier group is powerful if some of the following factors apply:

- The supplier industry is dominated by a few companies, but it sells to many (for example, the petroleum industry).

- Its product or service is unique and/or it has built up switching costs (for example, word processing software).

- Substitutes are not readily available (for example, electricity).

- Suppliers are able to integrate forward and compete directly with their present customers (for example, a microprocessor producer like Intel can make PCs).

- A purchasing industry buys only a small portion of the supplier group's goods and services and is thus unimportant to the supplier (for example, sales of lawn mower tires are less important to the tire industry than are sales of auto tires).

Relative Power of Other Stakeholders

A sixth force should be added to Porter's list to include a variety of stakeholder groups from the task environment. Some of these groups are governments (if not explicitly included elsewhere), local communities, creditors (if not included with suppliers), trade associations, special-interest groups, unions (if not included with suppliers), shareholders, and comple-mentors. According to Andy Grove, ex-CEO of Intel, a **complementor** is a company (e.g., Microsoft) or an industry whose product works well with another industry's or a firm's (e.g., Intel's) product and without which the product would lose much of its value.[21] Another example is the tire and automobile industries.

The importance of these stakeholders varies by industry. For example, environmental groups in Maine, Michigan, Oregon, and Iowa successfully fought to pass bills outlawing dis-posable bottles and cans, and thus deposits for most drink containers are now required. This effectively raised costs across the board, with the most impact on the marginal producers who could not internally absorb all of these costs. The traditionally strong power of national unions in the U.S. auto and railroad industries has effectively raised costs throughout these industries but are of little importance in computer software.

INDUSTRY EVOLUTION

Over time most industries evolve through a series of stages from growth through maturity to eventual decline. The strength of each of the six forces mentioned earlier varies according to the stage of industry evolution. The industry life cycle is useful for explaining and predicting trends among the six forces driving industry competition. For example, when an industry is new, people often buy the product regardless of price because it fulfills a unique need. This is probably a **fragmented industry**—no firm has large market share and each firm serves only a small piece of the total market in competition with others (for example, Chinese restaurants and cleaning services). As new competitors enter the industry, prices drop as a result of com-petition. Companies use the experience curve (to be discussed in Chapter 4) and economies of scale to reduce costs faster than the competition. Companies integrate to reduce costs even further by acquiring their suppliers and distributors. Competitors try to differentiate their products from one another's in order to avoid the fierce price competition common to a maturing industry.

By the time an industry enters maturity, products tend to become more like commodities. This is now a **consolidated industry**—dominated by a few large firms, each of which struggles to differentiate its products from the competition. As buyers become more sophisticated over time, purchasing decisions are based on better information. Price becomes a dominant con-cern, given a minimum level of quality and features. One example of this trend is the video-cassette recorder industry. By the 1990s, VCRs had reached the point where there were few major differences among them. Consumers realized that because slight improvements cost significantly more money, it made little sense to pay more than the minimum for a VCR. The same is true of gasoline.

As an industry moves through maturity toward possible decline, its products' growth rate of sales slows and may even begin to decrease. To the extent that exit barriers are low, firms will begin converting their facilities to alternate uses or will sell them to another firm. The industry tends to consolidate around fewer but larger competitors. In the case of the U.S. major home appliance industry, the industry changed from being a fragmented industry (pure competition) composed of hundreds of appliance manufacturers in the industry's early years to a consolidated industry (mature oligopoly) composed of five companies controlling over 98% of U.S. appliance sales. A similar consolidation is occurring now in European major home appliances.

CATEGORIZING INTERNATIONAL INDUSTRIES

According to Porter, world industries vary on a continuum from multidomestic to global (see **Figure 3–4**).[22] **Multidomestic industries** are specific to each country or group of countries. This type of international industry is a collection of essentially domestic industries, like retail-

Figure 3–4

Continuum of International Industries

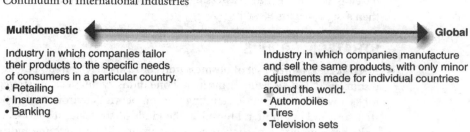

ing and insurance. The activities in a subsidiary of a multinational corporation (MNC) in this type of industry are essentially independent of the activities of the MNC's subsidiaries in other countries. Within each country, it has a manufacturing facility to produce goods for sale within that country. The MNC is thus able to tailor its products or services to the very specific needs of consumers in a particular country or group of countries having similar societal environments.

Global industries, in contrast, operate worldwide, with MNCs making only small adjustments for country-specific circumstances. A global industry is one in which an MNC's activities in one country are significantly affected by its activities in other countries. MNCs produce products or services in various locations throughout the world and sell them, making only minor adjustments for specific country requirements. Examples of global industries are commercial aircraft, television sets, semiconductors, copiers, automobiles, watches, and tires. The largest industrial corporations in the world in terms of dollar sales are, for the most part, multinational corporations operating in global industries.

The factors that tend to determine whether an industry will be primarily multidomestic or primarily global are:

1. *Pressure for coordination* within the multinational corporations operating in that industry
2. *Pressure for local responsiveness* on the part of individual country markets

To the extent that the pressure for coordination is strong and the pressure for local responsiveness is weak for multinational corporations within a particular industry, that industry will tend to become global. In contrast, when the pressure for local responsiveness is strong and the pressure for coordination is weak for multinational corporations in an industry, that industry will tend to be multidomestic. Between these two extremes lie a number of industries with varying characteristics of both multidomestic and global industries. The dynamic tension between these two factors is contained in the phrase: *Think globally, but act locally*.

INTERNATIONAL RISK ASSESSMENT

Some firms, such as American Can Company and Mitsubishi Trading Company, develop elaborate information networks and computerized systems to evaluate and rank investment risks. Small companies can hire outside consultants such as Chicago's Associated Consultants International or Boston's Arthur D. Little, Inc., to provide political-risk assessments. Among the many systems that exist to assess political and economic risks are the Political System Stability Index, the Business Environment Risk Index, Business International's Country Assessment Service, and Frost and Sullivan's World Political Risk Forecasts.[23] Business International provides subscribers with continuously updated information on conditions in 63 countries. A Boston company called International Strategies offers an Export Hotline (800 USA-XPORT) that faxes information to callers for only the cost of the call. (Contact

⟨ExportHotline.com⟩ for a free membership.) Regardless of the source of data, a firm must develop its own method of assessing risk. It must decide on its most important risk factors and then assign weights to each.

STRATEGIC GROUPS

A **strategic group** is a set of business units or firms that "pursue similar strategies with similar resources."[24] Categorizing firms in any one industry into a set of strategic groups is very useful as a way of better understanding the competitive environment.[25] Because a corporation's structure and culture tend to reflect the kinds of strategies it follows, companies or business units belonging to a particular strategic group within the same industry tend to be strong rivals and tend to be more similar to each other than to competitors in other strategic groups within the same industry.

For example, although McDonald's and Olive Garden are a part of the same restaurant industry, they have different missions, objectives, and strategies, and thus belong to different strategic groups. They generally have very little in common and pay little attention to each other when planning competitive actions. Burger King and Hardee's, however, have a great deal in common with McDonald's in terms of their similar strategy of producing a high volume of low-priced meals targeted for sale to the average family. Consequently they are strong rivals and are organized to operate similarly.

Strategic groups in a particular industry can be mapped by plotting the market positions of industry competitors on a two-dimensional graph using two strategic variables as the vertical and horizontal axes. (See **Figure 3–5**.)

1. Select two broad characteristics, such as price and menu, that differentiate the companies in an industry from one another.

2. Plot the firms using these two characteristics as the dimensions.

3. Draw a circle around those companies that are closest to one another as one strategic group, varying the size of the circle in proportion to the group's share of total industry sales. (You could also name each strategic group in the restaurant industry with an identifying title, such as quick fast food or buffet style service.)

Other dimensions, such as quality, service, location, or degree of vertical integration, can also be used in additional graphs of the restaurant industry to gain a better understanding of how the various firms in the industry compete. Keep in mind, however, that when choosing the two dimensions, they should not be highly correlated; otherwise, the circles on the map will simply lie along the diagonal, providing very little new information other than the obvious.

STRATEGIC TYPES

In analyzing the level of competitive intensity within a particular industry or strategic group, it is useful to characterize the various competitors for predictive purposes. A **strategic type** is a category of firms based on a common strategic orientation and a combination of structure, culture, and processes consistent with that strategy. According to Miles and Snow, competing firms within a single industry can be categorized on the basis of their general strategic orientation into one of four basic types.[26] This distinction helps explain why companies facing similar situations behave differently and why they continue to do so over a long period of time. These general types have the following characteristics:

■ **Defenders** are companies with a limited product line that *focus on improving the efficiency of their existing operations*. This cost orientation makes them unlikely to innovate in new areas.

Figure 3–5

Mapping Strategic Groups in the U.S. Restaurant Chain Industry

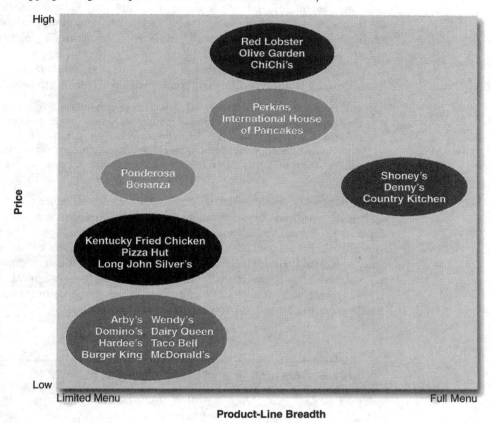

- **Prospectors** are companies with fairly broad product lines that *focus on product innovation and market opportunities*. This sales orientation makes them somewhat inefficient. They tend to emphasize creativity over efficiency.

- **Analyzers** are corporations that *operate in at least two different product–market areas*, one stable and one variable. In the stable areas, efficiency is emphasized. In the variable areas, innovation is emphasized.

- **Reactors** are corporations that *lack a consistent strategy–structure–culture relationship*. Their (often ineffective) responses to environmental pressures tend to be piecemeal strategic changes.

Dividing the competition into these four categories enables the strategic manager not only to monitor the effectiveness of certain strategic orientations, but also to develop scenarios of future industry developments (discussed later in this chapter).

HYPERCOMPETITION

Most industries today are facing an ever-increasing level of environmental uncertainty. They are becoming more complex and more dynamic. Industries that used to be multidomestic are becoming global. New flexible, aggressive, innovative competitors are moving into established markets to erode rapidly the advantages of large previously dominant firms. Distribution channels vary from country to country and are being altered daily through the use of sophisticated information systems. Closer relationships with suppliers are being forged to reduce costs, increase quality, and gain access to new technology. Companies learn to quickly imitate the successful strategies of market leaders, and it becomes harder to sustain any competitive advantage for very long. Consequently, the level of competitive intensity is increasing in most industries.

Richard D'Aveni contends that as this type of environmental turbulence reaches more industries, competition becomes **hypercompetition**. According to D'Aveni:

> In hypercompetition the frequency, boldness, and aggressiveness of dynamic movement by the players accelerates to create a condition of constant disequilibrium and change. Market stability is threatened by short product life cycles, short product design cycles, new technologies, frequent entry by unexpected outsiders, repositioning by incumbents, and tactical redefinitions of market boundaries as diverse industries merge. In other words, environments escalate toward higher and higher levels of uncertainty, dynamism, heterogeneity of the players and hostility.[27]

In hypercompetitive industries such as computers, competitive advantage comes from an up-to-date knowledge of environmental trends and competitive activity coupled with a willingness to risk a current advantage for a possible new advantage. Companies must be willing to **cannibalize** their own products (replacing popular products before competitors do so) in order to sustain their competitive advantage. As a result, industry or competitive intelligence has never been more important. See the boxed example to learn how Microsoft is operating in the hypercompetitive industry of computer software. (Hypercompetition is discussed in more detail in **Chapter 5.**)

Microsoft Operates in a Hypercompetitive Industry

Microsoft is a hypercompetitive firm operating in a hypercompetitive industry. It has used its dominance in operating systems (DOS and Windows) to move into a very strong position in application programs like word processing and spreadsheets (Word and Excel). Even though Microsoft held 90% of the market for personal computer operating systems in 1992, it still invested millions in developing the next generation—Windows 95 and Windows NT. Instead of trying to protect its advantage in the profitable DOS operating system, Microsoft actively sought to replace DOS with various versions of Windows. Before hypercompetition, most experts argued against *cannibalization* of a company's own product line because it destroys a very profitable product instead of harvesting it like a "cash cow." According to this line of thought, a company would be better off defending its older products. New products would be introduced only if it could be proven that they would not take sales away from current products. Microsoft was one of the first companies to disprove this argument against cannibalization.

Bill Gates, Microsoft's Cofounder, Chairman, and CEO, realized that if his company didn't replace its own DOS product line with a better product, someone else would (such as IBM with OS/2 Warp). He knew that success in the software industry depends not so much on company size but on moving aggressively to the next competitive advantage before a competitor does. "This is a hypercompetitive market," explained Gates. "Scale is not all positive in this business. Cleverness is the position in this business." By 2000, Microsoft still controlled over 90% of operating systems software and had achieved a dominant position in applications software as well.

Source: R. A. D'Aveni, *Hypercompetition* (New York: Free Press, 1994), p. 2.

Table 3–3   Industry Matrix

Key Success Factors	Weight	Company A Rating	Company A Weighted Score	Company B Rating	Company B Weighted Score
1	2	3	4	5	6
Total	1.00				

Source: T. L. Wheelen and J. D. Hunger, "Industry Matrix." Copyright © 2001 by Wheelen and Hunger Associates. Reprinted by permission.

USING KEY SUCCESS FACTORS TO CREATE AN INDUSTRY MATRIX

Within any industry there usually are certain variables—key success factors—that a company's management must understand in order to be successful. **Key success factors** are those variables that can affect significantly the overall competitive positions of all companies within any particular industry. They typically vary from industry to industry and are crucial to determining a company's ability to succeed within that industry. They are usually determined by the economic and technological characteristics of the industry and by the competitive weapons on which the firms in the industry have built their strategies.[28] For example, in the major home appliance industry, a firm must achieve low costs, typically by building large manufacturing facilities dedicated to making multiple versions of one type of appliance, such as washing machines. Since 60% of major home appliances in the United States are sold through "power retailers" like Sears and Best Buy, a firm must have a strong presence in the mass merchandiser distribution channel. It must offer a full line of appliances and provide a just-in-time delivery system to keep store inventory and ordering costs to a minimum. Because the consumer expects reliability and durability in an appliance, a firm must have excellent process R&D. Any appliance manufacturer that is unable to deal successfully with these key success factors will not long survive in the U.S. market.

Key success factors are different from strategic factors. *Key success factors* deal with an entire industry; whereas, *strategic factors* deal with a particular company.

An **industry matrix** summarizes the key success factors within a particular industry. As shown in **Table 3–3**, the matrix gives a weight for each factor based on how important that factor is for success within the industry. The matrix also specifies how well various competitors in the industry are responding to each factor. To generate an industry matrix using two industry competitors (called A and B), complete the following steps for the industry being analyzed:

1. In **Column 1** (Key Success Factors) list the 8 to 10 factors that appear to determine current and expected success in the industry.

2. In **Column 2** (Weight) assign a weight to each factor from **1.0** (Most Important) to **0.0** (Not Important) based on that factor's probable impact on the overall industry's current and future success. (**All weights must sum to 1.0 regardless of the number of strategic factors.**)

3. In **Column 3** (Company A Rating) examine a particular company within the industry—for example, Company A. Assign a rating to each factor from **5.0** (Outstanding) to **1.0** (Poor) based on Company A's current response to that particular factor. Each rating is a judgment regarding how well that company is currently dealing with each key success factor.

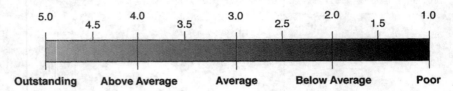

4. In **Column 4** (Company A Weighted Score) multiply the weight in **Column 2** for each factor times its rating in **Column 3** to obtain that factor's weighted score for Company A. This results in a weighted score for each key success factor ranging from **5.0** (Outstanding) to **1.0** (Poor) with **3.0** as the average.

5. In **Column 5** (Company B Rating) examine a second company within the industry—in this case, Company B. Assign a rating to each key success factor from **5.0** (Outstanding) to **1.0** (Poor) based on Company B's current response to each particular factor.

6. In **Column 6** (Company B Weighted Score) multiply the weight in **Column 2** for each factor times its rating in **Column 5** to obtain that factor's weighted score for Company B.

Finally, add the weighted scores for all the factors in **Columns 4** and **6** to determine the total weighted scores for companies A and B. The total weighted score indicates how well each company is responding to current and expected key success factors in the industry's environment. The industry matrix can be expanded to include all the major competitors within an industry simply by adding two additional columns for each additional competitor.

3.3 Competitive Intelligence

Much external environmental scanning is done on an informal and individual basis. Information is obtained from a variety of sources—suppliers, customers, industry publications, employees, industry experts, industry conferences, and the Internet.[29] For example, scientists and engineers working in a firm's R&D lab can learn about new products and competitors' ideas at professional meetings; someone from the purchasing department, speaking with supplier-representatives' personnel, may also uncover valuable bits of information about a competitor. A study of product innovation found that 77% of all product innovations in the scientific instruments and 67% in semiconductors and printed circuit boards were initiated by the customer in the form of inquiries and complaints.[30] In these industries, the sales force and service departments must be especially vigilant.

Competitive intelligence is a formal program of gathering information on a company's competitors. Until recently, few U.S. corporations had fully developed competitive intelligence programs. In contrast, all Japanese corporations involved in international business and most large European companies have active intelligence programs.[31] This situation is changing, however. Competitive intelligence is now one of the fastest growing fields within strategic management.[32] At General Mills, for example, all employees have been trained to recognize and tap sources of competitive information. Janitors no longer simply place orders with suppliers of cleaning materials, they also ask about relevant practices at competing firms! A recent survey of large U.S. corporations revealed that 78% of them reported competitive intelligence activities within their firm.[33]

Most corporations rely on outside organizations to provide them with environmental data. Firms such as A. C. Nielsen Co. provide subscribers with bimonthly data on brand share, retail prices, percentages of stores stocking an item, and percentages of stock-out stores. Strategists can use this data to spot regional and national trends as well as to assess market share. Information on market conditions, government regulations, competitors, and new products can be bought from "information brokers" such as Marketresearch.com and Finsbury Data Services. Company and industry profiles are generally available from the Hoover's Online site on the Internet ⟨www.hoovers.com⟩. Many business corporations have established their own in-house libraries and computerized information systems to deal with the growing mass of available information.

Some companies, however, choose to use industrial espionage or other intelligence-gathering techniques to get their information straight from their competitors. According to the American Society of Industrial Security, there were more than 1,100 documented incidents of illegal economic espionage in 1997 alone.[34] Using current or former competitors' employees and by using private contractors, some firms attempt to steal trade secrets, technology, business plans, and pricing strategies. For example, Avon Products hired private investigators to retrieve from a public dumpster documents (some of them shredded) that Mary Kay Corporation had thrown away. Even Procter & Gamble, which defends itself like a fortress from information leaks, is vulnerable. A competitor was able to learn the precise launch date of a concentrated laundry detergent in Europe when one of its people visited the factory where machinery was being made. Simply asking a few questions about what a certain machine did, whom it was for, and when it would be delivered was all that was necessary.

To combat the increasing theft of company secrets, the U.S. government passed the Economic Espionage Act in 1996. The law makes it illegal (with fines up to $5 million and 10 years in jail) to steal any material that a business has taken "reasonable efforts" to keep secret and if the material derives its value from not being known.[35] The Society of Competitive Intelligence Professionals ⟨www.scip.org⟩ urges strategists to stay within the law and to act ethically when searching for information. The society states that illegal activities are foolish because the vast majority of worthwhile competitive intelligence is available publicly via annual reports, Web sites, and public libraries.

3.4 Forecasting

Environmental scanning provides reasonably hard data on the present situation and current trends, but intuition and luck are needed to predict accurately if these trends will continue. The resulting forecasts are, however, usually based on a set of assumptions that may or may not be valid.

DANGER OF ASSUMPTIONS

Faulty underlying assumptions are the most frequent cause of forecasting errors. Nevertheless many managers who formulate and implement strategic plans rarely consider that their success is based on a series of assumptions. Many long-range plans are simply based on projections of the current situation.

One example of what can happen when a corporate strategy rests on the very questionable assumption that the future will simply be an extension of the present is that of Tupperware, the company that originated air-tight, easy-to-use plastic food storage containers. Much of the company's success had been based on Tupperware parties in the 1950s when housewives gathered in each other's homes to socialize and play games while the local Tupperware lady demonstrated and sold new products. Management assumed during the following decades that Tupperware parties would continue being an excellent distribution channel. Its faith in this assumption blinded it to information about America's changing lifestyle (two-career families) and its likely impact on sales. Even in the 1990s, when Tupperware executives realized that their sales forecasts were no longer justified, they were unable to improve their forecasting techniques until they changed their assumption that the best way to sell Tupperware was at a Tupperware party. Consequently, Rubbermaid and other competitors, who chose to market their containers in grocery and discount stores continued to grow at the expense of Tupperware.[36]

USEFUL FORECASTING TECHNIQUES

Various techniques are used to forecast future situations. Each has its proponents and critics. A study of nearly 500 of the world's largest corporations revealed trend **extrapolation** to be the most widely practiced form of forecasting—over 70% use this technique either occasionally or frequently.[37] Simply stated, extrapolation is the extension of present trends into the future. It rests on the assumption that the world is reasonably consistent and changes slowly in the short run. Time-series methods are approaches of this type; they attempt to carry a series of historical events forward into the future. The basic problem with extrapolation is that a historical trend is based on a series of patterns or relationships among so many different variables that a change in any one can drastically alter the future direction of the trend. As a rule of thumb, the further back into the past you can find relevant data supporting the trend, the more confidence you can have in the prediction.

Brainstorming, expert opinion, and statistical modeling are also very popular forecasting techniques. **Brainstorming** is a nonquantitative approach requiring simply the presence of people with some knowledge of the situation to be predicted. The basic ground rule is to propose ideas without first mentally screening them. No criticism is allowed. Ideas tend to build on previous ideas until a consensus is reached. This is a good technique to use with operating managers who have more faith in "gut feel" than in more quantitative "number crunching" techniques. **Expert opinion** is a nonquantitative technique in which experts in a particular area attempt to forecast likely developments. This type of forecast is based on the ability of a knowledgeable person(s) to construct probable future developments based on the interaction of key variables. One application is the **Delphi technique** in which separated experts independently assess the likelihoods of specified events. These assessments are combined and sent back to each expert for fine tuning until an agreement is reached. **Statistical modeling** is a quantitative technique that attempts to discover causal or at least explanatory factors that link two or more time series together. Examples of statistical modeling are regression analysis and other econometric methods. Although very useful for grasping historic trends, statistical modeling, like trend extrapolation, is based on historical data. As the patterns of relationships change, the accuracy of the forecast deteriorates. Other forecasting techniques, such as *cross-impact analysis (CIA)* and *trend-impact analysis (TIA)*, have not established themselves successfully as regularly employed tools.

Scenario writing appears to be the most widely used forecasting technique after trend extrapolation. Originated by Royal Dutch Shell, scenarios are focused descriptions of different likely futures presented in a narrative fashion. The scenario thus may be merely a written description of some future state, in terms of key variables and issues, or it may be generated in combination with other forecasting techniques.

An **industry scenario** is a forecasted description of a particular industry's likely future. Such a scenario is developed by analyzing the probable impact of future societal forces on key groups in a particular industry. The process may operate as follows.[38]

1. Examine possible shifts in the societal variables globally.

2. Identify uncertainties in each of the six forces of the task environment (for example, potential entrants, competitors, likely substitutes, buyers, suppliers, and other key stakeholders).

3. Make a range of plausible assumptions about future trends.

4. Combine assumptions about individual trends into internally consistent scenarios.

5. Analyze the industry situation that would prevail under each scenario.

6. Determine the sources of competitive advantage under each scenario.

7. Predict competitors' behavior under each scenario.

8. Select the scenarios that are either most likely to occur or most likely to have a strong impact on the future of the company. Use these scenarios in strategy formulation.

3.5 Synthesis of External Factors—EFAS

After strategic managers have scanned the societal and task environments and identified a number of likely external factors for their particular corporation, they may want to refine their analysis of these factors using a form such as that given in **Table 3–4**. The **EFAS** (External Factors Analysis Summary) **Table** is one way to organize the external factors into the generally accepted categories of opportunities and threats as well as to analyze how well a particular company's management (rating) is responding to these specific factors in light of the perceived importance (weight) of these factors to the company. To generate an EFAS Table for the company being analyzed, complete the following steps:

- In **Column 1** (External Factors), list the 8 to 10 most important opportunities and threats facing the company.

- In **Column 2** (Weight), assign a weight to each factor from **1.0** (Most Important) to **0.0** (Not Important) based on that factor's probable impact on a particular company's current strategic position. The higher the weight, the more important is this factor to the current and future success of the company. (**All weights must sum to 1.0 regardless of the number of factors.**)

- In **Column 3** (Rating), assign a rating to each factor from **5.0** (Outstanding) to **1.0** (Poor) based on management's current response to that particular factor. Each rating is a judgment on how well the company's management is currently dealing with each specific external factor.

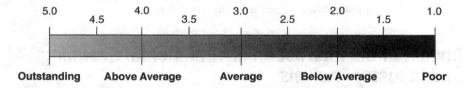

| 5.0 | 4.5 | 4.0 | 3.5 | 3.0 | 2.5 | 2.0 | 1.5 | 1.0 |

Outstanding   Above Average   Average   Below Average   Poor

- In **Column 4** (Weighted Score), multiply the weight in **Column 2** for each factor times its rating in **Column 3** to obtain each factor's weighted score. This results in a weighted score for each factor ranging from **5.0** (Outstanding) to **1.0** (Poor) with **3.0** as average.

- In **Column 5** (Comments), note why a particular factor was selected and/or how its weight and rating were estimated.

Finally, add the individual weighted scores for all the external factors in **Column 4** to determine the total weighted score for that particular company. The total weighted **score** indicates how well a particular company is responding to current and expected factors in its external environment. The score can be used to compare that firm to other firms in its industry. The total weighted score for an average firm in an industry is always 3.0.

Table 3-4 External Factor Analysis Summary (EFAS Table): Maytag as Example

External Factors	Weight	Rating	Weighted Score	Comments
	1	2	3	4	5
Opportunities				
· Economic integration of European Community	.20	4.1	.82	Acquisition of Hoover
· Demographics favor quality appliances	.10	5.0	.50	Maytag quality
· Economic development of Asia	.05	1.0	.05	Low Maytag presence
· Opening of Eastern Europe	.05	2.0	.10	Will take time
· Trend to "Super Stores"	.10	1.8	.18	Maytag weak in this channel
Threats				
· Increasing government regulations	.10	4.3	.43	Well positioned
· Strong U.S. competition	.10	4.0	.40	Well positioned
· Whirlpool and Electrolux strong globally	.15	3.0	.45	Hoover weak globally
· New product advances	.05	1.2	.06	Questionable
· Japanese appliance companies	.10	1.6	.16	Only Asian presence is Australia
Total Scores	**1.00**		**3.15**	

Notes:
1. List opportunities and threats (8–10) in column 1.
2. Weight each factor from 1.0 (Most Important) to 0.0 (Not Important) in Column 2 based on that factor's probable impact on the company's strategic position. **The total weights must sum to 1.00.**
3. Rate each factor from 5.0 (Outstanding) to 1.0 (Poor) in Column 3 based on the company's response to that factor.
4. Multiply each factor's weight times its rating to obtain each factor's weighted score in Column 4.
5. Use Column 5 (comments) for rationale used for each factor.
6. Add the individual weighted scores to obtain the total weighted score for the company in Column 4. This tells how well the company is responding to the strategic factors in its external environment.

Source: T. L. Wheelen and J. D. Hunger, "External Factors Analysis Summary (EFAS)." Copyright © 1991 by Wheelen and Hunger Associates. Reprinted by permission.

As an example of this procedure, **Table 3–4** includes a number of external factors for Maytag Corporation with corresponding weights, ratings, and weighted scores provided. This table is appropriate for 1995 before Maytag sold its European and Australian operations. Note that Maytag's total weight is 3.15, meaning that the corporation was slightly above average in the major home appliance industry at that time.

3.6 Impact of the Internet on Environmental Scanning and Industry Analysis

The Internet has changed the way the strategist engages in environmental scanning. It provides the quickest means to obtain data on almost any subject. A recent joint study of 77 companies by the American Productivity & Quality Center and the Society of Competitive Intelligence Professionals reveals that 73% of the firms ranked the Internet as being used to a "great" or "very great" extent. Other mentioned sources of information were competitor offerings & products (66%), industry experts (62%), personal industry contacts (60%), online databases (56%), market research (55%), and the sales force (54%).[39] Although the scope and quality of Internet information is increasing geometrically, it is also littered with "noise," misinformation, and utter nonsense. For example, a number of corporate Web sites are sending unwanted guests to specially constructed bogus Web sites![40]

Unlike the library, the Internet lacks the tight bibliographic control standards that exist in the print world. There is no ISBN or Dewey Decimal System to identify, search, and retrieve a document. Many Web documents lack the name of the author and the date of publication. A Web page providing useful information may be accessible on the Web one day and gone the next! Unhappy ex-employees, far-out environmentalists, and prank-prone hackers create Web sites to attack and discredit an otherwise reputable corporation. Rumors with no basis in fact are spread via chat rooms and personal Web sites. This creates a serious problem for the researcher. How can one evaluate the information found on the Internet?

A basic rule in intelligence gathering is that before a piece of information can be used in any report or briefing, it must first be evaluated in two ways. *First, the source of the information should be judged in terms of its truthfulness and reliability.* How trustworthy is the source? How well can a researcher rely upon it for truthful and correct information? One approach is to rank the reliability of the source on a scale from A (extremely reliable), B (reliable), C (unknown reliability), D (probably unreliable), to E (very questionable reliability). The reliability of a source can be judged on the basis of the author's credentials, the organization sponsoring the information, and past performance, among other factors. *Second, the information or data should be judged in terms of its likelihood of being correct.* The correctness of the data may be ranked on a scale from 1 (correct), 2 (probably correct), 3 (unknown), 4 (doubtful), to 5 (extremely doubtful). The correctness of a piece of data or information can be judged on the basis of its agreement with other bits of separately obtained information or with a general trend supported by previous data. For every piece of information found on the Internet, list not only the Web address of the Web page, but also the evaluation of the information from A1 (good stuff) to E5 (bad doodoo). Information found through library research in sources such as *Moody's Industrials*, *Standard & Poor's*, or *Value Line* can generally be evaluated as having a reliability of A. The correctness of the data can still range anywhere from 1 to 5, but in most instances is likely to be either 1 or 2, but probably no worse than 3 or 4. Other sources may be less reliable.

Sites such as those sponsored by the U.S. Securities and Exchange Commission (www.sec.gov) or Hoovers Online (www.hoovers.com) are extremely reliable. Company sponsored Web sites are generally reliable but are not the place to go for trade secrets, strategic plans, or proprietary information. For one thing, many firms think of their Web sites primarily in terms of marketing, and they provide little data aside from product descriptions and distribution channels. Other companies provide their latest financial statements and links to other useful Web sites. Nevertheless, some companies in very competitive industries may install software on their Web site to ascertain a visitor's Web address. Visitors from a competitor's domain name are thus screened before they are allowed to access certain Web sites. They may not be allowed beyond the product information page or they may be sent to a bogus Web site containing misinformation. Cisco Systems, for example, uses its Web site to send visitors from other high-tech firms to a special Web page asking if they would like to apply for a job at Cisco!

Time searching the Internet can be saved by using search engines—Web sites that search the Internet for names and products typed in by the user. The search engines most used by competitive intelligence professionals are AltaVista (50%), Yahoo! (25%), and Lycos (15%). Others are WebCrawler (7.5%), Switchboard (7.5%), Infoseek (5%), and Metacrawler (5%).[41]

Although information about publicly held corporations is widely available, it is much harder to obtain information on privately held companies. For a comparison of the type of information generally available on publicly and privately held companies, see the ▓ **Internet Issue** feature for competitor information available on the Internet.

Internet Issue

Competitor Information Available on the Internet

Type of Information	Likelihood of Finding Data on the Net for Publicly Held Company	Likelihood of Finding Data on the Net for Privately Held Company
Total Annual Sales	Very high	Very low
Sales and Profitability by Product Line or Distribution Channel	Very low	Very low
Market Sizes in Segments of Interest	Depends on the market: High for large companies, low for small "niche" firms	Same as for publicly held
Trends in Marketing, Technology, Distribution	Same as above	Same as for publicly held
Prices, Including the Lowest Prices to Best Customers	Very low	Very low
Marketing Strategy	Some information available from trade articles and analyst reports, but incomplete and dated	Even less than for publicly held
Sales and Technical Literature on Products	Strong likelihood, but often incomplete; less chance for detailed technical information	Even less than for publicly held
Number of Employees Working on Certain Products or in Particular Departments	Highly unlikely	Highly unlikely
Compensation Levels	Top management generally available; others unlikely	Will not be found
Customer Opinions Regarding Strengths and Weaknesses	Available from trade articles and industry reports; at best, may be incomplete and dated	Less likely than for publicly held
Feedback on Firm's Own Products and Services	Will not be found; look for independent user chat rooms	Same as for publicly held

Source: Adapted from C. Klein, "Overcoming 'Net Disease,'" *Competitive Intelligence Magazine* (July–September 1999), p. 31.

Projections for the 21st Century

- From 1994 to 2010, the number of people living in poverty will increase from 3.7 billion to 3.9 billion.
- From 1994 to 2010, the average number of children per woman will decrease from 3.2 to 2.7.[42]

Discussion Questions

1. Discuss how a development in a corporation's societal environment can affect the corporation through its task environment.

2. According to Porter, what determines the level of competitive intensity in an industry?

3. According to Porter's discussion of industry analysis, is Pepsi-Cola a substitute for Coca-Cola?

4. How can a decision maker identify strategic factors in the corporation's external international environment?

5. Compare and contrast trend extrapolation with the writing of scenarios as forecasting techniques.

Strategic Practice Exercise

What are the forces driving industry competition in the airline industry? Read the following paragraphs. Using Porter's approach to industry analysis, evaluate each of the six forces to ascertain what drives the level of competitive intensity in this industry.

In recent years, the airline industry has become increasingly competitive. Since being deregulated during the 1970s in the United States, long established airlines such as Pan American and Eastern have gone out of business as new upstarts like Midwest Express and Southwest have successfully entered the market. It appeared that almost anyone could buy a few used planes to serve the smaller cities that the larger airlines no longer wanted to serve. These low-cost, small-capacity commuter planes were able to make healthy profits in these markets where it was too expensive to land large jets. Rail and bus transportation either did not exist or was undesirable in many locations. Eventually the low-cost local commuter airlines expanded service to major cities and grabbed market share from the majors by offering cheaper fares with no-frills service. In order to be competitive with these lower cost upstarts, United Airlines and Northwest Airlines offered stock in the company and seats on the Board of Directors to their unionized employees in exchange for wage and benefit reductions. Delta and American Airlines, among other major carriers, reduced their costs by instituting a cap on travel agent commissions. Travel agencies were livid at this cut in their livelihood, but they needed the airlines' business in order to offer customers a total travel package.

Globally it seemed as though every nation had to have its own airline for national prestige. These state-owned airlines were expensive, but the governments subsidized them with money and supporting regulations. For example, a foreign airline was normally allowed to fly only into one of a country's airports, forcing travelers to switch to the national airline to go to other cities. During the 1980s and 1990s, however, many countries began privatizing their airlines as governments tried to improve their budgets. To be viable in an increasingly global industry, national or regional airlines were forced to form alliances and even purchase an airline in another country or region. For example, the Dutch KLM Airline acquired half interest in the U.S Northwest Airlines in order to obtain not only U.S. destinations, but also Northwest's Asian travel routes, thus making it one of the few global airlines.

Costs were still relatively high for all of the world's major airlines because of the high cost of new airplanes. Just one new jet plane costs anywhere from $25 million to $100 million. By 2001, only two airplane manufacturers provided almost all of the large commercial airliners: Boeing and Airbus. Major airlines were forced to purchase new planes because they were more fuel efficient, safer, and easier to maintain. Airlines that chose to stay with an older fleet of planes had to deal with higher fuel and maintenance costs—factors that often made it cheaper to buy new planes.

1. Evaluate each of the forces currently driving competition in the airline industry:

Threat of New Entrants	High, Medium, or Low?	_____
Rivalry Among Existing Firms	High, Medium, or Low?	_____
Threat of Substitutes	High, Medium, or Low?	_____
Bargaining Power of Buyers/Distributors	High, Medium, or Low?	_____
Bargaining Power of Suppliers	High, Medium, or Low?	_____
Relative Power of Other Stakeholders	High, Medium, or Low?	_____

   Such as_____

2. Which of these forces is changing? What will this mean to the overall level of competitive intensity in the airline industry in the future? Would you invest or look for a job in this industry?

Key Terms

brainstorming (p. 72)
cannibalize (p. 68)
competitive intelligence (p. 70)
complementor (p. 64)
consolidated industry (p. 64)
Delphi technique (p. 72)
EFAS Table (p. 73)
entry barrier (p. 61)
environmental scanning (p. 52)
environmental uncertainty (p. 52)
exit barriers (p. 62)
expert opinion (p. 72)
external strategic factors (p. 60)
extrapolation (p. 72)

fragmented industry (p. 64)
global industry (p. 65)
hypercompetition (p. 68)
industry (p. 60)
industry analysis (p. 53)
industry matrix (p. 69)
industry scenario (p. 72)
issues priority matrix (p. 59)
key success factors (p. 69)
multidomestic industry (p. 64)
multinational corporation (MNC) (p. 56)
new entrants (p. 61)

purchasing power parity (PPP) (p. 58)
repatriation of profits (p. 53)
scenario writing (p. 72)
societal environment (p. 52)
statistical modeling (p. 72)
strategic group (p. 66)
strategic myopia (p. 59)
strategic type (p. 66)
substitute products (p. 62)
task environment (p. 53)
Triad (p. 56)
trigger point (p. 58)

Notes

1. D. Phillips, "Special Delivery," *Entrepreneur* (September 1996), pp. 98–100; B. Saporito, "What's for Dinner?" *Fortune* (May 15, 1995), pp. 50–64.
2. J. B. Thomas, S. M. Clark, and D. A. Gioia, "Strategic Sensemaking and Organizational Performance: Linkages Among Scanning, Interpretation, Action, Outcomes," *Academy of Management Journal* (April 1993), pp. 239–270; J. A. Smith, "Strategies for Start-Ups," *Long Range Planning* (December 1998), pp. 857–872.
3. P. Lasserre and J. Probert, "Competing on the Pacific Rim: High Risks and High Returns," *Long Range Planning* (April 1994), pp. 12–35.
4. W. E. Halal, "The Top 10 Emerging Technologies," *Special Report* (World Future Society, 2000).
5. F. Dobbin and T. J. Dowd, "How Policy Shapes Competition: Early Railroad Foundings in Massachusetts," *Administrative Science Quarterly* (September 1997), pp. 501–529.
6. A. Shleifer and R. W. Viskny, "Takeovers in the 1960s and the 1980s: Evidence and Implications," in *Fundamental Issues in Strategy: A Research Agenda*, edited by R. P. Rumelt, D. E. Schendel, and D. J. Teece (Boston: Harvard Business School Press, 1994), pp. 403–418.
7. J. Wyatt, "Playing the Woofie Card," *Fortune* (February 6, 1995), pp. 130–132.
8. J. Greco, "Meet Generation Y," *Forecast* (May/June, 1996), pp. 48–54; J. Fletcher, "A Generation Asks: 'Can the Boom Last?'" *Wall Street Journal* (June 14, 1996), p. B10.
9. "Alone in America," *Futurist* (September–October 1995), pp. 56–57.
10. "Population Growth Slowing as Nation Ages," (Ames, IA) *Daily Tribune* (March 14, 1996), p. A7.
11. L. M. Grossman, "After Demographic Shift, Atlanta Mall Restyles Itself as Black Shopping Center," *Wall Street Journal* (February 26, 1992), p. B1.
12. J. Naisbitt, *Megatrends Asia* (New York: Simon & Schuster, 1996), p. 79.
13. K. Ohmae, "The Triad World View," *Journal of Business Strategy* (Spring 1987), pp. 8–19.
14. B. K. Boyd and J. Fulk, "Executive Scanning and Perceived Uncertainty: A Multidimensional Model," *Journal of Management*, Vol. 22, No. 1 (1996), pp. 1–21.

15. R. A. Bettis and C. K. Prahalad, "The Dominant Logic: Retrospective and Extension," *Strategic Management Journal* (January 1995), pp. 5–14; J. M. Stofford and C. W. F. Baden-Fuller, "Creating Corporate Entrepreneurship," *Strategic Management Journal* (September 1994), pp. 521–536; J. M. Beyer, P. Chattopadhyay, E. George, W. H. Glick, D. Pugliese, "The Selective Perception of Managers Revisited," *Academy of Management Journal* (June 1997), pp. 716–737.
16. H. I. Ansoff, "Strategic Management in a Historical Perspective," in *International Review of Strategic Management*, Vol. 2, No. 1 (1991), edited by D. E. Hussey (Chichester, England: Wiley, 1991), p. 61.
17. M. E. Porter, *Competitive Strategy* (New York: Free Press, 1980), p. 3.
18. This summary of the forces driving competitive intensity is taken from Porter, *Competitive Strategy*, pp. 7–29.
19. P. N. Avakian, "Political Realities in Strategy," *Strategy & Leadership* (October, November, December 1999), pp. 42–48.
20. Porter, *Competitive Strategy*, p. 23.
21. A. S. Grove, "Surviving a 10x Force," *Strategy & Leadership* (January/February 1997), pp. 35–37.
22. M. E. Porter, "Changing Patterns of International Competition," *California Management Review* (Winter 1986), pp. 9–40.
23. T. N. Gladwin, "Assessing the Multinational Environment for Corporate Opportunity," in *Handbook of Business Strategy*, edited by W. D. Guth (Boston: Warren, Gorham and Lamont, 1985), pp. 7.28–7.41.
24. K. J. Hatten and M. L. Hatten, "Strategic Groups, Asymmetrical Mobility Barriers, and Contestability," *Strategic Management Journal* (July–August 1987), p. 329.
25. A. Fiegenbaum and H. Thomas, "Strategic Groups as Reference Groups: Theory, Modeling and Empirical Examination of Industry and Competitive Strategy," *Strategic Management Journal* (September 1995), pp. 461–476; H. R. Greve, "Managerial Cognition and the Mimetic Adoption of Market Positions: What You See Is What You Do," *Strategic Management Journal* (October 1998), pp. 967–988.
26. R. E. Miles and C. C. Snow, *Organizational Strategy, Structure, and Process* (New York: McGraw-Hill, 1978).
27. R. A. D'Aveni, *Hypercompetition* (New York: The Free Press, 1994), pp. xiii–xiv.

28. C. W. Hofer and D. Schendel, *Strategy Formulation: Analytical Concepts* (St. Paul, MN: West Publishing Co., 1978), p. 77.
29. "Information Overload," *Journal of Business Strategy* (January–February 1998), p. 4.
30. E. Von Hipple, *Sources of Innovation* (New York: Oxford University Press, 1988), p. 4.
31. L. Kahaner, *Competitive Intelligence* (New York: Simon & Schuster, 1996).
32. S. M. Shaker and M. P. Gembicki, *WarRoom Guide to Competitive Intelligence* (New York: McGraw-Hill, 1999), p. 10.
33. R. G. Vedder, "CEO and CIO Attitudes about Competitive Intelligence," *Competitive Intelligence Magazine* (October–December 1999), pp. 39–41.
34. S. M. Shaker and M. P. Gembicki, *WarRoom Guide to Competitive Intelligence* (New York: McGraw-Hill, 1999), p. 202.
35. B. Flora, "Ethical Business Intelligence Is NOT Mission Impossible," *Strategy & Leadership* (January/February 1998), pp. 40–41.
36. L. M. Grossman, "Families Have Changed But Tupperware Keeps Holding Its Parties," *Wall Street Journal* (July 21, 1992), pp. A1, A13.
37. H. E. Klein and R. E. Linneman, "Environmental Assessment: An International Study of Corporate Practices," *Journal of Business Strategy* (Summer 1984), p. 72.
38. This process of scenario development is adapted from M. E. Porter, *Competitive Advantage* (New York: Free Press, 1985), pp. 448–470.
39. S. H. Miller, "Developing a Successful CI Program: Preliminary Study Results," *Competitive Intelligence Magazine* (October–December 1999), p. 9.
40. S. H. Miller, "Beware Rival's Web Site Subterfuge," *Competitive Intelligence Magazine* (January–March 2000), p. 8.
41. S. M. Shaker and M. P. Gembicki, *WarRoom Guide to Competitive Intelligence* (New York: McGraw-Hill, 1999), pp. 113–115.
42. J. Warner, "21st Century Capitalism: Snapshot of the Next Century," *Business Week* (November 18, 1994), p. 194

chapter 4

Internal Scanning: Organizational Analysis

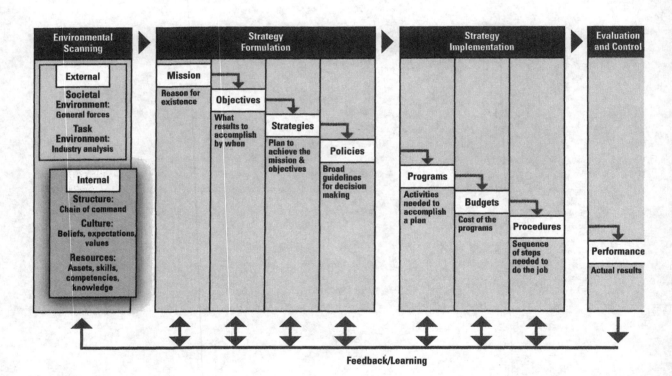

Environmental Scanning	Strategy Formulation	Strategy Implementation	Evaluation and Control

External

Societal Environment: General forces

Task Environment: Industry analysis

Internal

Structure: Chain of command

Culture: Beliefs, expectations, values

Resources: Assets, skills, competencies, knowledge

Mission

Reason for existence

Objectives

What results to accomplish by when

Strategies

Plan to achieve the mission & objectives

Policies

Broad guidelines for decision making

Programs

Activities needed to accomplish a plan

Budgets

Cost of the programs

Procedures

Sequence of steps needed to do the job

Performance

Actual results

Feedback/Learning

On November 17, 2000, United Airlines increased domestic fares by $50 for trips of less than 1,500 miles and $100 for flights over 1,500 miles. Continental, Delta, and American Airlines quickly followed with their own fare increases. Northwest Airlines and TWA stated that they were considering fare hikes. In contrast (and as usual), Dallas-based Southwest Airlines ignored the increase. "We are aware of it, but we are not taking any action," stated Southwest's spokesman Ed Stewart. He added that management hoped that the price increases by other airlines would drive more traffic to Southwest.[1]

Southwest is the undisputed master of the low fare. It is America's most efficient and profitable airline. Other airlines have tried many times to match or beat Southwest's low fares but have failed. For example, United Airlines used to dominate the California market before Southwest replaced it in the 1990s. To regain this lucrative market, United launched its own

80

low-cost carrier, Shuttle by United. It tried to imitate what it thought were Southwest's advantages. It used a fleet of Boeing 737s, the same plane Southwest used at that time. It was able to obtain looser union work rules and a lower wage scale from those at its United Airlines' parent. To compete effectively, the Shuttle aimed to reduce United's cost of flying from the main airline's 10.5¢ to 7.4¢ per passenger mile. It planned to fly planes longer, speed up passenger boarding and takeoffs, and reduce idle time on the ground. Sixteen months later, however, Shuttle by United had been able to reduce its costs only to 8¢ per passenger mile contrasted with Southwest's 7.1¢ in California. (Southwest's overall cost-per-passenger mile was the lowest in the industry at 6.43¢ compared to American Airlines' 12.95¢ per passenger mile—the highest in the industry.)[2] To keep from losing money, Shuttle by United was forced to raise fares and to pull out of all routes that did not connect with the carrier's hubs in San Francisco and Los Angeles. Even United's most loyal customers were taking Southwest for shorter flights. United's fare from San Francisco to Southern California was often $30 more than Southwest's rate of $69. Southwest had not only regained traffic it had lost initially to the Shuttle, it had actually increased its share of the California market!

In addition to Southwest's reputation for having the lowest costs in the industry, it has a well-earned reputation for flying passengers safely to their destination on time. What gave Southwest Airlines this kind of advantage in a very competitive industry? So far no U.S. airline seems able to copy the secret of its success.

4.1 A Resource-Based Approach to Organizational Analysis

Scanning and analyzing the external environment for opportunities and threats is not enough to provide an organization a competitive advantage. Analysts must also look within the corporation itself to identify **internal strategic factors**—those critical strengths and weaknesses that are likely to determine if the firm will be able to take advantage of opportunities while avoiding threats. This internal scanning is often referred to as **organizational analysis** and is concerned with identifying and developing an organization's resources.

A **resource** is an asset, competency, process, skill, or knowledge controlled by the corporation. A resource is a strength if it provides a company with a competitive advantage. It is something the firm does or has the potential to do particularly well relative to the abilities of existing or potential competitors. A resource is a weakness if it is something the corporation does poorly or doesn't have the capacity to do although its competitors have that capacity. Barney, in his **VRIO framework** of analysis, proposes 4 questions to evaluate each of a firm's key resources:

1. **Value:** Does it provide competitive advantage?
2. **Rareness:** Do other competitors possess it?
3. **Imitability:** Is it costly for others to imitate?
4. **Organization:** Is the firm organized to exploit the resource?

If the answer to these questions is "yes" for a particular resource, that resource is considered a strength and a distinctive competence.[3]

Evaluate the importance of these resources to ascertain if they are internal strategic factors—those particular strengths and weaknesses that will help determine the future of the company. This can be done by comparing measures of these resources with measures of (1) the company's past performance, (2) the company's key competitors, and (3) the industry as a whole. To the extent that a resource (such as a firm's financial situation) is significantly different from the firm's own past, its key competitors, or the industry average, the resource is likely to be a strategic factor and should be considered in strategic decisions.

USING RESOURCES TO GAIN COMPETITIVE ADVANTAGE

Proposing that a company's sustained competitive advantage is primarily determined by its resource endowments, Grant proposes a five-step, resource-based approach to strategy analysis.

1. Identify and classify the firm's resources in terms of strengths and weaknesses.

2. Combine the firm's strengths into specific capabilities. **Corporate capabilities** (often called **core competencies**) are the things that a corporation can do exceedingly well. When these capabilities/competencies are superior to those of competitors, they are often called **distinctive competencies**.

3. Appraise the profit potential of these resources and capabilities in terms of their potential for sustainable competitive advantage and the ability to harvest the profits resulting from the use of these resources and capabilities.

4. Select the strategy that best exploits the firm's resources and capabilities relative to external opportunities.

5. Identify resource gaps and invest in upgrading weaknesses.[4]

As indicated in Step 2, when an organization's resources are combined, they form a number of capabilities. In the earlier example, Southwest Airlines has two identifiable capabilities: low costs per passenger mile, and the capability of energizing its people to provide safe, on-time flight service. To ensure highly motivated employees, Southwest spends an inordinate amount of time and money on hiring and promoting, using a system to identify prospective employees who will fit into the company's corporate culture while retaining their individualism.[5]

DETERMINING THE SUSTAINABILITY OF AN ADVANTAGE

Just because a firm is able to use its resources and capabilities to develop a competitive advantage does not mean it will be able to sustain it. Two characteristics determine the sustainability of a firm's distinctive competency(ies): durability and imitability.

Durability is the rate at which a firm's underlying resources and capabilities (core competencies) depreciate or become obsolete. New technology can make a company's core competency obsolete or irrelevant. For example, Intel's skills in using basic technology developed by others to manufacture and market quality microprocessors was a crucial capability until management realized that the firm had taken current technology as far as possible with the Pentium chip. Without basic R&D of its own, it would slowly lose its competitive advantage to others.

Imitability is the rate at which a firm's underlying resources and capabilities (core competencies) can be duplicated by others. To the extent that a firm's distinctive competency gives it competitive advantage in the marketplace, competitors will do what they can to learn and imitate that set of skills and capabilities. Competitors' efforts may range from **reverse engineering** (taking apart a competitor's product in order to find out how it works), to hiring employees from the competitor, to outright patent infringement. A core competency can be easily imitated to the extent that it is transparent, transferable, and replicable.

- **Transparency** is the speed with which other firms can understand the relationship of resources and capabilities supporting a successful firm's strategy. For example, Gillette has always supported its dominance in the marketing of razors with excellent R&D. A competitor could never understand how the Sensor or Mach 3 razor was produced simply by taking one apart. Gillette's Sensor razor design, in particular, was very difficult to copy, partially because the manufacturing equipment needed to produce it was so expensive and complicated.

- **Transferability** is the ability of competitors to gather the resources and capabilities necessary to support a competitive challenge. For example, it may be very difficult for a wine maker to duplicate a French winery's key resources of land and climate, especially if the imitator is located in Iowa.

- **Replicability** is the ability of competitors to use duplicated resources and capabilities to imitate the other firm's success. For example, even though many companies have tried to imitate Procter & Gamble's success with brand management by hiring brand managers away from P&G, they have often failed to duplicate P&G's success. The competitors failed to identify less visible P&G coordination mechanisms or to realize that P&G's brand management style conflicted with the competitor's own corporate culture. Another example is Wal-Mart's sophisticated cross-docking system, which provides the company a substantial cost advantage by improving its ability to reduce shipping and handling costs. While Wal-Mart has the same resources in terms of retail space, employee skills, and equipment as many other discount chains, it has the unique capability to manage its resources for maximum productivity.[6]

It is relatively easy to learn and imitate another company's core competency or capability if it comes from **explicit knowledge**, that is, knowledge that can be easily articulated and communicated. This is the type of knowledge that competitive intelligence activities can quickly identify and communicate. **Tacit knowledge**, in contrast, is knowledge that is *not* easily communicated because it is deeply rooted in employee experience or in a corporation's culture.[7] Tacit knowledge is more valuable and more likely to lead to a sustainable competitive advantage than is explicit knowledge because it is much harder for competitors to imitate. The knowledge may be complex and combined with other types of knowledge in an unclear fashion in such a way that even management cannot clearly explain the competency.[8] Because Procter & Gamble's successful approach to brand management is primarily composed of tacit knowledge, the firm's top management is very reluctant to make any significant modifications to it, fearing that they might destroy the very thing they are trying to improve!

An organization's resources and capabilities can be placed on a continuum to the extent they are durable and can't be imitated (that is, aren't transparent, transferable, or replicable) by another firm. This **continuum of sustainability** is depicted in **Figure 4–1**. At one extreme are slow-cycle resources, which are sustainable because they are shielded by patents, geography, strong brand names, or tacit knowledge. These resources and capabilities are distinctive competencies because they provide a sustainable competitive advantage. Gillette's Sensor

Figure 4–1

Continuum of Resource Sustainability

	Level of Resource Sustainability	
High (Hard to Imitate)		**Low** (Easy to Imitate)
Slow-Cycle Resources	**Standard-Cycle Resources**	**Fast-Cycle Resources**
• Strongly shielded • Patents, brand name • Gilette: Sensor razor	• Standardized mass production • Economies of scale Complicated processes • Chrysler: Minivan	• Easily duplicated • Idea driven • Sony: Walkman

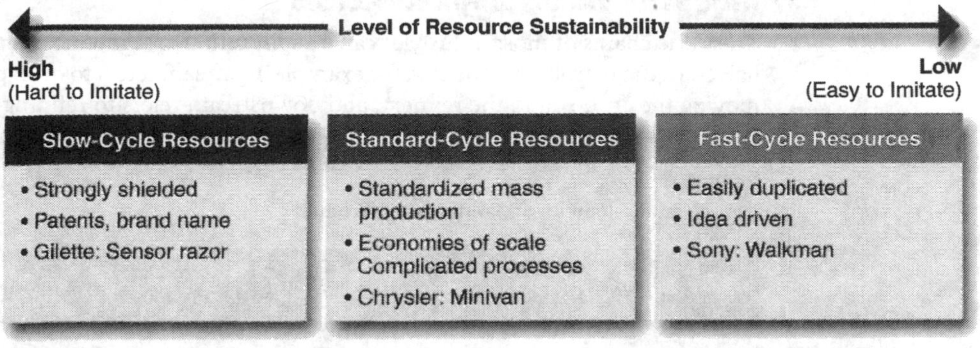

Source: Suggested by J. R. Williams, "How Sustainable Is Your Competitive Advantage?" *California Management Review* (Spring 1992), p. 33. Copyright © 1992 by the Regents of the University of California. Reprinted by permission of the Regents.

razor is a good example of a product built around slow-cycle resources. The other extreme includes fast-cycle resources, which face the highest imitation pressures because they are based on a concept or technology that can be easily duplicated, such as Sony's Walkman. To the extent that a company has fast-cycle resources, the primary way it can compete successfully is through increased speed from lab to marketplace. Otherwise, it has no real sustainable competitive advantage.

With its low-cost position, reputation for safe, on-time flights, and its dedicated workforce, Southwest Airlines has successfully built a sustainable competitive advantage based on relatively slow-cycle resources—resources that are durable and can't be easily imitated because they lack transparency, transferability, and replicability.

4.2 Value Chain Analysis

A good way to begin an organizational analysis is to ascertain where a firm's products are located in the overall value chain. A **value chain** is a linked set of value-creating activities beginning with basic raw materials coming from suppliers, moving on to a series of value-added activities involved in producing and marketing a product or service, and ending with distributors getting the final goods into the hands of the ultimate consumer. See **Figure 4–2** for an example of a typical value chain for a manufactured product. The focus of value chain analysis is to examine the corporation in the context of the overall chain of value-creating activities, of which the firm may be only a small part.

Very few corporations include a product's entire value chain. Ford Motor Company did when it was managed by its founder, Henry Ford I. During the 1920s and 1930s, the company owned its own iron mines, ore-carrying ships, and a small rail line to bring ore to its mile-long River Rouge plant in Detroit. Visitors to the plant would walk along an elevated walkway where they could watch iron ore being dumped from the rail cars into huge furnaces. The resulting steel was poured and rolled out onto a moving belt to be fabricated into auto frames and parts while the visitors watched in awe. As a group of visitors walked along the walkway, they observed an automobile being built piece by piece. Reaching the end of the moving line, the finished automobile was driven out of the plant into a vast adjoining parking lot. Ford trucks would then load the cars for delivery to dealers. Although the Ford dealers were not employees of the company, they had almost no power in the arrangement. Dealerships were awarded by the company and taken away if a dealer was at all disloyal. Ford Motor Company at that time was completely vertically integrated, that is, it controlled (usually by ownership) every stage of the value chain from the iron mines to the retailers.

INDUSTRY VALUE CHAIN ANALYSIS

The value chains of most industries can be split into two segments, *upstream* and *downstream* halves. In the petroleum industry, for example, upstream refers to oil exploration, drilling, and moving the crude oil to the refinery, and downstream refers to refining the oil plus the trans-

Figure 4–2
Typical Value Chain for a Manufactured Product

Source: Suggested by J. R. Galbraith, "Strategy and Organization Planning," in *The Strategy Process: Concepts, Contexts, Cases,* 2nd ed., edited by H. Mintzberg and J. B. Quinn (Upper Saddle River, NJ: Prentice Hall, 1991), p. 316. Reprinted by permission of Pearson Education, Inc., Upper Saddle River, NJ.

porting and marketing of gasoline and refined oil to distributors and gas station retailers. Even though most large oil companies are completely integrated, they often vary in the amount of expertise they have at each part of the value chain. Texaco, for example, has its greatest expertise downstream in marketing and retailing. Others, such as British Petroleum (now BP Amoco), are more dominant in upstream activities like exploration.

An industry can be analyzed in terms of the profit margin available at any one point along the value chain. For example, the U.S. auto industry's revenues and profits are divided among many value chain activities, including manufacturing, new and used car sales, gasoline retailing, insurance, after-sales service and parts, and lease financing. From a revenue standpoint, auto manufacturers dominate the industry, accounting for almost 60% of total industry revenues. Profits are, however, a different matter. Auto leasing is the most profitable activity in the value chain, followed by insurance and auto loans. The core activities of manufacturing and distribution, however, earn significantly smaller shares of the total industry profits than they do of total revenues. For example, since auto sales have become marginally profitable, dealerships are now emphasizing service and repair. As a result of various differences along the industry value chain, manufacturers have moved aggressively into auto financing. Ford, for example, generates nearly half its profits from financing, even though financing accounts for less than 20% of the company's revenues.[9]

In analyzing the complete value chain of a product, note that even if a firm operates up and down the entire industry chain, it usually has an area of primary expertise where its primary activities lie. A company's **center of gravity** is the part of the chain that is most important to the company and the point where its greatest expertise and capabilities lie—its core competencies. According to Galbraith, a company's center of gravity is usually the point at which the company started. After a firm successfully establishes itself at this point by obtaining a competitive advantage, one of its first strategic moves is to move forward or backward along the value chain in order to reduce costs, guarantee access to key raw materials, or to guarantee distribution.[10] This process is called *vertical integration* and is discussed in more detail in Chapter 6.

In the paper industry, for example, Weyerhauser's center of gravity is in the raw materials and primary manufacturing parts of the value chain in **Figure 4–2**. Weyerhauser's expertise is in lumbering and pulp mills, which is where the company started. It integrated forward by using its wood pulp to make paper and boxes, but its greatest capability still lay in getting the greatest return from its lumbering activities. In contrast, Procter & Gamble is primarily a consumer products company that also owned timberland and operated pulp mills. Its expertise is in the product producer and marketer distributor parts of the **Figure 4–2** value chain. P&G purchased these assets to guarantee access to the large quantities of wood pulp it needed to expand its disposable diaper, toilet tissue, and napkin products. P&G's strongest capabilities have always been in the downstream activities of product development, marketing, and brand management. It has never been as efficient in upstream paper activities as Weyerhauser. It had no real distinctive competence on that part of the value chain. When paper supplies became more plentiful (and competition got rougher), P&G gladly sold its land and mills to focus more on that part of the value chain where it could provide the greatest value at the lowest cost—creating and marketing innovative consumer products.

CORPORATE VALUE CHAIN ANALYSIS

Each corporation has its own internal value chain of activities. See **Figure 4–3** for an example of a corporate value chain. Porter proposes that a manufacturing firm's **primary activities** usually begin with inbound logistics (raw materials handling and warehousing), go through an operations process in which a product is manufactured, and continue on to outbound logistics (warehousing and distribution), marketing and sales, and finally to service (installa-

Figure 4–3
A Corporation's Value Chain

Source: Adapted/reprinted with the permission of The Free Press, an imprint of Simon & Schuster, from *Competitive Advantage: Creating and Sustaining Superior Performance* by Michael E. Porter, p. 37. Copyright © 1985, 1988 by Michael E. Porter.

tion, repair, and sale of parts). Several **support activities**, such as procurement (purchasing), technology development (R&D), human resource management, and firm infrastructure (accounting, finance, strategic planning), ensure that the primary value-chain activities operate effectively and efficiently. Each of a company's product lines has its own distinctive value chain. Because most corporations make several different products or services, an internal analysis of the firm involves analyzing a series of different value chains.

The systematic examination of individual value activities can lead to a better understanding of a corporation's strengths and weaknesses. According to Porter, "Differences among competitor value chains are a key source of competitive advantage."[11] Corporate value chain analysis involves the following three steps:

1. *Examine each product line's value chain in terms of the various activities involved in producing that product or service.* Which activities can be considered strengths (core competencies) or weaknesses (core deficiencies)? Do any of the strengths provide competitive advantage and can thus be labeled distinctive competencies?

2. *Examine the "linkages" within each product line's value chain.* **Linkages** are the connections between the way one value activity (for example, marketing) is performed and the cost of performance of another activity (for example, quality control). In seeking ways for a corporation to gain competitive advantage in the marketplace, the same function can be performed in different ways with different results. For example, quality inspection of 100% of output by the workers themselves instead of the usual 10% by quality control inspectors might increase production costs, but that increase could be more than offset by the savings obtained from reducing the number of repair people needed to fix defective products and increasing the amount of salespeople's time devoted to selling instead of exchanging already-sold, but defective, products.

3. *Examine the potential synergies among the value chains of different product lines or business units.* Each value element, such as advertising or manufacturing, has an inherent economy of scale in which activities are conducted at their lowest possible cost per unit of output. If a particular product is not being produced at a high enough level to reach economies of scale in distribution, another product could be used to share the same distribution channel. This is an example of **economies of scope**, which result when the value chains of two separate products or services share activities, such as the same marketing channels or manufacturing facilities. For example, the cost of joint production of multiple products can be less than the cost of separate production.

4.3 Scanning Functional Resources

The simplest way to begin an analysis of a corporation's value chain is by carefully examining its traditional functional areas for potential strengths and weaknesses. Functional resources include not only the financial, physical, and human assets in each area, but also the ability of the people in each area to formulate and implement the necessary functional objectives, strategies, and policies. The resources include the knowledge of analytical concepts and procedural techniques common to each area as well as the ability of the people in each area to use them effectively. If used properly, these resources serve as strengths to carry out value-added activities and support strategic decisions. In addition to the usual business functions of marketing, finance, R&D, operations, human resources, and information systems, we also discuss structure and culture as key parts of a business corporation's value chain.

BASIC ORGANIZATIONAL STRUCTURES

Although there is an almost infinite variety of structural forms, certain basic types predominate in modern complex organizations. **Figure 4–4** illustrates three basic **organizational structures**. The conglomerate structure is a variant of divisional structure and is thus not depicted as a fourth structure. Generally speaking, each structure tends to support some corporate strategies over others.

- **Simple structure** has no functional or product categories and is appropriate for a small, entrepreneur-dominated company with one or two product lines that operates in a reasonably small, easily identifiable market niche. Employees tend to be generalists and jacks-of-all-trades.

- **Functional structure** is appropriate for a medium-sized firm with several related product lines in one industry. Employees tend to be specialists in the business functions important to that industry, such as manufacturing, marketing, finance, and human resources.

- **Divisional structure** is appropriate for a large corporation with many product lines in several related industries. Employees tend to be functional specialists organized according to product/market distinctions. General Motors, for example, groups its various auto lines into the separate divisions of Chevrolet, Pontiac, Saturn, Oldsmobile, Buick, and Cadillac. Management attempts to find some synergy among divisional activities through the use of committees and horizontal linkages.

- **Strategic business units (SBUs)** are a recent modification to the divisional structure. Strategic business units are divisions or groups of divisions composed of independent product-market segments that are given primary responsibility and authority for the management of their own functional areas. *An SBU may be of any size or level, but it must have (1) a unique mission, (2) identifiable competitors, (3) an external market focus, and (4) control of its business functions.*[12] The idea is to decentralize on the basis of strategic elements rather than on the basis of size, product characteristics, or span of control and to create

Figure 4-4
Basic Organizational Structures

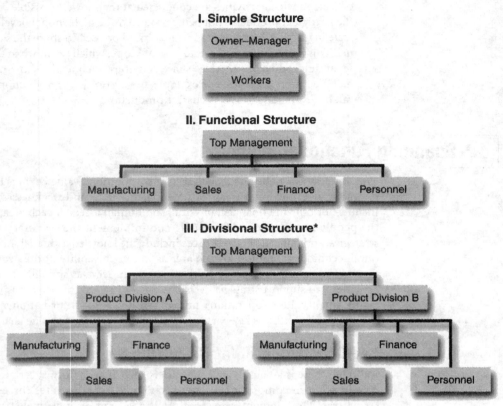

*Conglomerate structure is a variant of the divisional structure.

horizontal linkages among units previously kept separate. For example, rather than organize products on the basis of packaging technology like frozen foods, canned foods, and
bagged foods, General Foods organized its products into SBUs on the basis of consumer-
oriented menu segments: breakfast food, beverage, main meal, dessert, and pet foods.

■ **Conglomerate structure** is appropriate for a large corporation with many product lines in
several unrelated industries. A variant of the divisional structure, the conglomerate structure (sometimes called a holding company) is typically an assemblage of legally independent firms (subsidiaries) operating under one corporate umbrella but controlled through
the subsidiaries' boards of directors. The unrelated nature of the subsidiaries prevents any
attempt at gaining synergy among them.

If the current basic structure of a corporation does not easily support a strategy under
consideration, top management must decide if the proposed strategy is feasible or if the structure should be changed to a more advanced structure such as the matrix or network.
(Advanced structural designs such as the matrix and network are discussed in Chapter 7.)

CORPORATE CULTURE: THE COMPANY WAY

There is an oft-told story of a person new to a company asking an experienced coworker what
an employee should do when a customer calls. The old-timer responded: "There are three
ways to do any job—the right way, the wrong way, and the company way. Around here, we

always do things the company way." In most organizations, the "company way" is derived from the corporation's culture. **Corporate culture** is the collection of beliefs, expectations, and values learned and shared by a corporation's members and transmitted from one generation of employees to another. The corporate culture generally reflects the values of the founder(s) and the mission of the firm.[13] It gives a company a sense of identity: *This is who we are. This is what we do. This is what we stand for.* The culture includes the dominant orientation of the company, such as research and development at Hewlett-Packard, customer service at Nordstrom, or product quality at Maytag. It often includes a number of informal work rules (forming the "company way") that employees follow without question. These work practices over time become part of a company's unquestioned tradition.

Corporate culture has two distinct attributes, intensity and integration.[14] **Cultural intensity** is the degree to which members of a unit accept the norms, values, or other culture content associated with the unit. This shows the culture's depth. Organizations with strong norms promoting a particular value, such as quality at Maytag, have intensive cultures, whereas new firms (or those in transition) have weaker, less intensive cultures. Employees in an intensive culture tend to exhibit consistent behavior, that is, they tend to act similarly over time. **Cultural integration** is the extent to which units throughout an organization share a common culture. This is the culture's breadth. Organizations with a pervasive dominant culture may be hierarchically controlled and power oriented, such as a military unit, and have highly integrated cultures. All employees tend to hold the same cultural values and norms. In contrast, a company that is structured into diverse units by functions or divisions usually exhibits some strong subcultures (for example, R&D versus manufacturing) and a less integrated corporate culture.

Corporate culture fulfills several important functions in an organization:

1. Conveys a sense of identity for employees
2. Helps generate employee commitment to something greater than themselves
3. Adds to the stability of the organization as a social system
4. Serves as a frame of reference for employees to use to make sense out of organizational activities and to use as a guide for appropriate behavior[15]

Corporate culture shapes the behavior of people in the corporation. Because these cultures have a powerful influence on the behavior of people at all levels, they can strongly affect a corporation's ability to shift its strategic direction. A strong culture should not only promote survival, but it should also create the basis for a superior competitive position. For example, a culture emphasizing constant renewal may help a company adapt to a changing, hypercompetitive environment.[16] To the extent that a corporation's distinctive competence is embedded in an organization's culture, it will be a form of tacit knowledge and very difficult for a competitor to imitate.[17] See the 🌐 **Global Issue** feature to see how the Swiss company ABB Asea Brown Boveri AG uses its corporate culture to obtain competitive advantage in a global industry.

A change in mission, objectives, strategies, or policies is not likely to be successful if it is in opposition to the accepted culture of the firm. Foot-dragging and even sabotage may result as employees fight to resist a radical change in corporate philosophy. Like structure, if an organization's culture is compatible with a new strategy, it is an internal strength. But if the corporate culture is not compatible with the proposed strategy, it is a serious weakness.

STRATEGIC MARKETING ISSUES

The marketing manager is the company's primary link to the customer and the competition. The manager, therefore, must be especially concerned with the market position and marketing mix of the firm.

Global Issue

ABB Uses Corporate Culture as a Competitive Advantage

Zurich-based ABB Asea Brown Boveri AG is a worldwide builder of power plants, electrical equipment, and industrial factories in 140 countries. By establishing one set of values throughout its global operations, ABB's management believes that the company will gain an advantage over its rivals Siemens AG of Germany, France's Alcatel-Alsthom NV, and the United State's General Electric Company.

Percy Barnevik, Swedish Chairman of ABB, managed the merger that created ABB from Sweden's Asea AB and Switzerland's BBC Brown Boveri Ltd. At that time both companies were far behind the world leaders in electrical equipment and engineering. Barnevik introduced his concept of a company with no geographic base—one that had many "home" markets that could draw on expertise from around the globe. To do

this, he created a set of 500 global managers who could adapt to local cultures while executing ABB's global strategies. These people are multilingual and move around each of ABB's 5,000 profit centers in 140 countries. Their assignment is to cut costs, improve efficiency, and integrate local businesses with the ABB world view.

ABB requires local business units, such as Mexico's motor factory, to report both to one of ABB's traveling global managers and to a business area manager who sets global motor strategy for ABB. When the goals of the local factory conflict with worldwide priorities, it is up to the global manager to resolve it.

Few multinational corporations are as successful as ABB in getting global strategies to work with local operations. In agreement with the resource-based view of the firm, Barnevik states, "Our strength comes from pulling together. . . . If you can make this work real well, then you get a competitive edge out of the organization which is very, very difficult to copy."

Source: J. Guyon, "ABB Fuses Units with One Set of Values," *Wall Street Journal* (October 2, 1996), p. A15. Copyright © 1996 by the *Wall Street Journal.* Reprinted by permission of the *Wall Street Journal* via the Copyright Clearance Center.

Market Position and Segmentation
Market position deals with the question, "Who are our customers?" It refers to the selection of specific areas for marketing concentration and can be expressed in terms of market, product, and geographical locations. Through market research, corporations are able to practice **market segmentation** with various products or services so that managers can discover what niches to seek, which new types of products to develop, and how to ensure that a company's many products do not directly compete with one another.

Marketing Mix
The **marketing mix** refers to the particular combination of key variables under the corporation's control that can be used to affect demand and to gain competitive advantage. These variables are product, place, promotion, and price. Within each of these four variables are several subvariables, listed in **Table 4–1**, that should be analyzed in terms of their effects on divisional and corporate performance.

Product Life Cycle
One of the most useful concepts in marketing, insofar as strategic management is concerned, is that of the **product life cycle.** As depicted in **Figure 4–5**, the product life cycle is a graph showing time plotted against the dollar sales of a product as it moves from introduction through growth and maturity to decline. This concept enables a marketing manager to examine the marketing mix of a particular product or group of products in terms of its position in its life cycle.

Table 4–1   Marketing Mix Variables

Product	Place	Promotion	Price
Quality	Channels	Advertising	List price
Features	Coverage	Personal selling	Discounts
Options	Locations	Sales promotion	Allowances
Style	Inventory	Publicity	Payment periods
Brand name	Transport		Credit items
Packaging			
Sizes			
Services			
Warranties			
Returns			

Source: Philip Kotler, *Marketing Management: Analysis, Planning, and Control,* 4th ed. (Upper Saddle River, NJ: Prentice Hall, 1980), p. 89. Copyright © 1980. Reprinted by permission of Pearson Education, Inc., Upper Saddle River, NJ.

STRATEGIC FINANCIAL ISSUES

The financial manager must ascertain the best sources of funds, uses of funds, and control of funds. Cash must be raised from internal or external (local and global) sources and allocated for different uses. The flow of funds in the operations of the organization must be monitored. To the extent that a corporation is involved in international activities, currency fluctuations must be dealt with to ensure that profits aren't wiped out by the rise or fall of the dollar versus the yen, euro, or other currencies. Benefits in the form of returns, repayments, or products and services must be given to the sources of outside financing. All these tasks must be handled in a way that complements and supports overall corporate strategy. A firm's capital structure (amounts of debt and equity) can influence its strategic choices. For example, increased debt tends to increase risk aversion and decrease the willingness of management to invest in R&D.[18]

Figure 4–5
Product Life Cycle

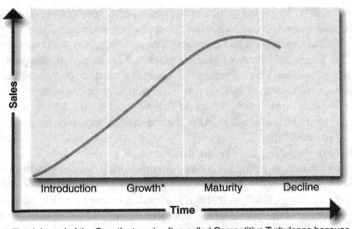

* The right end of the Growth stage is often called Competitive Turbulence because of price and distribution competition that shakes out the weaker competitors. For further information, see C.R. Wasson, *Dynamic Competitive Strategy and Product Life Cycles,* 3rd ed. (Austin, TX: Austin Press, 1978).

Financial Leverage

The mix of externally generated short-term and long-term funds in relation to the amount and timing of internally generated funds should be appropriate to the corporate objectives, strategies, and policies. The concept of **financial leverage** (the ratio of total debt to total assets) is helpful in describing how debt is used to increase the earnings available to common shareholders. When the company finances its activities by sales of bonds or notes instead of through stock, the earnings per share are boosted: The interest paid on the debt reduces taxable income, but fewer shareholders share the profits than if the company had sold more stock to finance its activities. The debt, however, does raise the firm's break-even point above what it would have been if the firm had financed from internally generated funds only. High leverage may therefore be perceived as a corporate strength in times of prosperity and ever-increasing sales, or as a weakness in times of a recession and falling sales. This is because leverage acts to magnify the effect on earnings per share of an increase or decrease in dollar sales. Research indicates that greater leverage has a positive impact on performance for firms in stable environments, but a negative impact for firms in dynamic environments.[19]

Capital Budgeting

Capital budgeting is the analyzing and ranking of possible investments in fixed assets such as land, buildings, and equipment in terms of the additional outlays and additional receipts that will result from each investment. A good finance department will be able to prepare such capital budgets and to rank them on the basis of some accepted criteria or hurdle rate (for example, years to pay back investment, rate of return, or time to break-even point) for the purpose of strategic decision making. Most firms have more than one hurdle rate and vary it as a function of the type of project being considered. Projects with high strategic significance, such as entering new markets or defending market share, will often have low hurdle rates.[20]

STRATEGIC RESEARCH AND DEVELOPMENT (R&D) ISSUES

The R&D manager is responsible for suggesting and implementing a company's technological strategy in light of its corporate objectives and policies. The manager's job, therefore, involves (1) choosing among alternative new technologies to use within the corporation, (2) developing methods of embodying the new technology in new products and processes, and (3) deploying resources so that the new technology can be successfully implemented.

R&D Intensity, Technological Competence, and Technology Transfer

The company must make available the resources necessary for effective research and development. A company's **R&D intensity** (its spending on R&D as a percentage of sales revenue) is a principal means of gaining market share in global competition. The amount spent on R&D often varies by industry. For example, the U.S. computer software industry spends an average of 13.5% of its sales dollar for R&D, whereas the paper and forest products industry spends only 1.0%.[21] A good rule of thumb for R&D spending is that a corporation should spend at a "normal" rate for that particular industry unless its strategic plan calls for unusual expenditures.

Simply spending money on R&D or new projects does not mean, however, that the money will produce useful results. For example, Pharmacia Upjohn spent more of its revenues on research than any other company in any industry (18%), but it was ranked low in innovation.[22] A company's R&D unit should be evaluated for **technological competence** in both the development and the use of innovative technology. Not only should the corporation make a consistent research effort (as measured by reasonably constant corporate expenditures that result in usable innovations), it should also be proficient in managing research personnel and integrating their innovations into its day-to-day operations. If a company is not proficient in

technology transfer, the process of taking a new technology from the laboratory to the marketplace, it will not gain much advantage from new technological advances. For example, Xerox Corporation has been criticized for failing to take advantage of various innovations (such as the mouse and the graphical user interface for personal computers) developed originally in its sophisticated Palo Alto Research Center. See the **boxed example** for a classic example of how Apple Computer's ability to imitate a core competency of Xerox gave it a competitive advantage (sustainable until Microsoft launched Windows 95).

R&D Mix

Basic R&D is conducted by scientists in well-equipped laboratories where the focus is on theoretical problem areas. The best indicators of a company's capability in this area are its patents and research publications. **Product R&D** concentrates on marketing and is concerned with product or product-packaging improvements. The best measurements of ability in this area are the number of successful new products introduced and the percentage of total sales and profits coming from products introduced within the past five years. **Engineering (or process) R&D** is concerned with engineering, concentrating on quality control and the development of design specifications and improved production equipment. A company's capability in this area can be measured by consistent reductions in unit manufacturing costs and by the number of product defects.

Most corporations will have a mix of basic, product, and process R&D, which varies by industry, company, and product line. The balance of these types of research is known as the **R&D mix** and should be appropriate to the strategy being considered and to each product's life cycle. For example, it is generally accepted that product R&D normally dominates the early stages of a product's life cycle (when the product's optimal form and features are still being debated), whereas process R&D becomes especially important in the later stages (when the product's design is solidified and the emphasis is on reducing costs and improving quality).

A Problem of Technology Transfer at Xerox Corporation

In the mid-1970s, Xerox Corporation's Palo Alto Research Center (PARC) had developed Alto, a new type of computer with some innovative features. Although Alto was supposed to serve as a research prototype, it became so popular among PARC personnel that some researchers began to develop Alto as a commercial product. Unfortunately this put PARC into direct conflict with Xerox's product development group, which was at the same time developing a rival machine called the Star. Because the Star was in line with the company's expressed product development strategy, top management, who placed all its emphasis on the Star, ignored Alto.

In 1979, Steve Jobs, Cofounder of Apple Computer, Inc., made a now-legendary tour of the normally very secretive PARC. Researchers gave Jobs a demonstration of the Alto. Unlike the computers that Apple was then building, Alto had the power of a minicomputer. Its user-friendly software generated crisp text and bright graphics. Jobs fell in love with the machine. He promptly asked Apple's engineers to duplicate the look and feel of Alto. The result was the Macintosh—a personal computer that soon revolutionized the industry.

Note: See the 1999 motion picture, *The Pirates of Silicon Valley,* for the full story of how Apple Computer imitated the features of the Alto and how Microsoft, in turn, imitated the "look and feel" of Apple's Macintosh.

Impact of Technological Discontinuity on Strategy

The R&D manager must determine when to abandon present technology and when to develop or adopt new technology. Richard Foster of McKinsey and Company states that the displacement of one technology by another (**technological discontinuity**) is a frequent and strategically important phenomenon. Such a discontinuity occurs when a new technology cannot simply be used to enhance the current technology but actually substitutes for that technology to yield better performance. For each technology within a given field or industry, according to Foster, the plotting of product performance against research effort/expenditures on a graph results in an S-shaped curve. He describes the process depicted in **Figure 4–6**:

> Early in the development of the technology a knowledge base is being built and progress requires a relatively large amount of effort. Later, progress comes more easily. And then, as the limits of that technology are approached, progress becomes slow and expensive. That is when R&D dollars should be allocated to technology with more potential. That is also—not so incidentally—when a competitor who has bet on a new technology can sweep away your business or topple an entire industry.[23]

Computerized information technology is currently on the steep upward slope of its S-curve in which relatively small increments in R&D effort result in significant improvement in performance. This is an example of Moore's Law, which states that silicon chips (microprocessors) double in complexity every 18 months. Proposed by Gordon Moore, Cofounder of Intel, in 1965, the law originally stated that processor complexity would double in one year, but Moore soon changed it to two years. Others changed it to 18 months—the number now generally accepted. In 1965, 16 components could be placed on a silicon chip. By 2000, that number had grown exponentially to 10 million. According to Moore, "Moore's Law has been the name given to everything that changes exponentially in the industry."[24]

Figure 4–6
Technological Discontinuity

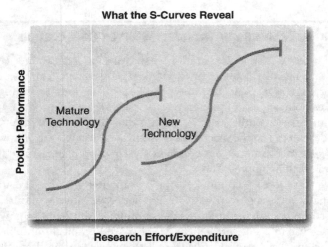

What the S-Curves Reveal

In the corporate planning process, it is generally assumed that incremental progress in technology will occur. But past developments in a given technology cannot be extrapolated into the future because every technology has its limits. The key to competitiveness is to determine when to shift resources to a technology with more potential.

Source: P. Pascarella, "Are You Investing in the Wrong Technology?" *Industry Week* (July 25, 1983), p. 38. Copyright © 1983 Penton Media, Inc., Cleveland, OH. All rights reserved. Reprinted with permission from *Industry Week.*

The presence of a technological discontinuity in the world's steel industry during the 1960s explains why the large capital expenditures by U.S. steel companies failed to keep them competitive with the Japanese firms that adopted the new technologies. As Foster points out, "History has shown that as one technology nears the end of its S-curve, competitive leadership in a market generally changes hands."[25]

Christensen explains in *The Innovator's Dilemma* why this transition occurs when a "disruptive technology" enters an industry. In a study of computer disk drive manufacturers, he explains that established market leaders are typically reluctant to move in a timely manner to a new technology. This reluctance to switch technologies (even when the firm is aware of the new technology and may have even invented it!) is because the resource allocation process in most companies gives priority to those projects (typically based on the old technology) with the greatest likelihood of generating a good return on investment—those projects appealing to the firm's current customers (whose products are also based on the characteristics of the old technology). For example, in the 1980s a disk drive manufacturer's customers (PC manufacturers) wanted a better (faster) 5¼″ drive with greater capacity. These PC makers were not interested in the new 3½″ drives based on the new technology because (at that time) the smaller drives were slower and had less capacity. Smaller size was irrelevant since these companies primarily made desktop personal computers that were designed to hold large drives.

The new technology is generally riskier and of little appeal to the current customers of established firms. Products derived from the new technology are more expensive and do not meet the customers' requirements, which are based on the old technology. New entrepreneurial firms are typically more interested in the new technology because it is one way to appeal to a developing market niche in a market currently dominated by established companies. Even though the new technology may be more expensive to develop, it offers performance improvements in areas that are attractive to this small niche, but of no consequence to the customers of the established competitors.

This was the case with the entrepreneurial manufacturers of 3½″ disk drives. These smaller drives appealed to the PC makers who were trying to increase their small PC market share by offering laptop computers. Size and weight were more important to these customers than were capacity and speed. By the time the new technology was developed to the point that the 3½″ drive matched and even surpassed the 5¼″ drive in terms of speed and capacity (in addition to size and weight), it was too late for the established 5¼″ disk drive firms to switch to the new technology. Once their customers begin demanding smaller products using the new technology, the established firms were unable to respond quickly and lost their leadership position in the industry. They were able to remain in the industry (with a much reduced market share) only if they were able to utilize the new technology to be competitive in the new product line.[26]

STRATEGIC OPERATIONS ISSUES

The primary task of the operations (manufacturing or service) manager is to develop and operate a system that will produce the required number of products or services, with a certain quality, at a given cost, within an allotted time. Many of the key concepts and techniques popularly used in manufacturing can be applied to service businesses.

In very general terms, manufacturing can be intermittent or continuous. In **intermittent systems** (job shops), the item is normally processed sequentially, but the work and sequence of the process vary. An example is an auto body repair shop. At each location, the tasks determine the details of processing and the time required for them. These job shops can be very labor intensive. For example, a job shop usually has little automated machinery and thus a small amount of fixed costs. It has a fairly low break-even point, but its variable cost line (composed of wages and costs of special parts) has a relatively steep slope. Because most of the costs associated with the product are variable (many employees earn piece-rate wages), a job shop's variable costs are higher than those of automated firms. Its advantage over other firms is that it can operate at low levels and still be profitable. After a job shop's sales reach breakeven, however, the huge variable costs as a percentage of total costs keep the profit per unit at a relatively low level. In terms of strategy, this firm should look for a niche in the marketplace for which it can produce and sell a reasonably small quantity of goods.

In contrast, **continuous systems** are those laid out as lines on which products can be continuously assembled or processed. An example is an automobile assembly line. A firm using continuous systems invests heavily in fixed investments such as automated processes and highly sophisticated machinery. Its labor force, relatively small but highly skilled, earns salaries rather than piece-rate wages. Consequently this firm has a high amount of fixed costs. It also has a relatively high break-even point, but its variable cost line rises slowly. This is an example of **operating leverage**, the impact of a specific change in sales volume on net operating income. The advantage of high operating leverage is that once the firm reaches breakeven, its profits rise faster than do those of less automated firms having lower operating leverage. Continuous systems reap benefits from economies of scale. In terms of strategy, this firm needs to find a high-demand niche in the marketplace for which it can produce and sell a large quantity of goods. However, a firm with high operating leverage is likely to suffer huge losses during a recession. During an economic downturn, the firm with less automation and thus less leverage is more likely to survive comfortably because a drop in sales primarily affects variable costs. It is often easier to lay off labor than to sell off specialized plants and machines.

Experience Curve

A conceptual framework that many large corporations have used successfully is the experience curve (originally called the learning curve). The **experience curve** suggests that unit production costs decline by some fixed percentage (commonly 20% to 30%) each time the total accumulated volume of production in units doubles. The actual percentage varies by industry and is based on many variables: the amount of time it takes a person to learn a new task, scale economies, product and process improvements, and lower raw materials costs, among others. For example, in an industry with an 85% experience curve, a corporation might expect a 15% reduction in unit costs for every doubling of volume. The total costs per unit can be expected to drop from $100 when the total production is 10 units, to $85 ($100 × 85%) when production increases to 20 units, and to $72.25 ($85 × 85%) when it reaches 40 units. Achieving these results often means investing in R&D and fixed assets; higher fixed costs and less flexibility thus result. Nevertheless the manufacturing strategy is one of building capacity ahead of demand in order to achieve the lower unit costs that develop from the experience curve. On the basis of some future point on the experience curve, the corporation should price the product or service very low to preempt competition and increase market demand. The resulting high number of units sold and high market share should result in high profits, based on the low unit costs.

Management commonly uses the experience curve in estimating the production costs of (1) a product never before made with the present techniques and processes or (2) current products produced by newly introduced techniques or processes. The concept was first applied in the airframe industry and can be applied in the service industry as well. For example, a cleaning company can reduce its costs per employee by having its workers use the same equipment and techniques to clean many adjacent offices in one office building rather than just cleaning a few offices in multiple buildings. Although many firms have used experience curves extensively, an unquestioning acceptance of the industry norm (such as 80% for the airframe industry or 70% for integrated circuits) is very risky. The experience curve of the industry as a whole might not hold true for a particular company for a variety of reasons.

Flexible Manufacturing for Mass Customization

Recently the use of large, continuous, mass-production facilities to take advantage of experience-curve economies has been criticized. The use of **Computer-Assisted Design and Computer-Assisted Manufacturing (CAD/CAM)** and robot technology means that learning times are shorter and products can be economically manufactured in small, customized batches in a process called **mass customization**—the low-cost production of individually customized goods and services.[27] **Economies of scope** (in which common parts of the manufacturing activities of various products are combined to gain economies even though small numbers of each product are made) replace **economies of scale** (in which unit costs are reduced by making large numbers of the same product) in flexible manufacturing. **Flexible manufacturing** permits the low-volume output of custom-tailored products at relatively low unit costs through economies of scope. It is thus possible to have the cost advantages of continuous systems with the customer-oriented advantages of intermittent systems.

STRATEGIC HUMAN RESOURCE MANAGEMENT (HRM) ISSUES

The primary task of the manager of human resources is to improve the match between individuals and jobs. A good HRM department should know how to use attitude surveys and other feedback devices to assess employees' satisfaction with their jobs and with the corporation as a whole. HRM managers should also use job analysis to obtain job description information about what each job needs to accomplish in terms of quality and quantity. Up-to-date job descriptions are essential not only for proper employee selection, appraisal, training, and development for wage and salary administration, and for labor negotiations, but also for summarizing the corporatewide human resources in terms of employee-skill categories. Just as a company must know the number, type, and quality of its manufacturing facilities, it must also know the kinds of people it employs and the skills they possess. The best strategies are meaningless if employees do not have the skills to carry them out or if jobs cannot be designed to accommodate the available workers. Hewlett-Packard, for example, uses employee profiles to ensure that it has the right mix of talents to implement its planned strategies.

Use of Teams

Management is beginning to realize that it must be more flexible in its utilization of employees in order for human resources to be a strength. Human resource managers, therefore, need to be knowledgeable about work options such as part-time work, job sharing, flex-time, extended leaves, contract work, and especially about the proper use of teams. Over two-thirds of large U.S. companies are successfully using **autonomous (self-managing) work teams** in which a group of people work together without a supervisor to plan, coordinate, and evaluate their own work.[28] Northern Telecom found productivity and quality to increase with work teams to such an extent that it was able to reduce the number of quality inspectors by 40%.[29]

As a way to move a product more quickly through its development stage, companies like Motorola, Chrysler, NCR, Boeing, and General Electric are using **cross-functional work teams.** Instead of developing products in a series of steps—beginning with a request from sales, which leads to design, then to engineering and on to purchasing, and finally to manufacturing (and often resulting in a costly product rejected by the customer)—companies are tearing down the traditional walls separating the departments so that people from each discipline can get involved in projects early on. In a process called **concurrent engineering**, the once-isolated specialists now work side by side and compare notes constantly in an effort to design cost-effective products with features customers want. Taking this approach enabled Chrysler Corporation to reduce its product development cycle from 60 to 36 months.[30] For such cross-functional work teams to be successful, the groups must receive training and coaching.

Otherwise, poorly implemented teams may worsen morale, create divisiveness, and raise the level of cynicism among workers.[31]

Union Relations and Temporary Workers

If the corporation is unionized, a good human resource manager should be able to work closely with the union. Union membership in the United States has dropped to 13.9% overall and to less than 12% of private sector workers in the mid 1990s from more than one-third a few decades earlier.[32] To save jobs, U.S. unions are increasingly willing to support employee involvement programs designed to increase worker participation in decision making.

Outside the United States, the average proportion of unionized workers among major industrialized nations is around 50%. European unions tend to be militant, politically oriented, and much less interested in working with management to increase efficiency. Nationwide strikes can occur quickly. Japanese unions are typically tied to individual companies and are usually supportive of management. These differences among countries have significant implications for the management of multinational corporations.

To increase flexibility, avoid layoffs, and reduce labor costs, corporations are using more temporary workers. From the 1980s to the 1990s, the employment of temporary (also known as contingent) workers in the U.S. increased 250% compared to a 20% increase in overall employment. Ninety percent of U.S. firms use temporary workers in some capacity; 43% now use them in professional and technical functions. Approximately 10% of the U.S. workforce (over 12 million individuals) are now temporary workers.[33] The percentage is even higher in some European countries, such as France. Labor unions are concerned that companies use temps to avoid hiring costlier unionized workers. At United Parcel Service, for example, 80% of the jobs created from 1993 to 1997 were staffed by part-timers, whose pay rates hadn't changed since 1982. Fully 10% of the company's 128,000 part-timers work 30 hours or more per week, but are still paid at a lower rate than are full-time employees.[34] According to John Kinloch, vice-president of Communications Workers of America Local 1058, "Corporations are trying to create a disposable workforce with low wages and no benefits."[35]

Quality of Work Life and Human Diversity

Human resource departments have found that to reduce employee dissatisfaction and unionization efforts (or, conversely, to improve employee satisfaction and existing union relations), they must consider the **quality of work life** in the design of jobs. Partially a reaction to the traditionally heavy emphasis on technical and economic factors in job design, quality of work life emphasizes improving the human dimension of work. The knowledgeable human resource manager, therefore, should be able to improve the corporation's quality of work life by (1) introducing participative problem solving, (2) restructuring work, (3) introducing innovative reward systems, and (4) improving the work environment. It is hoped that these improvements will lead to a more participative corporate culture and thus higher productivity and quality products. Ford Motor Company, for example, is rebuilding and modernizing its famous River Rouge plant using flexible equipment and new processes. Employees will work in teams and use Internet-connected PCs on the shop floor to share their concerns instantly with suppliers or product engineers. Workstations are being redesigned to make them more ergonomic and to reduce repetitive-strain injuries. "If you feel good while you're working, I think quality and productivity will increase, and Ford thinks that too, otherwise, they wouldn't do this," observed Jerry Sullivan, President of United Auto Worker Local 600.[36]

Human diversity refers to the mix in the workplace of people from different races, cultures, and backgrounds. This is a hot issue in HRM. Realizing that the demographics are changing toward an increasing percentage of minorities and women in the U.S. workforce, companies are now concerned with hiring and promoting people without regard to ethnic background. According to a study reported by *Fortune* magazine, companies that pursue diversity outperform the S&P 500.[37] Good human resource managers should be working to ensure that people are treated fairly on the job and not harassed by prejudiced coworkers or managers. Otherwise, they may find themselves subject to lawsuits. Coca-Cola Company, for example, agreed to pay $192.5 million because of discrimination against African American salaried employees in pay, promotions, and evaluations from 1995 and 2000. According to Chairman and CEO Douglas Daft, "Sometimes things happen in an unintentional manner. And I've made it clear that can't happen anymore."[38]

An organization's human resources are especially important in today's world of global communication and transportation systems. For example, on a visit to China during Spring 2000, one of Coca-Cola Company's executives was challenged by Chinese reporters regarding the company's racial problems. Advances in technology are copied almost immediately by competitors around the world. People are not as willing to move to other companies in other countries. This means that the only long-term resource advantage remaining to corporations operating in the industrialized nations may lie in the area of skilled human resources. Research does reveal that competitive strategies are more successfully executed in those companies with a high level of commitment to their employees than in those firms with less commitment.[39]

STRATEGIC INFORMATION SYSTEMS/TECHNOLOGY ISSUES

The primary task of the manager of information systems/technology is to design and manage the flow of information in an organization in ways that improve productivity and decision making. Information must be collected, stored, and synthesized in such a manner that it will answer important operating and strategic questions. The growth of the global Internet economy is forcing corporations to make significant investments in this functional area. (See the Internet Issue feature.) Corporate investments in information systems/technology are growing 11% annually even though 70% of all investments are either not completed or exceed cost projections by nearly 200%.[40]

Internet Issue

The Growing Global Internet Economy

Electronic commerce is poised to grow rapidly throughout the world to a total of $6.9 trillion in Internet sales by 2004. According to a report by Forrester Research entitled, *Global eCommerce Approaches Hypergrowth*, Internet sales in the United States should increase to $3.2 trillion by 2004 and account for 46.4% of the global Internet economy. The Asia-Pacific region should grow to $1.6 trillion in sales and account for 23.2% of the total Internet sales. Western Europe should reach $1.5 trillion in sales

(21.7% of the total) by 2004. After a slow start, Latin America's Internet sales should total $82.9 billion and account for 1.2% of total world Internet sales. Technologically, Latin America lags behind North America and Western Europe, but is being pushed by trading partners who are sophisticated Internet users to invest in crucial technology infrastructure such as phone lines, computers, Internet hosts, and cell phones. With Brazil and Argentina leading the way in liberalizing trade, the economic climate is rapidly improving. By 2004, Brazil should generate $64 billion on its own in online sales. Eastern Europe, Africa, and the Middle East are still facing the same problems that Latin America is now overcoming and will account for only $68.6 billion in sales, a mere 0.9% of the total world sales. The rest of the world's Internet sales will total $450 billion for the remaining 6.6% of total world sales.

Source: "Hypergrowth for E-Commerce?" *The Futurist* (September–October 2000), p. 15.

A corporation's information system can be a strength or a weakness in all elements of strategic management. It can not only aid in environmental scanning and in controlling a company's many activities, it can also be used as a strategic weapon in gaining competitive advantage. For example, American Hospital Supply (AHS), a leading manufacturer and distributor of a broad line of products for doctors, laboratories, and hospitals, developed an order entry distribution system that directly linked the majority of its customers to AHS computers. The system was successful because it simplified ordering processes for customers, reduced costs for both AHS and the customer, and allowed AHS to provide pricing incentives to the customer. As a result, customer loyalty was high and AHS's share of the market became large.

Information systems/technology offers four main contributions to corporate performance. *First* (beginning in the 1970s with main frame computers), it is used to automate existing back-office processes, such as payroll, human resource records, accounts payable and receivable, and to establish huge databases. *Second* (beginning in the 1980s), it is used to automate individual tasks, such as keeping track of clients and expenses, through the use of personal computers with word processing and spreadsheet software. Corporate databases are accessed to provide sufficient data to analyze the data and create what-if scenarios. These first two contributions tend to focus on reducing costs. *Third* (beginning in the 1990s), it is used to enhance key business functions, such as marketing and operations. This third contribution focuses on productivity improvements. The system provides customer support and help in distribution and logistics. For example, FedEx found that by allowing customers to directly access its package-tracking database via its Internet Web site instead of their having to ask a human operator, the company saved up to $2 million annually.[41] Business processes are analyzed to increase efficiency and productivity via reengineering. Enterprise resource planning application software, by firms such as SAP, PeopleSoft, Oracle, Baan, and J.D. Edwards, are used to integrate worldwide business activities so that employees need to enter information only once and that information is available to all corporate systems (including accounting) around the world. *Fourth* (beginning in 2000), it is used to develop competitive advantage. The focus is now on taking advantage of opportunities via supply chain management, electronic commerce, and knowledge management. Currently, most companies devote 85% of their IS/IT budget to the first two utility functions, 12% to productivity enhancement, and only 3% to efforts to gain competitive advantage.[42]

A current trend in corporate information systems is the increasing use of the Internet for marketing, intranets for internal communication, and extranets for logistics and distribution. An **intranet** is an information network within an organization that also has access to the external worldwide Internet. Intranets typically begin as ways to provide employees with company information such as lists of product prices, fringe benefits, and company policies. They are then converted into extranets for supply chain management. An **extranet** is an information network within an organization that is available to key suppliers and customers. The key issue in building an extranet is the creation of "fire walls" to block extranet users from accessing the firm's or other users' confidential data. Once this is accomplished, companies can allow employees, customers, and suppliers to access information and conduct business on the Internet in a completely automated manner. By connecting these groups, companies hope to obtain a competitive advantage by reducing the time needed to design and bring new products to market, slashing inventories, customizing manufacturing, and entering new markets.[43]

4.4 The Strategic Audit: A Checklist for Organizational Analysis

One way of conducting an organizational analysis to ascertain a company's strengths and weaknesses is by using the Strategic Audit found in **Appendix 10.A of Chapter 10**. The audit provides a checklist of questions by area of concern. For example, Part IV of the audit examines corporate structure, culture, and resources. It looks at resources in terms of the functional areas of marketing, finance, R&D, operations, human resources, and information systems, among others.

4.5 Synthesis of Internal Factors: IFAS

After strategists have scanned the internal organizational environment and identified factors for their particular corporation, they may want to summarize their analysis of these factors using a form such as that given in **Table 4–2**. This **IFAS** (Internal Factor Analysis Summary) **Table** is one way to organize the internal factors into the generally accepted categories of strengths and weaknesses as well as to analyze how well a particular company's management is responding to these specific factors in light of the perceived importance of these factors to the company. Use the VRIO framework (**V**alue, **R**areness, **I**mitability, and **O**rganization) to assess the importance of each of the factors that might be considered strengths. Except for its internal orientation, this IFAS Table is built the same way as the EFAS Table described in **Chapter 3** (in **Table 3–4**). To use the IFAS Table, complete the following steps:

- In **Column 1** (Internal Factors), list the 8 to 10 most important strengths and weaknesses facing the company.

- In **Column 2** (Weight), assign a weight to each factor from **1.0** (Most Important) to **0.0** (Not Important) based on that factor's probable impact on a particular company's current strategic position. The higher the weight, the more important is this factor to the current and future success of the company. All weights must sum to 1.0 regardless of the number of factors.

- In **Column 3** (Rating), assign a rating to each factor from **5.0** (Outstanding) to **1.0** (Poor) based on management's current response to that particular factor. Each rating is a judgment regarding how well the company's management is currently dealing with each internal factor.

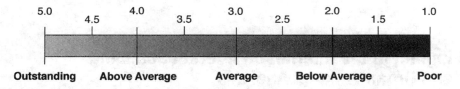

- In **Column 4** (Weighted Score), multiply the weight in **Column 2** for each factor times its rating in **Column 3** to obtain each factor's weighted score. This results in a weighted score for each factor ranging from **5.0** (Outstanding) to **1.0** (Poor) with **3.0** as Average.

- In **Column 5** (Comments), note why a particular factor was selected and/or how its weight and rating were estimated.

Finally, add the individual weighted scores for all the internal factors in **Column 4** to determine the total weighted score for that particular company. The **total weighted score** indicates how well a particular company is responding to current and expected factors in its internal environment. The score can be used to compare that firm to other firms in its industry. The total weighted score for an average firm in an industry is always 3.0.

As an example of this procedure, **Table 4–2** includes a number of internal factors for Maytag Corporation in 1995 (before Maytag sold its European and Australian operations) with corresponding weights, ratings, and weighted scores provided. Note that Maytag's total weighted score was 3.05, meaning that the corporation was about average compared to the strengths and weaknesses of others in the major home appliance industry at that time.

Table 4-2 Internal Factor Analysis Summary (IFAS Table): Maytag as Example

Internal Factors	Weight	Rating	Weighted Score	Comments
	1	2	3	4	5
Strengths				
• Quality Maytag culture	.15	5.0	.75	Quality key to success
• Experienced top management	.05	4.2	.21	Know appliances
• Vertical integration	.10	3.9	.39	Dedicated factories
• Employee relations	.05	3.0	.15	Good, but deteriorating
• Hoover's international orientation	.15	2.8	.42	Hoover name in cleaners
Weaknesses				
• Process-oriented R&D	.05	2.2	.11	Slow on new products
• Distribution channels	.05	2.0	.10	Superstores replacing small dealers
• Financial position	.15	2.0	.30	High debt load
• Global positioning	.20	2.1	.42	Hoover weak outside the United Kingdom and Australia
• Manufacturing facilities	.05	4.0	.20	Investing now
Total Scores	1.00		3.05	

Notes:
1. List strengths and weaknesses (8–10) in Column 1.
2. Weight each factor from 1.0 (Most Important) to 0.0 (Not Important) in Column 2 based on that factor's probable impact on the company's strategic position. **The total weights must sum to 1.00.**
3. Rate each factor from 5.0 (Outstanding) to 1.0 (Poor) in Column 3 based on the company's response to that factor.
4. Multiply each factor's weight times its rating to obtain each factor's weighted score in Column 4.
5. Use Column 5 (comments) for rationale used for each factor.
6. Add the individual weighted scores to obtain the total weighted score for the company in Column 4. This tells how well the company is responding to the strategic factors in its internal environment.

Source: T. L. Wheelen and J. D. Hunger, "Internal Factor Analysis Summary (IFAS)." Copyright © 1991 by Wheelen and Hunger Associates. Reprinted by permission.

4.6 Impact of the Internet on Internal Scanning and Organizational Analysis

The expansion of the marketing-oriented Internet into intranets and extranets is making significant contributions to organizational performance through supply chain management and virtual teams. **Supply chain management** is the forming of networks for sourcing raw materials, manufacturing products or creating services, storing and distributing the goods, and delivering them to customers and consumers.[44] Industry leaders are integrating modern information systems into their corporate value chains to harmonize companywide efforts and to achieve competitive advantage. For example, Heineken Beer distributors input actual depletion figures and replenishment orders to the Netherlands brewer through their linked Web pages. This interactive planning system generates time-phased orders based on actual usage rather than on projected demand. Distributors are then able to modify plans based on local conditions or changes in marketing. Heineken uses these modifications to adjust brewing and supply schedules. As a result of this system, lead times have been reduced from the traditional 10 to 12 weeks to 4 to 6 weeks. This time savings is especially useful in an industry competing on product freshness. In another example, Procter & Gamble participates in an information network to move the company's line of consumer products through Wal-Mart's many stores. As part of the network with Wal-Mart, P&G

knows by cash register and by store what products have passed through the system each day. The network is linked by satellite communications on a real-time basis. With actual point-of-sale information, products are replenished to meet current demand and minimize stockouts while maintaining exceptionally low inventories.[45]

Virtual teams are groups of geographically and/or organizationally dispersed coworkers that are assembled using a combination of telecommunications and information technologies to accomplish an organizational task.[46] Internet, intranet, and extranet systems are combining with other new technologies such as desktop videoconferencing and collaborative software to create a new workplace in which teams of workers are no longer restrained by geography, time, or organizational boundaries. As more companies outsource some of the activities previously conducted internally, the traditional organizational structure is being replaced by a series of virtual teams, which rarely, if ever, meet face-to-face. Such teams may be established as temporary groups to accomplish a specific task or may be more permanent to address continuing issues such as strategic planning. Membership on these teams is often fluid, depending upon the task to be accomplished. They may include not only employees from different functions within a company, but also members of various stakeholder groups, such as suppliers, customers, and law or consulting firms. The use of virtual teams to replace traditional face-to-face work groups is being driven by five trends:

1. Flatter organizational structures with increasing cross-functional coordination needs

2. Turbulent environments requiring more interorganizational cooperation

3. Increasing employee autonomy and participation in decision making

4. Higher knowledge requirements derived from a greater emphasis on service

5. Increasing globalization of trade and corporate activity[47]

Projections for the 21st Century

- From 1994 to 2010, the average income per capita in the developed nations will rise from $16,610 to $22,802.
- From 1994 to 2010, the average income per capita in the developing nations will increase from $950 to $2,563.[48]

Discussion Questions

1. What is the relevance of the resource-based view of the firm to strategic management in a global environment?

2. How can value-chain analysis help identify a company's strengths and weaknesses?

3. In what ways can a corporation's structure and culture be internal strengths or weaknesses?

4. What are the pros and cons of management's using the experience curve to determine strategy?

5. How might a firm's management decide whether it should continue to invest in current known technology or in new, but untested technology? What factors might encourage or discourage such a shift?

Strategic Practice Exercise

Can you analyze a corporation using the Internet? Try the following exercise.

1. Form teams of around five people. Find the Internet 100 Index from the latest copy of *USA Today.* (**Check this publisher's Web site for a recent listing of the**

Internet 100.) The index is divided into the e-Commerce 50 and the e-Business 50. The e-Commerce 50 is composed of four subindustries: e-Retail, e-Finance, e-New Media, and e-Service Providers. The e-Business 50 is composed of three subindustries: e-Infrastructure, e-Services/Solutions, and e-Advertising.

2. Each team selects four companies plus one assigned by the instructor. (The list of companies from which assignments will be made is Amazon.com, E-loan, Cisco Systems, AOL, Yahoo!, and DoubleClick.) Provide the instructor with your list.

3. Conduct research on each of your five companies *using the Internet only*.

4. Write a three to six page double-spaced typed report for each of the five companies. The report should include the following:

   a. Does the firm have any core competencies? Are any of these distinctive (better than the competition)

competencies? Does the firm have any competitive advantage? Provide a SWOT analysis using EFAS and IFAS Tables.

b. What is the likely future of this firm? Will the company survive industry consolidation?

c. Would you buy stock in this company? Assume that your team has $25,000 to invest. Allocate the money among your five companies. Be specific. List the five companies, the number of shares purchased of each, the cost of each share as of a given date, and the total cost for each purchase assuming a typical commission used by an Internet broker, such as E-Trade. (This part of your report will be common to all members of your team.)

Key Terms

autonomous (self-managing) work teams (p. 97)
basic R&D (p. 93)
capital budgeting (p. 92)
center of gravity (p. 85)
concurrent engineering (p. 97)
conglomerate structure (p. 88)
continuous systems (p. 96)
continuum of sustainability (p. 83)
core competencies (p. 82)
corporate capabilities (p. 82)
cross-functional work teams (p. 97)
corporate culture (p. 89)
cultural integration (p. 89)
cultural intensity (p. 89)
distinctive competencies (p. 82)
divisional structure (p. 87)
durability (p. 82)
economies of scale (p. 97)
economies of scope (p. 87)
engineering (or process) R&D (p. 93)
experience curve (p. 96)

explicit knowledge (p. 83)
extranet (p. 100)
financial leverage (p. 92)
flexible manufacturing (p. 97)
functional structure (p. 87)
human diversity (p. 98)
IFAS Table (p. 101)
imitability (p. 82)
intermittent systems (p. 95)
internal strategic factors (p. 81)
intranet (p. 100)
linkages (p. 86)
market position (p. 90)
market segmentation (p. 90)
marketing mix (p. 90)
mass customization (p. 97)
operating leverage (p. 96)
organizational analysis (p. 81)
organizational structures (p. 87)
primary activities (p. 85)
product life cycle (p. 90)
product R&D (p. 93)

quality of work life (p. 98)
R&D intensity (p. 92)
R&D mix (p. 93)
replicability (p. 83)
resource (p. 81)
reverse engineering (p. 82)
simple structure (p. 87)
strategic business units (SBUs) (p. 87)
support activities (p. 86)
supply chain management (p. 102)
tacit knowledge (p. 83)
technological competence (p. 92)
technological discontinuity (p. 94)
technology transfer (p. 93)
transferability (p. 82)
transparency (p. 82)
value chain (p. 84)
VRIO framework (p. 81)
virtual teams (p. 103)

Notes

1. M. Babineck, "United Airlines Increases Fares; Others Follow," *Des Moines Register* (November 18, 2000), p. 6D.
2. R. Roach & Associates, cited in *Air Transport World* (June 1996), p. 1.
3. J. B. Barney, *Gaining and Sustaining Competitive Advantage* (Reading, MA: Addison-Wesley, 1997), pp. 145–164.
4. R. M. Grant, "The Resource-Based Theory of Competitive Advantage: Implications for Strategy Formulation," *California Management Review* (Spring 1991), pp. 114–135.
5. M. Brellis, "Simple Strategy Makes Southwest Successful," (Ames) *Daily Tribune* (November 9, 2000), p. B7.
6. J. E. McGee and L. G. Love, "Sources of Competitive Advantage for Small Independent Retailers: Lessons from the Neighborhood Drugstore," *Association for Small Business & Entrepreneurship*, Houston, Texas (March 10–13, 1999), p. 2.
7. M. Polanyi, *The Tacit Dimension* (London: Routledge & Kegan Paul, 1966).

8. P. E. Bierly III, "Development of a Generic Knowledge Strategy Typology," *Journal of Business Strategies* (Spring 1999), p. 3.

9. O. Gadiesh and J. L. Gilbert, "Profit Pools: A Fresh Look at Strategy," *Harvard Business Review* (May–June, 1998), pp. 139–147.

10. J. R. Galbraith, "Strategy and Organization Planning," in *The Strategy Process: Concepts, Contexts, and Cases*, 2nd ed., edited by H. Mintzberg and J. B. Quinn (Upper Saddle River, NJ: Prentice Hall, 1991), pp. 315–324.

11. M. Porter, *Competitive Advantage: Creating and Sustaining Superior Performance* (New York: The Free Press, 1985), p. 36.

12. M. Leontiades, "A Diagnostic Framework for Planning," *Strategic Management Journal* (January–March 1983), p. 14.

13. E. H. Schein, *The Corporate Culture Survival Guide* (San Francisco: Jossey-Bass, 1999), p. 12; L. C. Harris and E. Ogbonna, "The Strategic Legacy of Company Founders," *Long Range Planning* (June 1999), pp. 333–343.

14. D. M. Rousseau, "Assessing Organizational Culture: The Case for Multiple Methods," in *Organizational Climate and Culture*, edited by B. Schneider (San Francisco: Jossey-Bass, 1990), pp. 153–192.

15. L. Smircich, "Concepts of Culture and Organizational Analysis," *Administrative Science Quarterly* (September 1983), pp. 345–346.

16. K. E. Aupperle, "Spontaneous Organizational Reconfiguration: A Historical Example Based on Xenophon's Anabasis," *Organization Science* (July–August 1996), pp. 445–460.

17. Barney, p. 155.

18. R. L. Simerly and M. Li, "Environmental Dynamism, Capital Structure and Performance: A Theoretical Integration and an Empirical Test," *Strategic Management Journal* (January 2000), pp. 31–49.

19. R. L. Simerly and M. Li, "Environmental Dynamism, Capital Structure and Performance: A Theoretical Integration and an Empirical Test," *Strategic Management Journal* (January 2000), pp. 31–49.

20. J. M. Poterba and L. H. Summers, "A CEO Survey of U.S. Companies' Time Horizons and Hurdle Rates," *Sloan Management Review* (Fall 1995), pp. 43–53.

21. "R&D Scoreboard," *Business Week* (June 27, 1994), pp. 81–103.

22. B. O'Reilly, "The Secrets of America's Most Admired Corporations: New Ideas and New Products," *Fortune* (March 3, 1997), p. 62.

23. P. Pascarella, "Are You Investing in the Wrong Technology?" *Industry Week* (July 25, 1983), p. 37.

24. D. J. Yang, "Leaving Moore's Law in the Dust," *U.S. News & World Report* (July 10, 2000), pp. 37–38; R. Fishburne and M. Malone, "Laying Down the Laws: Gordon Moore and Bob Metcalfe in Conversation," *Forbes ASAP* (February 21, 2000), pp. 97–100.

25. Pascarella., p. 38.

26. C. M. Christensen, *The Innovator's Dilemma* (Boston: Harvard Business School Press, 1997).

27. B. J. Pine, *Mass Customization: The New Frontier in Business Competition* (Boston: Harvard Business School Press, 1993).

28. E. E. Lawler, S. A. Mohrman, and G. E. Ledford, Jr., *Creating High Performance Organizations* (San Francisco: Jossey-Bass, 1995), p. 29.

29. A. Versteeg, "Self-Directed Work Teams Yield Long-Term Benefits," *Journal of Business Strategy* (November/December 1990), pp. 9–12.

30. R. Sanchez, "Strategic Flexibility in Product Competition," *Strategic Management Journal* (Summer 1995), p. 147.

31. A. R. Jassawalla and H. C. Sashittal, "Building Collaborative Cross-Functional New Product Teams," *Academy of Management Executive* (August 1999), pp. 50–63.

32. E. E. Lawler, S. A. Mohrman, and G. E. Ledford, Jr., *Creating High Performance Organizations* (San Francisco: Jossey-Bass, 1995), p. 123. The percentage of unionized government employees is 38.7%. See "Uncle Sam Gompers," *Wall Street Journal* (October 25, 1994), p. A20.

33. S. F. Matusik and C. W. L. Hill, "The Utilization of Contingent Work, Knowledge Creation, and Competitive Advantage," *Academy of Management Executive* (October 1998), pp. 680–697.

34. A. Bewrnstein, "At UPS, Part-Time Work Is a Full-Time Issue," *Business Week* (June 16, 1997), pp. 88–90.

35. D. L. Boroughs, "The New Migrant Workers," *U.S. News & World Report* (July 4, 1994), p. 53.

36. J. Muller, "A Ford Redesign," *Business Week* (November 13, 2000), Special Report.

37. G. Colvin, "The 50 Best Companies for Asians, Blacks, and Hispanics," *Fortune* (July 19, 1999), pp. 53–58.

38. J. Bachman, "Coke to Pay $192.5 Million to Settle Lawsuit," *The* (Ames) *Tribune* (November 20, 2000), p. D4.

39. J. Lee and D. Miller, "People Matter: Commitment to Employees, Strategy, and Performance in Korean Firms," *Strategic Management Journal* (June 1999), pp. 579–593.

40. B. Rosser, "Making IT Investments Cost Effective," *Executive Edge* (September 1998), pp. 50–54.

41. A. Cortese, "Here Comes the Intranet," *Business Week* (February 26, 1996), p. 76.

42. B. Rosser, "Making IT Investments Cost Effective," *Executive Edge* (September 1998), pp. 50–54.

43. D. Bartholomew, "Blue-Collar Computing," *InformationWeek* (June 19, 1995), pp. 34–43.

44. C. C. Poirier, *Advanced Supply Chain Management* (San Francisco: Berrett-Koehler Publishers, 1999), p. 2.

45. C. C. Poirer, pp. 3–5.

46. A. M. Townsend, S. M. DeMarie, and A. R. Hendrickson, "Virtual Teams" Technology and the Workplace of the Future," *Academy of Management Executive* (August 1998), pp. 17–29.

47. Townsend, DeMarie, and Hendrickson, p. 18.

48. J. Warner, "21st Century Capitalism: Snapshot of the Next Century," *Business Week* (November 18, 1994), p. 194.

chapter 5

Strategy Formulation: Situation Analysis and Business Strategy

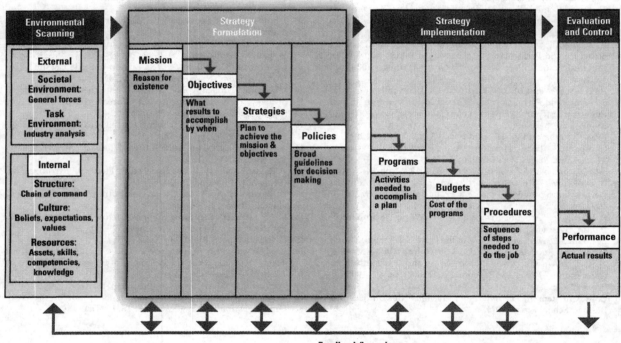

Feedback/Learning

When Donald Lamberti incorporated Casey's General Stores in 1967 in Des Moines, Iowa, he formulated a strategy unknown at that time in the convenience store industry. Instead of targeting the large, growing metropolitan areas of the eastern, western, and southern United States where potential sales were high, he chose to focus on the small towns in the agricultural heartland of the Midwest. Contrary to all the conventional wisdom arguing against beginning a business in a declining market, Lamberti avoided direct competition with 7-Eleven and moved into these increasingly ignored small markets. The company expanded its offerings from just gasoline and basic groceries to include fast food and bakeries. In many small Midwestern towns, Casey's was now the only retail business left. These were towns too small for even Wal-Mart to covet. Like any convenience store, prices were somewhat higher

108

than in larger, more specialized stores in the cities. But people from small towns did not want to have to drive 10 to 20 miles for a loaf of bread or a pizza.

By 2001, Casey's had opened over 1,100 stores in the upper midwestern United States. At a time when other convenience stores were struggling to show a profit and avoid bankruptcy, Casey's recorded continuing growth and profitability. (For further information, see <www.caseys.com>.)

Casey's General Stores is successful because its strategic managers formulated a new strategy designed to give it an advantage in a very competitive industry. Casey's is an example of a differentiation focus competitive strategy in which a company focuses on a particular market area to provide a differentiated product or service. This strategy is one of the business competitive strategies discussed in this chapter.

5.1 Situational Analysis: SWOT Analysis

Strategy formulation is often referred to as strategic planning or long-range planning and is concerned with developing a corporation's mission, objectives, strategies, and policies. It begins with situation analysis: the process of finding a strategic fit between external opportunities and internal strengths while working around external threats and internal weaknesses. As shown in the *Strategic Decision-Making Process* in **Figure 1–5** on pages 20–21, this is step 5(a): analyzing strategic factors in light of the current situation using SWOT analysis. **SWOT** is an acronym used to describe the particular **S**trengths, **W**eaknesses, **O**pportunities, and **T**hreats that are strategic factors for a specific company. SWOT analysis should not only result in the identification of a corporation's **distinctive competencies**—the particular capabilities and resources that a firm possesses and the superior way in which they are used—but also in the identification of opportunities that the firm is not currently able to take advantage of due to a lack of appropriate resources. Over the years, SWOT analysis has proven to be the most enduring analytical technique used in strategic management. For example, a survey of 113 manufacturing and service companies in the United Kingdom reported the five most-used tools and techniques in strategic analysis to be (1) spreadsheet "what if" analysis, (2) analysis of key or critical success factors, (3) financial analysis of competitors, (4) SWOT analysis, and (5) core capabilities analysis.[1] It is very likely that these have a similar rate of usage in the rest of the world.

It can be said that the essence of strategy is opportunity divided by capacity.[2] An opportunity by itself has no real value unless a company has the capacity (i.e., resources) to take advantage of that opportunity. This approach, however, considers only opportunities and strengths when considering alternative strategies. By itself, a distinctive competency in a key resource or capability is no guarantee of competitive advantage. Weaknesses in other resource areas can prevent a strategy from being successful. SWOT can thus be used to take a broader view of strategy through the formula SA = O/(S − W) (Strategic Alternative equals Opportunity divided by Strengths minus Weaknesses). This reflects an important issue facing strategic managers: *Should we invest more in our strengths to make them even stronger (a distinctive competence), or should we invest in our weaknesses to at least make them competitive?*

SWOT analysis, by itself, is not a panacea. Some of the primary **criticisms of SWOT** analysis are:

- It generates lengthy lists.
- It uses no weights to reflect priorities.
- It uses ambiguous words and phrases.
- The same factor can be placed in two categories (e.g., a strength may also be a weakness).
- There is no obligation to verify opinions with data or analysis.
- It requires only a single level of analysis.
- There is no logical link to strategy implementation.[3]

Table 4-2 Internal Factor Analysis Summary (IFAS): Maytag as Example
(Selection of Strategic Factors)*

Internal Strategic Factors	Weight	Rating	Weighted Score	Comments
	1	2	3	4	5
Strengths				
S1 Quality Maytag culture	.15	5.0	.75	Quality key to success
S2 Experienced top management	.05	4.2	.21	Know appliances
S3 Vertical integration	.10	3.9	.39	Dedicated factories
S4 Employee relations	.05	3.0	.15	Good, but deteriorating
S5 Hoover's international orientation	.15	2.8	.42	Hoover name in cleaners
Weaknesses				
W1 Process-oriented R&D	.05	2.2	.11	Slow on new products
W2 Distribution channels	.05	2.0	.10	Superstores replacing small dealers
W3 Financial position	.15	2.0	.30	High debt load
W4 Global positioning	.20	2.1	.42	Hoover weak outside the United Kingdom and Australia
W5 Manufacturing facilities	.05	4.0	.20	Investing now
Total Scores	1.00		3.05	

Table 3-4 External Factor Analysis Summary (EFAS): Maytag as Example
(Selection of Strategic Factors)*

External Strategic Factors	Weight	Rating	Weighted Score	Comments
	1	2	3	4	5
Opportunities				
O1 Economic integration of European Community	.20	4.1	.82	Acquisition of Hoover
O2 Demographics favor quality appliances	.10	5.0	.50	Maytag quality
O3 Economic development of Asia	.05	1.0	.05	Low Maytag presence
O4 Opening of Eastern Europe	.05	2.0	.10	Will take time
O5 Trend to "Super Stores"	.10	1.8	.18	Maytag weak in this channel
Threats				
T1 Increasing government regulations	.10	4.3	.43	Well positioned
T2 Strong U.S. competition	.10	4.0	.40	Well positioned
T3 Whirlpool and Electrolux strong globally	.15	3.0	.45	Hoover weak globally
T4 New product advances	.05	1.2	.06	Questionable
T5 Japanese appliance companies	.10	1.6	.16	Only Asian presence is Australia
Total Scores	1.00		3.15	

*The most important external and internal factors are identified in the EFAS and IFAS tables as shown here by shading these factors.

GENERATING A STRATEGIC FACTORS ANALYSIS SUMMARY (SFAS) MATRIX

The EFAS and IFAS Tables plus the SFAS Matrix have been developed to deal with the above criticisms of SWOT analysis. When used together, they are a powerful set of analytical tools for strategic analysis. The **SFAS (Strategic Factors Analysis Summary) Matrix** summarizes an organization's strategic factors by combining the external factors from the EFAS Table with the

Figure 5–1

Strategic Factor Analysis Summary (SFAS) Matrix

Strategic Factors (Select the most important opportunities/threats from EFAS, Table 3–4 and the most important strengths and weaknesses from IFAS, Table 4–2)	Weight	Rating	Weighted Score	SHORT	INTERMEDIATE	LONG	Comments
	1	**2**	**3**	**4** Duration		**5**	**6**
S1 Quality Maytag culture (S)	.10	5.0	.50			X	Quality key to success
S5 Hoover's international orientation (S)	.10	2.8	.28	X	X		Name recognition
W3 Financial position (W)	.10	2.0	.20	X	X		High debt
W4 Global positioning (W)	.15	2.2	.33				Only in N.A., U.K., and Australia
01 Economic integration of European Community (O)	.10	4.1	.41		X	X	Acquisition of Hoover
02 Demographics favor quality (O)	.10	5.0	.50		X		Maytag quality
05 Trend to super stores (O + T)	.10	1.8	.18	X			Weak in this channel
T3 Whirlpool and Electrolux (T)	.15	3.0	.45	X			Dominate industry
T5 Japanese appliance companies (T)	.10	1.6	.16			X	Asian presence
Total Scores	**1.00**		**3.01**				

Notes:
1. List each of the most important factors developed in your IFAS and EFAS tables in Column 1.
2. Weight each factor from 1.0 (Most Important) to 0.0 (Not Important) in Column 2 based on that factor's probable impact on the company's strategic position. **The total weights must sum to 1.00.**
3. Rate each factor from 5.0 (Outstanding) to 1.0 (Poor) in Column 3 based on the company's response to that factor.
4. Multiply each factor's weight times its rating to obtain each factor's weighted score in Column 4.
5. For duration in Column 5, check appropriate column (short term—less than 1 year; intermediate—1 to 3 years; long term—over 3 years).
6. Use Column 6 (comments) for rationale used for each factor.

Source: T. L. Wheelen and J. D. Hunger, "Strategic Factors Analysis Summary (SFAS)." Copyright © 1997 by Wheelen and Hunger Associates. Reprinted by permission.

internal factors from the IFAS Table. The EFAS and IFAS examples given of Maytag Corporation (as it was in 1995) in **Tables 3–4** and **4–2** list a total of 20 internal and external factors. These are too many factors for most people to use in strategy formulation. The SFAS Matrix requires the strategic decision maker to condense these strengths, weaknesses, opportunities, and threats into fewer than 10 strategic factors. This is done by reviewing and revising the weight given each factor. The revised weights reflect the priority of each factor as a determinant of the company's future success. The highest weighted EFAS and IFAS factors should appear in the SFAS Matrix.

As shown in **Figure 5–1**, you can create an SFAS Matrix by following these steps:

- In the **Strategic Factors** column (column 1), list the most important (in terms of weight) EFAS and IFAS items. After each factor, indicate whether it is a strength (S), weakness (W), opportunity (O), threat (T), or a combination.

- In the **Weight** column (column 2), enter the weights for all of the internal and external strategic factors. As with the EFAS and IFAS Tables, the **weight column must still total 1.00**. This means that the weights calculated for EFAS and IFAS will probably have to be adjusted.

- In the **Rating** column (column 3), enter the ratings of how the company's management is responding to each of the strategic factors. These ratings will probably (but not always) be the same as those listed in the EFAS and IFAS Tables.

- In the **Weighted Score** column (column 4), calculate the weighted scores as done earlier for EFAS and IFAS.

- In the new **Duration** column (column 5), depicted in **Figure 5–1**, indicate **short-term** *(less than 1 year)*, **intermediate-term** *(1 to 3 years)*, or **long-term** *(3 years and beyond)*.

- In the **Comments** column (column 6), repeat or revise your comments for each strategic factor from the EFAS and IFAS Tables.

The resulting SFAS Matrix is a listing of the firm's external and internal strategic factors in one table. The example given is that of Maytag Corporation in 1995 before the firm sold its European and Australian operations. The SFAS Matrix includes only the most important factors gathered from environmental scanning and thus provides the information essential for strategy formulation. The use of EFAS and IFAS Tables together with the SFAS Matrix deal with many of the criticisms of SWOT analysis.

FINDING A PROPITIOUS NICHE

One desired outcome of analyzing strategic factors is identifying a niche where an organization can use its core competencies to take advantage of a particular market opportunity. A niche is a need in the marketplace that is currently unsatisfied. The goal is to find a **propitious niche**—an extremely favorable niche—that is so well suited to the firm's internal and external environment that other corporations are not likely to challenge or dislodge it.[4] A niche is propitious to the extent that it currently is just large enough for one firm to satisfy its demand. After a firm has found and filled that niche, it is not worth a potential competitor's time or money to also go after the same niche.

Finding such a niche is not always easy. A firm's management must be always looking for a **strategic window**, that is, a unique market opportunity that is available only for a particular time. The first firm through a strategic window can occupy a propitious niche and discourage competition (if the firm has the required internal strengths). One company that has successfully found a propitious niche is Frank J. Zamboni & Company, the manufacturer of the machines that smooth the ice at ice skating rinks. Frank Zamboni invented the unique tractorlike machine in 1949 and no one has found a substitute for what it does. Before the machine was invented, people had to clean and scrape the ice by hand to prepare the surface for skating. Now hockey fans look forward to intermissions just to watch "the Zamboni" slowly drive up and down the ice rink turning rough, scraped ice into a smooth mirror surface—almost like magic. So long as Zamboni's company is able to produce the machines in the quantity and quality desired at a reasonable price, it's not worth another company's time to go after Frank Zamboni & Company's propitious niche.

As the niche grows, so can the company within that niche—by increasing its operations' capacity or through alliances with larger firms. The key is to identify a market opportunity in which the first firm to reach that market segment can obtain and keep dominant market share. For example, Church & Dwight was the first company in the United States to successfully market sodium bicarbonate for use in cooking. Its Arm & Hammer brand baking soda is still found in 95% of all U.S. households. The propitious niche concept is crucial to the software industry. Small initial demand in emerging markets allows new entrepreneurial ventures to go after niches too small to be noticed by established companies. When Microsoft developed its first disk operating system (DOS) in 1980 for IBM's personal computers, for example, the demand for such open systems software was very small—a small niche for a then very small Microsoft. The company was able to fill that niche and to successfully grow with it.

Niches can also change—sometimes faster than a firm can adapt to that change. A company's managers may discover in their situation analysis that they need to invest heavily in the firm's capabilities to keep them competitively strong in a changing niche. South African Breweries (SAB), for example, took this approach when management realized that the only way to keep competitors out of its market was to continuously invest in increased productivity and infrastructure in order to keep its prices very low. See the **Global Issue** feature to see how SAB was able to successfully defend its market niche during significant changes in its environment.

Global Issue

SAB Defends Its Propitious Niche

Out of 50 beers consumed by South Africans, 49 are brewed by South African Breweries (SAB). Founded more than a century ago, SAB controlled most of the local beer market by 1950 with brands like Castle and Lion. When the government repealed the ban on the sale of alcohol to blacks in the 1960s, SAB and other brewers competed for the rapidly growing market. SAB fought successfully to retain its dominance of the market. With the end of apartheid, foreign brewers have been tempted to break SAB's near-monopoly, but have been deterred by the entry barriers SAB has erected.

Entry Barrier #1

Every year for the past two decades SAB has reduced its prices. The "real" (adjusted for inflation) price of its beer is now half what it was during the 1970s. SAB has been able to achieve this through a continuous emphasis on productivity improvements—boosting production while cutting the workforce almost in half. Keeping prices low has been key to SAB's avoiding charges of abusing its monopoly.

Entry Barrier #2

In South Africa's poor and rural areas, roads are rough and electricity is undependable. SAB has long experience in transporting crates to remote villages along bad roads and making sure that distributors have refrigerators (and electricity generators if needed). Many of its distributors are former employees who have been helped by the company to start their own trucking businesses.

Entry Barrier #3

Most of the beer sold in South Africa is sold through unlicensed pubs called *shebeens*, most of which date back to apartheid when blacks were not allowed licenses. Although the current government of South Africa would be pleased to grant pub licenses to blacks, the shebeen-owners don't want them. They enjoy not paying any taxes. SAB cannot sell directly to the shebeens, but it does so indirectly through wholesalers. The government, in turn, ignores the situation, preferring that people drink SAB beer than potentially deadly moonshine.

To break into South Africa, a new entrant would have to build large breweries and a substantial distribution network. SAB would, in turn, probably reduce its prices still further to defend its market. The difficulties of operating in South Africa are too great, the market is growing too slowly, and (given SAB's low-cost position) the likely profit margin is too low to justify entering the market. Some foreign brewers, such as Heineken, would rather use SAB to distribute their products throughout South Africa. As a result, SAB is now the world's fifth largest brewer by volume. With its home market secure, SAB's management considered acquiring a global brewer such as Bass in June 2000, but decided against it because of the high price.

Source: "Big Lion, Small Cage," *The Economist* (August 12, 2000), p. 56. Reprinted with permission.

5.2 Review of Mission and Objectives

A reexamination of an organization's current mission and objectives must be made before alternative strategies can be generated and evaluated. Even when formulating strategy, decision makers tend to concentrate on the alternatives—the action possibilities—rather than on a mission to be fulfilled and objectives to be achieved. This tendency is so attractive because it is much easier to deal with alternative courses of action that exist right here and now than to really think about what you want to accomplish in the future. The end result is that we often choose strategies that set our objectives for us, rather than having our choices incorporate clear objectives and a mission statement.

Problems in performance can derive from an inappropriate statement of mission, which may be too narrow or too broad. If the mission does not provide a *common thread* (a unifying theme) for a corporation's businesses, managers may be unclear about where the company is heading. Objectives and strategies might be in conflict with each other. Divisions might be competing against one another, rather than against outside competition, to the detriment of the corporation as a whole.

A company's objectives can also be inappropriately stated. They can either focus too much on short-term operational goals or be so general that they provide little real guidance. There may be a gap between planned and achieved objectives. When such a gap occurs, either the strategies have to be changed to improve performance or the objectives need to be adjusted downward to be more realistic. Consequently, objectives should be constantly reviewed to ensure their usefulness. This is what happened at Toyota Motor Corporation when top management realized that its "Global 10" objective of aiming for 10% of the global vehicle market was no longer feasible. Emphasis was then shifted from market share to profits. Interestingly, at the same time that both Toyota and General Motors were de-emphasizing market share as a key corporate objective, Ford Motor Company was stating that it wanted to be Number 1 in sales worldwide. No longer content with being in second place, Alexander Trotman, Ford's Chairman of the Board, contends: "Have you ever seen a team run out on the field and say, 'We're going to be Number 2?'"[5]

5.3 Generating Alternative Strategies Using a TOWS Matrix

Thus far we have discussed how a firm uses SWOT analysis to assess its situation. SWOT can also be used to generate a number of possible alternative strategies. The **TOWS Matrix** (TOWS is just another way of saying SWOT) illustrates how the external opportunities and threats facing a particular corporation can be matched with that company's internal strengths and weaknesses to result in four sets of possible strategic alternatives. (See **Figure 5–2**.) This is a good way to use brainstorming to create alternative strategies that might not otherwise be considered. It forces strategic managers to create various kinds of growth as well as retrenchment strategies. It can be used to generate corporate as well as business strategies.

To generate a TOWS Matrix for Maytag Corporation in 1995, for example, use the *External Factor Analysis Summary* (EFAS) listed in **Table 3–4** from **Chapter 3** and the *Internal Factor Analysis Summary* (IFAS) listed in **Table 4–2** from **Chapter 4**. To build **Figure 5–3**, take the following steps:

1. In the **Opportunities (O)** block, list the external opportunities available in the company's or business unit's current and future environment from the EFAS Table (**Table 3–4**).

2. In the **Threats (T)** block, list the external threats facing the company or unit now and in the future from the EFAS Table (**Table 3–4**).

Figure 5–2
TOWS Matrix

INTERNAL FACTORS (IFAS) EXTERNAL FACTORS (EFAS)	Strengths (S) List 5 – 10 *internal* strengths here	Weaknesses (W) List 5 – 10 *internal* weaknesses here
Opportunities (O) List 5 – 10 *external* opportunities here	SO Strategies Generate strategies here that use strengths to take advantage of opportunities	WO Strategies Generate strategies here that take advantage of opportunities by overcoming weaknesses
Threats (T) List 5 – 10 *external* opportunities here	ST Strategies Generate strategies here that use strengths to avoid threats	WT Strategies Generate strategies here that minimize weaknesses and avoid threats

Source: Reprinted from *Long-Range Planning*, April 1982. H. Weihrich, "The TOWS Matrix—A Tool for Situational Analysis," p. 60. Copyright 1982, with permission from Elsevier Science.

3. In the **Strengths (S)** block, list the specific areas of current and future strength for the company or unit from the IFAS Table (**Table 4–2**).

4. In the **Weaknesses (W)** block, list the specific areas of current and future weakness for the company or unit from the IFAS Table (**Table 4–2**).

5. Generate a series of possible strategies for the company or business unit under consideration based on particular combinations of the four sets of factors:

   - **SO Strategies** are generated by thinking of ways in which a company or business unit could use its strengths to take advantage of opportunities.

   - **ST Strategies** consider a company's or unit's strengths as a way to avoid threats.

   - **WO Strategies** attempt to take advantage of opportunities by overcoming weaknesses.

   - **WT Strategies** are basically defensive and primarily act to minimize weaknesses and avoid threats.

The TOWS Matrix is very useful for generating a series of alternatives that the decision makers of a company or business unit might not otherwise have considered. It can be used for the corporation as a whole (as was done in **Figure 5–3** with Maytag Corporation before it sold Hoover Europe), or it can be used for a specific business unit within a corporation (like Hoover's floor-care products). Nevertheless the TOWS Matrix is only one of many ways to generate alternative strategies. Another approach is to evaluate each business unit within a corporation in terms of possible competitive and cooperative strategies.

5.4 Business Strategies

Business strategy focuses on improving the competitive position of a company's or business unit's products or services within the specific industry or market segment that the company or business unit serves. Business strategy can be competitive (battling against all competitors for

Table 4–2 Internal Factor Analysis Summary (IFAS): Maytag as Example (Selection of Strategic Factors)*

Internal Strategic Factors	Weight	Rating	Weighted Score	Comments
	1	2	3	4	5
Strengths				
S1 Quality Maytag culture	.15	5.0	.75	Quality key to success
S2 Experienced top management	.05	4.2	.21	Know appliances
S3 Vertical integration	.10	3.9	.39	Dedicated factories
S4 Employee relations	.05	3.0	.15	Good, but deteriorating
S5 Hoover's international orientation	.15	2.8	.42	Hoover name in cleaners
Weaknesses				
W1 Process-oriented R&D	.05	2.2	.11	Slow on new products
W2 Distribution channels	.05	2.0	.10	Superstores replacing small dealers
W3 Financial position	.15	2.0	.30	High debt load
W4 Global positioning	.20	2.1	.42	Hoover weak outside the United Kingdom and Australia
W5 Manufacturing facilities	.05	4.0	.20	Investing now
Total Scores	1.00		3.05	

Table 3–4 External Factor Analysis Summary (EFAS): Maytag as Example (Selection of Strategic Factors)*

External Strategic Factors	Weight	Rating	Weighted Score	Comments
	1	2	3	4	5
Opportunities				
O1 Economic integration of European Community	.20	4.1	.82	Acquisition of Hoover
O2 Demographics favor quality appliances	.10	5.0	.50	Maytag quality
O3 Economic development of Asia	.05	1.0	.05	Low Maytag presence
O4 Opening of Eastern Europe	.05	2.0	.10	Will take time
O5 Trend to "Super Stores"	.10	1.8	.18	Maytag weak in this channel
Threats				
T1 Increasing government regulations	.10	4.3	.43	Well positioned
T2 Strong U.S. competition	.10	4.0	.40	Well positioned
T3 Whirlpool and Electrolux strong globally	.15	3.0	.45	Hoover weak globally
T4 New product advances	.05	1.2	.06	Questionable
T5 Japanese appliance companies	.10	1.6	.16	Only Asian presence is Australia
Total Scores	1.00		3.15	

*The most important external and internal factors are identified in the EFAS and IFAS tables as shown here by shading these factors.

Figure 5–3
Generating a TOWS Matrix for Maytag Corporation

Strengths
Weaknesses

Internal Factors (IFAS Table 4–2) External Factors (EFAS Table 3–4)	Strengths (S) S1 Quality Maytag culture S2 Experienced top management S3 Vertical integration S4 Employee relations S5 Hoover's international orientation	Weaknesses (W) W1 Process-oriented R&D W2 Distribution channels W3 Financial position W4 Global positioning W5 Manufacturing facilities
Opportunities (O) O1 Economic integration of European Community O2 Demographics favor quality O3 Economic development of Asia O4 Opening of Eastern Europe O5 Trend toward super stores	**SO Strategies** • *Use worldwide Hoover distribution channels to sell both Hoover and Maytag major appliances.* • *Find joint venture partners in Eastern Europe and Asia.*	**WO Strategies** • *Expand Hoover's presence in continental Europe by improving Hoover quality and reducing manufacturing and distribution costs.* • *Emphasize superstore channel for all non-Maytag brands*
Threats (T) T1 Increasing government regulation T2 Strong U.S. competition T3 Whirlpool and Electrolux positioned for global economy T4 New product advances T5 Japanese appliance companies	**ST Strategies** • *Acquire Raytheon's appliance business to increase U.S. market share.* • *Merge with a Japanese major home appliance company.* • *Sell off all non-Maytag brands and strongly defend Maytag's U.S. niche.*	**WT Strategies** • *Sell off Dixie-Narco Division to reduce debt.* • *Emphasize cost reduction to reduce break-even point.* • *Sell out to Raytheon or a Japanese firm.*

advantage) and/or cooperative (working with one or more competitors to gain advantage against other competitors). Just as corporate strategy asks what industry(ies) the company should be in, business strategy asks how the company or its units should compete or cooperate in each industry.

PORTER'S COMPETITIVE STRATEGIES

Competitive strategy raises the following questions:

- Should we compete on the basis of low cost (and thus price), or should we differentiate our products or services on some basis other than cost, such as quality or service?

- Should we compete head to head with our major competitors for the biggest but most sought-after share of the market, or should we focus on a niche in which we can satisfy a less sought-after but also profitable segment of the market?

Michael Porter proposes two "generic" competitive strategies for outperforming other corporations in a particular industry: lower cost and differentiation.[6] These strategies are called generic because they can be pursued by any type or size of business firm, even by not-for-profit organizations.

- **Lower cost strategy** is the ability of a company or a business unit to design, produce, and market a comparable product more efficiently than its competitors.

- **Differentiation strategy** is the ability to provide unique and superior value to the buyer in terms of product quality, special features, or after-sale service.

Porter further proposes that a firm's competitive advantage in an industry is determined by its **competitive scope**, that is, the breadth of the company's or business unit's target market. Before using one of the two generic competitive strategies (lower cost or differentiation), the firm or unit must choose the range of product varieties it will produce, the distribution channels it will employ, the types of buyers it will serve, the geographic areas in which it will sell, and the array of related industries in which it will also compete. This should reflect an understanding of the firm's unique resources. Simply put, a company or business unit can choose a broad target (that is, aim at the middle of the mass market) or a narrow target (that is, aim at a market niche). Combining these two types of target markets with the two competitive strategies results in the four variations of generic strategies depicted in **Figure 5–4**. When the lower cost and differentiation strategies have a broad mass market target, they are simply called *cost leadership* and *differentiation*. When they are focused on a market niche (narrow target), however, they are called *cost focus* and *differentiation focus*. Although research does indicate that established firms pursuing broad-scope strategies outperform firms following narrow-scope strategies in terms of ROA, new entrepreneurial firms have a better chance of surviving if they follow a narrow-scope over a broad-scope strategy.[7]

Cost leadership is a low-cost competitive strategy that aims at the broad mass market and requires "aggressive construction of efficient-scale facilities, vigorous pursuit of cost reduc-

Figure 5–4
Porter's Generic Competitive Strategies

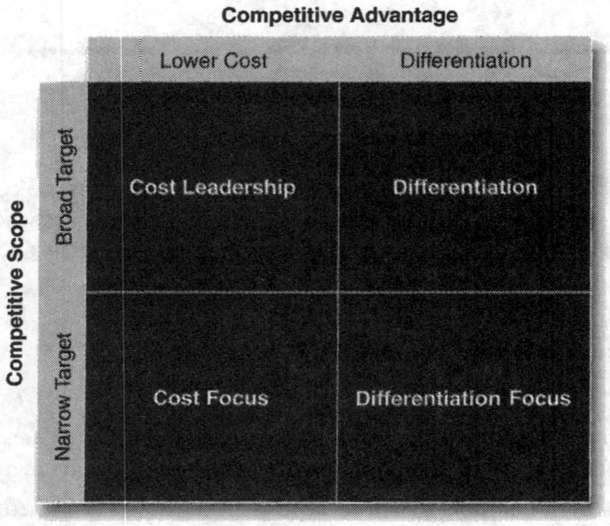

Source: Reprinted with permission of The Free Press, an imprint of Simon & Schuster, from *The Competitive Advantage of Nations* by Michael E. Porter, p. 39. Copyright © 1990 by Michael E. Porter.

tions from experience, tight cost and overhead control, avoidance of marginal customer accounts, and cost minimization in areas like R&D, service, sales force, advertising, and so on."[8] Because of its lower costs, the cost leader is able to charge a lower price for its products than its competitors and still make a satisfactory profit. Some companies successfully following this strategy are Wal-Mart, Alamo Rent-A-Car, Southwest Airlines, Timex, and Gateway 2000. Having a low-cost position also gives a company or business unit a defense against rivals. Its lower costs allow it to continue to earn profits during times of heavy competition. Its high market share means that it will have high bargaining power relative to its suppliers (because it buys in large quantities). Its low price will also serve as a barrier to entry because few new entrants will be able to match the leader's cost advantage. As a result, cost leaders are likely to earn above-average returns on investment.

Differentiation is aimed at the broad mass market and involves the creation of a product or service that is perceived throughout its industry as unique. The company or business unit may then charge a premium for its product. This specialty can be associated with design or brand image, technology, features, dealer network, or customer service. Differentiation is a viable strategy for earning above-average returns in a specific business because the resulting brand loyalty lowers customers' sensitivity to price. Increased costs can usually be passed on to the buyers. Buyer loyalty also serves as an entry barrier—new firms must develop their own distinctive competence to differentiate their products in some way in order to compete successfully. Examples of the successful use of a differentiation strategy are Walt Disney Productions, Maytag appliances, Nike athletic shoes, Apple Computer, and Mercedes-Benz automobiles. Research does suggest that a differentiation strategy is more likely to generate higher profits than is a low-cost strategy because differentiation creates a better entry barrier. A low-cost strategy is more likely, however, to generate increases in market share.[9]

Cost focus is a low-cost competitive strategy that focuses on a particular buyer group or geographic market and attempts to serve only this niche, to the exclusion of others. In using cost focus, the company or business unit seeks a cost advantage in its target segment. A good example of this strategy is Fadal Engineering. Fadal focuses its efforts on building and selling no-frills machine tools to small manufacturers. Fadal achieved cost focus by keeping overhead and R&D to a minimum and by focusing its marketing efforts strictly on its market niche. The cost focus strategy is valued by those who believe that a company or business unit that focuses its efforts is better able to serve its narrow strategic target more efficiently than can its competition. It does, however, require a tradeoff between profitability and overall market share.

Differentiation focus, like cost focus, concentrates on a particular buyer group, product line segment, or geographic market. This is the strategy successfully followed by Casey's General Stores, Morgan Motor Car Company (manufacturer of classic British sports cars), and local health food stores. In using differentiation focus, the company or business unit seeks differentiation in a targeted market segment. This strategy is valued by those who believe that a company or a unit that focuses its efforts is better able to serve the special needs of a narrow strategic target more effectively than can its competition. This is the strategy being effectively used by Inner City Entertainment (ICE), a company focusing on building new high quality movie theaters in inner-city locations aimed primarily at African Americans. Owned and managed by Alisa and Donzell Starks, ICE has successfully opened numerous theaters in Chicago's South Side. The company uses urban radio stations to promote its films and offers special screenings of films with high interest, such as *Amistad*. "I want to be the first black-owned theater chain," states Mr. Starks, the company's CEO. "No ifs, ands, or buts."[10]

Risks in Competitive Strategies

No one competitive strategy is guaranteed to achieve success, and some companies that have successfully implemented one of Porter's competitive strategies have found that they could not sustain the strategy. As shown in **Table 5–1**, each of the generic strategies has its risks. For

Table 5-1 Risks of Generic Competitive Strategies

Risks of Cost Leadership	Risks of Differentiation	Risks of Focus
Cost leadership is not sustained: • Competitors intimate. • Technology changes. • Other bases for cost leadership erode.	Differentiation is not sustained: • Competitors imitate. • Bases for differentiation become less important to buyers.	The focus strategy is imitated. The target segment becomes structurally unattractive: • Structure erodes. • Demand disappears.
Proximity in differentiation is lost.	Cost proximity is lost.	Broadly targeted competitors overwhelm the segment: • The segment's differences from other segments narrow. • The advantages of a broad line increase.
Cost focusers achieve even lower cost in segments.	Differentiation focusers achieve even greater differentiation in segments.	New focusers subsegment the industry.

Source: Adapted/reprinted with permission of The Free Press, an imprint of Simon & Schuster, from *Competitive Advantage: Creating and Sustaining Superior Performance* by Michael E. Porter, p. 21. Copyright © 1985 by Michael E. Porter.

example, a company following a differentiation strategy must ensure that the higher price it charges for its higher quality is not priced too far above the competition, otherwise customers will not see the extra quality as worth the extra cost. This is what is meant in **Table 5-1** by the term **cost proximity**. Procter & Gamble's use of R&D and advertising to differentiate its products had been very successful for many years until customers in the value-conscious 1990s turned to cheaper private brands. As a result, P&G was forced to reduce costs until it could get prices back in line with customer expectations.

Issues in Competitive Strategies

Porter argues that to be successful, a company or business unit must achieve one of the preceding generic competitive strategies. It is especially difficult to move between a narrow target strategy and a broad target strategy. Otherwise, the company or business unit is **stuck in the middle** of the competitive marketplace with no competitive advantage and is doomed to below-average performance. An example of a business unit that may be stuck in the middle is Hewlett-Packard's (HP) personal computer division. For years, HP was a niche player following a differentiation focus strategy in personal computers. Its Vectra personal computers were cherished by engineers and scientists for their high quality and for HP's solid service support. The computers were also expensive. HP's management decided in the mid-1990s to leave the niche and to compete instead in the broad-target market. The objective became high market share. In order to compete with its lower cost rivals such as Dell and Gateway, HP reduced prices. The plan worked. With more than 40% sales growth in 2000, it even outpaced Dell, the industry leader. Nevertheless, HP's reputation for high quality and exceptional service support (as reported in *PC Magazine* and *PC World*) declined from the years when it was a quality niche player. HP's switch from a narrow-target to a broad-target competitive strategy had its down side. As of 2000, the computer unit generated 43% of HP's revenues, but only a 4.6% operating margin, the lowest of HP's business units. In contrast, the printer and imaging division, which also accounted for 43% of HP's annual revenues, generated a 12% operating margin.[11] In moving to the mass market, HP had not kept up its quality image (thus losing its differentiation) and had thus far failed to achieve the lower cost position.

Although it may be difficult to move from a narrow- to a broad-target scope strategy (and vice versa) successfully, research does not support the argument that a firm or unit must choose between differentiation and lower cost in order to have success.[12] What of companies that attempt to achieve *both* a low-cost and a high-differentiation position? The Japanese auto

Table 5-2   The Eight Dimensions of Quality

1. **Performance**	Primary operating characteristics, such as a washing machine's cleaning ability
2. **Features**	"Bells and whistles," like cruise control in a car, that supplement the basic functions
3. **Reliability**	Probability that the product will continue functioning without any significant maintenance
4. **Conformance**	Degree to which a product meets standards. When a customer buys a product out of the warehouse, it will perform identically to that viewed on the showroom floor.
5. **Durability**	Number of years of service a consumer can expect from a product before it significantly deteriorates. Differs from reliability in that a product can be durable, but still need a lot of maintenance.
6. **Serviceability**	Product's ease of repair
7. **Aesthetics**	How a product looks, feels, sounds, tastes, or smells
8. **Perceived Quality**	Product's overall reputation. Especially important if there are no objective, easily used measures of quality.

Source: Adapted from D. A. Garvin, *Managing Quality: The Strategic and Competitive Edge* (New York: Free Press, 1988).

companies of Toyota, Nissan, and Honda are often presented as examples of successful firms able to achieve both of these generic strategies. Thanks to advances in technology, a company may be able to design quality into a product or service in such a way that it can achieve both high quality and high market share, thus lowering costs.[13] Although Porter agrees that it is possible for a company or a business unit to achieve low cost and differentiation simultaneously, he continues to argue that this state is often temporary.[14] Porter does admit, however, that many different kinds of potentially profitable competitive strategies exist. Although there is generally room for only one company to successfully pursue the mass market cost leadership strategy (because it is so dependent on achieving dominant market share), there is room for an almost unlimited number of differentiation and focus strategies (depending on the range of possible desirable features and the number of identifiable market niches). Quality, alone, has 8 different dimensions—each with the potential of providing a product with a competitive advantage (see **Table 5-2**).

Most entrepreneurial ventures follow focus strategies. The successful ones differentiate their product from those of other competitors in the areas of quality and service, and they focus the product on customer needs in a segment of the market, thereby achieving a dominant share of that part of the market. Adopting guerrilla warfare tactics, these companies go after opportunities in market niches too small to justify retaliation from the market leaders. Veteran entrepreneur Norm Brodsky argues that it's often much easier for a small company to compete against a big company than against a well-run small company. "We beat the giants on service. We beat them on flexibility. We beat them on location and price."[15]

Industry Structure and Competitive Strategy

Although each of Porter's generic competitive strategies may be used in any industry, certain strategies are more likely to succeed than others in some instances. In a **fragmented industry**, for example, where many small- and medium-sized local companies compete for relatively small shares of the total market, focus strategies will likely predominate. Fragmented industries are typical for products in the early stages of their life cycle. If few economies are to be gained through size, no large firms will emerge and entry barriers will be low, allowing a stream of new entrants into the industry. Chinese restaurants, veterinary care, used-car sales, and funeral homes are examples. As recently as 1996, over 85% of funeral homes in the United States were independently owned.[16]

If a company is able to overcome the limitations of a fragmented market, however, it can reap the benefits of a broadly targeted cost leadership or differentiation strategy. Until Pizza Hut was able to use advertising to differentiate itself from local competitors, the pizza fast-food business was a fragmented industry composed primarily of locally owned pizza parlors, each with its own distinctive product and service offering. Subsequently Domino's used the cost leader strategy to achieve U.S. national market share.

As an industry matures, fragmentation is overcome and the industry tends to become a **consolidated industry** dominated by a few large companies. Although many industries begin fragmented, battles for market share and creative attempts to overcome local or niche market boundaries often increase the market share of a few companies. After product standards become established for minimum quality and features, competition shifts to a greater emphasis on cost and service. Slower growth, overcapacity, and knowledgeable buyers combine to put a premium on a firm's ability to achieve cost leadership or differentiation along the dimensions most desired by the market. Research and development shifts from product to process improvements. Overall product quality improves, and costs are reduced significantly.

The **strategic rollup** was developed in the mid-1990s as an efficient way to quickly consolidate a fragmented industry. With the aid of money from venture capitalists, an entrepreneur acquires hundreds of owner-operated small businesses. The resulting large firm creates economies of scale by building regional or national brands, applies best practices across all aspects of marketing and operations, and hires more sophisticated managers than the small businesses could previously afford. Rollups differ from conventional mergers and acquisitions in three ways: (1) They involve large numbers of firms, (2) the acquired firms are typically owner operated, and (3) the objective is not to gain incremental advantage, but to reinvent an entire industry.[17] Rollups are currently underway in the funeral industry led by Service Corporation International, Stewart Enterprises, the Loewen Group and in the veterinary care industries by Veterinary Centers of America. Of the 16,000 pet hospitals in the United States, Veterinary Centers of American had acquired around 160 by 1997 and was in the process of buying at least 25 more each year for the foreseeable future.[18]

Once consolidated, the industry has become one in which cost leadership and differentiation tend to be combined to various degrees. A firm can no longer gain high market share simply through low price. The buyers are more sophisticated and demand a certain minimum level of quality for price paid. The same is true for firms emphasizing high quality. Either the quality must be high enough and valued by the customer enough to justify the higher price or the price must be dropped (through lowering costs) to compete effectively with the lower priced products. This consolidation is taking place worldwide in the automobile, airline, and home appliance industries.

Hypercompetition and Competitive Strategy

In his book *Hypercompetition*, D'Aveni proposes that it is becoming increasingly difficult to sustain a competitive advantage for very long. "Market stability is threatened by short product life cycles, short product design cycles, new technologies, frequent entry by unexpected outsiders, repositioning by incumbents, and tactical redefinitions of market boundaries as diverse industries merge."[19] Consequently a company or business unit must constantly work to improve its competitive advantage. It is not enough to be just the lowest cost competitor. Through continuous improvement programs, competitors are usually working to lower their costs as well. Firms must find new ways not only to reduce costs further, but also to add value to the product or service being provided.

The same is true of a firm or unit that is following a differentiation strategy. Maytag Company (a unit of Maytag Corporation), for example, was successful for many years by offering the most durable brand in major home appliances. It was able to charge the highest prices for Maytag brand washing machines. When other competitors improved the quality of their products, however, it became increasingly harder for customers to justify Maytag's significantly higher price. Consequently Maytag Company was forced not only to add new features to its products, but also to reduce costs through improved manufacturing processes so that its prices were no longer out of line with those of the competition.

D'Aveni contends that when industries become **hypercompetitive**, they tend to go through escalating stages of competition. Firms initially compete on cost and quality until an abundance of high-quality, low-priced goods result. This occurred in the U.S. major home appliance industry by 1980. In a second stage of competition, the competitors move into untapped markets. Others usually imitate these moves until the moves become too risky or expensive. This epitomized the major home appliance industry during the 1980s and 1990s as firms moved first to Europe and then into Asia and South America.

According to D'Aveni, firms then raise entry barriers to limit competitors. Economies of scale, distribution agreements, and strategic alliances made it all but impossible for a new firm to enter the major home appliance industry by the end of the 20th century. After the established players have entered and consolidated all new markets, the next stage is for the remaining firms to attack and destroy the strongholds of other firms. Maytag's 1995 decision to divest its European division and concentrate on improving its position in North America could be a prelude to building a North American stronghold while Whirlpool, GE, and Electrolux are distracted by European and worldwide investments. Eventually, according to D'Aveni, the remaining large global competitors work their way to a situation of perfect competition in which no one has any advantage and profits are minimal.

Before hypercompetition, strategic initiatives provided competitive advantage for many years, perhaps for decades. This is no longer the case. According to D'Aveni, as industries become hypercompetitive, there is no such thing as a sustainable competitive advantage. Successful strategic initiatives in this type of industry typically last only months to a few years. According to D'Aveni, the only way a firm in this kind of dynamic industry can sustain any competitive advantage is through a continuous series of multiple short-term initiatives aimed at replacing a firm's current successful products with the next generation of products before the competitors can do so. Intel and Microsoft are taking this approach in the hypercompetitive computer industry.

Hypercompetition views competition, in effect, as a distinct series of ocean waves on what used to be a fairly calm stretch of water. As industry competition becomes more intense, the waves grow higher and require more dexterity to handle. Although a strategy is still needed to sail from point A to point B, more turbulent water means that a craft must continually adjust course to suit each new large wave. One danger of D'Aveni's concept of hypercompetition, however, is that it may lead to an overemphasis on short-term tactics (to be discussed in the next section) over long-term strategy. Too much of an orientation on the individual waves of hypercompetition could cause a company to focus too much on short-term temporary advantage and not enough on achieving its long-term objectives through building sustainable competitive advantage.

Which Competitive Strategy Is Best?

Before selecting one of Porter's generic competitive strategies for a company or business unit, management should assess its feasibility in terms of company or business unit resources and capabilities. Porter lists some of the commonly required skills and resources as well as organizational requirements, in **Table 5–3**.

Competitive Tactics

Studies of decision making report that half the decisions made in organizations fail because of poor tactics.[20] A **tactic** is a specific operating plan detailing how a strategy is to be implemented in terms of when and where it is to be put into action. By their nature, tactics are nar-

Table 5-3 Requirements for Generic Competitive Strategies

Generic Strategy	Commonly Required Skills and Resources	Common Organizational Requirements
Overall Cost Leadership	• Sustained capital investment and access to capital • Process engineering skills • Intense supervision of labor • Products designed for ease of manufacture • Low-cost distribution system	• Tight cost control • Frequent, detailed control reports • Structured organization and responsibilities • Incentives based on meeting strict quantitative targets
Differentiation	• Strong marketing abilities • Product engineering • Creative flair • Strong capability in basic research • Corporate reputation for quality or technological leadership • Long tradition in the industry or unique combination of skills drawn from other businesses • Strong cooperation from channels	• Strong coordination among functions in R&D, product development, and marketing • Subjective measurement and incentives instead of quantitative measures • Amenities to attract highly skilled labor, scientists, or creative people
Focus	• Combination of the above policies directed at the particular strategic target	• Combination of the above policies directed at the particular strategic target

Source: Adapted/reprinted with permission of The Free Press, an imprint of Simon & Schuster, from *Competitive Strategy: Techniques for Analyzing Industries and Competitors* by Michael E. Porter, pp. 40–41. Copyright © 1980, 1988 by The Free Press.

rower in their scope and shorter in their time horizon than are strategies. Tactics, therefore, may be viewed (like policies) as a link between the formulation and implementation of strategy. Some of the tactics available to implement competitive strategies are **timing tactics** (when) and **market location tactics** (where).

Timing Tactics: When to Compete

The first company to manufacture and sell a new product or service is called the **first mover** (or **pioneer**). Some of the advantages of being a first mover are that the company is able to establish a reputation as an industry leader, move down the learning curve to assume the cost leader position, and earn temporarily high profits from buyers who value the product or service very highly. A successful first mover can also set the standard for all subsequent products in the industry. A company that sets the standard "locks in" customers and is then able to offer further products based on that standard.[21] Microsoft was able to do this in software with its Windows operating system, and Netscape garnered over 80% share of the Internet browser market by being first to commercialize the product successfully. Research does indicate that moving first or second into a new industry or foreign country results in greater market share and shareholder wealth than does moving later.[22] This is only true, however, if the first mover has sufficient resources to both exploit the new market and to defend its position against later arrivals with greater resources.[23]

Being a first mover does, however, have its disadvantages. These disadvantages can be, conversely, advantages enjoyed by late mover firms. **Late movers** may be able to imitate the technological advances of others (and thus keep R&D costs low), keep risks down by waiting until a new market is established, and take advantage of the first mover's natural inclination to ignore market segments.[24] Once Netscape had established itself as the standard for Internet browsers, Microsoft used its huge resources to directly attack Netscape's position. It did not want Netscape to also set the standard in the developing and highly lucrative intranet market inside corporations. Nevertheless, research suggests that the advantages and disadvantages of first and late movers may not always generalize across industries because of differences in entry barriers and the resources of the specific competitors.[25]

Market Location Tactics: Where to Compete

A company or business unit can implement a competitive strategy either offensively or defensively. An **offensive tactic** usually takes place in an established competitor's market location. A **defensive tactic** usually takes place in the firm's own current market position as a defense against possible attack by a rival.[26]

Offensive Tactics   Some of the methods used to attack a competitor's position are:

- **Frontal Assault:** The attacking firm goes head to head with its competitor. It matches the competitor in every category from price to promotion to distribution channel. To be successful, the attacker must not only have superior resources, but also the willingness to persevere. This is generally a very expensive tactic and may serve to awaken a sleeping giant (as MCI and Sprint did to AT&T in long-distance telephone service), depressing profits for the whole industry.

- **Flanking Maneuver:** Rather than going straight for a competitor's position of strength with a frontal assault, a firm may attack a part of the market where the competitor is weak. Cyrix Corporation followed this tactic with its entry into the microprocessor market—a market then almost totally dominated by Intel. Rather than going directly after Intel's microprocessor business, Cyrix developed a math co-processor for Intel's 386 chip that would run 20 times faster than Intel's microprocessor. To be successful, the flanker must be patient and willing to carefully expand out of the relatively undefended market niche or else face retaliation by an established competitor.

- **Bypass Attack:** Rather than directly attacking the established competitor frontally or on its flanks, a company or business unit may choose to change the rules of the game. This tactic attempts to cut the market out from under the established defender by offering a new type of product that makes the competitor's product unnecessary. For example, instead of competing directly against Microsoft's Windows 95 operating system, Netscape chose to use Java "applets" in its Internet browser so that an operating system and specialized programs were no longer necessary to run applications on a personal computer.

- **Encirclement:** Usually evolving out of a frontal assault or flanking maneuver, encirclement occurs as an attacking company or unit encircles the competitor's position in terms of products or markets or both. The encircler has greater product variety (a complete product line ranging from low to high price) and/or serves more markets (it dominates every secondary market). As a late mover into Internet browsers, Microsoft followed this tactic when it attacked Netscape's business with its "embrace and extend" strategy. By embracing Netscape's use of cross-platform Internet applets and quickly extending it into multiple applications, Microsoft worked to dominate the browser market.

- **Guerrilla Warfare:** Instead of a continual and extensive resource-expensive attack on a competitor, a firm or business unit may choose to "hit and run." Guerrilla warfare is characterized by the use of small, intermittent assaults on different market segments held by the competitor. In this way, a new entrant or small firm can make some gains without seriously threatening a large, established competitor and evoking some form of retaliation. To be successful, the firm or unit conducting guerrilla warfare must be patient enough to accept small gains and to avoid pushing the established competitor to the point that it must respond or else lose face. Microbreweries, which make beer for sale to local customers, use this tactic against national brewers like Anheuser-Busch.

Defensive Tactics According to Porter, defensive tactics aim to lower the probability of attack, divert attacks to less threatening avenues, or lessen the intensity of an attack. Instead of increasing competitive advantage per se, they make a company's or business unit's competitive advantage more sustainable by causing a challenger to conclude that an attack is unattractive. These tactics deliberately reduce short-term profitability to ensure long-term profitability.[27]

- **Raise Structural Barriers**: Entry barriers act to block a challenger's logical avenues of attack. Some of the most important according to Porter are to:

  1. Offer a full line of products in every profitable market segment to close off any entry points (for example, Coca-Cola offers unprofitable noncarbonated beverages to keep competitors off store shelves).

  2. Block channel access by signing exclusive agreements with distributors.

  3. Raise buyer switching costs by offering low-cost training to users.

  4. Raise the cost of gaining trial users by keeping prices low on items new users are most likely to purchase.

  5. Increase scale economies to reduce unit costs.

  6. Foreclose alternative technologies through patenting or licensing.

  7. Limit outside access to facilities and personnel.

  8. Tie up suppliers by obtaining exclusive contracts or purchasing key locations.

  9. Avoid suppliers that also serve competitors.

  10. Encourage the government to raise barriers such as safety and pollution standards or favorable trade policies.

- **Increase Expected Retaliation**: This tactic is any action that increases the perceived threat of retaliation for an attack. For example, management may strongly defend any erosion of market share by drastically cutting prices or matching a challenger's promotion through a policy of accepting any price-reduction coupons for a competitor's product. This counter-attack is especially important in markets that are very important to the defending company or business unit. For example, when Clorox Company challenged Procter & Gamble Company in the detergent market with Clorox Super Detergent, P&G retaliated by test marketing its liquid bleach, Lemon Fresh Comet, in an attempt to scare Clorox into retreating from the detergent market.

- **Lower the Inducement for Attack**: A third type of defensive tactic is to reduce a challenger's expectations of future profits in the industry. Like Southwest Airlines, a company can deliberately keep prices low and constantly invest in cost-reducing measures. With prices kept very low, there is little profit incentive for a new entrant.

COOPERATIVE STRATEGIES

Competitive strategies and tactics are used to gain competitive advantage within an industry by battling against other firms. These are not, however, the only business strategy options available to a company or business unit for competing successfully within an industry. **Cooperative strategies** can also be used to gain competitive advantage within an industry by working with other firms.

Collusion

The two general types of cooperative strategies are collusion and strategic alliances. **Collusion** is the active cooperation of firms within an industry to reduce output and raise prices in order to get around the normal economic law of supply and demand. Collusion may be explicit, in which firms cooperate through direct communication and negotiation, or tacit, in which firms cooperate indirectly through an informal system of signals. Explicit collusion is illegal in most countries. For example, Archer Daniels Midland (ADM), the large U.S. agricultural products firm, has been accused of conspiring with its competitors to limit the sales volume and raise the price of the food additive lysine. Executives from three Japanese and South Korean lysine manufacturers admitted meeting in hotels in major cities throughout the world to form a "lysine trade association." The three companies were fined more than $20 million by the U.S. federal government. Although ADM had earlier agreed to pay $25 million to settle a lawsuit on behalf of 600 lysine customers, U.S. federal prosecutors pursued a grand jury indictment of the company and two of its senior executives.[28]

Collusion can also be tacit, in which there is no direct communication among competing firms. According to Barney, tacit collusion in an industry is most likely to be successful if (1) there are a small number of identifiable competitors, (2) costs are similar among firms, (3) one firm tends to act as the "price leader," (4) there is a common industry culture that accepts cooperation, (5) sales are characterized by a high frequency of small orders, (6) large inventories and order backlogs are normal ways of dealing with fluctuations in demand, and (7) there are high entry barriers to keep out new competitors.[29]

Even tacit collusion can, however, be illegal. For example, when General Electric wanted to ease price competition in the steam turbine industry, it widely advertised its prices and publicly committed not to sell below these prices. Customers were even told that if GE reduced turbine prices in the future, it would give customers a refund equal to the price reduction. GE's message was not lost on Westinghouse, the major competitor in steam turbines. Both prices and profit margins remained stable for the next 10 years in this industry. The U.S. Department of Justice then sued both firms for engaging in "conscious parallelism" (following each other's lead to reduce the level of competition) in order to reduce competition.

Strategic Alliances

A **strategic alliance** is a partnership of two or more corporations or business units to achieve strategically significant objectives that are mutually beneficial.[30] Alliances between companies or business units have become a fact of life in modern business. More than 20,000 alliances occurred between 1992 and 1997, quadruple the total five years earlier.[31] Some alliances are very short term, only lasting long enough for one partner to establish a beachhead in a new market. Over time, conflicts over objectives and control often develop among the partners. For these and other reasons, between 30% and 50% of all alliances perform unsatisfactorily.[32] Others are more long lasting and may even be the prelude to a full merger between two companies. A study by Cooper and Lybrand found that firms involved in strategic alliances had 11% higher revenue and 20% higher growth rate than did companies not involved in alliances.[33]

Companies or business units may form a strategic alliance for a number of reasons, including:

1. **To obtain technology and/or manufacturing capabilities**: For example, Intel formed a partnership with Hewlett-Packard to use HP's capabilities in RISC technology in order to develop the successor to Intel's Pentium microprocessor.

2. **To obtain access to specific markets**: Rather than buy a foreign company or build breweries of its own in other countries, Anheuser-Busch chose to license the right to brew and market Budweiser to other brewers, such as Labatt in Canada, Modelo in Mexico, and Kirin in Japan.

3. **To reduce financial risk**: For example, because the costs of developing a new large jet airplane were becoming too high for any one manufacturer, Boeing, Aerospatiale of France, British Aerospace, Construcciones Aeronáuticas of Spain, and Deutsche Aerospace of Germany planned a joint venture to design such a plane.

4. **To reduce political risk**: To gain access to China while ensuring a positive relationship with the often restrictive Chinese government, Maytag Corporation formed a joint venture with the Chinese appliance maker, RSD.

5. **To achieve or ensure competitive advantage**: General Motors and Toyota formed Nummi Corporation as a joint venture to provide Toyota a manufacturing facility in the United States and GM access to Toyota's low-cost, high-quality manufacturing expertise.[34]

Cooperative arrangements between companies and business units fall along a continuum from weak and distant to strong and close. (See **Figure 5–5**.) The types of alliances range from mutual service consortia to joint ventures and licensing arrangements to value-chain partnerships.[35]

Mutual Service Consortia   A **mutual service consortium** is a partnership of similar companies in similar industries who pool their resources to gain a benefit that is too expensive to develop alone, such as access to advanced technology. For example, IBM of the United States, Toshiba of Japan, and Siemens of Germany formed a consortium to develop new generations of computer chips. As part of this alliance, IBM offered Toshiba its expertise in chemical mechanical polishing to help develop a new manufacturing process using ultraviolet lithography to etch tiny circuits in silicon chips. IBM then transferred the new technology to a facility in the United States.[36] The mutual service consortia is a fairly weak and distant alliance—appropriate for partners who wish to work together but not share their core competencies. There is very little interaction or communication among the partners.

Joint Venture   A **joint venture** is a "cooperative business activity, formed by two or more separate organizations for strategic purposes, that creates an independent business entity and allocates ownership, operational responsibilities, and financial risks and rewards to each member, while preserving their separate identity/autonomy."[37] Along with licensing arrangements, joint ventures lay at the midpoint of the continuum and are formed to pursue an opportunity that needs a capability from two companies or business units, such as the technology of one and the distribution channels of another.

Joint ventures are the most popular form of strategic alliance. They often occur because the companies involved do not want to or cannot legally merge permanently. Joint ventures provide a way to temporarily combine the different strengths of partners to achieve an outcome of value to both. For example, Toys "R" Us and Amazon.com formed a joint venture in August 2000 called Toysrus.com to act as an online toy store. Amazon was to include the joint venture on its Web site, ship the products, and handle customer service. In turn, Toys "R" Us was to choose and buy the toys, using its parent's purchasing power to get the most desired toys at the best price.[38]

Figure 5–5
Continuum of Strategic Alliances

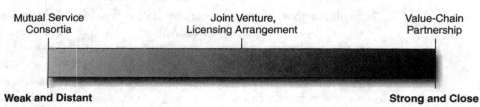

Mutual Service Consortia	Joint Venture, Licensing Arrangement	Value-Chain Partnership
Weak and Distant		**Strong and Close**

Source: Suggested by R. M. Kanter, "Collaborative Advantage: The Art of Alliances," *Harvard Business Review* (July–August 1994), pp. 96–108. Copyright © 2001 by the President and Fellows of Harvard College, all rights reserved.

Extremely popular in international undertakings because of financial and political-legal constraints, joint ventures are a convenient way for corporations to work together without losing their independence. Disadvantages of joint ventures include loss of control, lower profits, probability of conflicts with partners, and the likely transfer of technological advantage to the partner. Joint ventures are often meant to be temporary, especially by some companies who may view them as a way to rectify a competitive weakness until they can achieve long-term dominance in the partnership. Partially for this reason, joint ventures have a high failure rate. Research does indicate, however, that joint ventures tend to be more successful when both partners have equal ownership in the venture and are mutually dependent on each other for results.[39]

Licensing Arrangement   A **licensing arrangement** is an agreement in which the licensing firm grants rights to another firm in another country or market to produce and/or sell a product. The licensee pays compensation to the licensing firm in return for technical expertise. Licensing is an especially useful strategy if the trademark or brand name is well known, but the MNC does not have sufficient funds to finance its entering the country directly. Anheuser-Busch uses this strategy to produce and market Budweiser beer in the United Kingdom, Japan, Israel, Australia, Korea, and the Philippines. This strategy also becomes important if the country makes entry via investment either difficult or impossible. The danger always exists, however, that the licensee might develop its competence to the point that it becomes a competitor to the licensing firm. Therefore, a company should never license its distinctive competence, even for some short-run advantage.

Value-Chain Partnership   The **value-chain partnership** is a strong and close alliance in which one company or unit forms a long-term arrangement with a key supplier or distributor for mutual advantage. To improve the quality of parts it purchases, companies in the U.S. auto industry, for example, have decided to work more closely with fewer suppliers and to involve them more in product design decisions. Activities that had been previously done internally by an auto maker are being outsourced to suppliers specializing in those activities.

Such partnerships are also a way for a firm to acquire new technology to use in its own products. For example, Maytag Company was approached by one of its suppliers, Honeywell's Microswitch Division, which offered its expertise in fuzzy logic technology—a technology Maytag did not have at that time. The resulting partnership in product development resulted in Maytag's new IntelliSense™ dishwasher. Unlike previous dishwashers that the operator had to set, Maytag's fuzzy logic dishwasher automatically selected the proper cleaning cycle based on a series of factors such as the amount of dirt and presence of detergent. According to Paul Ludwig, business development manager for Honeywell's Microswitch division, "Had Maytag not included us on the design team, we don't believe the two companies would have achieved the same innovative solution, nor would we have completed the project in such a short amount of time."[40] The benefits of such relationships do not just accrue to the purchasing firm. Research suggests that suppliers who engage in long-term relationships are more profitable than suppliers with multiple short-term contracts.[41] For an example of an Internet value-chain partnership between Cisco Systems and its suppliers, see the ▨ **Internet Issue** feature.

All forms of strategic alliances are filled with uncertainty. There are many issues that need to be dealt with when the alliance is initially formed and others that emerge later. Many problems revolve around the fact that a firm's alliance partners may also be its competitors, either now or in the future. According to Peter Lorange, an authority in strategy, one thorny issue in any strategic alliance is how to cooperate without giving away the company or business unit's core competence. "Particularly when advanced technology is involved, it can be difficult for partners in an alliance to cooperate and openly share strategic know-how, but it is mandatory if the joint venture is to succeed."[42] It is therefore important that a company or business unit that is interested in joining or forming a strategic alliance consider the strategic alliance success factors listed in **Table 5–4**.

Internet Issue

Business to Business at Cisco Systems

Every day Cisco Systems, successful manufacturer of Internet servers, posts its requirements for components on an extranet, the dedicated Internet-based network connecting the company to 32 manufacturing plants. Although Cisco does not own these plants, each plant has completed a lengthy process of certification ensuring that each meets Cisco's quality and other standards. Within hours of the posting, these suppliers respond with a price, a delivery time, and a record of their recent performance in terms of reliability and product quality. Cisco then chooses which bid to select and the deal is finalized.

This process has replaced 50 purchasing agents who used to assemble the same information using telephones and faxes. The operation, which used to take three to four days, now takes only hours. The purchasing agents are instead managing the quality of the components.

Three aspects of Cisco's supply system are especially significant. *One* is the use of the electronic market to set prices. This is characteristic of online auctions and of business to business (B2B) value chain relationships. A *second* is the exchange of information between buyer and seller. The Internet allows the inexpensive flow of information in a way never before realized. *Third* is the extent to which Cisco outsources activities that many other companies do internally. The ability of the Internet to connect multiple departments together with suppliers and distributors in other companies makes outsourcing both effective and efficient.

Source: "Trying to Connect You," *The Economist E-Management Survey* (November 11, 2000), p. 28. Reprinted with permission.

Table 5-4 Strategic Alliance Success Factors

- Have a clear strategic purpose. Integrate the alliance with each partner's strategy. Ensure that mutual value is created for all partners.
- Find a fitting partner with compatible goals and complementary capabilities.
- Identify likely partnering risks and deal with them when the alliance is formed.
- Allocate tasks and responsibilities so that each partner can specialize in what it does best.
- Create incentives for cooperation to minimize differences in corporate culture or organization fit.
- Minimize conflicts among the partners by clarifying objectives and avoiding direct competition in the marketplace.
- If an international alliance, ensure that those managing it should have comprehensive cross-cultural knowledge.
- Exchange human resources to maintain communication and trust. Don't allow individual egos to dominate.
- Operate with long-term time horizons. The expectation of future gains can minimize short-term conflicts.
- Develop multiple joint projects so that any failures are counterbalanced by successes.
- Agree upon a monitoring process. Share information to build trust and keep projects on target. Monitor customer responses and service complaints.
- Be flexible in terms of willingness to renegotiate the relationship in terms of environmental changes and new opportunities.
- Agree upon an exit strategy for when the partners' objectives are achieved or the alliance is judged a failure.

Sources: Compiled from B. Gomes-Casseres, "Do You Really Have an Alliance Strategy?" *Strategy & Leadership* (September/October 1998), pp. 6–11; L. Segil, "Strategic Alliances for the 21st Century," *Strategy & Leadership* (September/October 1998), pp. 12–16; A. C. Inkpen and K-Q Li, "Joint Venture Formation: Planning and Knowledge Gathering for Success," *Organizational Dynamics* (Spring 1999), pp. 33–47. Inkpen and Li provide a checklist of 17 questions on p. 46.

5.5 Impact of the Internet on Business Strategy

The initial impact of the Internet was on marketing. **Business to consumer (B2C)** described the many dot-com start-ups selling items directly to consumers via their Web sites. The most well-known of these first entrants or pioneers was Amazon.com, the successful marketer of books and related merchandise. Not wanting to be disadvantaged late entrants, established manufacturers became active participants on the Internet. They supplemented their current distribution network with direct selling through their own Internet site or formed marketing alliances with technologically competent Web-based businesses. One such alliance is the joint venture between Toys "R" Us and Amazon.com to form Toysrus.com.

Business to business (B2B) describes the launching of Web portals aimed at electronically connecting buyers with suppliers, strengthening collective purchasing activities, and auctioning inventory. Dick Hunter, head of Dell Computer's supply chain management, states that one purpose of B2B is for information to replace inventory. For example, the companies supplying Dell with metal and plastic boxes for Dell's computers are located within 90 miles of Dell's assembly plant. They have access to Dell's real-time information on its use of their products. On the basis of Dell's usage of their parts, they make more and ship them as needed to Dell's plant. In turn, the suppliers keep only a day's worth of finished stock on hand. "If our information was 100% right," asserts Hunter, "the only inventory that would exist would be in transit."[43]

The B2B consortium is a recent example of the use of cooperative strategies to obtain competitive advantage. Traditional competitors are forming Internet consortia to centralize many activities, such as purchasing, which had been previously done internally. General Motors, Ford, and Chrysler have established an auto parts exchange called Covisint. Boeing, Lockheed Martin, Raytheon, and BAE Systems have formed the Global Aerospace & Defense Trading Exchange. Hewlett-Packard, Compaq, and 10 other computer makers have created Ehitex.com. Goodyear, Michelin, Bridgestone, and 4 other tire makers have formed Rubbernetwork.com. Although these consortia are being formed with great expectations, the reality has problems. For example, Covisint has three project leaders (one for each auto maker) who are battling over what to charge and how much trading data to allow users to access. The U. S. Federal Trade Commission is reviewing these consortia among erstwhile competitors for antitrust issues. Since Covisint's owners collectively dominate the North American automobile market, there could easily be collusion. According to Dana Corporation, an auto components supplier, "We're concerned about how big this gorilla is going to be. There's only so much room to squeeze prices."[44]

Although B2B is still in its initial stages, Hau Lee, director of the Global Supply Chain Management Forum at Stanford University proposes that business-to-business commerce will move through 4 stages of development.

Stage 1: *Information, such as demand forecasts and sales data, is exchanged.* Companies work to define common standards for inventory and point-of-sale to allow better planning.

Stage 2: *Companies move beyond data transfer to exchanging information.* For example, when Wal-Mart's Florida stores ran out of mosquito repellant during a heat wave, the company discovered that Warner Lambert, its supplier, was able to track weather forecasts to predict future peaks in demand. The sharing of this information enabled both companies to do better.

Stage 3: *Companies exchange the right to make decisions.* For example, since Wal-Mart sells disposable diapers made by P&G, which use sticky tape made by 3M, the three companies are experimenting with a system allowing one person instead of three to make the ordering decision for all three companies.

Stage 4: *Companies exchange work and roles.* The manufacturer becomes a retailer and the retailer moves to a support role. For example, companies such as VooDooCycles and Cannondale, makers of sport bicycles, are increasingly taking customers' orders directly and only then building the bicycles. Since a high quality bike needs last minute adjustments before it is ready for the customer, bicycle retailers are needed to perform this crucial service as well as to offer last minute purchases of helmets or other paraphernalia.[45]

Projections for the 21st Century

- From 1994 to 2010, the average life expectancy for women will rise from 67 to 71 and for men will increase from 63 to 67.
- From 1994 to 2010, the number of AIDS cases worldwide will increase from 20 million to 38 million.[46]

Discussion Questions

1. What industry forces might cause a propitious niche to disappear?

2. Is it possible for a company or business unit to follow a cost leadership strategy and a differentiation strategy simultaneously? Why or why not?

3. Is it possible for a company to have a sustainable competitive advantage when its industry becomes hyper-competitive?

4. What are the advantages and disadvantages of being a first mover in an industry? Give some examples of first mover and late mover firms. Were they successful?

5. Why are many strategic alliances temporary?

Strategic Practice Exercise

Following is an Internet case focusing upon strategic alliances. To begin the exercise, you will need a computer with Internet access. The rest is up to you!

Amy's Bread at Chelsea Market: A Web Discovery Case

CATHLEEN S. BURNS, UNIVERSITY OF MISSOURI, AND PAULA S. WEBER, ST. CLOUD STATE UNIVERSITY

COMPANY BACKGROUND AND HISTORY

In 1992, Amy Scherber opened her own business, "Amy's Bread." Amy's Bread is a retail and wholesale bakery in the Hell's Kitchen area of Manhattan. Amy's Bread has now expanded to a second Manhattan location in Chelsea Market, an innovative mall full of other entrepreneurs selling both food and nonfood items.

AMY'S DILEMMA

While Amy's Bread is doing well in Chelsea Market, profits are less than desired and the bakery has excess capacity. Amy is trying to decide what strategic alliances with other tenants in the mall would help her boost profits and absorb excess production capacity. You will help formulate Amy's emerging marketing strategy during your Web-based search process.

First Activity: Get familiar with Internet searches (if you are not already).

1. Check out a Web site that provides information on search engines and searching:
   - ⟨www.pbs.org/uti/begin.html⟩
   - ⟨www.microsoft.com/insider/internet/default.htm⟩
   - ⟨www.itrc.ucf.edu⟩ [search "search engines"]
   - ⟨www.zdnet.com/pccomp/features/fea1096/sub2.html⟩

- ⟨www.cl.ais.net/egsmlib/crawler.html⟩
- ⟨www.hamline.edu/library/bush/handouts/worms.html⟩

2. Search the Internet for Amy's Bread using at least three search engines:
   - ⟨yahoo.com⟩
   - ⟨altavista.com⟩
   - ⟨excite.com⟩
   - ⟨infoseek.com⟩
   - your choice

3. Search the Internet for Amy's Bread using one mega-search engine:
   - ⟨askjeeves.com⟩
   - ⟨metacrawler.com⟩

4. **Class discussion opportunity**: Share with the class (or your team) what you discovered about how search engines search the Internet. What differences exist in the data accessed by each search engine?

Second Activity: Get familiar with Amy's Bread's homepage.

   Class discussion opportunity: Share with the class (or your team) what information is included in Amy's Bread's Web site.
   - ⟨amysbread.com/sitemap.htm⟩

Third Activity: Prepare a brief Strengths/Weaknesses/Opportunities/Threats (SWOT) analysis for Amy's Bread.

1. **The Owner**: How did Amy prepare herself to be an entrepreneur?
   - ⟨amysbread.com/bio/htm⟩

2. **The Products**: How does Amy differentiate her bread products from low cost breads?
   - ⟨amysbread.com/chelsea.htm⟩

3. **The Media**: How does the media differentiate Amy's bread products from other bakeries' products?
   - ⟨amysbread.com/news.htm⟩

4. **The Locations**: How many Amy's Bread locations are there and how are they different or the same?
   - ⟨amysbread.com/locate.htm⟩
   - ⟨library.northernlight.com/SG19990714170000046.html?cb=13&sc=0⟩
   [The Web site above has some interesting history on Oreo cookies and the Chelsea Market location.]

5. **The Competition**: How many competitors does Amy's Bread have in the Manhattan area?
   - ⟨go-newyork.city.com/food/index.html⟩
   - ⟨www.womenshands.com/artisans/chelsea_market/related_story.htm⟩
   - ⟨www.womenshands.com/artisans/chelsea_market⟩

- ⟨store.yahoo.com/cmb/aboutcm.html⟩
- ⟨www.chelseamarketbaskets.com⟩
- ⟨www.elizabar.com⟩

6. **The Customers**: What can you discover about Chelsea Market customers? What do you think pedestrian traffic is like in that area? What are some of the demographics of New York City citizens that would affect their bakery purchases? For example, New Yorkers tend to walk or use public transportation; how does this impact their grocery shopping? New Yorkers tend to live in small apartments or condos; how does this impact their interest in dining out? What options exist for dining out in New York as opposed to a medium-sized city in your area?
   - ⟨www.demographia.com/dm-nyc.htm⟩ [Population density in NYC]
   - ⟨stats.bls.gov/csxmsa.htm⟩ [Consumer Expenditure Data by Metropolitan Statistical Area]

Fourth Activity: Consider strategic alliances that would be appropriate for Amy's Bread to pursue.

1. Using the textbook or Web resources, define what is meant by "strategic alliances." What are the advantages and disadvantages of strategic alliances?
   - ⟨www.e-marketing.com.au/documents/strategicalliances.htm⟩

2. On a macro level, what businesses has the developer, Irwin Cohen, included in the Chelsea Market commercial development?
   - ⟨store.yahoo.cmb/aboutcm.html⟩
   - ⟨westvillage.about.com/cities/midatlanticus/westvillage/ library/weekly/aa050499.htm⟩
   - ⟨www.womenshands.com/artisans/chelsea_market/related_story.htm⟩

3. Use the information in #2 above and your creativity to answer this question. On a more micro level, which of the Chelsea Market tenants appear to have potential for strategic alliances with Amy's Bread? Why?

4. Using the information in #2 above and your creativity, what other businesses (non-Chelsea Market tenants) can you imagine would have potential for strategic alliances with Amy's Bread? Why?

5. If the Chelsea Market developer asked you, Amy Scherber, for input on potential new mall tenants, what mall tenants would you recommend that the developer add to the mall? Why? What would be some of the decision factors the developer would consider in selecting tenants?

Source: This exercise was written as a case by Cathleen S. Burns of the University of Missouri, Columbia, and Paula S. Weber of St. Cloud State University and presented to the North American Research Association, October 2000. Copyright © 2000 by Cathleen S. Burns and Paula S. Weber. Reprinted by permission.

Key Terms

business strategy (p. 115)
business to business (B2B) (p. 131)
business to consumer (B2C) (p. 131)
collusion (p. 126)
competitive scope (p. 118)
competitive strategy (p. 117)
consolidated industry (p. 122)
cooperative strategies (p. 126)
cost focus (p. 119)
cost leadership (p. 118)
cost proximity (p. 120)
criticism of SWOT (p. 109)
defensive tactic (p. 125)
differentiation (p. 119)

differentiation focus (p. 119)
differentiation strategy (p. 118)
distinctive competencies (p. 109)
first movers (p. 124)
fragmented industry (p. 121)
hypercompetitive (p. 123)
joint venture (p. 128)
late movers (p. 124)
licensing arrangement (p. 129)
lower cost strategy (p. 118)
market location tactics (p. 124)
mutual service consortium (p. 128)
offensive tactic (p. 125)
pioneer (p. 124)

propitious niche (p. 112)
SFAS (Strategic Factors Analysis Summary) Matrix (p. 110)
SO, ST, WO, WT Strategies (p. 115)
strategic alliance (p. 127)
strategic rollup (p. 122)
strategic window (p. 112)
stuck in the middle (p. 120)
SWOT (p. 109)
tactic (p. 123)
timing tactics (p. 124)
TOWS Matrix (p. 114)
value-chain partnership (p. 129)

Notes

1. K. W. Glaister and J. R. Falshaw, "Strategic Planning: Still Going Strong?" *Long Range Planning* (February 1999), pp. 107–116.
2. T. Brown, "The Essence of Strategy," *Management Review* (April 1997), pp. 8–13.
3. T. Hill and R. Westbrook, "SWOT Analysis: It's Time for a Product Recall," *Long Range Planning* (February 1997), pp. 46–52.
4. W. H. Newman, "Shaping the Master Strategy of Your Firm," *California Management Review*, Vol. 9, No. 3 (1967), pp. 77–88.
5. R. L. Simpson and O. Suris, "Alex Trotman's Goal: To Make Ford No. 1 in World Auto Sales," *Wall Street Journal* (July 18, 1995), p. A5.
6. M. E. Porter, *Competitive Strategy* (New York: The Free Press, 1980), pp. 34–41 as revised in M. E. Porter, *The Competitive Advantage of Nations* (New York: The Free Press, 1990), pp. 37–40.
7. J. O. DeCastro and J. J. Chrisman, "Narrow-Scope Strategies and Firm Performance: An Empirical Investigation," *Journal of Business Strategies* (Spring 1998), pp. 1–16; T. M. Stearns, N. M. Carter, P. D. Reynolds, and M. L. Williams, "New Firm Survival: Industry, Strategy, and Location," *Journal of Business Venturing* (January 1995), pp. 23–42.
8. Porter, *Competitive Strategy*, p. 35.
9. R. E. Caves and P. Ghemawat, "Identifying Mobility Barriers," *Strategic Management Journal* (January 1992), pp. 1–12.
10. R. O. Crockett, "They're Lining Up for Flicks in the 'Hood," *Business Week* (June 8, 1998), pp. 75–76.
11. D. P. Hamilton, "H-P's First Breakdown of Profit Shows Under 25% Is from Computer Business," *Wall Street Journal* (November 28, 2000), p. B8; P. Burrows, "Can Fiorina Reboot HP?" *Business Week* (November 27, 2000), p. 59.
12. C. Campbell-Hunt, "What Have We Learned About Generic Competitive Strategy? A Meta Analysis," *Strategic Management Journal* (February 2000), pp. 127–154.
13. M. Kroll, P. Wright, and R. A. Heiens, "The Contribution of Product Quality to Competitive Advantage: Impacts on Systematic Variance and Unexplained Variance in Returns," *Strategic Management Journal* (April 1999), pp. 375–384.
14. R. M. Hodgetts, "A Conversation with Michael E. Porter: A 'Significant Extension' Toward Operational Improvement and Positioning," *Organizational Dynamics* (Summer 1999), pp. 24–33.

15. N. Brodsky, "Size Matters," *INC.* (September 1998), pp. 31–32.
16. R. Tomsho, "Funeral Parlors Become Big Business," *Wall Street Journal* (September 18, 1996), pp. B1, B4.
17. P. F. Kocourek, S. Y. Chung, and M. G. McKenna, "Strategic Rollups: Overhauling the Multi-Merger Machine," *Strategy + Business* (2nd Qtr 2000), pp. 45–53.
18. J. A. Tannenbaum, "Acquisitive Companies Set Out to 'Roll Up' Fragmented Industries," *Wall Street Journal* (March 3, 1997), pp. P. A1, A6.
19. R. A. D'Aveni, *Hypercompetition* (New York: The Free Press, 1994), pp. xiii–xiv.
20. P. C. Nutt, "Surprising But True: Half the Decisions in Organizations Fail," *Academy of Management Executive* (November 1999), pp. 75–90.
21. Some refer to this as the economic concept of "increasing returns." Instead of reaching a point of diminishing returns when a product saturates a market and the curve levels off, the curve continues to go up as the company takes advantage of setting the standard to spin off new products that use the new standard to achieve higher performance than competitors. See J. Alley, "The Theory That Made Microsoft," *Fortune* (April 29, 1996), pp. 65–66.
22. H. Lee, K. G. Smith, C. M. Grimm, and A. Schomburg, "Timing, Order and Durability of New Product Advantages with Imitation," *Strategic Management Journal* (January 2000), pp. 23–30; Y. Pan and P. C. K. Chi, "Financial Performance and Survival of Multinational Corporations in China," *Strategic Management Journal* (April 1999), pp. 359–374; R. Makadok, "Can First-Mover and Early-Mover Advantages Be Sustained in an Industry with Low Barriers to Entry/Imitation?" *Strategic Management Journal* (July 1998), pp. 683–696; B. Mascarenhas, "The Order and Size of Entry Into International Markets," *Journal of Business Venturing* (July 1997), pp. 287–299.
23. G. J. Tellis and P. N. Golder, "First to Market, First to Fail? Real Causes of Enduring Market Leadership," *Sloan Management Review* (Winter 1996), pp. 65–75.
24. For an in-depth discussion of first and late mover advantages and disadvantages, see D-S. Cho, D-J. Kim, and D. K. Rhee, "Latecomer Strategies: Evidence from the Semiconductor Industry in Japan and Korea," *Organization Science* (July–August 1998), pp. 489–505.

25. T. S. Schoenecker and A. C. Cooper, "The Role of Firm Resources and Organizational Attributes in Determining Entry Timing: A Cross-Industry Study," *Strategic Management Journal* (December 1998), pp. 1127–1143.

26. Summarized from various articles by L. Fahey in *The Strategic Management Reader*, edited by L. Fahey (Englewood Cliffs, N.J.: Prentice-Hall, 1989), pp. 178–205.

27. This information on defensive tactics is summarized from M. E. Porter, *Competitive Advantage* (New York: Free Press, 1985), pp. 482–512.

28. T. M. Burton, "Archer-Daniels Faces a Potential Blow as Three Firms Admit Price-Fixing Plot," *Wall Street Journal* (August 28, 1996), pp. A3, A6; R. Henkoff, "The ADM Tale Gets Even Stranger," *Fortune* (May 13, 1996), pp. 113–120.

29. Much of the content on cooperative strategies was summarized from J. B. Barney, *Gaining and Sustaining Competitive Advantage* (Reading, Mass.: Addison-Wesley, 1997), pp. 255–278.

30. E. A. Murray, Jr., and J. F. Mahon, "Strategic Alliances: Gateway to the New Europe?" *Long Range Planning* (August 1993), p. 103.

31. H. Meyer, "My Enemy, My Friend," *Journal of Business Strategy* (September–October 1998), pp. 42–46.

32. T. K. Das and B-S Teng, "Instabilities of Strategic Alliances: An Internal Tensions Perspective," *Organization Science* (January–February 2000), pp. 77–101.

33. L. Segil, "Strategic Alliances for the 21st Century," *Strategy & Leadership* (September/October 1998), pp. 12–16.

34. E. A. Murray, Jr., and J. F. Mahon, "Strategic Alliances: Gateway to the New Europe?" *Long Range Planning* (August 1993), pp. 105–106.

35. R. M. Kanter, "Collaborative Advantage: The Art of Alliances," *Harvard Business Review* (July–August 1994), pp. 96–108.

36. B. Bremner, Z. Schiller, T. Smart, and W. J. Holstein, "Keiretsu Connections," *Business Week* (July 22, 1996), pp. 52–54.

37. R. P. Lynch, *The Practical Guide to Joint Ventures and Corporate Alliances* (New York: John Wiley and Sons, 1989), p. 7.

38. H. Green, "Double Play," *Business Week E-Biz* (October 23, 2000), pp. EB42–EB46.

39. L. L. Blodgett, "Factors in the Instability of International Joint Ventures: An Event History Analysis," *Strategic Management Journal* (September 1992), pp. 475–481; J. Bleeke and D. Ernst, "The Way to Win in Cross-Border Alliances," *Harvard Business Review* (November–December 1991), pp. 127–135; J. M. Geringer, "Partner Selection Criteria for Developed Country Joint Ventures," in *International Management Behavior*, 2nd ed., edited by H. W. Lane, and J. J. DiStephano (Boston: PWS-Kent, 1992), pp. 206–216.

40. S. Stevens, "Speeding the Signals of Change," *Appliance* (February 1995), p. 7.

41. K. Z. Andrews, "Manufacturer/Supplier Relationships: The Supplier Payoff," *Harvard Business Review* (September–October 1995), pp. 14–15.

42. P. Lorange, "Black-Box Protection of Your Core Competencies in Strategic Alliances," in *Cooperative Strategies: European Perspectives*, edited by P. W. Beamish and J. P. Killing (San Francisco: The New Lexington Press, 1997), pp. 59–99.

43. "Enter the Eco-System," *The Economist E-Management Survey* (November 11, 2000), p. 30.

44. N. Weinberg, "Herding Cats," *Forbes* (July 24, 2000), pp. 108–110.

45. "Enter the Eco-System," *The Economist E-Management Survey* (November 11, 2000), p. 34.

46. J. Warner, "21st Century Capitalism: Snapshot of the Next Century," *Business Week* (November 18, 1994), p. 194.

Business Environment

Phil Bowers
The University of Edinburgh
Management School

Introduction

Introduction to the Module

The approach to economics will NOT be the standard approach; economists will have some advantages but should not overestimate them unless they really understand their subject.

The Module aims:

- to provide an understanding of the key business goal, which is to 'make money'.
- to relate this to economics as usually taught, adapting it to business circumstances, so that it is understandable outside the context of pure economic theory.

The structure of the module is set out in Fig 1 below; the numbers in brackets in this paragraph refer to the numbered boxes in the flow chart.

- We look initially at the basic goal of making money, which in the context of the firm means 'making a profit' and thus 'profit maximisation' (1). As we are now in an era when even 'socialists' seem to accept the market as a means of social organisation, we also look at some of its limitations as a means of social organisation.
- 'Opportunity Cost' (2) is the underlying concept of cost used in *The Goal* and in economic theory, and finance.
- But 'Marginal Cost' (3) is often more useful. It is a particular form of opportunity cost. We shall see that traditional economic theory is often misleading about the nature of Marginal Cost.
- The structure of industry cannot be understood without an understanding of 'economies of scale' (4).
- These concepts provide a basis for understanding costs, but profits are made by selling at a price above the costs of production. We therefore look next at 'Marginal Revenue' (5), and how it relates to decisions whether to cut prices or not.
- Next we look at the factors behind Marginal Revenue, and relating to 'Demand' (6).
- To finish we will show how these elements combine to help us to understand the problems faced by British Energy in 2002.

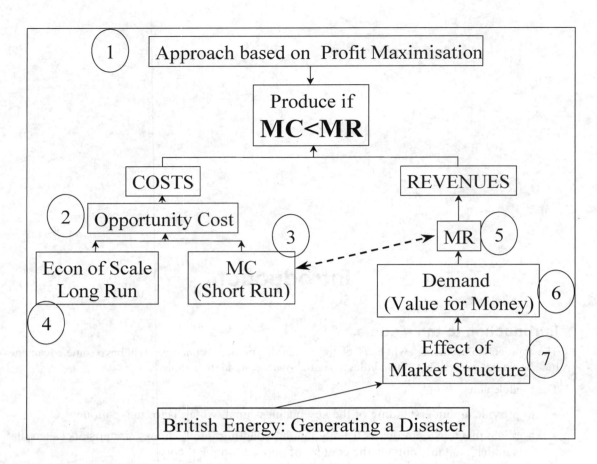

Note on reading for this section of the course:

Fairly frequent references are made to:

E. Goldratt and J. Cox (1993) *The Goal*, 2nd edition, Gower Publishing, Aldershot ISBN: 0-566-07418-4 Paperback.

This is a 'didactic novel' which gives a lively and realistic picture of an American manufacturing company wrestling with the problems of inappropriate control mechanisms and the chaos and losses that they cause. It will give you a feel for the reality of business life that is otherwise difficult to achieve. It therefore helps to put these lectures into a context of real life, and we use situations from the book to discuss theoretical issues, i.e. issues where the ideas have wider application to business life.

This book is also recommended reading for the Part-time MBA programme, which is made up of executives from the area around Edinburgh, most of them from service industries including the financial sector. Most of them see the lessons from *The Goal* as immediately applicable to their work situation, and so neither its age, nor the fact that it is about manufacturing, have made it irrelevant to today.

The Goal: Making Money

Profit maximising

Introduction:

We will:

- Engage with the issue of whether 'making money', and by implication as much money as possible, is 'the Goal' of business.

- Discuss whether it can be viewed 'as simply as that' – is it just one goal among many?

- Does it matter stating the wrong goal?

- Is this goalof making profits immoral?

Making money – profit maximising?

If as a company you do not make money, you go bankrupt. In other words: if the amount of money flowing out of the business is greater than the amount coming in, sooner or later the money runs out. Small firms are more vulnerable than divisions of large firms, because they cannot get support from the large company, and furthermore the bank knows this and the bank has less to lose from calling in any loans. However, we shall see that large companies may be impatient with divisions that do not make as much profit as headquarters believe to be right, and that this has the often painful result that the parent company closes the division or sells it. So at very least, you must not make losses, and as it is difficult to make a real profit, it is useful to start with the idea that the function of business is to make as much money as possible – in other words, to profit maximise.

What are profits?

They are the surplus cash after all expenses have been met. This is accounting profit; it is needed to make sure you avoid a cash flow crisis, as described above, where the money runs out. Such a cash flow crisis is called 'insolvency' – you cannot pay the money you owe to your workers and suppliers, and cannot borrow to pay. The bank, or other firms, may 'call in' your debt, the money you owe the bank for loans and overdrafts, but you will be unable to do so, and you go into 'receivership'. You lose the right to run your business and 'receivers' are appointed to take over with a view to recovering as much of the various debts as possible. They do this either by selling it 'as a going concern' to another set of managers who believe they can make money from it, or by selling off its assets to whoever will pay most for each item, known as 'liquidation'.

Profits are measured in 3 ways:

Net profits – in money terms

Return on investment: $\dfrac{\text{net profit}}{\text{Capital invested}}$

Net Cash Flow = Cash coming in less expenses

The first tells you how much you are making. The second tells you whether you are spending too much in the form of capital invested to make those profits. The third tells you whether you can stay in business, because even if by the end of the year you would make a handsome profit, if you can't pay your debts at the end of 6 months, you might be insolvent and so closed before the end of the year.

Economists define profit more narrowly; it should include as part of costs, the implicit costs of land and capital owned by the firm, and the proper value of the owner manager. In the example of the Sale of Assets, in the box on the next page, Souter (of Stagecoach) was working on economic profits and assets, whereas the sellers of

Southampton Bus Company were working on the accounting figures of cash flow only. Equally, economic profit would estimate the pay of the general manager as if that manager were in her 'next best opportunity' as a cost, and any excess over this as part of profit. Although this makes calculation of profit difficult, it is useful in giving guidance over the fundamental principle of competitive markets:

> **Where there is an opportunity for profitable trading, some person or firm will enter the market to take up that opportunity.**

'Profitable trading' includes the opportunity to make a product or provide a service, not just exchanging existing goods. And profit in that context has to be seen from a firm starting from nothing, and so the manager will be recruited at his or her market rate, not at a rate reflecting years of good performance.

The simple view that firms make money only by the excess of revenues from sales less their costs, is clearly not sufficient in an era that has seen the purchase of the giant National Westminster Bank by the relatively small Royal Bank of Scotland. How is money being made here? By replacing the management of the National Westminster, who did not enjoy the confidence of the City, with the management of the Royal Bank of Scotland who had a good reputation for keeping costs down, and being adventurous, it was hoped that the profits of the National Westminster would increase – and they did. In other cases, the same logic means that firms are making money by selling parts of the firm, because the purchaser will be willing to pay more, as they can make more money from the assets of the part of they firm they buy.

An example of the sale of a division of a company

In Edinburgh, there is a very well-known medical publishing 'company', **Churchill Livingstone**, with a substantial portfolio of best-selling medical books. It was part of Longmans, who published a wide range of textbooks. Longmans more or less left Churchill Livingstone to get on with the job they knew best. However, Longmans itself was not thought to be as profitable as it could be, and so was taken over by Pearson (owners of the Financial Times).

Pearson first moved the London Office of CL from Holborn to Clerkenwell, and then closed it down! They then sold the whole of CL to Brace, Harcourt, Jehanovic – a large US company specialising in this sort of publishing, in other words to a company where Churchill Livingstone is in their 'core area'.

The accidental purchase of the company was bad for morale at CL, but reflected some logic at the Group level of Pearson International, since the rest of Longmans is largely in their core area. The decisions about CL's London office reflected a lack of clarity about Pearson's goals for CL, and can only be regarded as bad management, since it costs money both to move offices and to close them down.

An example of sale of assets

Stagecoach started with a long distance coach service from Scotland to London. Their first big breakthrough came when they bought Southampton Bus Company for about £3m. – a fair price for the bus company given its buses and profits. What Mr Souter, MD and owner of Stagecoach, had spotted and the sellers had not, was that the bus depot in Southampton was prime commercial land and worth about £3m. So Mr Souter bought the Bus Company; sold the city centre depot; moved servicing to another depot on the outskirts, and thus got the bus operations – which have been decently profitable– for nothing!

Smart purchase! why sell? Because Souter was not a property developer. He would probably have made less money from developing the city centre bus station than someone who was practiced in property development.

Making a Profit

Implies selling products or services at a profit i.e. total costs must be lower than total revenues. This means that you must

    a)   have a sufficiently desirable product to attract enough people to buy at the price at which you are offering, and

    b)   have costs low enough make a profit.

A product is sufficiently desirable if **compared to other products on offer** it suits at least a proportion of the potential purchasers better than other products. Thus a product must be competitive as far as the consumers are concerned. This is the same as saying it must be '**good value for money**' to some consumers. Thus built into the market system is continual competition to find what consumers desire and ways to produce it and deliver it at a cost that makes it 'good value for money'.

In thinking about making profits, it is useful to distinguish revenues and costs, because the revenues are controlled by the consumers, and the costs by the firm

$$\text{Profit} = \text{Total Revenue} - \text{Total Costs}$$

$$\text{TR} = \text{Price x Quantity Sold} = \textit{Throughput}$$

The <u>firm</u> 'controls' product specifications and price, but the <u>customers</u> have the choice of buying or not, and so determine the quantity, and it is therefore the customers that are the key to the firm's revenue.

$$\text{TC} = \text{Fixed costs} + (\text{Variable Cost x Quantity Produced})$$

$$\textit{TC} = \textit{Overheads} + \textit{Inventory Costs} + \textit{Operating Costs}$$

The firm is however entirely responsible for the costs it incurs. It may face rising costs because some input becomes scarce, because it has to import its inputs and the value of the currency is falling, or because it is using the inputs inefficiently. However, the customer is not worried about this, and the firm is responsible for finding a solution to problems of higher costs than rival companies.

Profits from Sales of Assets

Equally large firms may decide to close or sell a division even when it is making money, either because it is not making enough, or because some other firm is willing to pay more for the division than the parent firm thinks it is worth to them. This is the mechanism by which the management of the National Westminster Bank were replace by that of the Royal Bank of Scotland; the Royal Bank of Scotland bought the National Westminster. The way companies can be valued is part of the subject of the Finance Module. This buying and selling of companies or parts of them is still a money-making activity, and it usually has some combination of the following motives:

a)   to get rid of divisions which the company cannot manage as well as another company thinks it could because they are not in the 'core business'.
b)   To give the company cash it can use – either to get out of trouble, or to invest in equipment, or to purchase companies, or divisions which it can manage better than their original owners (As in the Natwest case).

The logic of this activity is often justified by the notion of 'sticking to the knitting' or restricting the firm's activities to its 'Core business'. That is the areas about which management knows enough to be able to run them more profitably than other firms. A unit not in a company's core business should therefore be worth more to a company whose core business is the same as that of the unit.

Other Goals

*   'Maximising market share' to get into a dominant position is a very dangerous goal; it can push you to selling unprofitably. This was very popular in the 1970s after the Boston Consulting group had done a very large study which showed that the firms with the largest market shares were also normally the most profitable. The alternative explanation, that getting a better product gives you the largest market share, and thus higher profits was not investigated! It is now thought to be a more likely explanation. This goal also became very popular with the advent of the dot.com company, and we know what happened to most of them.
*   'Maximising quality' equally dangerous – it can push up costs to the point where a profitable price is unattainable. Even though this is the logic of the explanation of being both the largest and most profitable above, the danger in following this goal, is that the wording is wrong. 'A better product' is one whose combination of qualities and price suits the largest number of consumers, not one whose quality is maximised.

- 'Minimising costs' is perhaps the most dangerous of all. Poor quality or old technology are not good for sales.
- Maximising output in order to reduce costs: Arthur Scargill's fallacy. He used to say 'British Coal produces the cheapest deep-mined coal in the world.' But it was piling up in heaps unsold, because it was too expensive. If you have very large fixed costs (like the costs of developing a deep coal mine and equipping it), the more you produce, the lower the average cost – the cost per tonne – but if you are not selling it, producing more still increases the cost per unit sold, because each extra tonne adds a bit to cost, and what should be of interest is the cost of items sold, not the cost of production. The problem was that it is much more economical to produce coal by strip mining.

People will often succeed in meeting the target set; thus setting the wrong target, even where it is seen as a means to an end, is dangerous. Equally, not explaining what affects quality as far as the customer is concerned, and focussing only on cash flows is equally perverse.

Goals for Units within the Firm

'Making money' – maximising profits – will mean little to an operative making one small part of a machine. Thus their goals need to be spelt out. But the less the understanding of the overall goal and how they fit in, the more chance of wrong interpretations. Specifying goals that do not in fact contribute to making money is well illustrated in *the Goal* particularly the insistence by HQ of 'operational efficiencies' as the measurement of performance for the plant – this is the subject of the next session. [i]

Is the Market System Immoral?

It is often objected that the market system is 'immoral', and that maximising profits is therefore wrong. Firstly, in order to thrive markets need social order – otherwise theft is the best policy because it is usually cheaper to steal someone else's product than to produce yourself. If they invest in defense, that pushes up the cost of stealing. But it should still be possible to invest in arms so that while both sides now have the expense of weaponry and 'an army', the producer still has the cost of production as well. The tendency is for production to decline to that which keeps you alive, and the costs of defending your production to soar; the effects can be seen in almost any lawless state. The market therefore requires an ethical framework. In a stable, law abiding environment, there are still good reasons why the desire to make money may need to be controlled to safeguard society as a whole. The most important are probably:

- **Shifting costs e.g. pollution;**if the firm does not pay for the pollution it causes, either in production or in the use of its products, it is shifting the cost to society, and that seems close to a form of theft. For example, in the production of a car, an enormous amount of water is used, often requiring land to be flooded for reservoirs; the production of the steel uses enormous amounts of energy, and these in turn cause pollution by producing carbon dioxide (greenhouse gas) and other more directly unpleasant things like soot, some of which causes cancer, sulphur dioxide and nitrogen oxides, both of which cause acid rain. The carmaker does not pay for these damaging accidental outputs of the production process, any more than the motorist pays for the carbon dioxide and nitrogen oxides produced by running the car. Thus at very least, the exchange is not a fair one; costs are imposed on people without any compensation. The normal way to overcome these problems is to tackle them by making regulations; for example, by requiring cars to have catalytic converters which at least reduce the nitrogen oxides. The box below shows how tricky it is to set up controls that work well. A more recent example comes from European legislative attempts to ensure that we are not creating too much pollution in the form of waste from manufactured products, in this example electrical products. Refrigerators create considerable waste disposal problems both from the chemicals used, and from the bulk of material left. Sweden has had legislation on recycling in place for the last 3 years. Each Swede gets through 16kgs of electrical goods. Producers are expected to pay; and that means that all European producers must face the same legislation, or the ones with the weakest legislation will have an advantage because they will be able to produce more cheaply. This would not only favour the 'dirty' producers, but of course relatively increase pollution since the increased demand for the cheaper products would cause that dirty producer to produce more dirt along with the products. The potential for bad legislation caused by failure to look at the lifetime pollution of the product was discussed on The Today Programme on BBC Radio 4 on 31 May 2004. They gave the example of a Class A Electrolux fridge; this relies on substantial amounts of polyurethane foam as insulating material, but the foam cannot be recycled. Proposed legislation demands that 75% of large products, such as fridges, will need to be recycled, and this may make this level of insulation less viable, and so we risk having perverse incentives which will reduce insulation and so increase pollution by large amounts because of higher energy use through the product's life.

> There was an interesting example in *New Scientist* (20 Sept 1997 p13) showing that catalytic converters may not reduce pollution because of the pollution produced in making the platinum, palladium and rhodium, mined in Canada, South Africa and Russia. These precious metals occur in very low concentrations as sulphides in ores that also contain copper and nickel. The processing therefore emits tonnes of sulphur dioxide, which causes acid rain. Russian plants emit 10.9 kg of SO_2 per gram of precious metal, whereas Canadian plants only emit 1.7 kg. Canadian plants are fitted with 'scrubbers' water jets with added lime, which absorbs the SO_2 and gives gypsum, as a byproduct. The Russian plant in Norilsk emits more SO_2 than all the power plants in the US!. Catalytic converters have to travel 25000 km before the reduction in acid from the exhaust makes up for the creation of acid from the mining! The Russians particularly are avoiding the costs of cleaning up the acid rain by shifting them to the environment.

- **Exploiting workers**: if there is too little demand for workers because of depressed conditions, the owners/managers can demand inhuman working conditions, knowing that the alternative is no income. As labour costs are important, shifts to areas where workers are at a disadvantage is always possible. This mobility is constrained by relocation costs, including the preferences of key personnel, transport costs, and the 'efficiency of the workers' – high levels of education or training may be needed to operate efficiently. Secondly, in many such low income countries, the social infrastructure and industrial infrastructure is so poor that this raises costs, so the shift of work to those countries is likely to be much slower than some people imaging. Shifting low skilled production to such areas benefits the areas in question, and probably has adverse effects on the unskilled groups in the 'exporting' country. We can see the same thing happening within Europe –the high levels of taxation on companies for each employee in Belgium almost certainly contributed to the closure of the Renault plant there, but these high levels of taxation were partly to fund the welfare provisions for those workers. In each case, we gain as consumers from the 'inhuman' working conditions. But without that mechanism, there is no reason to move production to those countries, and so little incentive to improve the conditions in those very needy countries.

- **Exploiting the public by provision of bad products or services**, or selling under false pretences can cause complete market breakdown. It is not worth buying anything if you are too likely to be ripped off. Thus guarantees and fair trading laws are used to prevent this. Where this sort of exploitation does occur, it may be 'punished' by the market by breakdown or by consumers avoiding all products produced by that firm. It is not therefore an attractive strategy for companies who have substantial amounts of capital invested. Marks and Spencer would scarcely get over the difficulties caused by the problems with styling by selling shoddy materials.

- **Excess profits**: BT for example. These are generally attributable to lack of competition, which is what is meant by 'monopoly power'. It can certainly be argued that it is too weakly controlled, and that companies like British Airways and Microsoft compete on an unfair basis and make excessive profits as a result. Governments do however try to control this by legislation, but it is always a difficult field as it is difficult to show whether it is unfair competition or simply a better product that is reaping the rewards in the form of high profits.

The Market: An Inhuman System?

It is much easier to support the proposition that the market is inhuman than that it is directly immoral. It is impossible to operate a system as complex as a modern market economy on the basis of personal relationships. A modern car has in excess of 15,000 parts, largely made by different companies or units, and so even the simple idea of the managing director of the car manufacturer knowing all the managing directors of the component manufacturers is difficult to imagine, and even if he knew them, it would certainly not be on the basis of intimate friendships. Furthermore though we work in a market system and this is characterised by a mode of operation often called 'exit', other social contexts require different and more human approaches to social interaction.

1. **'Exit'** the freedom to just walk away from a transaction is the key market mechanism. People will 'exit' if a product does not give value for money, it therefore disciplines firms to provide the right goods at the right price. It is a characteristic of such market situations that the sellers have no 'right' to ask why a

customer is not purchasing. Pressure to purchase applied in this way is at very least rude. This is a problem for labour relations, workers are 'bought' i.e. paid to do a job; but the bosses can 'exit' from the relationship by firing the worker, or the worker can exit by walking out. Both boss and worker are subject to a market discipline. If the worker is not as good as others who could be employed, (s)he is at risk. If the worker can find another job and if the boss provides bad working conditions, whether because of excessive demands on the worker, dirty of noisy surroundings, or because of bad personal relations or harassment, then the worker is likely to exit. The firms whose workers are a valuable human resource with all sorts of special knowledge relating to the firm need therefore to be careful about how they treat their workers. Thus all sorts of 'humanising' elements have to be brought in, so that they do not exit.

2. **'Voice'** is the mechanism for political decisions. The insult here is to fail to give a member of the group a say, and/or not to listen to them. This means they have to be convinced and vigorous argument is acceptable – though not bullying which is an attempt to force, not to convince. Political decisions in this sense include those within the firm; there, decisions are made to follow certain courses of action – one cannot mix different approaches to design of a product for example – and so agreement i.e. 'voice' not 'exit' becomes the appropriate mechanism. We can see therefore, that there is an interesting conflict of principles in terms of relationships with workers and between workers. Both elements of the impersonal principle of 'Exit' and the personal interactions implied by 'Voice' apply. In fact it is even more complex than this; our next category also applies.

3. **'Fraternity'** i.e. sharing and mutual support, may be a more appropriate form of behaviour in personal relationships, where support and intimacy are the key factors, and this may well extend to personal relationships at work. If you know that a colleague is having real difficulties at home, it is neither sensible nor humanly acceptable to assume that (s)he will be as tough and resilient as usual, and to indulge in vigorous argument; care and support may be more appropriate to retain good relationships with a valued colleague.

The inhuman operation of the market by forcing firms to compete in the relatively inhuman mode of operation of 'exit' is probably necessary to create the prosperity that opens up so many opportunities to you; it gives consumers and workers the freedom to choose, and so puts pressure on companies to provide what consumers want, at a reasonable cost. It also gives workers the right to exit from jobs which do not pay them enough. Paradoxically however, within the firm, the mode of operation is actually a combination of 'exit' – if relations have got so bad that the situation is 'take it or leave it' – 'voice' because in most situations the firm has to work as a team not as independent individuals working as if in a market, and hence also perhaps 'fraternity' mutual support and forebearance that characterise personal relationships.

Question for thought:

A colleague is not 'pulling his weight. This becomes serious enough for action to be taken. The line managers discuss what is to be done, and come up with the following options: institute disciplinary hearings; challenge the colleague in a meeting of all the staff; or get his immediate superior, who has always had friendly relations with him, to have a quiet word to find out what is going on.

Should the option chosen be influenced by what sort of job the person is doing — a professional in a team, a computer programmer, or a tele-sales operative? And how does this relate to 'Exit'. 'Voice', and 'Fraternity'?

Summary:
- Firms in the market sector are devoted to 'making money' approximately: increasing profits.
- Profits are defined as revenue less costs, but the rate of return and net cash flows are vital measures of viability.
- Profits are usually thought to depend only on the sales revenue less the production costs BUT
- Large firms may make money by selling profitable units to other firms where the unit can make even more money for its new parent company. In the process 'foul ups' are quite likely.
- Rival goals to profit maximisation are likely to be misleading and dangerous, particularly if applied to units within the firm – to be explored further in the next section.

- Both the morality and inhumanity of a market system are criticised – potentially but by no means necessarily inappropriately.

---

[i] Jonah's plant level rules (p59) – explanation of the terminology used in *The Goal*

'**Throughput** is the rate at which the system generates money through sales.

Inventory is all the money that the system has invested in purchasing things which it intends to sell.

Operational Expense is all the money the system spends in order to turn inventory into throughput.'

And the aim is to increase throughput and decrease inventory and operational expense. This is exactly equivalent to maximising profits.

Opportunity Cost

Aims:

- Examine the general insight from Economics that good decisions are based on comparison with alternatives available, and thus the OPPORTUNITES FOREGONE when one course of action is taken.
- Apply this to production problems to derive: the Opportunity cost of bottleneck time, and the Opportunity cost of non-bottleneck time.
- Provide a critical view of Opportunity Cost as a subjective measure, which cannot be generalised.

Choices as Opportunities Foregone

Perhaps the easiest context in which to think of opportunity cost is an auction for a city centre site. Each bidder will have different plans for the site, and from those plans an estimate of the profits that can be made from developing and reselling the site. Let us for simplicity assume that the developer includes in the costs of development the minimum pay that (s)he is willing to accept for the work involved. Any money over and above this is therefore a real profit. Unfortunately, the successful bidder has to pay for the site! How much would they be willing to pay? How much will the winner have to pay?

Each bidder has included his or her own 'pay' for the work in the estimate of costs of the development, and so each would be willing to pay up to the profits they expect. So the one with the most profitable scheme will be willing to pay most.

How much will the one with the most profitable scheme have to pay? Presumably just enough to outbid the second most profitable scheme.

What is the **opportunity cost of the site**? The market price, **which is the amount the second most profitable scheme – the one that will not be built – would be willing to pay**.

It is the opportunity to construct this second most profitable scheme that society is doing without – hence the term 'Opportunity cost'.

Questions to ask in attempting to get a value for opportunity cost:

All questions involve assessing the changes brought about by an action; what do we lose? What would we gain?

1. If we produce this unit (say sell an extra bed-night in a hotel), what costs will be actually incurred in doing so? Note: this immediately eliminates from consideration any costs that will not change as the result of the decision, such as capital investments, management time among others, and restricts you to looking at the actual loss of opportunity to enjoy the cash instead.

2. Following a course of action, for example if a motor manufacturer decides to invest in the development of a significantly higher performance version of a car, what additional costs will the firm incur, and what additional benefits will they gain – net of the losses from reducing sales of the existing line? Opportunity cost of not doing this: the net benefits foregone. Opportunity cost of doing it: the direct investment costs, the production costs involved, and the losses in profit from reduced sales. This opportunity cost would then be compared to the expected revenues, and if the revenues are greater, it would pay to invest.

3. In an auction for a city centre site, what profits would I not get if I fail to get the site? This means a complex consideration of profits obtainable at alternative sites, including the potential availability of sites not on themarket. It is often easy to exaggerate the uniqueness of the site. There may in fact be many morecoming onto the market.

Very often market prices are the best estimate of 'opportunity cost'. The opportunity cost of a tonne of wheat is the price of that tonne of wheat, since another tonne of wheat is a perfect substitute, and you could buy it at the market price. This is generally true where there are markets without significant market power – the ability to restrict the output, so as to drive up price – or constraints on output. (Example of that sort of constraint:when the licensing lawswere first introduced, they resulted in a virtual stop on construction of new pubs. This created the opportunity for the big brewers to buy up the pubs, and so have a captive market for their beer. This reduced the supply of pubs to the rest, who started to bid more for them. This made a pub more valuable than the cost of the building, equipment, and supplies which would be required to open a pub.)

Opportunity cost of time on a bottleneck

What is a bottleneck? The machine that dictates whether or not production of a given unit of output can be produced. The word also used in *The Goal* is a 'Constraint'.

In *The Goal*, there are two major constraints on production:

> the New robot: the NCX-10

> The heat treatment plant.

How do they find them? By the great piles of work waiting to go through. This is a characteristic of almost all bottlenecks:

> road traffic – traffic queues, build up at the most constricting junction.

> water through a bridge – standing waves in front of the piers show the level of constriction;

> services – applications waiting for processing; waiting lists for appointments

(Note it may be difficult to trace the bottleneck in a Hospital, because the waiting list is by department, not by function. Thus the bottleneck might be beds, might be surgeons, might be anaesthetist, or nursing staff, or operating theatre time, or simply cash for medicines.)

According to Jonah, the management consultant friend of the plant manager, the opportunity cost of time lost on a bottleneck is the total running-cost of the plant. The output of the bottleneck machines determine the total output. Loss of time on that bottleneck must therefore be equivalent to the resulting loss of total output, and as we are considering costs, that means the total cost of the plant.

However that is defining "the opportunity foregone" as the cost of production. But it might be better to define it as the number of units of output lost x their value added (i.e. their price less the savings made by not producing them[1]) – Why is this a better measure? Because the costs of running the plant are not being lost or saved - it is the ability to ship output that is lost - hence the net value of the output is the "opportunity cost" of time lost on the bottlenecks. (You may wish to learn the term 'profit contribution', which is used for the conceptof net value in accountancy.)

Is time saved on a bottleneck of equal value to time lost?

In general yes, provided that the time saved does not turn the 'bottleneck' into a 'non-bottleneck'. Thus *'Elevating the constraints'*, i.e. improving the performance of the bottlenecks is vital and potentially very profitable.

Modelling to find bottlenecks

This is theoretically possible, and it may be done by the use of linear programming or one of the other simulation techniques. In practice it is often not possible since it requires a complete mathematical model of every production process, which might set the decision back by several years (see pp 140-147 in *The Goal*). Furthermore, models can only be constructed according to some theory, because only then do you know what you are looking for. Thus a model that could not take set-up time into account and was based on some average time to produce an item would be useless. If your implicit theory (e.g. maximisation of machine efficiency as a goal for the plant) is wrong, you will only have the correct information on which to base a model by pure chance. However, attempting to make a model will very often show you the illogical basis on which you are working. When modelled, the garbageyou get out, makes you realise you are putting garbage into the model.

Opportunity Cost of Non-Bottleneck Time

is zero; unless so much time is wasted that it becomes a bottleneck.

---

1 In this context that saving is usually just the bought inputs required. But it might include any knock on effects. For example the knock on effects of late delivery might involve losing the contract for producing parts for a particular customer.

It is tempting to use non-bottleneck machinery to keep up machine utilisation or to make parts for inventory. This overproduction, i.e. production that can't be sold, is creation of expense, not profit. There may be no alternative use for the workers or machines involved. Thus time is not important. The way of operating may be; e.g.If as in *The Goal*, complete runs of production have to be completed before any item is delivered to the next workstation, cutting the run length, that is the number of any particular item to be made before changing the set up, may help to reduce the inventory costs by reducing work in progress, and may help to speed a shipment by delivering parts to the bottleneck more quickly.This is however, an apparently illogical way of running the plant. Making parts for inventory, and future use, is highly dangerous. There are usually significant storage costs, and there is a high probability that models will change before the part is used. If so the extracosts involved in the production of those parts is pure expense, with no benefits.

A critical look at the concept of 'opportunity cost'

Presenting the general principle of 'looking for the alternatives available', i.e. what opportunities you foreclose if you choose a particular course of action, does not help to define these opportunities.

Examples:

1. If you believe the opportunity cost (the foreclosed option) of running non-bottlenecks with very short production runs is lost 'machine efficiency', you will conclude that there is a high opportunity cost of non-bottleneck time.

2. If you believe that all you lose when a bottleneck machine is out of action the cost is the combined value of the labour actually tending that machine and the value of the machine expressed as an hourly rate, you underestimate your opportunity cost. If it is expensive to get the machine repaired quickly, you are likely to leave it out of action while slow repairs are carried out, and so lose a lot of money.

3. Jonah's estimate of the value of lost production due to a bottleneck as being the total cost of the plant, is itself a wrong estimate. The opportunity foregone is lost sales net of input costs. Costs are things to avoid, not opportunities.

4. Each one of you probably has a different opportunity cost of coming to this course, and even more different opportunities in deciding to study at this university.

The last two examples provide both a key to estimating Opportunity Cost appropriately, and the major critique of the concept.

1. **Estimates should be global**; i.e. include the full set of consequences of the action. This goes some way to correcting wrong estimates. *The Goal* can be seen as a crusade against the use of 'local optima' as opposed to 'global optima', i.e. consequences always need to be specified for the situation (or organisation in the case of a firm) as a whole.

2. But the more global the estimate, the more difficult it will be to specify the consequences, and hence the less precisely one can estimate the value of the Opportunity Cost.

3. Opportunity Cost in practice measures perceived opportunities foregone, thus it is a subjective measure, and cannot be used for empirical analysis.

An alternative way of looking at the last point: unless you know the full details about a firm's constraints and opportunities, including the constraint that comes from their ability to spot opportunities, you cannot estimate their opportunity costs at the time. The last point is not true where the choice in question is BETWEEN different units of a homogeneous product i.e. where each unit is identical. In these cases, it is unambiguously the market price; e.g. the opportunity cost of shares in a particular company, or tonnes of standard grades of wheat or other commodities is the money with which you can buy other shares in that company etc.

Marginal Cost

But first:

Why do we want to know about costs?

> To see if we are going to make a profit?

> No, an accountant needs to forecast that with all the assumptions that forecasts imply, or to record it after the event.

> To see if we are going to make a profit on the particular transaction?

> That is not possible to know, profit requires all costs and all revenues to be calculated, and we will see that is almost never possible for a particular item.

We need cost data to help us to decide WHETHER TO COMPETE IN THAT MARKET.

Marginal cost

Aims:

- To get a more specific approach to the issue of Global Opportunity Cost.
- To understand a key term in economics, of immense general operational importance.
- To understand what lies behind the relationship between Marginal Cost and the level of the plant's output – will MC rise as output rises, remain constant, be zero at all levels, or be unstable?
- To develop an approach fully in accord with *The Goal*, and stressed in traditional economics.
- Examine the right sort of cost measurement to decide whether to produce (=to enter the market) in the 'short run'.

The Context: 'Short Run' decisions

The 'Short Run' has a particular meaning in economics. It refers to a context in which major aspects of production are fixed. Products have been developed, and plant installed; the initial advertising has been undertaken, the sales force, and management is in place. This is the situation described in *The Goal*. The contrasting situation is the 'long run' in which everything can be varied by further investments.

This is an unfortunate use of language as 'long run decisions' may not take a long time to come into effect. The key characteristic is that they involve taking decisions which will affect many units of output in the future. For example, advertising is an investment decision, that is a 'long run decision'; you advertise in order to influence a block of future orders. In that way, it is no different from investing in further machines. Once you have invested, it either works, and brings you more trade, or it doesn't; in the same way as a computer upgrade may improve your output, or may cause chaos, but you invest in that upgrade in advance of the results which will affect many units of output.

Marginal Cost is essentially a short run concept[1].

Making Money: Jonah's plant level rules (*The Goal* p59)

Let us consider an alternative approach to that found in economics text books to discussing costs. In *The Goal*, the term used for total revenue is: **"Throughput"** and "Throughput is the rate at which the system generates money through sales."

Costs are classified as either:

---

1 There is a concept 'long run marginal cost'. It is however, a very abstract notion, referring to the cost of an additional unit of output when all elements in the production process can be varied. As many elements are difficult to divide up into optimal amounts for a single unit of output, this concept is best left to advanced theoretical discussions.

Inventory which is all the money that the system has invested in purchasing things which it intends to sell. Or:

Operational Expense which is all the money the system spends in order to turn inventory into throughput.

And the aim is to <u>increase</u> throughput and <u>decrease</u> inventory and operational expense.

Note 1: these definitions apply for the firm as a whole, and not the plant, the 'global' not the 'local' values.

Note 2: To make money you **increase** throughput, and **decrease** inventory and operational expense; in other words you derive rules for **changes** in costs and revenues.

Marginal Cost is this change in Total Costs.

Formal definition of MC

> Marginal Cost (MC) is the increase in Total Costs required to produce another unit.

That is the same as saying: 'the extra cost of producing the unit of output in question.'

There is no general reason that suggests Marginal Cost should remain the same however many units you are producing , and it may also vary depending on other products you are producing if (as in *The Goal*) it is a multi-product firm – and very few firms are single product companies today.

A Useful Approximation to MC: Incremental Cost

> Incremental cost is the average **Extra** cost of a group of units of output.

In *The Goal,* when the contract with Mr Djangler in France is being considered, it is wisely being thought of as an all or nothing quantity – raising further complications in such negotiations may not be clever, as it calls into question the cost structure of the whole deal. It is therefore useful to think of the entire quantity wanted as 'the marginal unit'. In that particular case, the cost is the same for all units and so there is no problem of estimation of the average cost. But even if the extra output had required hiring more workers or some investment in machinery, the extra cost could have been estimated for all the units required, and then expressed as a cost per unit. That would be an 'incremental cost'.

Usefulness of MC

Marginal Cost is defined as the change in total cost from producing an extra unit. It is therefore the relevant cost if you are considering whether producing another unit is worthwhile.

Taking a local example:

> If deciding whether to accept another student in the Faculty of Arts, the fact that there are huge overhead costs in the Faculty of Science with expensive laboratories, high cost chemicals etc. is clearly irrelevant. The extra costs for the Faculty of Arts however are not irrelevant. If the **extra** costs to the Faculty of Arts are less than the **extra revenue** they will get from taking the student, then taking the extra student is going to lessen the constraints they face through shortage of cash.
>
> Even for the Faculty of Arts, however, the student is not going to require an extra professor, and is unlikely to influence the number of books required in the library. So for that decision, we can ignore the costs which will not vary with the number of students. Such costs are called '**Fixed Costs**'. The key factor in the use of the term in economics is whether the costs vary with the level of output; if they do not, they are Fixed Costs. In the decision, the Faculty of Arts should use only the Marginal Costs.

Marginal costs is the appropriate measure of cost to use in decisions about output levels when we have a given level of capacity (as in *The Goal*). To increase profits, we need to add to costs by less than we add to revenue. It is the **additional** cost and revenue that we need to consider. Averages hide information about such additional elements since they include all the existing costs. This is the key idea in understanding why we use Marginal Cost.

It is also convenient to use marginal cost for decision-making. It avoids issues of valuing fixed costs - those that do not vary with output. Many of the items needed for production may be very difficult to value. Firstly, the fall in value of plant and machinery is very difficult to estimate. It is only the same as 'depreciation' as accepted by the tax man by chance. If old machinery is being used, you could not replace it in its original form; it would be both very expensive and usually very inefficient – modern machinery is often better, and is certainly built using very difficult principles. So you cannot value it by its historic cost; its replacement cost implies a completely different machine.

A further reason why machinery is often difficult to value is because many of the fixed costs are 'joint costs'; that is the same costly item or service is used for different products (for example in *The Goal* the NC10-X is used in the production of many different products; the heat treatment plant is also likely to be used for all metal that has been machined, and therefore to be used for many different products.) Allocating the cost of such items to any particular product can be shown to be possible only by an arbitrary rule. The box below shows why it is arbitrary. Using marginal cost **may** therefore avoid problems of joint costs; many of the joint costs are things like machinery used for many products, and the overheads of HQ, marketing, etc. All of which are fixed costs.

But using marginal cost is not a solution to all problems relating to valuing joint costs; joint production costs are also common: e.g. Petrol comes from Petroleum along with many other products, some pure pollution (unwanted by-products), some useful by-products but which are surplus to requirements (which therefore become unwanted by-products), and many products which can be sold. By using marginal costs you at least avoid the problem of allocating fixed costs, and may have only low joint marginal costs, or it may turn out that much of the production process would be carried out anyway, and that the item only requires a little extra work to turn it from an unwanted by-product to a saleable item. In this case, what is its Marginal Cost? The costs involved in that extra work only. That is likely to be much easier to estimate than the full costs of the whole process; indeed on the logic of joint costs that 'full cost' may be impossible to estimate.

PUPA Hospital Plastic Surgery Unit – costs and survival

The hospital accountant has calculated that the Plastic Surgery Unit has total costs of £2,000,000. This includes surgeons, nurses, operating theatres and special equipment, bed-spaces in the wards and nursing staff. It treated only 500 patients in the year. These patients brought in revenues of only £1,000,000 – or £2000 on average each. Clearly however they were costing £4000 each. At a board meeting the Head of Orthopaedics had seized on the figures and suggested that they should either double the price, or close the unit down because it was making losses.

The head of the Plastic Surgery division, recruited only the year before to run this prestigious new venture was incandescent. The conservative and well established head of orthopaedics, whose special expertise was in hip replacements, tried to keep the smirk off his face, having opposed the setting up of the Plastic Surgery Unit, and detesting the 'flash young ***' who had been offered a higher salary than his. Their relationship had not been improved when the older man had suggested that the 'unnecessary and dangerous interventions' of plastic surgeons were causing harm to patients and were unethical. The younger man had replied something to the effect, that with his success rate at hip operations it was a wonder that they had not been sued.

The facts however, were that the plastic surgery unit had only started 3 months into the year; it had not been well-advertised, and that the normal pattern of development was that in the first year a unit would only get ¼ of the patients that it would treat in the third year. That implies that they would be expecting to treat 2000 patients in the third year, and if neither the costs nor the average revenue changed, they would therefore be operating at an average cost of £1000 per patient and an average revenue of £2000, and making profits of £2,000,000!

Average costs will vary considerably just with the number of patients (formally put: 'with the level of demand') where there are large amounts of fixed costs, and here there might be a staff complement that would not vary with output, as well as substantial investments in machinery and accommodation. So the calculated fixed cost element, will vary with the number of units produced, and is thus 'arbitrary' as it does not guide future costing accurately, since the future numbers will have changed.

A further intervention came from the Head of Nursing, who revealed that the operating theatres, nurses and bed-spaces had in fact been used for orthopaedic patients, for whom there had been insufficient space elsewhere. Thus even without taking the excellent profit potential into account, there was an issue of how much of the costs should be allocated to the orthopaedic unit. Allocating such costs, the joint costs, has the same problem of numbers as the fixed costs, and additionally it has insoluble problems of the share of such costs to be allocated to

each operation. Our calculation of fixed costs relied simply on the number of operations. That is in itself arbitrary; a knee replacement is considerably more difficult and risky than a hip replacement; a 'nose job', or the removal of wrinkles is much less risky and much less difficult than surgery to reconstruct a jaw… Perhaps we should allocate costs on the basis of the overall cost of the operation. Or perhaps it should be based on the time in the operating theatre. Or perhaps, the time on the wards better reflects the amount of resources being used… An endless waste of senior management time is possible if attempts are made to calculate average costs, and it will affect morale, as each unit will feel they are being robbed to finance others.. The important questions are:

Is the decision about whether a particular patient should be accepted for a particular operation? If so, the question is simply, will this increase revenue by more than cost – or alternatively phrased: is marginal cost less than marginal revenue?

Is the decision about extra resources, whether new equipment or extra staff? Both of these are effectively investment decisions, and the question is: will those increases bring in sufficient extra profits in the form of extra revenue less extra running costs, to justify the expenditure?

Conclusion: you can allocate fixed, and joint costs any way you please – after the event. But do not use them to make decisions. (And if you are not making decisions on the basis of the allocations, why waste time allocating, and getting into arguments. In the real world, all facts are politically loaded and will often be used to try to gain political advantage or settle personal scores, or both together. Remember, firms are political organisations devoted to economic ends.)

Text Book Economics VS Theory of Constraints – Different types of Marginal Cost

Rising Marginal Costs

Text book economics derives largely from agriculture where the LAW OF DIMINISHING RETURNS applies. Examples of the law of diminishing returns can be found throughout even modern agriculture. If you add more and more fertiliser to a crop, initially the yield will increase by large amounts, but as you add yet more, the extra yield gets less and less, until it actually decreases the total amount produced. The same is true when applied to the density of planting; initially you get so few plants that they may not do well at all. With higher density, there are enough similarly sized plants to protect from the wind and excessive evaporation from sun on the soil, and the plants are superb specimens if treated right, real competition winning stuff. However, if you want to maximise the yield, in terms of useful crop per hectare, a higher density of sowing is needed. This yields smaller plants but many more of them. Beyond this point, the plants get so small, that total yield is reduced. This can be applied to pesticides, herbicides and other forms of weeding, and the care applied to harvesting. In the general definition below, we call the inputs 'Factors of Production'. Which factors of production are fixed, depends on the situation. It might be the field if no planting or preparation has been done; once the seed is planted, the field and the seed are fixed etc.

> The Law of Diminishing Returns states that adding more and more of a variable factor to a set of fixed factors will result in a lower increase in output per unit increase of the variable factor.

The law of diminishing returns may apply to simple processes, particularly if they are dependent on natural laws, such as the output of power from the addition of extra fuel in an engine or the agricultural examples above, but very often machinery has a fixed speed of operation which means diminishing returns are complete or zero - adding an extra man-hour yields nothing (because the machine is already working full time and at the constant speed) or it adds just as much as the previous man-hour, (because you extend the time at which it runs at full-speed.) The same is not true if the task actually depends on the effort, whether physical or intellectual, put in by the worker. For example, working too few hours at the university will lead to underperformance; extra hours may yield increased learning, and even a more than proportionately increased learning, as there seems to be a threshold in understanding most things whereby failure to reach the threshold leaves little benefit; just exceeding it, may give solid benefits which can nevertheless be much increased by extra effort since then things will really 'click into place'. Beyond a certain point however, extra effort yields increasingly little extra understanding; the task may already be well done; boredom sets in and with it comes distraction, and finally, fatigue undermines further learning. In many tasks involving teamwork, such as producing computer programmes that require many programmers, an additional aspect contributes to rising marginal cost: the more programmers, the higher the effort that needs to be made on planning and controlling them, and checking the compatibility of each one's work.

The law of diminishing returns also implies that you can buy as much or as little of the relevant input as required – unlike in *The Goal*, where labour is essentially fixed unless overtime has to be worked.

Diminishing returns and the Rising Marginal Cost of text book economics

By adding progressively more labour you get progressively less extra output, until eventually you actually decrease the amount of output as the workers get in each other's way. This implies that the cost per extra unit produced is increasing.

> EXAMPLE: On a wheat farm, weeding the field with hoes, putting in 10 man hours gives 1 extra tonne (compared with no weeding); a second lot of 10 man hours: ¾ of a tonne; a third lot: ½ a tonne; etc. So the cost per tonne is rising, since if man hours cost 12 pence per 10 man hours, the first tonne costs 12 pence, the second $12 \div ¾ = 16$ pence; the third $12 \div ½ = 24$ pence etc.

Even in agriculture with modern technology this becomes less obvious; a tractor or combine harvester going over the field will probably have to work at a certain pace, and so a certain amount of work can be done per hour, so diminishing returns will set in, but in relation to the number of times the work is done, or the amount of chemical used per hectare.

Constant Marginal Cost with constant returns

In *The Goal* output depends critically on the speed of the robot NCX-10, which will be more or less fixed for a given item, and the heat treatment plant, which will again be fixed by how fast it can be loaded and heated. Furthermore, labour is purchased on the basis of a minimum number of hours per week. Up to those minimum hours, more labour can be devoted to a task, but it will cost no more. In *The Goal.* once the constraints have been 'elevated' – i.e. the plant can deliver anything and still have spare capacity with the existing machinery and labour – all costs are fixed except the material inputs that the firm buys in from elsewhere. So the only change to total cost of producing an extra unit of output, the marginal cost, is the cost of material inputs. This is exactly the calculation made by Rogo in the decisions relating to the French contract.

All this assumes that the labour has to be hired for a certain time. Discretionary hiring (e.g. overtime) means that the extra output is generating further extra cost. This is partly what 'flexible labour forces' are supposed to achieve. Labour is more adaptable to the particular pattern of production than the situation set out in *The Goal*. It may even be possible to hire the 'right amount of labour' at all times. In this case, the extra output will almost certainly involve extra labour costs, and if so, marginal cost will include those labour costs, as well as materials used up. (To check this ask the question: 'if we did not produce that unit, could we avoid this cost?')

What are the marginal costs, to Tesco for example, of an extra tin of baked beans sold? The shop, fittings, checkouts, and staff all have to be there anyway, and so the cost of those staff cannot be avoided whether or not the extra can of beans is sold. Thus the marginal cost is the cost to Tesco of the can of beans.

What is the marginal cost of an extra passenger on a train? Presumably nothing; the extra weight is scarcely going to alter the amount of energy required. All the other facilities are present. Indeed, the extra passenger may make an additional contribution to profits if he or she buys something at the bar. The same logic applies to additional customers in a swimming pool. This has led some pool managers to realise that they should treat the marginal cost as negative, and so charge a low price for entry, and make it up by charging more in the cafeteria and making that attractive so that they get as much profit as possible from it.

Marginal Cost under Constraints – unstable marginal cost

Once we exceed the capacity of the plant, we face a completely different situation. When capacity is constrained so that we can produce no more, marginal cost is the opportunity cost of producing one particular item rather than another. It cannot meaningfully be calculated using 'cost' figures (such as labour, materials, and a 'profits allocation'), and diminishing returns do not set in; it is a problem of the opportunity cost of producing one product rather than another since both cannot be produced.

Relation of opportunity Cost to Marginal Cost

Under capacity constraints MC is the Opportunity Cost of producing an extra item.

Thus we might think if the whole plant's operating cost is $3405 per hour and it takes 100th of an hour to process the part of the product that goes through the NCX-10, that product costs $34.05 plus the material costs. Because it is preventing output to the value of the plant being produced.

Correct? No not really; what is the opportunity foregone? The production of some other product, which can be sold. We therefore have to calculate the value to the company of a unit of output:

	Product 1	Product 2
Sale Price:	1000	1500
Cost of materials	300	400
Profit contribution (=VA)	700	1100

So if they both absorb the same amount of 'Bottleneck time', produce only Product 2 (other things like goodwill being equal.). If Product 1 uses less than 7/11 of the Bottleneck time taken by Product 2, it will be the more profitable, and so only it should be produced up to the point where no more is needed…

Conclusion: In cases where output depends not on one's ability to provide more materials but is limited by the capacity of the plant, MC (the cost of producing an extra unit) will be unstable because it depends on the opportunity cost at that particular time. The opportunity cost depends on the SALE value less the cost of purchased inputs of the next most profitable potential output.

Some Other Cases of MC

1.   What is the Marginal Cost of carrying an extra passenger on a train, bus, or aeroplane that is not full?

Zero, except for extra fuel in plane, and extra meals etc. if provided.

Their presence might bring in revenue that is not included in the price if the passenger buys stufffrom the bar on the trip and this is profitable for the company.

2.   Cost of extra sales in a shop?

The cost of the purchased input – i.e. the amount the shop paid for the goods, assuming that extra staff cannot be hired.

3.   Cost to the University of an extra student?

Very difficult; includes the extra paper etc. and opportunity costs of staff time if that prevents staff getting research grants etc.

4.   Cost of an extra guest in an unfilled hotel?

Extra cost of laundry (if any) and of cleaning the room, less any extra profit due to consumption of food and drink etc. (There would be no extra cost if the staff are all already in place so as to be able to service the hotel even when full.) – it is exactly analogous to the carrying of an extra passenger.

In all services the initial cost of an extra customer is usually very small in terms of extra resources required. However, more customers gradually reduce the quality of service, until the service provided becomes worse value for money than that of another provider; customers then shift to that other provider, and a decline in profits ensues. It is therefore common in services to get 'deficiency gains' where profit increases because the staff and facilities work harder, but it is not a tenable situation in the long run. Both staff and facilities become sub-standard, and clients find better quality elsewhere.

Should Price = MC?

Only in a world of perfect competition – but it is difficult to find one. It probably used to exist in agricultural products. Now with Agro-industry facing the might of the supermarkets it almost certainly does not.

Even in such a market, for the company, we cannot alter the price; it is set by the market. Marginal Cost enables us to decide whether we want to produce more – or less – given that price.

In other sorts of market, Marginal Cost has the same function. Given the demand, do we want to produce, or not?

In investment decisions, costs also determine whether we want to invest in order to enter that market.

Summary:

Marginal Cost is the increase in total costs required to produce another unit.

There are three very different situations in relation to Marginal Cost.

1. With continuously variable inputs (i.e. you can buy any quantity of the relevant input) and diminishing returns, marginal costs will increase as you try to produce more from a given set of fixed resources. (Clear applications in agriculture - it is also true in computer programming.)

2. With machinery working at a fixed speed, marginal cost may well be constant. If in addition labour is a 'fixed cost', then MC will be equal to the costs of the purchased inputs used by the extra unit of output.

3. Where (several products are produced and) the firm is short of capacity, marginal costs are determined by the net profits foregone on the next most profitable use of the machine.

Economies of Scale

We shall discuss how:

- Economies of Scale focus on the reductions of cost due to producing at large scales.
- What causes them?
- How they account for the following:
    1. Large firms often seem to dominate the economy and
    2. Trade between countries within an industry has grown at 9% per annum, much faster than the rate of growth of each of the countries themselves.
- How they are often used to justify mergers.
- Whether they are present everywhere in industry and the service sector, or are there 'diseconomies of scale'?

The Goal and Economies of Scale – Short run decisions and long run decisions.

The Goal is concerned with short run decisions, i.e. decisions which do not involve investments. Economies of Scale deal essentially with situations in which firms are able to adapt entirely by investment to the situation in which they find themselves. The question is then whether there are factors which will cause larger firms, or larger production runs to have lower costs per unit? i.e. Economies of Scale. (The Pupa Hospital example above showed the distinction clearly also: the short run decision about whether a particular patient was worth admitting, and thus whether the MC<MR; the long run investment decisions about opening or closing whole departments).

Economies of Scale

In contrast to *The Goal*, we consider a situation where you can scale up the whole operation so as to produce output at the lowest feasible cost.

Economies of scale exist if costs per unit costs decline when the size of the plant or firm is increased.

i.e. Economies of Scale refer to the situation where you can invest just the right amount, organise your R&D, and advertising to be at the right levels for sales. So it is about the situation when firms are working as efficiently as they can potentially do, (a '**Long Run**' situation in the terminology of economics not a '**Short Run**' situation.)

It is not the situation (described in *the Goal*) where they are making the best of a bad job, and muddling through to get as low a set of costs as they can, given the existing machinery.

Potential causes of Economies of Scale

a)   Indivisibilities:

Basic idea: investments can only be made in a discrete amount, that is significantly expensive compared to total costs. So that the larger the scale the smaller these costs on average. For example:

- If Research and Development (R&D) to achieve a certain improvement costs at least £10m (say) and lower scales of expenditure will not be effective, for small levels of output (100 units say) that is a significant expense (you need a contribution to profits of £10,000 for each unit of output to cover that particular investment). For 10 million units, you only need a contribution of £1 per unit.
- Advertising campaigns for a particular product are likely to gain in efficiency if they are expensively made and use national television because they will probably generate more sales per unit cost than local advertising.

- Production processes involve the use of very fast, but very expensive machines, (e.g. the NCX-10, or very fast printing presses, or paper manufacturing machinery) will require large scales of output or the average cost of the machine will be high. (remember, the average cost is the cost of the machine divided by the number of units produced.)

- The cost of control in processes like petroleum refining, may relate to the number of processes, not the amount they produce. Similarly, on a modern ship the size of crew relates to skills needed for certain processes, not the tonnage carried. Therefore, as the size of crew largely determine the costs, the more tonnes carried the lower the cost per tonne.

b) **Vessels: – economics of dimensions.**

- A vessel (ship, reaction vessels in petrochemicals, trucks etc) can handle a quantity related to its volume, whereas its construction cost usually only goes up in proportion to its surface area. Doubling the size of a cube would result in increases in volumes and surface areas shown below:

Side length	1	2	4
Volume	1	8	64
Surface area	6	24	96
Ratio of surface area to volume (giving relative costs)	6	3	1.5

- The operating costs may also vary with surface area: heat loss in a vessel is proportional to its surface area; the power required to keep a tanker moving is related to the friction of the surface of the vessel in the water.

c) **Specialisation**

Workers and management may gain efficiency if they can dedicate themselves to a limited range of tasks.

d) **Spreading risk:**

If selling to many markets, it is unlikely all will collapse together. If you have a few types of machine you only have to hold a limited number of spares as not all models are likely to have the same problem at the same time - (predictable breakdowns should be part of routine maintenance).

e) **Learning by Doing: the Learning Curve.**

Gruber 1992 showed that computer memory chips had a '78% learning curve', i.e. at each doubling of output of a particular chip the costs fall by 22%. Chips are produced in batches using expensive silicon coated with substances, then etched. The more they produced, the higher the proportion of useable chips they obtained, and so the lower the cost per chip.

c) **Network Economies**

These are really on the demand side. They refer to the increase in usefulness from such things as telephones, that you get when there are lots of others who own phones and can therefore be contacted by 'phone. The same is true of the internet, cars from the point of view of servicing facilities, computer programmes (such as Microsoft Word and Excel) where the more people use them, the easier it is to get support – formal and informal and the more people can read a file from disk or mail attachment, and hence the more useful they are. This encourages firms in industries with network economies to try to maximise market share if the networks are incompatible, or to join the most heavily used network if they have to choose.

> **Example of Economies of Scale in Operation:**
>
> Volvo and Renault were discussing a merger. Through the combination of a) and c) they expected to be able to save considerable marketing costs (The argument being that effective advertising of one car - say a Clio - would rub off on the other cars made by the same maker - e.g. a Volvo 850 replacement!). They also hoped to save on expenses involved in dealership networks – both makes being sold by one dealer might be cheaper than having rivals in each place. But above all they also hoped to save considerable production costs - estimated at $5.3bn, through specialisation of parts manufacture with different cars having common components produced at larger scales. Some of these savings would simply be better prices at the expense of the supplier, but much would be through the supplier having longer production runs of the same part. Inventory costs could be reduced by stocking less different parts, and the numbers of parts held in reserve might decline considerably through economies of risk spreading.
>
> The merger failed largely because of personality conflicts between the senior managers!

Domination of the market by large firms

Clearly the presence of economies of scale allows larger firms to produce more cheaply, and hence to undercut the other firms. Thus firms achieving large scales of output, presumably at least partly by providing good value for money to large numbers of consumers, will reinforce their dominance by their lower costs, and hence potentially lower prices, or if they keep prices the same, they will get higher profits.

The dangers of pursuing Economies of Scale – Diseconomies of Scale

1. **Compatibility with the existing production processes – global vs local again.**

   If the new machine is not matched by the performance of other machines, these other machines will be bottlenecks and it will not be possible to produce at the large scale of output planned.

2. **Dangers of inflexibility in the face of market changes:**

   Do you really produce so many before a change is needed? Is the market for a particular item that large - or will the market for that sort of item be segmented into lots of smaller markets? British Steel again failed to foresee the change to much more specialised steel alloys, or the opening up of the Brazilian and Indian steel industries, which reduced the size of market they could sell to.

3. **Loss of control.**

   As firms get larger, it becomes more and more difficult to control the different elements within them. This is particularly the case if the knowledge required to operate them ceases to be the same. ICI split the firm into two - ICI which retained bulk chemicals, paints, fertilisers etc and Zeneca which specialises in pharmaceuticals and Bio-engineering. Originally the pharmaceuticals were related products to the bulk chemicals and so had common bases in production and research. However as time went on the needs for R&D in Zeneca and a different approach to marketing meant that it required managers with different experience and training to operate the two firms. Hence they split, but only under threat from the corporate raider Hanson.

Economies of scale are limited by the scope of the market. A larger vessel may be cheaper to operate if full, but it is likely to be more expensive than a ship half its size if that is all that can be filled. Thus if economies of scale are as widespread in modern industries as one would expect, it would account for the increase in international trade, and particularly the apparently fruitless exchange of similar goods (the shipment of Rover cars to Japan when they ship Hondas here for example). This allows a large market by making the market nearly global, while catering for different tastes, which would otherwise limit the size of the market.

Marginal (Incremental) Revenue

Aim:

revenue is not just on the extra items sold, but also on the price cut on existing sales.

Context from *the Goal* pp307-308

Rogo has got the various illogical approaches to production sorted out. He has made sure that nothing wasteful is processed by the "constraints" by putting quality control before as well as after, and making sure that only required parts are made. He has also "elevated the constraints" by ensuring that they are manned at all times, and by improving the technology in the core of the heat treatment plant by pre-loading or taking out earlier on steel pallets. He has therefore been able to meet all delivery dates and now has some 20% spare capacity. The dialogue below takes place at a meeting with sales - Johnny being the chief salesman and Dick one of his assistants. Rogo is speaking:

"Johnny, do they sometimes demand prices that are lower than our cost?"

"Sometimes? All the time."

"And what do you do?" I continue.

"What can I do?" he laughs. "I try to explain the best I can. Sometimes it even works."

I swallow hard and say, "I'm ready to accept orders for ten percent below cost."

Johnny doesn't hurry to answer. His peoples' bonuses are based on total sales dollars. Finally he says, "Forget it."

"Why?"

He doesn't answer. I persist, "Why should I forget it?"

"Because it's stupid, because it doesn't make any business sense," he says in a hard voice, and then softer, "Alex, I don't know what tricks you have in mind but let me tell you, all those tricks have a very short life span before they explode in your face. Why do you want to ruin a promising career? You've done an outstanding job, why go and mess it up? Besides, if we lower prices for one client, it's just a matter of time until the others find out and demand the same. What then?"

He has a point. The last argument shows that the light at the end of the tunnel was just a train.

Help comes from an unexpected side.

"Djangler is not connected to our regular customers," Dick says hesitantly. "Besides, with the quantities he's asking for, we can always claim we gave him a volume discount."

"Forget it," Johnny is practically shouting. "That bastard is asking us to give him the goods for basically nothing, not to mention that he wants us to ship to France at our expense."

Turning to me he says, "This French guy has chutzpah, it's unbelievable. We negotiated for three months. We established each other's credibility, we agreed on terms and conditions. It all takes time. He asked for every technical detail that you can imagine, and we're not talking about one or two products, it's for almost the entire range. All this time not even a peep about prices. At the end, just two days ago, when everything is agreed, he faxes me that our prices are not acceptable and sends his counter offer. I was expecting the usual thing, asking for price reductions of ten percent, maybe fifteen percent considering the large quantities that he is willing to buy, but no, those Europeans probably have a different perception. For example, Model Twelve, the one that you pulled such a miracle on. Our price is nine hundred and ninety-two dollars. We sell it to Burnside for eight hundred and twenty-seven dollars; they're a big client and they consume very large quantities of this particular product. The bastard had the nerve to offer seven hundred and one dollars. Did you hear that! Seven hundred and one dollars. Now you understand?"

I turn to Ralph, "What's our material cost for Model Twelve?"

"Three hundred thirty-four dollars and seven cents," Lou answers without any hesitation.

"Johnny, are you sure that accepting this order will not have any impact on our domestic clients?"

"Not unless we go out, and sing it from the rooftops. On this point Dick is right, no impact. But the whole idea is ridiculous. Why are we wasting our time?"

I look at Lou, he nods.

"We'll take it," I say.

When Johnny doesn't respond, I repeat, "We'll take it."

"Can you explain what is going on?" he finally says, between gritted teeth.

"It's very simple," I answer. "I told you that I have spare capacity. If we take this order, the only out-of-pocket cost to produce these products will be the cost of the materials. We'll get seven hundred and one dollars, and we'll pay three hundred and thirty-four dollars. That's three hundred seventy-eight dollars to the bottom line per unit."

"It's three hundred sixty-six ninety-three pence per unit, and you forgot the freight," Lou corrects me.

"Thank you. How much is the air freight per unit?" I ask Johnny.

"I don't remember, but it's not more than thirty bucks."

"Can we see the details of that deal?" I ask him. "What I'm particularly interested in is the products, the quantities per month, and the prices."

The situation:

Key factors: The markets are separate; the offer price is way below present prices in the home market, but well above materials cost; it is a large order.

Is price above MC? – MC is assumed by Rogo to be materials cost. Why? What about salesmen, headquarters staff, mangers in the plant and all the work that goes into the product? In the context of the Goal, because of the labour contractsthey face which guarantee a minimum working week of 35 hours, these are FIXED COSTS. So MC = materials cost + delivery cost.

Is price above "the Real cost"? Not a good question; all the overheads are joint; and allocating them to particular products is by an arbitrary rule.

The real question is: "Does it further our goal of making money? Does it **increase** Throughput (Total Revenue) by more than it increases Operating and Inventory Costs?"

Is that equivalent to: 'Is price greater than Marginal Cost?' Answer: *in this case* YES.

BUT is Marginal Revenue above Marginal Cost?

Marginal Revenue:

MR is the increase in total revenue when you increase sales by one unit.

This is only equal to the price, if you can sell as many units as you want at that fixed price.

If you have to cut the price to sell more, and cannot separate the markets, so that you have to cut the price on the units you would have sold if you were still charging the higher price, the Marginal Revenue will be below the price, and might be negative. The situation would occur if you had to reduce the advertised price on all units of the product.

Where this is the case, the marginal revenue is:

> The price (**P**), plus the number of units sold (**Q**) multiplied by the change in price required to sell another unit ($\frac{dP}{dQ}$).

when written as an equation:

$$MR = P + Q\frac{dP}{dQ}$$

Example:

> Suppose that if you cut your price by £1 to £10, you can increase your sales from 100 units to 120 units.
>
> Your change in price is -£1, and the number of extra units sold is 20, so the change in price price required to sell one extra unit is **-£0.05,** if there is a constant change for all units between the two prices.

In the above formula $\frac{dP}{dQ} = -0.05$. So at 100 units and a price of £11,

> MR = 11+(100 x –0.05) = £6. At 120 units MR = £4, and one can calculate the units in between, for example at 110 units with a price of £10.50, MR = £5.

Incremental Revenue

> Incremental Revenue is the average change in total revenue from selling a larger number of units.

Example: Following the above example, (that if you cut your price by £1 to £10, you can increase your sales from 100 units to 120 units.)

Change in total revenue   = (20 x £10) - (100 x £1)

> = (Increase in sales (20) x their price) less (the previous number of units sold (100) x fall in price)

> = +£100

You gain £100 in total revenue, i.e. £5 per unit on average (I.e. Incremental Revenue = £5) - Note that this is only ½ of the £10 selling price - because of the cut in price on units you would have sold at £11 each. (but also note that it is not always ½ of the selling price); secondly, it is no accident that this is the 'average' of the marginal revenues for 100 units and for 120 units.

The French Contract:

Rogo is assured that there will be NO effect on the existing US customers. So losses from price cuts to existing sales do not have to be taken into account, and so PRICE = INCREMENTAL REVENUE, and since it is a 'take it or leave it' price, it is also equal to Marginal Revenue, because he cannot increase the quantity by reducing the price further.

Thus if Price is above Marginal Cost, the deal is increasing total revenue by more than total costs, and it is 'profitable'; i.e. it increases profits.

So why do the 'Marketing people' not understand? Because they are not thinking about maximising profits - making money - but obeying company rules that items are not to be sold below "Cost", by which they mean average cost. The company has created a rule which is a 'perverse incentive'; even though the rule was set up to prevent sales people from failing to take MR as opposed to Price into account in markets where a price cut to one customer would lead to demands for price cuts from all the others.

(Note 1: this is a difficult problem of organisation in the firm. If salesmen are paid purely by salary, they may not put as much energy and ingenuity into selling as they should, and as a result sales and profits fall. Thus they are often paid on commission, as a proportion of total sales. But once this is done, they have a strong incentive to maximise total sales revenue rather than profits - basically because they are not responsible for the costs. Thus they might well cut their prices too far, hence the sort of rule prevailing in *The Goal*.)

(Note 2: increasing sales will actually alter the average cost, since the fixed costs will now be shared over a larger number of units of output, but even if a sale such as this were below the new average cost, it would still increase profits as long as its marginal revenue is above marginal costs.)

Summary:

The SHORT RUN pricing rule is that you can cut your price down to the point where
$$MR = MC.$$

Further Examples of contexts where MR is not equal to price:

Explain:

1) Student Bar: cutting the price of beer or spirits - would a price cut be likely to increase the quantity sold by a greater proportion? Not usually; students bars are usually the cheapest places around, and so they are already benefiting from those who want to drink cheaply.

2) Models of a car: e.g. Ford Fiesta:

   a) apply above logic to Ford Fiestas – are they already the cheapest, or does the fall in price make them better value for money than some previously cheaper car.

   b) Consider how much of the increased demand will come from diversion of sales from other Fords – will a cheaper Fiesta takes sales away from the Ka? (This is often called 'cannibalisation').

   c) is the effect likely to last or will other manufacturers follow suit? And if so, will their customers flow back to them?

3) If the price cut is just for certain models within the range: e.g. Ford Fiesta e.g. Ford Fiesta LX, would the critical factor possibly be the losses of sales to other Ford Fiestas? If so why would any motor manufacturer do that?

4) Public transport fares: with empty seats, the MC of carrying an extra traveller is zero. But the cost of cutting the price depends on the marginal revenue -if MR is negative, because the gain in numbers of tickets sold at the lower price does not yield enough revenue to offset the revenue losses from the fall in price to existing users, then it is not profitable to try to fill the train by cutting prices.

Further Examples of contexts where MR is equal to price:

Wheat, Share prices, cattle at auction, MR=P because substitution between units of the product is perfect, and the seller does not control the market and so cannot create scarcity.

The general principle:

1. Where cutting price is a means to increase sales, MR is not equal to P

2. Where the product is standardised (homogeneous) and the market large, cutting price will not increase sales, and so MR = P. (Though the price may fall as the result of falls in demand or increases in supply, making a cut from the expected price essential if the item is to be sold.)

3. Marginal revenue will be positive when the percentage change in sales (quantity sold) is greater than the percentage fall in price.

Remember though that MR must be greater than the Marginal Cost for the change to be profitable. Thus up to the point where MR = MC it will be profitable to cut prices.

MR is not a viable concept in the context of Price Wars, that is where rivals respond to your price cuts with price cuts of their own. In that case it is impossible to estimate the likely marginal revenue since it depends on how much they cut their prices (and other things – see next lecture).

Demand in Modern Context

Aim:

To introduce another major insight into the nature of demand: that it is related to substitutes not just to the 'inherent desirability of the product.'

To show that the presence of substitutes is likely to be a major influence on the Marginal Revenue.

To explore the other elements that influence the quantity likely to be sold, such as incomes, prices of other related goods, and tastes.

Value for Money

- The decision to buy is the result of the consumer's view that the product or service provides value for money.
- There are thus two elements: the inherent value, and the price of purchase (and costs of use).
- However, if there are alternatives with equal inherent value, but at lower price, then the consumer would be irrational not to switch to the lower price alternative. Hence we might view:

Demand in relation to substitution

For many purchases, one unit (a car, washing machine, sitting room carpet…) is all that is needed. Thus the concept of opportunity cost applies directly. Purchasing any particular item involves considering the relative advantages of that as compared to others – and one of those relative advantages is the price. Thus demand (the quantity you sell at any particular price) depends on what consumers see as substitutes.

- Early Black and White TVs cost the equivalent of £1200! But no substitute was available.
- The first Sony Walkman was introduced at about £100 in 1979 Prices, which is about £150 at today's prices, for a specification equivalent to those costing £15 now – Dolby was not available. Prices fell when patents ran out and others entered the market thus providing substitutes.
- In contrast, with cars of similar type and price there is rich potential for substitution between new cars.
- And with cars of similar price, but different ages and types, there is likely to be an alternative form of substitution in the second hand market.

The traditional economists' approach to demand is based on making the product better value for money by cutting the price. This implies presence of substitutes, or the power of the consumer to substitute other products – ideas very appropriate to a world of homogeneous products, like wheat or flour, where substitution is very easy. Hence the concentration in economics texts on Price, and thus Marginal Revenue.

Marginal Revenue and substitution

Marginal Revenue depends on the outcome of the effect of increase in sales (the change is quantity sold x the new price) and the fall in price on existing sales (change in price x number of units sold at the old price). The availability of substitutes affects the increase in the number of units sold if the price is cut. Logically we should expect:

- A large increase in quantity if the price is cut when value for money of rival products is almost the same as the firm's product at the previous price.
- A large decrease in quantity when the other firms cut their prices in the above situation - or if the firm tries to raise its price.
- Rather little change if there is a large difference in value for money between the firm's and rivals' products, at least until the price and quality combination becomes a closer substitute.

Example:

> A senior transport engineer was proudly reporting that they had slashed public transport travel time to half its previous level. He also ruefully said that it had made no difference to the numbers of people travelling.
>
> Why?
>
> In transport studies it has been found that if you want a usable estimate of "price" or "cost" to the user, you have to include both the out of pocket expenses and an estimate of the value of time to the user. In other words the "cost of transport" is the fare and the value of the time spent for public transport, and the petrol, parking charges and the value of the time taken for the car. If you only have one of those measures available, it is usually time that gives a better estimate than cost, i.e. the time costs are more significant to the user than the out of pocket expenses. When asked how long it took to make a typical trip by the new speedy public transport as compared to going by car, he replied: "About twice as long."
>
> In other words the "new public transport system" was still not competitive - it did not compare in terms of value for money to going by car.

This means that there is a strong likelihood of price cuts to try to gain market if the products are very similar. The limiting case of this is that of pure commodities: coffee, tea, wheat, barley, potatoes, or mineral ores or refined products of a particular quality, where given that quality there is no difference from the consumer's point of view as to the source. These commodity markets tend to have a 'market price', often quoted on the relevant exchange. The company basically accepts that price (or less if stupid) or does not sell.

In these markets the price may be literally fixed by auction, and may fluctuate quite dramatically depending on the conditions of supply and demand. For example, if there is a failure in the Brazilian coffee crop, the price of coffee is likely to rise dramatically as the result of relatively constant demand and lower quantity supplied.

Suppliers work out what they think the price will be, and aim to maximise profits given that price, i.e. produce up to the point where marginal cost is equal to the price. As most commodities involve natural products, the law of diminishing returns (See the section on Marginal Cost) is likely to apply.

The 'Other Factors' affecting demand

If incomes rise, and people are confident, there is likely to be a large increase in house buying and selling; with this goes a boom in consumer durables, furnishings and furniture, as well as things like heating systems, and double glazing. New cars are bought, often with higher specifications etc.

We have already mentioned the effect of the prices of other products in relation to the effect of price changes by those products. An interesting example of the way such effects work is in the effect of petroleum price rises in the past. In 1974 the price of petroleum doubled, there was little change in demand, because in the short run, it is very difficult to find substitutes. In the longer run, the rise in the price of petrol seemed to completely alter the previous pattern of increased petroleum usage in the face of rising GDP (Gross Domestic Product – the value of all that is produced in a country, and hence a good measure of total incomes). From 1947 to 1974 the quantity of petroleum used increased more rapidly than, but consistently with, increased national income. After 1974, for at least a decade, there was no increase in petroleum use in spite of rises in national income. The effect of the price rises, and the shortages that went with it, had been to make people realise that saving fuel was a good idea; boilers, heating systems, cars etc all became more efficient. However, in general, these all take time to replace and so it was a gradual process. It also almost killed the US automobile industry, which had been producing ever more grotesque gas-guzzlers. The smaller much higher specification Japanese cars simply took over.

For changes in tastes: consider the collapse in demand for beef as the BSE crisis emerged, or the horrific effects of the terrorist bomb on Bali's tourist industry in 2001.

The modern context of product differentiation

"Product differentiation" is where products are deliberately made with differing characteristics so as to appeal to different groups of consumers, although the products clearly serve the same function.

Thus rather than alter price, it may pay the firm to alter characteristics, to fit some part of market better.

The more homogeneous the product before the change, the larger the shift in demand for small shifts in product characteristics, because when all products are the same, it only takes a small difference to make one significantly better than the rest.

> e.g. in a world of similar super-markets: extra checkout operators/ extra shelf fillers may make one supermarket much superior to the others, or in the context of similar models of cars a sun roof included, may cause purchasers to switch in that firm's favour.

To maximise profits: the increase in total cost from introducing the characteristic must be less than the increase in total revenue. (Note the calculations could be complicated: the increase in cost could come from both investments and operating costs, and the increase in revenue could come from both an increase in price of each unit and an increase in the number of units sold. Furthermore the increases in number of units sold could come from reductions in sales of other products produced by the same company.)

Role of advertising

(a) to inform of presence.

(b) to inform of characteristics,

(c) to change perception of product - correct misperceptions -- or give some non-existent flavour, i.e. to alter attributes while leaving characteristics constant. The "Gold Blend soap-opera" series of adverts reportedly increased the market share of Gold Blend from 10% to 30%.

(d) to assure customers of the quality and seriousness of the product and company: if you advertise, it encourages new purchases. If this does not encourage purchasers to recommend it to others, and both to repurchase, the advertising is likely to be too expensive. Thus incurring the cost of advertising, is a sort of guarantee of quality.

To decide on the appropriate level of advertising: increase the amount of advertising until the diminishing returns from advertising means that Cost of the Advert = increase in revenue less the marginal costs of production of the extra units due to the advert.

Industrial contracts

The situation in *the Goal* would involve the search for new contracts by the sales force, trade fairs etc., hopefully for large quantities of their products. Salesmen need to go out and find customers; prices are often not published, but settled by negotiation along with very important terms of the contract - delivery dates, quality guarantees, liability if changes in specification are required etc. and the intellectual property rights to the designs, which are often a combined effort of the purchaser and the producer.

In many cases the demand may be locked into the organisation of rival producers. Thus a small firm may produce on contract for one of the final users e.g. it might produce the sensors for heating systems, whereas rival final users may produce their own. This may seriously limit the market open to the small independent company.

What determines demand?

(a) the basic need of the purchaser for the product.

(b) the value for money of the product compared to rivals, which depends importantly upon:

(c) the ability of the producer to match or improve upon the quality, and convenience of the original terms of contract, i.e. the relationship between the producer and supplier.

This need for focus to ensure that the company is providing the best value for money is a theme of *Herman Simon **Hidden Champions** Lessons from 500 of the World's Best Unknown Companies,* Harvard Business School Press 1996

He shows the way German companies concentrate on one narrow area e.g. Dishwashers for Hotels **NOT** hospitals, Kärcher High Pressure Cleaners, Stihl Chain Saws, the printing of banknotes etc. All concentrate on technical excellence, so that value for money is not based on price; all provide substantial training and service backup, often by subsidiaries located in the customer's country.

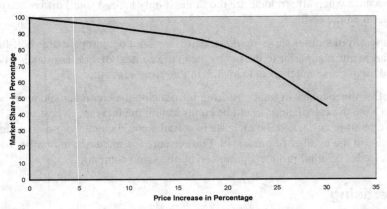

Effect of Price Increase on Hidden Champions' Market Share

Source: *Herman Simon* **Hidden Champions** *Lessons from 500 of the World's Best Unknown Companies,* Harvard Business School Press 1996, p114

Price wars

- Not a danger where many small firms compete, since each firm is too small to affect the rest.
- A major danger where a few firms are rivals and thus each feels the effect of any aggressive price cuts by a rival on its own market share. Hence the concern in *the Goal* about the potential for a response by French companies to the aggressive price being offered for the products see pp 309-310 in the previous section.

Ways of forestalling price war: by announcing that you are 'Never knowingly undersold.' Thus if rival starts, it knows it can expect an immediate response. The version: 'If you find a cheaper supplier, we will refund double the difference in price' would probably fall foul of fair trade laws, because it is such a strong warning to rivals not to try a price war that it is a means of keeping prices up!

Characteristic wars?

Perfectly possible; consider the enormous improvement in specification of most cars since Japanese cars entered the market with many 'options' as standard e.g. central locking, power steering, electric windows….

These are more likely to be profitable for the firm than a price war as it should take rivals longer to imitate than a cut in price, and so the firm should enjoy the extra profits for longer.

British Energy

Generating a disaster,

But is it a Nuclear Disaster?

Outline:

The case of British energy is interesting because:

1. it provides a good example of how markets work, particularly in attracting extra capacity if prices are high.
2. It shows the relationship between fixed costs and viability.
3. Possible cures to its bankruptcy would leave the government with serious problems, or would do nothing to resolve the difficulties in the electricity industry.

The situation .

British energy in the early 2001 was losing £40 for each megawatt hour of generation. This was the result of two things, firstly, there was overcapacity in the industry, and this led to falling prices. Secondly, on top of this, the government had introduced NETA, the New Electricity Trading Arrangements, which had forced prices down still further. British Energy was the company to go bankrupt because of the huge liabilities imposed on it by the need to decommission its nuclear plants. It was unable to go to the banks to reschedule the debt, and it had to go to the government for help. This took the form of a loan of some £600 million.

Whose responsibility was this? There is much blame attached to the management. Firstly, they appear to have failed to maintain the power stations, and this led to both power stations at Torness failing; this caused a reduction of 6% in British energy's generating capacity, with consequent losses of revenue. Secondly, the management had taken no precautions against their exposure to the stock market, which came in two forms. 75% of the Nuclear Decommissioning Fund was invested in the stock market, and about 70% of their pension fund. In the year leading up to 1 March 2002, the FTSE 100 had fallen by 25%. The pension fund a loan needed £13 million extra.(FT 9 Oct 2002) Thirdly, they had failed to diversify their activities, and so remained pure generators of electricity. As a result, when electricity prices fell, they were entirely vulnerable, whereas, if they had had some distribution capacity, they would have been selling at relatively fixed prices to consumers. With fixed prices to the consumers, and low prices for the electricity they generated, they would have been making high profits on distribution, which would have cancelled out at least some of their losses on generation. In the previous era, distribution had been relatively unprofitable, and generation had been very profitable thanks to the collusion that had been taking place between the three generating companies. This accounts for their lack of distribution capacity, but shows their lack of appreciation of the change in economic climate. Fourthly, they bought Eggborough power station at the peak price. This meant that they made losses even on that efficient coal powered station. They had also bought Bruce power in Canada, another nuclear station, but which remained profitable at the price they paid. Being profitable, it is one of the things they had to sell when they got into difficulties.

Government policies were also to blame. Firstly, when the electricity industry was privatised, the government separated the generating capacity into three large companies. British Energy was unique among these in that it had only nuclear power stations. The effect of this privatisation was to make it very easy for these three generating companies to work together (to collude) and so raise prices. As it was part of the approach to privatisation to permit the building of new generating capacity, new companies built gas turbine generating sets to take advantage of the high prices, and so considerably increased capacity. In this way, the government indirectly caused both the high prices after privatisation, and the resultant fall in prices after the new capacity was built. This fall in prices was then reinforced by the New Electricity Trading Arrangements. In addition, the government put in place a climate levy, supposedly to reduce carbon dioxide emissions, but applied it to British Energy as well as the conventional generating capacity. In addition, they quite rightly imposed the requirement to set up a fund to pay for the decommissioning of the nuclear plants. This naturally imposed further costs on the nuclear generator.

Low prices

When they talk about £40 loss per megawatt hour generated, they are talking about the loss based on average costs. The question is immediately comes, "should it be average costs, or marginal costs?" In this case, since we are talking about the ability to pay debt, we are talking about the need to cover fixed costs. The appropriate measure is therefore based on a measure of costs that includes these, and so average costs are correct. Note that it would almost certainly pay British Energy to continue generating in spite of these losses since the marginal costs of nuclear power are very low, and almost certainly below the marginal revenue. Each MW generated would therefore contribute to profits. The issue of generating for storage or inventory is not relevant since in general electricity cannot be stored.

Prices had fallen by 27% since the introduction of NETA in March 2001, and by 40% since 1998 (Financial Times 9 September 2002). The effect of overcapacity on prices can therefore be seen before the introduction of NETA. During this period, there had already been a tendency for distribution companies, those companies that sell electricity direct to final consumers, to buy into electricity generation. Generation companies like PowerGen, and Electricité de France had also bought into distribution companies. This meant that many companies were working on long-term internal contracts for the delivery of power. It also meant that if the prices paid for electricity generation fell, the relatively stable prices paid by consumers would have a large profit margin, which kept profits high for the companies that had both generation and distribution. As mentioned above, British energy did not do this.

NETA operates on futures contracts. These contracts were for the delivery of a certain amount of electricity at a certain time in the future. And they were between the generating company and distribution company. As this implies a lot of contracts it is potentially more difficult to collude and so keep prices high. This therefore accounts for some of the fall in prices. This effect, of course is much worse if many of the companies are already trading inside the company. This leaves the remaining companies facing surpluses that are greater compared with demand than they would be if the whole market demand were traded on the exchange. This is what is meant by an 'illiquid' market; illiquid markets always tend to increase the magnitude of any change in prices because a small excess of supply over demand may require a large fall in price to tempt someone to buy it, and conversely if there is a shortage, there is less likelihood that a participating generating company will have easily available spare capacity, and so the price would rise a lot before the demand was satisfied. (A note on terminology: in papers read by professionals of the finance sector you would probably not see the following statement: "Small markets tend to have large price fluctuations." You would see: "Illiquid markets are volatile." Both refer to the same phenomenon.)

What if British Energy had been sold as a company?

There are really two possibilities here. Firstly British energy could have been sold as a going concern. This would imply that another company would buy it up a price that was sufficiently low to make it profitable. The banks and shareholders would have to accept a very substantial loss. However, this would still leave the same capacity available for generating electricity. The overall prices would therefore presumably have remained very low. As British energy, or the company that bought it, would now have an advantage because their capital cost less, they would stay in business, and somebody else would go bankrupt. Selling the company as a going concern is therefore not a viable option if one were looking for a solution to the spare capacity in industry.

The second possibility is that the company might have been broken up, and the generating stations sold separately. Many of the power stations might have been closed down, and would not have found a buyer. This would help to solve the problem of overcapacity in industry, but would probably increase the losses to the government, the banks, and shareholders. The workers who had committed funds to the British energy pension fund would probably have lost their pensions.

As both of those options seem very unattractive, what did actually happen? The government extended its loan, and this gave enough time for the banks and shareholders to agree a rescue package. In other words, the first option was chosen, but no new company was brought in to run the assets. The chairman, and chief executive, naturally lost their jobs. This solution was possible because many of the other companies had decided to reduce the capacity available by "mothballing" many generating plants. This was profitable for them because during this period there was a lot of merger activity, which meant that there were only six companies left in the generation and distribution of electricity. Each company therefore could see the benefit from reducing capacity and from having spare capacity, which it could take out of mothballs if prices started to rise, or if new companies threatened to come into the industry. The mothballed capacity therefore acted as a deterrent against new companies entering the industry, and this allows the six existing companies to continue in their profitable ways.

Finance

Chapters from:
Corporate Financial Management
2nd Edition

Glen Arnold

Chapter 1

THE FINANCIAL WORLD

INTRODUCTION

Before getting carried away with specific financial issues and technical detail, it is important to gain a broad perspective by looking at the fundamental questions and the place of finance in the overall scheme of things. The finance function is a vital one, both within an individual organisation and for society as a whole. In the UK, for example, the financial services industry accounts for about as large a proportion of national output as the whole of manufacturing industry. This shift in demand and resource has accelerated rapidly since 1970 and, if the trend continues, it will not be long before finance employs more people and attracts more purchasing power than all the manufacturing industries put together. To some this is a cause of great alarm and regret but, given that this trend has occurred at a time when free choice in the market-place largely dictates what is produced, presumably there must be something useful that financial firms are providing. We will examine the key role played by financial intermediaries and markets in a modern economy, and how an efficient and innovative financial sector contributes greatly to the ability of other sectors to produce efficiently. One of the vital roles of the financial sector is to encourage the mobilisation of savings to put them to productive use through investment. Without a vibrant and adaptable finance sector all parts of the economy would be starved of investment and society would be poorer.

This chapter also considers the most fundamental question facing anyone trying to make decisions within an organisation – what is the objective of the business? Without clarity on this point it is very difficult to run a business in a purposeful and effective manner. The resolution of this question is somewhat clouded in the large, modern corporation by the tendency for the owners to be distant from the running of the enterprise. Professional managers are usually left in control and they have objectives which may or may not match those of the owners.

Finally, to help the reader become orientated, a brief rundown is given of the roles, size and activities of the major types of financial institutions and markets. A little bit of jargon-busting early on will no doubt be welcomed.

Learning objectives

It is no good learning mathematical techniques and theory if you lack an overview of what finance is about. At the end of this chapter the reader will have a balanced perspective on the purpose and value of the finance function, at both the corporate and the national level. More specifically, the reader should be able to:

- describe alternative views on the purpose of the business and show the importance to any organisation of clarity on this point;

- describe the impact of the divorce of corporate ownership from day-to-day managerial control;

- explain the role of the financial manager;

- detail the value of financial intermediaries;

- show an appreciation of the function of the major financial institutions and markets.

THE OBJECTIVE OF THE FIRM

Cadbury Schweppes has a clear statement of its objective in the 1999 Annual Report – see Case study 1.1.

CASE STUDY 1.1

Cadbury Schweppes

Cadbury Schweppes' objective is growth in shareowner value. The strategy by which it will achieve this objective is:

- Focusing on its core growth markets of beverages and confectionery
- Developing robust, sustainable market positions which are built on a platform of strong brands with supported franchises
- Expanding its market share through innovation in products, packaging and route to market where economically profitable
- Enhancing its market positions by acquisitions or disposals where they are on strategy, value-creating and available

Managing for Value is the process which supports the achievement of this strategy.

The Chairman in 1999, Sir Dominic Cadbury, expands on the theme of the purpose of the Company in his letter in the Business Review 1999:

> 'In the latter half of the 1990s we focused more closely on the creation of shareowner value through the adoption of Managing for Value ("MFV") in 1997. During 1999 our MFV programme was extended throughout the Group, establishing a new discipline to, and understanding of, our management of the business. Growth and scale are important; but in global markets, where competition is intense, a complete understanding of value-creation is essential.
>
> With a clear vision of what value-creation means, we are confident of achieving sustainable earnings growth in 2000 and beyond.
>
> Our value analysis has already had far-reaching consequences. The sale of our beverages brands recognised the comparative disadvantage they suffered in smaller markets. It was in shareowners' best interest to obtain optimum value for them by finding the most appropriate owner.'

Source: Cadbury Schweppes Annual Report and Form 20-F 1999. Reprinted with permission.

This book is all about practical decision making in the real world. When people have to make choices in the harsh environment in which modern businesses have to operate, it is necessary to be clear about the purpose of the organisation; to be clear about what objective is set for management to achieve. A multitude of small decisions are made every day; more importantly, every now and then major strategic commitments of resources are made. It is imperative that the management teams are aware of, respect and contribute to the fundamental objective of the firm in all these large and small decisions. Imagine the chaos and confusion that could result from the opposite situation where there is no clear, accepted objective. The outcome of each decision, and the direction of the firm, will become random and rudderless. One manager on one occasion will decide to grant long holidays and a shorter working week, believing that the purpose of the institution's existence is to benefit employees; while on another occasion a different manager sacks 'surplus' staff and imposes lower wages, seeing the need to look after the owner's interests as a first priority. So, before we can make decisions in the field of finance we need to establish what it is we are trying to achieve.

You have probably encountered elsewhere the question, 'In whose interests is the firm run?' This is largely a political and philosophical question and many books have been written on the subject. Here we will provide a brief overview of the debate because of its central importance to making choices in finance. The list of interested parties in Exhibit 1.1 could be extended, but no doubt you can accept the point from this shortened version that there are a number of claimants on a firm.

Sound financial management is necessary for the survival of the firm and for its growth. Therefore all of these stakeholders, to some extent, have an interest in seeing sensible financial decisions being taken. Many business decisions do not involve a conflict between the objectives of each of the stakeholders. However, there are occasions when someone has to decide which claimants are to have their objectives maximised, and which are merely to be satisfied – that is, given just enough of a return to make their contributions.

There are some strong views held on this subject. The pro-capitalist economists, such as Friedrich Hayek and Milton Friedman, believe that making shareholders' interests the paramount objective will benefit both the firm and society at large. This approach is not quite as extreme as it sounds because these thinkers generally accept that unbridled

Exhibit 1.1 A company has responsibilities to a number of interested parties

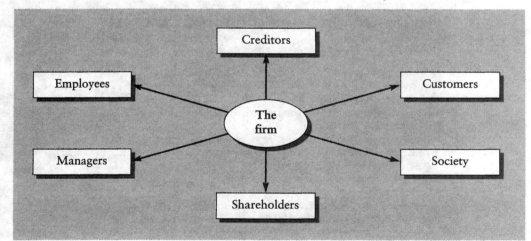

pursuit of shareholder returns, to the point of widespread pollution, murder and extortion, will not be in society's best interest and so add the proviso that maximising shareholder wealth is the desired objective provided that firms remain within 'the rules of the game'.

At the opposite end of the political or philosophical spectrum are the left-wing advocates of the primacy of workers' rights and rewards. The belief here is that labour should have its rewards maximised. The employees should have all that is left over, after the other parties have been satisfied. Shareholders are given just enough of a return to provide capital, suppliers are given just enough to supply raw materials and so on.

Standing somewhere in the middle are those keen on a balanced stakeholder approach. Here the (often conflicting) interests of each of the claimants is somehow maximised but within the constraints set by the necessity to compromise in order to provide a fair return to the other stakeholders.

Some possible objectives

A firm can choose from an infinitely long list of possible objectives. Some of these will appear noble and easily justified, others remain hidden, implicit, embarrassing, even subconscious. The following represent some of the most frequently encountered.

- *Achieving a target market share* In some industrial sectors to achieve a high share of the market gives high rewards. These may be in the form of improved profitability, survival chances or status. Quite often the winning of a particular market share is set as an objective because it acts as a proxy for other, more profound objectives, such as generating the maximum returns to shareholders. On other occasions matters can get out of hand and there is an obsessive pursuit of market share with only a thin veneer of shareholder wealth espousement – *see* Exhibit 1.2.

- *Keeping employee agitation to a minimum* Here, return to the organisation's owners is kept to a minimum necessary level. All surplus resources are directed to mollifying employees. Managers would be very reluctant to admit publicly that they place a high priority on reducing workplace tension, encouraging peace by appeasement and thereby, it is hoped, reducing their own stress levels, but actions tend to speak louder

Exhibit 1.2

Profits fall 39% on scheduled flights

FT

By Kevin Done, Aerospace Correspondent

International airlines last year suffered a 39 per cent fall in the net profits of their scheduled services to $1.9bn, the lowest level for five years, according to the International Air Transport Association (Iata).

Pierre Jeanniot, Iata director-general, warned that airlines should 'stop chasing the chimera of endless traffic growth at any price'.

'If governments are no longer going to subsidise such folly,' he said, 'why should we?'

The net profitability of international scheduled services fell to $1.9bn last year from $3.1bn in 1998 and $5bn in 1997, under pressure from rising fuel costs and falling yields resulting from widespread overcapacity.

Mr Jeanniot warned that most airline strategies continued to be based on market growth and on increasing market share instead of being driven by profits. Airline shareholders should be moved 'to the top of the priority list for rewards'.

Source: Financial Times, 5 April 2000, p. 13. Reprinted with permission.

than words. An example of this kind of prioritisation was evident in a number of state-owned UK industries in the 1960s and 1970s. Unemployment levels were low, workers were in a strong bargaining position and there were, generally, state funds available to bail out a loss-making firm. In these circumstances it was easier to buy peace by acquiescing to union demands than to fight on the picket lines.

- *Survival* There are circumstances where the overriding objective becomes the survival of the firm. Severe economic or market shock may force managers to focus purely on short-term issues to ensure the continuance of the business. They end up paying little attention to long-term growth and return to owners. However this focus is clearly inadequate in the long run – there must be other goals. If survival were the only objective then putting all the firm's cash reserves into a bank savings account might be the best option. When managers say that their objective is survival what they generally mean is the avoidance of large risks which endanger the firm's future. This may lead to a greater aversion to risk, and a rejection of activities that shareholders might wish the firm to undertake. Shareholders are in a position to diversify their investments: if one firm goes bankrupt they may be disappointed but they have other companies' shares to fall back on. However the managers of that one firm may have the majority of their income, prestige and security linked to the continuing existence of that firm. These managers may deliberately avoid high-risk/high-return investments and therefore deprive the owners of the possibility of large gains.
- *Creating an ever-expanding empire* This is an objective which is rarely openly discussed, but it seems reasonable to propose that some managers drive a firm forward, via organic growth or mergers, because of a desire to run an ever-larger enterprise. Often these motives become clearer with hindsight; when, for instance, a firm meets a calamitous end the *post mortem* often reveals that profit and efficiency were given second place to growth. The volume of sales, number of employees or overall stock market value of the firm have a much closer correlation with senior executive salaries, perks and status than do returns to shareholder funds. This may motivate some individuals to promote growth.
- *Maximisation of profit* This is a much more acceptable objective, although not everyone would agree that maximation of profit should be the firm's purpose.
- *Maximisation of long-term shareholder wealth* While many commentators concentrate on profit maximisation, finance experts are aware of a number of drawbacks of profit. The maximisation of the returns to shareholders in the long term is considered to be a superior goal. We look at the differences between profit maximisation and wealth maximisation later.

This list of possible objectives can easily be extended but it is not possible within the scope of this book to examine each of them. Suffice it to say, there can be an enormous variety of objectives and a large potential for conflict and confusion. We have to introduce some sort of order.

The assumed objective for finance

The company should make investment and financing decisions with the aim of maximising long-term shareholder wealth. Throughout the remainder of this book we will assume that the firm gives primacy of purpose to the wealth of shareholders. This assumption is made mainly on practical grounds, but there are respectable theoretical justifications too.

The practical reason

If one may assume that the decision-making agents of the firm (managers) are acting in the best interests of shareholders then decisions on such matters as which investment projects to undertake, or which method of financing to use, can be made much more simply. If the firm has a multiplicity of objectives, imagine the difficulty in deciding whether to introduce a new, more efficient machine to produce the firm's widgets, where the new machine both will be more labour efficient (thereby creating redundancies), and will eliminate the need to buy from one half of the firm's suppliers. If one focuses solely on the benefits to shareholders a clear decision can be made. This entire book is about decision-making tools to aid those choices. These range from whether to produce a component in-house, to whether to buy another company. If for each decision scenario we have to contemplate a number of different objectives or some vague balance of stakeholder interests, the task is going to be much more complex. Once the basic decision-making frameworks are understood within the tight confines of shareholder wealth maximisation, we can allow for complications caused by the modification of this assumption. For instance, shareholder wealth maximisation is clearly not the only consideration motivating actions of organisations such as Body Shop or the Co-operative Bank, each with publicly stated ethical principles. GlaxoSmithKline is coming under pressure from some of its shareholders to balance its shareholder wealth objective with generosity to AIDS victims – *see* Exhibit 1.3. It may be that the positive image created by providing cheap drugs to Africans is good for shareholders. On the other hand, it could be that the directors have to make a trade-off decision – greater generosity means less for shareholders. Real-world decision making can be agonisingly hard.

The theoretical reasons

The 'contractual theory' views the firm as a network of contracts, actual and implicit, which specify the roles to be played by various participants in the organisation. For instance, the workers make both an explicit (employment contract) and an implicit (show initiative, reliability, etc.) deal with the firm to provide their services in return for salary and other benefits, and suppliers deliver necessary inputs in return for a known payment. Each party has well-defined rights and pay-offs. Most of the participants bargain for a limited risk and a fixed pay-off. Banks, for example, when they lend to a firm, often strenuously try to reduce risk by making sure that the firm is generating sufficient cash flow to repay, that there are assets that can be seized if the loan is not repaid and so on. The bankers' bargain, like that of many of the parties, is a low-risk one and so, the argument goes, they should be rewarded with just the bare minimum for them to provide their service to the firm. Shareholders, on the other hand, are asked to put money into the business at high risk. The deal here is, 'You give us your £10,000 nest egg that you need for your retirement and we, the directors of the firm, do not promise that you will receive a dividend or even see your capital again. We will try our hardest to produce a return on your money but we cannot give any guarantees. Sorry.' Thus the firm's owners are exposed to the possibilities that the firm may go bankrupt and all will be lost. Because of this unfair balance of risk between the different potential claimants on a firm's resources it seems only fair that the owners should be entitled to any surplus returns which result after all the other parties have been satisfied. Another theoretical reason hinges on the practicalities of operating in a free market system. In such a capitalist system, it is argued, if a firm chooses to reduce returns to shareholders because, say, it wishes to direct more of the firm's surplus to the workers, then this firm will find it difficult to survive. Some shareholders will sell their

Exhibit 1.3

GSK under pressure over drugs for poor

Investors support Oxfam campaign to secure cheaper medicines for developing countries

By David Pilling in London

Large institutional investors in GlaxoSmithKline will this week throw their weight behind a campaign to force the newly merged Anglo-American drugs group to do more to make vital medicines available in developing countries.

Among those backing the campaign, to be launched today by Oxfam, is Friends Ivory Simes, which has £30bn under management and about £1bn invested in GSK. Oxfam is singling out GSK, the £120bn pharmaceutical giant, as part of a campaign focused on what it sees as the abuse of drug patents in denying poor countries access to cheaper medicines.

The issue of access to drugs has been highlighted by the HIV epidemic, which threatens to kill at least 30m people. It has been championed by Médecins sans Frontières, as well as by the author John Le Carré, whose novel *The Constant Gardener* portrays an industry devoid of morality.

Campaigners have accused drug companies of putting profits before lives in the developing world.

Craig Mackenzie, director of governance of Friends Ivory Simes, which manages Friends Provident's pension money, said 'If millions of Africans are dying of preventable diseases and one reason is that drug companies are charging too much, you have a serious reputational risk.'

Mr Mackenzie said institutional investors were taking ethical issues more seriously following last year's Pensions Act, which requires funds to detail their stance on such matters.

Mr Mackenzie said several large investors would meet on Wednesday to discuss how GSK could do more.

Oxfam, part of whose pension fund is also invested in GSK, accused the company of systematically using patent rules to 'squeeze low-cost copies of branded medi-

cines off the market'. It urged GSK to forego patents in Ghana, Uganda and South Africa where it said the company was using legal manoeuvres to block imports of cheap medicines.

GSK said it was disappointed that its 'extensive' drug donation programmes – dismissed by Oxfam as 'islands of philanthropy' – had not been acknowledged. It said it had offered to slash the cost of Aids medicine in Africa, but that governments had been slow to respond.

The company said patents were essential to stimulate investment in research. To argue that breaking or selectively applying patents would solve health disparities was naive, it said.

'If you start having patents in one country but not in another, it undermines the whole patent system. Where do you draw the line?'

Source: Financial Times, 12 February 2001, p. 23. Reprinted with permission.

shares and invest in other firms more orientated towards their benefit. In the long run those individuals who do retain their shares may be amenable to a takeover bid from a firm which does concentrate on shareholder wealth creation. The acquirer will anticipate being able to cut costs, not least by lowering the returns to labour. In the absence of a takeover the company would be unable to raise more finance from shareholders and this might result in slow growth and liquidity problems and possibly corporate death, throwing all employees out of work. For over 200 years it has been argued that society is best served by businesses focusing on returns to the owner. Adam Smith (1776) expressed the argument very effectively:

> The businessman by directing ... industry in such a manner as its produce may be of the greatest value, intends only his own gain, and he is in this, as in many other cases, led by an invisible hand to promote an end which was no part of his intention. Nor is it always the worse for society that it was no part of it. By pursuing his own interest he frequently promotes that of the society more effectually than when he really intends to promote it. I have never known much good done by those who affected to trade for the public good. It is an affectation, indeed, not very common among merchants.

Source: Adam Smith, *The Wealth of Nations*, 1776, p. 400.

One final, and powerful reason for advancing shareholders' interests above all others (subject to the rules of the game) is very simple: they own the firm and therefore deserve any surplus it produces.

This is not the place to advocate one philosophical approach or another which is applicable to all organisations at all times. Many organisations are clearly not shareholder wealth maximisers and are quite comfortable with that. Charities, government departments and other non-profit organisations are fully justified in emphasising a different set of values to those espoused by the commercial firm. The reader is asked to be prepared for two levels of thought when using this book. While it focuses on corporate shareholder wealth decision making, it may be necessary to make small or large modifications to be able to apply the same frameworks and theories to organisations with different goals.

Football clubs are organisations that often have different objectives from commercial organisations. As Exhibit 1.4 shows, many fans of Newcastle United believe that the objectives of their club changed for the worse when it became a company quoted on the London Stock Exchange. A confusion of objectives can make decision making complex and suspect.

Exhibit 1.4

It's not all black and white for Newcastle

Disgruntled fans are blaming the 'plc' for the club's lack of success

By Patrick Harverson

At professional football clubs, when things start to go badly wrong on the pitch it is traditional to blame the manager, the chairman, or the board of directors.

Not any more. As more and more clubs have begun to list their shares on the stock market, the 'plc' has slowly emerged as the favoured scapegoat of the disgruntled fans.

Take Newcastle United, a team lying six points above the Premiership's relegation zone after losing five of its last six league games. Despite its precarious position, the club has continued to sell some of its best players, and seems in no hurry to buy any replacements.

Although Kenny Dalglish, the team manager, has been criticised for the club's predicament, most of the blame has been heaped on the publicly quoted company that owns the club, and the institutional shareholders which hold shares in that company.

The fans believe Dalglish has been forced to sell players by the board of the plc, which is under pressure from City institutions to tighten its financial belt ahead of the planned £42m redevelopment of its St James' Park ground. Consequently, even though a net £12.5m has been raised from player sales in the past 12 months, there is still not enough money available to improve the playing squad.

The fans also think that if the club had remained private and in the hands of its former chairman, Sir John Hall – the local millionaire whose wealth provided the foundation for the club's rebirth in the 1990s – the team would still be buying new players and challenging for the Premiership title.

It is a persuasive argument, but is it true? And is it inevitable that quoted clubs will always remain vulnerable to the suspicion that they are running the business primarily for the benefit of the shareholders, and not the supporters?

With £31m of cash in the bank at the end of its last financial year,

Newcastle is certainly not short of money. The situation, explains Ms Dixon, is that Mr Dalglish has the funds to spend on players, but has been unable to get the ones he wanted.

Of course, the manager does not have a blank cheque. 'Like any business we have a strategy and we operate within a budget,' says Ms Dixon. 'We would have that whether we were private or public.'

Mark Edwards of the financial public relations firm Buchanan Communications advises several top clubs. He says: 'When a club announces plans to float, the first thing that comes up in the local press is the question of what happens if there's a choice between paying a dividend to shareholders or buying a player. These sorts of questions are being raised, but they are probably not being answered fully enough by the clubs.'

Source: Financial Times, 24/25 January 1998, p. 18. Reprinted with permission.

Exhibit 1.5 illustrates that a major debate is taking place in Germany about the objective of the firm.

Exhibit 1.5

Whirlwinds of change

FT

Vodafone AirTouch's takeover of Mannesmann will be a landmark in Germany's momentous journey towards a different model of capitalism, says John Plender

Vodafone AirTouch's victory in its bid to control Germany's Mannesmann is of profound historical importance.

At one level it suggests that, in the global competition between national political systems and economic institutions, the adversarial Anglo-American style of capitalism has won ground at the expense of the consensual German stakeholder model. The rules of the post-war German settlement between capital and labour are being radically rewritten from the outside, to the advantage of shareholders.

At another level Germany's 'insider' financial system, in which the banks have played a dominant role, has been opened up to a genuine market in corporate control. For good measure Vodafone, the

British telecommunications group, deployed the hostile bid techniques deplored earlier by Chancellor Gerhard Schröder.

The question now is how far convergence between the different systems will go. In one specific sense the Germans have already overtaken the US. Klaus Esser, Mannesmann's chairman, has shown himself far more sensitive to shareholder interests in the course of the bid battle than is usually the case with hostile bids in the US.

There are also limits to the speed of Germany's retreat from stakeholding. Gerhard Fels, Jürgen Matthes and Claus Schnabel argue in a recent paper for the think-tank that deeply embedded values are likely to prevent full convergence on the US model.

Companies, they say, 'are regarded as social institutions, not just as the property of their shareholders. Employees, trade unions and various other stakeholders have a strong say in corporate governance and in labour relations through legal requirements for power-sharing and through the traditional principle of consensus-seeking.'

A . . . worrying outcome might be that, with business, politicians and public differing so markedly in their respective appetites for reform, Germany could end up with the worst of both worlds: Anglo-American governance increasing the pressure for efficiency, while German labour market practice ensures that globally acceptable returns, and thus new jobs, could still only be generated abroad.

Source: Financial Times, 4 February 2000, p. 18. Reprinted with permission.

What is shareholder wealth?

Maximising wealth can be defined as maximising purchasing power. The way in which an enterprise enables its owners to indulge in the pleasures of purchasing and consumption is by paying them a dividend. The promise of a flow of cash in the form of dividends is what prompts investors to sacrifice immediate consumption and hand over their savings to a management team through the purchase of shares. Shareholders are interested in a flow of dividends over a long time horizon and not necessarily in a quick payback. Take the electronics giant Philips: it could raise vast sums for short-term dividend payouts by ceasing all research and development (R&D) and selling off surplus sites. But this would not maximise shareholder wealth because, by retaining funds within the business, it is believed that new products and ideas, springing from the R&D programme, will produce much higher dividends in the future. Maximising shareholder wealth means maximising the flow of dividends to shareholders *through time* – there is a long-term perspective.

If a company's shares are quoted on a stock exchange, and that stock exchange, through the actions of numerous buyers and sellers, prices shares appropriately given the firm's potential, then the prospective future dividend flow should be reflected in the share price. Thus, on this assumption of efficient share pricing we may take the current share price as our measure of shareholder wealth. (This assumption is examined in Chapter 14 when we look at the efficient markets hypothesis.) Thus, if the actions of directors, in their investment decisions, are beneficial to shareholders the share price will rise. If they make poor investments in real assets then future dividends will be reduced, and the share price will fall. The comments in Exhibit 1.6 from the *Financial Times* introduce the concept of shareholder value which is discussed in Chapters 15 and 16 – note for now that it involves more than good performance in product markets.

Exhibit 1.6

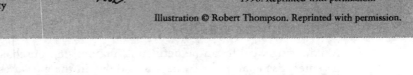

Never mind the price, feel the value

When you say 'shareholder value', do you sound convincing?

If you do, you're on your way to the top, or there already. It's one of those tests for modern business people: you just *have* to take shareholder value seriously.

But saying it with appropriate reverence, even writing mission statements about it, is easy. The hard work only starts when you try to put it into practice.

How *can* companies create shareholder value? And how they can make sure the world realises what they're doing?

The two questions are closely linked. The concept of shareholder value straddles two different markets: the product market in which a company's goods and services trade; and the stock market, in which its equity changes hands.

The snag is that a company can do well in its product market but still fail to realise its potential shareholder value.

There's no substitute for good product-market performance, of course; and any multi-line business also has to allocate capital properly between its subsidiaries.

But that may not be enough. If the share price is to reflect that success, investors must believe in the company's current management and future prospects. And if they don't you can kiss shareholder value goodbye.

How do you get investors to believe in you and your future? Talking to them helps. So does a convincing annual report.

Source: Financial Times, 17 January 1996. Reprinted with permission.

Illustration © Robert Thompson. Reprinted with permission.

Profit maximisation is not the same as shareholder wealth maximisation

Profit is a concept developed by accountants to aid decision-making, one decision being to judge the quality of stewardship shown over the owner's funds. The accountant has to take what is a continuous process, a business activity stretching over many years, and split this into accounting periods of say, a year, or six months. To some extent this exercise is bound to be artificial and fraught with problems. There are many reasons why accounting profit may not be a good proxy for shareholder wealth. Here are five of them:

■ *Prospects* Imagine that there are two firms that have reported identical profits but one firm is more highly valued by its shareholders than the other. One possible reason for this is that recent profit figures fail to reflect the relative potential of the two firms. The stock market will give a higher share value to the company which shows the greater future growth outlook. Perhaps one set of managers have chosen a short-term approach and raised their profits in the near term but have sacrificed long-term prospects. One way of achieving this is to raise prices and slash marketing spend – over the subsequent year profits might be boosted as customers are unable to switch suppliers immediately. Over the long term, however, competitors will respond and profits will fall.

■ *Risk* Again two firms could report identical historic profit figures and have future prospects which indicate that they will produce the same average annual returns. However one firm's returns are subject to much greater variability and so there will be years of losses and, in a particularly bad year, the possibility of bankruptcy. Exhibit 1.7 shows two firms which have identical average profit but Volatile Joe's profit is subject to much greater risk than that of Steady Eddie. Shareholders are likely to value the firm with stable income flows more highly than one with high risk.

Exhibit 1.7 Two firms with identical average profits but different risk levels

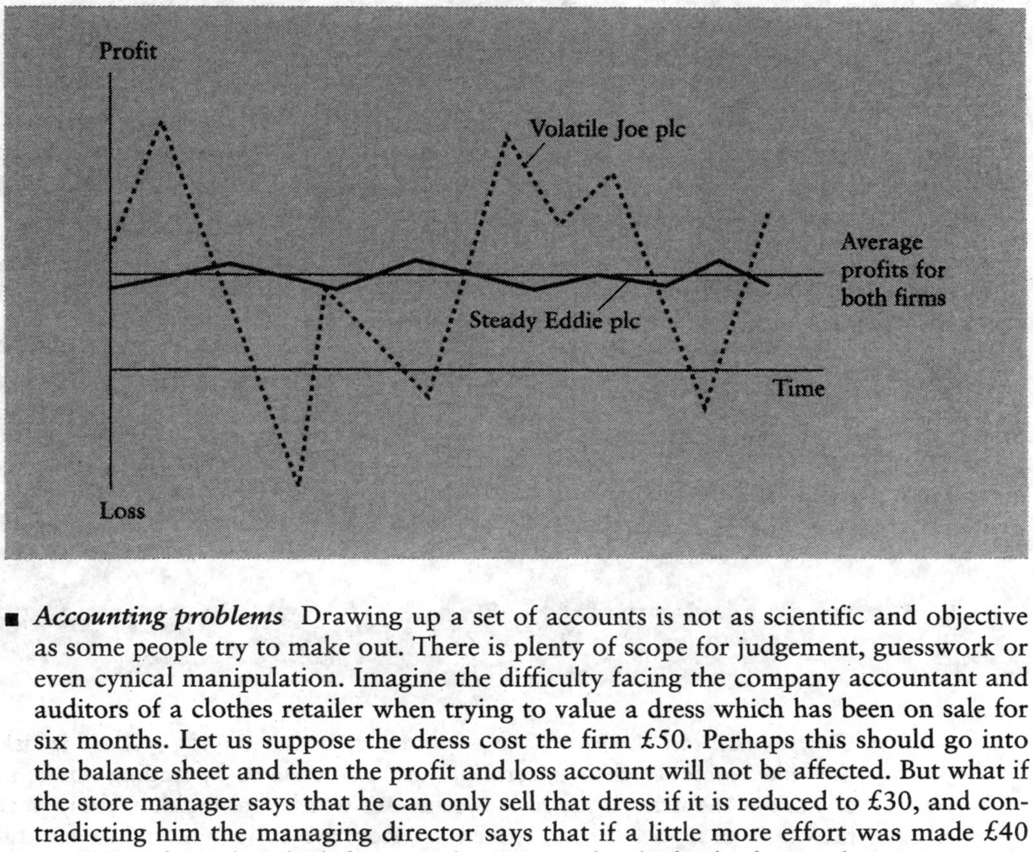

■ *Accounting problems* Drawing up a set of accounts is not as scientific and objective as some people try to make out. There is plenty of scope for judgement, guesswork or even cynical manipulation. Imagine the difficulty facing the company accountant and auditors of a clothes retailer when trying to value a dress which has been on sale for six months. Let us suppose the dress cost the firm £50. Perhaps this should go into the balance sheet and then the profit and loss account will not be affected. But what if the store manager says that he can only sell that dress if it is reduced to £30, and con-tradicting him the managing director says that if a little more effort was made £40 could be achieved? Which figure is the person who drafts the financial accounts going to take? Profits can vary significantly depending on a multitude of small judgements like this. Another difficult accounting issue is demonstrated in Exhibit 1.8 – just when does a sale add to profits?

Exhibit 1.8

Opening a blind eye to tech stocks' figure-flattering

Investors and analysts are concerned some companies are exploiting holes in accounting rules, say Caroline Daniel and Michael Peel

Investors and analysts are growing increasingly concerned that some companies are exploiting holes in accounting rules to give their turnover a more flattering look.

Institutions complain that their search for potential winners in volatile markets is hindered by companies that confuse the issue by booking tomorrow's sales today.

'In a strongly growing period, markets tend to be blind to some of these accounting issues,' says one UK technology fund manager. 'But when top line growth decelerates there is more emphasis on the financial details.'

Last month, shares in Lucent, the telecommunications equipment maker, fell sharply after it said it had overstated turnover because of a suspected accounting irregularity. The company refused to reveal further details of what it called a 'revenue recognition issue' until an investigation had been completed.

The question of revenue recognition is at the heart of the British debate, which revolves around the question of when a sale becomes a sale. For many companies, such as traditional retailers, the answer is easy – the sale is a sale once the goods have been passed to the customer.

But the boundaries become more blurred in sectors such as software, where companies might have ongoing obligations to provide customers with services such as advice and upgrades.

Some software businesses, such as Logica, take a prudent approach and recognise the sales in increments as they complete their contract.

But others take the more adventurous option of booking the full value of the sale as soon as product is handed over, even though their obligations may continue for many months.

Changes in revenue recognition policies can have a big impact, as ITNet, the computer services company, illustrated last month.

The group announced it would take a profits write-off of between £10m and £11m this year as a result of changing its accounting policy for long-term contracts.

A key point is that companies taking an aggressive line on accounting are not contravening any regulations, because Britain lacks clear standards on revenue recognition.

Source: Financial Times, 1 December 2000, p. 26. Reprinted with permission.

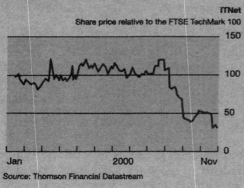

ITNet
Share price relative to the FTSE TechMark 100

Source: Thomson Financial Datastream

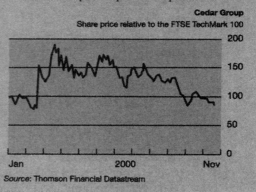

Cedar Group
Share price relative to the FTSE TechMark 100

Source: Thomson Financial Datastream

■ *Communication* Investors realise and accept that buying a share is risky. However they like to reduce their uncertainty and nervousness by finding out as much as they can about the firm. If the firm is reluctant to tell shareholders about such matters as the origin of reported profits, then investors generally will tend to avoid those shares. Fears are likely to arise in the minds of poorly informed investors: did the profits come from the most risky activities and might they therefore disappear next year? Is the company being used to run guns to unsavoury regimes abroad? The senior executives of large quoted firms spend a great deal of time explaining their strategies, sources of income and future investment plans to the large institutional shareholders to make sure that these investors are aware of the quality of the firm and its prospects. Firms that ignore the importance of communication and image in the investment community may be doing their shareholders a disservice as the share price might fall. Barclays seems to be aware of its responsibilities in this respect – see Exhibit 1.9.

Exhibit 1.9 More information leads to higher shareholder value . . .

Barclays to separate its revenue sources

Barclays plans to disclose significantly more information about earnings from different operations this year in an effort to improve its stock market valuation.

Mr Martin Taylor, chief executive, intends to publish revenues and costs from operations within investment banking and UK retail banking.

Until now, the bank has only given the overall figures for these divisions.

In its interim results announcement later this summer, the bank is likely to list separately revenues from investment banking, asset management, UK personal retail banking, and small and medium-sized business banking in the UK.

Mr Taylor hopes investors will be able to value the bank's earnings more accurately

from these figures. Asset management earnings are relatively high quality because they tend to be more consistent than those in investment banking.

Barclays also hopes that by showing the exact extent of its small business lending it will be able to reassure investors. Three-quarters of its earnings volatility in the past 15 years have come from bad debts on this lending.

A split between personal and small business banking would put Barclays among the leading banks in terms of disclosure. National Westminster only splits earnings between NatWest Markets, its investment bank, and its UK retail bank.

Source: John Gapper, Banking Editor, *Financial Times*, 14 May 1996, p. 22. Reprinted with permission.

The London Stock Exchange encourages companies to improve their communication with shareholders – *see* Exhibit 1.10.

Exhibit 1.10

Stock exchange in shareholder relations advice

By David Blackwell

The stock exchange is today sending every listed small company a guide to improving relations with shareholders.

Its main recommendation is for a Statement of Prospects to be published in the annual report. It also urges companies to explore the internet and other ways of making available information that will enable potential investors to make value judgements more easily.

The move follows the increasing pressure on small companies as they fall off investors' radar screens. They are becoming less important to institutions that are increasing in size as the financial services industry consolidates.

Source: Financial Times, 8 February 1999, p. 21. Reprinted with permission.

■ *Additional capital* Profits can be increased simply by making use of more shareholders' money. If shareholders inject more money into the company or the firm merely retains profits (which belong to shareholders) their future profits can rise, but the return on shareholders' money may fall to less than what is available elsewhere for the same level of risk. This is shareholder wealth destructive.

OWNERSHIP AND CONTROL

■ The problem

In theory the shareholders, being the owners of the firm, control its activities. In practice, the large modern corporation has a very diffuse and fragmented set of shareholders and control often lies in the hands of directors. It is extremely difficult to marshall thousands of shareholders, each with a small stake in the business, to push for change. Thus in many firms we have what is called a separation, or a divorce, of ownership and control. In times past the directors would usually be the same individuals as the owners. Today, however, less than 1 per cent of the shares of most of the UK's 100 largest quoted firms are owned by the directors and only four out of 10 directors of listed companies own any shares in their business.

The separation of ownership and control raises worries that the management team may pursue objectives attractive to them, but which are not necessarily beneficial to the shareholders – this is termed 'managerialism'. This conflict is an example of the principal–agent problem. The principals (the shareholders) have to find ways of ensuring that their agents (the managers) act in their interests. This means incurring costs, 'agency costs', to (a) monitor managers' behaviour, and (b) create incentive schemes and controls for managers to encourage the pursuit of shareholders' wealth maximisation. These costs arise in addition to the agency cost of the loss of wealth caused by the extent to which prevention measures do not work and managers continue to pursue non-shareholder wealth goals.

■ Some solutions?

Various methods have been used to try to align the actions of senior management with the interests of shareholders, that is, to achieve 'goal congruence'.

■ *Linking rewards to shareholder wealth improvements* A technique widely employed in UK industry is to grant directors and other senior managers share options. These permit managers to purchase shares at some date in the future at a price which is fixed now. If the share price rises significantly between the date when the option was granted and the date when the shares can be bought the manager can make a fortune by buying at the pre-arranged price and then selling in the market-place. For example in 2002 managers might be granted the right to buy shares in 2007 at a price of £1.50. If the market price moves to say £2.30 in 2007 the managers can buy and then sell the shares, making a gain of 80p. The managers under such a scheme have a clear interest in achieving a rise in share price and thus congruence comes about to some extent. An alternative method is to allot shares to managers if they achieve certain performance targets, for example, growth in earnings per share or return on assets.

■ *Sackings* The threat of being sacked with the accompanying humiliation and financial loss may encourage managers not to diverge too far from the shareholders' wealth path. However this method is employed in extreme circumstances only. It is sometimes difficult to implement because of difficulties of making a co-ordinated shareholder effort.

■ *Selling shares and the takeover threat* Over 60 per cent of the shares of the typical companies quoted on the London stock market are owned by financial institutions such as pension and insurance funds. These organisations generally are not prepared to put large resources into monitoring and controlling all the hundreds of firms of which they own a part. Quite often their first response, if they observe that management is not acting in what they regard as their best interest, is to sell the share rather than intervene. This will result in a lower share price, making the raising of funds more difficult. If this process continues the firm may become vulnerable to a merger bid by another group of managers, resulting in a loss of top management posts. Fear of being taken over can establish some sort of backstop position to prevent shareholder wealth considerations being totally ignored.

■ *Corporate governance regulations* There is a considerable range of legislation and other regulatory pressures designed to encourage directors to act in shareholders' interests. The Companies Acts require certain minimum standards of behaviour, as does the Stock Exchange. There is the back-up of the Serious Fraud Office (SFO) and the financial industry regulators – *see* Chapter 9. Following a number of financial scandals, such as the Maxwell affair, the Cadbury, Greenbury and Hampel reports on corporate governance attempted to improve the accountability of powerful directors. Under these non-statutory proposals, the board of directors should no longer be dominated by a single individual acting as both the chairman and chief executive. Also the non-executive directors should have more power to represent shareholder interests; in particular, at least three independently minded non-executives should be on the board of a large company and they should predominate in decisions connected with directors' remuneration and auditing of the firm's accounts.

■ *Information flow* The accounting profession, the stock exchange and the investing institutions have conducted a continuous battle to encourage or force firms to release more accurate, timely and detailed information concerning their operations. The quality of corporate accounts and annual reports has generally improved, as has the availability of other forms of information flowing to investors and analysts, such as company briefings and press announcements. This all helps to monitor firms, and identify any wealth-destroying actions by wayward managers early, but as a number of recent scandals have shown, matters are still far from perfect.

Corporate governance in other countries

The UK and other so-called Anglo-Saxon economies – the USA, Australia, etc. – are much more stock-market orientated than many other countries and a very strong distinction is made between investors and managers. In many continental European countries the stock exchange plays a less pivotal role in providing finance and influencing the actions of directors. Much heavier emphasis is placed on debt finance and this entails a slightly different set of principal–agent restraints, in that there tend to be more rules and legal restrictions. It is said that the Anglo-Saxon reliance on an active stock market and the takeover mechanism is an inefficient way of encouraging management to modify their actions. German companies have two boards to supervise the firm's strategy and operations. The supervisory board has a wide range of outside directors representing the numerous interest groups, not least of which are the bankers. Below this is the executive board, which implements the strategy. The information, power and influence that the banks have in Germany is often significantly greater than it is for their counterparts in the more financial-market-orientated economies.

In some countries the interests of shareholders are often placed far below those of the controlling managers. However progress is being made, as the article in Exhibit 1.11 demonstrates.

Exhibit 1.11

A big voice for the small man

John Plender meets a campaigner for the rights of shareholders in Korea's chaebol

In global corporate governance, South Korea is frontier territory in spite of its status as a member of the Organisation for Economic Co-operation and Development. So Professor Jang Hasung of Korea University, an outspoken campaigner for shareholder rights, has taken on one of the world's more stressful law and order jobs.

Working under the banner of the People's Solidarity for Participatory Democracy (PSPD), a Korean civic group campaigning against the abuse of power by government, the judiciary and big business, he has targeted the country's big five *chaebol*. These sprawling, opaque conglomerates are notorious for the abuse of conflicts of interest between their controlling families and minority shareholders.

'What we want is a fair outcome of the market process,' says the professor. 'We did a great job in Korea on development, but for 30 years fairness has been lacking because of cronyism and the rest. So the rich are not respected and the average person is very negative about the *chaebol*.' ...

One of his earliest targets was Korea First Bank. Large sums had been lent illegally to the failed Hanbo Steel Group, which was involved in a loans-for-bribes scandal. In 1998, the PSPD's legal action forced the bank's former management to reimburse Won 40bn (£23m) for losses arising from mismanagement and abuse of power.

But Professor Jang's biggest victory has been at SK Telekom, Korea's leading mobile phone group, where he wanted to prevent this very profitable part of the SK *chaebol* from bailing out weaker sister companies.

Here he succeeded in securing the appointment of outside directors and amending the company articles to increase transparency and impose a Won 10bn ceiling on deals with SK sister companies. The chief officer and president of the company even apologised to minority shareholders for excessive profit-taking and insider trading.

Since then, the professor's chief priority has been to secure change at Samsung Electronics, the jewel in the crown of Korea's second-ranked *chaebol*.

It is a tougher target. Prof Jang negotiated improvements in corporate governance with management before the last annual shareholders' meeting. There was give and take, he says. 'But to my despair, one day before the meeting, I was told the chairman did not like the negotiated deal.' The directors then proposed a Won 1,000bn threshold for deals with sister companies.

'This was outrageous,' he says. 'I have never seen anything like it – a mere pretence.' While outside directors were appointed to the board, PSPD's nominee was rejected.

But the professor did not give up, even though many of the foreign investors, with 52 per cent of the equity, failed to back him. A shareholders' meeting that was expected to last 20 minutes ran for 13 hours, as he drilled the executives over hidden subsidies made to the group's failed car company.

He also began legal action calling for the Samsung chairman and other executives to reimburse Won 300bn to the group for other incestuous and illegal transactions.

The activist professor acknowledges that traditional corporate governance remedies are imperfect in a Korean context. Non-executive directors may well be golf partners of the executives. The web of obligations that bind Koreans is a hindrance in persuading non-executive directors to play a proper monitoring role. 'When shareholder value issues arise,' he says, 'the problem is they never raise a voice on the board.'

The professor has concentrated on shareholder value because an immediate priority in dealing with the *chaebol* has been to prevent shareholders being robbed. 'If shareholders' rights are not protected,' he asserts, 'no other stakeholders will be protected. With shareholder rights, others get a safety net.'

But the overriding aim is to legitimise the workings of capitalism in Korea. So far, the impact of the professor and his small group of supporters has been out of all proportion to their numbers and resources.

Source: Financial Times, 4 May 2000, p. 15. Reprinted with permission.

In the absence of good corporate governance it is difficult for a firm to obtain funds for expansion – *see* the trouble Russian companies are having in Exhibit 1.12.

Exhibit 1.12

S&P plans new type of rating for Russian groups

By Arkady Ostrovsky in Moscow

Standard & Poor's, the international credit rating agency, will next month launch a product allowing the rating of Russian companies according to corporate governance standards.

Poor standards of corporate governance are among the most pressing issues in the Russian economy, which analysts say slow down foreign and domestic investment and undermine Russian growth.

The new product, whose launch will coincide with the OECD's round table on corporate governance, will rank companies according to their compliance with standards of governance rather than their financial position.

Investors say any instrument allowing measurement of corporate governance risk could be of great value.

The lack of transparency, poor business practices and disrespect for minority shareholders are among the biggest risks for investors in Russia. Last month Norilsk Nickel, one of Russia's largest commodity companies, came under fire from minority shareholders for failing to inform them about the company's restructuring plan and diluting their stakes.

Nick Bradley, director of corporate governance services at S&P, said companies would be evaluated according to four main criteria, including the transparency of the ownership structure, relationship with investors, financial transparency and level of disclosure, and the structure of the board of directors.

Mr Bradley said the service could be paid for by a company itself, or by a foreign investor who is interested in taking a stake in a Russian company.

Source: Financial Times, 11 October 2000, p. 37. Reprinted with permission.

PRIMITIVE AND MODERN ECONOMIES

A simple economy

Before we proceed to discuss the role of the financial manager and the part played by various financial institutions it is useful to gain an overview of the economy and the place of the financial system within society. To see the role of the financial sector in perspective it is, perhaps, of value to try to imagine a society without any financial services. Imagine how people would go about their daily business in the absence of either money or financial institutions. This sort of economy is represented in Exhibit 1.13. Here there are only two sectors in society. The business sector produces goods and services, making use of the resources of labour, land and commodities which are owned by the household sector. The household sector is paid with the goods and services produced by the business sector. (In such a simple economy we do not have to concern ourselves with a government sector or a foreign trade sector.)

In this economy there is no money and therefore there are two choices open to the household sector upon receipt of the goods and services:

1 *Consumption* Commodities can be consumed now either by taking those specific items provided from the place of work and enjoying their consumption directly, or, under a barter system, by exchanging them with other households to widen the variety of consumption.

2 *Investment* Some immediate consumption could be foregone so that resources can be put into building assets which will produce a higher level of consumption in the

Exhibit 1.13 **Flows within a simple economy – production level**

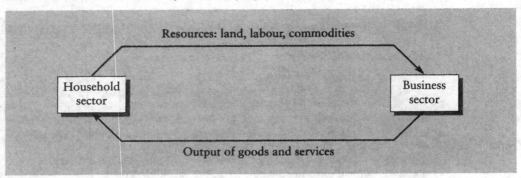

future. For instance, a worker takes payment in the form of a plough so that in future years when he enters the productive (business) sector he can produce more food per acre.

The introduction of money

Under a barter system much time and effort is expended in searching out other households interested in trade. It quickly becomes apparent that a tool is needed to help make transactions more efficient. People will need something into which all goods and services received can be converted. That something would have to be small and portable, it would have to hold its value over a long period of time and have general acceptability. This will enable people to take the commodities given in exchange for, say, labour and then avoid the necessity of, say, carrying the bushels of wheat to market to exchange them for bricks. Instead money could be paid in exchange for labour, and money taken to the market to buy bricks. Various things have been used as a means of exchange ranging from cowry shells to cigarettes (in prisons particularly) but the most popular has been a metal, usually gold or silver. The introduction of money into the system creates monetary as well as real flows of goods and services – *see* Exhibit 1.14.

Exhibit 1.14 **Flows within a simple economy – production level plus money**

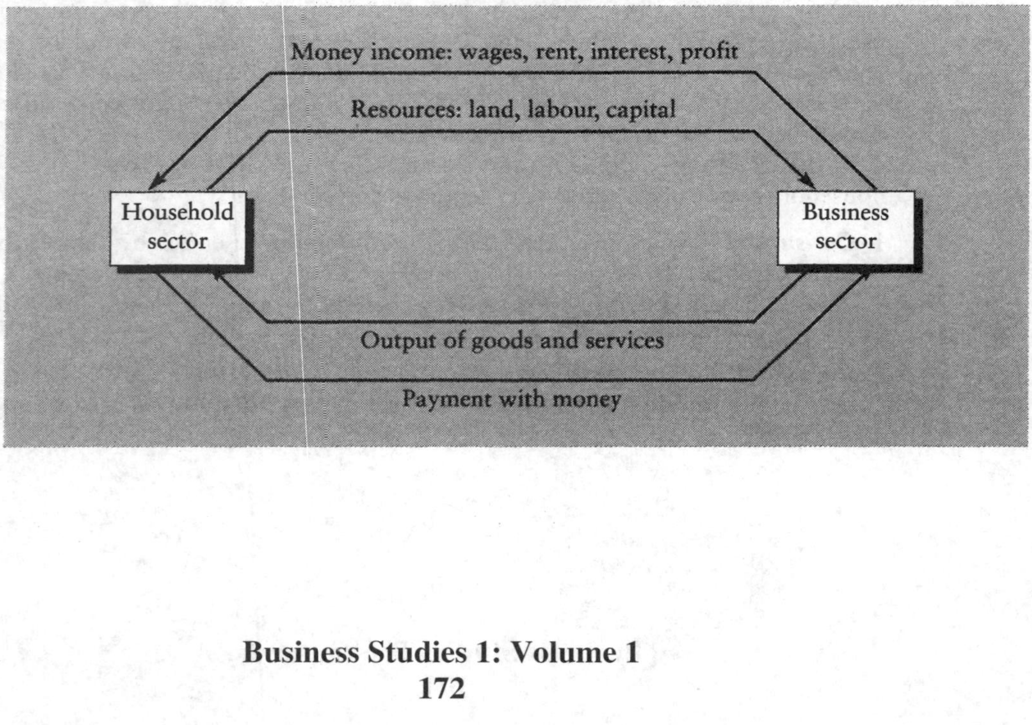

Investment in a money economy

Investment involves resources being laid aside now to produce a return in the future, for instance, today's consumption is reduced in order to put resources into building a factory and the creation of machine tools to produce goods in later years. Most investment takes place in the business sector but it is not the business sector consumption which is reduced if investment is to take place, as all resources are ultimately owned by households. Society needs individuals who are prepared to sacrifice consumption now and to wait for investments to come to fruition. These capitalists are willing to defer consumption and put their funds at risk within the business sector but only if they anticipate a suitable return. In a modern, sophisticated economy there are large-scale flows of investment resources from the ultimate owners (individuals who make up households) to the business sector. Even the profits of previous years' endeavours retained within the business belong to households – they have merely permitted firms to hold on to those resources for further investments on their behalf.

Investment in the twenty-first century is on a grand scale and the time gap between sacrifice and return has in many cases grown very large. This has increased the risks to any one individual investor and so investments tend to be made via pooled funds drawing on the savings of many thousands of households. A capital market has developed to assist the flow of funds between the business and household sectors. Amongst their other functions the financial markets reduce risk through their regulatory regimes and insistence on a high level of disclosure of information. In these more advanced financial structures businesses issue securities which give the holder the right to receive income in specified circumstances. Those that hold debt securities have a relatively high certainty of receiving a flow of interest. Those that buy a security called a share have less surety about what they will receive but, because the return is based on a share of profit, they expect to gain a higher return than if they had merely lent money to the firm.

In Exhibit 1.15 we can see household savings going into business investment. In exchange for this investment the business sector issues securities which show the claims that households have over firms. This exhibit shows three interconnected systems. The

Exhibit 1.15 Flows within a modern economy

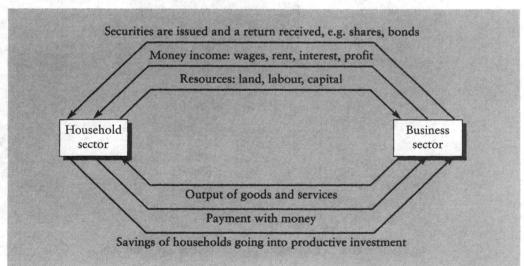

first is the flow of real goods and services. The second is a flow of money. The third is the investment system which enables production and consumption to be increased in the future. It is mainly in facilitating the flow of investment finance that the financial sector has a role in our society. The financial system increases the efficiency of the real economy by encouraging the flow of funds to productive uses.

THE ROLE OF THE FINANCIAL MANAGER

To be able to carry on a business a company needs real assets. These real assets may be tangible, such as buildings, plant, machinery, vehicles and so on. Alternatively a firm may invest in intangible real assets, for example patents, expertise, licensing rights, etc. To obtain these real assets corporations sell financial claims to raise money; to lenders a bundle of rights are sold within a loan contract, to shareholders rights over the ownership of a company are sold as well as the right to receive a proportion of profits produced. The financial manager has the task of both raising finance by selling financial claims and advising on the use of those funds within the business. This is illustrated in Exhibit 1.16.

Exhibit 1.16 The flow of cash between capital markets and the firm's operations

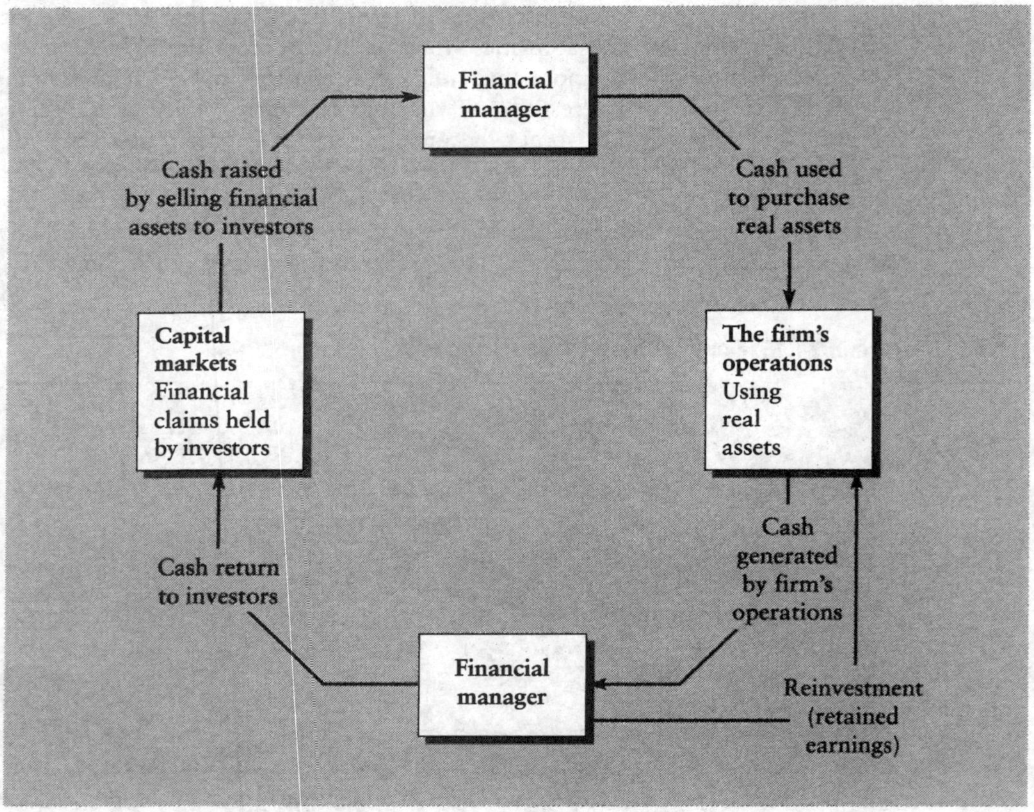

The financial manager plays a pivotal role in the following:

Interaction with the financial markets

In order to raise finance a knowledge is needed of the financial markets and the way in which they operate. To raise share (equity) capital awareness of the rigours and processes involved in 'taking a new company to market' might be useful. For instance, what is the role of an issuing house? What services do brokers, accountants, solicitors, etc. provide to a company wishing to float? Once a company is quoted on a stock market it is going to be useful to know about ways of raising additional equity capital – what about rights issues and open offers?

Knowledge of exchanges such as the Alternative Investment Market (UK) or the European market Euronext might be valuable. If the firm does not wish to have its shares quoted on an exchange perhaps an investigation needs to be made into the possibility of raising money through the venture capital industry.

Understanding how shares are priced and what it is that shareholders are looking for when sacrificing present consumption to make an investment could help the firm to tailor its strategy, operations and financing decisions to suit their owners. These, and dozens of other equity finance questions, are part of the remit of the finance expert within the firm.

Another major source of finance comes from banks. Understanding the operation of banks and what concerns them when lending to a firm may enable you to present your case better, to negotiate improved terms and obtain finance which fits the cash-flow patterns of the firm. Then there are ways of borrowing which by-pass banks. Bonds could be issued either domestically or internationally. Medium-term notes, commercial paper, leasing, hire purchase and factoring are other possibilities.

Once a knowledge has been gained of each of these alternative financial instruments and of the operation of their respective financial markets, then the financial manager has to consider the issue of the correct balance between the different types. What proportion of debt to equity? What proportion of short-term finance to long-term finance and so on?

Perhaps you can already appreciate that the finance function is far from a boring 'bean-counting' role. It is a dynamic function with a constant need for up-to-date and relevant knowledge. The success or failure of the entire business may rest on the quality of the interaction between the firm and the financial markets. The financial manager stands at the interface between the two.

Investment

Decisions have to be made concerning how much to invest in real assets and which specific projects to undertake. In addition to providing analytical techniques to aid these sorts of decisions the financial expert has to be aware of a wide variety of factors which might have some influence on the wisdom of proceeding with a particular investment. These range from corporate strategy and budgeting restrictions to culture and the commitment of individuals likely to be called upon to support an activity.

Treasury management

The management of cash may fall under the aegis of the financial manager. Many firms have large sums of cash which need to be managed properly to obtain a high return for shareholders. Other areas of responsibility might include inventory control, creditor and debtor management and issues of solvency and liquidity.

Risk management

Companies that enter into transactions abroad, for example exporters, are often subject to risk: they may be uncertain about the sum of money (in their own currency) that they will actually receive on the deal. Three or four months after sending the goods they may receive a quantity of yen or dollars but at the time the deal was struck they did not know the quantity of the home currency that could be bought with the foreign currency. Managing and reducing exchange rate risk is yet another area calling on the skills of the finance director.

Likewise, exposure to interest rate changes and commodity price fluctuations can be reduced by using hedging techniques. These often employ instruments such as futures, options, swaps and forward agreements. Misunderstanding these derivatives and their appropriate employment can lead to disaster – for example, the Barings Bank fiasco, in which a major bank was brought to bankruptcy through the misuse and misunderstanding of derivatives.

Strategy

Managers need to formulate and implement long-term plans to maximise shareholder wealth. This means selecting markets and activities in which the firm, given its resources, has a competitive edge. Managers need to distinguish between those products or markets that generate value for the firm and those that destroy value. The financial manager has a pivotal role in this strategic analysis.

Exhibit 1.17 demonstrates the centrality of the finance function.

Exhibit 1.17

More than just a number cruncher

Ask a well-informed private investor for views on chief executives and you'll get enough material to fill four filing cabinets. But pose the same question about finance directors and you'll be lucky if the answers fit on an envelope.

Finance directors have been comparatively low profile (mostly) men and (occasionally) women, ignored by the press unless, like hapless Stuart Straddling, finance director of Wickes, they're thrust into the limelight by a messy accounting scandal.

But dig a little deeper and you discover that while finance directors may not have public images, they're often the quiet voice of authority in a company.

Richard Lapthorne, finance director of British Aerospace, commands huge respect in the City and is viewed by some analysts as being the power behind the throne. Richard Brooke, finance director of BSkyB, may not be as colourful as that company's boss, Sam Chisholm, but he is regarded as a heavyweight who knows as much about the satellite broadcasting business as his chief executive.

There are two types of finance director: the chief finance officer who has been bred by the company, man and boy, and the 'career finance director' who is parachuted in at board level.

A good example of the first category is Rob Rowley at Reuters, who joined as an assistant financial manager in 1978, moved up via various financial positions and was named finance director in 1990.

A more flamboyant career path was taken by Roy Gardner, who joined British Gas as group finance director in 1994 and has recently been named chief executive designate of British Gas Energy.

Money, skills and politics too

Before reaching those Olympian heights, the finance director has to master accounting, treasury functions, City and investor relations and tax. International exposure, takeover experience and ability to handle pan-European acquisitions can be handy for a job with a multinational or a conglomerate. Political savvy is a useful attribute, too.

In theory, these skills are portable and finance directors can move between industries – Simon Moffat, finance director of drug developer Celltech, has a food-manufacturing background. Gerald Corbett, Grand Metropolitan's finance director, did the same job at Redland, the buildings-material supplier, and cut his managerial teeth at retailer Dixons.

But most finance directors stay in the same industry. Rebecca Winnington Ingram, of investment bank Morgan Stanley, says: 'A finance director may be great at performing treasury swaps but, if he knows nothing about the underlying industry, he's not much use.'

Given the weight of the role – closeness to the chief executive, input into corporate strategy and detailed knowledge of the company – the finance director might seem an obvious successor to the chief executive. That is borne out by some recent senior appointments in industry. Derek Bonham, chief executive of Hanson, was Hanson's former finance director, and Nigel Stapleton, finance director of Reed Elsevier, has recently been named chief executive.

'The FD will speak for the company in the chief executive's absence, might even be likened to a deputy chief executive,' he says, pointing to Tomkins's Greg Hutchins (chief executive) and Ian Duncan (finance director) as one such pairing, Sir Richard Greenbury and Keith Oates at Marks and Spencer as another.

Source: Tracy Hofman, *Investors Chronicle*, 16 August 1996. Reprinted with kind permission of *Investors Chronicle*.

THE FLOW OF FUNDS AND FINANCIAL INTERMEDIATION

Exhibit 1.16 looked at the simple relationship between a firm and investors. Unfortunately the real world is somewhat more complicated and the flow of funds within the financial system involves a number of other institutions and agencies. Exhibit 1.18 is a more realistic representation of the financial interactions between different groups in society.

Households generally place the largest proportion of their savings with financial institutions. These organisations then put that money to work. Some of it is lent back to members of the household sector in the form of, say, a mortgage to purchase a house, or as a personal loan. Some of the money is used to buy securities issued by the business sector. The institutions will expect a return on these loans and shares which flows back in the form of interest and dividends. However they are often prepared for businesses to retain profit within the firm for further investment in the hope of greater returns in the future. The government sector enters into the financial system in a number of ways, two of which are shown in Exhibit 1.18. Taxes are taken from businesses and this adds a further dimension to the financial manager's job – for example, taking taxation into account when selecting sources of finance and when approving investment proposals. Second, governments usually fail to match their revenues with their expenditure and therefore borrow significant sums from the financial institutions. The diagram in Exhibit 1.18 remains a gross simplification, it has not allowed for overseas financial transactions, for example, but it does demonstrate a crucial role for financial institutions in an advanced market economy.

Primary investors

Typically the household sector is in financial surplus. This sector contains the savers of society. It is these individuals who become the main providers of funds used for investment in the business sector. Primary investors tend to prefer to exchange their cash for financial assets which (a) allow them to get their money back quickly should they need to (with low transaction cost of doing so) and (b) have a high degree of certainty over the amount they will receive back. That is, primary investors like high liquidity and low risk. Lending directly to a firm with a project proposal to build a North Sea oil platform which will not be sold until five years have passed is not a high-liquidity and low-risk investment. However, putting money into a sock under the bed is (if we exclude the possibility of the risk of sock theft).

Exhibit 1.18 The flow of funds and financial intermediation

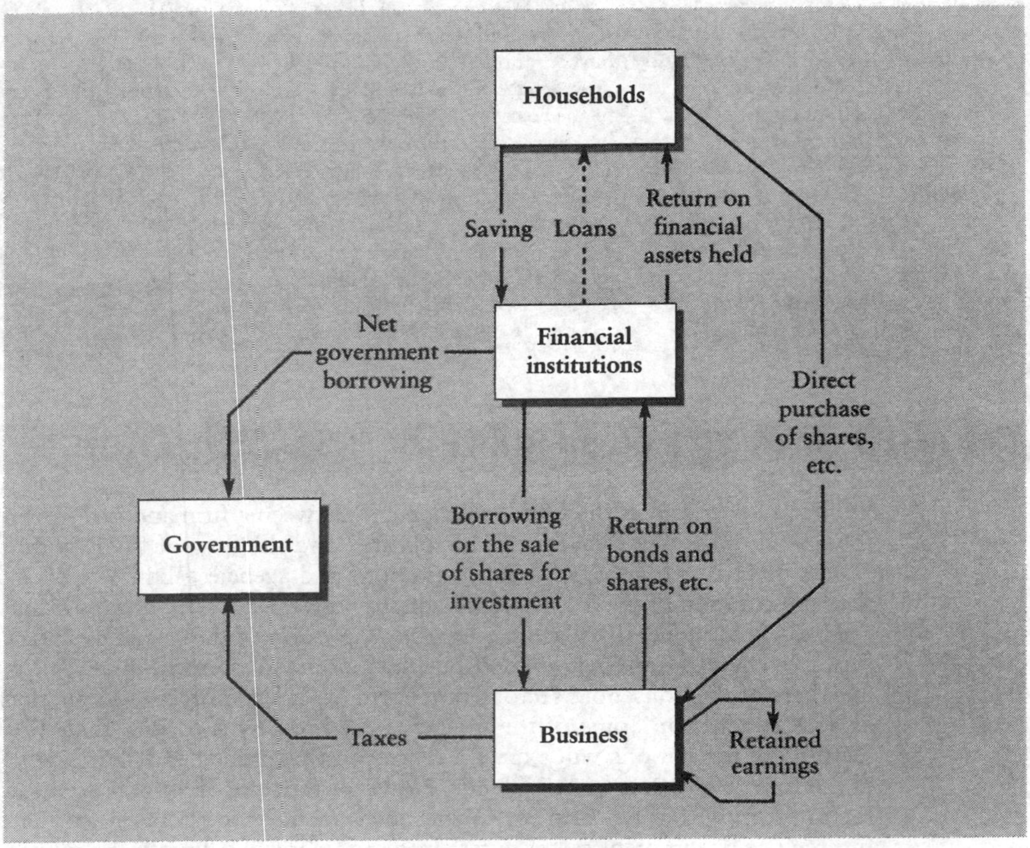

Ultimate borrowers

In our simplified model the ultimate borrowers are in the business sector. These firms are trying to maximise the wealth generated by their activities. To do this companies need to invest in real plant, equipment and other assets, often for long periods of time. The firms, in order to serve their social function, need to attract funds for use over many years. Also these funds are to be put at risk, sometimes very high risk. (Here we are using the term 'borrower' broadly to include all forms of finance, even 'borrowing' by selling shares.)

Conflict of preferences

We have a conflict of preference between the primary investors wanting low-cost liquidity and certainty, and the ultimate borrowers wanting long-term risk-bearing capital. A further complicating factor is that savers usually save on a small scale, £100 here or £200 there, whereas businesses are likely to need large sums of money. Imagine some of the problems that would occur in a society which did not have any financial intermediaries. Here lending and share buying will occur only as a result of direct contact and negotiation between two parties. If there were no organised market where financial securities could be sold on to other investors the fund provider, once committed, would be trapped in an illiquid investment. Also the costs that the two parties might incur in

Exhibit 1.19 Savings into investment in an economy without financial intermediaries

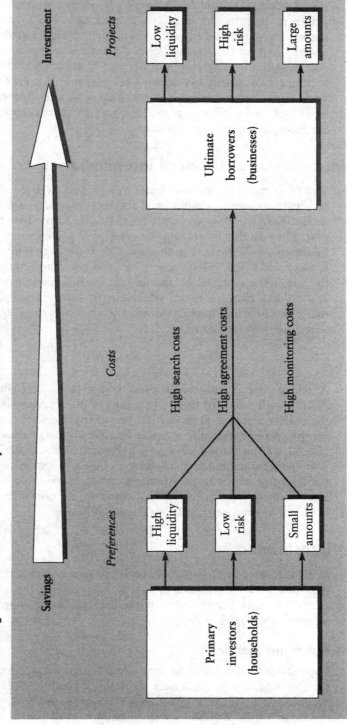

searching to find each other in the first place might be considerable. Following contact a thorough agreement would need to be drawn up to safeguard the investor, and additional expense would be incurred obtaining information to monitor the firm and its progress. In sum, the obstacles to putting saved funds to productive use would lead many to give up and to retain their cash. Those that do persevere will demand exceptionally high rates of return from the borrowers to compensate them for poor liquidity, risk, search costs, agreement costs and monitoring costs. This will mean that few firms will be able to justify investments because they cannot obtain those high levels of return when the funds are invested in real assets. As a result few investments take place and the wealth of society fails to grow. Exhibit 1.19 shows (by the top arrow) little money flowing from saving into investment.

The introduction of financial intermediaries

The problem of under-investment can be alleviated greatly by the introduction of financial institutions (e.g. banks) and financial markets (e.g. a stock exchange). Their role is to facilitate the flow of funds from primary investors to ultimate borrowers at a low cost. They do this by solving the conflict of preferences. There are two types of financial intermediation; the first is an agency or brokerage type operation which brings together lenders and firms, the second is an asset-transforming type of intermediation, in which the conflict is resolved by creating intermediate securities which have the risk, liquidity and volume characteristics which the investors prefer. The financial institution raises money by offering these securities, and then uses the acquired funds to purchase primary securities issued by firms.

Brokers

At its simplest an intermediary is a 'go-between', someone who matches up a provider of finance with a user of funds. This type of intermediary is particularly useful for reducing the search costs for both parties. Stockbrokers, for example, make it easy for investors wanting to buy shares in a newly floated company. Brokers may also have some skill at collecting information on a firm and monitoring its activities, saving the investor time. They also act as middlemen when an investor wishes to sell to another, thus enhancing the liquidity of the fund providers. Another example is the Post Office which enables individuals to lend to the UK government in a convenient and cheap manner by buying National Savings certificates or Premium Bonds.

Asset transformers

Intermediaries, by creating a completely new security, the intermediate security, increase the opportunities available to savers, encouraging them to invest and thus reducing the cost of finance for the productive sector. The transformation function can act in a number of different ways.

Risk transformation

For example, instead of an individual lending directly to a business with a great idea, such as digging a tunnel under the English Channel, a bank creates a deposit or current account with relatively low risk for the investor's savings. Lending directly to the firm the saver would demand compensation for the probability of default on the loan and therefore the business would have to pay a very high rate of interest which would inhibit investment. The bank acting as an intermediary creates a special kind of security called a bank account agreement. The intermediary then uses the funds attracted by the new financial asset to buy a security issued by the tunnel owner (the primary security) when it obtains long-term debt capital. Because of the extra security that a lender has by holding a bank account as a financial asset rather than by making a loan direct to a firm, the lender is prepared to accept a lower rate of interest and the ultimate borrower obtains funds at a relatively low cost. The bank is able to reduce its risk exposure to any one project by diversifying its loan portfolio amongst a number of firms. It can also reduce risk by building up expertise in assessing and monitoring firms and their associated risk. Another example of risk transformation is when unit or investment trusts take savers' funds and spread these over a wide range of company shares.

Maturity (liquidity) transformation

The fact that a bank lends long term for a risky venture does not mean that the primary lender is subjected to illiquidity. Liquidity is not a problem because banks maintain sufficient liquid funds to meet their liabilities when they arise. You can walk into a bank and take the money from your account at short notice because the bank, given its size, exploits economies of scale and anticipates that only a small fraction of its customers will withdraw their money on any one day. Banks and building societies play an important role in borrowing 'short' and lending 'long'.

Volume transformation

Many institutions gather small amounts of money from numerous savers and re-package these sums into larger bundles for investment in the business sector. Apart from the banks and building societies, unit trusts are important here. It is uneconomic for an investor with, say, £50 per month, who wants to invest in shares, to buy small quantities periodically. Unit trusts gather together hundreds of individuals' monthly savings and invest them in a broad range of shares, thereby exploiting economies in transaction costs.

Intermediaries' economies of scale

The intermediary is able to accept lending to (and investing in shares of) companies at a lower rate of return because of the economies of scale enjoyed compared with the primary investor. These economies of scale include:

(a) *Efficiencies in gathering information* on the riskiness of lending to a particular firm. Individuals do not have access to the same data sources or expert analysis.
(b) *Risk spreading* Intermediaries are able to spread funds across a large number of borrowers and thereby reduce overall risk. Individual investors may be unable to do this.
(c) *Transaction costs* They are able to reduce the search, agreement and monitoring costs that would be incurred by savers and borrowers in a direct transaction. Banks, for example, are convenient, safe locations with standardised types of securities. Savers do not have to spend time examining the contract they are entering upon when, say, they open a bank account. How many of us read the small print when we opened a bank account?

The reduced information costs, convenience and passed-on benefits from the economies of operating on a large scale mean that primary investors are motivated to place their savings with intermediaries.

Exhibit 1.20 Savings into investment in an economy with financial intermediaries and financial markets

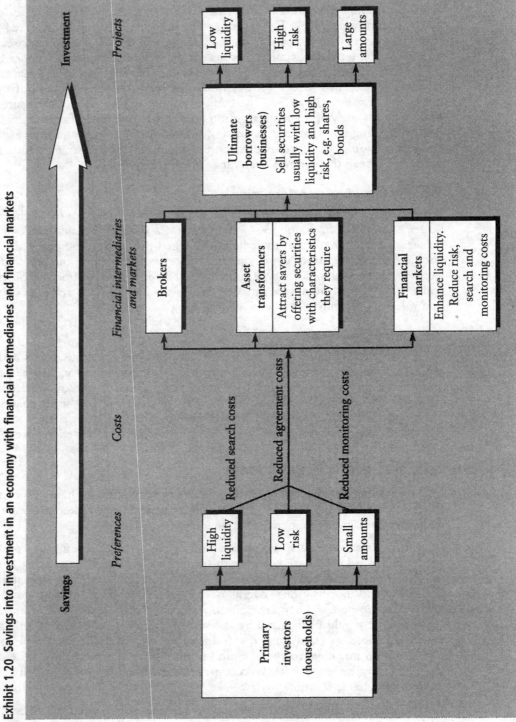

Financial markets

A financial market, such as a stock exchange, has two aspects; there is the *primary market* where funds are raised from investors by the firm, and there is the *secondary market* in which investors buy and sell shares, bonds, etc. between each other. These securities are generally long term and so it is beneficial for the original buyer to be able to sell on to other investors. In this way the firm achieves its objective of raising finance that will stay in the firm for a lengthy period and the investor has retained the ability to liquidate (turn into cash) a holding by selling to another investor. In addition a well-regulated exchange encourages investment by reducing search, agreement and monitoring costs – *see* Exhibit 1.20.

GROWTH IN THE FINANCIAL SERVICES SECTOR

The financial services sector has grown rapidly in the post-war period. It now represents a significant proportion of total economic activity, not just in the UK, but across the world. We define the core of the financial sector as banking (including building societies), insurance and various investment services. There are one or two other activities, such as accounting, which may or may not be included depending on your perspective. Firms operating in the financial services sector have, arguably, been the most dynamic, innovative and adaptable companies in the world over the past 20 years.

Some reasons for the growth of financial services in the UK

There are a number of reasons for the growth of the financial services sector. These include:

1 *High income elasticity*. This means that as consumers have become increasingly wealthy the demand for financial services has grown by a disproportionate amount. Thus a larger share of national income is devoted to paying this sector fees, etc. to provide services because people desire the benefits offered. Firms have also bought an ever-widening range of financial services from the institutions which have been able to respond quickly to the needs of corporations.

2 *International comparative advantage*. London is the world's leading financial centre in a number of markets, for instance international share trading and Eurobond dealing. It is the place where the most currency transactions take place – over £400bn per day. It is also a major player in the fund management, insurance and derivative markets. It is certainly Europe's leading financial centre. One of the reasons for London's maintaining this dominance is that it possesses a comparative advantage in providing global financial services. This advantage stems, not least, from the critical mass of collective expertise which it is difficult for rivals to emulate – *see* Exhibit 1.21.

Dynamism, innovation and adaptation – three decades of change

Since the 1970s there has been a remarkably proactive response by the financial sector to changes in the market environment. New financial instruments, techniques of intermediation and markets have been developed with impressive speed. Instruments which even in the early 1980s did not exist have sprung to prominence to create multi-billion pound markets, with thousands of employees serving that market.

Exhibit 1.21

London is 'gateway to euro-zone'

Clementi says City outpacing Frankfurt and Paris

By Alan Beattie, Economics Correspondent

London will continue to act as the gateway for investment into the euro-zone, David Clementi, deputy governor of the Bank of England, said yesterday.

Speaking in Tokyo, Mr Clementi said London had tightened its grip on euro-denominated markets since the launch of the euro two years ago, despite not having joined the single currency.

'The City of London does not depend on the currency used by the UK,' Mr Clementi said.

'Financial activity will be carried on where it can be carried on most conveniently, profitably and efficiently.'

Mr Clementi said that London's dominance in foreign exchange, derivatives, cross-border bank lending and euro-denominated international bond markets meant that it was outpacing Frankfurt and Paris as an international financial centre.

'Deep and liquid euro markets have become well established in London,' he said. 'They have replaced the previous, more segmented markets in the old national currencies like the Deutschemark and the French franc.'

Mr Clementi, the deputy governor with responsibility for promoting the UK as a financial centre, said that London's success rested on its flexible labour laws, low tax levels and 'non-bureaucratic but rigorous', approach to financial regulation.

His verdict on the first two years of trading in the euro throws weight behind the argument that the UK's position as a global financial centre has survived unscathed its decision not to participate in the first wave of monetary union. The effect on the competitive position of the UK's financial services industry is one of the Treasury's five tests for entry into the euro.

More than half of underwritten euro-denominated international bonds were issued in London, which also has a 70 per cent share of secondary trading in the market, the deputy governor said.

He added that the capitalisation of the London Stock Exchange was nearly double that of either Frankfurt or Paris.

Source: Financial Times, 14 February 2000, p. 6. Reprinted with permission.

Until the mid-1970s there were clearly delineated roles for different types of financial institutions. Banks did banking, insurance firms provided insurance, building societies granted mortgages and so on. There was little competition between the different sectors, and cartel-like arrangements meant that there was only limited competition within each sector. Some effort was made in the 1970s to increase the competitive pressures, particularly for banks. The arrival of large numbers of foreign banks in London helped the process of reform in the UK but the system remained firmly bound by restrictions, particularly in defining the activities firms could undertake.

The real breakthrough came in the 1980s. The guiding philosophy of achieving efficiency through competition led to large-scale deregulation of activities and pricing. There was widespread competitive invasion of market segments. Banks became much more active in the mortgage market and set up insurance operations, stockbroking arms, unit trusts and many other services. Building societies, on the other hand, started to invade the territory of the banks and offered personal loans, credit cards, cheque accounts. They even went into estate agency, stockbroking and insurance underwriting. The ultimate invasion happened when Abbey National decided to convert from a building society to a bank in 1989. The Stock Exchange was deregulated in 1986 (in what is known as 'Big bang') and this move enabled it to compete more effectively on a global scale and reduce the costs of dealing in shares, particularly for the large institutional investors.

The 1970s and early 1980s were periods of volatile interest rates and exchange rates. This resulted in greater uncertainty for businesses. New financial instruments were developed to help manage risk. The volume of trading in LIFFE (the London International Financial Futures and Options Exchange) has rocketed since it was opened in 1982 – it now handles over £358bn worth of business every day.[1] Likewise the volume of swaps, options, futures, etc. traded in the informal 'over-the-counter' market (i.e. not on a regulated exchange) has grown exponentially.

Through the 1980s the trend towards globalisation in financial product trading and services continued apace. Increasingly a world-wide market was established. It became possible for a company to have its shares quoted in New York, London, Frankfurt and Tokyo as well as its home exchange in Africa. Bond selling and trading became global and currencies were traded 24 hours a day. International banking took on an increasingly high profile, not least because the multinational corporations demanded that their banks provide multi-faceted services ranging from borrowing in a foreign currency to helping manage cash. The globalisation trend was assisted greatly by the abolition of exchange controls in 1979 in the UK, followed by other leading economies during the 1980s. (Before 1979 UK residents were restricted in the amount of foreign assets they could buy because of limits placed on the purchase of foreign currency.)

Vast investments have been made in computing and telecommunications systems to cut costs and provide improved services. Automated teller machines (ATMs), banking by telephone, and payment by EFTPOS (electronic funds transfer at point of sale) are now commonplace and taken for granted by consumers. A more advanced use of technological innovation is in the global trading of the ever-expanding range of financial instruments. It became possible to sit on a beach in the Caribbean and trade pork belly futures in Chicago, interest rate options in London and shares in Singapore. In the 1990s there was a continuation of the blurring of the boundaries between different types of financial institutions to the point where organisations such as J.P. Morgan Chase, and Barclays are referred to as 'financial supermarkets' (or 'universal banks') offering a wide range of services. The irony is that just as this title was being bandied about, the food supermarket giants such as Sainsbury's and Tesco set up comprehensive banking services, following a path trodden by a number of other non-banking corporations. Marks and Spencer provide credit cards, personal loans and even pensions. Virgin Direct sells life insurance, pensions and Individual Savings Accounts (ISAs) over the telephone. Also, a number of large building societies (e.g. Halifax, Alliance and Leicester and the Woolwich) decided to follow Abbey National and become banks. This has enabled them to undertake an even wider range of activities and to tap further the wholesale financial markets for funds. The internet has provided a new means of supplying financial services and lowered the barrier to entry into the industry. New banking, stockbroking and insurance services have sprung up. The internet allows people to trade millions of shares at the touch of a button from the comfort of their home, to transfer the proceeds between bank accounts and to search websites for data, company reports, newspaper reports, insurance quotations and so on – all much more cheaply than ever before.

The globalisation of business and investment decisions has continued making national economies increasingly interdependent. Borrowers use the international financial markets to seek the cheapest funds, and investors look in all parts of the globe for the highest returns. Some idea of the extent of global financial flows can be gained by contrasting the *daily* turnover of foreign exchange (approximately £1,500bn)[2] with the *annual* output of all the goods and services produced by the people in the UK (£950bn).[3]

Exhibit 1.22 Main features of change in financial services

1970s	• Roles strictly demarcated

1980s	• Deregulation • Competitive invasions of market segments • Globalisation

1990s and 2000s	• Continuation of boundary blurring • Increasing international focus • Disintermediation • New products (e.g. ever more exotic derivatives) • Internet services/trading

Another feature of recent years has been the development of disintermediation. This means borrowing firms by-passing the banks and obtaining debt finance by selling debt securities, such as bonds, in the market. The purchasers can be individuals but are more usually the large savings institutions such as pension funds and insurance funds. Banks, having lost some interest income from lending to these large firms, have concentrated instead on fee income gained by arranging the sale and distribution of these securities as well as underwriting their issue.

A summary of the history of the financial services sector is provided in Exhibit 1.22.

THE FINANCIAL SYSTEM

To assist with orientating the reader within the financial system and to carry out more jargon-busting, a brief outline of the main financial services sectors and markets is given here.

The institutions

The banking sector

Retail banks

Put at its simplest, the retail banks take (small) deposits from the public which are re-packaged and lent to businesses and households. This is generally high-volume and low-value business which contrasts with wholesale banking which is low volume but each transaction is for high value. The distinction between retail and wholesale banks has become blurred over recent years as the large institutions have diversified their operations. The retail banks operate nationwide branch networks and a subset of banks provide a cheque clearance system (transferring money from one account to another) – these are the *clearing* banks. The five largest UK clearing banks are Barclays, Lloyds TSB, Royal Bank of Scotland (including NatWest), HSBC and Abbey National. Loans, overdrafts and mortgages are the main forms of retail bank lending and total lending amounted to £1,284bn in mid-2000.[4] The trend has been for retail banks to reduce their reliance on retail deposits and raise more wholesale funds from the money markets. They also get together with other banks if a large loan is required by a borrower (say £150m) rather than provide the full amount themselves as this would create an excessive exposure to one customer – this is called syndicate lending, discussed in Chapter 11.

Wholesale banks

The terms wholesale bank, merchant bank and investment bank are often used inter-changeably. There are subtle differences but for most practical purposes they can be regarded as the same. These institutions tend to deal in large sums of money – at least £250,000 – although some have set up retail arms. They concentrate on dealing with other large organisations, corporations, institutional investors and governments. While they undertake some lending their main focus is on generating commission income by providing advice and facilitating deals. There are five main areas of activity:

■ *Raising external finance for companies* These banks provide advice and arrange finance for corporate clients. Sometimes they provide loans themselves, but often they assist the setting up of a bank syndicate or make arrangements with other institutions. They will advise and assist a firm issuing a bond, they have expertise in helping firms float on the Stock Exchange and make rights issues. They may 'underwrite' a bond or share issue. (This means that they will buy any part of the issue not taken up by other investors – *see* Chapter 10). This assures the corporation that it will receive the funds it needs for its investment programme.

■ *Broking and dealing* They act as agents for the buying and selling of securities on the financial markets, including shares, bonds and Eurobonds. Some also have market-making arms which assist the operation of secondary markets (*see* Chapter 9). They also trade in the markets on their own account and assist companies with export finance.

■ *Fund management (asset management)* The investment banks offer services to rich individuals who lack the time or expertise to deal with their own investment strategies. They also manage unit and investment trusts as well as the portfolios of some pension funds and insurance companies. In addition corporations often have short-term cash flows which need managing efficiently (treasury management).

■ *Assistance in industrial restructuring* Merchant banks earn large fees from advising acquirers on mergers and assisting with the merger process. They also gain by helping target firms avoid being taken over too cheaply. Advising governments on privatisations has become an important source of fee income. Indeed, the expertise built up in the UK in the 1980s led to a major export industry as governments around the world needed to draw on the bankers' body of knowledge to help privatise large chunks of state-controlled industries. Corporate disposal programmes, such as selling off a division in a management buyout (MBO), may also need the services of a whole-sale bank.

■ *Assisting risk management using derivatives* Risk can be reduced through hedging strategies using futures, options, swaps and the like. However this is a complex area with large room for error and terrible penalties if a mistake is made (*see* Chapter 21). The banks may have specialist knowledge to offer in this area.

International banks

There are two types of international banking:

■ *Foreign banking* transactions in sterling with non-UK residents (lending/borrowing, etc.) by UK banks.

■ *Eurocurrency banking* for transactions in a currency other than that of the host country. Thus for UK banks this involves transactions in currencies other than sterling with both residents and non-residents (Chapter 11 considers this further).

The major part of international banking these days is borrowing and lending in foreign currencies. There are over 550 non-UK banks operating in London, the most prominent of which are American, German and Japanese. Their initial function was mainly to provide services for their own nationals, for example for export and import transactions, but nowadays their main emphasis is in the Eurocurrency market. Often funds are held in the UK for the purpose of trading and speculation on the foreign exchange market.

Building societies

Building societies collect funds from millions of savers by enticing them to put their money in interest-bearing accounts. The vast majority of that deposited money is then lent to people wishing to buy a home – in the form of a mortgage. Thus, they take in short-term deposits and they lend money for long periods, usually for 25 years. More recently building societies have diversified their sources of finance (e.g. using the wholesale financial markets) and increased the range of services they offer. In 2000 they had loans outstanding to house buyers and other borrowers of about £134bn.[5] The moves by the biggest societies to convert to banks has diminished building societies' significance in the mortgage market.

Finance houses

Finance houses are responsible for the financing of hire purchase agreements and other instalment credit, for example, leasing. If you buy a large durable good such as a car or a washing machine you often find that the sales assistant also tries to get you interested in taking the item on credit, so you pay for it over a period of, say, three years. It is usually not the retailer that provides the finance for the credit. The retailer usually works in conjunction with a finance house which pays the retailer the full purchase price of the good and therefore becomes the owner. You, the customer, get to use the good, but in return you have to make regular payments to the finance house, including interest. Under a hire purchase agreement, when you have made enough payments you will become the owner. Under leasing the finance house retains ownership (for more detail *see* Chapter 12). Finance houses also provide factoring services – providing cash to firms in return for receiving income from the firms' debtors when they pay up. Most of the large finance houses are subsidiaries of the major conglomerate banks. The size of the market is in the region of £10bn–£12bn (new finance provided by Finance and Leasing Association members each year).[6]

Long-term savings institutions

Pension funds

Pension funds are set up to provide pensions for members. For example, the University Superannuation Scheme (USS), to which university lecturers belong, takes about

6.35 per cent of working members' salaries each month and puts it into the fund. In addition the employing organisation pays money into the scheme. When a member retires the USS will pay a pension. Between the time of making a contribution and retirement, which may be decades, the pension trustees oversee the management of the fund. They may place some or all of the fund with specialist investment managers. This is a particularly attractive form of saving because of the generous tax relief provided. The long time horizon of the pension business means that large sums are built up and available for investment. In 2001 this sum had reached over £800bn. A typical allocation of a fund is:

■ 50–70 per cent in UK shares;

■ 10 per cent lending to UK government by buying bonds and bills;

■ 5 per cent property;

■ 10–20 per cent overseas securities;

■ 5–10 per cent other.

Insurance funds

Insurance companies engage in two types of activities:

■ *General insurance* This is insurance against specific contingencies such as fire, theft, accident, generally for a one-year period. The money collected in premiums is mostly held in financial assets which are relatively short term and liquid so that short-term commitments can be met.

■ *Life assurance* With *term assurance*, your life is assured for a specified period. If you die your beneficiaries get a pay-out. If you live you get nothing at the end of the period. With *whole-of-life* policies, the insurance company pays a capital sum upon death whenever this occurs. *Endowment* policies are more interesting from a financial systems perspective because they act as a savings vehicle as well as cover against death. The premium will be larger but after a number of years have passed the insurance company pays a substantial sum of money even if you are still alive. The life company has to take the premiums paid over, say, 10 or 25 years, and invest them wisely to satisfy its commitment to the policy holder. Millions of UK house buyers purchase with an endowment mortgage. They simply pay interest to the lender (e.g. a building society) while also placing premiums into an endowment fund. The hope is that after 25 years or so the value of the accumulated fund will equal or be greater than the capital value of the loan.

Life assurance companies also provide *annuities*. Here a policy holder pays an initial lump sum and in return receives regular payments in subsequent years. They have also moved into personal pensions.

Life assurance companies had over £900bn under management in 2001.[7] A typical fund allocation is:

■ 40–50 per cent UK shares;

■ 20 per cent lending to UK government;

■ 10 per cent property;

■ 10–15 per cent overseas securities;

■ 5–10 per cent other.

The risk spreaders

These institutions allow small savers a stake in a large diversified portfolio.

Unit trusts

Unit trusts are 'open-ended' funds, so the size of the fund and the number of units depends on the amount of money investors wish to put into the fund. If a fund of one million units suddenly doubled in size because of an inflow of investor funds it would become a fund of two million units through the creation and selling of more units. The buying and selling prices of the units are determined by the value of the fund. So if a two-million unit fund is invested in £2m worth of shares in the UK stock market the value of each unit will be £1. If over a period the value of the shares rises to £3m, the units will be worth £1.50 each. Unit holders sell units back to the managers of the unit trust if they want to liquidate their holding. The manager would then either sell the units to another investor or sell some of the underlying investments to raise cash to pay the unit holder. The units are usually quoted at two prices depending on whether you are buying (higher) or selling. There is also usually an initial charge and an on-going management charge for running the fund. Trustees supervise the funds to safeguard the interests of unit holders but employ managers to make the investment decisions – *see* Exhibit 1.23.

Exhibit 1.23 Unit trust investors, trustees and managers

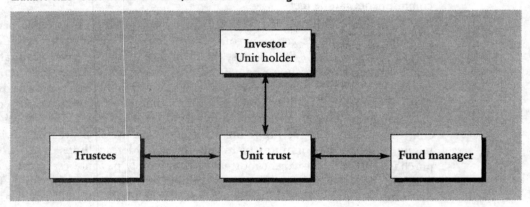

There is a wide choice of unit trust (over 1,000) specialising in different types of investments ranging from Japanese equities to privatised European companies. Of the £260bn (2001) invested, 50–60 per cent is devoted to UK company securities with the remainder mostly devoted to overseas company securities. Instruments similar to unit trusts are called mutual funds in other countries. For an example of a unit trust *see* Exhibit 1.24.

Investment trusts

Investment trusts differ from unit trusts by virtue of the fact that they are companies (rather than trusts!) able to issue shares and other securities. Investors can purchase these securities when the investment trust is first launched or purchase shares in the secondary market from other investors. These are known as closed-end funds because the company itself is closed to new investors – if you wished to invest your money you would go to an existing investor and not buy from the company. Investment trusts usu-

Exhibit 1.24 Unit trust offered by one of the 150+ managers

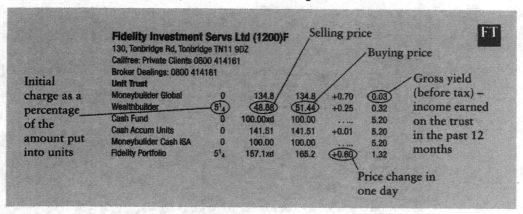

Source: *Financial Times*, 9 March 2001. Reprinted with permission.

ally spread the investors' funds across a range of other companies' shares. They are also more inclined to invest in a broader range of assets than unit trusts – even property and unlisted shares. Approximately one-half of the money devoted to UK investment trusts (£65bn) is put into UK securities, with the remainder placed in overseas securities. The managers of these funds are able to borrow in order to invest. This has the effect of increasing returns to shareholders when things go well. Correspondingly if the value of the underlying investments falls the return to shareholders falls even more, because of the obligation to meet interest charges.

Open-ended investment companies (OEICs)

Open-ended investment companies are hybrid risk-spreading instruments which allow an investment in an open-ended fund. Designed to be more flexible and transparent than either investment or unit trusts, OEICs have just one price. However, as with unit trusts, OEICs can issue more shares, in line with demand from investors, and they can borrow.

The markets

The money markets

The money markets are wholesale markets (usually involving transactions of £500,000 or more) which enable borrowing on a short-term basis (less than one year). The banks are particularly active in this market – both as lenders and as borrowers. Large corporations, local government bodies and non-banking financial institutions also lend when they have surplus cash and borrow when short of money.

The bond markets

A bond is merely a document which sets out the borrower's promise to pay sums of money in the future – usually regular interest plus a capital amount upon the maturity of the bond. These are long-dated securities (in excess of one year) issued by a variety of organisations including governments and corporations. The UK bond markets are over three centuries old and during that time they have developed very large and sophisticated primary and secondary sub-markets encompassing gilts (UK government bonds),

Exhibit 1.25 Some of the investment trusts (companies) listed in the *Financial Times*

Investment companies	Notes	Price	+ or −	52 week high	52 week low	Yield	NAV	Dis or Pm(−)
3i	♣†	1333	(−11)	1797	1001	0.9	1017.1	−31.1
3i Bioscience	♣	543	−7	$757\frac{1}{2}$	$357\frac{1}{2}$	−	593.7	8.5
3i European Technology	...	$57\frac{1}{2}$	$-\frac{1}{4}$	$136\frac{1}{2}$	53	−	56.2	−2.3
3i Smlr Quoted Cos	...†	243	+1	318	215	1.7	282.4	13.9
3i UK Select	...	110xd	$+\frac{1}{2}$	119	103	2.5	128.3	14.3
ACM Euro Enhanced	...	89	$+\frac{1}{2}$	106	86	10.1	84.0	−6.0
AIM Distribution	...ts	115	......	163	110	2.0	135.5	15.2
AIM Trust	♣	363	......	491	285	−	352.5	−3.0
AIM VCT	s	$176\frac{1}{2}$xd	......	270	170	0.8	183.3	8.7
AIM VCT 2	...	$92\frac{1}{2}$	......	120	85	−	96.1	3.8
Aberdeen Asian Smlr	...♣	$93\frac{1}{2}$	......	119	88	1.3	(113.4)	17.5
Warrants	...	$35\frac{3}{4}$	......	53	$32\frac{1}{2}$	−	−	−
Aberdeen Convertible	...♣	97	$+\frac{1}{2}$	111	96	8.4	86.3	−12.4
Aberdeen Devlpt Capital	♣†	$72\frac{1}{2}$	......	$77\frac{1}{2}$	$58\frac{1}{2}$	4.8	70.4	−3.0
Zero Div Pref	...	71	......	73	$61\frac{1}{2}$	−	64.4	−10.3
Aberdeen Emrg Ecos	...♣	$67\frac{3}{4}$	$+\frac{3}{4}$	78	60	−	83.6	18.9
Warrants	...	17	+1	$22\frac{1}{2}$	$12\frac{3}{4}$	−	−	−
Aberdeen High Inc	...♣†	$86\frac{1}{2}$	......	118	$85\frac{1}{2}$	11.6	70.5	−22.7
Aberseen Latin Amer	...♣	$66\frac{1}{2}$	......	$77\frac{1}{4}$	$58\frac{1}{2}$	−	83.2	20.1
Warrants	...	$15\frac{3}{4}$	......	26	$15\frac{1}{2}$	−	−	−
Aberdeen New Dawn	...♣	185	......	$195\frac{1}{2}$	$152\frac{1}{2}$	0.9	220.1	16.0
Aberdeen New Thai	...♣	$40\frac{1}{2}$	$-\frac{3}{4}$	$48\frac{1}{2}$	$33\frac{1}{2}$	0.6	45.6	11.2
Aberdeen Pfd	...♣	116	......	153	$115\frac{1}{2}$	15.2	88.5	−31.1
$5\frac{5}{8}$pc RPI Deb 2007	...	£$114\frac{3}{16}$	$-\frac{3}{32}$	£$116\frac{5}{16}$	£113	4.8	−	−
Units $8\frac{1}{4}$pc Ln' 23	...	£$102\frac{29}{32}$	$-\frac{15}{32}$	£$105\frac{3}{8}$	£$98\frac{23}{32}$	8.0	−	−
Aberdeen Pfd Zero Dv Pf	...	$272\frac{1}{2}$	......	$277\frac{1}{2}$	$245\frac{3}{4}$	−	269.9	−1.0
Aberdeen Pf Scs ZDv Pf 08		110	......	$111\frac{3}{4}$	101	−	102.7	−7.2
Aberforth Smlr	...	(337½)	......	338	$233\frac{3}{4}$	(2.6)	378.4	(10.8)

Annotations on the exhibit:

Change in price in one day

Net asset value. The value of the investment owned by the investment trust per share

The discount on the trust's share price compared with it NAV per share as a percentage

Closing price

Gross yield: dividend income before tax as a percentage of the share price

Source: Financial Times, 9 March 2001. Reprinted with permission.

corporate bonds, local authority bonds and Eurobonds, amongst others. The annual turnover of gilt-edged stocks alone is over £1,692bn and the government has over £380bn (2001) of bond debt outstanding. Bonds as a source of finance for firms will be examined in Chapter 11.

The foreign exchange markets (Forex or FX)

The foreign exchange markets are the markets in which one currency is exchanged for another. They include the *spot* market where currencies are bought and sold for 'immediate' delivery (in reality, two days later) and the *forward* markets, where the deal is agreed now to exchange currencies at some fixed point in the future. Also currency *futures* and *options* and other forex derivatives are employed to hedge risk and to speculate. The forex markets are dominated by the major banks, with dealing taking place 24 hours a day around the globe. Chapter 22 looks at how a company could use the forex market to facilitate international trade and reduce the risk attached to business transactions abroad.

The share markets

The London Stock Exchange is an important potential source of long-term equity (ownership) capital. Firms can raise finance in the primary market by a new issue, a rights issue, open offer, etc., either in the main listed London Market (the Official List), the techMARK, or on the Alternative Investment Market. Subsequently investors are able to buy and sell to each other on the very active secondary market. Chapters 9 and 10 examine stock markets and the raising of equity capital.

The derivative markets

A derivative is a financial instrument derived from other financial securities or some other underlying asset. For example, a future is the right to buy something (e.g. currency, shares, bond) at some date in the future at an agreed price. This *right* becomes a saleable derived financial instrument. The performance of the derivative depends on the behaviour of the underlying asset. These markets are concerned with the management and transfer of risk. They can be used to reduce risk (hedging) or to speculate. The London International Financial Futures and Options Exchange (LIFFE) trades options and futures in shares, bonds and interest rates. This used to be the only one of the markets listed here to have a trading floor where face-to-face dealing took place on an open outcry system (traders shouting and signalling to each other, face-to-face in a trading pit, the price at which they are willing to buy and sell). Now all the financial markets (money, bond, forex, derivative and share markets) are conducted using computers (and telephones) from isolated trading rooms located in the major financial institutions. In the derivative markets a high proportion of trade takes place on what is called the over-the-counter (OTC) market rather than on a regulated exchange. The OTC market flexibility allows the creation of tailor-made derivatives to suit a client's risk situation. The practical use of derivatives is examined in Chapter 21.

CONCLUDING COMMENTS

We now have a clear guiding principle set as our objective for the myriad financial decisions discussed later in this book: maximise shareholder wealth. Whether we are considering a major investment programme, or trying to decide on the best kind of finance to use, the criterion of creating value for shareholders over the long run will be paramount. A single objective is set primarily for practical reasons to aid exposition in this text, and anyone wishing to set another goal should not be discouraged from doing so. Many of the techniques described in later chapters will be applicable to organisations with other purposes as they stand, others will need slight modification.

There is an old joke about financial service firms: they just shovel money from one place to another making sure that some of it sticks to the shovel. The implication is that they contribute little to the well-being of society. Extremists even go so far as to regard these firms as parasites on the 'really productive' parts of the economies. And yet very few people avoid extensive use of financial services. Most have bank and building society accounts, pay insurance premiums and contribute to pension schemes. People do not put their money into a bank account unless they get something in return. Likewise building societies, insurance companies, pension funds, unit trusts, merchant banks and so on can only survive if they offer a service people find beneficial and are willing to pay for. Describing the mobilisation and employment of money in the service of productive investment as pointless or merely 'shovelling it around the system' is as logical as saying that the transport firms which bring goods to the high street do not provide a valuable service because there is an absence of a tangible 'thing' created by their activities.

Final thought

If 200 years ago, when the economy was mainly agrarian, you had told people that one day less than 2 per cent of the working population would produce all the food required for a population of 59 million you would have been laughed out of town. Given the lessons of the history of the last 200 years, where will the balance of economic power go over the next few decades in terms of employment and output?

KEY POINTS AND CONCEPTS

- Firms should clearly define the **objective** of the enterprise to provide a focus for decision making.

- **Sound financial management** is necessary for the achievement of all **stakeholder** goals.

- Some stakeholders will have their returns **satisficed** – given just enough to make their contribution. One (or more) group(s) will have their returns **maximised** – given any surplus after all others have been satisfied.

- The assumed objective of the firm for finance is to **maximise shareholder wealth**. Reasons:
  - **practical**, a single objective leads to clearer decisions;
  - the **contractual theory**;
  - **survival** in a competitive world;
  - it is better for **society**;
  - they **own** the firm.

- **Maximising shareholder wealth** is **maximising purchasing power** or **maximising the flow of discounted cash flow** to shareholders over a long time horizon. In an efficient stock market this equates to **maximising the current share price**.

- **Profit maximisation** is not the same as shareholder wealth maximisation. Some factors a profit comparison does not allow for:
  - future prospects;
  - risk;
  - accounting problems;
  - communication;
  - additional capital.

- Large corporations usually have a **separation of ownership and control**. This may lead to **managerialism** where the agent (the managers) take decisions primarily with their interests in mind rather than those of the principals (the shareholders). This is a **principal–agent problem**. Some solutions:
  - link managerial rewards to shareholder wealth improvement;
  - sackings;
  - selling shares and the takeover threat;
  - corporate governance regulation;
  - improve information flow.

- The efficiency of production and the well-being of consumers can be improved with the introduction of **money** to a **barter economy**.

- **Financial institutions and markets** encourage growth and progress by **mobilising savings** and encouraging investment.

- Financial managers contribute to firms' success primarily through **investment and finance decisions**. Their knowledge of financial markets, investment appraisal methods, treasury and risk management techniques are vital for company growth and stability.

- Financial institutions encourage the flow of saving into investment by acting as **brokers** and **asset transformers**, thus alleviating the **conflict of preferences** between the **primary investors** (households) and the **ultimate borrowers** (firms).

- **Asset transformation** is the creation of an intermediate security with characteristics appealing to the primary investor to attract funds, which are then made available to the ultimate borrower in a form appropriate to them. Types of asset transformation:
  - risk transformation;
  - maturity transformation;
  - volume transformation.

- Intermediaries are able to transform assets and encourage the flow of funds because of their **economies of scale** *vis-à-vis* the individual investor:
  - efficiencies in gathering information;
  - risk spreading;
  - transaction costs.

- The **secondary markets** in financial securities encourage investment by enabling investor liquidity (being able to sell quickly and cheaply to another investor) while providing the firm with long-term funds.

- The **financial services sector** has grown to be of great economic significance in the UK. Reasons:
  - high income elasticity;
  - international comparative advantage.

- The financial sector has shown remarkable **dynamism, innovation and adaptability** over the last three decades. Deregulation, new technology, globalisation and the rapid development of new financial products have characterised this sector.

- **Banking sector:**
  - **Retail banks** – high-volume and low-value business.
  - **Wholesale banks** – low-volume and high-value business. Mostly fee based.
  - **International banks** – mostly Eurocurrency transactions.
  - **Building societies** – still primarily small deposits aggregated for mortgage lending.
  - **Finance houses** – hire purchase, leasing, factoring.

- **Long-term savings institutions:**
  - **Pension funds** – major investors in financial assets.
  - **Insurance funds** – life assurance and endowment policies provide large investment funds.

- **The risk spreaders:**
  - **Unit trusts** – genuine trusts which are open-ended investment vehicles.
  - **Investment trusts** – companies which invest in other companies' financial securities, particularly shares.
  - **Open-ended investment companies** (OEICs) – a hybrid between unit and investment trusts.

- **The markets:**
  - **The money markets** are short-term wholesale lending and/or borrowing markets.
  - **The bond markets** deal in long-term bond debt issued by corporations, governments, local authorities and so on, and usually have a secondary market.
  - **The foreign exchange market** – one currency is exchanged for another.
  - **The share market** – primary and secondary trading in companies' shares takes place on the official list of the London Stock Exchange, techMARK and the Alternative Investment Market.
  - **The derivatives market** – LIFFE dominates the 'exchange-traded' derivatives market in options and futures. However there is a flourishing over-the-counter market.

REFERENCES AND FURTHER READING

Anthony, R.N. (1960) 'The trouble with profit maximisation', *Harvard Business Review*, Nov.–Dec., pp. 126–34. Challenges the conventional economic view of profit maximisation on grounds of realism and morality.

Arnold, G.C. (2000) 'Tracing the development of value-based management'. In Glen Arnold and Matt Davies (eds), *Value-based Management: Context and Application*. London: Wiley. A more detailed discussion of the objective of the firm is presented.

Blake, D. (2000) *Financial Market Analysis*. 2nd edn. London: Wiley. A more detailed introduction to the financial markets.

Brett, M. (2000) *How to Read the Financial Pages*, 5th edn. London: Random House. A well-written simple guide to the financial markets.

Buckle, M. and Thompson, J. (1995) *The UK Financial System*. 2nd edn. Manchester: Manchester University Press. Clear, elegant and concise description.

'The Cadbury Report' (1992) *Report of the Committee on the Financial aspects of Corporate Governance*. London: Gee. The first and most thorough of the three reports on corporate governance – easy to read.

Cannon, T. (1994) *Social Responsibility*. London: Pitman Publishing. A clear discussion of the corporate objective and governance.

Copeland, T., Koller, T. and Murrin, J. (1996) *Valuation*. 2nd edn. New York: McKinsey and Co. Inc. Contends that shareholder wealth should be the focus of managerial actions.

Donaldson, G. (1963) 'Financial goals: management vs. stockholders', *Harvard Business Review*, May–June, pp. 116–29. Clear and concise discussion of the conflict of interest between managers and shareholders.

Doyle, P. (1994) 'Setting business objectives and measuring performance', *Journal of General Management*, Winter, pp. 1–19. Western firms are over-focused on short-term financial goals (profit, ROI). Reconciling the interests of stakeholders should not be difficult as they are 'satisficers' rather than maximisers.

Fama, E.F. (1980) 'Agency problems and the theory of the firm', *Journal of Political Economy*, Spring, pp. 288–307. Explains how the separation of ownership and control can lead to an efficient form of economic organisation.

Friedman, M. (1970) 'The social responsibility of business is to increase its profits', *New York Times Magazine*, 30 Sept. A viewpoint on the objective of the firm.

Galbraith, J. (1967) 'The goals of an industrial system' (excerpt from *The new industrial state*). Reproduced in H.I. Ansoff, *Business Strategy*, London: Penguin, 1969. Survival, sales and expansion of the 'technostructure' are emphasised as the goals in real-world corporations.

Gardiner, E. and Molyneux, P. (eds) (1996) *Investment banking: theory and practice*. London: Euromoney Books. An overview of merchant banking.

'The Greenbury Report' (1995) *Directors' remuneration: report of a Study Group chaired by Sir Richard Greenbury*. London: Gee. One of the three reports designed to improve corporate governance.

Grinyer, J.R. (1986) 'An alternative to maximisation of shareholder wealth in capital budgeting decisions', *Accounting and Business Research*, Autumn, pp. 319–26. Discusses the maximisation of monetary surplus as an alternative to shareholder wealth.

'The Hampel Report' (1998) *The Committee on Corporate Governance, Final report*. London: Gee. The final report attempting to improve corporate behaviour.

Hart, O.D. (1995a) *Firms, Contracts and Financial Structure*. Oxford: Clarendon Press. A clear articulation of the principal–agent problem.

Hart, O.D. (1995b) 'Corporate governance: some theory and implications'. *Economic Journal*, 105, pp. 678–9. Principal–agent problem discussed.

Hayek, F.A. (1969) 'The corporation in a democratic society: in whose interests ought it and will it be run?' Reprinted in H.I. Ansoff, *Business Strategy*, London: Penguin, 1969. Objective should be long-run return on owners' capital subject to restraint by general legal and moral rules.

Jensen, M.C. (1986) 'Agency costs of free cash flow, corporate finance and takeovers', *American Economic Review*, 76, pp. 323–9. Agency cost theory applied to the issue of the use to which managers put business cash inflows.

Jensen, M.C. and Meckling, W.H. (1976) 'Theory of the firm: managerial behavior, agency costs and ownership structure', *Journal of Financial Economics*, Oct., Vol. 3, pp. 305–60. Seminal work on agency theory.

Keasey, K., Thompson, S. and Wright, M. (1997) *Corporate Governance: Economic, Management and Financial Issues*. Oxford: Oxford University Press. An edited collection of monographs, some of which deal with the question of the objective of the firm.

Levinson, M. (1999) *Guide to Financial Markets*. London: The Economist Books. A clear, brief account of modern financial markets.

Sheridan, T. and Kendall, N. (1992) *Corporate Governance*. London: Pitman Publishing. Discussion of the way in which modern corporations are directed and governed.

Simon, H.A. (1959) 'Theories of decision making in economics and behavioural science', *American Economic Review*, June. Traditional economic theories are challenged, drawing on psychology. Discusses the goals of the firm: satisficing vs. maximising.

Simon, H.A. (1964) 'On the concept of organisational goals', *Administrative Science Quarterly*, 9(1), June, pp. 1–22. Discusses the complexity of goal setting.

Smith, A. (1776) *The Wealth of Nations*. Reproduced in 1910 in two volumes by J.M. Dent, London. An early viewpoint on the objective of the firm.

Vaitilingam, R. (2001) *The Financial Times Guide to using the Financial Pages*. 4th edn. London: Financial Times Prentice Hall. Good introductory source of information. Clear and concise.

Williamson, O. (1963) 'Managerial discretion and business behaviour', *American Economic Review*, 53, pp. 1033–57. Managerial security, power, prestige, etc. are powerful motivating forces. These goals may lead to less than profit maximising behaviour.

WEBSITES

Association of British Insurers www.abi.org.uk

Association of Investment Trust Companies www.aitc.co.uk

Association of Unit Trusts and Investment Funds www.autif.org.uk

Bank of England www.bankofengland.co.uk

British Bankers Association www.bankfacts.org.uk

British Venture Capital Association www.bvca.co.uk

Building Societies Association www.bsa.org.uk

Chartered Institute of Bankers www.cib.org.uk

Companies House www.companieshouse.gov.uk

Finance and Leasing association www.fla.org.uk

Financial Times www.FT.com

National Association of Pension Funds www.napf.co.uk

London International Financial Futures and Options Exchange www.liffe.com or www.liffe.co.uk

London Stock Exchange www.londonstockexchange.com

SELF-REVIEW QUESTIONS

1 Why is it important to specify a goal for the corporation?

2 How can 'goal congruence' for managers and shareholders be achieved?

3 How does money assist the well-being of society?

4 What are the economies of scale of intermediaries?

5 Distinguish between a primary market and a secondary market. How does the secondary market aid the effectiveness of the primary market?

6 Illustrate the flow of funds between primary investors and ultimate borrowers in a modern economy. Give examples of intermediary activity.

7 List as many financial intermediaries as you can. Describe the nature of their intermediation and explain the intermediate securities they create.

8 What is the principal–agent problem?

9 What is the 'contractual theory'? Do you regard it as a strong argument?

10 What difficulties might arise in state-owned industries in making financial decisions?

11 Briefly describe the following types of decisions (give examples):
  a Financing
  b Investment
  c Treasury
  d Risk management
  e Strategic.

12 Briefly explain the role of the following:
   a The money markets
   b The bond markets
   c The foreign exchange markets
   d The share markets
   e The derivatives market.

QUESTIONS AND PROBLEMS

1 Explain the rationale for selecting shareholder wealth maximisation as the objective of the firm. Include a consideration of profit maximisation as an alternative goal.

2 What benefits are derived from the financial services sector which have led to its growth over recent years in terms of employment and share of GDP?

3 What is managerialism and how might it be incompatible with shareholder interests?

4 Why has an increasing share of household savings been channelled through financial intermediaries?

5 Discuss the relationship between economic growth and the development of a financial services sector.

6 Firm A has a stock market value of £20m (number of shares in issue x share price), while firm B is valued at £15m. The firms have similar profit histories:

	Firm A	Firm B
1997	1.5	1.8
1998	1.6	1.0
1999	1.7	2.3
2000	1.8	1.5
2001	2.0	2.0

Provide reasons why, despite the same total profit over the last five years, shareholders regard firm A as being worth £5m more (extend your thoughts beyond the numbers in the table).

7 The chief executive of Geight plc receives a salary of £80,000 plus 4 per cent of sales. Will this encourage the adoption of decisions which are shareholder wealth enhancing? How might you change matters to persuade the chief executive to focus on shareholder wealth in all decision-making?

ASSIGNMENTS

1 Consider the organisations where you have worked in the past and the people you have come into contact with. List as many objectives as you can, explicit or implicit, that have been revealed to, or suspected, by you. To what extent was goal congruence between different stakeholders achieved? How might the efforts of all individuals be channelled more effectively?

2 Review all the financial services you or your firm purchase. Try to establish a rough estimate of the cost of using each financial intermediary and write a balanced report considering whether you or your firm should continue to pay for that service.

CHAPTER NOTES

1 LIFFE: www.liffe.co.uk
2 BIS.
3 Office for National Statistics, *UK National Accounts (The Blue Book)*.
4 Office for National Statistics, *Financial Statistics*.
5 Office for National Statistics, *Financial Statistics*.
6 Finance and Leasing Association.
7 Office for National Statistics, *Financial Statistics*.
8 Bank of England.

Chapter 2

PROJECT APPRAISAL: NET PRESENT VALUE AND INTERNAL RATE OF RETURN

INTRODUCTION

Shareholders supply funds to a firm for a reason. That reason, generally, is to receive a return on their precious resources. The return is generated by management using the finance provided to invest in real assets. It is vital for the health of the firm and the economic welfare of the finance providers that management employ the best techniques available when analysing which of all the possible investment opportunities will give the best return.

Someone (or a group) within the organisation may have to take the bold decision on whether it is better to build a new factory or extend the old; whether it is wiser to use an empty piece of land for a multi-storey car park or to invest a larger sum and build a shopping centre; whether shareholders would be better off if the firm returned their money in the form of dividends because shareholders can obtain a better return elsewhere, or whether the firm should pursue its expansion plan and invest in that new chain of hotels, or that large car showroom, or the new football stand.

These sorts of decisions require not only brave people, but informed people; individuals of the required calibre need to be informed about a range of issues: for example, the market environment and level of demand for the proposed activity, the internal environment, culture and capabilities of the firm, the types and levels of cost elements in the proposed area of activity, and, of course, an understanding of the risk and uncertainty appertaining to the project.

Kingfisher presumably considered all these factors before making their multi-million pound investments – *see* Case study 2.1.

Kingfisher

The 2000 annual report for Kingfisher shows that the company spent £817m investing in the business. The chairman, Sir John Banham, comments:

> This year was characterized by record organic growth and a wide range of innovations and investments . . . including the £23.3 million costs of e-commerce and other new channel development . . . We also grew our business in new markets, for example expanding rapidly in Poland, a fast growing DIY market, and we opened our first store, a B&Q, in China. Overall the group opened 120 new stores . . . we have also gained massively from our investment in LibertySurf, the French Internet Service Provider.

Kingfisher not only invested in stores around the world. It had investment projects in: building strong retail brands; improving sourcing and supply chain management systems; e-commerce channels to customers and suppliers; fulfilment and delivery; property; and in a whole host of other assets and activities designed to create value for shareholders.

Bravery, information, knowledge and a sense of proportion are all essential ingredients when undertaking the onerous task of investing other people's money, but there is another element which is also of crucial importance, that is, the employment of an investment appraisal technique which leads to the 'correct' decision; a technique which takes into account the fundamental considerations.

In this chapter we examine two approaches to evaluating investments within the firm. Both emphasise the central importance of the concept of the time value of money and are thus described as Discounted Cash Flow (DCF) techniques. Net present value (NPV) and internal rate of return (IRR) are in common usage in most large commercial organisations and are regarded as more complete than the traditional techniques of payback and accounting rate of return (e.g. Return on Capital Employed – ROCE). The relative merits and demerits of these alternative methods are discussed in Chapter 4 in conjunction with a consideration of some of the practical issues of project implementation. In this chapter we concentrate on gaining an understanding of how net present value and internal rate of return are calculated, as well as their theoretical under-pinnings.

Learning objectives

By the end of the chapter the student should be able to demonstrate an understanding of the fundamental theoretical justifications for using discounted cash flow techniques in analysing major investment decisions, based on the concepts of the time value of money and the opportunity cost of capital. More specifically the student should be able to:

- calculate net present value and internal rate of return;

- show an appreciation of the relationship between net present value and internal rate of return;

- describe and explain at least two potential problems that can arise with internal rate of return in specific circumstances;

- demonstrate awareness of the propensity for management to favour a percentage measure of investment performance and be able to use the modified internal rate of return.

VALUE CREATION AND CORPORATE INVESTMENT

The objective of investment within the firm is to create value for its owners, the shareholders. The purpose of allocating money to a particular division or project is to generate a cash inflow in the future, significantly greater than the amount invested. Thus, put most simply, the project appraisal decision is one involving the comparison of the amount of cash put into an investment with the amount of cash returned. The key phrase and the tricky issue is 'significantly greater than'. For instance, would you, as part-owner of a firm, be content if that firm asked you to swap £10,000 of your hard-earned money for some new shares so that the management team could invest it in order to hand back to you, in five years, the £10,000 plus £1,000? Is this a significant return? Would you feel that your wealth had been enhanced if you were aware that by investing the £10,000 yourself, by, for instance, lending to the government, you could have received a 5 per cent return per year? Or that you could obtain a return of 15 per cent per annum by investing in other shares on the stock market? Naturally, you would feel let down by a management team that offered a return of less than 2 per cent per year when you had alternative courses of action which would have produced much more.

This line of thought is leading us to a central concept in finance and, indeed, in business generally – the time value of money. Investors have alternative uses for their funds and they therefore have an opportunity cost if money is invested in a corporate project. The *investor's opportunity cost* is the sacrifice of the return available on the forgone alternative.

Investments must generate at least enough cash for all investors to obtain their required returns. If they produce less than the investor's opportunity cost then the wealth of shareholders will decline.

Exhibit 2.1 summarises the process of good investment appraisal. The acheivement of value or wealth creation is determined not only by the future cash flows to be derived from a project but also by the timing of those cash flows and by making an allowance for the fact that time has value.

Exhibit 2.1 Investment appraisal: objective, inputs and process

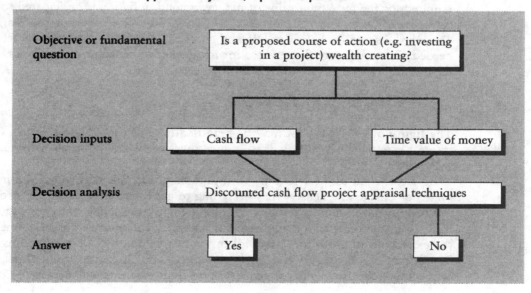

The time value of money

When people undertake to set aside money for investment something has to be given up now. For instance, if someone buys shares in a firm or lends to a business there is a sacrifice of consumption. One of the incentives to save is the possibility of gaining a higher level of future consumption by sacrificing some present consumption. Therefore, it is apparent that compensation is required to induce people to make a consumption sacrifice. Compensation will be required for at least three things:

- *Time* That is, individuals generally prefer to have £1.00 today than £1.00 in five years' time. To put this formally: the utility of £1.00 now is greater than £1.00 received five years hence. Individuals are predisposed towards *impatience to consume*, thus they need an appropriate reward to begin the saving process. The rate of exchange between certain future consumption and certain current consumption is the *pure rate of interest* – this occurs even in a world of no inflation and no risk. If you lived in such a world you might be willing to sacrifice £100 of consumption now if you were compensated with £104 to be received in one year. This would mean that your pure rate of interest is 4 per cent.

- *Inflation* The price of time (or the interest rate needed to compensate for time preference) exists even when there is no inflation, simply because people generally prefer consumption now to consumption later. If there is inflation then the providers of finance will have to be compensated for that loss in purchasing power as well as for time.

- *Risk* The promise of the receipt of a sum of money some years hence generally carries with it an element of risk; the payout may not take place or the amount may be less than expected. Risk simply means that the future return has a variety of possible values. Thus, the issuer of a security, whether it be a share, a bond or a bank account, must be prepared to compensate the investor for time, inflation and risk involved, otherwise no one will be willing to buy the security.

Take the case of Mrs Ann Investor who is considering a £1,000 one-year investment and requires compensation for three elements of time value. First, a return of 4 per cent is required for the pure time value of money. Second, inflation is anticipated to be 10 per cent over the year. Thus, at time zero (t_0) £1,000 buys one basket of goods and services. To buy the same basket of goods and services at time t_1 (one year later) £1,100 is needed. To compensate the investor for impatience to consume and inflation the investment needs to generate a return of 14.4 per cent, that is:

$$(1 + 0.04)\,(1 + 0.1) - 1 = 0.144$$

The figure of 14.4 per cent may be regarded here as the risk-free return (RFR), the interest rate which is sufficient to induce investment assuming no uncertainty about cash flows.

Investors tend to view lending to reputable governments through the purchase of bonds or bills as the nearest they are going to get to risk-free investing, because these institutions have unlimited ability to raise income from taxes or to create money. The RFR forms the bedrock for time value of money calculations as the pure time value and the expected inflation rate affect all investments equally. Whether the investment is in property, bonds, shares or a factory, if expected inflation rises from 10 per cent to 12 per cent then the investor's required return on all investments will increase by 2 per cent.

However, different investment categories carry different degrees of uncertainty about the outcome of the investment. For instance, an investment on the Russian stock market, with its high volatility, may be regarded as more risky than the purchase of a share in BP with its steady growth prospects. Investors require different risk premiums on top of the RFR to reflect the perceived level of extra risk. Thus:

> Required return = RFR + Risk premium
> (Time value of money)

In the case of Mrs Ann Investor, the risk premium pushes up the total return required to, say, 19 per cent, thus giving full compensation for all three elements of the time value of money.

Discounted cash flow

The net present value and internal rate of return techniques, both being discounted cash flow methods, take into account the time value of money. Exhibit 2.2, which presents Project Alpha, suggests that on a straightforward analysis, Project Alpha generates more cash inflows than outflows. An outlay of £2,000 produces £2,400.

Exhibit 2.2 Project Alpha, simple cash flow

Points in time (yearly intervals)	Cash flows (£)
0 Now	–2,000
1 (1 year from now)	+600
2	+600
3	+600
4	+600

However, we may be foolish to accept Project Alpha on the basis of this crude methodology. The £600 cash flows occur at different times and are therefore worth different amounts to a person standing at time zero. Quite naturally, such an individual would value the £600 received in one year more highly than the £600 received after four years. In other words, the present value of the pounds (at time zero) depends on when they are received.

It would be useful to convert all these different 'qualities' of pounds to a common currency, to some sort of common denominator. The conversion process is achieved by discounting all future cash flows by the time value of money, thereby expressing them as an equivalent amount received at time zero. The process of discounting relies on a variant of the compounding formula:

$$F = P (1 + i)^n$$

where F = future value
  P = present value
  i = interest rate
  n = number of years over which compounding takes place

> **Note**
>
> It will be most important for many readers to turn to Appendix 2.1 at this point to get to grips with the key mathematical tools which will be used in this chapter and throughout the rest of the book. Readers are also strongly advised to attempt the Appendix 2.1 exercises (answers for which are provided in Appendix VI at the end of the book).

Thus, if a saver deposited £100 in a bank account paying interest at 8 per cent per annum, after three years the account will contain £125.97:

$$F = 100 (1 + 0.08)^3 = £125.97$$

This formula can be changed so that we can answer the following question: 'How much must I deposit in the bank now to receive £125.97 in three years?'

$$P = \frac{F}{(1 + i)^n} \text{ or } F \times \frac{1}{(1 + i)^n}$$

$$P = \frac{125.97}{(1 + 0.08)^3} = 100$$

In this second case we have discounted the £125.97 back to a present value of £100. If this technique is now applied to Project Alpha to convert all the money cash flows of future years into their present value equivalents the result is as follows (assuming that the time value of money is 19 per cent).

Exhibit 2.3 Project Alpha, discounted cash flow

Points in time (yearly intervals)	Cash flows (£)	Discounted cash flows (£)
0	–2,000	–2,000.00
1	+600	$\frac{600}{1 + 0.19} = +504.20$
2	+600	$\frac{600}{(1 + 0.19)^2} = +423.70$
3	+600	$\frac{600}{(1 + 0.19)^3} = +356.05$
4	+600	$\frac{600}{(1 + 0.19)^4} = +299.20$

We can see that, when these future pounds are converted to a common denominator, this investment involves a larger outflow (£2,000) than inflow (£1,583.15). In other words the return on the £2,000 is less than 19 per cent.

Technical aside

If your calculator has a 'powers' function (usually represented by x^y or y^x) then compounding and discounting can be accomplished relatively quickly. Alternatively, you may obtain discount factors from the table in Appendix II at the end of the book. If we take the discounting of the fourth year's cash flow for Alpha as an illustration:

Calculator: $\dfrac{1}{(1 + 0.19)^4} \times 600$

Input 1.19
Press y^x (or x^y)
Input 4
Press =
Display 2.0053
Press $^1/_x$
Display 0.4987
Multiply by 600
Answer 299.20.

Using Appendix II, look down the column 19% and along the row 4 years to find discount factor of 0.4987:

$0.4987 \times 600 = 299.20$

NET PRESENT VALUE AND INTERNAL RATE OF RETURN

Net present value: examples and definitions

The conceptual justification for, and the mathematics of, the net present value and internal rate of return methods of project appraisal will be illustrated through an imaginary but realistic decision-making process at the firm of Hard Decisions plc. This example, in addition to describing techniques, demonstrates the centrality of some key concepts such as opportunity cost and time value of money and shows the wealth-destroying effect of ignoring these issues.

Imagine you are the finance director of a large publicly quoted company called Hard Decisions plc. The board of directors have agreed that the objective of the firm should be shareholder wealth maximisation. Recently, the board appointed a new director, Mr Brightspark, as an 'ideas' man. He has a reputation as someone who can see opportunities where others see only problems. He has been hired especially to seek out new avenues for expansion and make better use of existing assets. In the past few weeks Mr Brightspark has been looking at some land that the company owns near the centre of Birmingham. This is a ten-acre site on which the flagship factory of the firm once stood; but that was 30 years ago and the site is now derelict. Mr Brightspark announces to a board meeting that he has three alternative proposals concerning the ten-acre site.

Mr Brightspark stands up to speak: Proposal 1 is to spend £5m clearing the site, cleaning it up, and decontaminating it. [The factory that stood on the site was used for chemical production.] It would then be possible to sell the ten acres to property developers for a sum of £12m in one year's time. Thus, we will make a profit of £7m over a one-year period.

Proposal 1: Clean up and sell – Mr Brightspark's figures

Clearing the site plus decontamination payable, t_0	–£5m
Sell the site in one year, t_1	£12m
Profit	£7m

The chairman of the board stops Mr Brightspark at that point and turns to you, in your capacity as the financial expert on the board, to ask what you think of the first proposal. Because you have studied assiduously on your Financial Management course you are able to make the following observations:

Point 1 This company is valued by the stock market at £100m because our investors are content that the rate of return they receive from us is consistent with the going rate for our risk class of shares; that is, 15 per cent per annum. In other words, the opportunity cost for our shareholders of buying shares in this firm is 15 per cent. (Hard Decisions is an all-equity firm, no debt capital has been raised.) The alternative to investing their money with us is to invest it in another firm with similar risk characteristics yielding 15 per cent per annum. Thus, we may take this *opportunity cost of capital* as our minimum required return from any project we undertake. This idea of opportunity cost can perhaps be better explained by the use of a diagram (*see* Exhibit 2.4).

If we give a return of less than 15 per cent then shareholders will lose out because they can obtain 15 per cent elsewhere and will, thus, suffer an opportunity cost.

We, as managers of shareholders' money, need to use a discount rate of 15 per cent for any project of the same risk class that we analyse. The discount rate is the opportunity cost of investing in the project rather than the capital markets, for example, buying shares in other firms giving a 15 per cent return. Instead of accepting this project the firm can always give the cash to the shareholders and let them invest it in financial assets.

Exhibit 2.4 The investment decision: alternative uses of firm's funds

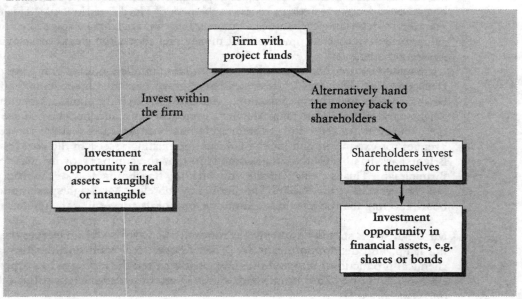

Point 2 I believe I am right in saying that we have received numerous offers for the ten-acre site over the past year. A reasonable estimate of its immediate sale value would be £6m. That is, I could call up one of the firms keen to get its hands on the site and squeeze out a price of about £6m. This £6m is an opportunity cost of the project, in that it is the value of the best alternative course of action. Thus, we should add to Mr Brightspark's £5m of clean-up costs the £6m of opportunity cost because we are truly sacrificing £11m to put this proposal into operation. If we did not go ahead with Mr Brightsparks' proposal, but sold the site as it is, we could raise our bank balance by £6m, plus the £5m saved by not paying clean-up costs.

Proposal 1: Clean up and sell – Year t_0 cash flows

Immediate sale value (opportunity cost)	£6m
Clean up, etc.	£5m
Total sacrifice at t_0	£11m

Point 3 I can accept Mr Brightspark's final sale price of £12m as being valid in the sense that he has, I know, employed some high quality experts to do the sum, but I do have a problem with comparing the initial outlay *directly* with the final cash flow on a simple *nominal* sum basis. The £12m is to be received in one year's time, whereas the £5m is to be handed over to the clean-up firm immediately, and the £6m opportunity cost sacrifice, by not selling the site, is being made immediately.

If we were to take the £11m initial cost of the project and invest it in financial assets of the same risk class as this firm, giving a return of 15 per cent, then the value of that investment at the end of one year would be £12.65m. Investing this sum in alternative investments:

$$F = P (1 + k)$$

where k = the opportunity cost of capital:

$$11 (1 + 0.15) = £12.65m$$

This is more than the return promised by Mr Brightspark.

Another way of looking at this problem is to calculate the net present value of the project. We start with the classic formula for net present value:

$$NPV = F_0 + \frac{F_1}{(1 + k)^n}$$

where F_0 = cash flow at time zero (t_0), and
   F_1 = cash flow at time one (t_1), one year after time zero:

$$NPV = -11 + \frac{12}{1 + 0.15} = -11 + 10.43 = -0.56m$$

All cash flows are expressed in the common currency of pounds at time zero. Thus, everything is in present value terms. When the positives and negatives are netted out we have the *net* present value. The decision rules for net present value are:

$NPV \geq 0$	Accept
$NPV < 0$	Reject

An investment proposal's net present value is derived by discounting the future net cash receipts at a rate which reflects the value of the alternative use of the funds, summing them over the life of the proposal and deducting the initial outlay.

In conclusion, Ladies and Gentlemen, given the choice between:

(a) selling the site immediately raising £6m and saving £5m of expenditure – a total of £11m, or

(b) developing the site along the lines of Mr Brightspark's proposal,

I would choose to sell it immediately because £11m would get a better return elsewhere.
The chairman thanks you and asks Mr Brightspark to explain Project Proposal 2.

Mr Brightspark: Proposal 2 consists of paying £5m immediately for a clean-up. Then, over the next two years, spending another £14m building an office complex. Tenants would not be found immediately on completion of the building. The office units would be let gradually over the following three years. Finally, when the office complex is fully let, in six years' time, it would be sold to an institution, such as a pension fund, for the sum of £40m (*see* Exhibit 2.5).

Proposal 2: Office complex – Mr Brightspark's figures

Exhibit 2.5

Points in time (yearly intervals)	Cash flows (£m)	Event
0 (now)	–5	Clean-up costs
0 (now)	–6	Opportunity cost
1	–4	Building cost
2	–10	Building cost
3	+1	Net rental income $\frac{1}{4}$ of offices let
4	+2	Net rental income $\frac{1}{2}$ of offices let
5	+4	Net rental income All offices let
6	+40	Office complex sold
TOTAL	+22	Inflow £47m Outflow £25m
PROFIT	22	

(*Note*: Mr Brightspark has accepted the validity of your argument about the opportunity cost of the alternative 'project' of selling the land immediately and has quickly added this –£6m to the figures.)

Mr Brightspark claims an almost doubling of the money invested (£25m invested over the first two years leads to an inflow of £47m).

The chairman turns to you and asks: Is this project really so beneficial to our shareholders?

You reply: The message rammed home to me by my finance textbook was that the best method of assessing whether a project is shareholder wealth enhancing is to discount all its cash flows at the opportunity cost of capital. This will enable a calculation of the net present value of those cash flows.

$$\text{NPV} = F_0 + \frac{F_1}{1 + k} + \frac{F_2}{(1 + k)^2} + \frac{F_3}{(1 + k)^3} \cdots + \frac{F_n}{(1 + k)^n}$$

So, given that Mr Brightspark's figures are true cash flows, I can calculate the NPV of Proposal 2 – *see* Exhibit 2.6.

Proposal 2: Net present values

Exhibit 2.6

Points in time (yearly intervals)	Cash flows (£m)		Discounted cash flows (£m)
0	−5		−5
0	−6		−6
1	−4	$\dfrac{-4}{(1 + 0.15)}$	−3.48
2	−10	$\dfrac{-10}{(1 + 0.15)^2}$	−7.56
3	1	$\dfrac{1}{(1 + 0.15)^3}$	0.66
4	2	$\dfrac{2}{(1 + 0.15)^4}$	1.14
5	4	$\dfrac{4}{(1 + 0.15)^5}$	1.99
6	40	$\dfrac{40}{(1 + 0.15)^6}$	17.29
Net present value			−0.96

Because the NPV is less than 0, we would serve our shareholders better by selling the site and saving the money spent on clearing and building and putting that money into financial assets yielding 15 per cent per annum. Shareholders would end up with more in Year 6.

The chairman thanks you and asks Mr Brightspark for his third proposal.

Mr Brightspark: Proposal 3 involves the use of the site for a factory to manufacture the product 'Worldbeater'. We have been producing 'Worldbeater' from our Liverpool factory for the past ten years. Despite its name, we have confined the selling of it to the UK market. I propose the setting up of a second 'Worldbeater' factory which will serve the European market. The figures are as follows (*see* Exhibit 2.7).

Proposal 3: Manufacture of 'Worldbeater' – Mr Brightspark's figures

Exhibit 2.7

Points in time (yearly intervals)	Cash flows (£m)	Event
0	–5	Clean-up
0	–6	Opportunity cost
1	–10	Factory building
2	0	
3 to infinity	+5	Net income from additional sales of 'Worldbeater'

Note: Revenue is gained in Year 2 from sales but this is exactly offset by the cash flows created by the costs of production and distribution. The figures for Year 3 and all subsequent years are net cash flows, that is, cash outflows are subtracted from cash inflows generated by sales.

The chairman turns to you and asks your advice.

You reply: Worldbeater is a well-established product and has been very successful. I am happy to take the cash flow figures given by Mr Brightspark as the basis for my calculations, which are as follows (*see* Exhibit 2.8).

Proposal 3: Worldbeater manufacturing plant

This project gives an NPV which is positive, and therefore is shareholder wealth enhancing. The third project gives a rate of return which is greater than 15 per cent per annum. It provides a return of 15 per cent plus a present value of £5.5m. Based on these figures I would recommend that the board looks into proposal 3 in more detail.

The chairman thanks you and suggests that this proposal be put to the vote.

Mr Brightspark (interrupts): Just a minute, are we not taking a lot on trust here? Our finance expert has stated that the way to evaluate these proposals is by using the NPV method, but in the firms where I have worked in the past, the internal rate of return (IRR) method of investment appraisal was used. I would like to see how these three proposals shape up when the IRR calculations are done.

The chairman turns to you and asks you to explain the IRR method, and to apply it to the figures provided by Mr Brightspark.

Exhibit 2.8

Points in time (yearly intervals)	Cash flows (£m)		Discounted cash flows (£m)
0	−11		−11
1	−10	$\dfrac{-10}{(1+0.15)}$	−8.7
2	0		
3 to infinity	5	Value of perpetuity at time t_2: $P = \dfrac{F}{k} = \dfrac{5}{0.15} = 33.33.$	
		This has to be discounted back two years: $\dfrac{33.33}{(1+0.15)^2}$	= 25.20
Net present value			+5.5

Note: If these calculations are confusing you are advised to read the mathematical Appendix 2.1 at the end of this chapter.

Before continuing this boardroom drama it might be useful at this point to broaden the understanding of NPV by considering two worked examples.

Worked example 2.1 Camrat plc

Camrat plc requires a return on investment of at least 10 per cent per annum over the life of a project in order to meet the opportunity cost of its shareholders (Camrat is financed entirely by equity). The dynamic and thrusting strategic development team have been examining the possibility of entering the new market area of mosaic floor tiles. This will require an immediate outlay of £1m for factory purchase and tooling-up which will be followed by *net* (i.e. after all cash outflows, e.g. wages, variable costs, etc.) cash inflows of £0.2m in one year, and £0.3m in two years' time. Thereafter, annual net cash inflows will be £180,000.

Required
Given these cash flows, will this investment provide a 10 per cent return (per annum) over the life of the project? Assume for simplicity that all cash flows arise on anniversary dates.

Answer
First, lay out the cash flows with precise timing. (Note: the assumption that all cash flows arise on anniversary dates allows us to do this very simply.)

Points in time (yearly intervals)	0	1	2	3 to infinity
Cash flows (£)	−1m	0.2m	0.3m	0.18m

Second, discount these cash flows to their present value equivalents.

Points in time	0	1	2	3 to infinity
	F_0	$\dfrac{F_1}{1 + k}$	$\dfrac{F_2}{(1 + k)^n}$	$\dfrac{F_3}{k} \times \dfrac{1}{(1 + k)^2}$
	$-1m$	$\dfrac{0.2}{1 + 0.1}$	$\dfrac{0.3}{(1 + 0.1)^2}$	$\dfrac{0.18}{0.1}$
				This discounts back two years: $\dfrac{0.18/0.1}{(1 + 0.1)^2}$
	$-1m$	0.1818	0.2479	$\dfrac{1.8}{(1.1)^2} = 1.4876$

Note

The perpetuity formula can be used on the assumption that the first payment arises one year from the time at which we are valuing. So, if the first inflow arises at time 3 we are valuing the perpetuity as though we are standing at time 2. The objective of this exercise is not to convert all cash flows to time 2 values, but rather to time 0 value. Therefore, it is necessary to discount the perpetuity value by two years.

Third, net out the discounted cash flows to give the net present value.

	-1.0000
	$+0.1818$
	$+0.2479$
	$+1.4876$
Net present value	$+0.9173$

Conclusion

The positive NPV result demonstrates that this project gives not only a return of 10 per cent per annum but a large surplus above and beyond a 10 per cent per annum return. This is an extremely attractive project: on a £1m investment the surplus generated beyond the opportunity cost of the shareholders (their time value of money) is £917,300; thus by accepting this project we would increase shareholder wealth by this amount.

Worked example 2.2 Actarm plc

Actarm plc is examining two projects, A and B. The cash flows are as follows:

	A £	B £
Initial outflow, t_0	240,000	240,000
Cash inflows:		
Time 1 (one year after t_0)	200,000	20,000
Time 2	100,000	120,000
Time 3	20,000	220,000

Using discount rates of 8 per cent, and then 16 per cent, calculate the NPVs and state which project is superior. Why do you get a different preference depending on the discount rate used?

Answer

Using 8 per cent as the discount rate:

$$NPV = F_0 + \frac{F_1}{1+k} + \frac{F_2}{(1+k)^2} + \frac{F_3}{(1+k)^3}$$

Project A

$$-240,000 + \frac{200,000}{1+0.08} + \frac{100,000}{(1+0.08)^2} + \frac{20,000}{(1+0.08)^3}$$

$$-240,000 + 185,185 + 85,734 + 15,877 = +£46,796$$

Project B

$$-240,000 + \frac{20,000}{1+0.08} + \frac{120,000}{(1+0.08)^2} + \frac{220,000}{(1+0.08)^3}$$

$$-240,000 + 18,519 + 102,881 + 174,643 = +£56,043$$

Using an 8 per cent discount rate both projects produce positive NPVs and therefore would enhance shareholder wealth. However, Project B is superior because it creates more value than Project A. Thus, if the accepting of one project excludes the possibility of accepting the other then B is preferred.

Using 16 per cent as the discount rate:
Project A

$$-240,000 + \frac{200,000}{1.16} + \frac{100,000}{(1.16)^2} + \frac{20,000}{(1.16)^3}$$

$$-240,000 + 172,414 + 74,316 + 12,813 = +£19,543$$

Project B

$$-240,000 + \frac{20,000}{1.16} + \frac{120,000}{(1.16)^2} + \frac{220,000}{(1.16)^3}$$

$$-240,000 + 17,241 + 89,180 + 140,945 = +£7,366$$

With a 16 per cent discount rate Project A generates more shareholder value and so would be preferred to Project B. This is despite the fact that Project B, in pure undiscounted cash flow terms, produces an additional £40,000.

The different ranking (order of superiority) occurs because Project B has the bulk of its cash flows occurring towards the end of the project's life. These large distant cash flows, when discounted at a high discount rate, become relatively small compared with those of Project A, which has its high cash flows discounted by only one year.

We now return to Hard Decisions plc. The chairman has asked you to explain internal rate of return (IRR).

You respond: The internal rate of return is a very popular method of project appraisal and it has much to commend it. In particular it takes into account the time value of money. I am not surprised to find that Mr Brightspark has encountered this appraisal technique in his previous employment. Basically, what the IRR tells you is the rate of interest you will receive by putting your money into a project. It describes by how much the cash inflows exceed the cash outflows on an annualised percentage basis, taking account of the timing of those cash flows.

The internal rate of return is the rate of return which equates the present value of future cash flows with the outlay (or, for some projects, it equates discounted future cash outflows with initial inflow):

Outlay = Future cash flows discounted at rate r

Thus:

$$F_0 = \frac{F_1}{1+r} + \frac{F_2}{(1+r)^2} + \frac{F_3}{(1+r)^3} \cdots \frac{F_n}{(1+r)^n}$$

IRR is also referred to as the 'yield' of a project.

Alternatively, the internal rate of return, r, is the discount rate at which the net present value is zero. It is the value for r which makes the following equation hold:

$$F_0 + \frac{F_1}{1+r} + \frac{F_2}{(1+r)^2} + \frac{F_3}{(1+r)^3} \cdots \frac{F_n}{(1+r)^n} = 0$$

(*Note*: in the first formula F_0 is expressed as a positive number, whereas in the second it is usually a negative.)

These two equations amount to the same thing. They both require knowledge of the cash flows and their precise timing. The element which is unknown is the rate of interest which will make the time-adjusted outflows and inflows equal to each other.

I apologise, Ladies and Gentlemen, if this all sounds like too much jargon. Perhaps it would be helpful if you could see the IRR calculation in action. Let's apply the formula to Mr Brightspark's Proposal 1.

Proposal 1: Internal rate of return

Using the second version of the formula, our objective is to find an r which makes the discounted inflow at time 1 of £12m plus the initial £11m outflow equal to zero:

$$F_0 + \frac{F_1}{1+r} = 0$$

$$-11 + \frac{12}{1+r} = 0$$

The method I would recommend for establishing r is trial and error (assuming we do not have the relevant computer program available). So, to start with, simply pick an interest rate and plug it into the formula.

Let us try 5 per cent:

$$-11 + \frac{12}{1 + 0.05} = £0.42857\text{m} \quad \text{or} \quad £428,571$$

A 5 per cent rate is not correct because the discounted cash flows do not total to zero. The surplus of approximately £0.43m suggests that a higher interest rate will be more suitable. This will reduce the present value of the future cash inflow.

Try 10 per cent:

$$-11 + \frac{12}{1 + 0.1} = -0.0909 \quad \text{or} \quad -£90,909$$

Again, we have not hit on the correct discount rate.

Try 9 per cent:

$$-11 + \frac{12}{1 + 0.09} = +0.009174 \quad \text{or} \quad +£9,174$$

The last two calculations tell us that the interest rate which equates to the present value of the cash flows lies somewhere between 9 per cent and 10 per cent. The precise rate can be found through interpolation.

Interpolation for Proposal 1

First, display all the facts so far established (*see* Exhibit 2.9).

Exhibit 2.9 Interpolation

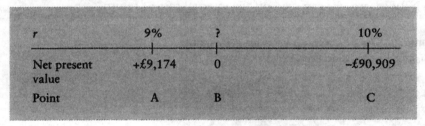

r	9%	?	10%
Net present value	+£9,174	0	−£90,909
Point	A	B	C

Exhibit 2.9 illustrates that there is a yield rate (r) which lies between 9 per cent and 10 per cent which will produce an NPV of zero. The way to find that interest rate is to first find the distance between points A and B, as a proportion of the entire distance between points A and C.

$$\frac{A \to B}{A \to C} = \frac{9,174 - 0}{9,174 + 90,909} = 0.0917$$

Thus the ? lies at a distance of 0.0917 away from the 9 per cent point.

Thus, IRR:

$$= 9 + \left(\frac{9{,}174}{100{,}083}\right) \times (10 - 9) = 9.0917 \text{ per cent}$$

To double-check our result:

$$-11 + \frac{12}{1 + 0.090917}$$

$$-11 + 11 = 0$$

Internal rate of return: examples and definitions

The rule for internal rate of return decisions is:

If $k > r$ reject

If the opportunity cost of capital (k) is greater than the internal rate of return (r) on a project then the investor is better served by not going ahead with the project and applying the money to the best alternative use.

If $k \le r$ accept

Here, the project under consideration produces the same or a higher yield than investment elsewhere for a similar risk level.

The IRR of Proposal 1 is 9.091 per cent, which is significantly below the 15 per cent opportunity cost of capital used by Hard Decisions plc. Therefore, using the IRR method as well as the NPV method, this project should be rejected.

It might be enlightening to consider the relationship between NPV and IRR. Exhibits 2.10 and 2.11 show what happens to NPV as the discount rate is varied between zero and 10 per cent for Proposal 1. At a zero discount rate the £12m received in one year is not discounted at all, so the NPV of £1m is simply the difference between the two cash flows. When the discount rate is raised to 10 per cent the present value of the year 1 cash flow becomes less than the current outlay. Where the line crosses the x axis, i.e. when NPV is zero, we can read off the internal rate of return.

Exhibit 2.10 The relationship between NPV and the discount rate (using Proposal 1's figures)

Discount rate (%)	NPV
10	−90,909
9.0917	0
9	9,174
8	111,111
7	214,953
6	320,755
5	428,571
4	538,461
3	650,485
2	764,706
1	881,188
0	1,000,000

Exhibit 2.11 The relationship between NPV and the discount rate for Project Proposal 1

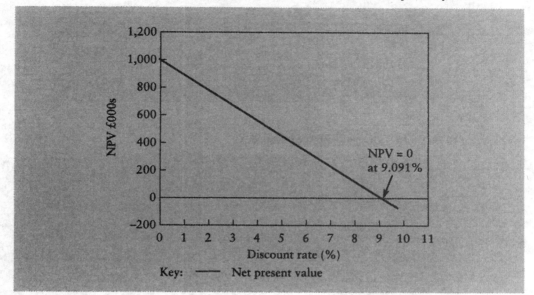

It should be noted that, in the case of Project Proposal 1 the NPV/discount rate relationship is nearly a straight line. This is an unusual case. When cash flows occur over a number of years the line is likely to be more curved and concave to the origin (at least for 'conventional cash flows' – conventional and non-conventional cash flows are discussed later in the chapter).

If the board will bear with me I can quickly run through the IRR calculations for Project Proposals 2 and 3.

Proposal 2: IRR

To calculate the IRR for Proposal 2 we first lay out the cash flows in the discount formula:

$$-11 + \frac{-4}{(1+r)} + \frac{-10}{(1+r)^2} + \frac{1}{(1+r)^3}$$

$$+ \frac{2}{(1+r)^4} + \frac{4}{(1+r)^5} + \frac{40}{(1+r)^6} = 0$$

Then we try alternative discount rates to find a rate, r, that gives a zero NPV:

Try 14 per cent:

NPV (approx.) = –£0.043 or –£43,000

    At 13 per cent:

NPV = £932,000

Interpolation[1] is required to find an internal rate of return accurate to at least one decimal place (*see* Exhibit 2.12).

$$13 + \frac{932,000}{975,000} \times (14 - 13) = 13.96\%$$

Exhibit 2.12 Interpolation

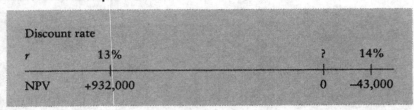

Discount rate				
r	13%		?	14%
NPV	+932,000		0	–43,000

Exhibit 2.13 Graph of NPV for Proposal 2

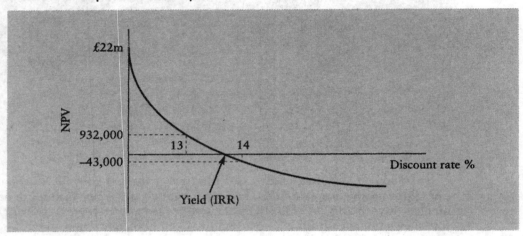

From Exhibit 2.13, we see that this project produces an IRR less than the opportunity cost of shareholders' funds; therefore it should be rejected under the IRR method. The curvature of the line is exaggerated to demonstrate the absence of linearity and emphasise the importance of having a fairly small gap in trial and error interest rates prior to interpolation. The interpolation formula assumes a straight line between the two discount rates chosen and this may lead to a false result. The effect of taking a wide range of interest rates can be illustrated if we calculate on the basis of 5 per cent and 30 per cent.

At 5 per cent, NPV of Project 2 = £11.6121m.
At 30 per cent, NPV of Project 2 = –£9.4743m.

$$5 + \left(\frac{11.6121}{11.6121 + 9.4743} \right) (30 - 5) = 18.77\%$$

Exhibit 2.14 Linear interpolation

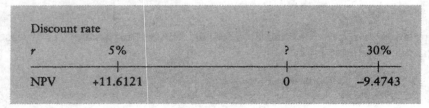

Discount rate				
r	5%		?	30%
NPV	+11.6121		0	–9.4743

Exhibit 2.15 Graph of NPV for Proposal 2 – using exaggerated linear interpolation

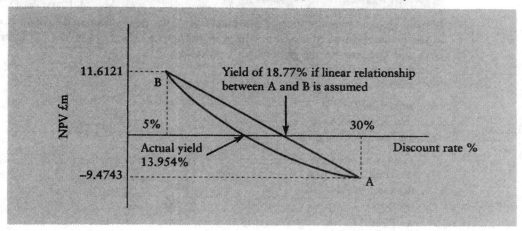

From Exhibit 2.15 we see that the non-linearity of the relationship between NPV and the discount rate has created an IRR almost 5 per cent removed from the true IRR. This could lead to an erroneous acceptance of this project given the company's hurdle rate of 15 per cent. In reality this project yields less than the company could earn by placing its money elsewhere for the same risk level.

Proposal 3: IRR

$$F_0 + \frac{F_1}{1 + r} + \frac{F_3/r}{(1 + r)^2} = 0$$

Try 19 per cent:

$$-11 + \frac{-10}{1 + 0.19} + \frac{5/0.19}{(1 + 0.19)^2} = -\pounds0.82\text{m}$$

Try 18 per cent:

$$-11 + \frac{-10}{1 + 0.18} + \frac{5/0.18}{(1 + 0.18)^2} = \pounds0.475\text{m}$$

Exhibit 2.16 Linear interpolation

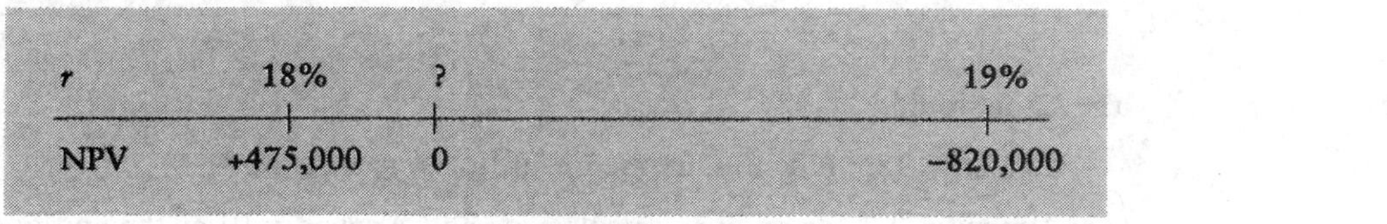

r	18%	?		19%
NPV	+475,000	0		–820,000

$$18 + \frac{475,000}{1,295,000} \times (19 - 18) = 18.37\%$$

Project 3 produces an internal rate of return of 18.37 per cent which is higher than the opportunity cost of capital and therefore is to be commended.

We temporarily leave the saga of Mr Brightspark and his proposals to reinforce understanding of NPV and IRR through the worked example of Martac plc.

Worked example 2.3 Martac plc

Martac plc is a manufacturer of *Martac-aphro*. Two new automated process machines used in the production of Martac have been introduced to the market, the CAM and the ATR. Both will give cost savings over existing processes:

£000s	CAM	ATR
Initial cost (machine purchase and installation, etc.)	120	250
Cash flow savings:		
At Time 1 (one year after the initial cash outflow)	48	90
At Time 2	48	90
At Time 3	48	90
At Time 4	48	90

All other factors remain constant and the firm has access to large amounts of capital. The required return on projects is 8 per cent.

Required
(a) Calculate the IRR for CAM.
(b) Calculate the IRR for ATR.
(c) Based on IRR which machine would you purchase?
(d) Calculate the NPV for each machine.
(e) Based on NPV which machine would you buy?
(f) Is IRR or NPV the better decision tool?

Answers
In this problem the total cash flows associated with the alternative projects are not given. Instead the incremental cash flows are provided, for example, the additional savings available over the existing costs of production. This, however, is sufficient for a decision to be made about which machine to purchase.

(a) IRR for CAM

$$F_0 + \frac{F_1}{1+r} + \frac{F_2}{(1+r)^2} + \frac{F_3}{(1+r)^3} + \frac{F_4}{(1+r)^4} = 0$$

Try 22 per cent:

$-120,000 + 48,000 \times$ annuity factor (af) for 4 years @ 22%

(*See* Appendix 2.1 for annuity calculations and Appendix III at the end of the book for an annuity table.)

The annuity factor tells us the present value of four lots of £1 received at four annual intervals. This is 2.4936, meaning that the £4 in present value terms is worth just over £2.49.

$-120,000 + 48,000 \times 2.4936 = -£307.20$

Try 21 per cent:

   −120,000 + 48,000 × annuity factor (af) for 4 years @ 21%

   −120,000 + 48,000 × 2.5404 = +£1,939.20

Exhibit 2.17   Interpolation

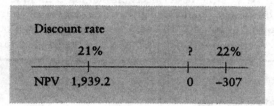

$$21 + \left(\frac{1939.2}{1939.2 + 307}\right) \times (22 - 21) = 21.86\%$$

(b) IRR for ATR

Try 16 per cent:

   −250,000 + 90,000 × 2.7982 = +£1,838

Try 17 per cent:

   −250,000 + 90,000 × 2.7432 = −£3,112

Exhibit 2.18   Interpolation

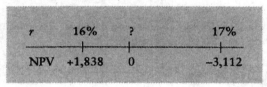

$$16 + \left(\frac{1,838}{1,838 + 3,112}\right) \times (17 - 16) = 16.37\%$$

(c) Choice of machine on basis of IRR

If IRR is the only decision tool available then as long as the IRRs exceed the discount rate (or cost of capital) the project with the higher IRR might appear to be the preferred choice. In this case CAM ranks higher than ATR.

(d) NPV for machines: CAM

   −120,000 + 48,000 × 3.3121 = +£38,981

NPV for ATR

   −250,000 + 90,000 × 3.3121 = +£48,089

(e) Choice of machine on basis of NPV

ATR generates a return which has a present value of £48,089 in addition to the minimum return on capital required. This is larger than for CAM and therefore ATR ranks higher than CAM if NPV is used as the decision tool.

(f) Choice of decision tool

This problem has produced conflicting decision outcomes, which depend on the project appraisal method employed. NPV is the better decision-making technique because it measures in absolute amounts of money. That is, it gives the increase in shareholder wealth available by accepting a project. In contrast IRR expresses its return as a percentage which may result in an inferior low-scale project being preferred to a higher-scale project.

Problems with internal rate of return

We now return to Hard Decisions plc.

Mr Brightspark: I have noticed your tendency to prefer NPV to any other method. Yet, in the three projects we have been discussing, NPV and IRR give the same decision recommendation. So, why not use IRR more often?

You reply: It is true that the NPV and IRR methods of capital investment appraisal are closely related. Both are 'time-adjusted' measures of profitability. The NPV and IRR methods gave the same result in the cases we have considered today because the problems associated with the IRR method are not present in the figures we have been working with. In the appraisal of other projects we may encounter the severe limitations of the IRR method and therefore I prefer to stick to the theoretically superior NPV technique.

I will illustrate two of the most important problems, multiple solutions and ranking.

Multiple solutions

There may be a number of possible IRRs. This can be explained by examining the problems Mr Flummoxed is having (*see* Worked example 2.4).

Worked example 2.4 Mr Flummoxed

Mr Flummoxed of Deadhead plc has always used the IRR method of project appraisal. He has started to have doubts about its usefulness after examining the proposal, 'Project Oscillation'.

Project Oscillation

Points in time (yearly intervals)	0	1	2
Cash flow	−3,000	+15,000	−13,000

Internal rates of return are found at 11.56 per cent *and* 288.4 per cent.

Given that Deadhead plc has a required rate of return of 20 per cent, it is impossible to decide whether to implement Project Oscillation using an unadjusted IRR methodology.

The cause of multiple solutions is unconventional cash flows. Conventional cash flows occur when an outflow is followed by a series of inflows or a cash inflow is followed by a series of cash outflows. Unconventional cash flows are a series of cash flows with more than one change in sign. In the case of Project Oscillation the sign changes from negative to positive once, and from positive to negative once. These two sign changes provide a clue to the number of possible solutions or IRRs. Multiple yields can be adjusted for whilst still using the IRR method, but the simplest approach is to use the NPV method.

Ranking

The IRR decision rule does not always rank projects in the same way as the NPV method. Sometimes it is important to find out, not only which project gives a positive return, but which one gives the greater positive return. For instance, projects may be mutually exclusive, that is, only one may be undertaken and a choice has to be made. The use of IRR alone sometimes leads to a poor choice (*see* Exhibit 2.19).

Exhibit 2.19 Ranking

Project	Cash flows £m		IRR%	NPV (at 15%)
	Time 0	One year later		
A	–20	+40	100%	+14.78m
B	–40	+70	75%	+20.87m

NPV at different discount rates		
Discount rate (%)	Project A	Project B
0	20	30
20	13.33	18.33
50	6.67	6.67
75	2.86	0
100	0	–5
125	–2.22	–8.89

From Exhibit 2.20 (p. 76), it is clear that the ranking of the projects by their IRRs is constant at 75 per cent and 100 per cent, regardless of the opportunity cost of capital (discount rate). Project A is always the better. On the other hand, ranking the projects by the NPV method is not fixed. The NPV ranking depends on the discount rate assumed. Thus, if the discount rate used in the NPV calculation is higher than 50 per cent, the ranking under both IRR and NPV would be the same, i.e. Project A is superior. If the discount rate falls below 50 per cent, Project B is the better choice. One of the major elements leading to the theoretical dominance of NPV is that it takes into account the scale of investment; thus the shareholders are made better off by undertaking Project B by £20.87m because the initial size of the project was larger. NPVs are measured in absolute amounts.

The board of directors of Hard Decisions are now ready for a coffee break and time to digest these concepts and techniques. The chairman thanks you for your clarity and rigorous analysis. He also thanks Mr Brightspark for originating three imaginative and thought-provoking proposals to take the business forward towards its goal of shareholder wealth enhancement.

Exhibit 2.20 **NPV at different discount rates**

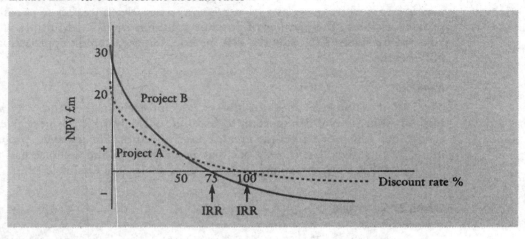

Summary of the characteristics of NPV and IRR

Exhibit 2.21 summarises the characteristics of NPV and IRR.

Exhibit 2.21 **Characteristics of NPV and IRR**

NPV	IRR
■ It recognises that £1 today is worth more than £1 tomorrow.	■ Also takes into account the time value of money.
■ In conditions where all worthwhile projects can be accepted (i.e. no mutual exclusivity) it maximises shareholder utility. Projects with a positive NPV should be accepted since they increase shareholder wealth, while those with negative NPVs decrease shareholder wealth.	■ In situations of non-mutual exclusivity, shareholder wealth is maximised if all projects with a yield higher than the opportunity cost of capital are accepted, while those with a return less than the time value of money are rejected.
■ It takes into account investment size – absolute amounts of wealth change.	■ Fails to measure in terms of absolute amounts of wealth changes. It measures percentage returns and this may cause ranking problems in conditions of mutual exclusivity, i.e. the wrong project may be rejected.
■ This is not as intuitively understandable as a percentage measure.	■ It is easier to communicate a percentage return than NPV to other managers and employees, who may not be familiar with the details of project appraisal techniques. The appeal of quick recognition and conveyance of understanding should not be belittled or underestimated.
■ It can handle non-conventional cash flows.	■ Non-conventional cash flows cause problems, e.g. multiple solutions.
■ Additivity is possible: because present values are all measured in today's £s they can be added together. Thus the returns (NPVs) of a group of projects can be calculated.	■ Additivity is not possible.

MODIFIED INTERNAL RATE OF RETURN

The fourth characteristic listed for IRR in Exhibit 2.21 is a powerful force driving its adoption in the practical world of business where few individuals have exposed themselves to the rigours of financial decision-making models, and therefore may not comprehend NPV. These issues are examined in more detail in Chapter 4, but it is perhaps worth explaining now the consequences of sticking rigidly to IRR.

One problem centres on the reinvestment assumption. With NPV it is assumed that cash inflows arising during the life of the project are reinvested at the opportunity cost of capital. In contrast the IRR implicitly assumes that the cash inflows that are received, say, half-way through a project, can be reinvested elsewhere at a rate equal to the IRR until the end of the project's life. This is intuitively unacceptable. In the real world, if a firm invested in a very high-yielding project and some cash was returned after a short period, this firm would be unlikely to be able to deposit this cash elsewhere until the end of the project and reach the same extraordinary high yield, and yet this is what the IRR implicitly assumes. The more likely eventuality is that the intra-project cash inflows will be invested at the 'going rate' or the opportunity cost of capital. In other words, the firm's normal discount rate is the better estimate of the reinvestment rate. The effect of this erroneous reinvestment assumption is to inflate the IRR of the project under examination.

For example, Project K below has a very high IRR, at 61.8 per cent; thus the £1,000 received after one year is assumed to be taken back into the firm and then placed in another investment, again yielding 61.8 per cent until time 2. This is obviously absurd: if such an investment existed why has the firm not already invested in it – given its cost of capital of only 15 per cent?

Project K (required rate of return 15 per cent)

Points in time (yearly intervals)	0	1	2
Cash flows (£)	–1,000	+1,000	+1,000

IRR

Try 60 per cent: NPV = 15.63.
Try 62 per cent: NPV = –1.68.

Interpolation

Exhibit 2.22 Interpolation, Project K

r	60%	?	62%
NPV	15.63	0	–1.68

$$60 + \left(\frac{15.63}{15.63 + 1.68} \right) \times (62 - 60) = 61.8\%$$

The reinvestment assumption of 61.8 per cent, for the £1,000 receivable at time 1, is clearly unrealistic, especially in light of the fact that most investors can only obtain a return of 15 per cent for taking this level of risk.

The IRR of Project K assumes the following:

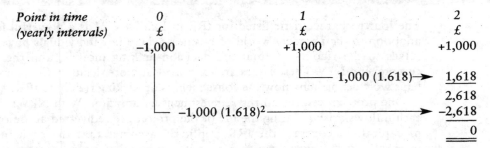

Point in time (yearly intervals)	0 £	1 £	2 £
	−1,000	+1,000	+1,000
		1,000 (1.618)→	1,618
			2,618
	−1,000 (1.618)²	→	−2,618
			0

The £2,618 compounded cash flows at the terminal date of the project are equivalent to taking the original investment of £1,000 and compounding it for two years at 61.8 per cent. However, an NPV calculation assumes that the intra-project cash inflow is invested at 15 per cent:

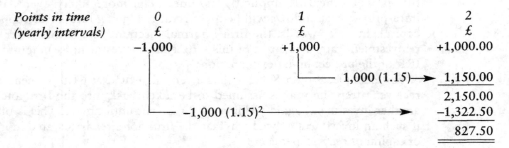

Points in time (yearly intervals)	0 £	1 £	2 £
	−1,000	+1,000	+1,000.00
		1,000 (1.15)→	1,150.00
			2,150.00
	−1,000 (1.15)²	→	−1,322.50
			827.50

Discounting £827.50 back two years gives the NPV of £625.71.

If, for reasons of pragmatism or communication within the firm, it is necessary to describe a project appraisal in terms of a percentage, then it is recommended that the modified internal rate of return (MIRR) is used. This takes as its starting point the notion that, for the sake of consistency with NPV, any cash inflows arising during the project are reinvested at the opportunity cost of funds. That is, at the rate of return available on the next best alternative use of the funds in either financial or real assets. The MIRR is the rate of return, m, which, if used to compound the initial investment amount (the original cash outlay) produces the same terminal value as the project cash inflows. The value of the project's cash inflows at the end of the project's life after they have been expressed in the terminal date's £s is achieved through compounding. In other words, the common currency this time is not time 0 £s, but time 4, or time 6, or time 'n' £s.

What we are attempting to do is find that rate of compounding which will equate the terminal value of the intra-project cash flows with the terminal value of the initial investment.

Modified internal rate of return for Project K

First, calculate the terminal value of the cash flows excluding the t_0 investment using the opportunity cost of capital.

			Terminal value (£)
t_1	1,000 (1.15)		1,150.00
t_2	1,000	already expressed as a terminal value because it occurs on the date of termination	1,000.00
		Total terminal value	2,150.00

The modified internal rate of return is the rate of compounding applied to the original investment necessary to produce a future (terminal) value of £2,150.00 two years later.

$$1,000 (1 + m)^2 = 2,150.00$$

Solve for m. (The mathematical tools – *see* Appendix 2.1 – may be useful here.) Divide both sides of the equation by 1,000:

$$(1 + m)^2 = \frac{2,150}{1,000}$$

Then, take roots to the power of 2 of both sides of the equation:

$$\sqrt[2]{(1 + m)^2} = \sqrt[2]{\frac{2,150}{1,000}}$$

$$m = \sqrt[2]{\frac{2,150}{1,000}} - 1 = 0.466 \text{ or } 46.6\%$$

or more generally:

$$m = \sqrt[n]{\frac{F}{P}} - 1$$

Thus, the MIRR is 46.6 per cent compared with the IRR of 61.8 per cent. In the case of Project K this reduced rate is still very high and the project is accepted under either rule. However, in a number of situations, the calculation of the MIRR may alter the decision given under the IRR method. This is true in the worked example of Switcharound plc for projects Tic and Cit, which are mutually exclusive projects and thus ranking is important.

Worked example 2.5 Switcharound plc

The business development team of Switcharound plc has been working to find uses for a vacated factory. The two projects it has selected for further consideration by senior management both have a life of only three years, because the site will be flattened in three years when a new motorway is constructed. On the basis of IRR the business development team is leaning towards acceptance of Cit but it knows that the key Senior Manager is aware of MIRR and therefore feels it is necessary to present the data calculated through both techniques. The opportunity cost of capital is 10 per cent.

Cash flows

Points in time (yearly intervals)	0	1	2	3	IRR
Tic (£m)	−1	0.5	0.5	0.5	23.4%
Cit (£m)	−1	1.1	0.1	0.16	27.7%

However, on the basis of MIRR, a different preference emerges.

Tic: MIRR

		Terminal value £m
t_1	$0.5 \times (1.1)^2$	0.605
t_2	0.5×1.1	0.550
t_3	0.5	0.500
Total terminal value		1.655

$$1,000,000 \, (1 + m)^3 = 1,655,000$$

$$m = \sqrt[n]{\frac{F}{P}} - 1$$

$$m = \sqrt[3]{\frac{1,655,000}{1,000,000}} - 1 = 0.183 \text{ or } 18.3\%$$

Cit: MIRR

		Terminal value £m
t_1	$1.1 \times (1.1)^2$	1.331
t_2	0.1×1.1	0.110
t_3	0.16	0.16
Total terminal value		1.601

$$1,000,000 \, (1 + m)^3 = 1,601,000$$

$$m = \sqrt[n]{\frac{F}{P}} - 1$$

$$m = \sqrt[3]{\frac{1,601,000}{1,000,000}} - 1 = 0.17 \text{ or } 17\%$$

Of course, a more satisfactory answer can be obtained by calculating NPVs, but the result may not be persuasive if the senior management team do not understand NPVs.

NPVs for Tic and Cit

Tic $-1 + 0.5 \times$ annuity factor, 3 years @10%
$-1 + 0.5 \times 2.4868 = 0.243400$ or £243,400

Cit $-1 + \dfrac{1.1}{1 + 0.1} + \dfrac{0.1}{(1 + 0.1)^2} + \dfrac{0.16}{(1 + 0.1)^3} = 0.202855$ or £202,855

Therefore, Tic contributes more towards shareholder wealth.

Summary table

Ranking

	NPV	*IRR*	*MIRR*
Tic	£243,400 (1)	23.4% (2)	18.3% (1)
Cit	£202,855 (2)	27.7% (1)	17.0% (2)

CONCLUDING COMMENTS

This chapter has provided insight into the key factors for consideration when an organisation is contemplating using financial (or other) resources for investment. The analysis has been based on the assumption that the objective of any such investment is to maximise economic benefits to the owners of the enterprise. To achieve such an objective requires allowance for the opportunity cost of capital or time value of money as well as robust analysis of relevant cash flows. Given that time has a value, the precise timing of cash flows is important for project analysis. The net present value (NPV) and internal rate of return (IRR) methods of project appraisal are both discounted cash flow techniques and therefore allow for the time value of money. However, the IRR method does present problems in a few special circumstances and so the theoretically preferred method is NPV. On the other hand, NPV requires diligent studying and thought in order to be fully understood, and therefore it is not surprising to find in the workplace a bias in favour of communicating a project's viability in terms of percentages. Most large organisations, in fact, use three or four methods of project appraisal, rather than rely on only one for both rigorous analysis and communication – *see* Chapter 4 for more detail. If a percentage approach is regarded as essential in a particular organisational setting then the MIRR is to be preferred to the IRR, or the distinctly poor accounting rate of return (e.g. return on capital employed). Not only does the MIRR rank projects more appropriately and so is useful in mutual exclusivity situations; it also avoids biasing upward expectations of returns from an investment. The fundamental conclusion of this chapter is that the best method for maximising shareholder wealth in assessing investment projects is net present value.

KEY POINTS AND CONCEPTS

- *Time value of money* has three component parts each requiring compensation for a delay in the receipt of cash:
  - the pure time value, or impatience to consume,
  - inflation,
  - risk.
- *Opportunity cost of capital* is the yield forgone on the best available investment alternative – the risk level of the alternative being the same as the project under consideration.
- Taking account of the time value of money and opportunity cost of capital in project appraisal leads to **discounted cash flow analysis (DCF)**.

- **Net present value** (NPV) is the present value of the future cash flows after netting out the initial cash flow. Present values are achieved by discounting at the opportunity cost of capital.

$$\text{NPV} = F_0 + \frac{F_1}{1+k} + \frac{F_2}{(1+k)^2} + \dots \frac{F_n}{(1+k)^n}$$

- **The net present value decision rules** are:

  NPV $\geqslant$ 0 accept
  NPV $<$ 0 reject

- **Internal rate of return** (IRR) is the discount rate which, when applied to the cash flows of a project, results in a zero net present value. It is an 'r' which results in the following formula being true:

$$F_0 + \frac{F_1}{1+r} + \frac{F_2}{(1+r)^2} + \dots \frac{F_n}{(1+r)^n} = 0$$

- **The internal rate of return decision rule** is:

  IRR $\geqslant$ opportunity cost of capital – accept
  IRR $<$ opportunity cost of capital – reject

- IRR is poor at handling situations of unconventional cash flows. **Multiple solutions can be the result.**

- There are circumstances when IRR ranks one project higher than another, whereas NPV ranks the projects in the opposite order. This **ranking problem** becomes an important issue in situations of mutual exclusivity.

- NPV measures in **absolute amounts of money.** IRR is a percentage measure.

- IRR assumes that intra-project cash flows can be invested at a rate of return equal to the IRR. This biases the IRR calculation.

- If a percentage measure is required, perhaps for communication within an organisation, then the **modified internal rate of return** (MIRR) is to be preferred to the IRR.

APPENDIX 2.1 MATHEMATICAL TOOLS FOR FINANCE

The purpose of this appendix is to explain essential mathematical skills that will be needed for the remainder of this book. The author has no love of mathematics for its own sake and so only those techniques of direct relevance to the subject matter of this textbook will be covered in this section.

Simple and compound interest

When there are time delays between receipts and payments of financial sums we need to make use of the concepts of simple and compound interest.

Simple interest

Interest is paid only on the original principal. No interest is paid on the accumulated interest payments.

Example 1

Suppose that a sum of £10 is deposited in a bank account that pays 12 per cent per annum. At the end of year 1 the investor has £11.20 in the account. That is:

$$F = P(1 + i)$$
$$11.20 = 10(1 + 0.12)$$

where F = Future value, P = Present value, i = Interest rate.
   At the end of five years:

$$F = P(1 + in)$$

where n = number of years. Thus,

$$16 = 10(1 + 0.12 \times 5)$$

The initial sum, called the principal, is multiplied by the interest rate to give the annual return. Note from the example that the 12 per cent return is a constant amount each year. Interest is not earned on the interest already accumulated from previous years.

Compound interest

The more usual situation in the real world is for interest to be paid on the sum which accumulates – whether or not that sum comes from the principal or from the interest received in previous periods. Interest is paid on the accumulated interest and principal.

Example 2

An investment of £10 is made at an interest rate of 12 per cent with the interest being compounded. In one year the capital will grow by 12 per cent to £11.20. In the second year the capital will grow by 12 per cent, but this time the growth will be on the accumulated value of £11.20 and thus will amount to an extra £1.34. At the end of two years:

$$F = P(1 + i)(1 + i)$$
$$F = 11.20(1 + i)$$
$$F = 12.54$$

Alternatively,

$$F = P(1 + i)^2$$

Exhibit 2.23 displays the future value of £1 invested at a number of different interest rates and for alternative numbers of years. This is extracted from Appendix I at the end of the book.

Exhibit 2.23 The future value of £1

	Interest rate (per cent per annum)				
Year	1	2	5	12	15
1	1.0100	1.0200	1.0500	1.1200	1.1500
2	1.0201	1.0404	1.1025	1.2544	1.3225
3	1.0303	1.0612	1.1576	1.4049	1.5209
4	1.0406	1.0824	1.2155	1.5735	1.7490
5	1.0510	1.1041	1.2763	1.7623	2.0113

From the second row of the table in Exhibit 2.23 we can read that £1 invested for two years at 12 per cent amounts to £1.2544. Thus, the investment of £10 provides a future capital sum 1.2544 times the original amount:

$$£10 \times 1.2544 = £12.544$$

Over five years the result is:

$$F = P (1 + i)^n$$
$$17.62 = 10(1 + 0.12)^5$$

The interest on the accumulated interest is therefore the difference between the total arising from simple interest and that from compound interest:

$$17.62 - 16.00 = 1.62$$

Almost all investments pay compound interest and so we will be using compounding throughout the book.

Present values

There are many occasions in financial management when you are given the future sums and need to find out what those future sums are worth in present-value terms today. For example, you wish to know how much you would have to put aside today which will accumulate, with compounded interest, to a defined sum in the future; or you are given the choice between receiving £200 in five years or £100 now and wish to know which is the better option, given anticipated interest rates; or a project gives a return of £1m in three years for an outlay of £800,000 now and you need to establish if this is the best use of the £800,000. By the process of discounting a sum of money to be received in the future is given a monetary value today.

Example 3

If we anticipate the receipt of £17.62 in five years' time we can determine its present value. Rearrangement of the compound formula, and assuming a discount rate of 12 per cent, gives:

$$P = \frac{F}{(1 + i)^n} \text{ or } P = F \times \frac{1}{(1 + i)^n}$$

$$10 = \frac{17.62}{(1 + 0.12)^5}$$

Alternatively, discount factors may be used, as shown in Exhibit 2.24 (this is an extract from Appendix II at the end of the book). The factor needed to discount £1 receivable in five years when the discount rate is 12 per cent is 0.5674.

Therefore the present value of £17.62 is:

$$0.5674 \times £17.62 = £10$$

Exhibit 2.24 The present value of £1

Year	Interest rate (per cent per annum)				
	1	5	10	12	15
1	0.9901	0.9524	0.9091	0.8929	0.8696
2	0.9803	0.9070	0.8264	0.7972	0.7561
3	0.9706	0.8638	0.7513	0.7118	0.6575
4	0.9610	0.8227	0.6830	0.6355	0.5718
5	0.9515	0.7835	0.6209	0.5674	0.4972

Examining the present value table in Exhibit 2.24 you can see that as the discount rate increases the present value goes down. Also the further into the future the money is to be received, the less valuable it is in today's terms. Distant cash flows discounted at a high rate have a small present value; for instance, £1,000 receivable in 20 years when the discount rate is 17 per cent has a present value of £43.30. Viewed from another angle, if you invested £43.30 for 20 years it would accumulate to £1,000 if interest compounds at 17 per cent.

CASE STUDY 2.2 The effect of compounding over long periods

Jacques Chirac's attempt to help Eurotunnel

In May 1996, when Eurotunnel seemed to be headed for bankruptcy, Jacques Chirac, the French president, urged that Eurotunnel's franchise to operate the Channel tunnel be extended by between 20 and 30 years. He was concerned at the impact of the financial problems on hundreds of thousands of small shareholders in the UK and France. In the spring of 1996 the concession was due to end in 2052. In the City the move was regarded as 'brilliant public relations' and it was thought that it might encourage other parties,

especially the bankers, to make concessions in the negotiation of a reprieve package. However, the impact on the company would be limited as one banker said, 'The value in current money of revenues in 60 or 70 years' time is actually quite low.' The *Financial Times* commented that 'Analysts estimated that a 30-year extension could increase the value of the company by £100m –£500m. This compares with the group's debts of £8.4bn.'

Source: Financial Times, 16 May 1996. Reprinted with permission.

Determining the rate of interest

Sometimes you wish to calculate the rate of return that a project is earning. For instance, a savings company may offer to pay you £10,000 in five years if you deposit £8,000 now, when interest rates on accounts elsewhere are offering 6 per cent per annum. In order to make a comparison you need to know the annual rate being offered by the savings company. Thus, we need to find i in the discounting equation.

To be able to calculate i it is necessary to rearrange the compounding formula. Since:

$$F = P(1 + i)^n$$

first, divide both sides by P:

$$F/P = (1 + i)^n$$

(The Ps on the right side cancel out.)

Second, take the root to the power n of both sides and subtract 1 from each side:

$$i = \sqrt[n]{[F/P]} - 1 \text{ or } i = [F/P]^{1/n} - 1$$

Example 4

In the case of a five-year investment requiring an outlay of £10 and having a future value of £17.62 the rate of return is:

$$i = \sqrt[5]{\frac{17.62}{10}} - 1 \quad i = 12\%$$
$$i = [17.62/10]^{1/5} - 1 \quad i = 12\%$$

Technical aside

You can use the $\sqrt[x]{y}$ or the $\sqrt[x]{x}$ button, depending on the calculator.

Alternatively, use the future value table, an extract of which is shown in Exhibit 2.23. In our example, the return on £1 worth of investment over five years is:

$$\frac{17.62}{10} = 1.762$$

In the body of the Future Value table look at the year 5 row for a future value of 1.762. Read off the interest rate of 12 per cent.

An interesting application of this technique outside finance is to use it to put into perspective the pronouncements of politicians. For example, in 1994 John Major made a speech to the Conservative Party conference promising to double national income (the total quantity of goods and services produced) within 25 years. This sounds impressive, but let us see how ambitious this is in terms of an annual percentage increase.

$$i = \sqrt[25]{\frac{F}{P}} - 1$$

F, future income, is double P, the present income.

$$i = \sqrt[25]{\frac{2}{1}} - 1 = 0.0281 \text{ or } 2.81\%$$

The result is not too bad compared with the previous 20 years. However, performance in the 1950s and 1960s was better and countries in the Far East have annual rates of growth of between 5 per cent and 10 per cent.

The investment period

Rearranging the standard equation so that we can find n (the number of years of the investment), we create the following equation:

$$F = P(1 + i)^n$$
$$F/P = (1 + i)^n$$
$$\log(F/P) = \log(1 + i)^n$$
$$n = \frac{\log(F/P)}{\log(1 + i)}$$

Example 5

How many years does it take for £10 to grow to £17.62 when the interest rate is 12 per cent?

$$n = \frac{\log(17.62/10)}{\log(1 + 0.12)} \text{ Therefore } n = 5 \text{ years}$$

An application outside finance

How many years will it take for China to double its real national income if growth rates continue at 10 per cent per annum?
Answer:

$$n = \frac{\log(2/1)}{\log(1 + 0.1)} = 7.3 \text{ years (quadrupling in less than 15 years)}$$

Annuities

Quite often there is not just one payment at the end of a certain number of years. There can be a series of identical payments made over a period of years. For instance:

- bonds usually pay a regular rate of interest;
- individuals can buy, from saving plan companies, the right to receive a number of identical payments over a number of years;
- a business might invest in a project which, it is estimated, will give regular cash inflows over a period of years;
- a typical house mortgage is an annuity.

An annuity is a series of payments or receipts of equal amounts. We are able to calculate the present value of this set of payments.

Example 6

For a regular payment of £10 per year for five years, when the interest rate is 12 per cent, we can calculate the present value of the annuity by three methods.

Method 1

$$P_{an} = \frac{A}{(1+i)} + \frac{A}{(1+i)^2} + \frac{A}{(1+i)^3} + \frac{A}{(1+i)^4} + \frac{A}{(1+i)^5}$$

where A = the periodic receipt.

$$P_{10,5} = \frac{10}{(1.12)} + \frac{10}{(1.12)^2} + \frac{10}{(1.12)^3} + \frac{10}{(1.12)^4} + \frac{10}{(1.12)^5} = £36.05$$

Method 2

Using the derived formula:

$$P_{an} = \frac{1 - 1/(1+i)^n}{i} \times A$$

$$P_{10,5} = \frac{1 - 1/(1 + 0.12)^5}{0.12} \times 10 = £36.05$$

Method 3

Use the 'Present Value of an Annuity' table. (*See* Exhibit 2.25, an extract from the more complete annuity table at the end of the book in Appendix III.) Here we simply look along the year 5 row and 12 per cent column to find the figure of 3.605. This refers to the present value of five annual receipts of £1. Therefore we multiply by £10:

$$3.605 \times £10 = £36.05$$

Exhibit 2.25 The present value of an annuity of £1 per annum

Year	Interest rate (per cent per annum)				
	1	5	10	12	15
1	0.9901	0.9524	0.9091	0.8929	0.8696
2	1.9704	1.8594	1.7355	1.6901	1.6257
3	2.9410	2.7232	2.4868	2.4018	2.2832
4	3.9020	3.5459	3.1699	3.0373	2.8550
5	4.8535	4.3295	3.7908	3.6048	3.3522

The student is strongly advised against using Method 1. This was presented for conceptual understanding only. For any but the simplest cases, this method can be very time consuming.

Perpetuities

Some contracts run indefinitely and there is no end to the payments. Perpetuities are rare in the private sector, but certain government securities do not have an end date; that is, the amount paid when the bond was purchased by the lender will never be repaid, only interest payments are made. For example, the UK government has issued Consolidated Stocks or War Loans which will never be redeemed. Also, in a number of project appraisals or share valuations it is useful to assume that regular annual payments go on forever. Perpetuities are annuities which continue indefinitely. The value of a perpetuity is simply the annual amount received divided by the interest rate when the latter is expressed as a decimal.

$$P = \frac{A}{i}$$

If £10 is to be received as an indefinite annual payment then the present value, at a discount rate of 12 per cent, is:

$$P = \frac{10}{0.12} = £83.33$$

It is very important to note that in order to use this formula we are assuming that the first payment arises 365 days after the time at which we are standing (the present time or time zero).

Discounting semi-annually, monthly and daily

Sometimes financial transactions take place on the basis that interest will be calculated more frequently than once a year. For instance, if a bank account paid 12 per cent nominal return per year, but credited 6 per cent after half a year, in the second half of the year interest could be earned on the interest credited after the first six months. This will mean that the true annual rate of interest will be greater than 12 per cent.

The greater the frequency with which interest is earned, the higher the future value of the deposit.

Example 7

If you put £10 in a bank account earning 12 per cent per annum then your return after one year is:

$$10(1 + 0.12) = £11.20$$

If the interest is compounded semi-annually (at a nominal annual rate of 12 per cent):

$$10(1 + [0.12/2])(1 + [0.12/2]) = 10(1 + [0.12/2])^2 = £11.236$$

In Example 7 the difference between annual compounding and semi-annual compounding is an extra 3.6p. After six months the bank credits the account with 60p in interest so that in the following six months the investor earns 6 per cent on the £10.60.

If the interest is compounded quarterly:

$$10(1 + [0.12/4])^4 = £11.255$$

Daily compounding:

$$10(1 + [0.12/365])^{365} = £11.2747$$

Example 8

If £10 is deposited in a bank account that compounds interest quarterly and the nominal return per year is 12 per cent, how much will be in the account after eight years?

$$10(1 + [0.12/4])^{4 \times 8} = £25.75$$

Continuous compounding

If the compounding frequency is taken to the limit we say that there is continuous compounding. When the number of compounding periods approaches infinity the future value is found by $F = Pe^{in}$ where e is the value of the exponential function. This is set as 2.71828 (to five decimal places, as shown on a scientific calculator).

So, the future value of £10 deposited in a bank paying 12 per cent nominal compounded continuously after eight years is:

$$10 \times 2.71828^{0.12 \times 8} = £26.12$$

Converting monthly and daily rates to annual rates

Sometimes you are presented with a monthly or daily rate of interest and wish to know what that is equivalent to in terms of Annual Percentage Rates (APR).

If m is the monthly interest or discount rate, then over 12 months:

$$(1 + m)^{12} = 1 + i$$

where i is the annual compound rate.

$$i = (1 + m)^{12} - 1$$

Thus, if a credit card company charges 1.5 per cent per month, the annual percentage rate (APR) is:

$$i = (1 + 0.015)^{12} - 1 = 19.56\%$$

If you want to find the monthly rate when you are given the APR:

$$m = (1 + i)^{1/12} - 1 \quad \text{or} \quad m = \sqrt[12]{(1 + i)} - 1$$
$$m = (1 + 0.1956)^{1/12} - 1 = 0.015 = 1.5\%$$

Daily rate:

$$(1 + d)^{365} = 1 + i$$

where d is the daily discount rate.

The following exercises will consolidate the knowledge gained by reading through this appendix (answers are provided at the end of the book in Appendix VI).

MATHEMATICAL TOOLS EXERCISES

1 The rate of interest is 8 per cent. What will a £100 investment be worth in three years' time if the rate of interest is 8 per cent, using: (a) simple interest? (b) annual compound interest?

2 You plan to invest £10,000 in the shares of a company.
(a) If the value of the shares increases by 5 per cent a year, what will be the value of the shares in 20 years?
(b) If the value of the shares increases by 15 per cent a year, what will be the value of the shares in 20 years?

3 How long will it take you to double your money if you invest it at: (a) 5 per cent? (b) 15 per cent?

4 As a winner of a lottery you can choose one of the following prizes:
(a) £1,000,000 now.
(b) £1,700,000 at the end of five years.
(c) £135,000 a year for ever, starting in one year.
(d) £200,000 for each of the next 10 years, starting in one year.
If the interest rate is 9 per cent, which is the most valuable prize?

5 A bank lends a customer £5,000. At the end of 10 years he repays this amount plus interest. The amount he repays is £8,950. What is the rate of interest charged by the bank?

6 The Morbid Memorial Garden company will maintain a garden plot around your grave for a payment of £50 now, followed by annual payments, in perpetuity, of £50. How much would you have to put into an account which was to make these payments if the account guaranteed an interest rate of 8 per cent?

7 If the flat (nominal annual) rate of interest is 14 per cent and compounding takes place monthly, what is the effective annual rate of interest (the Annual Percentage Rate)?

8 What is the present value of £100 to be received in 10 years' time when the interest rate (nominal annual) is 12 per cent and (a) annual discounting is used? (b) semi-annual discounting is used?

9 What sum must be invested now to provide an amount of £18,000 at the end of 15 years if interest is to accumulate at 8 per cent for the first 10 years and 12 per cent thereafter?

10 How much must be invested now to provide an amount of £10,000 in six years' time assuming interest is compounded quarterly at a nominal annual rate of 8 per cent? What is the effective annual rate?

11 Supersalesman offers you an annuity of £800 per annum for 10 years. The price he asks is £4,800. Assuming you could earn 11 per cent on alternative investments would you buy the annuity?

12 Punter buys a car on hire purchase paying five annual instalments of £1,500, the first being an immediate cash deposit. Assuming an interest rate of 8 per cent is being charged by the hire purchase company, how much is the current *cash* price of the car?

REFERENCES AND FURTHER READING

Bierman, H. and Smidt, S. (1992) *The Capital Budgeting Decision*, 8th edn. New York: Macmillan. A clear introductory exposition of the concepts discussed in this chapter.

Dean, J. (1951) *Capital Budgeting*. New York: Columbia University Press. Dean introduced an analytical framework for a systemised approach to investment within the firm based on discounted cash flow. Easy to read.

Fama, E.F. and Miller, M.H. (1972) *The Theory of Finance*. New York: Holt, Rinehart & Winston. A more detailed consideration of IRR and NPV.

Fisher, I. (1930) *The Theory of Interest*. Reprinted in 1977 by Porcupine Press. Originator of the present value rule.

Hirshleifer, J. (1958) 'On the theory of optimal investment decision', *Journal of Political Economy*, 66 (August), pp. 329–52. Early theory.

Hirshleifer, J. (1961) 'Risk, the discount rate and investment decisions'. *American Economic Review*, May, pp. 112–20. Theoretical justification for the use of net present value.

McDaniel, W.R., McCarty, D.E. and Jessell, K.A. (1988) 'Discounted cash flow with explicit reinvestment rates: Tutorial and extension', *The Financial Review*, August. Modified internal rate of return discussed in more detail as well as other theoretical developments.

Solomon, E. (1963) *The Theory of Financial Management*. New York: Columbia University Press. An early advocate of net present value.

Wilkes, F.M. (1980) 'On multiple rates of return', *Journal of Business, Finance and Accounting*, 7(4). Theoretical treatment of a specific issue.

SELF-REVIEW QUESTIONS

1   What are the theoretical justifications for the NPV decision rules?

2   Explain what is meant by conventional and unconventional cash flows and what problems they might cause in investment appraisal.

3   Define the time value of money.

4   What is the reinvestment assumption for project cash flows under IRR? Why is this problematical? How can it be corrected?

5   Rearrange the compounding equation to solve for: (a) the annual interest rate, and (b) the number of years over which compounding takes place.

6   What is the 'yield' of a project?

7   Discuss the statement: 'The IRR method is better than the NPV method for choosing which projects to invest in because the cost of capital is not needed at the outset.'

8   Explain why it is possible to obtain an inaccurate result using the trial and error method of IRR when a wide difference of two discount rates is used for interpolation.

QUESTIONS AND PROBLEMS

1   Proast plc is considering two investment projects whose cash flows are:

Points in time (yearly intervals)	Project A	Project B
0	−120,000	−120,000
1	60,000	15,000
2	45,000	45,000
3	42,000	55,000
4	18,000	60,000

The company's required rate of return is 15 per cent.

a   Advise the company whether to undertake the two projects.

b   Indicate the maximum outlay in year 0 for each project before it ceases to be viable.

2   Highflyer plc has two possible projects to consider. It cannot do both – they are mutually exclusive. The cash flows are:

Points in time (yearly intervals)	Project A	Project B
0	−420,000	−100,000
1	150,000	75,000
2	150,000	75,000
3	150,000	0
4	150,000	0

Highflyer's cost of capital is 12 per cent. Assume unlimited funds. These are the only cash flows associated with the projects.

    a Calculate the internal rate of return (IRR) for each project.

    b Calculate the net present value (NPV) for each project.

    c Compare and explain the results in (a) and (b) and indicate which project the company should undertake and why.

3* Mr Baffled, the managing director of Confused plc, has heard that the internal rate of return (IRR) method of investment appraisal is the best modern approach. He is trying to apply the IRR method to two new projects.

	Cash flows		
Year	0	1	2
Project C	−3,000	+14,950	−12,990
Project D	−3,000	+7,500	−5,000

    a Calculate the IRRs of the two projects.

    b Explain why Mr Baffled is having difficulties with the IRR method.

    c Advise Confused whether to accept either or both projects. (Assume a discount rate of 25 per cent.)

4 Using a 13 per cent discount rate find the NPV of a project with the following cash flows:

Points in time (yearly intervals)	t_0	t_1	t_2	t_3
Cash flow (£)	−300	+260	−200	+600

How many IRRs would you expect to find for this project?

5† **a** Find the total terminal value of the following cash flows when compounded at 15 per cent. Cash flows occur at annual intervals and the fourth year's cash flow is the last.

Points in time (yearly intervals)	t_1	t_2	t_3	t_4
Cash flow (£)	+200	+300	+250	+400

    b If £900 is the initial cash outflow at time 0 calculate the compounding rate that will equate the initial cash outflow with the terminal value as calculated in (a) above.

    c You have calculated the modified internal rate of return (MIRR), now calculate the IRR for comparison.

6† **a** If the cost of capital is 14 per cent find the modified internal rate of return for the following investment and state if you would implement it.

Points in time (yearly intervals)	t_0	t_1	t_2	t_3	t_4
Cash flow	−9,300	5,400	3,100	2,800	600

    b Is this project to be accepted under the internal rate of return method?

7* Seddet International is considering four major projects which have either two- or three-year lives. The firm has raised all of its capital in the form of equity and has never borrowed money. This is partly due to the success of the business in generating income and partly due to an insistence by the dominant managing director that borrowing is to be avoided if at all possible. Shareholders in Seddet International regard the firm as relatively risky, given its existing portfolio of projects. Other firms' shares in this risk class have generally given a return of 16 per cent per annum and this is taken as the opportunity cost of capital for the investment projects. The risk level for the proposed projects is the same as that of the existing range of activities.

Project

Points in time (yearly intervals)	Net cash flows			
	t_0	t_1	t_2	t_3
A	−5,266	2,500	2,500	2,500
B	−8,000	0	0	10,000
C	−2,100	200	2,900	0
D	−1,975	1,600	800	0

Ignore taxation and inflation.

a The managing director has been on a one-day intensive course to learn about project appraisal techniques. Unfortunately, during the one slot given over to NPV he had to leave the room to deal with a business crisis, and therefore does not understand it. He vaguely understands IRR and insists that you use this to calculate which of the four projects should be proceeded with, if there are no limitations on the number which can be undertaken.

b State which is the best project if they are mutually exclusive (i.e. accepting one excludes the possibility of accepting another), using IRR.

c Use the NPV decision rule to rank the projects and explain why, under conditions of mutual exclusivity, the selected project differs from that under (b).

d Write a report for the managing director, detailing the value of the net present value method for shareholder wealth enhancement and explaining why it may be considered of greater use than IRR.

ASSIGNMENTS

1 Try to discover the extent to which NPV, IRR and MIRR are used in your organisation. Also try to gauge the degree of appreciation of the problems of using IRR.

2 If possible, obtain data on a real project, historical or proposed, and analyse it using the techniques learned in this chapter.

CHAPTER NOTE

1 Interpolation (with a conventional cash flow project) always overstates the actual IRR.

Chapter 3

PROJECT APPRAISAL: CASH FLOW AND APPLICATIONS

INTRODUCTION

The last chapter outlined the process of project evaluation. This required consideration of the fundamental elements; first, recognition of the fact that time has a value and that money received in the future has to be discounted at the opportunity cost of capital; second, the identification of relevant cash flows that are to be subject to the discounting procedure. It is to this second issue that we now turn.

This chapter examines the estimation of the cash flows appropriate for good decision-making. The relevant cash flows are not always obvious and easy to obtain and therefore diligent data collection and rigorous analysis are required. Defining and measuring future receipts and outlays accurately is central to successful project appraisal.

In the following Case study Airbus would have had to consider carefully which projected cash flows are, and are not, relevant to the decision whether to go ahead with producing an aircraft capable of carrying 555 passengers.

Having completed the essential groundwork the chapter moves on to demonstrate the practical application of the net present value (NPV) method. This deals with important business decisions, such as whether to replace a machine with a new more efficient (but expensive) version or whether it is better to persevere with the old machine for a few more years despite its rising maintenance costs and higher raw material inputs. Another area examined is replacement cycles, that is, if you have machinery which costs more to run as it gets older and you know that you will continue to need this type of machine and therefore have to replace it at some stage should you regularly replace after one year or two, three or four years? An example is a car hire company that replaces its fleet of cars on a regular cycle. Other topics include the make or buy decision and optimal timing for the implementation of a project.

Airbus's superjumbo

Surely one of the biggest investment appraisal decisions ever made was when Airbus decided to go ahead and produce the A380 superjumbo. This is one of those 'bet the company' type investments. A massive $10,700 million will be needed to create this monster aircraft.

It was touch and go all through 2000 as to whether Airbus would dare to invest so much money. Before they said 'yes let's do it' they had to have firm orders for at least 50 aircraft. Finally, just before Christmas the sixth major buyer signed up, to take the order book to 50 'definites' and 42 on option (the airlines have the right to buy, but not the obligation).

The A380 will be significantly larger than Boeing's highly successful 747. It will carry 555 passengers (compared with 416). It will also cut direct operating costs for the airlines by 15–20 per cent compared with Boeing's 747-400 and will be able to fly 10% further (8,150 nautical miles).

So, where is all the money on development and build going? This is a project at the cutting edge of technology. The remarkable innovations cost a tremendous amount in terms of up-front cost but the benefit will be spread out over many decades.

Here are some of the innovations:

- New, weight-saving materials.
- Better aerodynamics.
- Lower airframe weight.
- Carbon-fibre central wingbox.
- 40 per cent of the structure and components will be made from new carbon components and metal alloys.
- Upper fuselage shell is not to be aluminium but 'Glare', a laminate with alternative layers of aluminium and glass-fibre reinforced adhesive.
- Innovative hydraulic systems.
- Improved air conditioning.

Airbus reckon that they need to sell at least 250 aircraft to break even in cash-flow terms (presumably meaning that nominal cumulative cash inflows equal nominal cumulative cash

Rivalry in the skies: contrasting views

Traffic volume in 2019
Forecasts

Order evolution
% share of units ordered

Revenue passenger kilometres (bn) — 7,969.7

Very large aircraft — 1,550*, 500**

Including freighters — 315, 160

Airbus global market forecasts

Boeing current market outlook

Boeing

Airbus

1995 96 97 98 99 2000***

Profit potential

Passengers required to break even   Available profit seats

Airbus A3XX — 323†

Boeing B747-400 — 290††

* 500 seats and above ** Larger than 747 *** Includes announcements from Farnborough Air Show 2000
† Assuming same revenue per passenger as B747-400 †† Break-even load factor assumed for B747-400; 70%
Source: *Financial Times*, 2 November 2000, p. 28 Reprinted with permission. Data from Airbus.

outflows). To achieve a positive net present value would require the sale of hundreds more aircraft. Each aircraft has a list price of around $216m – $230m – but don't pay too much attention to that, as airlines receive substantial discounts. At full tilt something like 96,000 people will be working on this aircraft.

And yet it could so easily have been abandoned. Boeing had decided not to develop a superjumbo because it estimated the maximum market at 500 aircraft – they believe that airlines are generally content to continue using the 747. Airbus estimated the market for jumbos and superjumbos at 1,550. It expects to take two-thirds of that business, worth $400bn in today's prices.

This is a high impact project appraisal if ever there was one. Many of the techniques you have learned in Chapter 2 and will learn in this chapter will have been employed by the management of Airbus to help them decide whether or not to press the button to 'go' or the button to 'stop'.

Learning objectives

By the end of this chapter the reader will be able to identify and apply relevant and incremental cash flows in net present value calculations. The reader will also be able to recognise and deal with sunk costs, incidental costs and allocated overheads and be able to employ this knowledge to the following:

■ the replacement decision/the replacement cycle;

■ the calculation of annual equivalent annuities;

■ the make or buy decision;

■ optimal timing of investment;

■ fluctuating output situations.

QUALITY OF INFORMATION

Good decisions are born of good information. This principle applies to all types of business decisions but is especially appropriate in the case of capital investment decisions in which a substantial proportion of the firm's assets can be put at risk. Obtaining relevant and high-quality information reduces the extent of the risk for the enterprise. Information varies greatly in its reliability, which often depends upon its source. The financial manager or analyst is often dependent on the knowledge and experience of other specialists within the organisation to supply data. For example the marketing team may be able to provide an estimate of likely demand while the production team could help establish the costs per unit. Allowance will have to be made for any bias that may creep into the information passed on; for instance, a manager who is particularly keen on encouraging the firm to expand in a particular geographical area might tend to be over-optimistic concerning the market demand. Some aspects of project appraisal might be able to use high-quality information whereas other aspects have a lower quality. Take the case of the investment in a new lorry for a courier firm; the cost of purchase can be estimated with high precision, whereas the reaction of competitor firms is subject to much more uncertainty.

The sources of information which are useful as inputs for decision making vary widely; from accounting systems and special investigations, to those of the informal, 'just-between-you-and-me-and-the-gatepost' type. Whatever its source all information should, as far as possible, have the following characteristics:

- relevance;
- completeness;
- consistency;
- accuracy;
- reliability;
- timeliness;
- low cost of collection compared with benefit.

ARE PROFIT CALCULATIONS USEFUL FOR ESTIMATING PROJECT VIABILITY?

Accountants often produce a wealth of numerical information about an organisation and its individual operations. It is tempting to simply take the profit figures for a project and put these into the NPV formula as a substitute for cash flow. A further reason advanced for favouring profit-based evaluations is that managers are often familiar with the notion of 'the bottom line' and frequently their performance is judged using profit. However, as was noted in Chapter 1, determining whether a project is 'profitable' is not the same as achieving shareholder wealth maximisation.

Profit is a concept developed by accountants in order to assist them with auditing and reporting. Profit figures are derived by taking what is a continuous process, a change in a company's worth over time, and allocating these changes to discrete periods of time, say a year (see Exhibit 3.1). This is a difficult task. It is a complex task with rules, principles and conventions in abundance.

Exhibit 3.1 Business activity is a continuous process; this is difficult to capture in periodic accounts

Business activity				
A continuous process of change in a company's wealth . . .				
Year 1	Year 2	Year 3	Year 4	Year 5 . . .

Profit uses two carefully defined concepts: income and expenses. Income is not cash inflow, it is the amount earned from business activity whether or not the cash has actually been handed over. So, if a £1,000 sofa has been sold on two years' credit the accountant's income arises in the year of sale despite the fact that cash actually flows in two years later. Expense relates the use of an asset to a particular time period whether or not any cash outflow relating to that item occurs in that period. If a firm pays immediately for a machine which will have a ten-year useful life it does not write off the full cost of the machine against the first year's profit, but allocates a proportion of the cost to each of the next ten years. The cash outflow occurs in the first year but the expense (use) of the asset occurs over ten years.

Shareholders make current consumption sacrifices, or they give up the return available elsewhere when they choose to invest their money in a firm. They do this in anticipation of receiving more £s in the future than they laid out. Hence what is of interest to them are the future cash flows and the precise timing of these cash flows. The accountant does a difficult and important job but the profit figures produced are not suitable for project appraisal. Profit is a poor approach for two main reasons, first, depreciation and second, working capital.

Depreciation

Accounting profit is calculated after deducting depreciation, whereas what we are interested in is net cash inflows for a year. Depreciation should not be deducted to calculate net cash inflows. For example, if a firm buys a machine for £20,000 which is expected to be productive for four years and have a zero scrap value, the firm's accountant may allocate the depreciation on the machine over the four years to give the profit figures of say, a stable £7,000 per year. The reason for doing this may be so that the full impact of the £20,000 payout in the first year is not allocated solely to that year's profit and loss account, but is spread over the economic life of the asset. This makes good sense for calculating accounting profit. However, this is not appropriate for project appraisal based on NPV because these figures are not true cash flows. We need to focus on the cash flows at the precise time they occur and should not discount back to time zero the figure of £7,000, but cash flows at the time they occur. The contrast between profit figures and cash flow figures is shown in the example of Quarpro plc (*see* Exhibit 3.2).

Exhibit 3.2 Quarpro plc: An example of adjustment to profit and loss account

Machine cost £20,000, at time 0.		Productive life of four years.		
Accountant's figures				
Year	1	2	3	4
	£	£	£	£
Profit before depreciation	12,000	12,000	12,000	12,000
Depreciation	5,000	5,000	5,000	5,000
Profit after depreciation	7,000	7,000	7,000	7,000
Cash flow				
Point in time (yearly intervals)	0 £	1 £	2 £	3 £	4 £
Cash outflow	–20,000				
Cash inflow		12,000	12,000	12,000	12,000

Working capital

When a project is accepted and implemented the firm may have to invest in more than the large and obvious depreciable assets such as machines, buildings, vehicles and so forth. Investment in a new project often requires an additional investment in working capital, that is, the difference between short-term assets and liabilities. The main short-term assets are cash, inventories and debtors. The principal short-term liabilities are creditors.

So, a firm might take on a project which involves an increase in the requirements for one of these types of working capital. Each of these will be taken in turn.

Cash floats

It may be that the proposed project requires the firm to have a much higher amount of cash float. For instance, a firm setting up a betting shop may have to consider not only the cash outflow for building or refurbishment, but also the amount of extra cash float needed to meet unexpectedly large betting payouts. Thus, we have to take into account this additional aspect of cash inputs when evaluating the size of the initial investment. This is despite the fact that the cash float will be recoverable at some date in the future (for instance, when the shop is closed in, e.g., three years' time). The fact that this cash is being used and is therefore not available to shareholders means that a sacrifice has been made at a particular point. The owners of that money rightfully expect to receive a suitable return while that money is tied up and unavailable for them to use as they wish.

Stock (inventories)

Examples of stock are raw materials and finished goods. If a project is undertaken which raises the level of inventories then this additional cash outflow has to be allowed for. So, for a retail business opening a number of new shops the additional expenditure on stock is a form of investment. This extra cash being tied up will not be recognised by the profit and loss accounts because all that has happened is that one asset, cash, has been swapped for another, inventory. However the cash use has to be recognised in any NPV calculation. With some projects there may be a reduction in inventory levels. This may happen in the case of the replacement of an inefficient machine with a new piece of equipment. In this case the stock reduction releases cash and so results in a positive cash flow.

Debtors

Accounting convention dictates that if a sale is made during a year it is brought into the profit and loss account for that year. But in many cases a sale might be made on credit and all the firm has is a promise that cash will be paid in the future, the cash inflow has not materialised in the year the sale was recorded. Also, at the start of the financial year this firm may have had some outstanding debtors, that is, other firms or individuals owing this firm money, and in the early months of the year cash inflow is boosted by those other firms paying off their debt.

If we want to calculate the cash flow for the year then the annual profit figure has to be adjusted to exclude the closing balance of debtors (cash owed by customers at the end of the year but not yet paid over), and include the opening balance of debtors (cash owed by the customers at the beginning of the year which is actually received in this year for sales that took place the previous year).

Creditors

Creditors are suppliers to the firm to whom cash payment is due. If creditors rise as a result of a course of action then this is effectively an increase in lending by those firms to this firm, and the cash flow has improved. If the creditor level falls then this firm is effectively experiencing a reduction in cash flow.

Thus we may have four working capital adjustments to make to the profit and loss account figures to arrive at cash flow figures. The value of the firm's investment in net working capital, associated with a project, is found by the:

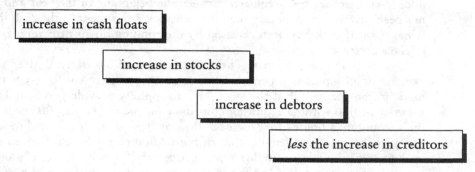

increase in cash floats

increase in stocks

increase in debtors

less the increase in creditors

Net operating cash flow

The net operating cash flow associated with a new investment is equal to the profit, with depreciation added back plus or minus any change in working capital. If the project results in an increase in working capital then:

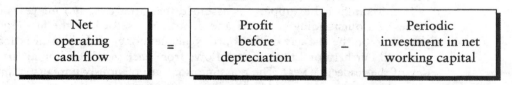

| Net operating cash flow | = | Profit before depreciation | − | Periodic investment in net working capital |

An example of the differences between profit and cash flow

We now turn to an example of a firm, ABC plc, carrying out a project appraisal. The finance manager has been provided with forecast profit and loss accounts and has to adjust these figures to arrive at cash flow. This project will require investment in machinery of £20,000 at the outset. The machinery will have a useful life of four years and a zero scrap value when production ceases at the end of the fourth year.

ABC's business involves dealing with numerous customers and the cash flows within any particular week are unpredictable. It therefore needs to maintain a cash float of £5,000 to be able to pay for day-to-day expenses. (Note: this cash float is not used up, and cannot therefore be regarded as a cost – in some weeks cash outflows are simply greater than cash inflows and to provide adequate liquidity £5,000 is needed for the firm to operate efficiently. The £5,000 will not be needed when output ceases.)

To produce the product it will be necessary to have a stock of raw materials close to hand. The investment in this form of inventory together with the cash committed to work in progress and finished goods amounts to £2,000 at the beginning of production. However, more cash (an extra £1,000) is expected to be required for this purpose at the end of the second year. When the new business is begun a large proportion of raw materials will come from suppliers who will grant additional credit. Therefore the level of creditors will rise by £1,000 over the period of the project.

To illustrate some of the differences between profit and cash flow there follows a conversion from projected accounting figures to cash flow. First it is necessary to add back the depreciation and instead account for the cost of the machine at time 0, the start date for the project when the cash actually left the firm. This is shown in Exhibit 3.3. To capture the cash flow effect of the investment in inventories (stock) we need to see if any additional cash has been required between the beginning of the year and its end. If cash has been invested in inventory then the net stock adjustment to the cash flow calculation is negative. If cash has been released by the running down of inventory the cash flow effect is positive.

Now we turn to creditors. The accounting profit is derived after subtracting the expense of all inputs in a period, whether or not the payment for those inputs has been made in that period. If at the start ABC's suppliers provide goods and services to the value of £1,000 without requiring immediate payment then £1,000 needs to be added to the accountant's figures for true cash flow at that point. If the creditor's adjustment is not made then we are denying that of the £2,000 of stock delivered on the first day of trading half is bought on credit. It is not necessary for ABC to pay £2,000 at the start to suppliers; they pay only £1,000 and thus the creditor adjustment shows a positive cash flow at time 0, offsetting the outflow on stock. (In other examples, later in the book, it may be assumed that all stock is bought on trade credit and therefore there would not be a cash outflow for stock payments at time 0. In these examples all creditor and debtor adjustments are made at the year ends and not at time 0.) In subsequent years the prior year's creditor debts actually paid match the amount outstanding at the year end, thus no net cash flow effect adjustment is necessary.

In this simplified example it is assumed that after exactly four years all production ceases and outstanding creditors and debtors are settled on the last day of the fourth year. Also on the last day of the fourth year the money tied up in cash float and stock is released. Furthermore, the net cash flows from each year's trading all arrive on the last day of the respective year. These assumptions are obviously unrealistic, but to make the example more realistic would add to its complexity.

Incremental cash flows

A fundamental principle in project appraisal is to include only incremental cash flows. These are defined as the cash flows dependent on the project's implementation. If a project is accepted only those cash flows that are induced by the investment at time 0 and in subsequent years are regarded as incremental. Some of these cash flows are easy to establish but others are much more difficult to pin down.

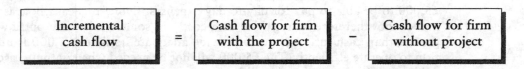

There follow some guide posts for finding relevant/incremental cash flows.

Exhibit 3.3 ABC plc: an example of profit to cash flow conversion

■ Machinery cost £20,000 at time 0, life of four years, zero scrap value.
■ Extra cash floats required: £5,000, at time 0.
■ Additional work in progress: £2,000 at time 0, £3,000 at time 2.
■ Increase in creditors: £1,000.

ABC plc	Accounting year				
Point in time (yearly intervals)	*0*	*1*	*2*	*3*	*4*
	£	£	£	£	£
Accounting profit		7,000	7,000	7,000	7,000
Add back depreciation		5,000	5,000	5,000	5,000
		12,000	12,000	12,000	12,000
Initial machine cost	−20,000				
Cash float	−5,000				5,000
Stock					
Closing stock	2,000	2,000	3,000	3,000	0
Opening stock		2,000	2,000	3,000	3,000
Net stock adjustment (Outflow −tive, Inflow +tive)	−2,000	0	−1,000	0	+3,000
Creditors					
End of year	1,000	1,000	1,000	1,000	0
Start of year		1,000	1,000	1,000	−1,000
Cash flow effect of creditors (Outflow −tive, Inflow +tive)	+1,000	0	0	0	−1,000
Net operating cash flow	−26,000	12,000	11,000	12,000	19,000
Point in time (yearly intervals)	*0*	*1*	*2*	*3*	*4*
Cash flow	−26,000	12,000	11,000	12,000	19,000

Cost of capital 12%

$$NPV = -26,000 + \frac{12,000}{(1 + 0.12)} + \frac{11,000}{(1 + 0.12)^2} + \frac{12,000}{(1 + 0.12)^3}$$

$$+ \frac{19,000}{(1 + 0.12)^4} = +£14,099$$

This project produces a positive NPV, i.e. it generates a return which is more than the required rate of 12%, and therefore should be accepted.

Include all opportunity costs

The direct inputs into a project are generally easy to understand and measure. However, quite often a project uses resources which already exist within the firm but which are in short supply and which cannot be replaced in the immediate future. That is, the project under consideration may be taking resources away from other projects. The loss of net cash flows from these other projects is termed an opportunity cost. For example, a firm may be considering a project that makes use of a factory which at present is empty. Because it is empty we should not automatically assume that the opportunity cost is zero. Perhaps the firm could engage in the alternative project of renting out the factory to another firm. The forgone rental income is a cost of the project under consideration.

Likewise if a project uses the services of specialist personnel this may be regarded as having an opportunity cost. The loss of these people to other parts of the organisation may reduce cash flows on other projects. If they cannot be replaced with equally able individuals then the opportunity cost will be the lost net cash flows. If equally able hired replacements are found then the extra cost imposed, by the additional salaries etc., on other projects should be regarded as an opportunity cost of the new project under consideration.

For a third example of opportunity cost, imagine your firm bought, when the price was low, a stock of platinum to use as a raw material. The total cost was £1m. It would be illogical to sell the final manufactured product at a price based on the old platinum value if the same quantity would now cost £3m. An alternative course of action would be to sell the platinum in its existing state, rather than to produce the manufactured product. The current market value of the raw platinum (£3m) would then be the opportunity cost.

Include all incidental effects

It is possible for a new project to either increase or reduce sales of other products of the company. Take the case of an airline company trying to decide whether to go ahead with a project to fly between the USA and Japan. The direct cash flows of selling tickets, etc. on these flights may not give a positive NPV. However, if the additional net revenue is included, from extra passengers choosing this airline firm for flights between, say, Europe and the USA, because it now offers a more complete world-wide service, the project may be viable.

On the other hand if a clothes retailer opens a second or a third outlet in the same town, it is likely to find custom is reduced at the original store. This loss elsewhere in the organisation becomes a relevant cash flow in the appraisal of the *new* project, that is, the new shop.

In the soft drink business the introduction of a new brand can reduce the sales of the older brands. This is not to say that a company should never risk any cannibalisation, only that if a new product is to be launched it should not be viewed in isolation. All incremental effects have to be allowed for, including those effects not directly associated with the new product or service.

Royal Dutch/Shell are to include the incidental effect of carbon emissions in all future projects – *see* Exhibit 3.4.

Exhibit 3.4

Environmental cost included in project appraisals

Royal Dutch/Shell, the Anglo-Dutch energy company, decided, in 2000, to include a cost for carbon emissions in all big projects. Each project is now required to achieve a satisfactory internal rate of return after the deduction of $5 per tonne of carbon dioxide in the years 2005–2009, rising to $20 per tonne in 2010.

Ignore sunk costs

Do not include sunk costs. For example, the project to build Concorde involved an enormous expenditure in design and manufacture. At the point where it had to be decided whether to put the aeroplane into service, the costs of development became irrelevant to the decision. Only incremental costs and inflows should be considered. The development costs are in the past and are bygones; they should be ignored. The money spent on development is irrecoverable, whatever the decision on whether to fly the plane. Similarly with Eurotunnel, the fact that the overspend runs into billions of pounds and the tunnel service is unlikely to make a profit does not mean that the incremental cost of using some electricity to power the trains and the cost of employing some train drivers should not be incurred. The £9bn+ already spent is irrelevant to the decision on whether to transport passengers and freight between France and the UK. So long as incremental costs are less than incremental benefits (cash flows when discounted) then the service should operate.

A common mistake in this area is to regard pre-project survey work already carried out or committed to (market demand screening, scientific study, geological survey, etc.) as a relevant cost. After all, the cost would not have been incurred but for the possibility of going ahead with the project. However, at the point of decision on whether to proceed, the survey cost is sunk – it will be incurred whether or not implementation takes place, and it therefore is not incremental. Sunk costs can be either costs for intangibles (such as research and development expenses), or costs for tangibles that may not be used for other purposes (such as the cost of the Eurotunnel). When dealing with sunk costs it is sometimes necessary to be resolute in the face of comments such as, 'good money is being thrown after bad' but always remember the 'bad' money outflow happened in the past and is no longer an input factor into a rigorous decision-making process.

Be careful with overheads

Overheads consist of such items as managerial salaries, rent, light, heat, etc. These are costs that are not directly associated with any one part of the firm or one project. An accountant often allocates these overhead costs amongst the various projects a firm is involved in. When trying to assess the viability of a project we should only include the incremental or extra expenses that would be incurred by going ahead with a project. Many of the general overhead expenses may be incurred regardless of whether the project takes place.

There are two types of overhead. The first type is truly incremental costs resulting from a project. For example, extra electricity, rental and administrative staff costs may be incurred by going ahead rather than abstaining. The second type of overhead consists of such items as head office managerial salaries, legal expertise, public relations, research and development and even the corporate jet. These costs are not directly associated with any one part of the firm or one project and will be incurred regardless of whether the project under consideration is embarked upon. The accountant generally charges a proportion of this overhead to particular divisions and projects. When trying to assess the viability of a project only the incremental costs incurred by going ahead are relevant. Those costs which are unaffected are irrelevant.

Dealing with interest

Interest on funds borrowed to invest does represent a cash outflow. However, it is wrong to include this element in the cash flow calculations. **To repeat, interest should not be deducted from the net cash flows.** This is because if it were subtracted this would amount to double counting because the opportunity cost of capital used to discount the cash flows already incorporates a cost of these funds. The net cash flows are reduced to a present value by allowing for the weighted average cost of finance to give a return to shareholders and lenders. If the un-discounted cash flows also had interest deducted there would be a serious understatement of NPV. For more details see Chapter 16 on the calculation of the firm's discount rate (cost of capital).

Worked example 3.1 Tamcar plc

The accountants at Tamcar plc, manufacturers of hairpieces, are trying to analyse the viability of a proposed new division, 'Baldies heaven'. They estimate that this project will have a life of four years before the market is swamped by the lifting of the present EU import ban on hairpieces. The estimated sales, made on three months' credit, are as follows:

Year	Sales (£)
20X1	1.5m
20X2	2.0m
20X3	2.5m
20X4	3.0m

Cash flows from sales may be regarded as occurring on the last day of the year and there are no bad debts.

Year	Cost of production (£)
20X1	0.75m
20X2	1.00m
20X3	1.25m
20X4	1.50m

Costs of production likewise can be assumed to be paid for on the last day of the year. There are no creditors.

At the start of the project an investment of £1m will be required in buildings, plant and machinery. These items will have a net worth of zero at the end of this project. The accountants depreciate the plant and machinery at 25 per cent per annum on a straight line basis.

A cash float of £0.5m will be required at the start. Also stocks will increase by £0.3m. These are both recoverable at the end of the project's life.

A £1m invoice for last year's scientific study of 'Baldies heaven' hairpiece technology (e.g. wind resistance and comb-ability) has yet to be paid.

The head office always allocates a proportion of central expenses to all divisions and projects. The share to be borne by 'Baldies heaven' is £500,000 per annum. The head office costs are unaffected by the new project.

The accountants have produced the following profit and loss accounts:

Year	20X1 £m	20X2 £m	20X3 £m	20X4 £m
Sales	1.50	2.00	2.50	3.00
Costs of production	0.75	1.00	1.25	1.50
Depreciation	0.25	0.25	0.25	0.25
Scientific survey	0.25	0.25	0.25	0.25
Head office	0.50	0.50	0.50	0.50
Profit/loss	−0.25	0	0.25	0.50

Accountants' summary
Investment: £2m   Return: £0.5m over 4 years

$$\text{Average Return on Investment (ROI)} = \frac{\text{Average profit}}{\text{Investment}} = \frac{0.5 \div 4}{2} = 0.0625 \text{ or } 6.25\%$$

Recommendation: do not proceed with this project as 6.25% is a poor return.

Required
Calculate the Net Present Value and recommend whether to accept this project or invest elsewhere.

Assume

- No inflation or tax.
- The return required on projects of this risk class is 11%.
- Start date of the project is 1.1.20X1.

Answer

- Depreciation is not a cash flow and should be excluded.
- The scientific survey is a sunk cost. This will not alter whether Tamcar chooses to go ahead or refuses to invest – it is irrelevant to the NPV calculation.
- Head office costs will be constant regardless of the decision to accept or reject the project, they are not incremental.

The sales figures shown in the first line of the table below are not the true cash receipts for each of those years because three months' credit is granted. Thus, in year one only three-quarters of £1.5m is actually received. An adjustment for debtors shows that one-quarter of the first year's sales are deducted. Thus £375,000 is received in the second year and therefore this is added to time 2's cash flow. However, one-quarter of the £2m of time 2's sales is subtracted because this is not received until the following year.

An assumption has been made concerning the receipt of debtor payments after production and distribution has ceased. In 20X4 sales are on the last day and given the three months' credit, cash is received after three months at time 4.25.

Tamcar cash flows

Time (annual intervals)	0	1	2	3	4	4.25
Year	20X1	20X1	20X2	20X3	20X4	20X5
Sales		+1.5	+2.0	+2.5	+3.0	
Buildings, plant, machinery	−1.0					
Cash float	−0.5				+0.5	
Stocks	−0.3				+0.3	
Costs of production		−0.75	−1.0	−1.25	−1.50	
Adjustment for debtors						
Opening debtors	0	0	0.375	0.500	0.625	0.75
Closing debtors	0	0.375	0.500	0.625	0.750	0
Cash flow adjustment for debtors		−0.375	−0.125	−0.125	−0.125	
Cash flow	−1.8	+0.375	+0.875	+1.125	+2.175	+0.75

$$\text{Net present value} \quad -1.8 + \frac{0.375}{(1.11)} + \frac{0.875}{(1.11)^2} + \frac{1.125}{(1.11)^3} + \frac{2.175}{(1.11)^4} + \frac{0.75}{(1.11)^{4.25}}$$

	−1.8	+0.338	0.710	0.823	+1.433	+0.481

NPV = + £1.985m

This is a project that adds significantly to shareholder wealth, producing £1.985m more than the minimum rate of return of 11 per cent required by the firm's finance providers.

Worked example 3.2 The International Seed Company (TISC)

As the newly appointed financial manager of TISC you are about to analyse a proposal for the marketing and distribution of a range of genetically engineered vegetable seeds which have been developed by a bio-technology firm. This firm will supply the seeds and permit TISC to market and distribute them under a licence.

Market research, costing £100,000, has already been carried out to establish the likely demand. After three years TISC will withdraw from the market because it anticipates that these products will be superseded by further bio-technological developments.

The annual payment to the bio-technology firm will be £1m for the licence; this will be payable at the end of each accounting year.

Also £500,000 will be needed initially to buy a fleet of vehicles for distribution. These vehicles will be sold at the end of the third year for £200,000.

There will be a need for a packaging and administrative facility. TISC is large and has a suitable factory with offices, which at present are empty. Head office has stated that they will let this space to your project at a reduced rent of £200,000 per annum payable at the end of the accounting year (the open market rental value is £1m p.a.).

The project would start on 1.1.20X1 and would not be subject to any taxation because of its special status as a growth industry. A relatively junior and inexperienced accountant has prepared forecast profit and loss accounts for the project as shown in the following table.

Year	20X1	20X2	20X3
Sales	5 (£m)	6 (£m)	6 (£m)
Costs			
Market research	0.1		
Raw material (seeds)	2.0	2.4	2.4
Licence	1.0	1.0	1.0
Vehicle fleet depreciation	0.1	0.1	0.1
Direct wages	0.5	0.5	0.5
Rent	0.2	0.2	0.2
Overhead	0.5	0.5	0.5
Variable transport costs	0.5	0.5	0.5
Profit	0.1	0.8	0.8

By expanding its product range with these new seeds the firm expects to attract a great deal of publicity which will improve the market position, and thus the profitability, of its other products. The benefit is estimated at £100,000 for each of the three years.

Head office normally allocates a proportion of its costs to any new project as part of its budgeting/costing process. This will be £100,000 for this project and has been included in the figures calculated for overhead by the accountant. The remainder of the overhead is directly related to the project.

The direct wages, seed purchases, overhead and variable transport costs can be assumed to be paid at the end of each year. Likewise, sales revenue may be assumed to be received at the end of each year. The firm will grant two months' credit to its customers. An initial cash float of £1m will be needed. This will be returned at the end of the third year.

Assume no inflation. An appropriate discount rate is 15 per cent.

Required

Assess the viability of the proposed project using the discounted cash flow technique you feel to be most appropriate.

Suggestion

Try to answer this question before reading the model answer.

Answer

Notes

- Market research cost is non-incremental.
- Opportunity cost of factory is £1m per annum.
- Vehicle depreciation does not belong in a cash flow calculation.
- The effect on TISC's other products is an incidental benefit.
- Head office cost apportionment should be excluded.

£m	*20X1 start*	*20X1 end*	*20X2 end*	*20X3 end*	*20X3 end*	*20X4 2 months*
Inflows						
Sales		5.0	6.0	6.0		
Benefit to divisions		0.1	0.1	0.1		
Cash at end					1.0	
Vehicles					0.2	
Total inflows	0	5.1	6.1	6.1	1.2	0
Outflows						
Licence		1.0	1.0	1.0		
Vehicles	0.5					
Property rent (opportunity cost)		1.0	1.0	1.0		
Raw materials		2.0	2.4	2.4		
Direct wages		0.5	0.5	0.5		
Overheads		0.4	0.4	0.4		
Variable transport		0.5	0.5	0.5		
Initial cash	1.0					
Cash flows after outflows	−1.5	−0.3	0.3	0.3	1.2	0
Adjustment for debtors						
Debtor: start		0	0.833	1.00		1.0
end		0.833	1.000	1.00		0
Cash flow effect of debtors		−0.833	−0.167	0	0	+1.0
Cash flows	−1.5	−1.133	+0.133	+0.3	+1.2	+1.0

Cash flows

Net present value

$$NPV = -1.5 \quad \frac{-1.133}{(1.15)} + \frac{0.133}{(1.15)^2} + \frac{0.3}{(1.15)^3}$$

$$+ \frac{1.2}{(1.15)^3} + \frac{1.00}{(1.15)^{3.167}}$$

$$NPV = -1.5 - 0.985 + 0.101 + 0.197 + 0.789 + 0.642 = -£0.756$$

Conclusion

Do not proceed with the project as it returns less than 15 per cent.

The Severn river crossing consortium had to pay a great deal of attention to the estimated relevant cash flows associated with building and operating the new bridge linking Wales and England. Many thought that they had overestimated the likely revenue and therefore would destroy shareholder wealth. Only time will tell. *See* Exhibit 3.5.

Exhibit 3.5

The New Severn River Crossing

One of the biggest UK projects in the mid-1990s was the construction of a second bridge linking South Wales and England. The £330m 3-mile bridge was constructed under the government's Private Finance Initiative (PFI). The deal is as follows: a franchise is awarded to the Severn River Crossing, plc (SRC) to operate and receive toll income on the two Severn bridges for a period of 30 years. In return SRC had to build and finance the second bridge and maintain both for the period of the franchise. SRC has four shareholders, Laing and GTM Entrepose with 35% each, Bank of America International Finance Corporation with 15%, and BZW, the investment bank, with 15%.

The first Severn bridge carried 19m vehicles in 1995/96, at a toll rate of £3.80 for a car, £7.70 for a small goods vehicle and £11.50 for a heavy goods vehicle to enter Wales (the eastward journey is toll free). The government has imposed caps on the rate of increase of these tolls to the retail price index. Also there is to be no subsidy from government. The construction consortium were criticised for making a cut-price bid to win the franchise. However, they are confident volumes will rise significantly over the next three decades to justify their investment.

Source: Based on *Financial Times*, 15 May 1996.

THE REPLACEMENT DECISION

In the dynamic and competitive world of business it is important to review operations continually to ensure efficient production. Technological change brings with it the danger that a competitor has reduced costs and has leaped ahead. Thus, it is often wise to examine, say, the machinery used in the production process to see if it should be replaced with a new improved version. This is a continual process in many industries, and the frustrating aspect is that the existing machine may have years of useful life left in it. Despite this the right decision is sometimes to dispose of the old and bring in the new. If your firm does not produce at lowest cost, another one will.

In making a replacement decision the increased costs associated with the purchase and installation of the new machine have to be weighed against the savings from switching to the new method of production. In other words the incremental cash flows are the focus of attention. The worked example of Amtarc plc demonstrates the incremental approach.

Worked example 3.3 Amtarc plc

Amtarc plc produces Tarcs with a machine which is now four years old. The management team estimates that this machine has a useful life of four more years before it will be sold for scrap, raising £10,000.

Q-leap, a manufacturer of machines suitable for Tarc production, has offered its new computer-controlled Q-2000 to Amtarc for a cost of £800,000 payable immediately.

If Amtarc sold its existing machine now, on the secondhand market, it would receive £70,000. (Its book value, after depreciation, is £150,000.) The Q-2000 will have a life of four years before being sold for scrap for £20,000.

The attractive features of the Q-2000 are its lower raw material wastage and its reduced labour requirements. Selling price and variable overhead will be the same as for the old machine.

The accountants have prepared the figures shown below on the assumption that output will remain constant at last year's level of 100,000 Tarcs per annum.

	Profit per unit of Tarc	
	Old machine	Q-2000
	£	£
Sale price	45	45
Costs		
Labour	10	9
Materials	15	14
Variable overhead	7	7
Fixed overhead		
factory admin., etc.	5	5
depreciation	0.35	1.95
Profit per Tarc	7.65	8.05

The depreciation per unit has been calculated as follows:

$$\frac{\text{Total depreciation for a year}}{\text{Output for a year}}$$

$$\text{Old machine:} \quad \frac{(150,000 - 10,000)/4}{100,000} = £0.35$$

$$\text{Q-2000:} \quad \frac{(800,000 - 20,000)/4}{100,000} = £1.95$$

An additional benefit of the Q-2000 will be the reduction in required raw material buffer stocks – releasing £120,000 at the outset. However, because of the lower labour needs, redundancy payments of £50,000 will be necessary after one year.

Assume
- No inflation or tax.
- The required rate of return is 10 per cent.
- To simplify the analysis sales, labour costs, raw material costs and variable overhead costs all occur on the last day of each year.

Required
Using the NPV method decide whether to continue using the old machine or to purchase the Q-2000.

Hints
Remember to undertake incremental analysis. That is, analyse only the difference in cash flow which will result from the decision to go ahead with the purchase. Remember to include the £10,000 opportunity cost of scrapping the old machine in four years if the Q-2000 is purchased.

Answers

Stage 1
Note the irrelevant information:

1 Depreciation is not a cash flow and should not be included.
2 The book value of the machine is merely an accounting entry and has little relationship with the market value. Theoretically book value has no influence on the decision. (In practice, however, senior management may be reluctant to write off the surplus book value through the profit and loss account as this may prejudice an observer's view of their performance – despite there being no change in the underlying economic position.)

Stage 2
Work out the annual incremental cost savings.

	Savings per Tarc		
	Old machine £	Q-2000 £	Saving £
Labour	10	9	1
Materials	15	14	1
Total saving			2

Total annual saving £2 × 100,000 = £200,000.

Stage 3 Incremental cash flow table

Time £000s	0	1	2	3	4
Purchase of Q-2000	−800				
Scrap of old machine	+70				
Raw material stocks	+120				
Opportunity cost (old machine)					−10
Redundancy payments		−50			
Sale of Q-2000					+20
Annual cost savings		+200	+200	+200	+200
	−610	+150	+200	+200	+210

Stage 4 Calculate NPV

Discounted cash flows

$$-610 \quad + \frac{150}{1.1} + \frac{200}{(1.1)^2} + \frac{200}{(1.1)^3} + \frac{210}{(1.1)^4}$$

NPV = −£14,660.

The negative NPV indicates that shareholder wealth will be higher if the existing machine is retained.

REPLACEMENT CYCLES

Many business assets, machinery and vehicles especially, become increasingly expensive to operate and maintain as they become older. This rising cost burden prompts the thought that there must be a point when it is better to buy a replacement than to face rising repair bills. Assets such as vehicles are often replaced on a regular cycle, say every two or three years, depending on the comparison between the benefit to be derived by delaying the replacement decision (that is, the postponed cash outflow associated with the purchase of new assets) and the cost in terms of higher maintenance costs (and lower secondhand value achieved with the sale of the used asset).

Consider the case of a car rental firm which is considering a switch to a new type of car. The cars cost £10,000 and a choice has to be made between four alternative (mutually exclusive) projects (four alternative regular replacement cycles). Project 1 is to sell the cars on the secondhand market after one year for £7,000. Project 2 is to sell after two years for £5,000. Projects 3 and 4 are three-year and four-year cycles and will produce £3,000 and £1,000 respectively on the secondhand market. The cost of maintenance rises from £500 in the first year to £900 in the second, £1,200 in the third and £2,500 in the fourth. The cars are not worth keeping for more than four years because of the bad publicity associated with breakdowns. The revenue streams and other costs are unaffected by which cycle is selected. We will focus on achieving the lowest present value of the costs.

If we make the simplifying assumption that all the cash flows occur at annual intervals then the relevant cash flows are as set out in Exhibit 3.6.

Exhibit 3.6 Relevant cash flows

Point in time (yearly intervals)		0	1	2	3	4
Project 1		£				
Replace after	Purchase cost	−10,000				
one year	Maintenance		−500			
	Sale proceeds		+7,000			
	Net cash flow	−10,000	+6,500			
Project 2						
Replace after	Purchase cost	−10,000				
two years	Maintenance		−500	−900		
	Sale proceeds			+5,000		
	Net cash flow	−10,000	−500	+4,100		
Project 3						
Replace after	Purchase cost	−10,000				
three years	Maintenance		−500	−900	−1,200	
	Sale proceeds				+3,000	
	Net cash flow	−10,000	−500	−900	+1,800	

▶

Exhibit 3.6 Relevant cash flows *continued*

Point in time (yearly intervals)		0	1	2	3	4
Project 4						
Replace after four years	Purchase cost	−10,000				
	Maintenance		−500	−900	−1,200	−2,500
	Sale proceeds					+1,000
	Net cash flow	−10,000	−500	−900	−1,200	−1,500

Assuming a discount rate of 10 per cent the Present Values (PVs) of costs of one cycle of the projects are:

$$PV_1 \quad -10,000 \quad + \quad \frac{6,500}{1.1} \qquad\qquad\qquad\qquad\qquad = -4,090.90$$

$$PV_2 \quad -10,000 \quad - \quad \frac{500}{1.1} \quad + \quad \frac{4,100}{(1.1)^2} \qquad\qquad\qquad = -7,066.12$$

$$PV_3 \quad -10,000 \quad - \quad \frac{500}{1.1} \quad + \quad \frac{900}{(1.1)^2} \quad + \quad \frac{1,800}{(1.1)^3} \qquad = -9,845.98$$

$$PV_4 \quad -10,000 \quad - \quad \frac{500}{1.1} \quad - \quad \frac{900}{(1.1)^2} \quad - \quad \frac{1,200}{(1.1)^3} \quad - \quad \frac{1,500}{(1.1)^4} = -13,124.44$$

At first sight the figures in Exhibit 3.6 might suggest that the first project is the best. Such a conclusion would be based on the normal rule with mutually exclusive projects of selecting the one with the lowest present value of costs. However, this is not a standard situation because purchases and sales of vehicles have to be allowed for far beyond the first round in the replacement cycle. If we can make the assumption that there are no increases in costs and the cars can be replaced with identical models on regular cycles in the future[1] then the pattern of cash flows for the third project, for example, are as shown in Exhibit 3.7.

Exhibit 3.7 Cash flows for Project 3

Time (years)	0	1	2	3	4	5	6	7 ...
Cash flows (£)								
1st generation	−10,000	−500	−900	+1,800				
2nd generation				−10,000	−500	−900	+1,800	
3rd generation							−10,000	−500 ...

One way of dealing with a long-lived project of this kind is to calculate the present values of numerous cycles stretching into the future. This can then be compared with other projects' present values calculated in a similarly time-consuming fashion.

Fortunately there is a much quicker technique available called the annual equivalent annuity method (AEA). This third project involves three cash outflows followed by a cash inflow within one cycle as shown in Exhibit 3.8.

Exhibit 3.8 Cash outflows and cash inflow in one cycle

Time (years)	0	1	2	3
Cash flows (£)	–10,000	–500	–900	+1,800

This produces a one-cycle present value of –£9,845.98. The annual equivalent annuity (AEA) method finds the amount that would be paid in each of the next three years if each annual payment were identical and the three payments gave the same (equivalent) present value of –£9,845.98, that is, the constant amount which would replace the ? in Exhibit 3.9.

Exhibit 3.9 Using the AEA

Time (years)	0	1	2	3	Present value
Actual cash flows (£)	–10,000	–500	–900	+1,800	–9,845.98
Annual equivalent annuity (£)		?	?	?	–9,845.98

(Recall that the first cash flow under an 'immediate' annuity arises after one year.)

To find the AEA we need to employ the annuity table in Appendix III. This table gives the value of a series of £1 cash flows occurring at annual intervals in terms of present money. Normally these 'annuity factors' (af) are multiplied by the amount of the cash flow that is received regularly, the annuity (A), to obtain the present value, PV. In this case we already know the PV and we can obtain the af by looking at the three-year row and the 10 per cent column. The missing element is the annual annuity.

$$PV = A \times af$$

$$\text{or } A = \frac{PV}{af}$$

In the case of the three-year replacement:

$$A = \frac{-£9,845.98}{2.4869} = -£3,959.14$$

Thus, two alternative sets of cash flows give the same present value (*see* Exhibit 3.10).

Exhibit 3.10 Present value, calculated by Cash flow 1 and cash flow 2

Time (years)	0 £	1	2	3
Cash flow 1	–10,000	–500	–900	+1,800
Cash flow 2		–3,959.14	–3,959.14	–3,959.14

The second generation of cars bought at the end of the third year will have a cost of –£9,845.98 when discounted to the end of the third year (assuming both zero inflation and that the discount rate remains at 10 per cent). The present value of the costs of this second generation of vehicle is equivalent to the present value of an annuity of –£3,959.14. Thus replacing the car every three years is equivalent to a cash flow of –£3,959.14 every year to infinity (see Exhibit 3.11).

Exhibit 3.11 Replacing the car every three years

Time (years)	0	1	2	3	4	5	6	7 ...
Cash flows (£)								
First generation	–10,000	–500	–900	+1,800				
Second generation				–10,000	–500	–900	+1,800	
Third generation							–10,000	–500 ...
Annual equivalent annuity		0 –3,959.14	–3,959.14	–3,959.14	–3,959.14	–3,959.14	–3,959.14	–3,959.14

If all the other projects are converted to their annual equivalent annuities a comparison can be made.

Exhibit 3.12 Using AEAs for all projects

Cycle	Present value of one cycle (PV)	Annuity factor (af)	Annual equivalent annuity (PV/af)
1 year	–4,090.90	0.9091	–4,500.00
2 years	–7,066.12	1.7355	–4,071.52
3 years	–9,845.98	2.4869	–3,959.14
4 years	–13,124.44	3.1699	–4,140.33

Thus Project 3 requires the lowest equivalent annual cash flow and is the optimal replacement cycle. This is over £540 per year cheaper than replacing the car every year.

A valid alternative to the annual equivalent annuity is the lowest common multiple (LCM) method. Here the alternatives are compared using the present value of the costs over a time-span equal to the lowest common multiple of the cycle lengths. So the cash flow for 12 cycles of Project 1 would be discounted and compared with six cycles of Project 2, four cycles of Project 3 and three cycles of Project 4. The AEA method is the simplest and quickest method in cases where the lowest common multiple is high. For instance the LCM of five-, six- and seven-year cycles is 35 years, and involves a great many calculations.

Worked example 3.4 Brrum plc

Suppose the firm Brrum has to decide between two machines, A and B, to replace an old worn-out one. Whichever new machine is chosen it will be replaced on a regular cycle. Both machines produce the same level of output. Because they produce exactly the same output we do not need to examine the cash inflows at all to choose between the machines; we can concentrate solely on establishing the lower-cost machine.

Brrum plc

- Machine A costs £30m, lasts three years and costs £8m a year to run.
- Machine B costs £20m, lasts two years and costs £12m a year to run.

Cash flows

Point in time (yearly intervals)	0	1	2	3	PV (6%)
Machine A (£m)	−30	−8	−8	−8	−51.38
Machine B (£m)	−20	−12	−12	–	−42.00

Because Machine B has a lower PV of cost, should we jump to the conclusion that this is the better option? Well, Machine B will have to be replaced one year before Machine A and therefore, there are further cash flows to consider and discount.

If we were to assume a constant discount rate of 6 per cent and no change in costs over a number of future years, then we can make a comparison between the two machines. To do this we need to convert the total PV of the costs to a cost per year. We convert the PV of the costs associated with each machine to the equivalent annuity.

Machine A

Machine A has a PV of −£51.38m. We need to find an annuity with a PV of −£51.38 which has regular equal costs occurring at years 1, 2 and 3.

Look in the annuity table along the row of three years and down the column of 6% to get the three-year annuity factor.

Machine A

PV = Annual annuity payment (A) × 3-year annuity factor (af)

−51.38 = A × 2.673

A = −51.38/2.673 = −£19.22m per year

Point in time (yearly intervals)	0	1	2	3	PV (6%)
Cash flows (£m)	−30	−8	−8	−8	−51.38
Equivalent 3-year annuity (£m)		−19.22	−19.22	−19.22	−51.38

When Machine A needs to be replaced at the end of the third year, if we can assume it is replaced by a machine of equal cost we again have a PV of costs for the Year 3 of £51.38m dated at Year 3. This too has an equivalent annuity of −£19.22m. Thus, the −£19.22m annual costs is an annual cost for many years beyond Year 3.

Machine B

PV = A × af

−42 = A × 1.8334

A = −42/1.8334 = −£22.908m

Point in time (yearly intervals)	0	1	2	PV (6%)
Cash flows (£m)	−20	−12	−12	−42
Equivalent 2-year annuity (£m)		−22.91	−22.91	−42

Again, if we assume that at the end of two years the machine is replaced with an identical one, with identical costs, then the annuity of –£22.91m can be assumed to be continuing into the future.

Comparing the annual annuities
Machine A: (£m) –19.22.
Machine B: (£m) –22.91.

When we compare the annual annuities we see that Machine A, in fact, has the lower annual cost and is therefore the better buy.

WHEN TO INTRODUCE A NEW MACHINE

Businesses, when switching from one kind of a machine to another, have to decide on the timing of that switch. The best option may not be to dispose of the old machine immediately. It may be better to wait for a year or two because the costs of running the old machine may amount to less than the equivalent annual cost of starting a regular cycle with replacements. However, eventually the old machine is going to become more costly due to its lower efficiency, increased repair bills or declining secondhand value. Let us return to the case of the car rental firm. It has been established that when a replacement cycle is begun for the new type of car, it should be a three-year cycle. The existing type of car used by the firm has a potential further life of two years. The firm is considering three alternative courses of action. The first is to sell the old vehicles immediately, raising £7,000 per car, and then begin a three-year replacement cycle with the new type of car. The second possibility is to spend £500 now to service the vehicles ready for another year's use. At the end of the year the cars could be sold for £5,200 each. The third option is to pay £500 for servicing now, followed by a further £2,000 in one year to maintain the vehicles on the road for a second year, after which they would be sold for £1,800. The easiest approach for dealing with a problem of this nature is to calculate NPVs for all the possible alternatives. We will assume that the revenue aspect of this car rental business can be ignored as this will not change regardless of which option is selected. The relevant cash flows are shown in Exhibit 3.13. Note that the annual equivalent annuity cash flow, rather than the actual cash flows for the three-year cycle of new cars, is incorporated and is assumed to continue to infinity. It is therefore a perpetuity.

(Note that the sums of £3,959.14 are perpetuities starting at Times 1, 2 and 3, and so are valued at Times 0, 1 and 2. The latter two therefore have to be discounted back one and two years respectively). The switch to the new cars should take place after one year. Thereafter the new cars should be replaced every three years. This policy is over £800 cheaper than selling off the old cars immediately.

The net present value calculations are as set out in Exhibit 3.14.

Exhibit 3.13 Cash flow per car (excluding operating revenues, etc.)

Point in time (yearly intervals)		0	1	2	3 → ∞
Option 1 – sell old car at time 0	Secondhand value	+7,000			
	New car		–3,959.14	–3,959.14	–3,959.14
	Net cash flow	+7,000	–3,959.14	–3,959.14	–3,959.14
Option 2 – sell old car after one year	Secondhand value		+5,200		
	Maintenance	–500			
	New car			–3,959.14	–3,959.14
	Net cash flow	–500	+5,200	–3,959.14	–3,959.14
Option 3 – sell old car after two years	Secondhand value			+1,800	
	Maintenance	–500	–2,000		
	New car				–3,959.14
	Net cash flow	–500	–2,000	+1,800	–3,959.14

Exhibit 3.14 NPV calculations

$$\text{Option 1} \quad + \quad 7,000 \quad - \quad \frac{3,959.14}{0.1} \quad = -£32,591.4$$

$$\text{Option 2} \quad -500 \quad + \quad \frac{5,200}{1.1} \quad - \quad \frac{3,959.14}{0.1} \times \frac{1}{1.1} \quad = -£31,764.91$$

$$\text{Option 3} \quad -500 \quad - \quad \frac{2,000}{1.1} \quad + \quad \frac{1,800}{(1.1)^2} \quad - \quad \frac{3,959.14}{0.1} \times \frac{1}{(1.1)^2} \quad = -£33,550.74$$

DRAWBACKS OF THE ANNUAL EQUIVALENT ANNUITY METHOD

It is important to note that annual equivalent annuity analysis relies on there being a high degree of predictability of cash flows stretching into the future. While the technique can be modified reasonably satisfactorily for the problems caused by inflation we may encounter severe problems if the assets in question are susceptible to a high degree of technical change and associated cash flows. An example here would be computer hardware where simultaneously, over short time periods both technical capability increases and cost of purchase decreases. The absence of predictability means that the AEA approach is not suitable in a number of situations. The requirement that identical replacement takes place can be a severe limitation but the AEA approach can be used for approximate analysis, which is sufficient for practical decisions in many situations – provided the analyst does not become too preoccupied with mathematical preciseness and remembers that good judgement is also required.

TIMING OF PROJECTS

In some industries the mutually exclusive projects facing the firm may simply be whether to take a particular course of action now or to make shareholders better off by considering another possibility, for instance, to implement the action in a future year. It may be that taking action now would produce a positive NPV and is therefore attractive. However, by delaying action an even higher NPV can be obtained. Take the case of Lochglen distillery. Ten years ago it laid down a number of vats of whisky. These have a higher market value the older the whisky becomes. The issue facing the management team is to decide in which of the next seven years to bottle and sell it. The table in Exhibit 3.15 gives the net cash flows available for each of the seven alternative projects.

Exhibit 3.15 Lochglen distillery's choices

		Year of bottling					
Point in time (yearly intervals)	*0*	*1*	*2*	*3*	*4*	*5*	*6*
Net cash flow £000s per vat	60	75	90	103	116	129	139
Percentage change on previous year		25%	20%	14.4%	12.6%	11.2%	7.8%

The longer the firm refrains from harvesting, the greater the size of the money inflow. However, this does not necessarily imply that shareholders will be best served by delaying as long as possible. They have an opportunity cost for their funds and therefore the firm must produce an adequate return over a period of time. In the case of Lochglen the assumption is that the firm requires a 9 per cent return on projects. The calculation of the NPVs for each project is easy (*see* Exhibit 3.16).

As shown in Exhibit 3.16, the optimal point is at Year 5 when the whisky has reached the ripe old age of 15. Note also that prior to the fifth year the value increased at an annual rate greater than 9 per cent. After Year 5 (or 15 years old) the rate of increase is less than the cost of capital. Another way of viewing this is to say that, if the whisky was sold when at 15 years old the cash received could be invested elsewhere (for the same level of risk) and receive a return of 9 per cent, which is more than the 7.8 per cent available by holding the whisky one more year.

Exhibit 3.16 NPVs for Lochglen distillery's choices

		Year of bottling					
Point in time (yearly intervals)	*0*	*1*	*2*	*3*	*4*	*5*	*6*
£000s per vat		$\frac{75}{1.09}$	$\frac{90}{(1.09)^2}$	$\frac{103}{(1.09)^3}$	$\frac{116}{(1.09)^4}$	$\frac{129}{(1.09)^5}$	$\frac{139}{(1.09)^6}$
Net present value	60	68.8	75.8	79.5	82.2	83.8	82.9

THE MAKE OR BUY DECISION

A perennial issue which many organisations have to address is whether it is better to buy a particular item, such as a component, from a supplier or to produce the item in-house. If the firm produces for itself it will incur the costs of set-up as well as the on-going annual costs. These costs can be avoided by buying in but this has the potential drawback that the firm may be forced to pay a high market price. This is essentially an incremented cash flow problem. We need to establish the difference between the costs of set-up and production in-house and the costs of purchase. Take the case of Davis and Davies plc who manufacture fishing rods. At the moment they buy in the 'eyes' for the rods from I'spies plc at £1 per set. They expect to make use of 100,000 sets per annum for the next few years. If Davis and Davies were to produce their own 'eyes' they would have to spend £40,000 immediately on machinery, setting up and training. The machinery will have a life of four years and the annual cost of production of 100,000 sets will be £80,000, £85,000, £92,000 and £100,000 respectively. The cost of bought-in components is not expected to remain at £1 per set. The more realistic estimates are £105,000 for Year 1, followed by £120,000, £128,000 and £132,000 for Years 2 to 4 respectively, for 100,000 sets per year. The new machinery will be installed in an empty factory the open market rental value of which is £20,000 per annum and the firm's cost of capital is 11 per cent. The extra cash flows associated with in-house production compared with buying in are as set out in Exhibit 3.17.

As the incremental NPV is negative Davis and Davies should continue to purchase 'eyes'. The present values of the future annual savings are worth less than the initial investment for self-production.

Exhibit 3.17 Cash flows for producing 'eyes' in-house

Points in time (yearly intervals) £000s	0	1	2	3	4
1 Cash flows of self-production	40	80	85	92	100
2 Plus opportunity costs		20	20	20	20
3 Relevant cash flows of making	40	100	105	112	120
4 Costs of purchasing component		105	120	128	132
Incremented cash flow due to making (line 4 – line 3)	–40	5	15	16	12

Net present value of incremental cash flows

$$-40 + \frac{5}{1.11} + \frac{15}{(1.11)^2} + \frac{16}{(1.11)^3} + \frac{12}{(1.11)^4}$$

NPV = –£3,717

FLUCTUATING OUTPUT

Many businesses and individual machines operate at less than full capacity for long periods of time. Sometimes this is due to the nature of the firm's business. For instance, electricity demand fluctuates through the day and over the year. Fluctuating output can produce some interesting problems for project appraisal analysis. Take the case of the Potato Sorting Company, which grades and bags potatoes in terms of size and quality. During the summer and autumn its two machines work at full capacity, which is the equivalent of 20,000 bags per machine per year. However, in the six months of the winter and spring the machines work at half capacity because fewer home grown potatoes need to be sorted. The operating cost of the machine per bag is 20 pence. The machines were installed over 50 years ago and can be regarded as still having a very long productive life. Despite this they have no secondhand value because modern machines called Fastsort now dominate the market. Fastsort has an identical capacity to the old machine but its running cost is only 10 pence per bag. These machines are also expected to be productive indefinitely, but they cost £12,000 each to purchase and install. The new production manager is keen on getting rid of the two old machines and replacing them with two Fastsort machines. She has presented the figures given in Exhibit 3.18 to a board meeting on the assumption of a cost of capital of 10 per cent.

The production manager has identified a way to save the firm £6,000 and is duly proud of her presentation. The newly appointed finance director thanks her for bringing this issue to the attention of the board but thinks that they should consider a third possibility. This is to replace only one of the machines. The virtue of this approach is that

Exhibit 3.18 Comparison of old machines with Fastsort

Cost of two old machines			
Output per machine = per year	rate of 20,000 p.a. for six months 20,000 × 0.5	=	10,000
+	rate of 10,000 p.a. for six months 10,000 × 0.5	=	$\dfrac{5,000}{15,000}$
15,000 bags @ 20p × 2 = £6,000.			
Present value of a perpetuity of £6,000:		$\dfrac{6,000}{0.1}$ =	£60,000
Cost of the Fastsorts			
Annual output – same as under old machines, 30,000 bags p.a.			
Annual operating cost 30,000 × 10p = £3,000			
Present value of operating costs $\dfrac{3,000}{0.1}$ =		£30,000	
Plus initial investment		£24,000	
Overall cost in present value terms		£54,000	

during the slack six months only the Fastsort will be used and can be supplemented with the old machine during the busy period, thus avoiding £12,000 of initial investment. The figures work out as set out in Exhibit 3.19.

Exhibit 3.19 Replacing only one old machine

	Fastsort	Old machine
Output	20,000 bags	10,000 bags
Initial investment	£12,000	
Operating costs	10p × 20,000 = £2,000	20p × 10,000 = £2,000
Present value of operating costs	$\dfrac{2,000}{0.1}$ = £20,000	$\dfrac{2,000}{0.1}$ = £20,000
Total present value	£12,000 + £20,000	+ £20,000 = £52,000

The board decides to replace only one of the machines as this saves £8,000 compared with £6,000 under the production manager's proposal.

CONCLUDING COMMENTS

Finding appropriate cash flows to include in a project appraisal often involves some difficulty in data collection and requires some thoughtfulness in applying the concepts of incremental cash flow. The reader who has diligently worked through this chapter and has overcome the barriers to understanding may be more than a little annoyed at being told that the understanding of these issues is merely one of the stages leading to successful application of net present value to practical business problems. The logical, mathematical and conceptual knowledge presented above has to be married to an appreciation of real-world limitations imposed by the awkward fact that it is people who have to be persuaded to act to implement a plan. This is an issue examined in the next chapter. Further real-world complications such as the existence of risk, of inflation and taxation and of limits placed on availability of capital are covered in subsequent chapters.

KEY POINTS AND CONCEPTS

- **Raw data** have to be checked for accuracy, reliability, timeliness, expense of collection, etc.

- **Depreciation** is not a cash flow and should be excluded.

- **Profit** is a poor substitute for cash flow. For example, working capital adjustments may be needed to modify the profit figures for NPV analysis.

- Analyse on the basis of **incremental cash flows**. That is the difference between the cash flows arising if the project is implemented and the cash flows if the project is not implemented:

- opportunity costs associated with, say, using an asset which has an alternative employment are relevant;
- incidental effects, that is, cash flow effects throughout the organisation, should be considered along with the obvious direct effects;
- sunk costs – costs which will not change regardless of the decision to proceed are clearly irrelevant;
- allocated overhead is a non-incremental cost and is irrelevant;
- interest should not be double counted by both including interest as a cash flow and including it as an element in the discount rate.

■ The replacement decision is an example of the application of incremental cash flow analysis.

■ Annual equivalent annuities (AEA) can be employed to estimate the optimal replacement cycle for an asset under certain restrictive assumptions. The lowest common multiple (LCM) method is sometimes employed for short-lived assets.

■ Whether to repair the old machine or sell it and buy a new machine is a very common business dilemma. Incremental cash flow analysis helps us to solve these types of problems. Other applications include the timing of projects, the issue of fluctuating output and the make or buy decision.

REFERENCES AND FURTHER READING

Bierman, H. and Smidt, S. (1992) *The Capital Budgeting Decision*, 8th edn. New York: Macmillan. Chapters 5 and 7 are particularly useful for a student at introductory level.

Carsberg, B.V. (1975) *Economics of Business Decisions*. Harmondsworth: Penguin. An economist's perspective on relevant cash flows.

Coulthurst, N.J. (1986) 'The application of the incremental principle in capital investment project evaluation', *Accounting and Business Research*, Autumn. A discussion of the theoretical and practical application of the incremental cash flow principle.

Damodaran, A. (1999) *Applied Corporate Finance*. New York: Wiley. A clear account of some of the issues discussed in this chapter.

Gordon, L.A. and Stark, A.W. (1989) 'Accounting and economic rates of return: a note on depreciation and other accruals', *Journal of Business Finance and Accounting*, 16(3), pp. 425–32. Considers the problem of depreciation – an algebraic approach.

Pohlman, R.A., Santiago, E.S. and Markel, F.L. (1988) 'Cash flow estimation practices of larger firms', *Financial Management*, Summer. Evidence on large US corporation cash flow estimation practices.

Reinhardt, U.E. (1973) 'Break-even analysis for Lockheed's Tristar: an application of financial theory', *Journal of Finance*, 28, pp. 821–38, September. An interesting application of the principle of the opportunity cost of funds.

Wilkes, F.M. (1983) *Capital Budgeting Techniques*, 2nd edn. Chichester: Wiley. Useful if your maths is up to scratch.

Wright, M.G. (1973) *Discounted Cash Flow*, 2nd edn. Maidenhead: McGraw-Hill. Chapter 4 deals with cash flows at an introductory level.

SELF-REVIEW QUESTIONS

1   Imagine the Ministry of Defence have spent £50m researching and developing a new guided weapon system. Explain why this fact may be irrelevant to the decision on whether to go ahead with production.

2   'Those business school graduates don't know what they are talking about. We have to allocate overheads to every department and activity. If we simply excluded this cost there would be a big lump of costs not written off. All projects must bear some central overhead.' Discuss this statement.

3   What is an annual equivalent annuity?

4   What are the two main techniques available for evaluating mutually exclusive projects with different lengths of life? Why is it not valid simply to use NPVs?

5   Arcmat plc owns a factory which at present is empty. Mrs Hambicious, a business strategist, has been working on a proposal for using the factory for doll manufacture. This will require complete modernisation. Mrs Hambicious is a little confused about project appraisal and has asked your advice about which of the following are relevant and incremental cash flows.

    a   The future cost of modernising the factory.

    b   The £100,000 spent two months ago on a market survey investigating the demand for these plastic dolls.

    c   Machines to produce the dolls – cost £10m payable on delivery.

    d   Depreciation on the machines.

    e   Arcmat's other product lines are expected to be more popular due to the complementary nature of the new doll range with these existing products – the net cash flow effect is anticipated at £1m.

    f   Three senior managers will be drafted in from other divisions for a period of a year.

    g   A proportion of the US head office costs.

    h   The tax saving due to the plant investment being offset against taxable income.

    i   The £1m of additional raw material stock required at the start of production.

    j   The interest that will be charged on the £20m bank loan needed to initiate this project.

    k   The cost of the utility services installed last year.

6   In a 'make or buy' type of decision should we also consider factors not easily quantified such as security of supply, convenience and the morale of the workforce? (This question is meant to start you thinking about the issues discussed in Chapter 4. You are not expected to give a detailed answer yet.)

7   'Depreciation is a cost recognised by tax authorities so why don't you use it in project appraisal?' Help the person who made this statement.

8   A firm is considering the implementation of a new project to produce slippers. The equipment to be used has sufficient spare capacity to allow this new production without affecting existing product ranges. The production manager suggests that because the equipment has been paid for it is a sunk cost and should not be included in the project appraisal calculations. Do you accept his argument?

QUESTIONS AND PROBLEMS

1   The Tenby-Sandersfoot Dock company is considering the reopening of one of its moth-balled loading docks. Repairs and new equipment will cost £250,000. To operate the new dock will require additional dockside employees costing £70,000 p.a. There will also be a need for additional administrative staff and other overheads such as extra stationery, insurance and telephone costs amounting to £85,000 p.a. Electricity and other energy used on the dock is anticipated to cost £40,000 p.a. The London head office will allocate £50,000 of its (unchanged) costs to this project. Other docks will experience a reduction in receipts of about £20,000 due to some degree of cannibalisation. Annual fees expected from the new dock are £255,000 p.a.

Assume
- all cash flows arise at the year end except the initial repair and equipment costs which are incurred at the outset;
- no tax or inflation;
- no sales are made on credit.

a   Lay out the net annual cash flow calculations. Explain your reasoning.

b   Assume an infinite life for the project and a cost of capital of 17 per cent. What is the net present value?

2   A senior management team at Railcam, a supplier to the railway industry, is trying to prepare a cash flow forecast for the years 20X1–20X5. The estimated sales are:

Year	20X1	20X2	20X3	20X4	20X5
Sales (£)	20m	22m	24m	21m	25m

These sales will be made on three months' credit and there will be no bad debts.

There are only three cost elements. First, wages amounting to £6m p.a. Second, raw materials costing one-half of sales for the year. Raw material suppliers grant three months of credit. Third, direct overhead at £5m per year.

Calculate the net operating cash flow for the years 20X2–20X4. Start date: 1.1.20X1.

3   (*Examination level*) Pine Ltd have spent £20,000 researching the prospects for a new range of products. If it were decided that production is to go ahead an investment of £240,000 in capital equipment on 1 January 20X1 would be required.

The accounts department has produced budgeted profit and loss statements for each of the next five years for the project. At the end of the fifth year the capital equipment will be sold and production will cease.

The capital equipment is expected to be sold for scrap on 31.12.20X5 for £40,000.

	Year end 31.12.20X1	Year end 31.12.20X2	Year end 31.12.20X3	Year end 31.12.20X4	Year end 31.12.20X5
Sales	400	400	400	320	200
Materials	240	240	240	192	120
Other variable costs	40	40	40	32	20
Fixed overheads	20	20	24	24	24
Depreciation	40	40	40	40	40
Net profit/(loss)	60	60	56	32	(4)

(All figures in £000s)

When production is started it will be necessary to raise material stock levels by £30,000 and other working capital by £20,000.

It may be assumed that payment for materials, other variable costs and fixed overheads are made at the end of each year.

Both the additional stock and other working capital increases will be released at the end of the project.

Customers receive one year's credit from the firm.

The fixed overhead figures in the budgeted accounts have two elements – 60 per cent is due to a reallocation of existing overheads, 40 per cent is directly incurred because of the take-up of the project.

For the purposes of this appraisal you may regard all receipts and payments as occurring at the year end to which they relate, unless otherwise stated. The company's cost of capital is 12 per cent.

Assume no inflation or tax.

Required

a Use the net present value method of project appraisal to advise the company on whether to go ahead with the proposed project.

b Explain to a management team unfamiliar with discounted cash flow appraisal techniques the significance and value of the NPV method.

4* (*Examination level*) Mercia plc owns two acres of derelict land near to the centre of a major UK city. The firm has received an invoice for £50,000 from consultants who were given the task of analysis, investigation and design of some project proposals for using the land. The consultants outline the two best proposals to a meeting of the board of Mercia.

Proposal 1 is to spend £150,000 levelling the site and then constructing a six-level car park at an additional cost of £1,600,000. The earthmoving firm will be paid £150,000 on the start date and the construction firm will be paid £1.4m on the start date, with the balance payable 24 months' later.

It is expected that the car park will be fully operational as from the completion date (365 days after the earthmovers first begin).

The annual income from ticket sales will be £600,000 to an infinite horizon. Operational costs (attendants, security, power, etc.) will be £100,000 per annum. The consultants have also apportioned £60,000 of Mercia's central overhead costs (created by the London-based head office and the executive jet) to this project.

The consultants present their analysis in terms of a commonly used measure of project viability, that of payback.

This investment idea is not original; Mercia investigated a similar project two years ago and discovered that there are some costs which have been ignored by the consultants. First, the local council will require a payment of £100,000 one year after the completion of the construction for its inspection services and a trading and environmental impact licence. Second, senior management will have to leave aside work on other projects, resulting in delays and reduced income from these projects amounting to £50,000 per year once the car park is operational. Also, the proposal is subject to depreciation of one- fiftieth (1/50) of the earthmoving and construction costs each year.

Proposal 2 is for a health club. An experienced company will, for a total cost of £9m payable at the start of the project, design and construct the buildings and supply all the equipment. It will be ready for Mercia's use one year after construction begins. Revenue from customers will be £5m per annum and operating costs will be £4m per annum. The consultants allocate £70,000 of central general head office overhead costs for each year from the start. After two years of operating the health club Mercia will sell it for a total of £11m.

Information not considered by the consultants for Proposal 2

The £9m investment includes £5m in buildings not subject to depreciation. It also includes £4m in equipment, 10 per cent of which has to be replaced each year. This has not been included in the operating costs.

A new executive will be needed to oversee the project from the start of the project – costing £100,000 per annum.

The consultants recommend that the board of Mercia accept the second proposal and reject the first.

Assume:

- If the site was sold with no further work carried out it would fetch £100,000.
- No inflation or tax.
- The cost of capital for Mercia is 10 per cent.
- It can be assumed, for simplicity of analysis, that all cash flows occur at year ends except those occurring at the start of the project.

Required

a   Calculate the net present value of each proposal.
    State whether you would recommend Proposal 1 or 2.

b   Calculate the internal rate of return for each proposed project.

5* (*Examination level*) Mines International plc
The Albanian government is auctioning the rights to mine copper in the east of the country. Mines International plc (MI) is considering the amount they would be prepared to pay as a lump sum for the five-year licence. The auction is to take place very soon and the cash will have to be paid immediately following the auction.

In addition to the lump sum the Albanian government will expect annual payments of £500,000 to cover 'administration'. If MI wins the licence, production would not start until one year later because it will take a year to prepare the site and buy in equipment. To begin production MI would have to commission the manufacture of specialist engineering equipment costing £9.5m, half of which is payable immediately, with the remainder due in one year.

MI has already conducted a survey of the site which showed a potential productive life of four years with its new machine. The survey cost £300,000 and is payable immediately.

The accounts department have produced the following projected profit and loss accounts.

Projected profit and loss (£m)	Year				
	1	2	3	4	5
Sales	0	8	9	9	7
Less expenses					
Materials and consumables	0.6	0.4	0.5	0.5	0.4
Wages	0.3	0.7	0.7	0.7	0.7
Overheads	0.4	0.5	0.6	0.6	0.5
Depreciation of equipment	0	2.0	2.0	2.0	2.0
Albanian govt. payments	0.5	0.5	0.5	0.5	0.5
Survey costs written off	0.3				
Profit (loss) excluding licence fee	(2.1)	3.9	4.7	4.7	2.9

The following additional information is available:

(a) Payments and receipts arise at the year ends unless otherwise stated.

(b) The initial lump sum payment has been excluded from the projected accounts as this is unknown at the outset.

(c) The customers of MI demand and receive a credit period of three months.

(d) The suppliers of materials and consumables grant a credit period of three months.

(e) The overheads contain an annual charge of £200,000 which represents an apportionment of head office costs. This is an expense which would be incurred whether or not the project proceeds. The remainder of the overheads relate directly to the project.

(f) The new equipment will have a resale value at the end of the fifth year of £1.5m.

(g) During the whole of Year 3 a specialised item of machinery will be needed, which is currently being used by another division of MI. This division will therefore incur hire costs of £100,000 for the period the machinery is on loan.

(h) The project will require additional cash reserves of £1m to be held in Albania throughout the project for operational purposes. These are recoverable at the end of the project.

(i) The Albanian government will make a one-off refund of 'administration' charges three months after the end of the fifth year of £200,000.

The company's cost of capital is 12 per cent.

Ignore taxation, inflation and exchange rate movements and controls.

Required

a Calculate the maximum amount MI should bid in the auction.

b What would be the Internal Rate of Return on the project if MI did not have to pay for the licence?

c The board of directors have never been on a finance course and do not understand any of the finance jargon. However, they have asked you to persuade them that the appraisal method you have used in (a) above can be relied on. Prepare a presentation for the board of directors explaining the reasoning and justification for using your chosen project appraisal technique and your treatment of specific items in the accounts. You will need to explain concepts such as the time value of money, opportunity cost and sunk cost in plain English.

6 Find the annual equivalent annuity at 13 per cent for the following cash flow:

Point in time (yearly intervals)	0	1	2	3
Cash flow (£)	−5,000	+2,000	+2,200	+3,500

7* (*Examination question if combined with question 8*) Reds plc is attempting to decide a replacement cycle for new machinery. This machinery costs £10,000 to purchase. Operating and maintenance costs for the future years are:

Point in time (yearly intervals)	0	1	2	3
Operating and maintenance costs (£)	0	12,000	13,000	14,000

The values available from the sale of the machinery on the secondhand market are:

Point in time (yearly intervals)	0	1	2	3
Second hand value (£)	0	8,000	6,500	3,500

Assume

– replacement by an identical machine to an infinite horizon;

– no inflation, tax or risk;

– the cost of capital is 11 per cent.

Should Reds replace this new machine on a one-, two- or three-year cycle?

8* The firm Reds plc in Question 7 has not yet purchased the new machinery and is considering postponing such a cash outflow for a year or two. If it were to replace the existing machine it could be sold immediately for £4,000. If the firm persevered with the old machine for a further year then £2,000 would have to be spent immediately to recondition it. The machine could then be sold for £3,000 in 12 months' time. The third possibility is to spend £2,000 now, on reconditioning, and £1,000 on maintenance in one year, and finally sell the machine for £1,500, 24 months from now. Assuming all other factors remain constant regardless of which option is chosen, which date would you recommend for the commencement of the replacement cycle?

9 Quite plc has an ageing piece of equipment which is less efficient than more modern equivalents. This equipment will continue to operate for another 15 years but operating and maintenance costs will be £3,500 per year. Alternatively it could be sold, raising £2,000 now, and replaced with its modern equivalent which costs £7,000 but has reduced operating and maintenance costs at £3,000 per year. This machine could be sold at the end of its 15-year life for scrap for £500. The third possibility is to spend £2,500 for an immediate overhaul of the old machine which will improve its efficiency for the rest of its life, so that operating and maintenance costs become £3,200 per annum. The old machine will have a zero scrap value in 15 years, whether or not it is overhauled. Quite plc requires a return of 9 per cent on projects in this risk class. Select the best course of action. (Assume that cash flows arise at the year ends.)

10* The managing director of Curt plc is irritated that the supplier for the component widgets has recently increased prices by another 10 per cent following similar rises for each of the last five years. Based on the assumption that this pattern will continue, the cost of these widgets will be:

Points in time (yearly intervals)	1	2	3	4	5
Payments for widgets (£)	100,000	110,000	121,000	133,100	146,410

The managing director is convinced that the expertise for the manufacture of widgets exists within Curt. He therefore proposes the purchase of the necessary machine tools and other items of equipment to produce widgets in-house, at a cost of £70,000. The net cash outflows associated with this course of action are:

Points in time (yearly intervals)	0	1	2	3	4	5
Cash outflows	70,000	80,000	82,000	84,000	86,000	88,000

Note: The figures include the £70,000 for equipment and operating costs, etc.

The machinery has a life of five years and can be sold for scrap at the end of its life for £10,000. This is not included in the £88,000 for year 5. The installation of the new machine will require the attention of the technical services manager during the first year. She will have to abandon other projects as a result, causing a loss of net income of £48,000 from those projects. This cost has not been included in the above figures.

The discount rate is 16 per cent, and all cash flows occur at year ends except the initial investment.

Help Curt plc to decide whether to produce widgets for itself. What other factors might influence this decision?

11† The Borough Company is to replace its existing machinery. It has a choice between two new types of machine having different lives. The machines have the following costs:

Points in time (yearly intervals)		Machine X	Machine Y
0	Initial investment	£20,000	£25,000
1	Operating costs	£5,000	£4,000
2	Operating costs	£5,000	£4,000
3	Operating costs	£5,000	£4,000
4	Operating costs		£4,000

Each machine will be replaced at the end of its life by identical machines with identical costs. This cycle will continue indefinitely. The cost of capital is 13 per cent.

Which machine should Borough buy?

12* Netq plc manufactures Qtrans, for which demand fluctuates seasonally. Netq has two machines, each with a productive capacity of 1,000 Qtrans per year. For four months of the year each machine operates at full capacity. For a further four months the machines operate at three-quarters of their full capacity and for the remaining months they produce at half capacity. The operating costs of producing a Qtran is £4 and the machines are expected to be productive to an indefinite horizon. Netq is considering scrapping the old machines (for which the firm will receive nothing) and replacing them with new improved versions. These machines are also expected to last forever if properly maintained but they cost £7,000 each. Operating costs (including maintenance) will, however, fall to £1.80 per Qtran. The firm's cost of capital is 13 per cent. Should Netq replace both of its machines, one of them, or neither? Assume output is the same under each option and that the new machines have the same productive capacity as the old.

13 Clipper owns 100 acres of mature woodland and is trying to decide when to harvest the trees. If it harvests immediately the net cash flow, after paying the professional loggers, will be £10,000. If it waits a year the trees will grow, so that the net cash flow will be £12,000. In two years, £14,000 can be obtained. After three years have elapsed, the cash flow will be £15,500, and thereafter will increase in value by £1,000 per annum.

Calculate the best time to cut the trees given a cost of capital of 10 per cent.

14* (*Examination level*) Opti plc operates a single machine to produce its output. The senior management are trying to choose between four possibilities. First, sell the machine on the secondhand market and buy a new one at the end of one year. Second, sell in the secondhand market and replace at the end of two years. The third is to replace after three years. Finally, the machine could be scrapped at the end of its useful life after four years. These replacement cycles are expected to continue indefinitely. The management team believe that all such replacements will be for financially identical equipment, i.e., the cash inflows produced by the new and old equipment are the same. However, the cost of maintenance and operations increases with the age of the machine. These costs are shown in the table, along with the secondhand and scrap values.

Points in time (yearly intervals)	0	1	2	3	4
Initial outlay (£)	20,000				
Operating and maintenance costs (£)		6,000	8,000	10,000	12,000
Secondhand/scrap value (£)		12,000	9,000	6,000	2,000

Assume

- The cost of capital is 10 per cent.
- No inflation.
- No technological advances.
- No tax.
- All cash flows occur on anniversary dates.

Required

Choose the length of the replacement cycle which minimises the present values of the costs.

15 (*Examination level*) Hazel plc produces one of the components used in the manufacture of car bumpers. The production manager is keen on obtaining modern equipment and he has come to you, the finance director, with details concerning two alternative machines, A and B.

The cash flows and other assumptions are as follows.

Points in time (yearly intervals)	0	£000s 1	£000s 2	£000s 3
Machine A	–200	+220	+242	0
Machine B	–240	+220	+242	+266

Machine A would have to be replaced by an identical machine on a two-year cycle.
Machine B would be replaced by an identical machine every three years.
It is considered reasonable to assume that the cash flows for the future replacements of A and B are the same as in the above table.
The opportunity cost of capital for Hazel is 15 per cent.
Ignore taxation.
The acceptance of either project would leave the company's risk unchanged.
The cash flows occur on anniversary dates.

Required

a Calculate the net present value of Machine A for its two-year life.

b Calculate the net present value of Machine B for its three-year life.

c Calculate the annual equivalent annuities for Machines A and B and recommend which machine should be selected.

d You are aware that the production manager gets very enthusiastic about new machinery and this may cloud his judgement. You suggest the third possibility, which is to continue production with Machine C which was purchased five years ago for £400,000. This is expected to produce +£160,000 per year. It has a scrap value now of £87,000 and is expected to last another five years. At the end of its useful life it will have a scrap value of £20,000.

Should C be kept for another five years?

e The production manager asks why you are discounting the cash flows. Briefly explain the time value of money and its components.

ASSIGNMENTS

1   Try to obtain budgeted profit and loss accounts for a proposed project and by combining these with other data produce cash flow estimates for the project. Calculate the NPV and contrast your conclusions on the viability of the project with that suggested by the profit and loss projections.

2   Examine some items of machinery (e.g. shop-floor machine tools, vehicles, computers). Consider whether to replace these items with the modern equivalent, taking into account increased maintenance costs, loss or gain of customer sales, secondhand values, higher productivity, etc.

3   Apply the technique of annual equivalent annuities to an asset which is replaced on a regular cycle. Consider alternative cycle lengths.

CHAPTER NOTE

1 This is a bold assumption. More realistic assumptions could be made, e.g. allowing for inflation, but the complexity that this produces is beyond the scope of this book.

Chapter 4

THE DECISION-MAKING PROCESS FOR INVESTMENT APPRAISAL

INTRODUCTION

An organisation may be viewed simply as a collection of projects, some of which were started a long time ago, some only recently begun, many are major 'strategic' projects and others minor operating-unit-level schemes. It is in the nature of business for change to occur, and through change old activities, profit centres and methods die, to be replaced by the new. Without a continuous process of regeneration firms will cease to progress and be unable to compete in a dynamic environment. It is vital that the processes and systems that lead to the development of new production methods, new markets and products, and so on are efficient. That is, both the project appraisal techniques and the entire process of proposal creation and selection lead to the achievement of the objective of the organisation. Poor appraisal technique, set within the framework of an investment process that does not ask the right questions and which provides erroneous conclusions, will destroy the wealth of shareholders.

The payback and accounting rate of return (ARR) methods of evaluating capital investment proposals have historically been, and continue to be, very popular approaches. This is despite the best efforts of a number of writers to denigrate them. It is important to understand the disadvantages of these methods, but it is also useful to be aware of why practical business people still see a great deal of merit in observing the outcome of these calculations.

The employment of project appraisal techniques must be seen as merely one of the stages in the process of the allocation of resources within a firm. The appraisal stage can be reached only after ideas for the use of capital resources have been generated and those ideas have been filtered through a consideration of the strategic, budgetary and business resource capabilities of the firm. Following the appraisal stage are the approval, implementation and post-completion auditing stages.

Any capital allocation system has to be viewed in the light of the complexity of organisational life. This aspect has been ignored in Chapters 2 and 3, where mechanical analysis is applied. The balance is corrected in this chapter. Investment, whether in intangible assets, as in the case of Noddy (*see* Case study 4.1), or tangible, as in the case of Bentley cars (*see* Case study 4.2), need to be thoroughly evaluated. This chapter considers the process of project development, appraisal and post-investment monitoring.

CASE STUDY 4.1

The Noddy and Big Ears project

In March 1996 Trocadero paid £13m for the copyright and trade marks of all the works of Enid Blyton. These include 700 books, 10,000 stories and a range of characters. The company believes that the Blyton stories have been under-exploited compared with Thomas the Tank Engine. The merchandising of Thomas brings in hundreds of millions whereas Noddy earned only £150,000 in merchandising in 1995/96. The Famous Five earned a mere £5,000.

The characters' popularity will be built upon in Japan and the USA. The BBC will continue to distribute the television series of Noddy as well as videos, audio tapes and associated books and magazines. Efforts to merchandise Noddy and other Enid Blyton characters will be stepped up including Blyton parades every day in the Trocadero in London, a travelling Noddy show and a deal with a big retail group to bring Noddy to every High Street.

Source: Based on *Financial Times*, May 1996.

CASE STUDY 4.2

Bentley output to rise on £600m investment

By John Griffiths

Production of Bentley cars, already due to leap from 2,000 to 9,000 annually over the next three years under a £600m investment programme, may be expanded further under plans being developed within Volkswagen group, Bentley's owner for the past three years.

'We have a huge vision for the brand in the long run – we certainly don't see 9,000 a year as the limiting factor,' said Tony Gott, the chief executive of Bentley Motor Cars.

Further expansion can be undertaken 'without taking Bentley downmarket', said Mr Gott.

Executives at the luxury carmaker, which currently manufactures Rolls-Royce as well as Bentley models at Crewe in Cheshire, are understood to be studying a number of other niches of the world car market in which the brand could compete.

These range from very high performance 'super-cars' to luxurious four-wheel-drive recreational vehicles.

Bentley could produce such vehicles without necessarily dropping prices below the £85,000-plus at which a 'cheaper' Bentley is expected to be priced when it is launched in 2003.

Some £500m is already being invested in new models, plus approaching £100m on doubling the size of assembly buildings and installing new research, development and engineering facilities.

Employment at the Crewe facility is to rise by about 1,000 people to 3,500 over the next three years.

Source: *Financial Times*, 23 January 2001, p. 6. Reprinted with permission.

Learning objectives

The main outcome expected from this chapter is that the reader is aware of both traditional and discounted cash flow investment appraisal techniques and the extent of their use. The reader should also be aware that these techniques are a small part of the overall capital-allocation planning process. This includes knowledge of:

- empirical evidence on techniques used;
- the calculation of payback, discounted payback and accounting rate of return (ARR);
- the drawbacks and attractions of payback and ARR;
- the balance to be struck between mathematical precision and imprecise reality;
- the capital-allocation planning process.

EVIDENCE ON THE EMPLOYMENT OF APPRAISAL TECHNIQUES

A number of surveys enquiring into the appraisal methods used in practice have been conducted over the past 20 years. The results from surveys conducted by Pike and by the author jointly with Panos Hatzopoulos are displayed in Exhibit 4.1. Some striking features emerge from these and other studies. Payback remains in wide use, despite the increasing application of discounted cash flow techniques. Internal rate of return is at least as popular as net present value. However, NPV is gaining rapid acceptance. Accounting rate of return continues to be the laggard, but is still used in over 50 per cent of large firms. One observation that is emphasised in many studies is the tendency for decision makers to use more than one method. In the 1997 study 67 per cent of firms use three or four of these techniques. These methods are regarded as being complementary rather than competitors.

There is an indication in the literature that while some methods have superior theoretical justification, other, simpler methods are used for purposes such as communicating project viability and gaining commitment throughout an organisation. It is also suggested that those who sponsor and advance projects within organisations like to have the option of presenting their case in an alternative form which shows the proposal in the best light.

Another clear observation from the literature is that small and medium-sized firms use the sophisticated formal procedures less than their larger brethren.

PAYBACK

The payback period for a capital investment is the length of time before the cumulated stream of forecasted cash flows equals the initial investment.

The decision rule is that if a project's payback period is less than or equal to a predetermined threshold figure it is acceptable.

Exhibit 4.1 Appraisal techniques used

	Proportion of companies using technique							
	Pike surveys[a]				Arnold and Hatzopoulos survey[b]			
	1975 %	1980 %	1986 %	1992 %	1997			
					Small %	Medium %	Large %	Total %
Payback	73	81	92	94	71	75	66	70
Accounting rate of return	51	49	56	50	62	50	55	56
Internal rate of return	44	57	75	81	76	83	84	81
Net present value	32	39	68	74	62	79	97	80

Capital budget (per year) for companies in Arnold and Hatzopoulos study approx.
Small: £1–50m. Medium: £1–100m. Large: £100m+

Notes
(a) Pike's studies focus on 100 large UK firms.
(b) In the Arnold and Hatzopoulos study (2000), 300 finance directors of UK companies taken from *The Times 1000* (London: Times Books), ranked according to capital employed (excluding investment trusts), were asked dozens of questions about project appraisal techniques, sources of finance and performance measurement. The first 100 (Large size) of the sample are the top 100; another 100 are in the rankings at 250–400 (Medium size); the final 100 are ranked 820–1,000 (Small size). The capital employed ranges between £1.3bn and £24bn for the large firms, £207m and £400m for the medium-sized firms, and £40m and £60m for the small companies. Ninety-six usable replies were received: 38 large, 24 medium and 34 small.

Sources: Pike (1988 and 1996) and Arnold and Hatzopoulos (2000).

Consider the case of Tradfirm's three mutually exclusive proposed investments (see Exhibit 4.2):

Exhibit 4.2 Tradfirm

| | Cash flows (£m) | | | | | | |
Points in time (yearly intervals)	0	1	2	3	4	5	6
Project A	–10	6	2	1	1	2	2
Project B	–10	1	1	2	6	2	2
Project C	–10	3	2	2	2	15	10

Note: Production ceases after six years, and all cash flows occur on anniversary dates.

There is a board room battle in Tradfirm, with older members preferring the payback rule. They set four years as the decision benchmark. For both A and B the £10m initial outflow is recouped after four years. In the case of C it takes five years for the cash inflows to cumulate to £10m. Thus payback for the three projects is as follows:

Project A: 4 years
Project B: 4 years
Project C: 5 years

If the payback rule is rigidly applied, the older members of the board will reject the third project, and they are left with a degree of indecisiveness over whether to accept A or B. The younger members prefer the NPV rule and are thus able to offer a clear decision.

Exhibit 4.3 Tradfirm: Net Present Values (£m)

$$\text{Project A} \quad -10 + \frac{6}{1.1} + \frac{2}{(1.1)^2} + \frac{1}{(1.1)^3} + \frac{1}{(1.1)^4} + \frac{2}{(1.1)^5} + \frac{2}{(1.1)^6} = £0.913m$$

$$\text{Project B} \quad -10 + \frac{1}{1.1} + \frac{1}{(1.1)^2} + \frac{2}{(1.1)^3} + \frac{6}{(1.1)^4} + \frac{2}{(1.1)^5} + \frac{2}{(1.1)^6} = -£0.293m$$

$$\text{Project C} \quad -10 + \frac{3}{1.1} + \frac{2}{(1.1)^2} + \frac{2}{(1.1)^3} + \frac{2}{(1.1)^4} + \frac{15}{(1.1)^5} + \frac{10}{(1.1)^6} = £12.208m$$

Note: The discount rate is 10 per cent.

Project A has a positive NPV and is therefore shareholder wealth enhancing. Project B has a negative NPV; the firm would be better served by investing the £10m in the alternative that offers a 10 per cent return. Project C has the largest positive NPV and is therefore the one that creates most shareholder wealth.

Drawbacks of payback

The first drawback of payback is that it makes no allowance for the time value of money. It ignores the need to compare future cash flows with the initial investment after they have been discounted to their present values. The second drawback is that receipts beyond the payback period are ignored. This problem is particularly obvious in the case of project C. A third disadvantage is the arbitrary selection of the cut-off point. There is no theoretical basis for setting the appropriate time period and so guesswork, whim and manipulation take over.

Discounted payback

With discounted payback the future cash flows are discounted prior to calculating the payback period. This is an improvement on the simple payback method in that it takes into account the time value of money. In Exhibit 4.4 the *discounted* cash inflows are added together to calculate payback. In the case of Project B the discounted cash inflows never reach the level of the cash outflow.

This modification tackles the first drawback of the simple payback method but it is still necessary to make an arbitrary decision about the cut-off date and it ignores cash flows beyond that date.

Reasons for the continuing popularity of payback

Payback remains a widely used project appraisal method despite its drawbacks. This requires some explanation. The first fact to note is that payback is rarely used as the primary investment technique, but rather as a secondary method which supplements the more sophisticated methods. Although it appears irrational to employ payback when the issue is examined in isolation, we may begin to see the logic behind its use if we take into account the organisational context and the complementary nature of alternative techniques. For example, payback may be used at an early stage to filter out projects which have clearly unacceptable risk and return characteristics. Identifying those proj-

Exhibit 4.4 Discounted payback: Tradfirm plc (£m)

Points in time (yearly intervals)	0	1	2	3	4	5	6	Discounted payback
Project A								
Undiscounted cash flow	−10	6	2	1	1	2	2	
Discounted cash flow	−10	5.45	1.65	0.75	0.68	1.24	1.13	Year 6
Project B								
Undiscounted cash flow	−10	1	1	2	6	2	2	Outflow −10m
Discounted cash flow	−10	0.909	0.826	1.5	4.1	1.24	1.13	Inflow +£9.7m
Project C								
Undiscounted cash flow	−10	3	2	2	2	15	10	
Discounted cash flow	−10	2.72	1.65	1.5	1.37	9.3	5.64	Year 5

Note: The discount rate is 10 per cent.

ects at a preliminary stage avoids the need for more detailed evaluation through a discounted cash flow method, thus increasing the efficiency of the appraisal process. This early sifting has to be carefully implemented so as to avoid premature rejection.

Payback also has one extraordinarily endearing quality to busy managers and hard-pressed students alike – it is simple and easy to use. Executives often admit that the payback rule, used indiscriminately, does not always give the best decisions, but it is the simplest way to communicate an idea of project profitability. NPV is difficult to understand and so it is useful to have an alternative measure which all managers can follow. In the workplace a project's success often relies on the gaining of widespread employee commitment. Discussion, negotiation and communication of ideas often need to be carried out in a simple form so that non-quantitative managers can make their contribution and, eventually, their commitment. Communication in terms of the sophisticated models may lead to alienation and exclusion and, ultimately, project failure.

Another argument advanced by practitioners is that projects which return their outlay quickly reduce the exposure of the firm to risk. In the world beyond the simplifications needed in academic exercises, as described in Chapters 2 and 3, there is a great deal of uncertainty about future cash flows. Managers often distrust forecasts for more distant years. Payback has an implicit assumption that the risk of cash flows is directly related to the time distance from project implementation date. By focusing on near-term returns this approach uses only those data in which management have greatest faith. Take the case of the Internet service provider industry. Here, competitive forces and technology are changing so rapidly that it is difficult to forecast for eight months ahead, let alone for eight years. Thus, managers may choose to ignore cash flow projections beyond a certain number of years. Those who advocate NPV counter this approach by saying that risk is accounted for in a better way in the NPV model than is done by simply excluding data. This is examined in Chapter 6.

A further advantage of payback, as perceived by many managers, is its use in situations of capital shortage. If funds are limited, there is an advantage in receiving a return on projects earlier rather than later, as this permits investment in other profitable opportunities. Theoretically this factor can be allowed for in a more satisfactory way with the NPV method; capital rationing is discussed in Chapter 5.

Finally, it is often claimed that the cash flows in the first few years of a project provide some indication of the cash flows in later years. In many cases it is reasonable to assume that the cash flow trends beyond the payback period are similar to those during the payback period, and so NPV and payback frequently give the same decision in relation to whether to accept or to reject. In Exhibit 4.5, X, Y and Z exhibit similar cash flow trends prior to year 4 and after year 4. Under both the payback and NPV decision rules X is accepted and Y and Z are rejected.

Exhibit 4.5 Payback and NPV

Points in time (yearly intervals)	*Cash flows (£m)*								
	0	1	2	3	4	5	6	7	
Project X	−35	10	10	10	10	10	10	10	No cash flows
Project Y	−35	13	10	7	4	3	2	1	after seventh
Project Z	−35	8	8	8	8	8	8	8	year

Payback decision (cut-off at 4 years)

- Project X   Accept
- Project Y   Reject
- Project Z   Reject

Net present value decision (discount rate of 20%)

		Decision
Project X	$-35 +$ annual annuity $\times$ annuity factor $=$ NPV	
	$-35 + 10 \times 3.6046 = +1.046$	Accept

Project Y $-35 + \dfrac{13}{1.2} + \dfrac{10}{(1.2)^2} + \dfrac{7}{(1.2)^3} + \dfrac{4}{(1.2)^4} + \dfrac{3}{(1.2)^5} + \dfrac{2}{(1.2)^6} + \dfrac{1}{(1.2)^7} =$ NPV

$-35 + 10.8 + 6.94 + 4.05 + 1.93 + 1.21 + 0.67 + 0.28 = -9.12$ Reject

Project Z $-35 +$ annual annuity $\times$ annuity factor $=$ NPV
$-35 + 8 \times 3.6046 = -6.16$ Reject

In this case, using the payback rule-of-thumb method led to the correct decision, but payback and NPV do not always give the same answer.

This section is not meant to promote the use of payback. It remains a theoretically inferior method to the discounted cash flow approaches. Payback has a number of valuable attributes, but the primary method of project appraisal in most organisations should take into account all of the relevant cash flows and then discount them.

ACCOUNTING RATE OF RETURN

The accounting rate of return (ARR) method may be known to readers by other names such as the return on capital employed (ROCE) or return on investment (ROI). The ARR is a ratio of the accounting profit to the investment in the project, expressed as a percentage.

The *decision rule* is that if the ARR is greater than, or equal to, a hurdle rate then accept the project.

This ratio can be calculated in a number of ways but the most popular approach is to take profit after depreciation and to regard any increases in working capital as adding to the investment required. Three alternative versions of ARR are calculated for Timewarp plc which give markedly different results (*see* Worked example 4.1). Note: these are just three of all the possible ways of calculating ARR – there are many more.

Worked example 4.1 Timewarp plc

Timewarp is to invest £30,000 in machinery for a project which has a life of three years. The machinery will have a zero scrap value and will be depreciated on a straight-line basis.

Accounting rate of return, version 1 (annual basis)

$$ARR = \frac{\text{Profit for the year}}{\text{Asset book value at start of year}} \times 100$$

Time (year)	1 £	2 £	3 £
Profit before depreciation	15,000	15,000	15,000
Less depreciation	10,000	10,000	10,000
Profit after depreciation	5,000	5,000	5,000
Value of asset (book value)			
Start of year	30,000	20,000	10,000
End of year	20,000	10,000	0

Accounting rate of return $\dfrac{5,000}{30,000} = 16.67\%$ $\quad \dfrac{5,000}{20,000} = 25\%$ $\quad \dfrac{5,000}{10,000} = 50\%$

On average the ARR is: $1/3 \times (16.67 + 25 + 50)\% = 30.55\%$.
Note the annual rise in apparent profitability despite the profits remaining constant.

Accounting rate of return, version 2 (total investment basis)

$$ARR = \frac{\text{Average annual profit}}{\text{Initial capital invested}} \times 100$$

$$ARR = \frac{(5,000 + 5,000 + 5,000)/3}{30,000} \times 100 = 16.67\%$$

Accounting rate of return, version 3 (average investment basis)

$$ARR = \frac{\text{Average annual profit}}{\text{Average capital invested}} \times 100$$

Average capital invested: $\dfrac{30,000}{2} = 15,000$

$$ARR = \frac{(5,000 + 5,000 + 5,000)/3}{15,000} \times 100 = 33.33\%$$

If we now make the example slightly more sophisticated by assuming that the machinery has a scrap value of £8,000 at the end of Year 3, then the average capital invested figure becomes:

>0.5 (initial outlay + scrap value)
>0.5 (30,000 + 8,000) = 19,000

The profit figures also change.

	Year 1 £	Year 2 £	Year 3 £
Profit before depreciation	15,000	15,000	15,000
Depreciation	7,333	7,333	7,333
Profit after depreciation	7,667	7,667	7,667

The ARR (version 3) is: $\dfrac{7,667}{19,000} \times 100 = 40.35\%$

Drawbacks of accounting rate of return

The number of alternative ARR calculations can be continued beyond the three possibilities described in Worked example 4.1. Each alternative would be a legitimate variant and would find favour with some managers and accountants. The almost wide-open field for selecting profit and asset definitions is a major weakness of ARR. This flexibility may tempt decision makers to abuse the technique to suit their purposes. Secondly, as explained in Chapter 3, the inflow and outflow of cash should be the focus of investment analysis appraisals. Profit figures are very poor substitutes for cash flow. The most important criticism of accounting rate of return is that it fails to take account of the time value of money. There is no allowance for the fact that cash received in Year 1 is more valuable than an identical sum received in Year 3. Also there is a high degree of arbitrariness in defining the cut-off or hurdle rate.

Accounting rate of return can lead to some perverse decisions. For example, suppose that Timewarp use the second version, the total investment ARR, with a hurdle rate of 15 per cent, and the appraisal team discover that the machinery will in fact generate an additional profit of £1,000 in a fourth year. Common sense suggests that if all other factors remain constant this new situation is better than the old one, and yet the ARR declines to below the threshold level because the profits are averaged over four years rather than three and the project is therefore rejected.

The original situation is:

$$ARR = \frac{(5,000 + 5,000 + 5,000)/3}{30,000} = 16.67\%. \text{ Accepted}$$

The new situation is:

$$ARR = \frac{(5,000 + 5,000 + 5,000 + 1,000)/4}{30,000} = 13.33\%. \text{ Rejected}$$

Reasons for the continued use of accounting rate of returns

Exhibit 4.1 shows that over one-half of large firms calculate ARR when appraising projects and so the conclusion must be that, in the practical world of business, some merit is seen in this technique. One possible explanation is that managers are familiar with this ancient and extensively used profitability measure. The financial press regularly report accounting rates of return. Divisional performance is often judged on a profit-to-assets employed ratio. Indeed, the entire firm is often analysed and management evaluated on this ratio. Because performance is measured in this way, managers have a natural bias towards using it in appraising future projects. Conflicting signals are sometimes sent to managers controlling a division. They are expected to use a discounted cash flow approach for investment decisions, but find that their performance is being monitored on a profit-to-investment ratio basis. This dichotomy may produce a resistance to proposed projects which produce low returns in the early years and thus report a low ARR to head office. This may result in excellent long-term opportunities being missed. (Some additional reasons for the continued use of ARR and payback are given in the Arnold and Hatzopoulos (2000) paper.)

INTERNAL RATE OF RETURN: REASONS FOR CONTINUED POPULARITY

Exhibit 4.1 shows that firms use IRR as much as the theoretically superior NPV. Given the problems associated with IRR described in Chapter 2, this may seem strange. It is all the more perplexing if one considers that IRR is often more difficult to calculate manually than NPV (although, with modern computer programs, the computational difficulties virtually disappear). Some possible explanations follow.

- *Psychological* Managers are familiar with expressing financial data in the form of a percentage. It is intuitively easier to grasp what is meant by an IRR of 15 per cent than, say, an NPV of £2,000.

- *IRR can be calculated without knowledge of the required rate of return* Making a decision using the IRR involves two separate stages. Stage 1 involves gathering data and then computing the IRR. Stage 2 involves comparing this with the cut-off rate. By contrast, it is not possible to calculate NPV without knowing the required rate of return. The proposal has to be analysed in one stage only. Thus, in a large company it is possible for senior managers to request that profit centres and divisions appraise projects on the basis of their IRRs, while refusing to communicate in advance the rate of return required. This has at least two potential advantages. First, the required rate may change over time and it becomes a simple matter of changing the cut-off comparison rate at head office once the IRR computations are received from lower down the organisation. With NPV, each project's cash flows would need to be calculated again at the new discount rate. Secondly, managers are only human and there is a tendency to bias information passed upwards so as to achieve their personal goals. For instance, it has been known for ambitious managers to be excessively optimistic concerning the prospects for projects which would lead to an expansion of their domain. If they are provided with a cut-off rate prior to evaluating projects you can be sure that all projects they sponsor will have cash flows 'forecasted' to produce a return greater than the target. If the head office team choose not to communicate a cut-off rate, this leaves them free to adjust the required return to allow for factors such as over-optimisim. They may also adjust the minimum rate of return for perceived risk associated with particular projects or divisions.

- *Ranking* Some managers are not familiar with the drawbacks of IRR and believe that ranking is most accurately and most easily carried out using the percentage-based IRR method. This was, in Chapter 2, shown not to be the case.

THE 'SCIENCE' AND THE 'ART' OF INVESTMENT APPRAISAL

This book places strong emphasis on the formal methods of project appraisal, so a word of warning is necessary at this point. Mathematical technique is merely one element needed for successful project appraisal. The quantitative analysis is only the starting point for decision making. In most real-world situations there are many qualitative factors which need to be taken into account. The techniques described in Chapters 2 and 3 cannot be used in a mechanical fashion. Management is largely an art form with a few useful quantitative techniques to improve the quality of the art. For instance, in generating and evaluating major investments the firm has to take into account:

- *Strategy* The relationship between the proposed project and the strategic direction of the firm.

- *Social context* The effect on individuals is a crucial consideration. Projects require people to implement them. Their enthusiasm and commitment will be of central importance. Neglecting this factor may lead to resentment and even sabotage. Discussion and consensus on major project proposals may matter more than selecting the mathematically correct option. In many cases, quantitative techniques are avoided because they are precise. It is safer to sponsor a project in a non-quantifiable or judgemental way at an early stage in its development. If, as a result of discussion with colleagues and superiors, the idea becomes more generally accepted and it fits into the pervading view on the firm's policy and strategy, the figures are presented in a report. Note here the order of actions. First, general acceptance. Second, quantification. A proposal is usually discussed at progressively higher levels of management before it is 'firmed up' into a project report. One reason for this is that continuing commitment and support from many people will be needed if the project is to succeed. In order to engender support and to improve the final report it is necessary to start the process in a rather vague way, making room for modifications in the light of suggestions. Some of these suggestions will be motivated by shareholder wealth considerations, others will be motivated by goals closer to the hearts of key individuals. Allowing adaptability in project development also means that if circumstances change, say, in the competitive environment, the final formal appraisal takes account of this. The sponsor or promoter of a capital investment has to be aware of, and to adjust for, social sub-systems within the organisation.

- *Expense* Sophisticated project evaluation can cost a considerable amount of money. The financial experts' input is costly enough, but the firm also has to consider the time and trouble managers throughout the organisation might have to devote to provide good-quality data and make their contribution to the debate. In a firm of limited resources it may be more efficient to search for projects at an informal or judgement level, thus generating a multitude of alternative avenues for growth, rather than to analyse a few in greater quantitative depth.

■ *Stifling the entrepreneurial spirit* Excessive emphasis on formal evaluatory systems may be demotivating to individuals who thrive on free thinking, fast decision making and action. The relative weights given to formal approaches and entrepreneurialism will depend on the context, such as the pace of change in the market-place.

■ *Intangible benefits* Frequently, many of the most important benefits that flow from an investment are difficult to measure in money terms. Improving customer satisfaction through better service, quality or image may lead to enhanced revenues, but it is often difficult to state precisely the quantity of the increased revenue flow. Pepsi Cola, in 1996, spent $500m on a marketing and design campaign, switching the colour of its packaging from a predominant red to blue. Clearly, the benefits of such an action cannot be quantified in advance. It will be many years before the results can be assessed. Another example: new technology often provides a number of intangible benefits, such as reduced time needed to switch machine tools to the production of other products, thereby reducing risk in fluctuating markets, or a quicker response to customer choice. These non-quantifiable benefits can amount to a higher value than the more obvious tangible benefits. An example of how intangible benefits could be allowed for in project appraisal is shown through the example of Crowther Precision plc.

Worked example 4.2 Crowther Precision plc

Crowther Precision plc produces metal parts for the car industry, with machinery that is now more than 20 years old. With appropriate maintenance these machines could continue producing indefinitely. However, developments in the machine tool industry have led to the creation of computer-controlled multi-use machines. Crowther is considering the purchase of the Z200 which would provide both quantifiable and non-quantifiable benefits over the old machine. The Z200 costs £1.2m but would be expected to last indefinitely if maintenance expenditure were increased by £20,000 per annum.

The quantifiable benefits are:

(a) reduced raw material requirements, due to lower wastage, amounting to £35,000 per annum;
(b) labour cost savings of £80,000 per year.

These quantifiable benefits are analysed using the NPV method (*see* Exhibit 4.6).

Exhibit 4.6 Incremental net present value analysis of Z200

		Present value £
Purchase of machine		−1,200,000
Present value of raw material saving	$\dfrac{35,000}{0.1}$	+350,000
Present value of labour saving	$\dfrac{80,000}{0.1}$	+800,000
Less present value of increased maintenance costs	$\dfrac{20,000}{0.1}$	−200,000
Net present value		−250,000

Note: Assume discount rate of 10 per cent, no inflation, tax or risk, all cash flows arise at the year ends, zero scrap value of old machine.

Examining the quantifiable elements in isolation will lead to a rejection of the project to buy the Z200. However, the non-quantifiable benefits are:

- reduced time required to switch the machine from producing one version of the car component to one of the other three versions Crowther presently produces;
- the ability to switch the machine over to completely new products in response to changed industry demands, or to take up, as yet unseen, market opportunities in the future;
- improved quality of output leading to greater customer satisfaction.

It is true that the discounted cash flow analysis has failed to take into account all the relevant factors, but this should not lead to its complete rejection. In cases where non-quantifiable elements are present, the problem needs to be separated into two stages.

1 Analyse those elements that are quantifiable using NPV.
2 If the NPV from Stage 1 is negative, then managerial judgement will be needed to subjectively assess the non-quantifiable benefits. If these are judged to be greater than the 'loss' signalled in Stage 1 then the project is viable. For Crowther, if the management team consider that the intangible benefits are worth more than £250,000 they should proceed with the purchase of the Z200.

This line of thought is continued in Chapter 21, where operational and strategic decisions with options (real options) are considered. As the article in Exhibit 4.7 shows, the decision to commit to an investment means the loss of options.

Exhibit 4.7 Sacrificing options

Tyranny of time

By their very nature capital investment decisions threaten to place a straitjacket on companies. There is no easy way out.

By Peter Martin

When you make a capital investment decision, you freeze time. In fast-moving industries, this may be the most important aspect of the decision – more important than its actual content. But it is rarely assessed in this light.

There is any amount of theory about how to take capital investment decisions.

All such approaches assume that there are financial and easily quantifiable costs of taking the decision; and less measurable benefits to set against it. The techniques all revolve around ways of making imponderable future benefits more tangible. There is a reason for this: managers usually want to take

investment decisions while their superiors usually do not. So the techniques are ever more elaborate ways of capturing the discounted value of blue sky.

But there are also intangible costs of taking the decision, and they are not given the attention they deserve. The cost of freezing time is one of the most important.

Here is how it works. When you make a big capital investment decision, it will usually take between 18 months and five years to bring the plant fully into operation. The cost of tying up capital for that time is reflected in the investment appraisal. But the broader implications of tying up the company are not.

When you have committed yourself to a big new plant, you have not just signed a cheque for the money. You have also sold your soul to this technology, on this scale, in this site. That is what freezing time means. Until the plant is complete, and it is clear whether it works and whether there is a market for its products, time stands still. For you, but not for your rivals.

They are free to react, to adjust technology, to play around with the pricing and volume. You are not. Unless you have built an implausibly flexible new plant, you are on a convergence course with a straitjacket.

Once your new plant is up and running, you can start to adjust the

Exhibit 4.7 continued

pattern of its output, and strive to reduce its costs. But until then, your options are more limited: press on, or give up.

The semiconductor industry illustrates this dilemma in a big way. In the mid-1990s, the UK looked like a good home for a bunch of new chip plants. Siemens, LG Group and Hyundai all targeted the British regions for big state-of-the-art factories. One of them – Siemens' factory on Tyneside – opened and promptly shut down again. The other two have never made it into production, and look more questionable by the moment: the Asian crisis undermined their parents and their markets simultaneously.

The decisions all three companies had to make were unenviable, because they were all or nothing. Technology had moved on while the plants were being prepared. Once the Siemens plant came into production, it was clear that it was the wrong plant, making the wrong sort of chip, in the wrong place.

So the company shut it down, at vast cost – only to invest another huge sum in a different plant to make different chips in France. For LG and Hyundai the moment of decision comes even before they have had the satisfaction of seeing their plants up and running.

The problem is not so much the risk that a plant's technology may prove inappropriate, or that its markets may not meet expectations: these are the normal risks of doing business in a capital intensive industry. It is more that the process of building the factory shuts out other alternatives, freezing the company's options and its internal clock.

What can companies do to avoid this risk? First, look for investment decisions that can be made piece by piece, and implemented quickly, minimising the freezing effect. Engineers usually hate this approach, because it means they are never designing plants at the cutting edge of the technology, or at maximum efficient scale. That's tough.

Second, once an investment has been approved, managers must resist the temptation to make the decision sacrosanct. It needs revisiting, in the light of changing technology and markets, just as much as plants that are already operating. This is a difficult balance to strike, because every big investment decision usually had to be made in the teeth of the opposition of a faction that wanted something bigger, smaller, older, newer, or somewhere else. This group of dissidents will never be happy with the decision, and they may even be right.

Third, keep a close eye on the relationship between the product cycle time in your industry and the time it takes to get a new plant commissioned.

If the former is shrinking while the latter is lengthening – a common feature of any high-technology industry that has to cater to retail consumers – there will come a point at which the price of freezing time will outstrip the benefits of new plant.

If you cannot keep going by patching the old factory, it is time to think of some revolutionary new process that will replace one big capital investment decision with a lot of small ones. Or give up.

Source: Financial Times, 1 June 1999, p. 18. Reprinted with permission.

THE INVESTMENT PROCESS

There is a great deal more to a successful investment programme than simply project appraisal. As Exhibit 4.8 demonstrates, project appraisal is one of a number of stages in the investment process. The emphasis in the academic world on ever more sophistication in appraisal could be seriously misplaced. Attention paid to the evolution of investment ideas, their development and sifting may produce more practical returns. Marrying the evaluation of projects once screened with strategic, resource and human considerations may lead to avoidance of erroneous decisions. Following through the implementation with a review of what went right, what went wrong, and why, may enable better decision making in the future.

Investment by a firm is a process often involving large numbers of individuals up and down an organisational hierarchy. It is a complex and infinitely adaptable process which is likely to differ from one organisation to another. However, we can identify some common threads.

Exhibit 4.8 The investment process

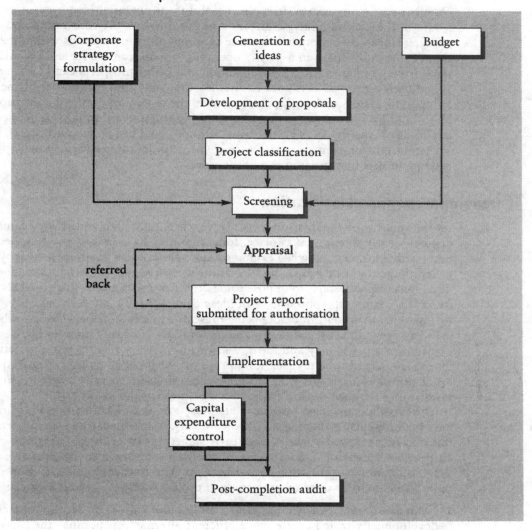

Generation of ideas

A firm is more likely to founder because of a shortage of good investment ideas than because of poor methods of appraisal. A good investment planning process requires a continuous flow of ideas to regenerate the organisation through the exploitation of new opportunities. Thought needs to be given to the development of a system for the encouragement of idea generation and subsequent communication through the firm. Indeed, one of the central tasks of senior management is to nurture a culture of search for and sponsorship of ideas. In the absence of a well-functioning system, the danger remains that investment proposals only arise in a reactive manner. For example, a firm examines new product possibilities only when it is realised that the old product is becoming, or has become, obsolete. Or else the latest technology is installed in reaction to its adoption by a competitor. A system and culture is needed to help the firm 'get ahead of the game' and be proactive rather than reactive.

One of the main inputs into a more systematic search for ideas is likely to be an environment-scanning process. It is also helpful if all potential idea-generators are made aware of the general strategic direction of the firm and the constraints under which it operates. Idea-generators often become sponsors of their proposals within the organisation. These individuals, in a poorly operating system, can see themselves taking a high risk for very little reward. Their reputation and career prospects can be intimately associated with a project. If it goes badly then they may find themselves blamed for that failure. In a system with such poor incentives the natural response of most people would be to hold back from suggesting ideas and pushing them through, and concentrate on day-to-day management. This defensive attitude could be bad for the organisation and it is therefore incumbent on senior management to develop reward systems that do not penalise project idea-generators and sponsors.

Development and classification

As the sponsor or the division-level team gather more data and refine estimates, some degree of early filtering takes place. Ideas that may have looked good in theory do not necessarily look so good when examined more closely. In a well-functioning system, idea generation should be propagated in an unstructured, almost random manner, but the development phase starts to impose some degree of order and structure. Many firms like to have a bottom-up approach, with ideas coming from plant level and being reviewed by divisional management before being presented to senior management. At the development stage the sponsor elaborates and hones ideas in consultation with colleagues. The divisional managers may add ideas, ask for information and suggest alternative scenarios. There may also be division-level projects which need further consideration. As the discussions and data gathering progress the proposal generally starts to gain commitment from a number of people who become drawn in and involved.

The classification stage involves matching projects to identified needs. Initially, there may be a long list of imaginative project ideas or solutions to a specific problem, but this may be narrowed down in these early stages to two or three. Detailed evaluation of all projects is expensive. Some types of project do not require the extensive search for data and complex evaluation that others do. The following classification may allow more attention to be directed at the type of project where the need is greatest:

1 *Equipment replacement* Equipment obsolescence can occur because of technological developments which create more efficient alternatives, because the old equipment becomes expensive to maintain or because of a change in the cost of inputs, making an alternative method cheaper (for example, if the oil price quadruples, taxi firms may shift to smaller cars).

2 *Expansion or improvement of existing products* These investments relate to increasing the volume of output and/or improving product quality and market position.

3 *Cost reduction* A continuous process of search and analysis may be necessary to ensure that the firm is producing at lowest cost. Small modifications to methods of production or equipment, as well as the introduction of new machines, may bring valuable incremental benefits.

4 *New products* Many firms depend on a regular flow of innovatory products to permit continued expansion. Examples are Intel, GlaxoSmithKline and 3M. These firms have to make huge commitments to research and development, market research and promotion. Vast investments are needed in new production facilities around the world.

5 *Statutory and welfare* Investments may be required by law for such matters as safety, or pollution control. These do not, generally, give a financial return and so the focus is usually to satisfy the requirement at minimum cost. Welfare investments may lead to some intangible benefits which are difficult to quantify, such as a more contented work-force. The Arnold and Hatzopoulos (2000) survey showed that 78 per cent of the firms undertook non-economic projects directed at health and safety issues; 74 per cent accepted projects motivated by legislation; and 54 per cent had paid for uneconomic projects for social and environmental reasons.

The management team have to weigh up the value of a more comprehensive analysis against the cost of evaluation. Regular equipment replacement, cost reduction and existing product expansion decisions are likely to require less documentation than a major strategic investment in a new product area. Also, the information needs are likely to rise in proportion to the size of the investment. A £100m investment in a new pharmaceutical plant is likely to be treated differently to a £10,000 investment in a new delivery vehicle.

Screening

At this stage, each proposal will be assessed to establish whether it is sufficiently attractive to receive further attention through the application of sophisticated analysis. The quality of information is generally rather poor and the payback method may feature predominantly at this point. Screening decisions should be made with an awareness of the strategic direction of the firm and the limitations imposed by the financial, human and other resources available. There should also be a check on the technical feasibility of the proposal and some preliminary assessment of risk.

Strategy

Capital allocation is a pivotal part of the overall strategic process. A good investment appraisal system must mesh with the firm's long-term plan. The managers at plant or division level may not be able to see opportunities at a strategic level, such as the benefits of combining two divisions, or the necessity for business unit divestment. Thus, the bottom-up flow of ideas for investment at plant level should complement the top-down strategic planning from the centre. Each vantage point has a valuable contribution to make.

Budget

Most large firms prepare capital budgets stretching over many years. Often a detailed budget for capital expenditure in the forthcoming year is set within the framework of an outline plan for the next five years. Individual projects are required to conform to the corporate budget. However, the budget itself, at least in the long run, is heavily influenced by the availability of project proposals. The Arnold and Hatzopoulos (2000) survey shows the use of budgets by UK firms – Exhibit 4.9.

Appraisal

It is at the appraisal stage that detailed cash flow forecasts are required as inputs to the more sophisticated evaluation methods, such as net present value. Manuals provide detailed checklists which help the project sponsor to ensure that all relevant costs and other factors have been considered. These manuals may explain how to calculate NPV and IRR and may also supply the firm's opportunity cost of capital. (If risk adjustment is made through the discount rate there may be more than one cost of capital and the

Exhibit 4.9 Capital expenditure budgets for UK firms

	Small firms %	Medium-sized firms %	Large firms %
Outline capital expenditure budgets are prepared for:			
1 year ahead	18	8	–
2 years ahead	18	25	13
3 years ahead	35	50	18
4 years ahead	9	–	5
More than 4 years ahead	21	13	61
Blank	–	4	3
Detailed capital expenditure budgets are prepared for:			
1 year ahead	70	79	55
2 years ahead	21	13	21
3 years ahead	9	4	8
4 years ahead	–	–	5
More than 4 years ahead	–	4	11

Note: 96 firms completed the survey questionnaire.

Source: Arnold and Hatzopoulos (2000).

sponsor then has to classify the project into, say, high, medium, or low risk categories – *see* Chapter 6.) The project promoter may seek the aid of specialists, such as engineers, accountants and economists, in the preparation of the formal analysis.

Report and authorisation

Many firms require that project proposals are presented in a specific manner through the use of capital appropriation request forms. Such forms will detail the nature of the project and the amount of finance needed, together with the forecasted cash inflows and the NPV, IRR, ARR or payback. Some analysis of risk and a consideration of alternatives to the proposed course of action may also be required.

Expenditure below a threshold, say £100,000, will gain authorisation at division level, while that above the threshold will need approval at corporate level. At head office a committee consisting of the most senior officers (chairman, chief executive, finance director, etc.) will meet on a regular basis to consider major capital projects. Very few investment proposals are turned down by this committee, mainly because these project ideas will have already been through a number of stages of review and informal discussion up and down the organisation, and the obviously non-viable will have been eliminated. Also, even marginally profitable projects may get approval to give a vote of confidence to the sponsoring management team. The alternative of refusal may damage motivation and may cause loss of commitment to developing other projects. If the senior management had had doubts about a proposal they would have influenced the sponsoring division(s) long before the proposal reached the final report stage. In most cases there is a long period of consultation between head office and division managers, and informal pressures to modify or drop proposals can be both more efficient and politically astute ways of proceeding than refusal at the last hurdle.

Implementation

Capital expenditure controls

Firms must keep track of investment projects so as to be quickly aware of delays and cost differences compared with the plan. When a project is authorised there is usually a specified schedule of expenditure, and the accountants and senior management will keep a watchful eye on cash outflows. During the installation, purchasing and construction phases, comparisons with original estimates will be made on a periodic basis. Divisions may be permitted to overspend by, say, 10 per cent before a formal request for more funds is required. A careful watch is also kept on any changes to the projected start and completion dates. Deviations from projected cash flows can be caused by one of two factors:

a inaccuracy in the original estimate, that is, the proposal report did not reflect reality perfectly;

b poor control of costs.

It is often difficult to isolate each of these elements. However, deviations need to be identified and explained as the project progresses. This may permit corrective action to be taken to avoid further overspending and may, in extreme circumstances, lead to the cancellation of the project.

Post-completion audit

Post-completion auditing is the monitoring and evaluation of the progress of a capital investment project through a comparison of the actual cash flows and other costs and benefits with those forecasted at the time of authorisation. Companies need a follow-up procedure which examines the performance of projects over a long time span, stretching over many years. It is necessary to isolate and explain deviations from estimated values.

Exhibit 4.10 shows the extent of the use of post-competition audits by UK companies.

Exhibit 4.10 Replies to the question: 'Does your company conduct post-audits of major capital expenditure?'

	Small %	Medium-sized %	Large %	Composite %
Always	41	17	24	28
Sometimes/on major projects	41	67	71	59
Rarely	12	17	5	10
Never	6	–		2

Note: 96 companies responded to the survey.
Source: Arnold and Hatzopoulos (2000).

There are three main reasons for carrying out a post-completion audit:

1 *Financial control mechanism* This monitoring process helps to identify problems and errors evident in a particular project. A comparison with the original projections establishes whether the benefits claimed prior to approval actually materialise. If a problem is encountered then modifications or abandonment may be possible before it is too late.

2 *Insight gained may be useful for future capital investment decisions* One benefit of auditing existing projects is that it might lead to the identification of failings in the capital investment process generally. It may be discovered that data collection systems are inadequate or that appraisal methods are poor. Regular post-completion auditing helps to develop better decision making. For instance, past appraisals may have paid scant regard to likely competitor reaction; once recognised this omission will be corrected for in all future evaluations.

3 *The psychological effect* If potential project sponsors are aware that implemented proposals are monitored and reviewed they may be encouraged to increase their forecasting accuracy. They may also be dissuaded from playing 'numbers games' with their project submission, designed to draw more resources to their divisions or pet schemes unjustifiably. In addition, they may take a keener interest in the implementation phase.

Senior management must conduct a careful balancing act because the post-completion audit may encourage another sort of non-optimal behaviour. For instance, if managers are judged on the extent to which project outcomes exceed original estimates, there will be a tendency to deliberately understate the forecast. Also, if the audit is too inquisitorial, or if it too forcefully apportions blame for results which are only partially under the control of managers, then they may be inclined to suggest only relatively safe projects with predictable outcomes. This may result in a loss of opportunities. Ideally, regular post-completion reviews are needed, but many firms settle for an audit one year after the asset has been put in place. This may be inadequate for projects producing returns over many years. Some firms do manage an annual review of progress, and some even go as far as monthly monitoring during the first year followed by annual reviews thereafter. On the other hand, many projects involve only minor commitment of resources and are routine in nature. The need for post-completion auditing is not as pressing for these as it would be for strategic projects requiring major organisational resource commitment. Given the costs involved in the auditing process, many firms feel justified in being highly selective and auditing only a small proportion. Another reason for not carrying out a post-completion audit in all cases is the difficulty of disentangling the costs and benefits of a specific project in a context of widespread interaction and interdependence.

CONCLUDING COMMENTS

The typical student of finance will spend a great deal of time trying to cope with problems presented in a mathematical form. This is necessary because these are often the most difficult aspects of the subject to absorb. However, readers should not be misled into thinking that complex computations are at the centre of project investment in the practical world of business. Managers are often either ignorant of the principles behind discounted cash flow techniques or choose to stress more traditional rule-of-thumb techniques, such as payback and accounting rate of return, because of their communicatory or other perceived advantages. These managers recognise that good investment decision making and implementation require attention to be paid to the social and psychological factors at work within an organisation. They also know that formal technical appraisal takes place only after a long process of idea creation and development in a suitably nurturing environment. There is also a long period of discussion and commitment forming, and continuous re-examination and refinement. The real art of management is in the process of project creation and selection and not in the technical appraisal stage.

KEY POINTS AND CONCEPTS

- **Payback and ARR** are widely used methods of project appraisal, but discounted cash flow methods are the most popular.

- Most large firms use **more than one appraisal method.**

- **Payback** is the length of time for cumulated future cash inflows to equal an initial outflow. Projects are accepted if this time is below an agreed cut-off point.

- **Payback has a few drawbacks:**

  - no allowance for the time value of money;
  - cash flows after the cut-off are ignored;
  - arbitrary selection of cut-off date.

- **Discounted payback** takes account of the time value of money.

- **Payback's attractions:**

  - it complements more sophisticated methods;
  - simple, and easy to use;
  - good for communication with non-specialists;
  - makes allowance for increased risk of more distant cash flows;
  - projects returning cash sooner are ranked higher. Thought to be useful when capital is in short supply;
  - often gives the same decision as the more sophisticated techniques.

- **Accounting rate of return** is the ratio of accounting profit to investment, expressed as a percentage.

- **Accounting rate of return has a few drawbacks:**

  - it can be calculated in a wide variety of ways;
  - profit is a poor substitute for cash flow;
  - no allowance for the time value of money;
  - arbitrary cut-off rate;
  - some perverse decisions can be made.

- **Accounting rate of return attractions:**

  - familiarity, ease of understanding and communication;
  - managers' performances are often judged using ARR and therefore they wish to select projects on the same basis.

- **Internal rate of return** is used more than NPV:

  - psychological preference for a percentage;
  - can be calculated without cost of capital;
  - thought (wrongly) to give a better ranking.

- **Mathematical technique is only one element** needed for successful project appraisal. Other factors to be taken into account are:

  - strategy;
  - social context;
  - expense;

- entrepreneurial spirit;
- intangible benefits.

■ The investment process is more than appraisal. It has many stages:

- generation of ideas;
- development and classification;
- screening;
- appraisal;
- report and authorisation;
- implementation;
- post-completion auditing.

REFERENCES AND FURTHER READING

Arnold, G.C. and Hatzopoulos, P.D. (2000) 'The theory practice gap in capital budgeting: evidence from the United Kingdom' *Journal of Business Finance and Accounting*, 27(5) and (6), June/July, pp. 603–26. Recent evidence of techniques used by UK firms, discussion of reasons for continued use of rule-of-thumb methods.

Arya, A., Fellingham, J.C. and Glover, J.C. (1998) 'Capital budgeting: some exceptions to the net present value rule', *Issues in Accounting Education*, 13(3), August, pp. 499–508. Discussion on the use of NPV.

Bhasker, K. (1979) 'A multiple objective approach to capital budgeting', *Accounting and Business Research*, Winter, Discussion of investment appraisal.

Bierman, H. (1988) *Implementing Capital Budgeting Techniques*, Revised edn. Cambridge Mass: Ballinger Publishing. Practical issues.

Boardman, C.M., Reinhard, W.J. and Celec, S.G. (1982) 'The role of the payback period in the theory and application of duration to capital budgeting', *Journal of Business Finance and Accounting*, 9(4), Winter, pp. 511–22. Payback critically assessed.

Bower, J.L. (1972) *Managing the Resource Allocation Process*. Illinois: Irwin. Provides insight into the managerial processes involved in investment decision-taking.

Bromwich, M. and Bhimani, A. (1991) 'Strategic investment appraisal', *Management Accounting*, March. Short article describing appraisal of non-quantifiable benefits of a project.

Chartered Institute of Public Finance and Accountancy (1983) 'Management of capital programmes' (*Financial System Review* 8). Advice on project processes in the public sector.

Christy, G.A. (1966) *Capital Budgeting – Current Practices and their Efficiency*, Bureau of Business and Economic Research, University of Oregon. More evidence of use.

Cooper, D.J. (1975) 'Rationality and investment appraisal', *Accounting and Business Research*, Summer, pp 198–202. Capital budgeting set in context.

Dean, J. (1951) *Capital Budgeting*: New York: Columbia University Press. The first comprehensive capital budgeting book. An early rejection of payback.

Demski, J.S. (1994) *Managerial Uses of Accounting Information*. Boston: Kluwer Academic Pub. Includes a discussion of the practical employment of NPV.

Dixit, A.K. and Pindyck, R.S. (1994), *Investment Under Uncertainty*. Princeton, NJ: Princeton University Press. Higher-level discussion.

Emmanuel, C., Otley, D. and Merchant, K. (1990) *Accounting for Management Control*, 2nd edn. London: Chapman and Hall. An advanced accounting text that deals with investment appraisal.

Finnie, J. (1988) 'The role of financial appraisal in decisions to acquire advanced manufacturing technology', *Accounting and Business Research*, 18(70), pp. 133–9. Argues that better management of the appraisal process is required for projects using advanced manufacturing technology.

Fisher, F.M. and McGowan, J.I. (1983) 'On the misuse of accounting rates of return to infer monopoly profits', *American Economic Review*, 73, March, pp. 82–97. Highlights a number of problems with ARR.

Gadella, J.W. (1992), 'Post-project appraisal', *Management Accounting*, March, pp. 52 and 58. Yet more on post-completion auditing

Gitman, L.J. and Forrester, J.R. (1977) 'A survey of capital budgeting techniques used by major US firms', *Financial Management*, Fall, pp. 66–76. Empirical evidence from the USA.

Gitman, L.J. and Maxwell, C.E. (1987) 'A longitudinal comparison of capital budgeting techniques used by major US firms: 1986 versus 1976', *The Journal of Applied Business Research*, Fall, pp. 41–50. Empirical evidence from the USA.

Gitman, L.J. and Mercurio, V.A. (1982) 'Cost of capital techniques used in major US firms', *Financial Management*, Winter, pp. 21–9. Empirical evidence from the USA.

Gordon, L.A. and Myers, M.D. (1991) 'Postauditing capital projects', *Management Accounting (US)*, January, pp. 39–42.

Grayson, C.J. (1966) 'The use of statistical techniques in capital budgeting', in A.A. Robichek, (ed.) *Financial Research and Management Decisions*. New York: Wiley, pp. 90–132. Early discussion.

Gurnani, C. (1984) 'Capital budgeting: theory and practice', *Engineering Economist*, Fall, pp. 19–46. Discussion of the theory–practice gap.

Hajdasinski, M.M. (1993) 'The payback period as a measure of profitability and liquidity', *The Engineering Economist*, 38(3), Spring, pp. 177–191. Payback's usefulness.

Haka, S.F., Gordon, L.A. and Pinches, G.E. (1985) 'Sophisticated capital budgeting selection techniques and firm performance', *Accounting Review*, October, pp. 651–69. Do firms that adopt textbook best practice perform the best?

Harris, M., Kriebel, C.H. and Raviv, A. (1982) 'Asymmetric information, incentives and intrafirm resource allocation', *Management Science*, 28(6), June, pp. 604–20. Explanations for the theory–practice gap.

Ho, S.M. and Pike, R.H. (1991) 'Risk analysis techniques in capital budgeting contexts', *Accounting and Business Research*, 21(83). Survey of 146 UK firms' project risk analysis practices.

Hodgkinson, L. (1987) 'The capital budgeting decision of corporate groups', Plymouth Business School Paper. An interesting survey of the capital investment process in medium-sized UK companies.

Jones, T.C. and Dugdale, D. (1994) 'Academic and practitioner rationality: the case of investment appraisal', *British Accounting Review*, 26, pp. 3–25. Theory-practice gap explored.

Kaplan, R.S. (1986) 'Must CIM be justified by faith alone?' *Harvard Business Review*, March/April, pp. 87–95. DCF analysis applied to computer-integrated manufacturing projects – interesting application of principles.

Kaplan, R.S. and Atkinson, A.A. (1998) *Advanced Management Accounting*, International Edition. Englewood Cliffs, NJ: Prentice-Hall. Theory–practice gap explored.

Kay, J.A. (1976) 'Accountants, too, could be happy in a golden age: the accountant's rate of profit and the internal rate of return', *Oxford Economic Papers*, 28, pp. 447–60. A technical/ mathematical consideration of the link between ARR and IRR.

Kee, R. and Bublitz, B. (1988), 'The role of payback in the investment process', *Accounting and Business Research*, 18(70), pp. 149–55. Value of payback discussed.

Kennedy, A. and Mills, R. (1992) 'Post completion auditing: a source of strategic direction?', *Management Accounting (UK)*, May, pp. 26–8. Post-completion auditing evidence.

Kennedy, A. and Mills, R. (1993a) 'Post completion auditing in practice', *Management Accounting*, October, pp. 22–5. Post-completion auditing evidence.

Kennedy, A. and Mills, R. (1993b) 'Experiences in operating a post-audit system', *Management Accounting*, November. Post-completion auditing evidence.

Kennedy, J.A. and Mills, R. (1990), *Post Completion Audit of Capital Expenditure Projects*. London: CIMA. Management Accounting Guide 9. Post-completion auditing evidence.

Kim, S.H. (1982) 'An empirical study of the relationship between capital budgeting practices and earning performance', *Engineering Economics*, 27(3), Spring, pp. 185–96. Does the adoption of theoretical best practice result in outperformance?

Kim, S.H. and Farragher, E.J. (1981) 'Current capital budgeting practices', *Management Accounting (US)*. June, pp. 26–33. Empirical evidence.

Kim, S.H., Crick, T. and Kim, S.H. (1986) 'Do executives practice what academics preach?', *Management Accounting (US)*. November, pp. 49–52. Theory–practice gap.

King, P. (1975), 'Is the emphasis of capital budgeting theory misplaced?' *Journal of Business Finance and Accounting*, 2(1), p. 69. Theory–practice gap.

Klammer, T., Koch, B. and Wilner, N. (1991) 'Capital budgeting practices – a survey of corporate use', *Journal of Management Accounting Research*, Fall, pp. 447–64. Empirical evidence.

Lawrence, A.G. and Myers, M.D. (1991) 'Post-auditing capital projects', *Management Accounting*, January, pp. 39–42. Survey of 282 large US firms' post-auditing objectives, method and thoroughness.

Lefley, F. (1996) 'Strategic methodologies of investment appraisal of AMT projects: a review and synthesis', *The Engineering Economist*, 41(4), Summer, pp. 345–61. Quantitative analysis and judgement are both needed in order to assess advanced manufacturing technology projects.

Lefley, F. (1997) 'The sometimes overlooked discounted payback method', *Management Accounting* (UK). November, p. 36. Payback's virtues.

Litzenberger, R.M. and Joy, O.M. (1975) 'Decentralized capital budgeting decisions and shareholder wealth maximisation'; *Journal of Finance*, 30(4), pp. 993–1002. Practical DCF.

Longmore, D.R. (1989) 'The persistence of the payback method: a time-adjusted decision rule perspective', *The Engineering Economist*, 43(3), Spring, pp. 185–94. Payback's use.

Lowenstein, L. (1991) *Sense and Nonsense in Corporate Finance*. Reading, MA: Addison Wesley. Criticism of over-preciseness in project appraisal and the underplaying of unquantifiable elements.

Lumijärvi, O.P. (1991) 'Selling of capital investments to top management'. *Management Accounting Research*, 2, pp. 171–88. Describes a real-world case of a lower-level manager influencing superiors so that desired investment funds are received.

McIntyre, A.D. and Coulthurst, N.J. (1986) *Capital Budgeting Practices in Medium-Sized Businesses – A Survey*. London: Institute of Cost and Management Accountants. Interesting survey of investment appraisal practices in UK medium-sized firms. More detailed than the later (1987) article.

McIntyre, A.D. and Coulthurst, N.J. (1987) 'Planning and control of capital investment in medium-sized UK companies', *Management Accounting*, March, pp. 39–40. Interesting summary of empirical work explaining the capital budgeting processes in 141 medium-sized firms with turnovers in the range £1.4m–£5.75m.

Mills, R.W. (1988) 'Capital budgeting techniques used in the UK and the USA', *Management Accounting*, January, pp. 26–7. Empirical evidence on investment appraisal methods used in practice.

Mills, R.W. and Herbert, P.J.A. (1987) 'Corporate and divisional influence in capital budgeting', Chartered Institute of Management Accountants, Occasional Paper Series. Internal issues associated with capital budgeting.

Mills, R., Robertson, J. and Ward, T. (1992) 'Why financial economics is vital in measuring business value', *Management Accounting (UK)*, January, pp. 39–42. Theoretical discussion.

Neale, B. and Holmes, D. (1988) 'Post-completion audits: the costs and benefits', *Management Accounting*, March, pp. 27–30. Post-completion audits discussion.

Neale, C.W. and Holmes, D.E.A. (1988) 'Post-completion audits: the costs and benefits', *Management Accounting*, 66(3). Benefits of post-completion auditing. Evidence from a survey of 384 UK and USA large firms.

Northcott, D. (1991) 'Rationality and decision making in capital budgeting', *British Accounting Review*, Sept., pp. 219–34. Theory–practice gap explored.

Patterson, C.S. (1989) 'Investment decision criteria used by listed New Zealand companies', *Accounting and Finance*, 29(2), November, pp. 73–89. Evidence from the Pacific.

Pike, R.H. (1982) *Capital Budgeting in the 1980s*. London: Chartered Institute of Management Accountants. Clearly describes evidence on the capital investment practices of major British companies.

Pike, R.H. (1983) 'A review of recent trends in formal capital budgeting processes', *Accounting and Business Research*, Summer, pp. 201–8. More evidence.

Pike, R.H. (1985) 'Owner-manager conflict and the role of payback', *Accounting and Business Research*, Winter, pp. 47–51. Comparison of methods.

Pike, R.H. (1988) 'An empirical study of the adoption of sophisticated capital budgeting practices and decision-making effectiveness', *Accounting and Business Research*, 18(72), Autumn, pp. 341–51. Observes the trend within 100 large UK firms over 11 years towards sophisticated methods – NPV, post-completion audits, probability analysis.

Pike, R.H. (1996) 'A longitudinal survey of capital budgeting practices', *Journal of Business Finance and Accounting*, 23(1), January. Excellent, short and clear article surveying appraisal methods in UK large firms.

Pike, R.H. and Wolfe, M. (1988) *Capital Budgeting in the 1990s*. London: Chartered Institute of Management Accountants. Some interesting evidence on appraisal methods used in practice. Clearly expressed.

Pinches, G.E. (1982) 'Myopia, capital budgeting and decision-making', *Financial Management*, Autumn, pp. 6–19.

Ross, S.A. (1995) 'Uses, abuses, and alternatives to the net-present-value rule', *Financial Management*, 24(3), Autumn, pp. 96–102 Discussion of the value of NPV.

Sangster, A. (1993), 'Capital investment appraisal techniques: a survey of current usage', *Journal of Business Finance and Accounting*, 20(3), April, pp. 307–33. Evidence of use.

Scapens, R.W. and Sale, J.T. (1981) 'Performance measurement and formal capital expenditure controls in divisionalised companies', *Journal of Business Finance and Accounting*, 8, pp. 389–420. The capital investment process in large UK and US firms.

Scapens, R.W., Sale, J.T. and Tikkas, P.A. (1982) *'Financial Control of Divisional Capital Investment*. London: Institute of Cost and Management Accountants, Occasional Papers Series. Good insight into the capital investment process in large UK and US companies.

Statman, M. (1982) 'The persistence of the payback method: a principle–agent perspective', *The Engineering Economist*, Summer, pp. 95–100. Payback's usefulness.

Statman, M. and Sepe, J.F. (1984) 'Managerial incentive plans and the use of the payback method', *Journal of Business Finance and Accounting*, 11(1), Spring, pp. 61–5. Payback's usefulness.

Tyrrall, D.E. (1998) 'Discounted cash flow: rational calculation or psychological crutch?', *Management Accounting (UK)*, February, pp 46–8. Discussion of theory–practice relationship.

Wardlow, A. (1994), 'Investment appraisal criteria and the impact of low inflation', *Bank of England Quarterly Bulletin*, 34(3), August, pp. 250–4. Discussion of the failure to adjust to a low and stable inflation environment. Easy to read.

Weingartner, H.M. (1969) 'Some new views on the payback period and capital budgeting', *Management Science*, 15, pp. 594–607. Why payback is frequently employed.

Weingartner, H.M. (1977) 'Capital rationing: *n* authors in search of a plot', *Journal of Finance*, December, pp. 1403–31. Critical discussion.

Zimmerman, J.L. (1997) *Accounting for Decision Making and Control*, 2nd edn. Boston: Irwin/McGraw-Hill. Contains a useful discussion on discounted cash flow methods.

SELF-REVIEW QUESTIONS

1 Payback is dismissed as unsound. Discuss.

2 Define accounting rate of return and compare it with net present value.

3 Describe discounted payback.

4 Do you believe the arguments for using IRR are strong enough to justify relying on this technique alone?

5 Why is investment project generation, selection and implementation closer to an art form than a science?

6 How would you appraise a project with a high proportion of non-quantifiable benefits?

7 If you were chief executive of a large corporation, how would you encourage project idea generation, communication and sponsorship?

8 Why is project screening necessary?

9 Invent five projects, each of which falls into a different project category.

10 Why are few projects rejected at the report stage?

11 When do capital expenditure controls and post-completion audits become an excessive burden, and when are they very important?

12 Comment on the following statement:

'The firm should choose the investment with a short payback rather than one with a larger net present value.'

QUESTIONS AND PROBLEMS

1 For the following cash flows, calculate the payback and the discounted payback.

Point in time (yearly intervals)	0 £	1 £	2 £	3 £	4 £	5 £	6 £	7 £
A	−3,000	500	500	500	500	500	500	500
B	−10,000	2,000	5,000	3,000	2,000	–	–	–
C	−15,000	5,000	4,000	4,000	5,000	10,000	–	–
D	−4,000	1,000	1,000	1,000	1,000	7,000	7,000	7,000
E	−8,000	500	500	500	2,000	5,000	10,000	–

The cost of capital is 12 per cent.

2† A project has a £10,000 initial investment and cash inflows of £3,334 per year over six years. What is the payback period? What will be the payback period if the receipts of £3,334 per year occur for only three years? Explain the significance of your answer.

3* (*Examination level*) Oakland plc is considering a major investment project. The initial outlay of £900,000 will, in subsequent years, be followed by positive cash flows, as shown below. (These occur on the anniversary dates.)

Year	1	2	3	4	5
Cash flow (£)	+50,000	+120,000	+350,000	+80,000	+800,000

After the end of the fifth year this business activity will cease and no more cash flows will be produced.

The initial £900,000 investment in plant and machinery is to be depreciated over the five-year life of the project using the straight-line method. These assets will have no value after Year 5.

The management judge that the cash inflows shown above are also an accurate estimation of the profit before depreciation for each of the years. They also believe that the appropriate discount rate to use for the firm's projects is 10 per cent per annum.

The board of directors are used to evaluating project proposals on the basis of a payback rule which requires that all investments achieve payback in four years.

As the newly appointed executive responsible for project appraisal you have been asked to assess this project using a number of different methods and to advise the board on the advantages and disadvantages of each. Do this in the following sequence.

(1) a Calculate the payback period.
    b Calculate the discounted payback period.
    c Calculate the accounting rate of return.
    d Calculate the internal rate of return.
    e Calculate the net present value.

(2) Compare the relative theoretical and practical merits and demerits of each of the methods used.

Assume: No tax or inflation.

4   A firm is considering investing in a project with the following cash flows:

Year	1	2	3	4	5	6	7	8
Net cash flow (£)	1,000	1,500	2,000	1,750	1,500	1,000	500	500

The initial investment is £6,250. The firm has a required rate of return of 10 per cent. Calculate:

a the payback period;
b the discounted payback;
c the net present value.

What are the main objections to the use of payback? Why does it remain a very popular method?

5* Maple plc is considering which of two mutually exclusive projects to accept, each with a five-year life. Project A requires an initial expenditure of £2,300,000 and is forecast to generate annual cash flows before depreciation of £800,000. The equipment purchased at time zero has an estimated residual value after five years of £300,000. Project B costs £660,000, has a residual value of £60,000 and cash inflows before depreciation of £250,000 per annum are anticipated. The company has a straight-line depreciation policy and a cost of capital of 15 per cent. You can assume that the cash flows are also equal to the profits before depreciation. Calculate:

a the accounting rate of return;
b the net present value.

What are the disadvantages of using ARR?

6   Explain why empirical studies show that, in practice, firms often prefer to evaluate projects using traditional methods.

7   Camelia plc has been run in an autocratic style by the chief executive and main shareholder, Mr Linedraw, during its 40-year history. The company is now too large for Mr Linedraw to continue being involved in all decisions. As part of its reforms the firm intends to set up a structured programme of capital investment. You have been asked to compile a report which will guide management. This will detail the investment process and will not be confined to appraisal techniques.

8   'The making of good investment decisions is as much about understanding human psychology as it is about mathematics.' Explain this statement.

Explain how each of the following can lead to a sub-optimal investment process:

a relying on top-down idea generation;
b managers being judged solely on accounting rate of return;
c a requirement that projects have a quick payback;
d post-auditing once only, one year after completion;
e post-auditing conducted by managers from 'rival' divisions;
f over-optimism of project sponsors.

ASSIGNMENT

Investigate the capital investment process in a firm you know well. Relate the stages and methods used to the process outlined in this chapter. Consider areas for improvement.

Chapter 9

STOCK MARKETS

CASE STUDY 9.1 Using the stock market both to create wealth and to treat disease

Oxford BioMedica

Alan and Sue Kingsman started an Oxford University-backed company called Oxford BioMedica in 1995. This company develops technologies to treat diseases including cancer, cystic fibrosis, Parkinson's disease and AIDS using gene therapy. The aim is to replace faulty genes.

Alan and Sue are biochemistry academics who lacked the finance needed for future research and development. They raised seed finance in June 1996 (small amounts of start-up money) and then sought several millions by floating on the Alternative Investment Market in December 1996.

Oxford BioMedica was upgraded to the Official List of the London Stock Exchange in April 2001 following a successful £35.5 million fund-raising. The company has two products in trial: MetXia(R) is in clinical trial for late stage breast cancer and ovarian cancer; TroVaxTM is in clinical trial for late stage colorectal cancer. The company has never made a profit, but shareholders are willing to wait. The potential rewards are huge, running into billions of pounds if a successful vaccine is produced. The rewards to patients could be beyond price.

Sources: Based on articles in the *Financial Times*, 3 June 1996, 18 August 1999 and 3 January 2001 and *Investors Chronicle*, 8 November 1996, and on Oxford BioMedica news releases, available at www.hemscott.com.

INTRODUCTION

This chapter is concerned with the role and value of stock markets in the modern economy. It also looks more specifically at the workings of the London Stock Exchange. Imagine the difficulties Sue and Alan Kingsman would have getting their venture off the ground in a world without some form of market where long-term risk capital can be raised from investors, and where those investors are able to sell on their holdings to other risk takers whenever they wish. There would certainly be a much smaller pool of money made available to firms with brilliant ideas and society would be poorer.

STOCK EXCHANGES AROUND THE WORLD

Stock exchanges are markets where government and industry can raise long-term capital and investors can buy and sell securities. Stock exchanges grew in response to the demand for funds to finance investment and (especially in the early days) ventures in overseas trade. The risky sea-voyage trading businesses of the sixteenth, seventeenth and eighteenth centuries often required the raising of capital from large numbers of investors. Until the Napoleonic Wars the Dutch capital markets were pre-eminent, raising funds for investment abroad, loans for governments and businesses, and developing a thriving secondary market in which investors could sell their financial securities to other investors. This transferability of ownership of financial assets was an important breakthrough for the development of sophisticated financial systems. It offered the investor liquidity, which encouraged the flow of funds to firms, while leaving the capital in the business venture untouched.

The Napoleonic Wars led to a rapid rise in the volume of British government debt sold to the public. Trading in this debt tended to take place in coffee houses in London and other cities. Much of the early industrialisation was financed by individuals or partnerships, but as the capital requirements became larger it was clear that joint-stock enterprises were needed, in which the money of numerous investors was brought together to give joint ownership with the promise of a share of profits. Canal corporations, docks companies, manufacturing enterprises, railways and insurance companies were added to the list of shares and bonds traded on the London Stock Exchange in the first half of the nineteenth century.

The second major breakthrough was the introduction of limited liability for shareholders in 1855.[1] This meant that the owners of shares were not responsible for the debts of the firm – once they had handed over the money to purchase the shares they could not be called on to contribute any further, regardless of the demands of creditors to a failed firm. This encouraged an even greater flow of funds into equity (ownership) capital and aided the spectacular rise of Victorian Britain as an economic powerhouse. Similar measures were taken in other European and North American countries to boost the flow of funds for investment. Outside the Western economies the value of a stock exchange was quickly recognised – for example, Bombay and Johannesburg opened stock markets in the nineteenth century.

Today the important contribution of stock exchanges to economic well-being has been recognised from Moldova to Shanghai. There are now over 90 countries with officially recognised exchanges and many of these countries have more than one exchange. Exhibit 9.1 focuses on the share trading aspect of a number of these markets. Shares will be the main concern of this and the following chapter, but it is important to note that stock markets often do much more than trade shares. Many also trade government debt securities and a wide array of financial instruments issued by firms, for example corporate bonds, convertibles, preference shares, warrants and eurobonds. (These will be examined in later chapters.) Total (or market) capitalisation is the total value, at market prices, of all the shares in issue of the companies quoted on the stock market.

The 1990s was a dynamic period for global financial markets. The shift in political and economic philosophies and policies towards free markets and capitalism produced a growing demand for capital. Following the successful example of the West and the 'Tiger' economies of Asia, numerous emerging markets promoted stock exchanges as a major pillar of economic progress. The liberalisation and the accelerating wave of privatisation pushed stock markets to the forefront of developing countries' tools of economic progress. The collapse of communism and the adoption of pro-market policies led to the rise of share exchanges in dozens of former anti-capitalist bastions. Even countries which still espouse communism, such as China and Vietnam, now have thriving and increasingly influential stock exchanges designed to facilitate the mobilisation of capital and its employment in productive endeavour, with – 'horror-of-horrors' to some hard-line communists – a return going to the capital providers. In the emerging countries alone there are now over 26,000 companies quoted on stock exchanges worth over £1,500,000,000. The total value of all companies quoted on all the stock exchanges in the world amounts to more than £25,000 billion.

Clearly stock markets are an important element in the intricate lattice-work of a modern and sophisticated society. Not only are they a vital meeting place for investors and a source of investment capital for businesses, they permit a more appropriate allocation of resources within society – that is, a more optimum mix of goods and services produced to satisfy people. Peruvians see a 'Shareholder mentality' as a worthy objective since this may help in 'boosting low levels of domestic savings' – *see* Exhibit 9.2.

There has been a remarkable increase in the number of officially recognised stock exchanges around the globe in the last five to ten years. As well as an increase in the significance of stock exchanges in the economies of developing countries, there has also been a notable increase in the size and importance of the older exchanges. This is illustrated by the fact that the market value of all the ordinary shares issued by companies (market capitalisation) listed on some exchanges exceeds the total output of goods and services produced by that country's citizens in a year (Gross Domestic Product). This applies to Canada, France, Japan, Sweden, the UK and the USA. In some countries (e.g. Finland, the Netherlands and Switzerland, and in Hong Kong) market capitalisation of quoted companies is more than double annual national output.

China is a wholehearted convert to the virtues of stock markets. Over 50 million Chinese hold shares in over 1,000 companies quoted either on the stock exchange in Shanghai or on the one in Shenzhen. The president of China, Jiang Zemin, no less, speaks with the fervour of the recent convert – *see* Exhibit 9.3.

Exhibit 9.1 Stock exchanges around the world

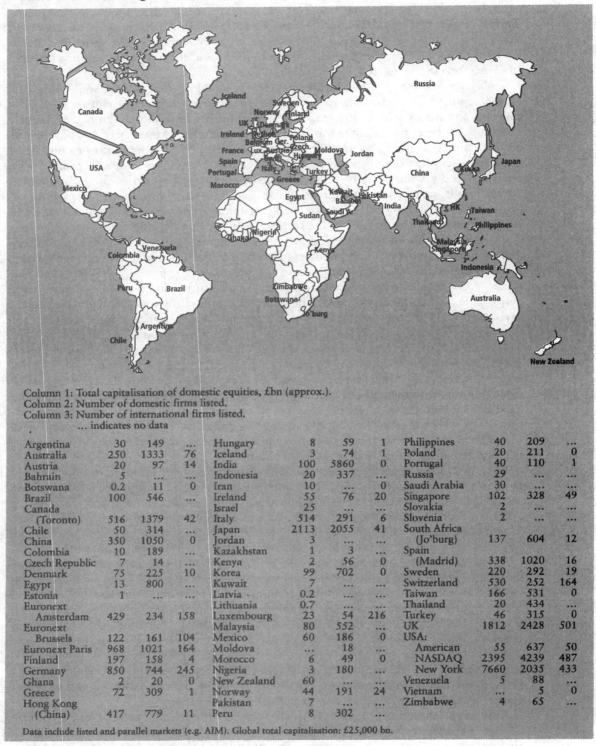

Column 1: Total capitalisation of domestic equities, £bn (approx.).
Column 2: Number of domestic firms listed.
Column 3: Number of international firms listed.
... indicates no data

Argentina	30	149	...	Hungary	8	59	1	Philippines	40	209	...
Australia	250	1333	76	Iceland	3	74	1	Poland	20	211	0
Austria	20	97	14	India	100	5860	0	Portugal	40	110	1
Bahrain	5	...	...	Indonesia	20	337	...	Russia	29	...	...
Botswana	0.2	11	0	Iran	10	...	0	Saudi Arabia	30	...	...
Brazil	100	546	...	Ireland	55	76	20	Singapore	102	328	49
Canada				Israel	25	...	...	Slovakia	2	...	...
(Toronto)	516	1379	42	Italy	514	291	6	Slovenia	2	...	...
Chile	50	314	...	Japan	2113	2055	41	South Africa			
China	350	1050	0	Jordan	3	...	...	(Jo'burg)	137	604	12
Colombia	10	189	...	Kazakhstan	1	3	...	Spain			
Czech Republic	7	14	...	Kenya	2	56	0	(Madrid)	338	1020	16
Denmark	75	225	10	Korea	99	702	0	Sweden	220	292	19
Egypt	13	800	...	Kuwait	7	...	...	Switzerland	530	252	164
Estonia	1	...	...	Latvia	0.2	...	...	Taiwan	166	531	0
Euronext				Lithuania	0.7	...	...	Thailand	20	434	...
Amsterdam	429	234	158	Luxembourg	23	54	216	Turkey	46	315	0
Euronext				Malaysia	80	552	...	UK	1812	2428	501
Brussels	122	161	104	Mexico	60	186	0	USA:			
Euronext Paris	968	1021	164	Moldova	...	18	...	American	55	637	50
Finland	197	158	4	Morocco	6	49	0	NASDAQ	2395	4239	487
Germany	850	744	245	Nigeria	3	180	...	New York	7660	2035	433
Ghana	2	20	0	New Zealand	60	...	...	Venezuela	5	88	...
Greece	72	309	1	Norway	44	191	24	Vietnam	...	5	0
Hong Kong				Pakistan	7	...	...	Zimbabwe	4	65	...
(China)	417	779	11	Peru	8	302	...				

Data include listed and parallel markets (e.g. AIM). Global total capitalisation: £25,000 bn.

Sources: London Stock Exchange Fact File 2001; Financial Times, various issues.

Exhibit 9.2

Peru's small investors given sell-off call

'Treat me with a bit of respect, my friend,' an oil-stained though cheery garage mechanic tells his customer. 'I'm going to be a shareholder.'

The television advertisement forms part of a multi-million dollar publicity campaign in Peru designed to persuade tens of thousands of middle-income Peruvians to buy shares this month in Telefónica del Perú, the former state telecommunications monopoly in which Telefónica Internacional of Spain acquired a controlling stake in February 1994.

Now Peru is putting the bulk of its retained 28.6 per cent stake, worth up to $1.4bn (£915m), on the market. Offers for the domestic tranche began last Monday, with applications from Peruvian institutional investors – mainly insurance companies and private pension funds – and individuals.

The complementary but larger international offering kicked off this weekend with a road

show, orchestrated by J.P. Morgan and Merrill Lynch, making presentations in 23 cities in the US, Europe and Japan. The price per share will be announced on July 1, but it is expected to prove one of Latin America's biggest equity offerings this year.

Citizen participation is geared to creating a shareholder mentality and boosting low levels of domestic savings. To encourage this, Peruvians who hang on to their investment for 18 months will get one free share for every 20 held.

'This is Peru's first large-scale privatisation and will form the basis for similar operations in the future,' says Mr Raimundo Morales, general manager of the Banco de Credito, Peru's largest bank and domestic co-ordinator of the offering. 'It will give the liberal economic model a permanence which is extremely important.'

Source: Sally Bowen, *Financial Times*, 10 June 1996. Reprinted with permission.

Exhibit 9.3

Jiang 'strongly endorses stock markets'

Jiang Zemin, China's president, has given an unprecedented, ringing endorsement of the country's stock markets and their role in fostering the development of an efficient private sector, witnesses said yesterday ...

'He spoke at great length about the development of the local stock markets,' said one person who heard him speak.

'I did not expect him to be so animated on this subject but he was very animated indeed.'

Mr Jiang made the point that robust stock markets were a vital component of a modern economy. He said that development of China's stock markets was important, adding that it would help foster the country's non-state sector, according to a summary of his comments provided by witnesses.

He also seemed to advocate the introduction of a culture of risk within the Chinese economy, saying at one point that Chinese people are inherently risk-takers. The president also mentioned his own role in helping to create the

Shanghai stock market during his time as Communist party secretary of China's biggest city in the late 1980's ...

Mr Jiang's comments represented the first time since Asia began to recover from the financial crisis that struck in 1997 that a top Chinese leader is known to have endorsed the promotion of the national stock markets.

His endorsement adds considerable weight to several indications over the past few weeks that Beijing is on the threshold of a crucial five years of financial reform ...

The number of financial institutions, including foreign joint ventures, that will be permitted to invest in local stock markets is set to rise significantly. The stock markets are also expected to offer an expanded range of investment options, including new indices and new boards oriented towards younger and more high-tech companies.

Source: James Kynge, *Financial Times*, 15 June 2000, p. 12. Reprinted with permission.

Traditionally many European countries, such as France and Germany, were less focused on equity capital markets than the Anglo-Saxon economies (the UK, the USA, Australia, etc.), but this is starting to change. Privatisation and a greater concern for generating shareholder value is leading to an increasing appreciation of equity markets. Exhibit 9.4 shows that, in France, shares are seen as having a role in the provision of pensions and in encouraging employees to take an interest in their company's profitability.

Exhibit 9.4

France joins the stakeholder revolution

The popularity of employee shareholding schemes at French companies is establishing an equity culture, says **Samer Iskandar**

Suez Lyonnaise des Eaux, the French utilities and environmental services group, yesterday joined the growing list of companies encouraging employees to invest in their shares.

Gérard Mestrallet, Suez Lyonnaise's chairman, is aiming to raise the share of the group's capital held by its 120,000 employees from less than 1 per cent to more than 5 per cent. Staff at Vivendi, Suez Lyonnaise's main domestic rival, increased their stake in the company from 2.5 per cent to more than 4 per cent in a similar scheme this year.

Equity investment has been relatively unpopular in France where, until recently, money market funds benefited from favourable tax treatment. Investors have started turning to shares only in the past few years, as interest rates fell to historic lows in the run-up to January's launch of the euro, reducing the risk-free returns previously available on cash and treasury bonds.

The fiscal treatment of shares, relative to bonds, has also been gradually relaxed by Dominique Strauss-Kahn, finance minister, in an attempt to both tackle the country's pensions shortfall (by encouraging personal investment) and to encourage 'productive investment' – investment leading to job creation.

Analysts are optimistic that the growing popularity of employee shareholding schemes will play a significant role in establishing an 'equity culture' in continental Europe – and in France, in particular.

French law is especially supportive of employee share ownership. As part of the 1986 privatisation laws, the government, led by the prime minster Jacques Chirac, allowed privatised companies to offer employees discounts of up to 20 per cent on their shares' market price. The aim was to soften trade union opposition to the privatisation programme and thereby avoid social unrest.

Source: Samer Iskandar, *Financial Times*, 21 May 1999, p. 35. Reprinted with permission.

Thailand too is keen to develop an 'equity culture' – *see* Exhibit 9.5.

It can be seen from the world map (*see* Exhibit 9.1) that the dominant financial centres form a 'golden triangle' in three different time zones: USA, London and Tokyo. America is the largest source of equity capital, providing over one-third of the world's total, but the finance raised is split between three exchanges. The New York Stock Exchange (NYSE) is the largest in terms of market capitalisation. However, the NASDAQ (National Association of Securities Dealers Automated Quotations) market has over twice as many companies listed, but its market capitalisation is much less. The laggard is the American Stock Exchange (which is now owned by NASDAQ). In terms of domestic company share trading the NASDAQ is the world leader. However, in terms of trading in non-domestic (foreign) shares, London is pre-eminent. This is shown in Exhibit 9.6.

There is great rivalry between London and the American exchanges in attracting companies from other countries to list shares on their exchanges. In addition to 500 or so

Exhibit 9.5 Thai Stock Exchange

A market appeals to the sceptical masses

Thailand wants to build an 'equity culture', especially among the young.
But doubts about the standards of corporate governance mean it faces an
uphill struggle, says **Amy Kazmin**.

During the recent school break, 15-year-old Soramon Prasirtphun spent three days at the Thai stock exchange.

It is all part of a campaign to create an 'equity culture' in Thailand, where less than 1 per cent of Thailand household savings are invested in stocks. As exchange officials struggle to breathe new life into a market valued at less than half of its 1994 all-time high, they say that attracting new money – and expanding the narrow domestic investor base – is crucial if the exchange is to be a viable venue for companies to raise capital.

So despite the market's seven-year downward slide – including a 44 per cent plunge last year – the exchange is out to convince a sceptical Thai public that buying stocks is not necessarily a losing gamble. A new Bt30m ($660,000) television advertising blitz contends that, like lighting a match, buying a diamond or growing a bonsai tree, investing in stocks can bring

benefits if it is done properly. The exchange will also host its first 'Investor Fair' next month, where brokers and mutual fund companies will attempt to woo new money into the market.

'There is an abundance of people out there who are potential investors, who may have a sense that it is too risky to come in,' says Vicharat Vichit-Vadakan, president of the Stock Exchange of Thailand ...

Thailand's equity market has always been a secondary part of the country's story of economic growth. As elsewhere in Asia, Thailand's boom during the 1980s and early 1990s was largely financed by corporate debt: Thais entrusted about 95 per cent of their savings into banks.

Although plenty of companies listed on the exchange during the growth years, many offerings were driven more by a desire for the status of being listed than by a real need for capital. Often, only small amounts of equity in family-run

companies were sold and most controlling share-owners continued to view their companies as private domain, even if they were listed.

But since the Asian crisis, Thai banks have shunned new lending, focusing instead on digging themselves out from beneath a pile of bad loans. That has put the spotlight on the need to strengthen the equity market as a forum for raising capital. Investors, too, are looking for new things to do with their savings, given the historically low deposit rates at banks now flush with unwanted liquidity.

While the stock exchange mounts its charm offensive, the government of Thaksin Shinawatra, the prime minister, has laid out plans to support the market by offering new tax incentives for companies that agree to list and by accelerating Thailand's stagnant privatisation programme.

Source: Amy Kazmin, *Financial Times*, 21 May 2001, p. 11. Reprinted with permission.

international companies with a listing in London, hundreds more are listed and regulated on their home exchanges are traded via the London international share dealing service, Stock Exchange Automated Quotation International (SEAQI). The essential features of this are an electronic market-place where share prices are quoted in the home currency and the transactions are settled (that is, the legal rights to shares are transferred from one investor to another) through the local settlement system, not through London. Trading in these shares can take place 24 hours a day. Over one-half of equity turnover in the UK is in non-UK equities (£1,767 billion compared with £1,231 billion for domestic shares in 2000).

When SEAQI was created in the mid-1980s most European markets were relatively inaccessible, and SEAQI was well received as a way of helping to satisfy Europe's investment needs and it expanded rapidly. By the mid-1990s many of these markets had matured, so the significance of SEAQI in creating a market to establish a share's price and permit share exchange was lessened. However, SEAQI is now turning to the needs of emerging markets (developing economies) for investment capital.

Exhibit 9.6 Domestic and foreign equity turnover on major exchanges, 2000

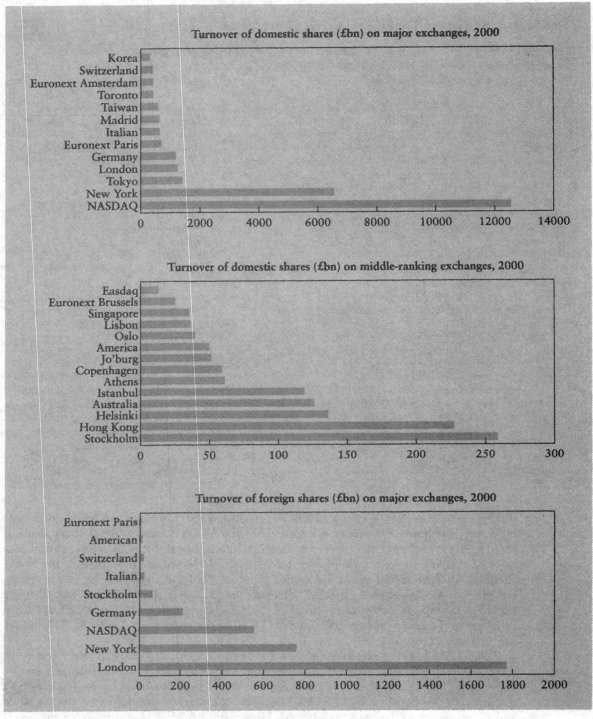

Note: London figures have been halved for comparison purposes for non-order book trading.

Source: *London Stock Exchange Fact File 2001.*

European stock exchanges

In Europe the trend is for stock exchanges to merge together or to form alliances. This is being encouraged by the major financial institutions which desire a seamless, less costly way of trading shares across borders. The ultimate ambition for some visionaries is a single highly liquid equity market allowing investors to trade and companies to raise capital, wherever it suits them. Ideally there would be no distortions in share price, costs of trading or regulation as investors cross from one country to another. Whether it is necessary to merge Europe's disparate stock exchanges to achieve frictionless pan-European trading is a matter that is currently hotly debated. Some argue that the absence of a single securities market damages the EU's competitive position *vis-à-vis* the huge, streamlined and highly liquid US capital market. Furthermore, they say, it prevents European companies and investors enjoying the full benefits of the euro.

On the other hand the cost of actually trading shares in Europe is extremely low. The major costs (90 per cent) arise in the processing of the transaction *after* the deal is done ('the back office'). These clearing and settlement activities (*see* later in the chapter for a definition) are usually carried out by organisations separate from the exchanges. The critics of the drive to merge argue that what is needed is pan-European transaction processing rather than one giant stock exchange.

Whatever the long-run outcome of the current arguments the state of play as in 2001 is as shown in Exhibit 9.7.

The most significant move toward integration has been the merger of the Brussels, Amsterdam and Paris markets to form Euronext. It is the largest market in the Euro-zone with a market capitalisation of over £1,500 billion, only slightly lower than that for London. The merger creates a genuine cross-border exchange with enhanced liquidity and lower cost for investors. It also promotes three exchanges from the second rank to a more prominent role in the European financial structure. Already Euronext is wooing other leading stock exchanges ('bourses'), notably Luxembourg, Milan and Zurich, to join. The Lisbon bourse has even entered talks with Euronext.

The Deutsche Börse is the third most significant stock exchange in Europe. With 989 companies listed and a growing interest in share investment among the German people the Deutsche Börse is in a strong position – and it is also ambitious. It has attempted to form mergers and alliances to create a dominant pan-European exchange. So far it has failed, most notably in the attempt to merge with the London Stock Exchange in 2000. In 1997 the Deutsche Börse created a market for shares in young, innovative and generally more risky companies, called Neuer Market. This has been very successful: it is the largest of its kind in Europe with 339 companies.

Neuer Markt has joined with a number of other stock markets aimed at risky growth companies to form a European network called Euro.NM. Its members are Le Nouveau Marché (of the Paris Stock Exchange), Nuovo Mercato (of Italy), Euro.NM Amsterdam and Euro.NM Belgium. The market capitalisation of the 400 or so Euro.NM companies is about €250 billion, and the combined daily turnover of shares is about €1 billion. The Neuer Markt accounts for the vast majority of this.

An important rival to Euro.NM for the listing and trading of innovative, young and fast-growing companies is Nasdaq Europe. This was created in 1999 but it did not become a serious competitor until, in 2001, it took 58 per cent ownership of the ailing pan-European exchange for technology companies, EASDAQ. The American exchange clearly has ambitions to create a global 24-hour stock market and the expansion of its presence in Europe will help achieve its aim (there is also a Nasdaq Japan). With only 62

Exhibit 9.7 Stock exchanges in Europe

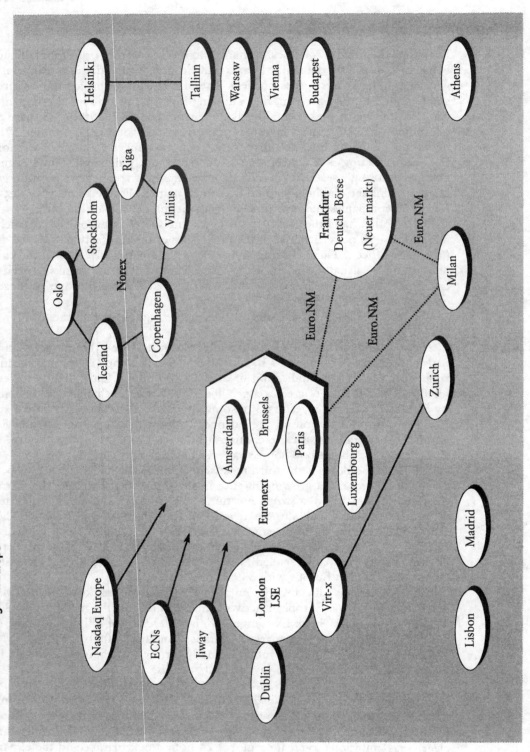

companies listed on Nasdaq Europe it starts from a low base but it has the resources and brand name to expand rapidly. This is a serious threat to the European exchanges. Angela Knight, chief executive of the London-based Association of Private Client Investment Managers and Stockbrokers, said Nasdaq Europe will increase competition between exchanges to the benefit of investors: 'Europe's exchanges are losing their national franchises, becoming listed companies, and now are facing an aggressive trading operation with a strong brand name. We are after a battle royal here'. (*Financial Times*, 28 March 2001, p. 36).

In 1998 the Stockholm and Copenhagen Exchanges formed the Norex Alliance. This was later to embrace Norway and Iceland. Latvia and Lithuania hope to join soon. The individual exchanges remain independent, and continue listing companies and supervising trading. However, the general rules and regulations are being harmonised to make cross-border trading simpler and cheaper. The larger market gives the smaller countries access to larger pools of capital and improves liquidity. Helsinki has chosen to remain outside the alliance. It has bought control of the Tallinn Stock Exchange and has increased its links with Deutsche Börse instead.

Tradepoint, started in 1995, became the second stock exchange permitted to trade shares in the UK. At first, it was thought to be a serious threat to the London Stock Exchange. However, in the 1990s it failed to take more than a 1 per cent of share transactions. In 2000 the Swiss stock exchange took a major stake and its name was changed to Virt-x. This is a London-based exchange, supervised by London's Financial Services Authority, that deals in all the large European company shares across the continent. The issuers of shares traded on Virt-x will remain listed in their chosen jurisdictions (e.g. on the Official List of the London Stock Exchange or the Deutsche Börse) and subject to the corporate governance and listing requirements of that jurisdiction. All trading in Swiss blue chips (leading companies), e.g. Nestlé, has been transferred to Virt-x together with 2,000 UK shares and the 230 largest European company shares. It plans to capture 20 per cent of European cross-border trading.

A major challenge to the traditional stock exchanges is the development of sophisticated electronic networks linking buyers and sellers of shares. Electronic Communication Networks (ECNs), such as Instinet and Island, have taken a considerable amount of share trading from NASDAQ and the NYSE in the USA. Some 30 per cent of trading in NASDAQ shares now takes place outside its organised market (the figure is 5 per cent for the NYSE).

So far ECNs have had little impact on European share trading. This is attributed to the efficiency of the traditional exchanges and, therefore, the low cost of trading. However, there is no room for complacency: Paul Walker-Duncalf, head of dealing in Europe of Merrill Lynch Investment Managers, said: 'It makes little difference where we trade. Most exchanges look the same. If I'm dealing in Paris, or London or Frankfurt, there are just a few visual differences and a few minor market differences. What matters is having a pool of liquidity' (*Financial Times Special Report on World Stocks and Derivative Exchanges*, 28 March 2001).

Another attempt to move share trading away from traditional exchanges is Jiway, launched in 2000. It does not list any shares; it merely offers a trading service across Europe and the USA for private investors (through their brokers). Instead of trading in ten different exchanges investors can execute trades in 6,000 shares (and transaction process) through Jiway. It is hoped that broker costs can be cut in half.

GLOBALISATION OF FINANCIAL FLOWS

Over the past twenty years there has been an increasing emphasis placed on share (equity) finance and stock exchanges. It seems that an 'equity culture' is spreading around the world. This trend toward equity has been given a name: 'equitisation'. Given that stock markets have been around for centuries, what has happened in the last twenty years to spark such a widespread interest? The first explanation is that a greatly increased number of companies have sought a stock market quotation for their shares and there have been deliberate attempts by governments to stimulate interest in share ownership. Following the Thatcher and Reagan privatisations, and the push for wider share ownership in 1980s Britain and the USA, hundreds of state-owned or privately held companies worldwide have floated their shares on stock exchanges. The issue of new shares globally has reached over £200 billion per year. Secondly, it became apparent that equities had provided good long-term returns over the first eighty years of the twentieth century – returns significantly ahead of inflation and those on bonds. So, increasingly, those with responsibility for providing pensions decades from now concentrated on buying shares. Thirdly, the 1980s and 1990s were one of the best periods ever for share returns. The bull market stimulated great interest from millions of investors who previously preferred to hold less risky, lower-return, securities, such as bonds. In America, for instance, almost one-half of all households now own shares (either directly or indirectly through mutual funds and self-select pension funds). In Australia, the level of ownership is higher still. One-quarter of British households own shares. The equity culture has grown so strongly in Germany that almost one-fifth of households hold shares (now, there are more share holders than trade union members). In the five years to mid-2001 there were more new companies joining the Deutsche Börse than in the previous fifty put together and there are over 10,000 German investment clubs. The Scandinavian countries and the Netherlands are even more 'equitised' than Germany.

Financial globalisation means the integration of capital markets throughout the world. The extent of the internationalisation of the equity markets is illustrated by the volume of foreign equity trades in the major financial centres (*see* Exhibit 9.6). It is also evident in the fact that a substantial proportion of pension fund and insurance fund money is invested in foreign equities (*see* Chapter 1). Also, today a corporation is not limited to raising funds in a capital market where it is domiciled. Three of the major elements encouraging cross-border financial activity are shown in Exhibit 9.8.

Exhibit 9.8 Globalisation of financial flows

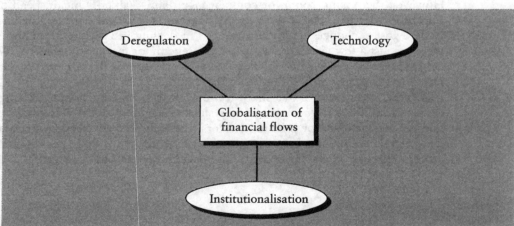

Deregulation

The 1980s and 1990s was a period when government deregulation of financial markets was seen as a way of enabling financial and corporate entities to compete in the global market-place and benefit consumers. The limits placed on the purchase and sale of foreign currency (foreign exchange controls) have been eliminated or lowered in most advanced economies. This has encouraged the flow of investment capital. Cartel-like arrangements for fixing the minimum commissions paid by investors for buying and selling shares have been eroded, as have the restrictions on ownership of financial firms and brokers by foreigners. Now, more than ever, domestic securities can be purchased by individuals and institutional funds from another country. Commercial banks have found the barriers preventing participation in particular markets being demolished. Tax laws have been modified so as not to discourage the flow of funds across borders for investment, and the previously statutorily enforced 'single-activity' financial institutions (in which, for example, banks did banking, building societies did mortgage lending) have ventured into each others' markets, increasing competition and providing a better deal for the consumer.

Technology

The rapid transmission of vast quantities of financial information around the globe has transformed the efficiency of financial markets. Securities can be monitored, analysed and dealt in on hundreds of share, bond, commodity and derivative exchanges at the touch of a button from almost anywhere in the world. The combination of powerful computers and extensive telecommunication networks allows accelerated integration, bringing with it complex trading strategies and enormous daily capital flows.

Institutionalisation

Thirty years ago most shares were owned by individuals. Today, the markets are dominated by financial institutions (pension funds, insurance companies and the 'mutual funds' such as unit and investment trusts). Whereas the individual, as a shareholder, tended to be more parochial and to concentrate on national company shares, the institutions have sufficient knowledge and strength to seek out the rewards from overseas investments. They also appreciate the diversification benefits which accrue due to the low level of correlation between some financial markets (*see* Chapter 7).

Why do companies list their shares on more than one exchange?

There are hundreds of companies which pay for the privilege of having their shares listed for trading on stock exchanges in other countries as well as on their local exchange. Exhibit 9.1 shows that the most popular secondary listings locations are the USA and the UK. There are also substantial numbers of foreign shares listed on most of the northern European exchanges, as well as on those of Canada, Australia, Japan and Singapore. This dual or triple listing can be a costly business and the regulatory environment can be stringent so there must be some powerful motivating factors driving managers to globalise their investor base. For British Telecom the costs and hassle of listing in four countries – the UK, the USA, Canada and Japan – when it floated in 1984 must have been a deterrent (the costs of maintaining a listing in Tokyo are over £100,000 per year alone).[2] Here are some reasons for listing abroad:

■ *To broaden the shareholder base* By inviting a larger number of investors to subscribe for shares it may be possible to sell those shares for a higher price and thus raise capital more cheaply (that is, a lower return will be required per £ invested).

■ *The domestic stock exchange is too small or the firm's growth is otherwise constrained* Some companies are so large relative to their domestic stock markets that they have no choice but to obtain equity finance from abroad. Ashanti Goldfields, the Ghanaian gold-mining company, was privatised in April 1994. It was valued at about $1.7 billion, which was more than ten times the capitalisation of the Accra stock market. A listing in London was a great success and the company has now expanded its activities in other African countries – it is now listed in New York, Toronto, Zimbabwe, Ghana and London. South African Breweries can raise money on a global basis and escape restrictions placed on it in South Africa by listing in London – *see* Exhibit 9.9.

Exhibit 9.9

SAB plans to raise up to £200m in London listing

South African Breweries, the world's fourth largest brewing group, plans to raise between £150m and £200m in a placing of new shares when it lists on the London Stock Exchange next month.

SAB is the latest in a flood of South African companies moving to London. They are seeking to escape the constraints of exchange controls at home and to gain access to global capital markets to fund growth outside South Africa where most have reached market saturation.

The cash SAB is raising will be used to finance the group's switch to London and to find expansion in emerging markets.

SAB, which controls more than 98 per cent of the South African beer market with brands such as Castle and Lion, has operations in 18 countries countries, including China, Russia, Poland and Ghana ...

Other South African groups that have announced their intention to seek a London listing include Anglo American, another mining group, and Old Mutual, the country's largest life assurance group.

Source: John Willman, *Financial Times*, 11 February 1999, p. 29. Reprinted with permission.

■ *To reward employees* Many employees of foreign-owned firms are rewarded with shares in the parent company. If these shares are locally listed these share-ownership plans can be better managed and are more appealing to employees.

■ *Foreign investors may understand the firm better* This point is illustrated with the case of Eidos (Exhibit 9.10).

Exhibit 9.10 'My shareholders don't understand me.'

Eidos

In November 1996 Eidos, a UK software developer, decided to offer its shares to US investors by obtaining a quotation on the NASDAQ market. It expected to raise an additional £50 million. The reason the company gave for this snub to UK investors is the 'knowledge and understanding of computer software companies by US investor groups'. On the NASDAQ market US computer games developers' shares are usually valued at least at double their turnover, whereas Eidos is valued at only 1.5 expected sales in London.

Source: Based on *Investors Chronicle*, 1 November 1996.

■ *To raise awareness of the company* For example, African Lakes listed on the Nairobi Stock Exchange as well as in London – *see* Exhibit 9.11.

Exhibit 9.11

African Lakes dips into Nairobi Stock Exchange

African Lakes, the internet services, information technology and automotive distribution group, yesterday became the first London listed company to raise money through a secondary listing on the Nairobi Stock Exchange.

The company, which owns Africa Online, the continent's most broadly based internet service provider, is raising Ks378m (£3.2m) through an open offer of 4m shares at Ks94.5 (80p) each.

Lesley Davey, finance director, said the company was still cash rich after raising £17.7m through a placing and open offer at 55p a share in London last September. It had gone to

Nairobi's exchange to enable African institutions to participate in the growth of the company and to raise its profile in eastern Africa.

Already operating in seven countries, Ms Davey said Africa Online was looking to double that number by the end of this year ...

The move will also give African Lakes substantial influence as the country's third-largest listed company

Source: David Blackwell and Mark Turner, *Financial Times*, 17 February 2000. Reprinted with permission.

■ *Discipline* This is illustrated through the example of Chinese banks (*see* Exhibit 9.12). The value of stock market discipline has reached the heart of a previously totalitarian centrally controlled economy. Not only have Chinese companies seen the benefit of tapping Western share capital, they have also been made aware of the managerial rigour demanded by stock markets and their investors.

Exhibit 9.12 'We need the discipline of the market.'

Plan mooted to list 'big four' Chinese banks

A senior Chinese state banker yesterday made the boldest official proposal yet for the listing of the 'big four' state banks, a move that would revolutionise the country's banking system and hasten the reform of China's socialist-era industries.

Fang Xinghai, general manager of the group co-ordination office at the China Construction Bank, one of the 'big four' banks that dominate the country's financial system, said that stock market flotations would be the only sure way to improve corporate governance at the banks.

'To establish a good governance and incentive system in banks, I see no other way but to list these banks on well functioning stock mar-

kets,' Mr Fang said in a statement seen by the Financial Times ...

A listing by one of the big four would have enormous consequences for China's economic reforms. The four banks are the pillars of the socialist economy, providing the loans that keep the inefficient but politically important state industrial sector in business.

Stock market listings could force the big four to apply commercial criteria to their lending, spelling an end to the indulgence that allows the state sector to swallow at least two-thirds of all bank loans to finance just one-third of industrial output.

Source: James Kynge, *Financial Times*, 19 April 2000, p. 10. Reprinted with permission.

■ *To understand better the economic, social and industrial changes occurring in major product markets.* This is illustrated by the Toyota article – *see* Exhibit 9.13.

Exhibit 9.13

Toyota to list in New York and London

Automotive effort to increase investor base will involve issuing 45m shares worth about Y162bn

Toyota, Japan's third-largest company by market capitalisation, plans to list its shares in New York and London this month.

The issue is aimed at attracting international investors, meeting the needs of the increasingly global industry and boosting Toyota's image, said Yuji Araki, senior managing director.

The move is the latest in a series of global offers by Japanese companies, which are aimed at increasing the international element of their shareholder base ...

Mr Araki said the company decided to list in New York and London not only to increase its investor base but also to be able to judge whether Toyota's performance met western standards.

'If they don't, we will have to change ourselves', he said.

Listing in the two cities would also help Toyota sense the changes in foreign stock markets more quickly and from those changes, the economic, social and industrial changes occurring in those markets, Mr Araki said.

Foreigners own a relatively low proportion of Toyota – just 8.8 per cent. But Mr Araki emphasised that the company had no fixed target for foreign shareholders ...

In addition to New York, Toyota decided to list in London because 'in order to attract international investors it is essential to list in London' he added ...

However, over the next two to three years, changes would be introduced in Japanese reporting requirements, which would bring them much closer to SEC standards, Mr Araki said.

Source: Michiyo Nakamoto and Paul Abrahams, *Financial Times*, 8 September 1999, p. 26. Reprinted with permission.

THE IMPORTANCE OF A WELL-RUN STOCK EXCHANGE

A well-run stock exchange has a number of characteristics. It is one where a 'fair game' takes place; that is, where some investors and fund raisers are not able to benefit at the expense of other participants – all players are on 'a level playing field'. It is a market which is well regulated to avoid abuses, negligence and fraud in order to reassure investors who put their savings at risk. It is also one on which it is reasonably cheap to carry out transactions. In addition, a large number of buyers and sellers are likely to be needed for the efficient price setting of shares and to provide sufficient liquidity, allowing the investor to sell at any time without altering the market price. There are six main benefits of a well-run stock exchange.

1 Firms can find funds and grow

Because investors in financial securities with a stock market quotation are assured that they are, generally, able to sell their shares quickly, cheaply and with a reasonable degree of certainty about the price, they are willing to supply funds to firms at a lower cost than they would if selling was slow, or expensive, or the sale price was subject to much uncertainty. Thus stock markets encourage investment by mobilising savings. As well as stimulating the investment of domestic savings, stock markets can be useful for attracting foreign savings and for aiding the privatisation process.

2 Allocation of capital

One of the key economic problems for a nation is finding a mechanism for deciding what mixture of goods and services to produce. An extreme solution has been tried and shown to be lacking in sophistication – that of a totalitarian directed economy where bureaucratic diktat determines the exact quantity of each line of commodity produced. The alternative method favoured in most nations (for the majority of goods and services) is to let the market decide what will be produced and which firms will produce it.

An efficiently functioning stock market is able to assist this process through the flow of investment capital. If the stock market was poorly regulated and operated then the mis-pricing of shares and other financial securities could lead to society's scarce capital resources being put into sectors which are inappropriate given the objective of maximising economic well-being. If, for instance, the market priced the shares of a badly managed company in a declining industrial sector at a high level then that firm would find it relatively easy to sell shares and raise funds for further investment in its business or to take over other firms. This would deprive companies with better prospects and with a greater potential contribution to make to society of essential finance.

To take an extreme example: imagine the year is 1910 and on the stock market are some firms which manufacture horse-pulled carriages. There are also one or two young companies which have taken up the risky challenge of producing motor cars. Analysts will examine the prospects of the two types of enterprise before deciding which firms will get a warm reception when they ask for more capital in, say, a rights issue. The unfavoured firms will find their share prices falling as investors sell their shares, and will be unable to attract more savers' money. One way for the older firm to stay in business would be to shift resources within the firm to the production of those commodities for which consumer demand is on a rising trend.

A more recent transfer of finance is discussed in Exhibit 9.14. A dramatic shift in resources occurred in the late 1990s as financial markets supplied hundreds of billions of dollars to high-technology industries.

Exhibit 9.14

Rebuilt by Wall Street

The US's dynamic stock market has directed resources into high-tech industries, giving the economy a huge advantage that other countries must strive to match, says **David Hale**.

The stock market boom has been part of a much larger process of reallocation of global resources resulting from the end of the cold war, the increasing role of information technology in the economy, and the leadership of US companies in utilising this technology.

Despite public perceptions to the contrary, there has not been a broad-based asset inflation in the US equity market during the past few years. The majority of the companies in the S & P 500 have experienced share price declines or only small gains since 1998. Nor has there been a visible expansion of margin debt or bank lending to finance stock market speculation ...

Rather, the stock market rise systems overwhelmingly from the take-off in the market capitalisation of the technology sector. It has mushroomed to $4,500bn (£2,700bn) from $300bn during the early 1990s. The resulting wealth creation has, in turn, redefined the US business cycle by combining a significant expansion of business investment with falling output prices. Moreover, the expansion – now the longest peacetime business cycle in US history – is unlikely to end in the foreseeable future because the technology revolu-

tion has helped it to develop several self-reinforcing growth characteristics that are apparent in both financial markets and the real economy.

First, there has been a dramatic improvement in the ability of small companies in the technology sector to obtain capital. In 1999 initial public offerings raised $69.2bn, compared with a previous peak of $49.9bn in 1996 and a grand total of $350.8bn since 1989. Second, the ability of small companies to go public has encouraged a dramatic expansion of the US venture capital industry. It raised funds at an annualised rate of $25bn during the first

Exhibit 9.14 continued

half of 1999, nearly twice as much as during all of 1998. About 66 per cent of the funds were placed in the information technology sector while 73 per cent of the IT component was placed with internet companies.

As a result, the technology share of the US stock market has expanded from 10 per cent in the early 1990s to about 33 per cent today. The US technology sector now has a market capitalisation of over $3,000bn, compared with $350bn for the entire global mining industry. Microsoft, alone has a market capitalisation of $535bn, making it the first US company to have a value larger than the GDP of Canada.

By contrast, the IT sector represents only 5.1 per cent of stock market capitalisation in Germany, 9.4 per cent in France, 4.9 per cent in Britain and 15 per cent in Japan. The countries that have IT sectors comparable to the stock market capitalisation of the US are Canada (29 per cent), Taiwan (21.9 per cent) Sweden (38.2 per cent) and Finland (more than 50 per cent).

As a result of the dramatic changes in the composition of the US stock market and the surge of IPO activity, the US economy has been able to reallocate resources on a large scale from traditional industries to new high-growth sectors linked to IT and the internet. But the impact of the technology revolution is also increasingly apparent in the real economy. Spending on research and development in the US has rebounded to 2.7

per cent of GDP after declining to 2.4 per cent during the mid-1990s. The number of patents issued during 1989 was about 140,000 – 29 per cent higher than during 1997 and 55 per cent higher than during 1990.

Human talent is flocking to the IT sector too: almost half the doctorates awarded in the US today are in technical subjects, up from a trough of 36 per cent during the late 1970s. Business investment has represented about one-third of the economy's growth since 1990, compared with only about one-sixth for all the output growth since 1950. The information technology share of output has increased to 5.8 per cent from 3.3 per cent in 1992.

The impact of technology on the real economy has enhanced productivity to such an extent that higher rates of non-inflationary growth are now possible. Most Federal Reserve governors now perceive that the economy's optimal non-inflationary growth rate is $3–3\frac{1}{2}$ per cent, compared with only $2–2\frac{1}{2}$ per cent a few years ago ...

It would have been difficult for the US to finance the rapid growth of the IT sector without a buoyant stock market because companies in this field need equity capital, not debt finance. The US has been able to play a leading role because of its ratio of stock market capitalisation to bank assets is almost 3 to 1, whereas in Japan and continental Europe bank assets are typically three to five times larger than stock market capitalisation. The rise of

the Neuer Markt in Germany and companies such as Softbank in Japan suggests that other countries could catch up with the US in the future, but the gap is still large today. In 1998 venture capital funding in Europe was only $6.8bn while in Japan the total value of all venture capital funds is about $6.7bn, compared with more than $100bn in the US.

It is not difficult to construct scenarios in which the US stock market could experience a correction and dampen the economy's momentum. The Federal Reserve will raise interest rates at least two or three times this year to slow the economy's growth rate to 3 per cent. As a result of the stock market boom, there is so much competition in America's high-tech sector that many companies may experience earnings disappointments and decline sharply.

But the main lesson of the US experience of the late 1990s is that a dynamic stock market can be a valuable national asset for mobilising capital and reallocating resources from low- to high-growth sectors. The stock market boom has given the US economy a huge advantage that will be difficult for other countries to follow until their stock markets promote entrepreneurial energy and creative destruction.

The author is global chief economist at Zurich Financial Services.

Source: David Hale, *Financial Times*, 25 January 2000, p. 22. Copyright © David Hale. Reprinted with permission.

3 For shareholders

Shareholders benefit from the availability of a speedy, cheap secondary market if they want to sell. Not only do shareholders like to know that they can sell shares when they want to, they may simply want to know the value of their holdings even if they have no intention of selling at present. By contrast, an unquoted firm's shareholders often find it very difficult to assess the value of their holding.

Founders of firms may be particularly keen to obtain a quotation for their firms. This will enable them to diversify their assets by selling a proportion of their holdings. Also, venture capital firms which fund unquoted firms during their rapid growth phase often press the management to aim for a quotation to permit the venture capitalist to have the option of realising the gains made on the original investment, or simply to boost the value of their holding by making it more liquid.

4 Status and publicity

The public profile of a firm can be enhanced by being quoted on an exchange. Banks and other financial institutions generally have more confidence in a quoted firm and therefore are more likely to provide funds at a lower cost. Their confidence is raised because the company's activities are now subject to detailed scrutiny. The publicity surrounding the process of gaining a quotation may have a positive impact on the image of the firm in the eyes of customers, suppliers and employees and so may lead to a beneficial effect on their day-to-day business.

5 Mergers

Mergers can be facilitated better by a quotation. This is especially true if the payments offered to the target firm's shareholders for their holdings are shares in the acquiring firm. A quoted share has a value defined by the market, whereas shares in unquoted firms are difficult to assess.

The stock exchange also assists what is called 'the market in managerial control'. That is a mechanism in which teams of managers are seen as competing for control of corporate assets. Or, to put it more simply, mergers through the stock market permit the displacement of inefficient management with a more successful team. Thus, according to this line of reasoning, assets will be used more productively and society will be better off. This 'market in managerial control' is not as effective as is sometimes claimed (it tends to be over-emphasised by acquiring managers) (*see* Chapter 20 for further discussion).

6 Improves corporate behaviour

If a firm's shares are traded on an exchange, the directors may be encouraged to behave in a manner conducive to shareholders' interests. This is achieved through a number of pressure points. For example, to obtain a quotation on a reputable exchange, companies are required to disclose a far greater range and depth of information than is required by accounting standards or the Companies Acts. This information is then disseminated widely and can become the focus of much public and press comment. In addition, investment analysts ask for regular briefings from senior managers and continuously monitor the performance of firms. Before a company is admitted to the Stock Exchange the authorities insist on being assured that the management team are sufficiently competent and, if necessary, additional directors are appointed to supplement the board's range of knowledge and skills. Directors are required to consult shareholders on important decisions, such as mergers, when the firm is quoted. They also have to be very careful to release price-sensitive information in a timely and orderly fashion and they are strictly forbidden to use inside information to make a profit by buying or selling the firm's shares.

THE LONDON STOCK EXCHANGE

The London Stock Exchange (LSE) started in the coffee houses of eighteenth-century London where the buying and selling of shares in joint stock companies took place. In 1773 the volume of trade was sufficiently great for the brokers to open a subscription room in Threadneedle Street. They called the building the Stock Exchange. (It began trading in its present form in 1801.) During the nineteenth century, over twenty other stock exchanges were formed in the rapidly expanding industrial towns of Britain. They amalgamated in 1973 to become a unified Stock Exchange. All of the old trading floors of the regional exchanges and in London, where market members would meet face to face to exchange shares, are now obsolete. Today, there is no physical market-place. The dealing rooms of the various finance houses are linked via telephone and computer, and trading takes place without physical contact.

Securities traded

The volume of trade has expanded enormously in recent years. There are three types of *fixed-interest securities* traded in London: gilts, sterling corporate bonds and Eurobonds. The government bond or 'gilts' market (lending to the UK government) is enormous, with an annual turnover in the secondary market of £1,595 billion in 2000. In that year the UK government raised a total of £8.2bn through gilt-edged securities. Sterling bonds issued by companies (corporate bonds) comprise a relatively small market – just a few billion. Specialist securities, such as warrants, are normally bought and traded by a few investors who are particularly knowledgeable in investment matters. (Warrants are discussed in Chapter 10.) During 2000, 1,826 new Eurobonds were listed in London, raising a total of £185.7 billion.

In addition foreign governments raised £2 billion by selling bonds on the LSE.

Exhibit 9.15 Types of financial securities sold on the London Stock Exchange

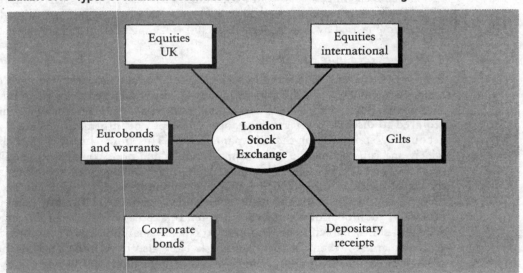

There has been the rapid development of the *depositary receipt* market since 1994. These are certificates which can be bought and sold, which represent evidence of ownership of a company's shares held by a depositary. Thus, an Indian company's shares could be packaged in, say, groups of five by a depositary (usually a bank) which then sells a certificate representing the bundle of shares. The depositary receipt can be denominated in a currency other than the corporation's domestic currency and dividends can be received in the currency of the depositary receipt rather than the currency of the original shares. These are attractive securities for sophisticated international investors because they may be more liquid and more easily traded than the underlying shares. They may also be used to avoid settlement, foreign exchange and foreign ownership difficulties which may exist in the company's home market. This market is large: for example, the China Petroleum and Chemical Corporation raised £2,435.9m when it issued its depositary receipts in London in 2000. Exhibit 9.16 discusses depositary receipts.

Exhibit 9.16

Stock markets are booming, call for the DRs

A natural beneficiary of the booming stock market is the business in depositary receipts, which has experienced a strong start this year thanks to the high numbers of European initial public offerings from the technology, media and telecommunications sectors.

Depositary receipts allow companies to list on foreign stock exchanges, usually in the US, through the sale of repackaged shares. But they are not just a recent product of globalisation. The first DR programme was set up for the UK department store Selfridges by J.P. Morgan in 1927.

The most common form is the American Depositary Receipt, whereby companies from the rest of the world can tap the demand from US equity investors.

For a foreign company to list in the US it must also have an ADR programme, although many companies use ADRs to raise cash without having to go through a complete listing.

Companies hope that by broadening the range of investors who take part in its IPO, there will be a greater demand for their shares and a higher valuation for stock. 'An ADR brings higher visibility, attracts higher valuation and brings the greater liquidity associated with the US market,' says Akbar Poonawala, global head of the client management group at Deutsche Bank in New York.

European companies have been the heaviest users of DRs, though emerging market companies have also been keen to broaden their investor base internationally through Global Depositary Receipts . . .

The role of the depositary receipt is expanding. When UK internet company e-bookers launched its IPO, it listed ADRs on the Nasdaq as well as the German Neuer Markt without a listing of any ordinary shares. The ADRs, despite being denominated in dollars, can now be traded on the Neuer Markt in euros thanks to an arrangement between

the clearing systems in the US and Germany. 'It is one of the first ever cases of a global ADR,' say Patrick Colle, head of ADRs for Europe, Middle East and Africa at J.P. Morgan. Another development has been the use of ADRs as an acquisition currency. In the cases of BP's takeover of Amoco and Vodafone's purchase of AirTouch, the UK companies paid the US companies' shareholders with ADRs. But despite the potential of ADRs in these situations, there have not been as many cases as expected . . .

But as other bankers point out, the number of new programmes is less important than their characteristics. Of the approximately 2,000 ADRs in existence, 50 account for 80 per cent of the value of the market. The others are dormant and illiquid programmes, the result of over-zealous marketing from depositary banks.

Source: Rebecca Bream, *Financial Times*, 3 April 2000, p. 35. Reprinted with permission.

Our main concern in this chapter is with the market in ordinary shares and it is to this we now turn. The London Stock Exchange is both a *primary market* and a *secondary market*. The primary market is where firms can raise new finance by selling shares to investors. The secondary market is where existing securities are sold by one investor to another (*see* Exhibit 9.17).

The primary market (equities)

Large sums of money flow from the savers in society via the Stock Exchange to firms wanting to invest and grow. At the beginning of 2001 there were 2,405 companies on the Official List (1,904 UK, and 501 foreign). There were also 524 companies on the Exchange's new market for smaller and younger companies, the Alternative Investment

Exhibit 9.17 Primary and secondary share markets

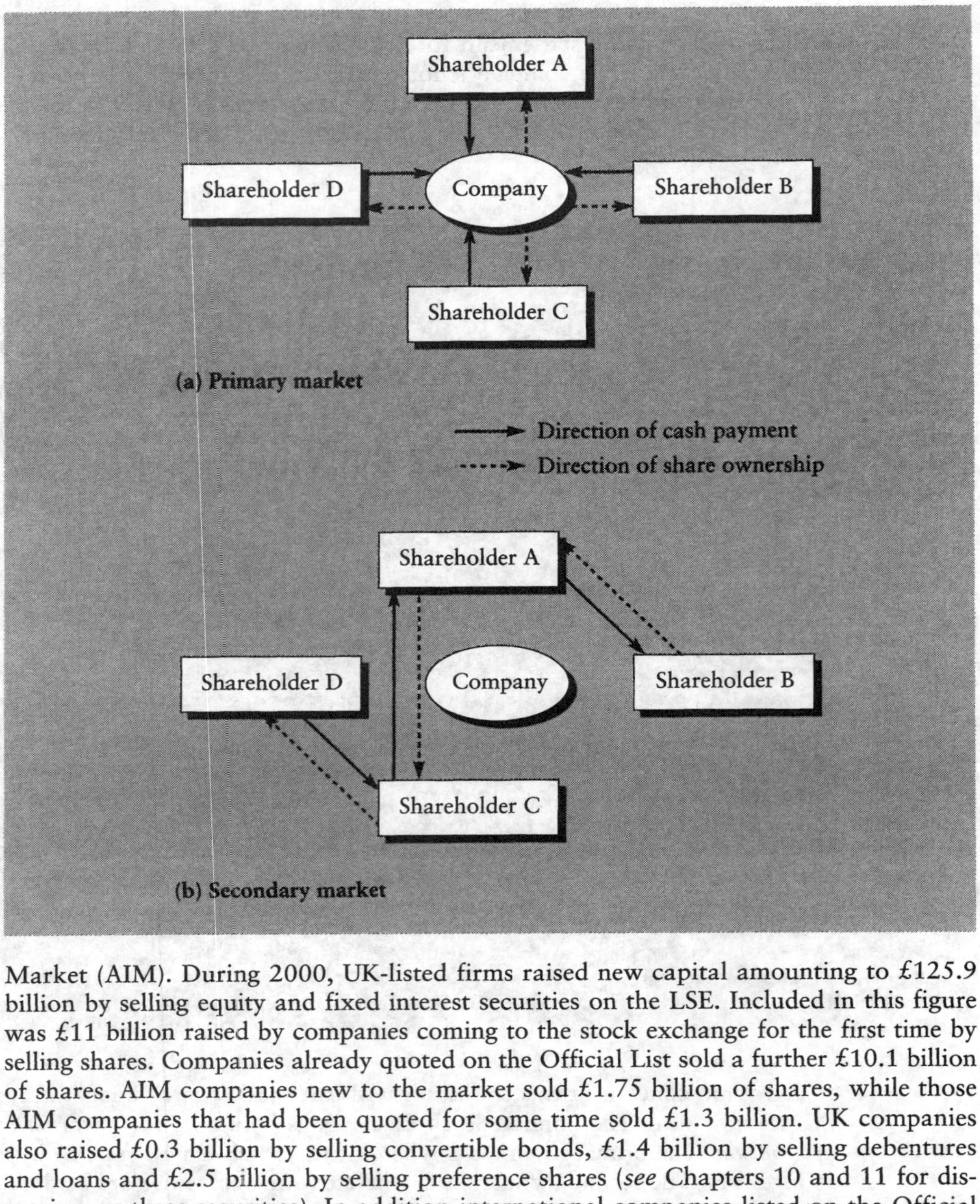

(a) Primary market

⟶ Direction of cash payment
┈┈⟶ Direction of share ownership

(b) Secondary market

Market (AIM). During 2000, UK-listed firms raised new capital amounting to £125.9 billion by selling equity and fixed interest securities on the LSE. Included in this figure was £11 billion raised by companies coming to the stock exchange for the first time by selling shares. Companies already quoted on the Official List sold a further £10.1 billion of shares. AIM companies new to the market sold £1.75 billion of shares, while those AIM companies that had been quoted for some time sold £1.3 billion. UK companies also raised £0.3 billion by selling convertible bonds, £1.4 billion by selling debentures and loans and £2.5 billion by selling preference shares (*see* Chapters 10 and 11 for discussion on these securities). In addition international companies listed on the Official List raised £99.7 billion through the sale of equities (£10.3 billion) and fixed interest securities, including preference shares, eurobonds and warrants (£89.4 billion). Also, UK companies raised another £97 billion by selling Eurobonds.

Each year there is great interest and excitement inside dozens of companies as they prepare for flotation. The year 2000 was a watershed year for 163 UK companies and 37 foreign companies which joined the Official List and 277 which joined AIM. The requirements for joining the Official List are stringent. The listing particulars should

Exhibit 9.18 Money raised by UK companies on the Official List (OL) and by UK and international companies on the Alternative Investment Market (AIM), 1996–2000

Year	Companies floating on OL during Year		Companies already listed selling more shares, e.g. rights issue	Companies floating on AIM during year		Companies already on AIM	Convertible bond issues (OL) £bn	Debentures and loans (OL) £bn	Preference shares (OL) £bn	Eurobonds (UK companies only) £bn
	No.	Amount raised selling shares £bn	£bn	No.	Amount raised selling shares £bn	Amount raised by selling more shares £bn				
1996	230	10.6	8.9	145	0.5	0.3	n/a	n/a	n/a	35.7
1997	132	6.9	4.2	107	0.3	0.4	0.7	1.2	0.6	43.6
1998	122	4.1	5.8	75	0.3	0.3	0.2	0.6	0.3	46.0
1999	96	4.9	8.9	102	0.3	0.6	0.2	0.5	0.7	82.4
2000	163	11.0	10.1	277	1.8	1.3	0.3	1.4	2.5	97.0

Sources: London Stock Exchange Fact File, 1997, 1998, 1999, 2000, 2001

give a complete picture of the company; its trading history, financial record, management and business prospects. It should (normally) have at least a three-year trading history and has to make at least 25 per cent of its ordinary shares publicly available. Given the costs associated with gaining a listing, it may be surprising to find that the total value of the ordinary shares of the majority of quoted companies is less than £100 million – *see* Exhibit 9.19.

The LSE is clearly an important source of new finance for UK corporations. However, it is not the most significant source. The most important source of funds is from within the firm itself (internal finance). This is the accumulated profits retained within the firm and not distributed as dividends. In an average year retained profits account for about one half of the new funds for UK firms. The sale of ordinary shares rarely accounts for a

Exhibit 9.19 Distribution of UK companies by equity market value at 31 December 2000

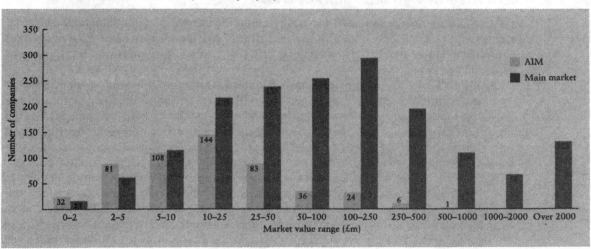

Source: London Stock Exchange Fact File, 2001. Reproduced with permission.

significant proportion of capital raised (it is usually less than 15 per cent of funds raised). Firms tend to vary greatly the proportion of finance obtained from bank loans. This is a form of finance that is most attractive when interest rates are low and retained earnings are insufficient to finance expansion. However, when interest rates are high and companies are reluctant to invest (as in the recession of the early 1990s) companies tend to repay loans rather than borrow more. The sale of bonds and preference shares combined generally accounts for less than 5 per cent of new capital put into UK companies.

The secondary market in equities

The LSE operates and regulates a secondary market for the buying and selling of UK shares between investors in which an average of 116,775 bargains, worth £7.5 billion, were completed in an average day in 2000 (average bargain value: £64,414). In addition to these domestic equities a further 44,845 bargains, worth £14.0 billion, of foreign shares were traded on a typical day (average bargain value: £311,457). The secondary market turnover far exceeds the primary market sales. This high level of activity ensures a liquid market enabling shares to change ownership speedily, at low cost and without large movements in price – one of the main objectives of a well-run exchange.

THE UK EQUITY MARKETS AVAILABLE TO COMPANIES

The Official List

Companies wishing to be listed have to sign a Listing Agreement which commits directors to certain high standards of behaviour and levels of reporting to shareholders. This is a market for medium and large established firms with a reasonably long trading history. The costs of launching even a modest new issue runs into hundreds of thousands of pounds and therefore small companies are unable to justify a full main market listing. Companies wishing to float are expected to have a trading history of three years and to put 25 per cent of the ordinary shares in public hands (that is, not in the hands of dominant shareholders or connected persons).

The Alternative Investment Market (AIM)

There is a long-recognised need for equity capital by small, young companies which are unable to afford the costs of full Official listing. Most developed stock exchanges have alternative equity markets that set less stringent rules and regulations for joining or remaining quoted.

Lightly regulated or unregulated markets have a continuing dilemma. If the regulation is too lax scandals of fraud or incompetence will arise, damaging the image and credibility of the market, and thus reducing the flow of investor funds to companies. On the other hand, if the market is more tightly regulated, with more company investigations, more information disclosure and a requirement for longer trading track records, the associated costs and inconvenience will deter many companies from seeking a quotation.

The driving philosophy behind AIM is to offer young and developing companies access to new sources of finance, while providing investors with the opportunity to buy and sell shares in a trading environment run, regulated and marketed by the LSE. Efforts were made to keep the costs down and make the rules as simple as possible. In contrast to the OL there is no requirement for AIM companies to be a minimum size, to have traded for a minimum period or for a set proportion of their shares to be in public hands. However, investors have some degree of reassurance about the quality of companies coming to the market. These firms have to appoint, and retain at all times, a nominated adviser and nominated broker. The nominated adviser ('nomad') is selected by the corporation from a Stock Exchange approved register of firms. These advisers have demonstrated to the Exchange that they have sufficient experience and qualifications to act as a 'quality controller', confirming to the LSE that the company has complied with the rules. Nominated brokers have an important role to play in bringing buyers and sellers of shares together. Investors in the company are reassured that at least one broker is ready to trade or do its best to match up buyers and sellers. The adviser and broker are to be retained throughout the company's life in AIM. They have high reputations and it is regarded as a very bad sign if either of them abruptly refuses further association with a firm. AIM companies are also expected to comply with strict rules regarding the publication of price-sensitive information and the quality of annual and interim reports. Upon flotation a detailed prospectus is required. This even goes so far as to state the directors' unspent convictions and all bankruptcies of companies where they were directors. The LSE charges companies £5,000 per year to maintain a quotation on AIM. If to this is added the cost of financial advisers and of management time spent communicating with institutions and investors the annual cost of being quoted on AIM runs into tens of thousands of pounds. This can be a deterrent for some companies.

Exhibit 9.20 The AIM market attracts the Moomins and Kenny Dalglish

Aim trickle becomes a torrent   FT

A surge in companies listing on Aim last week suggested the gloom that has been hanging over the new issues market since the beginning of the year may be lifting ...

Aim bucked the main board trend with a steady trickle of small offerings. Last week, however, that flow of issues grew into a stream with a spurt of offerings in sectors ranging from media to window manufacturing.

The Moomins landed on Aim on Monday, with the listing of Maverick Entertainment, which owns the intellectual property of children's characters and toys.

It is run by John Howson and Michael Diprose, who were involved in marketing Mr Blobby and Wallace and Gromit at the BBC. Shares were issued at 3p and the company, which had a market capitalisation of £4.3m at listing, raised £1.96m. They closed at 3¼p on Friday.

Proactive Sports, which manages footballers such as Andrew Cole and Stuart Pearce, listed on Aim on Thursday at 25p.

Shares in the company – 3 per cent of which is owned by Kenny Dalglish who also acts as a consultant – rose 62 per cent on Thursday and closed at 40½p on Friday, valuing the company at £40m.

Proactive was founded in 1990 by Paul Stretford, chief executive, and manages 150 professional footballers ...

Shares in Send Group, which was formed following TT Group's decision to demerge its Beatson Group and James Gibbons Format operations, rose from 40p to 68½p on its first day of listing on Aim on Tuesday an closed at 67p on Friday, valuing the company at £8.5m.

Send has four operating companies – Beatson Clark, which makes glass packaging, James Gibbons Format, a manufacturer of architectural ironmongery, James Gibbons, which manufactures and supplies aluminium windows and shop fronts and Rollalong, which makes modular accommodation for clients including the Ministry of Defence and NHS Trusts.

In 2000, these four businesses made pre-tax profits of £3.2m on turnover of £92.6m ...

Clover Corporation, which takes the oil out of tuna so it can be added to other food for those who don't like the taste of fish, listed at 10p on Wednesday. The company's market capitalisation was £14m and shares closed unchanged at 10p on Friday.

Dutch company Vema, which makes electro-magnetic locking devices for European banks and hospitals, raised £2.9m when it listed on Thursday. It had a market capitalisation at listing of £5.8m and shares were issued at 4p. By Friday's close they had risen to 4¾p.

Imprint Search & Selection, the recently established recruitment consultancy, raised £5m last Monday when it listed on Aim at 80p per share. Trading will begin on May 23.

Source: Sarah Ross, *Financial Times*, 21 May 2001, p. 23. Reprinted with permission.

Exhibit 9.20 continued

Recent issues

Name	Business	Date of first trading	Latest market capitalisation	Issue price	High	Low	Latest price
PC Medics Group	IT support	May-08	£2.9m	2p	3p	2p	2.5p
MoneyGuru	Wealth management	May-08	£8.7m	3.5p	4p	3.5p	4p
Maverick Entertainment	Intellectual property	May-14	£5.4m	3p	3.75p	3.75p	3.75p
Send	Packaging/building products	May-15	£8.5m	40p*	68.5p	40p	67p
Clover Corporation	Natural oils	May-16	£10m	8.5p	10p	8.5p	10p
Proactive Sports	Sports management	May-17	£40m	25p	40.5p	25p	40.5p
Verna	Security products	May-17	£5.9m	4p	4.75p	4p	4.75p
Wincanton	Logistics	May-18	£241m	225p	n.a.	n.a.	210p

Impending issues

Name	Business	Sponsor	Issue method	Market debut	Expected market capitalisation	Issue price	Market
Imprint Search & Selection	Recruitment	Altium Capital	Placing	May-23	£14m	80p	Aim
Pursuit Dynamics	Engineering	Numis	Placing	May-23	£20m	n.a.	Aim
Capcon Holdings	Private investigation	Charles Stanley	Placing	May-25	£6m	n.a.	Aim
Cytomyx	Biotechnology	Corporate Synergy	Placing	May-29	n.a.	n.a.	Aim
Akaei	Computer games	Hoodless Brennan	Placing	May	n.a.	n.a.	Aim
Atlantic Global	Software developer	Seymour Pierce	Placing	May	£5m	25p	Aim
Oxus Resources	Gold mining	Old Mutual Securities	Placing	June	£50m	n.a.	Aim
Photo Therapeutics	Medical equipment	Investec Hend. Crosth.	TBA	Q2 2001	£75m	n.a.	Main
Friends Provident	Financial services	Merrill Lynch	Offer	Jul-09	£3.7bn–£4.2bn	n.a.	Main

Sources: companies; FT   Compiled by Jamie Chisholm   e-mail: jamie.chisholm@ft.com   *opening price

techMARK

At the end of 1999, at the height of high technology fever, the London Stock Exchange launched a 'market-within-a-market' called techMARK. This is part of the Official List and is therefore technically not a separate market. It is a grouping of technology companies on the Official List. One of the reasons for its creation was that many companies lacking the minimum three-year account history required to join the Official List had relatively high market values and desired the advantages of being on a prestigious market. The LSE relaxed its rule and permitted a listing if only one year of accounts are available for techMARK companies. This allowed investors to invest through a well-regulated exchange in companies at an early stage of development, such as Freeserve and lastminute.com. The LSE does insist that all companies joining techMARK have a market capitalisation of at least £50m and they must sell at least £20m worth of new or existing shares when floating. Also at least 25 per cent of their shares must have a free float and they must publish quarterly reports of the company's activities, including financial and non-financial (e.g. number of visitors to the company website for dot.com companies) operating data.

Another reason for creating techMARK as a separate segment of the Official List is to give technology companies a higher profile and visibility, resulting in more attention from investors and research analysts, and enticing more technology-led companies to go for a public quote. The intention is to emulate the success of the NASDAQ in the USA, and to challenge the Neuer Markt in Germany in attracting these young fast-moving companies. Most of the companies on techMARK are firms that were previously on the general part of the Official List, such as Vodafone and AstraZeneca (no AIM companies were transferred). However it has attracted a few dozen young, fast-growing companies. In March 2001 there were 232 UK companies listed on techMARK and 12 international companies.

Critics say it is less like a market than an index (see a discussion on indices later in the chapter), and it has done little to address the issues to stimulate investment in technology. It was also seen as a competitor to AIM which is the home of some exciting technological companies – *see* Exhibit 9.21.

Exhibit 9.21

Companies' nursery shrugs off rival

FT

The launch of Techmark at the end of last year posed a threat to Aim but the LSE is optimistic that the two markets will complement each other

Just as the future had started to look brighter for the Alternative Investment Market (Aim), Britain's long-suffering junior market, a fresh menace appeared on the horizon.

The potential competitor was Techmark – a new forum for technology companies set up by the London Stock Exchange at the end of last year.

Having been the main victim of investors' dislike of small companies, Aim had started to establish itself as the nursery for promising UK companies – shedding its traditional image as the repository for small old-economy groups. As a result the exchange enjoyed the most successful 12 months in its five-year history, with the FTSE Aim index rising 141 per cent in 1999 – a performance bettered only by the Turkish stock market.

Techmark, some thought at the time, threatened to take Aim back to square one.

Although not a separate exchange, Techmark has more lenient listing requirements than the main exchange.

Techmark, therefore, appeared to threaten Aim's growing orientation towards high-tech stocks.

Aim currently plays host to some of the UK's best known and most promising technology companies, including Infobank International and Affinity International – both of which are capitalised at more than £1bn. Sixteen out of the top 20 companies on the market are technology companies.

The initial fear of some analysts when Techmark was launched was that promising high-tech companies would by-pass Aim and that some of the exchange's brightest lights would jump ship. Some even feared that Aim would be consigned to the dustbin of history, like the USM, its ill-fated predecessor.

In the event, neither appears to have happened and the London Stock Exchange is optimistic that Techmark and Aim will prove complementary to each other.

Theresa Wallis, chief operating officer of Aim, is convinced that the junior exchange will retain its appeal. 'Techmark should actually be good for Aim, providing a better branded environment for Aim's high-tech stocks to move on to,' she says.

Companies do not need the three-year record normally required of listed stocks.

'Insofar as Techmark has stimulated investor interest in technology shares it has actually been good for the exchange.'

Many companies, she argues, will continue to choose the more relaxed regulatory regime offered by Aim.

Although companies floating on Techmark do not need a three-year trading record, they do need to have a market capitalisation of £50m. Many extremely promising companies, Ms Wallis says, are likely to fall short of this requirement.

Aspiring Techmark companies will also have to meet tougher disclosure requirements.

An Aim listing also allows founders to hold on to a larger share of the business than Techmark, which requires a free-float of at least 25 per cent of the company's shares.

This is not all, says Ms Wallis.

Other burdens of a full listing, she says, include the rules on takeovers, which require companies to seek shareholder approval for acquisitions which represent more than 25 per cent of their market capitalisation.

The differentiation between a Techmark listing and an Aim listing, she argues, should prevent Aim going the way of the USM ...

So far so good, Aim has continued to attract companies. Since Techmark's birth in early November about 35 companies have come to the exchange.

►

Exhibit 9.21 continued

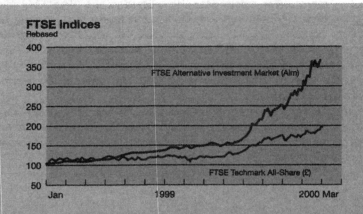

FTSE indices
Rebased

Investment bankers say there are many more in the pipeline.

Analysts, too, are now much more upbeat about the future of the exchange.

'Aim has been remarkably successful at rebranding as the home of young high-tech companies,' says Drew Edmonstone, editor of Durlacher's Aim Bulletin.

'While there will no doubt be companies that bypass it for Techmark, it would be wrong to think that Techmark has sounded

the death knell for Aim,' he added.

His views are echoed by other Aim-watchers.

'Aim's recent success has given it a scale which now makes it more of a force to be reckoned with,' argues Peter Ashworth, at Teather and Greenwood.

'The market is now capitalised at £16bn and is made up of 362 companies,' he adds.

But the future is unlikely to be plain sailing for Aim.

The battle to win the listings of

Europe's high-tech companies is hotting up.

The field of combatants – comprising Euro NM, an alliance of small-cap bourses, and Easdaq – has recently been joined by Nasdaq-Europe.

Richard Donner, managing director of information technology investment banking at Granville, says the future looks bleak both for Techmark and Aim.

'Most of Aim's recent success has been due to buoyant market conditions, which has put a premium on speed for companies wishing to come to the market,' he argues.

'As the froth subsides companies may think longer and harder about where they want to list.'

Nasdaq's association to the deepest and most liquid market in the world should give it an edge, he says.

'Techmark may prove little more than a short-term distraction.'

Source: Christopher Swann, *Financial Times,* 10 March 2000 (Special Survey: UK middle market companies). Reprinted with permission.

■ Ofex

Companies that do not want to pay the costs of an initial float (this can range from £100,000 to £1m) and the annual costs on AIM could go for a listing on Ofex. Ofex was set up by broker J.P. Jenkins in 1995. This is a dealing facility with few of the rules that apply to the OL or AIM. However, the annual fee for UK companies is £3,500. Ofex companies are generally very small and often brand new. However, some long-established and well-known firms also trade on Ofex, e.g. Weetabix and Arsenal Football Club.

J.P. Jenkins uses its electronic small company news service, Newstrack, as the basis for 'trading'. This runs on four of the City's main financial news services and acts as a noticeboard for company news. Jenkins makes a market in a company's share by posting on Newstrack two prices: a price at which it is willing to buy and a price at which it will sell. The spread between these prices is normally a maximum of around 5 per cent.

Ofex is a way for untried companies to gain access to capital without submitting to the rigour and expense of a listing on AIM. The only regulations are the basic requirements of company law and of the stockbroking watchdog, the Securities and Futures Authority (discussed later in this chapter) and the restrictions under the European Union's market abuse directive. However, companies raising fresh capital on Ofex must have a sponsor (e.g. a stockbroker, accountant or lawyer) and must produce a prospectus. In late 2001 Ofex asked the Treasury to amend the Financial Services and Markets Act so that it would be regulated by the Financial Services Authority. That will generally cost between £25,000 and £50,000. Exhibits 9.22 and 9.23 discuss the demand for the Ofex Facility.

Exhibit 9.22

Record demand for internet shares swamps Ofex market

The normally sleepy Ofex over-the-counter market for tiny company shares has been struggling to cope with record dealing levels after private investors discovered the high-risk internet shares quoted on it.

Stockbrokers trying to deal on Ofex faced long telephone waits this week after the unprecedented demand exposed flaws in the telephone system at J P Jenkins, the marketmaker that runs Ofex.

Ofex shares frequently go for months with no dealing at all, but more shares were dealt this week – almost all in internet companies – than in the whole of December 1998. This year's first day of trading, on Tuesday, was Ofex's busiest ever, despite the telephone problems.

The surge of interest has allowed Ofex internet shares to avoid the bloodletting in the internet sector,

with many showing rises yesterday despite further falls in 'dot com' stocks listed on the main market . . .

Stockbrokers are confounded by the interest in companies which many of them admit to never having heard of before, and are warning private investors that shares in tiny companies, particularly on the unregulated Ofex, are high risk.

But investors have ignored such warnings and acted on share tips in newspapers and on bulletin boards, driving huge leaps in the share prices of companies that few brokers can identify.

'Not only do we [brokers] not know much about these companies, but it is hard to see how anybody knows much about them,' said Justin Urquhart-Stewart, marketing director of Barclays Stockbrokers.

The biggest beneficiary is Silicon Valley, which saw its shares soar from 61.5p to £3.40 after a newspaper tip.

Mr Urquhart-Stewart said investors were looking for volatile internet shares. Because of the normally low levels of dealing on Ofex a few trades could move the share price sharply, so Ofex companies fitted their criteria perfectly.

However, there seems to be little risk of a consumer backlash if the internet bubble bursts, even though Ofex investors stand to lose the most. Private investors are not putting in large sums, with typical trades around £1,500–£2,000, described by one broker as 'punt money'.

Source: James Mackintosh, *Financial Times*, 7 January 2000, p. 2. Reprinted with permission.

Exhibit 9.23 Junior market breweries, breakfast and bulls add the 'bricks and mortar'

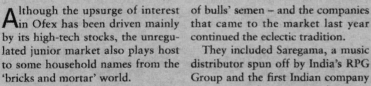

Exchange with eclectic tradition

Although the upsurge of interest in Ofex has been driven mainly by its high-tech stocks, the unregulated junior market also plays host to some household names from the 'bricks and mortar' world.

The biggest by market capitalisation is Weetabix, the breakfast cereals maker, at £389m, followed by two football clubs, Rangers and Arsenal, and brewing companies Daniel Thwaites and Shepherd Neame. But the majority of the companies are valued at less than £10m.

Overall, Ofex, set up in 1995, now lists 191 constituent companies and 205 tradeable securities with a total market capitalisation of £2.81bn.

The range of activity lower down the list is broad – extending as far as Genus, Britain's largest supplier

of bulls' semen – and the companies that came to the market last year continued the eclectic tradition.

They included Saregama, a music distributor spun off by India's RPG Group and the first Indian company on the exchange; Accidentcare, which provides a service to keep motorists on the road after a crash or other mishap; Wing Kong (Holdings), a Liverpool-based producer of frozen Chinese meals; and Mills Technology, which makes floor lighting strips for passenger aircraft.

During last year, 49 companies floated on Ofex – three up on 1998 – of whom the star performer was Easy-screen, the financial software provider that produces one of the leading computer interfaces used for trading electronically on the

London International Financial Futures and Options Exchange.

Barry Hocken of J P Jenkins, the main marketmaker to Ofex, said that nine out of 10 inquiries about possible listings were now from companies with internet links. 'We have a very healthy potential flow of new companies – we should be quite busy in the first quarter in comparison with last year.'

He attributed much of the renewed interest in Ofex to the relaunch of its web site in June to provide real-time prices. 'The private investor can now see the same information as the professional – that has made a huge difference.'

Source: David Blackwell, *Financial Times*, 7 January 2000, p. 2. Reprinted with permission.

TASKS FOR STOCK EXCHANGES

Traditionally, exchanges perform the following tasks in order to play their valuable role in a modern society:

- Supervision of trading to ensure fairness and efficiency
- The authorisation of market participants such as brokers and marketmakers
- Creation of an environment in which prices are formed efficiently and without distortion
- Organisation of the settlement of transactions (after the deal has been struck the buyer must pay for the shares and the shares must be transferred to the new owners)
- The regulation of the admission of companies to the exchange and the regulation of companies on the exchange
- The dissemination of information, e.g. trading data, prices and company announcements

In recent years there has been a questioning of the need for stock exchanges to carry out all these activities. In the case of the LSE the settlement of transactions was long ago handed over to CREST (discussed later in this chapter). In 2001 the responsibility for authorising the listing of companies was transferred to the Financial Services Authority (the principal UK regulator). Also in 2001 the LSE's Regulatory News Service (which distributes important company announcements) was told that it will have to compete with other distribution platforms outside the LSE's control. Listed companies are now able to choose between competing providers of news dissemination platforms. However the LSE still retains an important role in the distribution of trading and pricing information. In response to some of these changes, and the threat to its position as the leading European stock exchange, from the competitive actions of other exchanges, the LSE went through a modernisation process: in 2000 it ceased to be an organisation owned by its members (a few hundred marketmakers, brokers and financial institutions) to being a company with shares. In 2001 it floated this company on its own Official List so anyone can now own a portion of the LSE. This move also makes mergers with other stock exchanges easier – not least, because the vested interests of the old members will not weigh so heavily in any future deal; shareholder value will be placed ahead of, say, marketmakers' loss of business. Exhibit 9.24 discusses the changing role of stock exchanges.

TRADING SYSTEMS

Quote-driven systems

A few stock exchanges use a quote-driven system for trading shares. NASDAQ in the USA is the most notable.

Following the stock market reforms known as 'Big Bang' in 1986, the LSE adopted a quote-driven system, which remains the main method of buying or selling shares. At the centre of this system are about 40 *marketmakers* who post on the computerised system called SEAQ (Stock Exchange Automated Quotation) the prices at which they are willing to trade shares. These competing marketmakers feed in two prices. The 'bid' price is the price at which they are willing to buy. The 'offer' price is the price at which they will sell. Thus, for Tesco, one marketmaker might quote the bid–offer prices of 335p–338p, while another quotes 336p–339p. The spread between the two prices represents a hoped-for return to the marketmaker.

The SEAQ computer gathers together the bid–offer quotes from all the marketmakers that make a market in that particular share. These competing quotations are then avail-

Exhibit 9.24

Trading places

FT

After four centuries of providing a range of services for the business world, Europe's stock markets must be prepared to share their role

Europe's stock markets are engaged in a thinly disguised war for survival: against each other, against their customers and against their US rivals. But the struggle is frequently misunderstood.

The threat is not that Paris will beat London; or that Frankfurt plus the Nasdaq will beat them both; or that the New York Stock Exchange will triumph over all. Nor does the threat come from the euro or the arrival of rival high-technology exchanges.

Instead, the risk is of an unbundling of the clutch of services an exchange provides. Exchanges will continue to exist, but as humble performers of routine duties. The real action – and the real added value – will have moved elsewhere.

Stock exchanges have been a part of business life for nearly four centuries, their role unquestioned until recent decades. Now, forced at last to justify their existence, exchanges struggle to provide a simple answer. Perhaps the truth is that they have no single *raison d'être*. Instead, their importance lies in the way they have bundled together a range of services, wrapping them in a layer of respectability or legal authorisation.

These services include the provision of price-information mechanism; the supervision of trading; the settlement of transactions; the authorisation of market participants; the administration and regulation of company listings; and the publication of trade data, prices and stock market indices.

Not all exchanges have performed all these functions. In some countries governments or private-sector bodies perform one or more of these tasks. But everywhere, surviving stock exchanges combine enough of these roles to give them a central status in the country's equity markets.

It is this bundling-up that is under threat: from governments, from technology, and from the increasing power of participants on buy and sell sides. Other groups, usually operating on a cross-border basis, are performing the individual functions of the traditional exchange. They are acquiring scale and skills that exchanges – organised on a national basis – cannot match.

Here are some examples. The US Securities and Exchange Commission is in effect setting listing criteria for the world's big companies, using US accounting principles. Settlement consortia and global custodians are taking over the back-office functions that exchanges historically provided. Bodies such as the European Union, the Iosco group of securities regulators or the Basle committee of the Bank for International Settlements are setting standards for market participants

Trading behaviour is increasingly supervised by government-sponsored bodies, not exchanges. Even the exchanges' most sacred role, providing a home for prices to be set and orders to be executed, is slipping from their hands. Traders can be linked electronically, without a physical floor. Many trades are matched automatically. Others are carried out off-market, or handled internally by big broker-dealers and investment managers.

There is a remaining role for exchanges in most of these areas, for example in ensuring that the standards set by external regulators are observed. But it is much less rewarding – and less well rewarded ...

Within five years, it is likely that Europe's top tier of companies will have found a common home on an electronic exchange. Whether the technology is inherited from Frankfurt or Paris, London or Washington is unimportant. So is the location of this new Euro-bourse's head office. So is the language of its statutes, the nationality of its governing board. Above all, it does not matter which of today's European exchanges leads the coalition from which the new bourse emerges.

Of course, some individuals will be winners or losers. Some national *amour-propre* will be affected. But that is all. The real struggle, the one with economic impact, is over the location of the value-added services that surround the exchange. Where will the main regulatory decisions be made: Brussels, London, Paris, Berlin or Washington? Who will host the settlement process? Where will the dealers who handle complex trades be located? Which city will have the critical mass of analysts and corporate financiers? Which region will host the bulk of the programmers who write the software market participants require? Where will the intellectual content of the new pan-European indices come from?

In deciding these issues, the site of incorporation of the Euro-bourse, or the location of its computers and officials, will carry only a little weight. Much more important will be the imagination, depth of human resources, and diplomatic skills and leadership of Europe's financial community. Exploiting those assets properly will ensure that Europe retains the economic role its individual exchanges are losing.

Source: Peter Martin, *Financial Times*, 2 July 1998, p. 24. Reprinted with permission.

able to brokers and other financial institutions linked up to the SEAQ system. For frequently traded shares, such as those of Tesco, there may be 15–20 marketmakers willing to 'make a book' in those shares. For an infrequently traded share there may be only two or three marketmakers willing to quote prices.

The marketmakers are obliged to deal (up to a certain number of shares) at the price quoted, but they have the freedom to adjust prices after deals are completed. The investor or broker (on behalf of an investor) is able to see the best price available on their computer terminals linked up to SEAQ and is able to make a purchase or sale.

Transactions are generally completed by the broker speaking to the marketmaker on the telephone. All trades are reported to the central electronic computer exchange and are disseminated to market participants (usually within three minutes) so that they are aware of the price at which recent trades were completed (*see* Exhibit 9.26).

The large investing institutions (pension funds, etc.) have SEAQ screens in their offices. This allows them to see the best prices being offered by marketmakers and to trade without necessarily going through a broker, thus cutting out commission.

The underlying logic of the quote-driven system is that through the competitive actions of numerous marketmakers, investors are able to buy or sell at any time at the best price. A problem arises for some very small or infrequently traded firms. Marketmakers are reluctant to commit capital to holding shares in such firms, and so for some there may be only one marketmaker's quote, for others there may be none. The LSE has developed SEATS plus, the Stock Exchange Alternative Trading Service, on which a single marketmaker's quote can be displayed. If business is so infrequent that no marketmaker will make a continuous quote the computer screen will act as a 'bulletin board' on which member firms can display their buy and sell orders. If more than one marketmaker registers in a share on SEATS plus the security is transferred to SEAQ (except for AIM shares which remain on SEATS plus). Huntingdon Life Sciences shareholders faced the prospect of trading through SEATS plus in 2001 – *see* Exhibit 9.25.

Exhibit 9.25

Shareholders take stock at a testing time

The animal rights campaign against Huntindon Life Sciences now threatens to leave the drug-testing company's shareholders feeling isolated. With no marketmakers left offering trades in the shares yesterday, investors faced a trading system that resembled a lonely hearts column.

Those wishing to deal in the shares at the start of the week could have done so using the London Stock Exchange's computerised platform – Seaq. Some 3,000 companies are traded on the system, with each share requiring at least two brokers so that the price is formed through competing quotes.

When Winterflood Securities stepped down on Tuesday as one of HLS's two remaining marketmakers, the company was left with 10 days to find a replacement broker or be moved to the Seats Plus trading system. This platform lists some 600 shares, including Aim-listed companies regardless of the number of marketmakers and all other companies with only one or no broker.

Effectively, a sole marketmaker can set the prevailing share price, leaving investors with less choice and less liquidity.

If investors do not have confidence in this price-setting mechanism, they can resort to a virtual notice-board on their Seats Plus system, on which they can post an offer to buy or sell at their own price in the hope of eventually attracting a match.

These transactions would lack the immediacy offered by marketmakers and it is not impossible that share dealings could take weeks, depending on the number of orders posted.

This was the situation faced by HLS shareholders yesterday after Dresdner Kleinwort Wasserstein followed Winterflood in withdrawing because of a policy of not acting as the sole marketmaker. Dresdner's move not only forced HLS on to the Seats Plus platform but make it one of the 30 to 60 companies at any one time with no marketmaker at all.

Source: Gautam Malkani, *Financial Times*, 29 March 2001, p. 3. Reprinted with permission.

Exhibit 9.26 The SEAQ quote-driven system

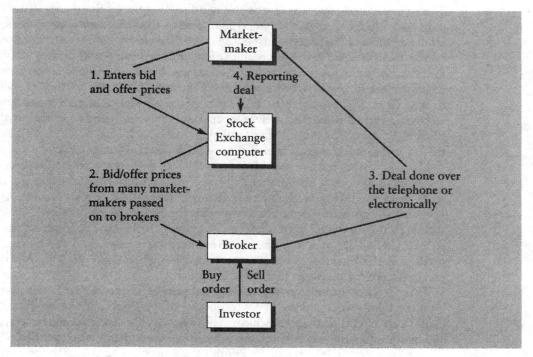

When a trade has been completed and reported to the exchange it is necessary to 'clear' the trade. That is, the exchange ensures that all reports of the trade are reconciled to make sure all parties are in agreement as to the number of shares traded and the price. Later the transfer of ownership from seller to buyer has to take place; this is called settlement (*see* Exhibit 9.27).

Exhibit 9.27 Settlement

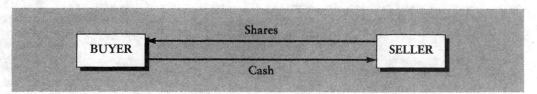

In 2001 the exchange moved to 'three-day rolling settlement' (Trading day +3, or T+3), which means that investors normally pay for shares three working days after the transaction date. Prior to 1996 the transfer of shares involved a tedious paper-chase between investors, brokers, company registrars, marketmakers and the Exchange. The new system, called CREST provides an electronic means of settlement and registration. This 'paperless' system is cheaper and quicker – ownership is transferred with a few strokes of a keyboard.

Under the CREST system shares are usually held in the name of a nominee company rather than in the name of the beneficial owner (i.e. the individual or organisation that actually bought them). Brokers and investment managers run these nominee accounts.

There might be dozens of investors with shares held by a particular nominee company. The nominee company appears as the registered owner of the shares as far as the company (say Marconi or BT) is concerned. Despite this, the beneficial owners will receive all dividends and the proceeds from the sale of the shares via the nominee company. One reason for this extra layer of complexity in the ownership and dealing of shares is that the nominee holdings are recorded in electronic form rather than in the form of a piece of paper (the inelegant word used for the move to electronic records is 'dematerialisation'). Thus, if a purchase or sale takes place a quick and cheap adjustment to the electronic record is all that is needed. Investors have no need to bother with share certificates. It is hoped that one day settlement can be achieved much more quickly than in the current three days once every investor holds shares electronically.

Many investors oppose the advance of CREST nominee accounts because under such a system they do not automatically receive annual reports and other documentation, such as an invitation to the annual general meeting. They also lose the right to vote (after all the company does not know who the beneficial owners are). Those investors who take their ownership of a part of a company seriously can insist on remaining outside of CREST. In this way they receive share certificates and are treated as the real owners of the business. This is more expensive when share dealing, but that is not a great concern for investors that trade infrequently.

There is a compromise position: personal membership of CREST. The investor is then both the legal owner and the beneficial owner of the shares, and also benefits from rapid (and cheap) electronic share settlement. The owner will be sent all company communications and retain voting rights. However, this is more expensive than the normal CREST accounts.

The *Financial Times* article in Exhibit 9.28 puts forward a case for reducing settlement delay to just one day.

Exhibit 9.28

Time running out for 'buy now, pay later'

If you are an investor in UK equities, you will be aware by now that, from today, the settlement cycle is being shortened from five days to three. In other words, you and your money will be parted after three days when you buy stocks listed on the London Stock Exchange, instead of five. Are you ready for this?

You should be. The stock market is one of the few places that still works on the 'buy now, pay later' principle. That is slowly changing. Across the world, the trend is towards ever-shorter time lags between buying shares and paying for them (or selling them and getting paid, which is just as important).

This trend is generally held to be a Good Thing. After all, the shorter the settlement cycle, the less risk there is of something going wrong between the execution and settlement of a transaction.

Stock markets are not exactly super-efficient, high-tech businesses. So there is a risk that something could go wrong, especially in cross-border equity trading, which is all the rage these days. The sharp rise in trading volumes also increases risk factors.

According to industry estimates, some 15 per cent of all cross-border trades fail. That means a buyer fails to pay up for shares on time (or at all), or a seller is not paid, or the shares go missing. A shorter settlement cycle is a good way to reduce the risk inherent in such trading.

In the US and much of Europe, the settlement cycle is three days (T+3: trading plus three days). So today's move by the London market brings it into line with its peers.

It has involved some reorganisation of back offices in the City. This costs money, and investors will no doubt be asked to pick up the bill. The argument, though, is that whatever the cost, it is outweighed by a parallel reduction in failed transactions and therefore in the risk inherent in exposure to a market.

Now that a certain global harmonisation has been achieved, the debate is about how far this process of shorter settlement cycles should go.

In theory, there is no reason why stock markets should not operate

Exhibit 9.28 continued

as other markets do. When you buy most goods you pay and go. Stock markets are not corner shops, however.

A particular problem in many markets is the need for paper share certificates to provide proof of ownership. Getting these bits of paper through the system is the reason for much of the grief of failed transactions.

The US, which has an efficient settlement and clearing infrastructure, had a plan to introduce T+1 settlement next year, at the urging of the Securities and Exchange Commission. But it has been put off until 2004 at the earliest.

In Europe, where the clearing and settlement infrastructure is not so joined up, there is no concerted push towards T+1, although there is an aspiration ...

Source: Vincent Boland, *Financial Times,* 5 February 2001, p. 25. Reprinted with permission.

The London Stock Exchange has a third quotation system sharing its Sequence platform along with SEAQ and SEATS plus. SEAQ International provides a linkage for quotations from competing international marketmakers in London. The 44 marketmakers, generally departments of major international securities houses, quote continuous two-way prices, usually in the home currency of the company. This is a market for professionals with an average bargain size in 2000 of £311,457 (compared with £64,414 for UK equities on SEAQ).

Order-driven systems

Most of the stock exchanges in the world operate order-driven markets, which do not require marketmakers to act as middlemen. These markets allow buy and sell orders to be entered on a central system, and investors are automatically matched (they are sometimes called matched-bargain systems). Shock-waves went through the financial markets when Tradepoint began and dozens of eminent City institutions signed up to take the service. Tradepoint (now renamed Virt-x) was designed to allow investors to avoid having to pay the marketmaker a spread for acting as an intermediary. It allowed institutional investors, in particular, to deal directly with each other at lower cost. Order-driven systems generally work as follows: All the buyers and sellers enter a price limit at which they are willing to deal (for most investors, without the computer systems, a broker would do this, for a commission). The computer calculates the price that permits the maximum quantity of sellers' and buyers' prices to be matched. So, in the stylised example shown in Exhibit 9.29, the equilibrium price is 98. At this price the sellers are willing to provide 9,000 shares (2,500 + 2,500 + 4,000). Some of these sellers would be content with 95 Euros, but set this merely as their price limit. At 98 euros there are buyers for 10,000 shares (3,000 + 2,000 + 5,000). At the market price of 98 as many orders as possible have been filled (9,000 shares). The unfilled orders at the market price are carried forward with 98 as the limit price.

The buyers and sellers orders and the recent market prices are continuously shown on the screen so a new buyer (or seller) can pitch the price they demand appropriately (*see* Exhibit 9.30).

The LSE initially responded to the Tradepoint threat by pointing out that a market-maker-centred system provides more liquidity than an order-driven system where investors may not be able to trade on demand. However, in October 1997 the Stock Exchange introduced its own order-driven service for the largest 100 quoted UK firms – this is called SETS (the Stock Exchange Trading Service). This now trades 189 large company shares. A typical screen is shown in Exhibit 9.31.

Exhibit 9.29

Buyers		Sellers	
Quantity of shares	Price limit (Euros)	Price limit (Euros)	Quantity of shares
3000	100	95	2500
2000	99	97	2500
5000	98	98	4000
1000	96	99	2000
2000	95	100	4000
6000	94	101	10,000

Exhibit 9.30 A Virt-x screen

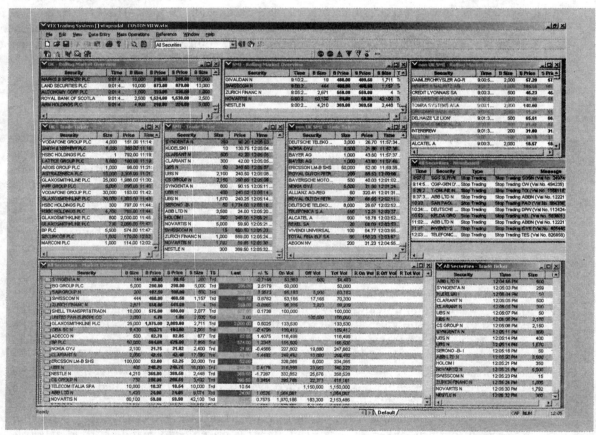

Source: Reproduced by courtesy of Virt-x Investment Exchange

The SETS system runs alongside the marketmaker system for the largest companies' shares. However, the medium-sized and small firms' shares are dealt with entirely through the marketmaker (quote-driven) system.

For SETS shares the London Stock Exchange has delegated clearing to the London Clearing House (LCH). The LCH has also become the counter-party in every SETS transaction. This means that it acts as the buyer to every seller and the seller to every buyer, thus guaranteeing that shares will be delivered against payment and vice versa. It also means that investors can trade anonymously. The article in Exhibit 9.32 discusses the introduction of the central counter-party (CCP).

Exhibit 9.31 SETS screen

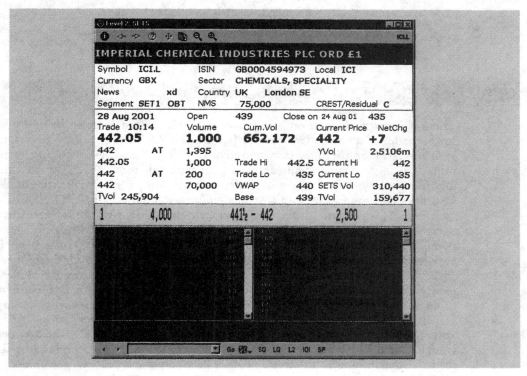

Source: Reproduced by courtesy of Thomson Financial.

Exhibit 9.32

LSE revamps trading structure

Intermediary service expected to provide strategic boost

The biggest shake-up in the structure of the UK equity market since the introduction of electronic trading – to be announced today – is expected to give a strategic boost to the London Stock Exchange.

The change involves the start of a 'central counter-party' (CCP) service to act as intermediary between buyers and sellers of shares.

Investors have been clamouring for years for the service, which offers enhanced risk management and guaranteed anonymity in trading. It will give the LSE a competitive advantage over Deutsche Börse. The LSE will be the second large European exchange to provide a CCP service, putting it on par with Euronext, the Euoprean exchange operator. Deutsche Börse and other European exchanges either do not have one or are developing the service.

The CCP is a joint initiative by the three institutions at the heart of London's financial markets – the stock exchange, the London Clearing House and Crest, which processes equity market transactions ...

Bankers and fund managers said the introduction of CCP was the most significant change to the way the stock market works since the Sets electronic trading system for

►

Exhibit 9.32 continued

blue-chip UK stocks was launched in 1997 ...

The CCP works by putting itself between the two parties involved in a stock market transaction – the buyer and the seller. It assumes the risk involved by becoming the buyer to every seller and the seller to every buyer. It also means buyers and sellers do not know each other's identity.

Large institution such as investment banks and fund management firms see this anonymity as an important advantage because it reduces the 'market impact cost' of other investors knowing that their competitors are active in the market at a particular time.

Source: Vincent Boland, *Financial Times*, 26 February 2001, p. 23. Reprinted with permission.

THE OWNERSHIP OF UK QUOTED SHARES

There was a transformation in the pattern of share ownership in Britain over the last four decades of the twentieth century (*see* Exhibit 9.33). The tax-favoured status of pension funds made them a very attractive vehicle for savings, resulting in billions of pounds being put into them each year. Most of this money was invested in equities, making pension funds the most influential investing group on the stock market. Insurance companies similarly rose in significance, doubling their share of quoted equities from 10 per cent to about 20 per cent by the early 1990s. The group which decreased in importance is ordinary individuals holding shares directly. They used to dominate the market, with 54 per cent of quoted shares in 1963. By the late 1980s this had declined to about 20 per cent. Investors tended to switch from direct investment to collective investment vehicles. They gain benefits of diversification and skilled management by putting their savings into unit and investment trusts or into endowment and other savings schemes offered by the insurance companies. Another factor was the increasing share of equities held by overseas investors: only 7 per cent in 1963, but over 16 per cent by the mid-1990s. While the proportion of the stock market owned by individuals plunged between the early 1960s and late 1980s, it has been broadly stable since then. A contributing factor to this halt is probably the spread of personal equity plans (PEPs) and Individual Savings Accounts (ISAs), which give some of the tax benefits available to pension schemes directly to individuals. Another major element has been the success of privatisation and building society conversions to public company status.

In 1980 only three million individuals held shares. After the privatisation programme, which included British Gas, British Telecom and TSB, the figure rose to nine million by 1988. By 1991 the flotations of Abbey National, the water companies and regional electricity companies had taken the numbers to 11 million. The stampede of building societies to market in 1997 produced a record 16 million individual shareholders.

Exhibit 9.33 Share ownership in Britain, distribution by sector (quoted shares) (%)

Sector	1963	1975	1989	1997
Individuals	54.0	37.5	17.7	20.5
Pension funds	6.4	16.8	34.2	27.9
Insurance cos.	10.0	15.9	17.3	23.1
Others (banks, public sector, unit trusts, overseas, etc.)	29.6	29.6	30.8	28.5

Source: Office for National Statistics. Crown Copyright 1997. Reproduced by permission of the Controller of HMSO and the Office for National Statistics.

Although the mode of investment has changed from direct to indirect, Britain remains a society with a deep interest in the stock market. Very few people are immune from the performance of the Exchange. The vast majority have a pension plan or endowment savings scheme, an ISA or a unit trust investment. Some have all four.

REGULATION

Financial markets need high-quality regulation in order to induce investors to place their trust in them. There must be safeguards against unscrupulous and incompetent operators. There must be an orderly operation of the markets, fair dealing and integrity. However, the regulations must not be so restrictive as to stifle innovation and prevent the markets from being competitive internationally.

London's financial markets have a unique blend of law, self-regulation and custom to regulate and supervise their members' activities. The Financial Services Act 1986 the Banking Act 1987 and the Financial Services and Markets Act 2000 created the present structure. The main burden of regulation falls upon self-regulatory bodies, but within a statutory (legal) framework. The Self-Regulatory Organisations (SROs) have the task of policing the investment business carried out by their members. Overseeing the SROs is the Financial Services Authority (FSA). The FSA has strong statutory powers. All individuals or organisations wishing to undertake 'investment business' have to be authorised to do so. The SROs have the duty to scrutinise their members to ensure their fitness to operate. It is a criminal offence to undertake investment business without being authorised.

There are three SROs reporting to the FSA:

- *The Securities and Futures Authority (SFA)* This covers dealing in securities (for example shares) as well as dealing in financial and commodity futures and dealing in international bonds from London. Thus, members of the LSE, the LIFFE futures and options market, the commodity markets and London Eurobond dealers are regulated by the SFA.

- *The Investment Management Regulatory Organisation (IMRO)* This regulates institutions managing pooled investments, for example managers of investment trusts, unit trusts and pension funds.

- *The Personal Investment Authority (PIA)* This covers insurance brokers, independent investment advisers and the marketing of pooled investment products (for example life assurance or unit trusts).

The FSA also recognises certain professional bodies whose members undertake investment business, primarily accountants and lawyers. A further responsibility of the FSA is the supervision of Recognised Investment Exchanges (RIE). A recognised exchange is exempt from the requirement of authorisation for anything done in its capacity as an RIE. However, the members of an exchange will need authorisation under, say, the SFA. To gain and retain the exalted status of an RIE an exchange has to convince the FSA that high standards are maintained through constant monitoring and enforcement of the rules of the exchange. The LSE is an RIE and, as such, it aims for the highest standards of integrity, fairness, transparency, efficiency and protection of shareholders.

For an overview of the regulation of the financial service industry, *see* Exhibit 9.34.

Outside the FSA structure there are numerous ways in which the conduct of firms and financial institutions is put under scrutiny and constraint. The media keep a watchful stance – always looking to reveal stories of fraud, greed and incompetence. There is legislation prohibiting insider dealing, fraud and negligence. Companies Acts regulate the

Exhibit 9.34 Financial service industry regulation

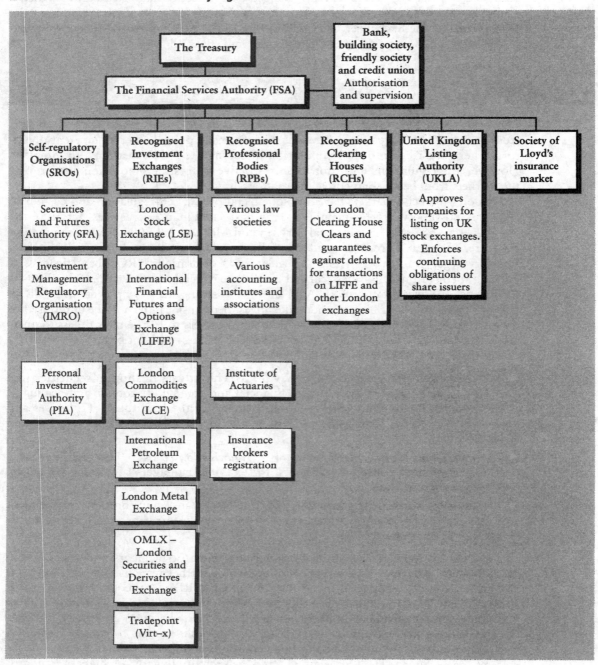

formation and conduct of companies and there are special Acts for building societies, insurance companies and unit trusts. The Competition Commission (CC) and the Office of Fair Trading (OFT) attempt to prevent abuse of market power. The Panel on Takeovers and Mergers determines the manner in which acquisitions are conducted for public companies (*see* Chapter 20). In addition European Union regulations are an increasing feature of corporate life. Accountants also function, to some extent, as regulators helping to ensure companies do not misrepresent their financial position. In addition any member of the public may access the account of any company easily and cheaply at Companies House (or via Companies House's website or the postal system).

UNDERSTANDING THE FIGURES IN THE FINANCIAL PAGES

Financial managers and investors need to be aware of what is happening on the financial markets, how their shares are affected and which measures are used as key yardsticks in evaluating a company. The financial pages of the broadsheet newspapers, particularly the *Financial Times*, provide some important statistics on company share price performance and valuation ratios. These enable comparisons to be made between companies within the same sector and across sectors. Exhibit 9.35 shows extracts from two issues of the *Financial Times* from the same week. The information provided in the Monday edition is different from that provided on the other days of the week.

Indices

Information on individual companies in isolation is less useful than information set in the context of the firm's peer group, or in comparison with quoted companies generally. For example, if ICI shares fall by 1 per cent on a particular day, an investor might be keen to learn whether the market as a whole rose or fell on that day, and by how much. The *Financial Times* (FT) joined forces with the Stock Exchange (SE) to create FTSE International in November 1995, which has taken over the calculation (in conjunction with the Faculty and Institute of Actuaries) of a number of equity indices. These indicate the state of the market as a whole or selected sectors of the market and consist of 'baskets' of shares so that the value of that basket can be compared at different times. Senior managers are often highly sensitive to the relative performance of their company's share price. One reason for this is that their compensation package may be linked to the share price and in extreme circumstances managers are dismissed if they do not generate sufficiently high relative returns.

The indices shown in Exhibit 9.36 are arithmetically weighted by market capitalisation. Thus, a 2 per cent movement in the share price of a larger company has a greater effect on an index than a 2 per cent change in a small company's share price. The characteristics of some of these indices are as follows.

■ *FTSE 100* The 'Footsie™' index is based on the 100 largest companies (generally over £3bn market capitalisation). Large and relatively safe companies are referred to as 'blue chips'. This index has risen six-fold since it was introduced at the beginning of 1984 at a value of 1,000. This is the measure most watched by international observers. It is calculated in real time (every 15 seconds) and so changes can be observed throughout the day. The other international benchmarks are: for the USA, the Dow Jones Industrial average (DJIA) (30 share) index, the Standard and Poors 500 index and the NASDAQ 100; for the Japanese market the Nikkei 225 index; for France the CAC-40; for Hong Kong the Hang Seng index and for Germany the Dax index. For Europe as a whole there is FTSE Eurotop 300 and for the world FTSE All-World Index.

■ *FTSE All-Share* This index is the most representative in that it reflects the average movements of nearly 800 shares representing 98 per cent of the value of the London market. This index is broken down into a number of industrial and commercial

Exhibit 9.35 London Share Service extracts: general retailers

FT

FRIDAY MAY 25 2001
GENERAL RETAILERS

	Notes	Price	+ or –	52 week high	52 week low	Volume '000s	yield	P/E
Alexon		126½	–8½	138½	47½	332	1.6	9.5
Allders	♣	161½	...	163	90	876	5.3	10.2
Arcadia		276½	–5½	299½	36	315	–	79.1
Arnotts 1£	♣	428¾	+11¾	457	364½	–	4.0	Φ
Ashley (Laura)		25½	...	27½	18¾	99	–	34.4
Austin Reed	♣	153½	+2½	157	82½	81	5.2	9.9
Beale	♣	112½	–1½	127½	69	20	4.7	10.0
Beattie (J)	♣	180xd	+½	186½	118½	144	6.4	11.1
Bentalls	♣	99xd	+4½	100	59½	344	4.1	41.7
Blacks Leisure	♣	179	+4	318½	136½	339	3.8	Φ
Body Shop		98½	...	132½	71½	7	6.4	11.6
Boots	†	585	+5	650	474	1,810	4.4	12.9
Brown & Jcksn		40½	–2	157½	27½	87	8.6	4.3
Brown (N)	q	291½	...	360	231½	304	1.8	21.9
Carpetright	♣†	600	...	682	428	61	4.1	16.6
Carphone Warehouse		140½	+4½	237½	110½	1,456	–	50.0
Cash Converters Units		1	...	5½	1	–	–	–
Clinton Cards		135xd	...	141	83½	292	4.4	6.7
Courts	♣†	327½	+5½	417½	272½	16	1.7	9.1
DFS Furniture	†s	487½xd	–1	490	297½	647	3.9	15.4
Debenhams	†	462	–2	485½	154	1,223	2.4	17.9
Dixons	†sP	250	+½	359	176	13,726	1.9	30.3
ebrokers.com		149	...	161½	97½	8	–	–
Electronics Boutique		92	+¾	95	30	1,299	0.7	Φ
Falkland Islands		146½	...	178½	130	4	3.0	12.1
Findel		276	+8½	288½	200½	203	4.2	Φ
Flying Brands Uts	♣q	130	...	132½	71½	4	5.7	15.8
Forminster		27	...	38½	24½	3	–	–
French Connect		857½xd	...	872½	642½	2	0.8	15.6
Gieves & Hawkes		20	...	25½	15½	3	–	–
Grampian	♣	75	+2	85	54½	242	11.5	Φ
Great Universal	♣	605	+14	607½	366½	5,280	3.4	18.2
Hamleys	a	127½	–3	168	112½	28	6.4	18.8
Harvey Nichols Grp	†	231	...	233½	116	3	3.2	11.6
Heal's		216	+1	217½	150	1	3.5	9.0
Homestyle	♣	459	–1	465	260	1,108	4.2	Φ

MONDAY MAY 21 2001
GENERAL RETAILERS

	Notes	Price	W'K% ch'nge	Div	Div cov.	Mkt cap£m	Last xd	City line
Alexon		118	13.5	2.0	6.6	73.9	11'93	1565
Allders	♣	155	4.7	8.4	1.6	120.4	15.1	2745
Arcadia		287½	4.5	–	–	544.0	1'0	2020
Arnotts 1£	♣	423¼	–.6	27.3c	Φ	76.8	18.9	–
Ashley (Laura)		26	2.0	–	–	155.2	5'97	1664
Austin Reed	♣	145	–2.4	7.75	1.9	45.5	30.10	3798
Beale	♣	114	...	5.3	2.1	23.2	28.2	5027
Beattie (J)	♣	177½xd	2.5	11.5	1.4	78.8	16.5	1784
Bentalls	♣	84xd	–4.0	4.05	0.6	34.4	9.5	1808
Blacks Leisure	♣	172½	...	6.65	Φ	71.4	18.12	1846
Body Shop		95	0.5	5.7	Φ	184.3	4.12	1864
Boots	†	583	–7.3	25.5	1.8	5,247	13.11	1876
Brown & Jcksn		42½	–24.8	3.5	2.7	71.3	13.11	1984
Brown (N)	q	280½	–1.9	5.2	2.5	820.7	27.11	1985
Carpetright	♣†	600	4.2	24.5	1.5	453.0	7.2	2464
Carphone Warehouse		128	1.6	–	–	1,048	–	2833
Cash Converters Units		1	...	–	–	1.51	11'98	2445
Clinton Cards		134½xd	3.5	5.88	3.4	92.4	9.5	4978
Courts	♣†	321	...	5.6	6.4	196.8	7.3	2256
DFS Furniture	†s	480xd	5.1	19.2	1.7	496.3	16.5	3588
Debenhams	†	478	2.4	11.1	2.3	1,769	20.11	2936
Dixons	†sP	244	0.1	4.8	1.7	4,672	29.1	2355
ebrokers.com		137½	...	–	–	63.9	–	–
Electronics Boutique		88	–4.3	0.66	Φ	306.0	30.10	3368
Falkland Islands		144	...	4.4	2.8	8.78	9.10	1615
Findel	†	251½	–1.4	10.65	1.3	182.6	18.12	2563
Flying Brands Uts	♣q	129	–1.9	7.35	1.1	34.7	28.2	2789
Forminster		27	...	–	–	8.94	11'99	2618
French Connect		865xd	0.6	6.5	8.4	183.5	21.3	2633
Gieves & Hawkes		20	–2.4	–	–	6.22	5.6	2694
Grampian	♣	72½	1.4	8.0	Φ	84.3	30.10	2751
Great Universal	♣	569	2.9	20.6	1.6	5,724	2.1	2740
Hamleys	a	122	0.4	8.15	1.1	25.6	18.12	4304
Harvey Nichols Grp	†	213½	3.6	7.5	2.6	117.4	8.1	1744
Heal's		205	6.5	7.8	3.2	25.0	7.2	2819

Market price: This is the mid-price (midway between the best buying and selling prices) quoted by marketmakers at 4.30 p.m. on the previous day; 'xd' (ex-dividend) means that new buyers of the share will not receive a recently announced dividend (it will go to the existing shareholders).

Change in closing price on Thursday compared with previous trading day.

The highest and lowest prices during the previous 52 weeks.

Dividend yield: The dividend divided by the current share price expressed as a percentage:

$$\frac{\text{dividend per share}}{\text{current share price}} \times 100$$

Market capitalisation is calculated by multiplying the number of shares issued by their market price.

Ex-dividend date is the last date on which the share went ex-dividend.

City line: up-to-the-second share prices available by telephone (call 0906 003 plus 4-digit code).

Price/earnings ratio (PER): Share price divided by the company's earnings (profits after tax) per share in the latest twelve-month period. A much examined and talked about measure (see Chapter 17):

$$\text{PER} = \frac{\text{share price}}{\text{earnings per share}}$$

Share price change over the previous week.

Dividend is the dividend paid in the company's last full year – it is the cash payment in pence per share.

Dividend cover: Profit after tax divided by the dividend payment, or earnings per share divided by dividend per share:

$$\text{Dividend cover} = \frac{\text{earnings per share}}{\text{dividend per share}}$$

Source: Financial Times, 21 and 25 May 2001. Reprinted with permission.

sectors, so that investors and companies can use sector-specific yardsticks, such as those for mining or chemicals. Companies in the FTSE All-Share index have market capitalisations above £35m.

- *FTSE 250* This index is based on 250 firms which are in the next size range after the top 100. Capitalisations are generally £350m–£3bn. (It is also calculated with investment trusts excluded.)

- *FTSE 350* This index is based on the largest 350 quoted companies. It combines the FTSE 100 and the FTSE 250. This cohort of shares is also split into two to give high and low dividend yield groups.

- *FTSE SmallCap* This index covers approximately 500–600 companies included in the FTSE All-Share but excluded from the FTSE 350, with a market capitalisation of between £35m and £350m.

- *FTSE Fledgling* This includes over 700 companies too small to be in the FTSE All-Share Index. This index is a mixture of Ordinary List and AIM shares.

- *FTSE AIM* Index of all AIM companies.

- *FTSE techMARK 100* Includes 100 techMARK companies with capitalisation less than £4bn.

- *FTSE techMARK All share* Includes all companies on the techMARK.

Exhibit 9.36 FTSE Actuaries Share Indices

FTSE Actuaries Share Indices UK series
Produced in conjunction with the Faculty and Institute of Actuaries

	£ Stlg May 24	Day's chge%	Euro Index	£ Stlg May 23	£ Stlg May 22	Year ago	Actual yield%	Cover	P/E ratio	Xd adj. ytd	Total Return
FTSE 100	5915.9	+0.3	7594.8	5897.8	5976.6	6231.1	2.25	1.98	22.44	67.86	2772.16
FTSE 250	6635.8	−0.4	8519.7	6663.7	6672.5	6153.8	2.59	1.89	20.37	74.18	3071.24
FTSE 250 ex Inv Co	6742.7	−0.4	8656.3	6773.1	6780.1	6173.4	2.73	1.97	18.60	80.19	3144.23
FTSE 350	2918.3	+0.2	3746.5	2912.1	2946.4	3020.6	2.30	1.97	22.14	33.35	2797.35
FTSE 350 ex Inv Co	2909.8	+0.2	3735.6	2903.4	2938.1	3014.5	2.32	1.98	21.83	33.69	1431.41
FTSE 350 Higher Yield	3279.4	+0.5	4210.1	3263.5	3282.5	2842.5	3.12	1.93	16.64	53.22	2762.38
FTSE 350 Lower Yield	2514.5	−0.2	3228.1	2519.0	2569.4	3231.4	1.15	2.11	41.36	11.47	1908.30
FTSE SmallCap	3146.56	+0.2	4039.55	3139.67	3142.88	3157.88	2.34	1.55	27.65	31.85	2965.82
FTSE SmallCap ex Inv Co	3118.80	+0.3	4003.91	3108.84	3111.92	3117.83	2.36	1.73	24.48	31.64	2982.76
FTSE All-Share	2864.51	+0.2	3677.46	2858.36	2890.91	2961.20	2.30	1.95	22.31	32.59	2787.74
FTSE All-Share ex Inv Co	2855.45	+0.2	3665.82	2849.03	2882.14	2954.66	2.32	1.97	21.90	32.92	1430.62
FTSE All-Share ex Multinational	984.09	+0.4	1047.11	981.07	991.50	1025.22	2.44	1.77	23.19	12.28	1025.82
FTSE Fledgling	2283.00	+0.1	2930.91	2280.50	2278.43	2073.45	3.13	0.49	65.82	24.52	2745.32
FTSE Fledgling ex Inv Co	2411.00	+0.1	3095.24	2408.09	2404.54	2128.66	3.06	0.41	79.97	24.76	2920.89
FTSE All-Small	1904.47	+0.2	2444.95	1900.74	1901.91	1873.00	2.50	1.27	31.52	19.51	2291.72
FTSE All-Small ex Inv Co	1937.24	+0.3	2487.03	1931.80	1932.79	1894.22	2.50	1.42	28.24	19.69	2355.81
FTSE AIM	1226.3	−0.2	1574.4	1228.8	1228.4	1609.8	0.55	‡	‡	2.69	1141.04
FTSE Actuaries Industry Sectors											
RESOURCES(15)	6524.31	+0.6	8375.90	6487.35	6554.80	5661.41	2.33	2.79	15.39	83.29	3246.80
Mining(5)	6363.93	−0.4	8170.01	6387.02	6480.08	4019.66	2.63	2.46	15.47	104.64	2233.30
Oil & Gas(10)	7201.43	+0.8	9245.18	7146.40	7214.29	6608.48	2.27	2.87	15.37	86.31	3673.74
BASIC INDUSTRIES(51)	2484.23	−0.6	3189.26	2500.22	2510.80	2072.62	3.37	1.83	16.24	34.96	1625.35
Chemicals(10)	2484.35	−1.4	3189.41	2519.25	2548.51	2302.02	4.20	1.79	13.29	29.46	1422.02
Construction & Bld Matls(39)	2349.42	−0.1	3016.19	2352.80	2356.55	1811.50	3.15	2.43	13.03	37.23	1430.91
Forestry & Paper(1)	8079.61	+1.9	10372.60	7926.20	7900.63	8100.83	5.44	2.01	9.13	143.18	4184.20
Steel & Other Metals(1)	1871.61	−3.4	2402.77	1937.81	1937.81	2256.77	1.29	‡	‡	0.00	1321.65

Exhibit 9.36 continued

	£ Stlg May 24	Day's chge%	Euro Index	£ Stlg May 23	£ Stlg May 22	Year ago	Actual yield%	Cover	P/E ratio	Xd adj. ytd	Total Return
GENERAL INDUSTRIALS(52)	2107.06	−1.4	2705.04	2136.23	2113.61	2489.14	3.64	1.71	16.09	31.66	1365.23
Aerospace & Defence(9)	2181.93	−1.2	2801.16	2208.12	2169.08	2373.47	2.71	1.73	21.34	30.27	1537.14
Electronic & Elect Equip(21)	4623.38	−1.6	5947.05	4708.38	4747.52	7355.89	3.99	1.52	16.52	24.95	2733.98
Engineering & Machinery(22)	2356.70	−1.5	3025.52	2392.70	2360.59	2413.22	5.23	1.82	10.53	59.79	1732.46
CYCLICAL CONSUMER GOODS(7)	5393.57	−0.1	6924.26	5401.44	5447.76	6089.85	2.93	2.36	14.49	91.04	2287.47
Automobiles & Parts(4)	3781.51	−0.3	4854.70	3794.54	3829.07	4365.61	2.64	2.56	14.81	64.18	2206.96
Household Goods & Texts(3)	2351.24	+2.0	3018.52	2305.29	2311.97	2120.44	6.01	1.42	11.73	37.31	1181.60
NON-CYCLICAL CONS GOODS(70)	6407.68	+0.7	8226.17	6359.99	6397.79	5847.36	2.17	1.80	25.64	60.55	2723.01
Beverages(7)	4111.71	+0.1	5278.61	4107.17	4043.07	3286.14	3.14	1.85	17.24	40.51	1777.88
Food Producers & Processors(13)	3174.66	−0.2	4075.62	3180.19	3164.41	2981.32	2.82	1.85	19.13	48.85	1675.50
Health(17)	3073.96	−0.3	3964.34	3083.21	3091.03	2660.37	1.40	2.83	25.27	22.99	2078.45
Packaging(5)	2393.21	+1.4	3072.40	2361.10	2397.69	1963.03	4.93	1.44	14.06	15.58	1262.93
Personal Care & Hse Prods(2)	2605.75	−0.9	3345.25	2628.49	2645.64	2170.78	2.79	1.13	31.61	35.76	1223.31
Pharmaceuticals(23)	11874.35	+1.1	15244.29	11746.80	11897.19	11259.29	1.60	1.73	36.25	70.35	4489.72
Tobacco(3)	7173.50	+1.3	9209.33	7079.51	7071.12	5609.31	5.11	1.88	10.43	250.59	2387.99
CYCLICAL SERVICES(219)	3558.95	−0.6	4568.98	3579.08	3618.60	3743.85	2.16	1.86	24.80	30.74	2083.61
Distributors(15)	2567.00	−3.6	3295.52	2662.67	2667.81	2652.72	2.92	1.86	18.39	12.70	1101.72
General Retailers(42)	1865.72	+0.7	2395.21	1856.36	1851.36	1744.78	2.97	1.70	19.80	11.93	1236.71
Leisure Entermt & Hotels(39)	3167.86	−0.4	4066.99	3180.46	3204.43	3299.20	2.41	2.56	16.19	45.22	1933.51
Media & Photography(48)	5959.17	−1.0	7650.38	6019.43	6167.02	7097.46	1.29	1.37	56.24	41.61	2354.09
Support Services(48)	5264.10	−0.3	6758.04	5278.35	5344.41	4942.18	1.45	2.78	24.88	40.87	3637.26
Transport(27)	2647.28	−1.2	3398.58	2678.17	2663.80	2701.50	3.80	1.59	16.60	28.20	1287.34
NON-CYCLICAL SERVICES(23)	2923.45	−0.4	3753.12	2936.51	3021.87	4486.07	0.94	1.74	61.00	6.38	1673.52
Food & Drug Retailers(9)	3367.47	+0.2	4323.15	3359.37	3361.39	2745.22	2.31	1.90	22.75	33.65	2477.02
Telecommunication Services(14)	4307.31	−0.8	5529.73	4331.67	4478.67	7184.31	0.70	1.65	80.80†	3.22	2166.33
UTILITIES(16)	3914.37	+1.1	5025.27	3873.65	3883.63	3566.76	3.99	1.23	20.40	58.48	2085.44
Electricity(8)	3999.13	+1.1	5134.08	3956.47	3979.95	3487.55	3.76	0.91	29.07	67.44	2637.61
Gas Distribution(2)	4100.72	+0.5	5264.50	4081.58	4082.31	4226.05	2.51	2.17	18.34	55.02	2518.15
Water(6)	2680.17	+1.8	3440.80	2633.21	2617.22	2346.07	6.85	1.37	10.70	27.35	1914.30
INFORMATION TECHNOLOGY(90)	1634.00	−0.9	2097.72	1648.26	1701.13	3106.53	0.62	3.24	49.75	2.90	1659.03
Information Tech Hardware(18)	3129.27	−1.6	4017.35	3178.79	3278.50	6351.01	0.69	2.93	35.56	4.95	3173.00
Software & Computer Services(72)	1478.28	−0.4	1897.81	1484.16	1532.48	2719.49	0.39	3.75	67.86	2.75	1499.59
NON FINANCIALS(543)	2804.18	...	3600.00	2802.84	2837.86	3068.47	2.10	2.01	23.77	25.40	2439.87
FINANCIALS(218)	6367.61	+0.7	8174.73	6323.00	6374.60	5492.58	2.89	1.83	18.94	115.37	3214.00
Banks(12)	10066.79	+0.9	12923.74	9978.77	10059.23	8043.32	3.07	2.24	14.55	209.50	3875.96
Insurance(9)	2363.94	+0.4	3034.82	2355.48	2415.74	2095.28	4.81	0.12	80.00†	74.13	2193.84
Life Assurance(7)	6616.22	+1.6	8493.90	6510.29	6612.76	7325.43	3.53	0.63	45.23	151.80	3227.68
Investment Companies(126)	4941.12	−0.1	6343.41	4947.82	4963.15	4943.46	1.64	0.91	67.01	29.57	1889.67
Real Estate(35)	2310.95	−0.1	2966.79	2313.82	2302.17	1904.41	2.32	1.77	24.41	13.95	1633.89
Speciality & Other Finance(29)	5451.34	−0.6	6998.42	5483.62	5531.56	4425.26	1.71	2.53	23.15	45.59	3538.25

■ Hourly movements	8.03	9.00	10.00	11.00	12.00	13.00	14.00	15.00	16.00	High/day	Low/day
FTSE 100	5898.0	5939.0	5933.7	5943.0	5922.9	5924.8	5924.3	5937.5	5925.6	5950.0	5889.3
FTSE 250	6652.3	6648.3	6644.4	6642.9	6637.5	6638.9	6637.1	6640.6	6639.6	6654.1	6633.8
FTSE SmallCap	3136.33	3136.88	3138.15	3138.82	3140.99	3142.71	3144.13	3146.05	3146.36	3146.61	3136.33
FTSE All-Share	2857.84	2874.18	2871.86	2875.58	2867.24	2868.14	2867.90	2873.45	2868.65	2878.43	2854.20

Time of FTSE 100 Day's high:10:15:15 Day's low: 8:21:15. FTSE 100 2001 High: 6334.5 (30/01/2001) Low: 5314.8 (22/03/2001)

Time of FTSE 100 All-Share Day's high:10:15:00 Day's low: 8:21:00. FTSE All-Share 2001 High: 3045.55 (30/01/2001) Low: 2573.07 (22/03/2201)

Further information is available on http://www.ftse.co,. © FTSE International Limited 2001. All Rights reserved.

'FTSE', 'FT-SE' and 'Footsie' are trade marks of the London Stock Exchange and The Financial Times and are used by FTSE International under licence. † Sector P/E ratios greater that 80 are not shown. − Values are negative.

Source: Financial Times, 25 May 2001. Reprinted with permission.

TAXATION AND CORPORATE FINANCE

Taxation impacts on financial decisions in at least three ways.

1 *Capital allowances* At one time it was possible for a firm to reduce its taxable profit by up to 100 per cent of the amount invested in certain fixed assets. So if a firm made a profit of £10m, and in the same year bought £10m worth of approved plant and equipment, the Inland Revenue would not charge any tax because the capital allowance of £10m could be subtracted from the profit to calculate taxable profit. The idea behind this generosity was to encourage investment and thus stimulate economic growth. Today, the capital allowance is generally 25 per cent of the value of the investment in the first year and 25 per cent on a declining balance for subsequent years.

Capital allowances in project appraisal were discussed in Chapter 5.

2 *Selecting type of finance* The interest paid on borrowed capital can be used to reduce the taxable profit and thus lower the tax bill. On the other hand, payments to shareholders, such as dividends, cannot be used to reduce taxable profit. This bias against share capital may have some impact on the capital structure decision – see Chapter 18.

3 *Distribution of profit* Companies pay corporation tax on profits. The profits are calculated after all costs have been deducted, including interest but excluding dividends. The proportion of taxable profit paid to the tax authorities is 30 per cent if taxable profit exceeds £1,500,000, and 20 per cent where it is less than £300,000 but above £50,000 (a sliding scale applies between £300,000 and £1.5 million). Very small companies with profits under £10,000 pay only 10 per cent tax, and a sliding scale applies between £10,000 and £50,000.

Standard-rate taxpayers (those with a marginal tax rate of 22 per cent on normal income) are liable to pay 10 per cent income tax on dividends. The rate of income tax on dividends for higher taxpayers is 32.5 per cent. The 10 per cent rate is deemed to be paid by the company when it pays corporation tax. Therefore, standard-rate taxpayers do not have to pay tax on dividends received. The higher-rate taxpayer can offset the 10 per cent tax paid against the total tax they are due to pay on dividends.

CONCLUDING COMMENTS

Stock markets are major contributors to the well-being of a modern financially sophisticated society. They have great value to a wide variety of individuals and institutions. For savers they provide an environment in which savings can be invested in real productive assets to yield a return both to the saver and to society at large. The powerful pension and insurance funds rely on a well-regulated and broadly based stock exchange to enable the generation of income for their members. The mobilisation of savings for investment is a key benefit of a well-run exchange; so too is the improved allocation of scarce resources in society which results in a more satisfying mixture of goods and services being produced. The stock market has a part to play in directing investment to those parts of the economy which will generate the greatest level of utility for consumers. If people want cars rather than horse-drawn transport then savings will be directed to permit investment in factories and production lines for cars. If they demand word processors rather than typewriters then the computer firm will find it easier to raise fresh finance than will the typewriter firm.

Companies value stock markets for their capacity to absorb new issues of financial securities permitting firms to expand, innovate and produce wealth. Entrepreneurs can reap the rewards of their efforts by having access to a flourishing secondary share market and employees can be rewarded with shares which become more appealing because they can be quickly valued by examining reports in the financial press on market prices. Managers often acknowledge the disciplinary benefits of a stock market which insists on high levels of information disclosure, integrity, competence and the upholding of shareholder interests. Governments are aware of the range of social benefits listed above and so should value an exchange on these grounds alone. However, they also see more direct advantages in a fit and proper market. For example, they are able to raise finance to cover the difference between taxes and expenditure, and they are able to tap the market in privatisations and thereby not only fill government coffers but encourage wider share ownership and allow the market to pressurise managers to run previously state-owned businesses in a more efficient manner.

Having gained some background knowledge of the workings of the London Stock Exchange, we now need to turn to the question of how equity funds are actually raised on the Official List and on AIM. The next chapter will examine this. It will also describe sources of equity finance available to firms which are not quoted.

KEY POINTS AND CONCEPTS

- **Stock exchanges** are markets where government and industry can raise long-term capital and investors can buy and sell securities.

- **Two breakthroughs in the rise of capitalism:**
  - thriving secondary markets for securities;
  - limited liability.

- **Over 90 countries now have stock markets.** They have grown in significance due to:
  - disillusionment with planned economies combined with admiration for Western and the 'tiger' economies;
  - recognition of the key role of stock markets in a liberal pro-market economic system.

- The **largest** domestic stock markets are in the USA, Japan and the UK. The **leading international equity market** is the London Stock Exchange.

- The **globalisation** of equity markets has been driven by:
  - deregulation;
  - technology;
  - institutionalisation.

- Companies **list on more than one exchange** for the following reasons:
  - to broaden the shareholder base and lower the cost of equity capital;
  - the domestic market is too small or the firm's growth is otherwise constrained;
  - to reward employees;
  - foreign investors may understand the firm better;
  - to raise awareness of the company;
  - to discipline the firm and learn to improve performance;
  - to understand better the economic, social and industrial changes occurring in major product markets.

- A well-run stock exchange:
  - allows a 'fair game' to take place;
  - is regulated to avoid negligence, fraud and other abuses;
  - allows transactions to take place cheaply;
  - has enough participants for efficient price setting and liquidity.

- **Benefits** of a well-run stock exchange:
  - firms can find funds and grow;
  - society can allocate capital better;
  - shareholders can sell speedily and cheaply. They can value their financial assets and diversify;
  - increase in status and publicity for firms;
  - mergers can be facilitated by having a quotation. The market in managerial control is assisted;
  - corporate behaviour can be improved.

- The **London Stock Exchange** regulates the trading of **equities** (domestic and international) and **debt instruments** (e.g. gilts, corporate bonds and Eurobonds, etc.) and **other financial instruments** (e.g. warrants, depository receipts and preference shares).

- The **primary market** is where firms can raise finance by selling shares (or other securities) to investors.

- The **secondary market** is where existing securities are sold by one investor to another.

- **Internal funds** are generally the most important source of long-term capital for firms. **Bank borrowing** varies greatly and **new share or bond issues** account for a minority of the funds needed for corporate growth.

- The **Official List (OL)** is the most heavily regulated UK exchange.

- The **Alternative Investment Market (AIM)** is the lightly regulated exchange designed for small, young companies.

- **techMARK** is the sector of the Official List focused on technology-led companies. The rules for listing are different for techMARK companies than for other OL companies.

- **Ofex** is an unregulated market.

- Stock exchanges undertake most or all of the following **tasks** to play their role in a modern society:
  - supervise trading;
  - authorise market participants (e.g. brokers, marketmakers);
  - assist price formation;
  - clear and settle transactions;
  - regulate the admission of companies to and companies on the exchange;
  - disseminate information.

- A **quote-driven** share trading system is one in which **marketmakers** quote a bid and an offer price for shares. An **order-driven** system is one in which investors' buy and sell orders are matched without the intermediation of marketmakers.

- The **ownership of quoted shares** has shifted from dominance by individual shareholders in the 1960s to dominance by institutions, particularly pension and insurance funds. This trend has been encouraged by the tax system and the recognition of the advantages of pooled investment vehicles, for example diversification and skilled investment management.

■ **High-quality regulation** generates confidence in the financial markets and encourages the flow of savings into investment.

■ The **Financial Services Authority** is at the centre of UK financial regulation. **Self-Regulatory Organisations** (SROs) supervise the activities of financial businesses. There are two **Recognised Investment Exchanges** (RIEs) trading shares in the UK – the London Stock Exchange and Virt-x.

■ **Dividend yield:**

$$\frac{\text{Dividend per share}}{\text{Share price}} \times 100$$

■ **Price-earnings ratio (PER):**

$$\frac{\text{Share price}}{\text{Earnings per share}}$$

■ **Dividend cover:**

$$\frac{\text{Earnings per share}}{\text{Dividend per share}}$$

■ **Taxation** impacts on financial decisions in at least three ways:
  – capital allowances;
  – selecting type of finance;
  – corporation tax.

REFERENCES AND FURTHER READING

Brett, M. (2000) *How to Read the Financial Pages.* 5th edn. London: Random House Business Books. An easy to read jargon-buster. Chapter 6 is particularly relevant.

Buckle, M. and Thompson, J. (1995) *The UK Financial System: Theory and Practice.* Manchester: Manchester University Press. Well written, succinct and clear account of the City.

Levine, R. and Zervos, S. (1996a) 'Capital control liberalisation and stock market development', *World Bank Policy Research Working Paper* No. 1622. World Bank. Some useful data.

Levine, R. and Zervos, S. (1996b) 'Stock markets, banks and economic growth', *World Bank Policy Research Working Paper*, World Bank. Background information with a worldwide perspective.

London Stock Exchange Annual Report. An excellent overview of the role and activities of the LSE. Great graphics and illustrations.

London Stock Exchange Fact File. (Annual.) This superbly produced book contains a wealth of useful information.

London Stock Exchange Publicity. A quarterly newsletter focused on AIM and techMARK.

London Stock Exchange quarterly magazine. Discusses recent events.

Vaitilingam, R. (2001) *The Financial Times Guide to Using the Financial Pages.* 4th edn. London: FT Prentice Hall. Excellent introduction to the mysteries of the financial pages.

Valdez, S. (2000) *An Introduction to Global Financial Markets.* 3rd edn. London: Macmillan Business. Chapter 7 discusses, in an easy to read fashion, many of the topics covered in this chapter.

WEBSITES

Companies House
  www.companieshouse.gov.uk

CREST www.crestco.co.uk

Financial Services Authority www.FSA.gov.uk

Financial Times www.ft.com

FTSE International www.ftse.com

Hemmington Scott www.hemscott.net

International Federation of Stock Exchanges
  www.FIBV.com

Investors Chronicle
  www.investorschronicle.co.uk

London Clearing House www.lch.co.uk

London Stock Exchange
  www.londonstockexchange.com

Morgan Stanley Capital www.MSCI.com

NASDAQ www.nasdaq.com

New York Stock Exchange www.nyse.com

OFEX www.ofex.co.uk

Office of National Statistics
  www.statistics.gov.uk

Proshare www.proshare.org

SELF-REVIEW QUESTIONS

1   Name the largest (by volume of share turnover on the secondary market) share exchanges in the USA, Europe and Asia.

2   What is SEAQI?

3   What is a depositary receipt and why are they created?

4   Explain why finance has been 'globalised' over the last 20 years.

5   What are the characteristics of, and who benefits from, a well-run exchange?

6   What securities, other than shares, are traded on the London Stock Exchange?

7   Why is a healthy secondary market good for the primary share market?

8   Explain the acronyms AIM, NASDAQ, SEAQ, OL, IMRO, SFA, PIA, SRO, RIE and FSA.

9   Does the origin of long-term finance for firms remain stable over time? If not, how does it change?

10 Why has it been necessary to have more share exchanges than simply the Official List in the UK?

11 Why is a nominated adviser appointed to a firm wishing to join AIM?

12 Why might you be more cautious about investing in a company listed by J.P. Jenkins on Ofex, than a company on the Official List of the London Stock Exchange?

13 What is SEATS plus?

14 What is CREST?

15 What have been the main trends in UK share ownership over the past 30 years?

16 Explain the following: FTSE 100, FT All-Share, FTSE Fledgling.

QUESTIONS AND PROBLEMS

1 'Stock markets are capitalist exploitative devices giving no benefit to ordinary people.' Write an essay countering this argument.

2 Describe what a badly run stock exchange would be like and explain how society would be poorer as a result.

3 Many countries, for example Peru and Germany, are encouraging small investors to buy quoted shares. Why are they doing this?

4 Explain why firms obtain a share listing in countries other than their own.

5 Describe the trading systems of the London Stock Exchange and outline the advantages and disadvantages of the alternative methods of trading shares.

6 In the USA some firms have completely bypassed the formal stock exchanges and have sold their shares directly to investors over the internet (e.g. Spring Street Brewing). What advantages are there to this method of raising funds compared with a regulated exchange? What are the disadvantages, for firms and shareholders?

7 Discuss some of the consequences you believe might follow from the shift in UK share ownership over the past 30 years.

8 Describe the network of controls and restraints on the UK financial system to prevent fraud, abuse, negligence, etc. Do you regard this system as preferable to a statutorily controlled system? Explain your answer.

9 Frame-up plc is considering a flotation on the Official List of the London Stock Exchange. The managing director has asked you to produce a 1,000-word report explaining the advantages of such a move.

10 Collasus plc is quoted on the London Stock Exchange. It is a large conglomerate with factories and sales operations in every continent. Why might Collasus wish to consider obtaining additional quotations in other countries?

11 'The City is still far too clubby and gentlemanly. They are not rigorous enough in rooting out wrongdoing. What we need is an American type of system where the government takes a lead in setting all the detailed rules of behaviour.' Consider the advantages and disadvantages of a self-regulatory system so decried by this speaker.

ASSIGNMENTS

1 Carry out a comparative study in your firm (or any quoted firm) using information provided by the *Financial Times*. Compare PERs, dividend yields, dividend cover and other key factors, with a peer group of firms and the stock market as a whole. Try to explain the differences.

2 If your firm has made use of the stock market for any reason, put together a report to explain the benefits gained and some estimate of the costs of membership.

CHAPTER NOTES

1 The first limited liability law was introduced in the USA in 1811.

2 BT delisted from the Tokyo Stock Exchange in 2001 as only a small proportion of its shares were held there.

Chapter 11

LONG-TERM DEBT FINANCE

INTRODUCTION

The concept of borrowing money to invest in real assets within a business is a straightforward one, yet in the sophisticated capital markets of today with their wide variety of financial instruments and forms of debt, the borrowing decision can be a bewildering one. Should the firm tap the domestic bond market or the Eurobond market? Would bank borrowing be best? If so, on what terms, fixed or floating rate interest, a term loan or a mortgage? And what about syndicated lending, mezzanine finance and high-yield bonds? The variety of methods of borrowing long-term finance is infinite. This chapter will outline the major categories and illustrate some of the fundamental issues a firm may consider when selecting its finance mix. As you can see from the extract from the annual accounts of Boots plc (Exhibit 11.1) a firm may need knowledge and understanding of a great many different debt instruments. The terms bonds, notes, commercial paper and Eurobond mentioned in the extract are explained in this chapter. Lease finance and overdrafts are examined in Chapter 12. Swaps are discussed in Chapter 21.

Learning objectives

An understanding of the key characteristics of the main categories of debt finance is essential to anyone considering the financing decisions of the firm. At the end of this chapter the reader will be able to:

- explain the nature and the main types of bonds, their pricing and their valuation;
- describe the main considerations for a firm when borrowing from banks;
- give a considered view of the role of mezzanine and high-yield bond financing as well as convertible bonds, sale and leaseback, securitisation and project finance;
- demonstrate an understanding of the value of the international debt markets;
- explain the term structure of interest rates and the reasons for its existence.

Exhibit 11.1 Loans and other borrowings for Boots plc

Borrowings	Notes	Group 2000 £m
Bank loans and overdrafts repayable on demand		103.1
Other bank loans and overdrafts	a	161.3
Variable rate notes – Sterling	b	11.8
– Irish punts	b	10.5
Commercial paper		–
10.125% bond 2017	c	47.6
5.5% eurobond 2009	d	300.0
Net liability under currency swaps	e	8.4
Obligations under finance leases		17.1
		659.8
Amounts included above repayable by instalments		187.4
Repayments fall due as follows:		
Within one year:		
– Bank loans and overdrafts		149.4
– Obligations under finance leases		6.9
– Other borrowings		54.5
		210.8
After more than one year:		
– Within one to two years		45.1
– Within two to five years		68.7
– After five years		335.2
		449.0
		659.8

Source: *The Boots Company Report and Accounts for the year ended 31st March 2000.*

SOME FUNDAMENTAL FEATURES OF DEBT FINANCE

Put at its simplest, debt is something that has to be repaid. Corporate debt repayments have taken the form of interest and capital payments as well as more exotic compensations such as commodities and shares. The usual method is a combination of a regular interest, with capital (principal) repayments either spread over a period or given as a lump sum at the end of the borrowing. Debt finance is less expensive than equity finance, not only because the costs of raising the funds (for example arrangement fees with a bank or the issue costs of a bond) are lower, but because the annual return required to attract investors is less than for equity. This is because investors recognise that investing in a firm via debt finance is less risky than investing via shares. It is less risky because interest is paid out before dividends are paid so there is greater certainty of receiving a return than there would be for equity holders. Also, if the firm goes into liquidation, the holders of a debt type of financial security are paid back before share-holders receive anything.

Offsetting these plus-points for debt are the facts that lenders do not, generally, share in the value created by an extraordinarily successful business and there is an absence of voting power – although debt holders are able to protect their position to some extent through rigorous lending agreements.

When a company pays interest the tax authorities regard this as a cost of doing business and therefore it can be used to reduce the taxable profit. This lowers the effective cost to the firm of servicing the debt compared with servicing equity capital through dividends which are not tax deductible (see Chapters 9 and 10). Thus to the attractions of the low required return on debt we must add the benefit of tax deductibility.

There are dangers associated with raising funds through debt instruments. Creditors are often able to claim some or all of the assets of the firm in the event of non-compliance with the terms of the loan. This may result in liquidation. Institutions which provide debt finance often try to minimise the risk of not receiving interest and their original capital. They do this by first of all looking to the earning ability of the firm, that is, the pre-interest profits in the years over the period of the loan. As a back-up they often require that the loan be secured against assets owned by the business, so that if the firm is unable to pay interest and capital from profits the lender can force the sale of the assets to receive their legal entitlement. The matter of security has to be thought about carefully before a firm borrows capital. It could be very inconvenient for the firm to grant a bank a fixed charge on a specific asset – say a particular building – because the firm is then limiting its future flexibility to use its assets as it wishes. For instance, it will not be able to sell that building, or even rent it without the consent of the bank or the bondholders.

BONDS

A bond is a long-term contract in which the bondholders lend money to a company. In return the company (usually) promises to pay the bond owners a series of interest payments, known as coupons, until the bond matures. At maturity the bondholder receives a specified principal sum called the par, face or nominal value of the bond. This is usually £100 in the UK and $1,000 in the USA. The time to maturity is generally between seven and 30 years although a number of firms, for example Disney, IBM and Reliance of India, have issued 100-year bonds.

Bonds may be regarded as merely IOUs (I owe you) with pages of legal clauses expressing the promises made. These IOUs can usually be traded in the secondary market through securities dealers on the Stock Exchange so that the investor who originally provided the firm with money does not have to hold on to the bond until the maturity date (the redemption date). The amount the investor receives in the secondary market might be more or less than what he paid. For instance, imagine an investor paid £99.80 for a bond which promised to pay a coupon of 9 per cent per year on a par value of £100 and to repay the par value in seven years. If one year after issue interest rates on similar bonds are 20 per cent per annum no one will pay £99.80 for a bond agreement offering £9 per year for a further six years plus £100 on the redemption date. We will look at a method for calculating exactly how much they might be willing to pay later in the chapter.

These negotiable (that is tradeable in a secondary market) instruments come in a variety of forms. The most common is the type described above with regular (usually semi-annual) fixed coupons and a specified redemption date. These are known as straight, plain vanilla or bullet bonds. Other bonds are a variation on this. Some pay coupons every three months, some pay no coupons at all (called zero coupon bonds – these are sold at a large discount to the par value and the investor makes a capital gain by holding the bond), some bonds do not pay a fixed coupon but one which varies depending on the level of short-term interest rates (floating-rate or variable-rate bonds), some have interest rates linked to the rate of inflation. In fact, the potential for variety and innovation is almost infinite. Bonds issued in the last few years have linked the interest rates paid or the principal payments to a wide variety of economic events, such as the price of silver, exchange-rate movements, stock market indices, the price of oil, gold, copper – even to the occurrence of an earthquake. These bonds were generally designed to let companies adjust their interest payments to manageable levels in the event of the firm being adversely affected by some economic variable changing. For example, a copper miner pays lower interest on its finance if the copper price falls. In 1999 Sampdoria, the Italian football club, issued a €3.5m bond that paid a higher rate of return if the club won promotion to the 'Serie A' division. If the club rose to the top four in Serie A the coupon would rise to 14 per cent.

Debentures and loan stocks

The most secured type of bond is called a debenture. They are usually secured by either a fixed or a floating charge against the firm's assets. A fixed charge means that specific assets are used as security which, in the event of default, can be sold at the insistence of the debenture bondholder and the proceeds used to repay them. Debentures secured on property may be referred to as mortgage debentures. A floating charge means that the loan is secured by a general charge on all the assets of the corporation. In this case the company has a large degree of freedom to use its assets as it wishes, such as sell them or rent them out, until it commits a default which 'crystallises' the floating charge. If this happens a receiver will be appointed with powers to dispose of assets and to distribute the proceeds to the creditors. Even though floating-charge debenture holders can force a liquidation, fixed-charge debenture holders rank above floating-charge debenture holders in the payout after insolvency.

The terms bond, debenture and loan stock are often used interchangeably and the dividing line between debentures and loan stock is a fuzzy one. As a general rule debentures are secured and loan stock is unsecured but there are examples which do not fit this classification. If liquidation occurs the unsecured loan stockholders rank beneath the debenture holders and some other categories of creditors such as the tax authorities. In the USA the definitions are somewhat different and this can be confusing. There a debenture is an unsecured bond and so the holders become general creditors who can only claim assets not otherwise pledged. In the USA the secured form of bond is referred to as the mortgage bond and unsecured shorter-dated issues (less than 15 years) are called notes.

Trust deeds and covenants

Bond investors are willing to lower the interest they demand if they can be reassured that their money will not be exposed to a high risk. This reassurance is conveyed by placing risk-reducing restrictions on the firm. A trust deed sets out the terms of the contract between bondholders and the company. The trustees ensure compliance with the contract throughout the life of the bond and have the power to appoint a receiver. The loan agreement will contain a number of affirmative covenants. These usually include the requirements to supply regular financial statements, interest and principal payments. The deed may also state the fees due to the lenders and details of what procedures are to be followed in the event of a technical default, for example non-payment of interest.

In addition to these basic covenants are the negative covenants. These restrict the actions and the rights of the borrower until the debt has been repaid in full. Some examples are as follows.

■ *Limits on further debt issuance* If lenders provide finance to a firm they do so on certain assumptions concerning the riskiness of the capital structure. They will want to ensure that the loan does not become more risky due to the firm taking on a much greater debt burden relative to its equity base, so they limit the amount and type of further debt issues – particularly debt which is higher (superior) ranking for interest payments and for a liquidation payment. Subordinated debt – with low ranking on liquidation – is more likely to be acceptable.

■ *Dividend level* Lenders are opposed to money being taken into the firm by borrowing at one end, while being taken away by shareholders at the other. An excessive withdrawal of shareholder funds may unbalance the financial structure and weaken future cash flows.

■ *Limits on the disposal of assets* The retention of certain assets, for example property and land, may be essential to reduce the lenders' risk.

■ *Financial ratios* A typical covenant here concerns the interest cover, for example: 'The annual pre-interest pre-tax profit will remain four times as great as the overall annual interest charge'. Other restrictions might be placed on working capital ratio levels, and the debt to net assets ratio. In the case of Photobition the interest cover threshold is 3.25 – *see* Exhibit 11.2.

Exhibit 11.2

Photobition cautions on covenants

Photobition, the Surrey-based graphics business, admitted yesterday it could breach banking covenants over the level of its interest cover if US advertising spending continued to slow down.

The company, which also reported a sharp fall in half-year profits, said net debt has risen to £103.5m (£77.3m) after a number of US acquisitions . . .

Analysts forecast that cover might fall to 2.43 times at the year-end in June, below the required minimum of 3.25.

'If they breach the bank covenants, they will be at the mercy of debt holders,' said one analyst. 'They could have to renegotiate their debt, or make some form of debt-equity conversion. They might also resort to a rights issue.'

Source: Florian Gimbel, *Financial Times*, 28 February 2001, p. 28. Reprinted with permission.

While negative covenants cannot provide completely risk-free lending they can influence the behaviour of the management team so as to reduce the risk of default. The lenders' risk can be further reduced by obtaining guarantees from third parties (for example guaranteed loan stock). The guarantor is typically the parent company of the issuer.

Despite a raft of safeguards the fact that bondholders are still exposed to some degree of risk was brought home painfully to the bondholders in Barings Bank in 1996. They had lent £100m on the understanding that the money would be used for standard merchant banking activities. When they lost their entire investment due to the extraordinary activities of Nick Leeson in the derivatives markets (*see* Chapter 21) their response was to issue writs for compensation from three stockbrokers and a dozen former Barings directors, claiming that misleading information was given about Barings' business when in January 1994 the bond issue was launched.

Repayments

The principal on many bonds is paid entirely at maturity. However, there are bonds which can be repaid before the final redemption date. One way of paying for redemption is to set up a sinking fund that receives regular sums from the firm which will be sufficient, with added interest, to redeem the bonds. A common approach is for the company to issue bonds where it has a range of dates for redemption; so a bond dated 2004–2008 would allow a company the flexibility to repay a part of the principal in cash in each of the four years. Another way of redeeming bonds is for the issuing firm to buy the outstanding bonds by offering the holder a sum higher than or equal to the amount originally paid. A firm is also able to purchase bonds on the open market.

Some bonds are described as 'irredeemable' as they have no fixed redemption date. From the investor's viewpoint they may be irredeemable but the firm has the option of repurchase and can effectively redeem the bonds.

Bond variations

Bonds which are sold at well below the par value are called deep discounted bonds, the most extreme form of which is the zero coupon bond. It is easy to calculate the rate of return offered to an investor on this type of bond. For example, if a company issues a bond at a price of £60 which is redeemable at £100 in eight years the annualised rate of return (r) is:

$$60(1 + r)^8 = 100$$

$$r = \sqrt[8]{\frac{100}{60}} - 1 = 0.066 \text{ or } 6.6\%$$

These bonds are particularly useful for firms with low cash flows in the near term, for example firms engaged in a major property development which will not mature for many years.

A major market has developed recently called the floating rate note (FRN) market (also called the variable-rate note market). Two factors have led to the rapid growth in FRN usage. First, the oscillating and unpredictable inflation of the 1970s and early 1980s caused many investors to make large real-term losses on fixed-rate bonds as the interest rate fell below the inflation rate. As a result many lenders became reluctant to lend at fixed rates on a long-term basis. Secondly, a number of corporations, especially financial institutions, hold assets which give a return that varies with the short-term interest rate level (for example bank loans and overdrafts) and so prefer to hold a similar floating-rate liability. These instruments pay an interest that is linked to a benchmark rate – such as the LIBOR (London Inter-Bank Offered Rate – the rate that banks charge each other for borrowed funds). The issuer will pay, say, 70 basis points (0.7 of a percentage point) over LIBOR. The coupon is set for (say) the first six months at the time of issue, after which it is adjusted every six months; so if LIBOR was 10 per cent, the FRN would pay 10.7 per cent for that particular six months.

There are many other variations on the basic vanilla bond, two of which will be examined later – high-yield bonds and convertible bonds. We now turn to another major source of long-term debt capital – bank borrowing.

BANK BORROWING

An alternative to going to the capital markets to raise money via a public bond issue or a private bond placement is to borrow directly from a bank. In this case a tradeable security is not issued. The bank makes the loan from its own resources and over time the borrowing company repays the bank with interest. Borrowing from banks is attractive to companies for the following reasons.

- *Administrative and legal costs are low* Because the loan arises from direct negotiation between borrower and lender there is an avoidance of the marketing, arrangement, regulatory and underwriting expenses involved in a bond issue.

- *Quick* The key provisions of a bank loan can be worked out speedily and the funding facility can be in place within a matter of hours.

- *Flexibility* If the economic circumstances facing the firm should change during the life of the loan banks are generally better equipped – and are more willing – to alter the terms of the lending agreement than bondholders. Negotiating with a single lender in a crisis has distinct advantages.

- *Available to small firms* Bank loans are available to firms of almost any size whereas the bond market is for the big players only.

Factors for a firm to consider

There are a number of issues a firm needs to address when considering bank borrowing.

Costs

The borrower may be required to pay an arrangement fee, say 1 per cent of the loan, at the time of the initial lending, but this is subject to negotiation. The interest rate can be either fixed or floating. If it is floating then the rate will generally be a certain percentage above the banks' base rate or LIBOR. For customers in a good bargaining position this may be 1 or 2 per cent 'over base'. For customers in a poorer bargaining position offering a higher risk proposal the rate could be 5 per cent or more over the base rate. The interest rate will be determined not only by the riskiness of the undertaking and the bargaining strength of the customer but also by the degree of security for the loan and the size of loan – economies of scale in lending mean that large borrowers pay a lower interest rate. A generation ago it would have been more normal to negotiate fixed-rate loans but sharp movements of interest rates in the 1970s and 1980s meant that banks and borrowers were less willing to make this type of long-term commitment. Most loans today are 'variable rate'.

Floating-rate borrowings have advantages for the firm over fixed-rate borrowings.

■ If interest rates fall the cost of the loan falls.
■ At the time of arrangement fixed rates are usually above floating rates (to allow for lenders' risk of misforecasting future interest rates).
■ Returns on the firm's assets may be positively related to times when higher interest rates reign therefore the risk of higher rates is offset.

However floating rates have some disadvantages.

■ The firm may be caught out by a rise in interest rates.
■ There will be uncertainty about the precise cash outflow impact of the interest.

Security

When banks are considering the provision of debt finance for a firm they will be concerned about the borrower's competence and honesty. They need to evaluate the proposed project and assess the degree of managerial commitment to its success. The firm will have to explain why the funds are needed and provide detailed cash forecasts covering the period of the loan. Between the bank and the firm stands the classic gulf called 'asymmetric information' in which one party in the negotiation is ignorant of, or cannot observe, some of the information which is essential to the contracting and decision-making process. The bank is unable to accurately assess the ability and determination of the managerial team and will not have a complete understanding of the market environment in which they propose to operate. Companies may overcome bank uncertainty to some degree by providing as much information as possible at the outset and keeping the bank informed of the firm's position as the project progresses.

The finance director and managing director need to consider both the quantity and quality of information flows to the bank. An improved flow of information can lead to a better and more supportive relationship. Any firm which has significant bank financing requirements to fund growth will be well advised to cultivate and strengthen understanding and rapport with its bank(s). The time to lay the foundations for subsequent borrowing is when the business does not need the money so that when loans are required there is a reasonable chance of being able to borrow the amount needed on acceptable terms.

Another way for a bank to reduce its risk is to ensure that the firm offers sufficient collateral for the loan. Collateral provides a means of recovering all or the majority of the bank's investment should the firm fail. If the firm is unable to meet its loan obligations then holders of fixed-charge collateral can seize the specific asset used to back the loan. Also, on liquidation, the proceeds of selling assets will go first to the secured loan holders, including floating-charge bank lenders. Collateral can include stocks, debtors and equipment as well as land, buildings and marketable investments such as shares in other companies. In theory banks often have this strong right to seize assets or begin proceedings to liquidate. In practice they are reluctant to use these powers because the realisation of full value from an asset used as security is sometimes difficult and such Draconian action can bring adverse publicity. Banks are careful to create a margin for error in the assignment of sufficient collateral to cover the loan because, in the event of default, assigned assets usually command a much lower price than their value to the company as a going concern. A quick sale at auction produces bargains for the buyers of liquidated assets and usually little for the creditors.

Another safety feature applied by banks is the requirement that the firm abide by a number of loan covenants which place restrictions on managerial action in a similar fashion to bond covenants (*see* section on bonds earlier in this chapter).

Finally, lenders can turn to the directors of the firm to provide additional security. They might be asked to sign personal guarantees that the firm will not default. Personal assets (such as homes) may be used as collateral. This erodes the principle of limited liability status and is likely to inhibit risk-taking productive activity. However for many smaller firms it is the only way of securing a loan and at least it demonstrates the commitment of the director to the success of the enterprise.

Repayment

A firm must carefully consider the period of the loan and the repayment schedules in the light of its future cash flows. It could be disastrous, for instance, for a firm engaging in a capital project which involved large outlays for the next five years followed by cash inflows thereafter to have a bank loan which required significant interest and principal payments in the near term. For situations like these repayment holidays or grace periods may be granted, with the majority of the repayment being made once cash flows are sufficiently positive.

It may be possible for a company to borrow by means of a mortgage on freehold property in which repayments of principal plus interest may be spread over long periods of time. The rate charged will be a small margin over the base interest rate or LIBOR. The main advantage of a mortgage is that ownership of the property remains with the mortgagee (the borrowing firm) and therefore the benefits which come from the ownership of an asset, which may appreciate, are not lost.

A term loan is a business loan with an original maturity of more than one year and a specified schedule of principal and interest payments. It may or may not be secured and has the advantage over the overdraft of not being repayable at the demand of the bank at short notice (*see* Chapter 12). The terms of the loan are usually tailored to the specific needs of the individual borrower and these are capable of wide variation. A proportion of the interest and the principal can be repaid monthly or annually and can be varied to correspond with the borrower's cash flows. It is rare for there to be no repayment of the principal during the life of the loan but it is possible to request that the bulk of the principal is paid in the later years. Banks generally prefer self-amortising term loans with a high proportion of the principal paid off each year. This has the advantage of reducing risk by imposing a programme of debt reduction on the borrowing firm.

The repayment schedule agreed between bank and borrower is capable of infinite variety – four possibilities are shown in Exhibit 11.3.

Exhibit 11.3 Example of loan repayment arrangements

£10,000 borrowed, repayable over four years with interest at 10% p.a. (assuming annual payments, not monthly)

(a) Time period (years)	1	2	3	4
Payment (£)	3,155	3,155	3,155	3,155
(b) Time period (years)	1	2	3	4
Payment (£)	1,000	1,000	1,000	11,000
(c) Time period (years)	1	2	3	4
Payment (£)	0	0	0	14,641
(d) Time period (years)	1	2	3	4
Payment (£)	0	1,000	6,000	6,831

The retail and merchant banks are not the only sources of long-term loans. Insurance companies and other specialist institutions such as 3i will also provide long-term debt finance.

SYNDICATED LOANS

For large loans a single bank may not be able or willing to lend the whole amount. To do so would be to expose the bank to an unacceptable risk of failure on the part of one of its borrowers. Bankers like to spread their lending to gain the risk-reducing benefits of diversification. They prefer to participate in a number of syndicated loans in which a few banks each contribute a portion of the overall loan. So, for a large multinational company loan of, say, £500m, a single bank may provide £30m, with perhaps 100 other banks contributing the remainder. The bank originating the loan will usually manage the syndicate and is called the lead manager (there might be one or more lead banks). This bank (or these banks) may invite a handful of other banks to co-manage and underwrite the loan. They help the process of forming the syndicate group of banks in the general syndication. Syndicated loans are available at short notice and can be provided discreetly (helpful if the money is to finance a merger bid, for example). Syndicated loans generally offer lower returns than bonds, but as they rank above most bonds on liquidation payouts there is less risk. The loans carry covenants similar to those on bond agreements. The volume of new international syndicated loans now runs into hundreds of billions of pounds per year.

Pearson needed $6bn of bank loans to finance its purchase of Simon & Schuster in 1998; this is far too much for any one bank to provide. So Goldman Sachs and HSBC put together a syndicated loan package involving a number of banks – *see* Exhibit 11.4. A revolving credit facility gives Pearson the right to draw down short-term loans up to a maximum of $2bn as and when the need arises – this it can do at a number of points over a five-year period. Note that the loans are expected to be tradeable (bought and sold) in a secondary market so banks can sell off some of their loans if they wish to.

Exhibit 11.4

Pearson signs up facility to finance US acquisition

Pearson, the UK media group which owns the *Financial Times*, has signed up $6bn of bank facilities to finance its acquisition of Simon & Schuster, the US publisher, and refinance outstanding syndicated loans. It is the latest in a line of substantial acquisitions to be financed through the syndicated loan market, following Texas Utilities' recent $11bn loan to fund its purchase of The Energy Group and jumbo loans from Imperial Chemical Industries and BAT Industries.

The new financing package has been put together by Goldman Sachs and HSBC and includes a $2.5bn five-year term loan, a $2bn five-year revolving credit and a $1.5bn 364-day loan. Investors expect the loans to be tradeable. This has become commonplace in the US but was only introduced to the euroloan market last year with the $8.5bn loan to ICI to finance its acquisition of Unilever's speciality chemicals business.

There has been considerable reluctance by European corporates to have bankers trading out of loans. The *quid pro quo*, in theory, is more attractive financing. Details of the terms of the loan were not available yesterday. A broader underwriting group will be put together in the next 10 days.

Pearson's credit rating from Standard & Poor's, the rating agency, has been put on negative outlook as a result of the acquisition, but its shares rose sharply yesterday.

Source: Simon Davies, *Financial Times*, 19 May 1998, p. 40. Reprinted with permission.

CREDIT RATING

Firms often pay to have their bonds rated by specialist credit-rating organisations. The debt rating depends on the likelihood of payments of interest and/or capital not being paid (that is, default) and on the extent to which the lender is protected in the event of a default by the loan contract (the recoverability of the debt). UK government gilts have an insignificant risk of default whereas unsecured subordinated corporate loan stock has a much higher risk. We would expect that firms which are in stable industries and have conservative accounting and financing policies and a risk-averse business strategy would have a low risk of default and therefore a high credit rating. Companies with a high total debt burden, a poor cash flow position, in a worsening market environment causing lower and more volatile earnings, will have a high default risk and a low credit rating. Several organisations provide credit ratings, including Moody's and Standard & Poor's (S&P) based in the USA and Fitch IBCA in Europe (owned by a French company). The highest rating is AAA or Aaa (triple-A rated). Such a rating indicates very high quality. The capacity to repay interest and principal is extremely strong. Single A indicates a strong capacity to pay interest and capital but there is some degree of susceptibility to impairment as economic events unfold. BBB indicates adequate debt service capacity but vulnerability to adverse economic conditions or changing circumstances. B and C rated debt has predominantly speculative characteristics. The lowest is D which indicates the firm is in default. Ratings of BBB– (or Baa3 for Moody's) or above are regarded as 'investment grade' – this is important because many institutional investors are permitted to invest in investment grade bonds only (*see* Exhibit 11.5). Bonds rated below this are called high-yield (or junk) bonds. The specific loan is rated rather than

Exhibit 11.5 A comparison of Moody's and Standard & Poor's rating scales

Standard & Poor's	Moody's	Comments
AAA	Aaa	
AA+	Aa1	
AA	Aa2	
AA–	Aa3	
A+	A1	
A	A2	Investment grade bonds
A–	A3	
BBB+	Baa1	
BBB	Baa2	
BBB–	Baa3	
BB+	Ba1	
BB	Ba2	
BB–	Ba3	
B+	B1	
B	B2	
B–	B3	Non-investment grade high-yield 'junk' bonds
CCC+	Caa1	
CCC	Caa2	
CCC–	Caa3	
CC	Ca	
C	C	

the borrower. If the loan does not have a rating it could be that the borrower has not paid for one, rather than implying anything sinister. Plus or minus signs, '+' or '−', may be appended to a rating to denote relative status within major rating categories.

The rating and re-rating of bonds is followed with great interest by borrowers and lenders and can give rise to some heated argument – *see* Exhibit 11.6.

Exhibit 11.6

UPC slams Moody's debt downgrade

UPC, the European cable communications company, on Friday strongly disputed a downgrade in its debt rating, but investor worries over its funding brought falls in its share and bond prices . . .

The agency downgraded its senior notes, already carrying junk-bond status at B2, to Caa1 and said the outlook for the rating remained negative. The move affects $8.4bn of UPC debt.

Mark Schneider, UPC chairman, said: 'We are very disappointed, and fundamentally disagree with this analysis.' The company continued to meet all its financial targets, he maintained, and had 'significant liquidity in place' to fund its operations.

He added that the rating revision would not affect either its interest bill or other terms of its existing credit facilities. UPC shares, down 13 per cent at one stage, rallied to close 2.2 per cent lower at €6.32 on Friday. However, they remain below their flotation level of two years ago.

UPC's euro-denominated bonds reacted immediately to the downgrade, falling 9 points on Friday to approximately 55 per cent of their face value. Traders said prices then rose towards the end of the day, to around 60 per cent of face value.

UPC's bonds have been trading at relatively low levels for many months, reflecting worries about the company's credit quality. Analysts said the bond market had expected a downgrade, but not one as aggressive as Moody's announced.

Source: Gordon Cramb, *Financial Times*, 23 April 2001, p. 31. Reprinted with permission.

Credit ratings are of great concern to the borrowing corporation because bonds with lower ratings tend to have higher costs. Even enormous telecommunication concerns can run into difficulties and increase the risk for their lenders – *see* Exhibit 11.7. Examples of ratings on long-term instruments are given in Exhibit 11.8.

Exhibit 11.7

Credit rating agencies show their teeth
Recent telecoms downgradings highlight more aggressive stance

Downgradings of the credit ratings of European telecommunications operators in the past six months has brought the work of Fitch, Moody's Investors Service and Standard & Poor's to the attention of a wider spectrum of spectators.

While fuelling demands for an insight into the agencies' inner workings and rating procedures, the downgradings have highlighted their shift towards a more aggressive ratings stance.

During the emerging market crisis of 1997/98, rating agencies were accused of being too slow to spot risks and were urged by the International Monetary Fund and others to change the way they rated countries.

Similar accusations were levelled last year about companies in the European telecoms sector, which took on tens of billions of new debt

Exhibit 11.7 continued

to pay the €100bn bill for acquiring third generation mobile phone licences in Europe.

But Chris Legge, head of corporate ratings at S&P, denies that agencies were not quick enough to downgrade telecoms companies during 2000.

'The two key elements of our work are to be right and to be early, but not necessarily to be first,' Mr Legge says . . .

Last September, Moody's downgraded companies including KPN and France Telecom and said it would give them 12–18 months to reduce their debt in line with their new ratings.

Soon after, equity markets became more hostile to telecoms companies and sensitive to their growing debt burdens, and the prospects of raising cash through asset disposals and initial public offerings receded.

After Orange's disappointing IPO, the rating agencies felt they could not wait any longer.

Further cuts from Fitch, Moody's and S&P have followed in the past few weeks, in some cases surprising the debt and equity markets.

When earlier this month Moody's cut France Telecoms rating just two days after assigning it a stable outlook, investors and bankers were angry that they were not given a warning.

Moody's say the cut was prompted by extra information from France Telecom but that the nature of the information had to be kept confidential . . .

The incident has led to accusations of opaqueness.

Although they pride themselves on their impartiality, agencies derive most of their income from the companies they rate. They frown on the practice of giving unsolicited ratings and depend on the fact that companies need to be rated to borrow in the corporate bond market.

Initial ratings are available for a standard cost in the region of €45,000. After that the cost of rat-

ings coverage depends on its size.

One issue of concern to investors is the extent to which agency analysts are subject to intense pressure from companies to accept their version of events.

In the telecoms industry, company chairman and chief executives have been the ones telling ratings analysts their strategies.

'Rating agencies are subject to a powerful lobby from the companies they rate, which needs to be taken into account,' says Mark Wauton, executive director of fixed income at UBS Asset Management.

However many investors feel ratings only exist as a guide, and fund managers should be able to do their own analysis. 'Rating agencies can be wrong, and fund managers are paid to make up their own minds and spot investment opportunities,' says Marino Valensise at Baring Asset Management.

Source: Aline van Duyn and Rebecca Bream, *Financial Times*, 27 February 2001, p. 34. Reprinted with permission.

Long-term credit ratings history

BT	S&P	Moody's	Deutsche Telekom	S&P	Moody's
Feb 2000	AA plus	Aa1	Feb 2000	AA minus	Aa2
Apr 24 2000	Put on neg watch	–	Apr 28 2000	Put on neg watch	–
May 4 2000	–	Put on neg watch	Jun 22 2000	–	Put on neg watch
Aug 24 2000	Cut to A	–	Oct 5 2000	–	Cut to A2
Sep 6 2000	–	Cut to A2	Oct 6 2000	Cut to A minus*	–
Feb 16 2001	Put on neg watch	–	**KPN**		
France Telecom			Feb 2000	AA, with neg watch	Aa1*
Feb 2000	AAminus	Aa2	May 22 2000	–	Cut to Aa2*
May 30 2000	–	Put on neg watch	Sep 1 2000	Cut to A minus*	–
Aug 23 2000	Cut to A*	–	Sep 7 2000	–	Cut to A3
Sep 18 2000	–	Cut to A1	Dec 13 2000	–	Put on watch
Feb 15 2001	–	Cut to A3	Jan 15 2001	Cut to BBB plus*	–
Feb 16 2001	Cut to A minus	–	Feb 13 2001	–	Cut to Baa2

*With a negative outlook

The ratings in Exhibit 11.8 are for June 2001 and will not necessarily be applicable in future years because the creditworthiness and the specific debt issue can change significantly in a short period. This was illustrated in Exhibit 11.7, which describes the removal of BT's double-A rating to a single A in August 2000. This was to fall to A– in May 2001. In the late 1990s BT had a triple-A rating. As a consequence its cost of borrowing rose considerably, compounding its problems.

Exhibit 11.8 Examples of ratings on long-term instruments in June 2001

	Currency of borrowing	*S&P*	*Moody's*
UK	€	AAA	Aaa
Spain (Kingdom of)	Yen	AA+	Aa2
Wal-Mart	US$	AA	Aa2
Halifax	£	AA	Aa1
Ford	US$	A	A2
GUS	£	A–	A2
Powergen	€	BBB+	A3
News Corp.	US$	BBB–	Baa3
NTL Comms	€	B–	B2
Argentina	US$	B–	Caa1
Jazztel	€	CCC+	Caa1

Source: *Financial Times*, 25 September 2001, p. 33. Reprinted with permission.

Exhibit 11.9 shows the default rates on bonds of different ratings over different time periods. Those bonds below investment grade have a much higher probability of default than high-grade bonds.

Before examining the data on default rates it is important to appreciate that default is a wide-ranging term, and could refer to any number of events from a missed payment to bankruptcy. For some of these events all is lost from the investor's perspective. For other events a very high percentage, if not all, of the interest and principal is recovered. Hickman (1958) observed that defaulted publicly held and traded bonds tended to sell for 40 cents on the dollar. This average recovery rate rule-of-thumb seems to have held over time. Standard & Poor's published a study of the recovery rates on defaulted bond issues in 1999. They obtained prices of defaulted bonds at the end of the default month for 533 S&P-rated straight-debt issues that defaulted between 1 January 1981 and 1 December 1997. Roughly, investors who liquidate a position in defaulted subordinated securities shortly after default can expect to recover, on average, 36–37 cents in the dollar.

Exhibit 11.9 Standard & Poor's average cumulative default rates by rating category (static pool), 1981–98 (percentage of bonds defaulting)

Rating	*After 1 year %*	*After 5 years %*	*After 10 years %*	*After 15 years %*
AAA	0.00	0.15	0.81	0.81
AA	0.00	0.24	0.78	0.87
A	0.04	0.48	1.53	1.98
BBB	0.22	1.75	3.52	4.06
BB	0.92	8.89	14.58	16.01
B	4.82	20.06	26.49	27.23
CCC	20.39	41.29	45.08	45.08
Investment grade	0.08	0.71	1.76	2.11
Speculative grade	3.83	16.08	22.01	23.03

Source: Standard & Poor's (1999) *Ratings Performance 1998: Stability and Transition*, January.

MEZZANINE DEBT AND HIGH-YIELD (JUNK) BONDS

Mezzanine debt is debt offering a high return with a high risk. It may be either unsecured or secured but ranking behind senior loans. This type of debt generally offers interest rates two to nine percentage points more than that on senior debt and frequently gives the lenders some right to a share in equity values should the firm perform well. It is a kind of hybrid finance ranking for payment below straight debt but above equity – it is thus described alternatively as *subordinated*, *intermediate*, or *low grade*. One of the major attractions of this form of finance for the investor is that it often comes with equity warrants (*see* Chapter 10) or share options attached which can be used to obtain shares in the firm – this is known as an 'equity kicker'. These may be triggered by an event such as the firm joining the stock market.

Mezzanine finance tends to be used when bank borrowing limits are reached and the firm cannot or will not issue more equity. The finance it provides is cheaper (in terms of required return) than would be available on the equity market and it allows the owners of a business to raise large sums of money without sacrificing control. It is a form of finance which permits the firm to move beyond what is normally considered acceptable debt : equity ratios (gearing or leverage levels).

Bonds with high-risk and high-return characteristics are called high-yield (junk) bonds (they are rated below investment grade by rating agencies with ratings of Bs and Cs). These may be bonds which started as apparently safe investments but have now become more risky ('fallen angels') or they may be bonds issued specifically to provide higher-risk finance instruments for investors. This latter type began its rise to prominence in the USA in the 1980s. The US junk bond market has grown from almost nothing in the early 1980s to over $120bn of new issues each year. This money has been used to spectacular effect in corporate America – the most outstanding event was the $25bn takeover of RJR Nabisco using primarily junk bonds. The rise of the US junk bond market meant that no business was safe from the threat of takeover, however large – *see* Case study 11.1 on Michael Milken.

CASE STUDY 11.1

The junk bond wizard: Michael Milken

While studying at Wharton Business School in the 1970s Michael Milken came to the belief that the gap in interest rates between safe bonds and high-yield bonds was excessive, given the relative risks. This created an opportunity for financial institutions to make an acceptable return from junk bonds, given their risk level. At the investment banking firm Drexel Burnham Lambert, Milken was able to persuade a large body of institutional investors to supply finance to the junk bond market as well as provide a service to corporations wishing to grow through the use of junk bonds. Small firms were able to raise billions of dollars to take over large US corporations. Many of these issuers of junk bonds had debt ratios of 90 per cent and above – for every $1 of share capital $9 was borrowed. These gearing levels concerned many in the financial markets. It was thought that companies were pushing their luck too far and indeed many did collapse under the weight of their debt. The market was dealt a particularly severe blow when Michael Milken was convicted of fraud, sent to jail and ordered to pay $600m in fines. Drexel was also convicted, paid $650m in fines and filed for bankruptcy in 1990. The junk bond market was in a sorry state in the early 1990s, with high levels of default and few new issues. However it did not take long for the market to recover. In 1993 $69.1bn was raised in junk bond issues and the annual amount raised has stayed well above $40bn since then.

The high-yield bond is much more popular in the USA than in Europe because of the aversion (constrained by legislation) to such instruments in the major financial institutions. The European high-yield bond market is in its infancy. The first high-yield bonds denominated in European currencies were issued as recently as 1997 when Geberit, a Swiss/UK manufacturer, raised DM 157.5m by selling 10-year bonds offering an interest rate which was 423 basis points higher than the interest rate on a 10-year German government bond (bund). Since then there have been over 100 issues. Nevertheless the European high-yield market remains about one-tenth the size of the US one. If the bond issue by Messer Griesheim (*see* Exhibit 11.10) is anything to go by, the European market will one day challenge the American one for leadership.

Exhibit 11.10

Messer Griesheim pulls off record high-yield bond

Messer Griesheim, the German industrial gases group spun off from Aventis has completed the largest ever deal in the European high-yield bond market.

Proceeds from the €550m bond issue will help finance Messer's €1.8bn ($1.57m) leveraged buy-out by Allianz Capital Partners and Goldman Sachs Private Equity in January, one of Europe's biggest buy-outs to date.

Conditions are ripe for new junk bond deals, analysts say, as investors are cash-rich and the flow of new issues has dwindled after a hectic New Year . . .

The bonds were priced at a spread of 548 basis points over German government bonds, a yield of almost 10.4 per cent, and traders said that on Friday they were already trading well above their issue price. The B2/B plus-rated issue was arranged by Goldman Sachs.

Other large European high-yield deals, such as KPN Qwest's €500m issue in January this year, have so far been confined to the telecoms sector and issues from industrial borrowers tend to be small and illiquid. The telecoms sector, having been largely responsible for the market's dismal performance in 2000, remains out of favour with investors.

Source: Rebecca Bream, *Financial Times*, 14 May 2001, p. 28. Reprinted with permission.

Even though the high-yield bond market has not developed as strongly on this side of the Atlantic there has been a rapid growth in mezzanine finance. It has proved to be particularly useful to managers involved in a management buyout (MBO) which by necessity requires high levels of debt, that is, leveraged buyouts (LBOs). A typical LBO would have a financial structure as follows:

■ 60 per cent from senior bank or other debt providers;

■ 25–30 per cent from subordinated debt – for example, mezzanine finance, unsecured low-ranking bonds and/or preference shares;

■ 10–15 per cent equity.

Fast-growing companies also make use of mezzanine finance. It has proved a particularly attractive source for cable television companies, telecommunications and some media businesses which require large investments in the near term but also offer a relatively stable profits flow in the long-term.

Exhibit 11.11 describes the importance of the mezzanine finance market in Europe.

Exhibit 11.11

Flexibility catches eye of investors

FT

Mezzanine investors take higher risks than bond buyers but get higher returns

While bond markets have been buffeted by volatility in recent months, private markets such as mezzanine debt have come into their own and impressed investors with their flexibility.

Mezzanine debt has long been used by mid-cap companies in Europe and the US as a funding alternative to high yield bonds or bank debt. This product ranks between senior bank debt and equity in a company's capital structure, and mezzanine investors take higher risks than bond buyers but are rewarded with equity-like returns . . .

Companies that are too small to tap the bond markets have been the traditional users of mezzanine debt, but it is increasingly being used as part of the financing package for larger leveraged acquisition deals. Although mezzanine has been more expensive for companies to use than junk bonds, the recent spread widening in the high yield debt markets has closed this source of funding and has made mezzanine look better value . . .

'There has been a lot of hype over the past few years about high yield bonds crowding out mezzanine debt, but now the situation is revers-

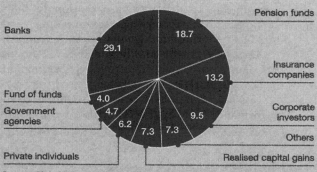

Sources of new funds raised
% (1999)

Source: Global Private Equity 2000

ing,' says Simon Collins, head of debt advisory services at KPMG . . .

The structures of leveraged finance transactions are evolving to cope with with the increased market volatility, and a greater use of mezzanine debt is part of this trend . . .

The characteristics of the mezzanine market make it well-suited to LBO deals – money can be raised quickly and discreetly as companies negotiate directly with mezzanine funds. 'There are inherent advantages to using mezzanine over high yield bonds. It is more flexible, offers better call protection and can be structured specifically for each deal,' says Mark Brunault, executive director at Pricoa.

New investors are being drawn to the European mezzanine market in search of higher returns, as illustrated by the burgeoning number of new funds established this year. In July, Mezzanine Management raised one of the largest independent mezzanine funds in the European market, worth $525m. Its first investment was a $12m mezzanine finance and equity injection into UK media monitoring company Xtreme Information . . .

Many of the funds in the mezzanine market are cash rich, because

of the popularity of the product and due to the current lack of major investment opportunities . . .

Mezzanine fund managers are unlikely to rush into deals, though, having recently been reminded of the risks involved in the mezzanine market. At the start of October Finelist, the car parts distributor that was bought by French rival Autodis in March, went into receivership. The €505m buy-out had been financed with leveraged loans and €275m of mezzanine debt, and had one of the largest deals in the European mezzanine market.

Finelist's collapse was triggered when it broke financial covenants on its debt, and receivers Ernst & Young have since been readying the business for sale and looking into allegations of financial irregularities. While the bank lenders have a good chance of recovering their money, the mezzanine lenders risk losing their subordinated investment. Goldman Sachs, which arranged the buy-out's financing, is thought to hold more than half of the imperilled mezzanine debt in its Mezzanine Partners II fund.

Source: Rebecca Bream, *Financial Times*, 3 November 2000, Leveraged Finance, p. 4. Reprinted with permission.

New European funds raised
€bn

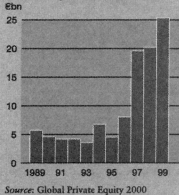

Source: Global Private Equity 2000

Mezzanine financing has been employed, not only by firms 'gearing themselves up' to finance merger activity, but also for leveraged recapitalisations. For instance, a firm might have run into trouble, defaulted and its assets are now under the control of a group of creditors, including bankers and bondholders. One way to allow the business to continue would be to persuade the creditors to accept alternative financial securities in place of their debt securities to bring the leverage to a reasonable level. They might be prepared to accept a mixture of shares and mezzanine finance. The mezzanine instruments permit the holders to receive high interest rates in recognition of the riskiness of the firm, and they open up the possibility of an exceptionally high return from warrants or share options should the firm get back to a growth path. The alternative for the lenders may be a return of only a few pence in the pound from the immediate liquidation of the firm's assets.

Mezzanine finance and high debt levels impose a high fixed cost on the firm and can be a dangerous way of financing expansion and therefore have their critics. On the other hand, some commentators have praised the way in which high gearing and large annual interest payments have focused the minds of managers and engendered extraordinary performance (*see* Chapter 18). Also, without this finance, many takeovers, buyouts and financial restructurings would not take place.

Financing a leveraged buyout

If the anticipated cash flows are reasonably stable then a highly leveraged buyout may give an exceptional return to the shareholders. Take the case of Sparrow, a subsidiary of Hawk plc. The managers have agreed a buyout price of £10m, equal to Sparrow's assets. They are able to raise £1m from their own resources to put into equity capital and have borrowed £9m. The debt pays an interest rate of 14 per cent and the corporate tax rate is 25 per cent (payable one year after year end). Profits before interest and tax in the first year after the buyout are expected to be £1.5m and will grow at 25 per cent per annum thereafter. All earnings will be retained within the business to pay off debt.

Exhibit 11.12 Sparrow – Profit and Loss Account and Balance Sheet (£000s)

				Years		
	1	2	3	4	5	6
Profit before interest and taxes (after depreciation)	1,500	1,875	2,344	2,930	3,662	4,578
Less interest	1,260	1,226	1,144	999	770	433
	240	649	1,200	1,931	2,892	4,145
Tax	0	60	162	300	483	723
Profits available to pay off debt	240	589	1,038	1,631	2,409	3,422

Balance Sheet				Year			
	Opening	1	2	3	4	5	6
Equity	1,000	1,240	1,829	2,867	4,498	6,907	10,329
Debt	9,000	8,760	8,171	7,133	5,502	3,093	0
Assets	10,000	10,000	10,000	10,000	10,000	10,000	10,329

Notes: Past tax liabilities have been accepted by Hawk. Money set aside for depreciation is used to replace assets to maintain £10m of assets throughout. Also depreciation equals capital allowances used for tax purposes.

In the first few years the debt burden absorbs a large proportion of the rapidly increasing profits. However it only takes six years for the entire debt to be retired. The shareholders then own a business with assets of over £10m, an increase of over tenfold on their original investment. The business is also producing a large annual profit which could make a stock market flotation attractive, in which case the value of the shares held by the management will probably be worth much more than £10m.[1]

CONVERTIBLE BONDS

Convertible bonds carry a rate of interest in the same way as vanilla bonds, but they also give the holder the right to exchange the bonds at some stage in the future into ordinary shares according to some prearranged formula. The owner of these bonds is not obliged to exercise this right of conversion and so the bond may continue until redemption as an interest-bearing instrument. Usually the *conversion price* is 10–30 per cent greater than the existing share price. So if a £100 bond offered the right to convert to 40 ordinary shares the conversion price would be £2.50 which, given the market price of the shares of, say, £2.20, would be a *conversion premium* of:

$$\frac{2.50 - 2.20}{2.20} = 0.136 \text{ or } 13.6\%$$

In a rising stock market it is reasonable to suppose that most convertible bonds issued with a small conversion premium will be converted to shares. However this is not always the case. Northern Foods (with the brand names Express Dairies, Eden Vale, Fox's Biscuits, Palethorpe Sausages, Pork Farms and Bowyers) issued convertible bonds in February 1993. The issue raised £91.28m. The bonds were to be redeemed in 15 years if they had not been converted before this and were priced at a par value of £100. The coupon was set at 6.75 per cent and the conversion price was at 326p per share. From this information we can calculate the *conversion ratio*:

$$\text{Conversion ratio} = \frac{\text{Nominal (par) value of bond}}{\text{Conversion price}} = \frac{£100}{£3.26} = 30.67 \text{ shares}$$

The conversion price was set at a premium of 18.11 per cent over the ordinary share price at the time of pricing which was 276p ((326 − 276)/276 = 18.11%). At the time of the issue many investors may have looked at the low interest rate on the convertible (for 15-year bonds in 1993) and said to themselves that although this was greater than the dividend yield on shares (4–5 per cent) it was less than that on conventional bonds, but offsetting this was the prospect of capital gains made by converting the bonds into shares. If the shares rose to, say, £4, each £100 bond could be converted to 30.67 shares worth 30.67 × £4 = £122.68. Unfortunately the share price by mid-2001 had fallen to about £1.54 and so the conversion right had not gained any intrinsic value – perhaps by the year 2008 it will be worthwhile exchanging the bonds for shares. In the meantime the investors at least have the comfort of a £6.75 coupon every year.

The value of a convertible bond (also called an 'equity-linked bond') rises as the value of ordinary shares increases, but at a lower percentage rate. If the share price rises above the conversion price the investor may exercise the option to convert if he/she anticipates that the share price will at least be maintained. If the share price rise is seen to be temporary the investor may wish to hold on to the bond. If the share price falls or rises by only a small amount the value of the convertible will be the same as a straight bond at maturity.

Exhibit 11.13 Summary of convertible bond technical jargon

- **Conversion ratio** This gives the number of ordinary shares into which a convertible bond may be converted:

$$\text{Conversion ratio} = \frac{\text{Nominal (par) value of bond}}{\text{Conversion price}}$$

- **Conversion price** This gives the price of each ordinary share obtainable by exchanging a convertible bond:

$$\text{Conversion price} = \frac{\text{Nominal (par) value of bond}}{\text{Number of shares into which bond may be converted}}$$

- **Conversion premium** This gives the difference between the conversion price and the market share price, expressed as a percentage:

$$\text{Conversion premium} = \frac{\text{Conversion price} - \text{Market share price}}{\text{Market share price}} \times 100$$

- **Conversion value** This is the value of a convertible bond if it were converted into ordinary shares at the current share price:

$$\text{Conversion value} = \text{Current share price} \times \text{Conversion ratio}$$

Most convertible bonds are unsecured but as the Case study on Greenhills shows, this is not always the case – a good thing for Hunter Ground.

CASE STUDY 11.2 Secured convertible debentures

Greenhills

The first AIM-traded company to go into receivership was Greenhills, the restaurant operator. A major investor, Hunter Ground, appointed administrative receivers on 4 December 1996. Hunter Ground held secured convertible debentures from Greenhills worth £506,000.

Source: Investors Chronicle, 20 December 1996, p. 11. Reprinted with kind permission of the Investors Chronicle.

Advantages to the company of convertible bonds

Convertible bonds have the following advantages to the company.

1 *Lower interest than on a similar debenture* The firm can ask investors to accept a lower interest on these debt instruments because the investor values the conversion right. This was a valuable feature for many dot.com companies in the late 1990s. Companies such as Amazon and AOL could pay 5–6 per cent on convertibles – less than half what they would have paid on straight bonds. In 1999 one-quarter of all US convertible issues were by internet companies.

2 *The interest is tax deductible* Because convertible bonds are a form of debt the coupon payment can be regarded as a cost of the business and can therefore be used to reduce taxable profit.

3 *Self liquidating* When the share price reaches a level at which conversion is worthwhile the bonds will (normally) be exchanged for shares so the company does not have to find cash to pay off the loan principal – it simply issues more shares. This has obvious cash flow benefits. However the disadvantage is that the other equity holders may experience a reduction in earnings per share and dilution of voting rights.

4 *Fewer restrictive covenants* The directors have greater operating and financial flexibility than they would with a secured debenture. Investors accept that a convertible is a hybrid between debt and equity finance and do not tend to ask for high-level security, impose strong operating restrictions on managerial action or insist on strict financial ratio boundaries – notwithstanding the case of Greenhills (*see* Case study 11.2).

5 *Underpriced shares* A company which wishes to raise equity finance over the medium term but judges that the stock market is temporarily underpricing its shares may turn to convertible bonds. If the firm does perform as the managers expect and the share price rises, the convertible will be exchanged for equity.

Advantages to the investor

The advantages of convertible bonds to the investor are as follows.

1 They are able to wait and see how the share price moves before investing in equity.

2 In the near term there is greater security for their principal compared with equity investment, and the annual coupon is usually higher than the dividend yield.

The terms associated with each issue of convertible bonds can vary considerably. In the case of BPB Industries, the plasterboard giant (*see* Case study 11.3) the bonds issued in 1993 offer the holders the right to convert between 1993 and 2008 while giving the company the power to redeem the bonds from 1998 to 2008.

CASE STUDY 11.3 Convertible subordinated bonds

BPB plc

'On 23 February 1993 the company issued £64 million 7.25 per cent convertible subordinated bonds, convertible at the bondholders' option into 24.8 million ordinary shares of the company at a price of 258p per share at any time from 27 April 1993 to 18 August 2008. The company may redeem the bonds, in full or in multiples of £5 million nominal, at any time from 8 September 1998 to 25 August 2008. The bonds are unsecured and rank after all creditors, but before ordinary shareholders.'

The reader may like to look up the current share price of BPB plc (formerly BPB Industries plc) and calculate a conversion value to gain some impression of the return made by the convertible bond investors in this instance.

Source: BPB Industries plc Annual Report 1996. Reprinted by permission of BPB plc. (Note that these bonds were withdrawn in 2000.)

The bonds sold may not give the right to conversion into shares of the issuers, but shares of another company held by the issuer – *see* the cases of Hutchison and Whampoa, Telecom Italia and France Telecom in Exhibit 11.14. Note that the term exchangeable bond is probably more appropriate in these cases.

Exhibit 11.14

Brakes applied to convertible bond market

One of Europe's most active periods of issuance has been slowed by volatile equities, writes **Rebecca Bream**

The European convertible bond market kicked off the year with the most active period for new issues that many can remember. Not only were there high volumes of business but the deals were among the biggest the market had seen. But since March the volatility in the equity markets has taken its toll, and the hectic pace of new issues has slowed.

The first quarter saw €13.8bn of European equity-linked issuance, up almost 50 per cent from the first quarter of 2000's figure of €9.2bn. This compares to about €37bn of convertible issuance globally, and a 16 per cent decrease of issuance in the US . . .

In January Hong Kong conglomerate Hutchison Whampoa sold $2.65bn of bonds exchangeable into shares of Vodafone, the UK mobile phone operator. Hutchison had been gradually divesting its stake in the UK group

since completing a $3bn exchangeable bond deal last September.

This was followed at the end of the month by Telecom Italia which sold €2bn of bonds exchangeable into shares of subsidiaries Telecom Italia Mobile and Internet operator Seat.

In February France Telecom sold €3.3bn of bonds exchangeable into shares of Orange, completed at the same time as the mobile unit's IPO, and one of the biggest exchangeable bond deals ever sold in Europe.

The deals were helped along by the fact that money had flowed into dedicated convertible bond funds at the end of 2000, both buy-and-hold accounts and arbitrage-driven hedge funds, and investor demand outstripped supply.

Source: Rebecca Bream, *Financial Times*, 6 April 2001, p. 35. Reprinted with permission.

VALUING BONDS

Bonds, particularly those which are traded in secondary markets such as the London Stock Exchange, are priced according to supply and demand. The main influences on the price of a bond will be the general level of interest rates for securities of that risk level and maturity. If the coupon is less than the current interest rate the bond will trade at less than the par value of £100. Take the case of an irredeemable bond with an annual coupon of 8 per cent. This financial asset offers to any potential purchaser a regular £8 per year for ever. When the bond was first issued general interest rates for this risk class may well have been 8 per cent and so the bond may have been sold at £100. However interest rates change over time. Suppose that the rate demanded by investors is now 10 per cent. Investors will no longer be willing to pay £100 for an instrument that yields £8 per year. The current market value of the bond will fall to £80 (£8/0.10) because this is the maximum amount needed to pay for similar bonds given the current interest rate of 10 per cent. If the coupon is more than the current market interest rate the market price of the bond will be greater than the nominal (par) value. Thus if markets rates are 6 per cent the irredeemable bond will be priced at £133.33 (£8/0.06).

The formula relating the price of an irredeemable bond, the coupon and the market rate of interest is:

$$P_D = \frac{i}{k_D}$$

where P_D = price of bond
   i = nominal annual interest (the coupon rate × nominal value of the bond)
   k_D = market discount rate, annual return required on similar bonds

Also:

$$V_D = \frac{I}{k_D}$$

where V_D = total market value of bonds
   I = total annual nominal interest

We may wish to establish the market rate of interest represented by the market price of the bond. For example, if an irredeemable bond offers an annual coupon of 9.5 per cent and is currently trading at £87.50, with the next coupon due in one year, the rate of return is:

$$k_D = \frac{i}{P_D} = \frac{9.5}{87.5} = 0.1086 \text{ or } 10.86\%$$

Redeemable bonds

A purchaser of a redeemable bond buys two types of income promise; first the coupon, second the redemption payment. The amount that an investor will pay depends on the amount these income flows are worth when discounted at the rate of return required on that risk class of debt. The relationships are expressed in the following formulae:

$$P_D = \frac{i_1}{1 + k_D} + \frac{i_2}{(1 + k_D)^2} + \frac{i_3}{(1 + k_D)^3} + \dots + \frac{R_n}{(1 + k_D)^n}$$

and:

$$V_D = \frac{I_1}{1 + k_D} + \frac{I_2}{(1 + k_D)^2} + \frac{I_3}{(1 + k_D)^3} + \dots + \frac{R^*_n}{(1 + k_D)^n}$$

where i_1, i_2 and i_3 = nominal interest per bond in years 1, 2 and 3
   I_1, I_2 and I_3 = total nominal interest in years 1, 2 and 3
   R_n and R^*_n = redemption value of a bond, and total redemption of
                all bonds in year n

The worked example of Blackaby illustrates the valuation of a bond when the market interest rate is given.

Worked example 11.1 Blackaby plc

Blackaby plc issued a bond with a par value of £100 in September 2001, redeemable in September 2007 at par. The coupon is 8% payable annually in September. The facts available from this are:

■ the bond might have a par value of £100 but this may not be what investors will pay for it;
■ the annual cash payment will be £8 (8 per cent of par);
■ in September 2007, £100 will be handed over to the bondholder.

Question 1

What is the price investors will pay for this bond at the time of issue if the market rate of interest for a security in this risk class is 7 per cent?

Answer

$$P_D = \frac{8}{1 + 0.07} + \frac{8}{(1 + 0.07)^2} + \frac{8}{(1 + 0.07)^3} + \dots \frac{8}{(1 + 0.07)^6} + \frac{100}{(1 + 0.07)^6}$$

$P_D = $ £8 annuity for 6 years @ 7 per cent = 4.7665×8 = 38.132

 plus $\dfrac{100}{(1 + 0.07)^6}$ = $\dfrac{66.634}{£104.766}$

Question 2

What is the bond's value in the secondary market in September 2004 if interest rates rise by 200 basis points between 2001 and 2004? (Assume the next coupon payment is in one year.)

Answer

$P_D = $ £8 annuity for 3 years @ 9 per cent = 2.5313×8 = 20.25

 plus $\dfrac{100}{(1 + 0.09)^3}$ = $\dfrac{77.22}{£97.47}$

Note that as interest rates rise the price of bonds falls.

To calculate the rate of return demanded by investors from a particular bond we can compute the internal rate of return. For example Bluebird plc issued a bond many years ago which is due for redemption at par of £100 in three years. The coupon is 6 per cent and the market price is £91. The rate of return now offered in the market by this bond is found by solving for k_D:

$$P_D = \frac{i_1}{1 + k_D} + \frac{i_2}{(1 + k_D)^2} + \frac{R_n + i_3}{(1 + k_D)^3}$$

$$91 = \frac{6}{1 + k_D} + \frac{6}{(1 + k_D)^2} + \frac{106}{(1 + k_D)^3}$$

To solve this requires the skills learned in calculating internal rates of return in Chapter 2. At an interest rate (k_D) of 9 per cent, the right side of the equation amounts to £92.41. At an interest rate of 10 per cent the right-hand side of the equation amounts to £90.05. Using linear interpolation:

Interest rate	9%	?	10%
Value of discounted cash flows	£92.41	£91	£90.05

$$k_D = 9\% + \frac{92.41 - 91}{92.41 - 90.05} \times (10 - 9) = 9.6\%$$

The two types of interest yield

The *Financial Times* quotes two yields for fixed-interest securities. The *interest yield* (also known as the flat yield, income yield and running yield) is the gross (before tax) interest amount divided by the current market price of the bond expressed as a percentage:

$$\frac{\text{Gross interest (coupon)}}{\text{Market price}} \times 100$$

Thus for a holder of Bluebird's bonds the interest yield is:

$$\frac{£6}{£91} \times 100 = 6.59\%$$

This is a gross yield. The after-tax yield will be influenced by the investor's tax position.

Net interest yield = Gross yield $(1 - T)$,

where T = the tax rate applicable to the bondholder

At a time when interest rates are higher than 6.59 per cent it is obvious that any potential purchaser of Bluebird bonds in the market will be looking for a return other than from the coupon. That additional return comes in the form of a capital gain over three years of £100 – £91. A rough estimate of this annual gain is $(9/91) \div 3 = 3.3$ per cent per year. When this is added to the interest yield we have an approximation to the second type of yield, the yield to maturity (also called the redemption yield). The yield to maturity of a bond is the discount rate such that the present value of all the cash inflows from the bond (interest plus principal) is equal to the bond's current market price. The rough estimate of 9.89 per cent (6.59% + 3.3%) has not taken into account the precise timing of the investor's income flows. When this is adjusted for, the yield to maturity is 9.6 per cent – the internal rate of return calculated above. Thus the yield to maturity includes both coupon payments and the capital gain or loss on maturity.

Semi-annual interest

The example of Bluebird given above is based on the assumption of annual interest payments. This makes initial understanding easier and reflects the reality for many types of bond, particularly internationally traded bonds. However UK companies usually issue domestic sterling bonds with semi-annual interest payments. A bond offering a coupon of 9 per cent would pay £4.50 half-way through the year and the remainder at the end. The rate of return calculation on these bonds is slightly more complicated. For example Redwing plc has an 11 per cent bond outstanding which pays interest semi-annually. It will be redeemed in two years at £100 and has a current market price of £96, with the next interest payment due in six months. The redemption yield on this bond is calculated as follows:

Cash flows

Point in time (years)	0.5	1	1.5	2.0	2.0
Cash flow	£5.5	£5.5	£5.5	£5.5	£100

The nominal interest rate over a six-month period is 5.5% (11%/2):

$$96 = + \frac{5.50}{1 + k_D/2} + \frac{5.50}{(1 + k_D/2)^2} + \frac{5.50}{(1 + k_D/2)^3} + \frac{5.50}{(1 + k_D/2)^4} + \frac{100}{(1 + k_D/2)^4}$$

At a rate of 6% for $k_D/2$ the right-hand side equals:

$$5.50 \times \text{4-period annuity @ 6\%} = 5.50 \times 3.4651 = 19.058$$

$$\text{plus } \frac{100}{(1 + 0.06)^4} = \underline{79.209}$$

$$\underline{\underline{£98.267}}$$

At a rate of 7% for $k_D/2$ the right-hand side equals:

$$5.50 \times \text{4-period annuity @ 7\%} = 5.50 \times 3.3872 = 18.630$$

$$\text{plus } \frac{100}{(1 + 0.07)^4} = \underline{76.290}$$

$$\underline{\underline{£94.920}}$$

The IRR of the cash flow equals:

$$6\% + \frac{98.267 - 96}{98.267 - 94.92} \times (7 - 6) = 6.68\%$$

The IRR needs to be converted from a half-yearly cash flow basis to an annual basis:

$$(1 + 0.0668)^2 - 1 = 0.1381 \text{ or } 13.81\%$$

INTERNATIONAL SOURCES OF DEBT FINANCE

Larger and more creditworthy companies have access to a wider array of finance than small firms. These companies can tap the *Euro-securities markets* which are informal (unregulated) markets in money held outside its country of origin. For example there is a large market in *Eurodollars*. These are dollar credits and deposits managed by a bank not resident in the USA. This has the distinct advantage of transactions not being subject to supervision and regulation by the authorities in the USA. So, for example, an Italian firm can borrow dollars from a Spanish bank in the UK and the US regulatory authorities have no control over the transaction. There is a vast quantity of dollars held outside the USA and this money is put to use by borrowers. The same applies to all the major currencies – the money is lent and borrowed outside its home base and therefore is beyond the reach of the domestic regulators. Today it is not unusual to find an individual holding a dollar account at a UK bank – a *Eurodeposit* account – which pays interest in dollars linked to general dollar rates. This money can be lent to firms wishing to borrow in Eurodollars prepared to pay interest and capital repayments in dollars. There are large markets in Euromarks, Eurosterling and Euroyen. The title 'Euro' is misleading as this market is not limited to the European currencies or European banks (and is unconnected with the European single currency, the euro). Nowadays, there is daily Eurosecurities business transacted in all of the major financial centres.

The companies which are large enough to use the Eurosecurities markets are able to put themselves at a competitive advantage *vis-à-vis* smaller firms. There are at least four advantages:

■ The finance available in these markets can be at a lower cost in both transaction costs and rates of return.

■ There are fewer rules and regulations.

■ There may be the ability to hedge foreign currency movements. For example, if a firm has assets denominated in a foreign currency it can be advantageous to also have liabilities in that same currency to reduce the adverse impact of exchange-rate movements (*see* Chapter 22).

■ National markets are often not able to provide the same volume of finance. The borrowing needs of some firms are simply too large for their domestic markets to supply. To avoid being hampered in expansion plans large firms can turn to the international market in finance.

For these internationally recognised firms there are three sources of debt finance:

a the domestic or national market;

b the financial markets of other countries which make themselves open to foreign firms – *the foreign debt market;*

c the Eurosecurities market which is not based in any one country and is not therefore regulated by any country.

Thus, for example, there are three bond markets available to some firms – as shown in Exhibit 11.15.

Exhibit 11.15 Bond markets

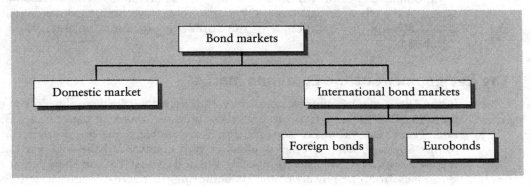

Foreign bonds

A foreign bond is a bond denominated in the currency of the country where it is issued when the issuer is a non-resident. For example, in Japan bonds issued by non-Japanese companies denominated in yen are foreign bonds. (The interest and capital payments will be in yen.) Foreign bonds have been given some amusing names: foreign bonds in Tokyo are known as Samurai bonds, foreign bonds issued in New York and London are called Yankees and Bulldogs respectively. The Netherlands allows foreigners to issue Rembrandt bonds and in Spain Matador bonds are traded. Foreign bonds are regulated by the authorities where the bond is issued. These rules can be demanding and an encumbrance to companies needing to act quickly and at low cost. The regulatory authorities have also been criticised for stifling innovation in the financial markets. The growth of the less restricted Eurobond market has put the once dominant foreign bond market in the shade.

Eurobonds

Eurobonds are bonds sold outside the jurisdiction of the country of the currency in which the bond is denominated. So, for example, the UK financial regulators have little influence over the Eurobonds denominated in Sterling, even though the transactions (for example interest and capital payments) are in pounds. They are medium- to long-term instruments. Eurobonds are not subject to the rules and regulations which are imposed on foreign bonds, such as the requirement to issue a detailed prospectus. More importantly they are not subject to an interest-withholding tax. In the UK most domestic bonds are subject to a withholding tax by which basic rate income tax is deducted before the investor receives interest. Interest on Eurobonds is paid gross without any tax deducted – which has attractions to investors keen on delaying, avoiding or evading tax. Moreover, Eurobonds are bearer bonds which means that the holders do not have to disclose their identity – all that is required to receive interest and capital is for the holder to have possession of the bond. In contrast, UK domestic bonds are registered, which means that companies and governments are able to identify the owners. Bearer bonds have to be kept in a safe place as a thief could benefit greatly from possession of a bearer bond.

Despite the absence of official regulation, the International Securities Market Association (ISMA), a self-regulatory body founded in 1969 and based in Switzerland, imposes some restrictions, rules and standardised procedures on Eurobond issue and trading.

Eurobonds are distinct from euro bonds, which are bonds denominated in euros and issued in the euro currency area. Of course, there have been euro-denominated bonds issued outside the jurisdiction of the authorities in the euro area. These are euro Eurobonds.

The development of the Eurobond market

In the 1960s many countries, companies and individuals held surplus dollars outside of the USA. They were reluctant to hold these funds in American banks under US jurisdiction. There were various reasons for this. For example, some countries, particularly the former Soviet Union and other communist bloc countries of the cold war era, thought their interests were best served by using the dollars they had on the international markets, away from the powers of the US authorities to freeze or sequestrate (seize) assets. More recently this sort of logic has applied to countries such as Iran, Iraq and Libya. Also in the 1960s the American authorities had some very off-putting tax laws and created a tough regulatory environment in their domestic financial markets. These encouraged investors and borrowers alike to undertake transactions in dollars outside the USA. London's strength as a financial centre, the UK authorities' more relaxed attitude to business, and its position in the global time zones, made it a natural leader in the Euro markets. The first Eurobond was issued in the early 1960s and the market grew modestly through the 1970s and then at a rapid rate in the 1980s. By then the Eurodollar bonds had been joined by bonds denominated in a wide variety of Eurocurrencies. The market was stimulated not only by the tax and anonymity benefits, which brought a lower cost of finance than for the domestic bonds, but also by the increasing demand from transnational companies and governments needing large sums in alternative currencies and with the potential for innovatory characteristics. It was further boosted by the recycling of dollars from the oil-exporting countries.

In 1979 less than $20bn worth of bonds were issued in a variety of currencies. As can be seen from Exhibit 11.16 the rate of new issuance is now over $1,900bn a year, with a

Exhibit 11.16 International bond issues

Year ($bn)	1998	1999	2000
Straights – fixed rate	846.9	1,231.5	1,252.7
Equity-related	47.1	52.1	56.5
Floating-rate issues	292.5	484.9	624.3
Total	1,186.4	1,768.5	1,933.5
Amount outstanding of fixed-rate bonds and floating-rate bonds	4,039.2	4,966.2	5,907.7

Source: Bank for International Settlements (BIS) *Quarterly Review*, www.BIS.org, November 2000, March 2001, June 2001, February 2000, March 1999.

total amount outstanding of over $5,900bn. In any one year approximately 30–50 per cent of new bonds are denominated in dollars. Euro-denominated issues account for 30–40 per cent of issues. The yen is the currency of issue for 10–20 per cent of international bonds. Sterling accounts for between 4 and 7 per cent. Even though the majority of Eurobond trading takes place through London, sterling is not one of the main currencies, and what is more, it tends to be large US and other foreign banks located in London which dominate the market.

Types of Eurobonds

The Eurobond market has been extraordinarily innovative in producing bonds with all sorts of coupon payment and capital repayment arrangements (for example, the currency of the coupon changes half-way through the life of the bond, or the interest rate switches from fixed to floating rate at some point). We cannot go into detail here on the rich variety but merely categorise the bonds into broad types.

1 *Straight fixed-rate bond* The coupon remains the same over the life of the bond. These are usually made annually, in contrast to domestic bond semi-annual coupons. The redemption of these bonds is usually made with a 'bullet' repayment at the end of the bond's life.

2 *Equity related* These take two forms:

   a *Bonds with warrants attached* Warrants are options which give the holder the right to buy some other asset at a given price in the future. An equity warrant, for example, would give the right, but not the obligation, to purchase shares. There are also warrants for commodities such as gold or oil, and for the right to buy additional bonds from the same issuer at the same price and yield as the host bond. Warrants are detachable from the host bond and are securities in their own right, unlike convertibles.

   b *Convertibles* The bondholder has the right (but not the obligation) to convert the bond into ordinary shares at a preset price.

3 *Floating-rate notes (FRNs)* Exhibit 11.16 shows the increasing importance of FRNs. These have a variable coupon reset on a regular basis, usually every three or six months, in relation to a reference rate, such as LIBOR. The size of the spread over LIBOR reflects the perceived risk of the issuer. The typical term for an FRN is about five to 12 years.

Within these broad categories all kinds of 'bells and whistles' can be attached to the bonds, for example *reverse floaters* – the coupon declines as LIBOR rises; *capped bonds* – the interest rate cannot rise above a certain level; *zero coupon* – a capital gain only is offered to the lender.

The majority of Eurobonds (more than 80 per cent) are rated AAA or AA and denominations are usually $1,000, $5,000 or $10,000 (or similar large sums in the currency of issue).

It is clear from Exhibit 11.17 that corporations account for a relatively small proportion of the international bond market. The biggest issuers are the banks. Issues by governments ('sovereign issues') and state agencies in the public sector account for about one-fifth of issues. Also strongly represented are governments and international agencies such as the World Bank, the International Bank for Reconstruction and Development and the European Investment Bank.

Exhibit 11.17 Issuers of international bond issues

	Year					
	1998		1999		2000	
	$bn	%	$bn	%	$bn	%
Banks and other financial institutions	596.1	50	896.8	51	1,021.4	53
Corporate issuers	261.2	22	476.5	27	478.5	25
Public sector	227.7	19	317.4	18	363.0	19
International institutions	101.4	9	77.8	4	70.7	3
Total	1,186.4	100	1,768.5	100	1,933.5	100

Source: Bank for International Settlements (BIS) *Quarterly Review*, www.BIS.org, November 2000, June 2001.

Issuing Eurobonds

The issuing of Eurobonds is similar to a placing. A bank (lead manager or book runner) or group of banks acting for the issuer invite a large number of other banks or other investors to buy some of the bonds. The managing group of banks is responsible for underwriting the issue and it may enlist a number of smaller institutions to use their extensive contacts to sell the bonds. Exhibit 9.18 on p. 357 in Chapter 9 gave some idea of the relative importance of the Eurobond market to UK-listed firms – in recent years the amount raised on the international market is greater than that raised through domestic debt and equity issues.

Eurobonds are traded on the secondary market through intermediaries acting as marketmakers. Most Eurobonds are listed on the London or Luxembourg stock exchanges but the market is primarily an over-the-counter one, that is, most transactions take place outside a recognised exchange. Deals are conducted using the telephone, computers, telex and fax. The ISMA set up Coredeal, an electronic trading platform for 6,000 international securities, in 2000. It is in competition with many other recently created electronic platforms. In 2002 ISMA plans to launch an internet-based market data service which will provide daily bid and offer quotes on more than 8,000 international debt issues. The extent to which electronic platforms will replace telephone dealing is as yet unclear. Exhibit 11.18 presents the advantages and disadvantages of Eurobonds.

Exhibit 11.18 Advantages and drawbacks of Eurobonds as a source of finance for corporations

Advantage	Drawback
1 Large loans for long periods are available.	1 Only for the largest companies – minimum realistic issue size is about £50m.
2 Often cheaper than domestic bonds. The finance provider receives the interest without tax deduction and retains anonymity and therefore supplies cheaper finance.	2 Bearer securities are attractive to thieves and therefore safe storage is needed.
3 Ability to hedge interest rate and exchange-rate risk.	3 Because interest and capital are paid in a foreign currency there is a risk that exchange-rate movements mean more of the home currency is required to buy the foreign currency than was anticipated.
4 The bonds are usually unsecured. The limitations placed on management are less than those for a secure bond.	4 The secondary market can be illiquid.
5 The lower level of regulation allows greater innovation and tailor-made financial instruments.	

To conclude the discussion of Eurobonds we will consider a few examples and deal with some of the jargon. The article, 'Russian bond issue raises $1bn' (Exhibit 11.19) describes the history-making return of Russia to the international bond market after an absence of 79 years. Note the high rate of interest Russia has to pay compared with the US Treasury – an extra 3.45 per cent per year. Once trading was under way the buyers pushed the market price of the bond up so that any secondary-market purchasers would only achieve a 3.38 per cent premium over US Treasury notes.

Exhibit 11.19

Russian bond issue raises $1bn

Chernomyrdin hails vote of confidence by international investors

Russia yesterday raised $1bn (£600m) in the bond markets, double the amount it originally thought it could raise, in its first international issue since the 1917 Bolshevik revolution . . .

J.P. Morgan and SBC Warburg, the investment banks that arranged the deal, said 44 per cent of the issue was placed with investors in the US, 30 per cent in Asia and 26 per cent in Europe.

The five-year bonds pay interest of 9.25 per cent semi-annually and were offered to investors at a yield of 9.36 per cent, 345 basis points more than the yield on US Treasury notes. That spread tightened to 338 basis points during trading yesterday on the high demand.

Source: Conner Middelmann and John Thornhill, *Financial Times*, 22 November 1996, p. 24. Reprinted with permission.

On Tuesday to Friday the *Financial Times* carries a small article giving a brief description of the new issues in the international bond market. The issues on Wednesday 13 June 2001 are described in Exhibit 11.20. Notice that a bond raising €800m is not regarded as particularly large (not a 'jumbo transaction'). The 'spread' mentioned is the yield to maturity above that on a government bond of similar maturity. So Washington

Exhibit 11.20

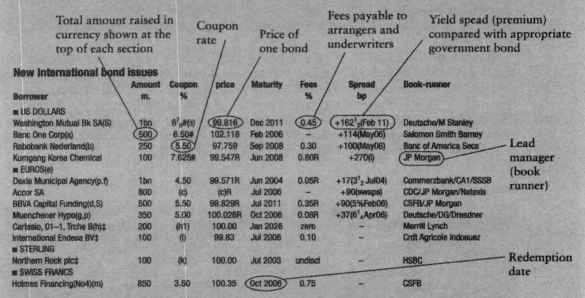

Accor launches €800m issue

The primary market took a breather yesterday, with no jumbo transactions appearing, although preparations for large issues continued.

The deals that were launched focused on the corporate and the bank debt sector. Accor, the French hotel operator rated BBB/BBB+, launched a €800m five-year bond.

It was the company's first bond and the size reflects the growing acceptance of Triple B rated credits in the euro-zone bond markets.

In the secondary market spreads were a touch wider as investors continued to take profits, on renewed concern about the telecommunications sector and ahead of the large amount of new supply in coming weeks.

Roadshows for Deutsche Telekom's euro-dominated bond issue, which could total up to €8bn, will start on June 25 and be completed by June 29. It will be the company's only large international bond sale this year.

Also in telecoms, roadshows for a £500m high-yield bond issue to finance the purchase of Yell, the business directory services firm bought from British Telecommunications in May, will start on July 9.

Source: Aline van Duyn, *Financial Times*, 14 June 2001, p. 32. Reprinted with permission.

Total amount raised in currency shown at the top of each section

Coupon rate

Price of one bond

Fees payable to arrangers and underwriters

Yield spread (premium) compared with appropriate government bond

New International bond issues

Borrower	Amount m.	Coupon %	price	Maturity	Fees %	Spread bp	Book-runner
■ US DOLLARS							
Washington Mutual Bk SA(S)	1bn	$6\frac{7}{8}$#(s)	99.816	Dec 2011	0.45	$+162\frac{1}{2}$(Feb 11)	Deutsche/M Stanley
Banc One Corp(a)	500	6.50#	102.118	Feb 2006	–	+114(May06)	Salomon Smith Barney
Rabobank Nederland(b)	250	5.50	97.759	Sep 2008	0.30	+100(May06)	Banc of America Secs
Kumgang Korea Chemical	100	7.625#	99.547R	Jun 2008	0.80R	+270(i)	JP Morgan
■ EUROS(e)							
Dexia Municipal Agency(p.f)	1bn	4.50	99.571R	Jun 2004	0.05R	$+17(3\frac{1}{2}$ Jul04)	Commerzbank/CA1/SSSB
Accor SA	800	(c)	(c)R	Jul 2006	–	+90(swaps)	CDC/JP Morgan/Natexis
BBVA Capital Funding(d,S)	500	5.50	99.829R	Jul 2011	0.35R	+90(5%Feb06)	CSFB/JP Morgan
Muenchener Hypo(g,p)	350	5.00	100.026R	Oct 2006	0.08R	$+37(6\frac{1}{4}$Apr06)	Deutsche/DG/Dresdner
Cartesio, 01–1, Trche B(h)‡	200	(h1)	100.00	Jan 2026	zero	–	Merrill Lynch
International Endesa BV‡	100	(i)	99.83	Jul 2006	0.10	–	Crdt Agricole Indosuez
■ STERLING							
Northern Rock plc‡	100	(k)	100.00	Jul 2003	undiscl	–	HSBC
■ SWISS FRANCS							
Holmes Financing(No4)(m)	850	3.50	100.35	Oct 2006	0.75	–	CSFB

Lead manager (book runner)

Redemption date

Final terms, non-callable unless stated. Yield spread (over relevant government bond) at launch supplied by lead manager. ‡ Floating-rate note. #Semi-annual coupon. R: fixed re-offer price: fees shown at re-offer level. a) Fungible with $2bn. Plus 139 days accrued. b) Fungible with $500m. Plus 280 days accrued. c) Priced today. d) Callable from 4/7/06 at par. If not called coupon steps to 3ME +110bp. e) Spreads relate to German govt bonds unless stated. f) Spread re French govt bonds. g) Fungible with €2bn. Plus 259 days accrued. h) Secured on loan to TAV, Italian state railway. Av life: 15.73 yrs. h1) 3-mth Euribor +10bp. i) Over interpolated yield. j) 3-mth Euribor +30bp. k) 3-mth Libor +5bp. m) Secured on UK residential mortgages by Abbey National. Legal maturity: 15/10/09. p) Secured on loans to public sector. s) Short 1st. S) Subordinated.

Source: *Financial Times*, 14 June 2001, p. 32.

Mutual pays 1.62 per cent per annum more interest than a US government bond on its $10\frac{1}{2}$-year bond.

The *Financial Times* also publishes a table showing a selection of secondary-market bid prices of actively traded international and emerging market bonds. This gives the reader some idea of current market conditions and rates of return demanded for bonds of different maturities, currencies and riskiness.

Exhibit 11.21

World bond prices

International bonds

Jun 11	Red date	Coupon	S&P* Rating	Moody's Rating	Bid price	Bid yield	Day's chge yield	Mth's chge yield	Spread vs Govts
■ US$									
Pac Bell	07/02	7.25	AA–	Aa3	102.8147	4.46	–0.03	–0.18	+4.46
NY Tel	08/25	7.00	A+	A1	92.3730	7.89	–0.06	–0.21	+2.00
CWE	05/08	8.00	A–	A3	105.7051	6.94	–0.07	–0.16	+1.65
GECC	05/07	8.75	AAA	Aaa	114.0138	5.91	–0.06	–0.14	+0.62
Banc One	08/02	7.25	A–	A1	103.1569	4.35	–0.02	–0.18	+4.35
CNA Fin	01/18	6.95	BBB	Baa1	85.4648	8.61	–0.05	–0.20	+2.92
Lucent	03/29	6.45	BBB–	Baa3	68.2678	9.79	–0.05	–0.49	+4.10
News Corp	10/08	7.38	BBB–	Baa3	100.8905	7.21	–0.06	–0.22	+1.92
TCI Comm	05/03	6.38	A	A3	101.4526	5.54	–0.06	–0.24	+1.45
FHLMC	04/09	5.86	N/A	Aaa	99.8138	5.88	–0.07	–0.21	+0.59
SLMA	05/04	7.01	N/A	Aaa	105.6619	4.88	–0.08	–0.21	+0.79
FNMA	08/28	6.16	N/A	Aaa	95.6238	6.50	–0.05	–0.18	+0.81
FFCB	05/02	5.25	N/A	Aaa	101.1131	3.95	–0.04	–0.24	+3.95
Charter Comm	04/09	8.63	B+	B2	95.5000	–	–	–	–
HMH Prop	08/08	7.88	BB	Ba2	96.5000	–	–	–	–
AMC Ent	02/11	9.50	CCC+	Caa3	90.0000	–	–	–	–
Jun 12									
IBRD	06/10	7.125	AAA	Aaa	107.9800	5.96	–0.07	–0.11	+0.72
Wal-Mart	08/09	6.875	AA	Aa2	104.9600	6.09	–0.05	–0.13	+0.89
Ford	06/10	7.875	A	A2	106.6700	6.87	–0.07	–0.15	+1.63
Viacom	07/10	7.700	A–	A3	106.4700	6.74	–0.04	–0.08	+1.50
■ C$									
Inter Am Dev Bk	06/09	5.625	AAA	Aaa	97.2800	6.06	–0.03	–0.13	+0.44
JP Morgan	03/04	6.875	A+	A2	101.7960	6.13	–0.02	–0.09	+1.03
Prov of Ontario	01/06	7.500	AA	Aa3	107.5900	5.60	–0.07	–0.05	+0.14
Quebec Hydro	07/22	9.625	A+	A2	133.7100	6.63	–0.03	–0.18	+0.72
■ £									
EIB	12/11	5.500	AAA	Aaa	97.4000	5.83	+0.09	+0.15	+0.61
GUS	07/09	6.375	A–	A2	97.0500	6.86	+0.12	+0.09	+1.53
Gallaher	05/09	6.625	BBB+	Baa2	97.3253	7.07	+0.13	+0.22	+1.74
Halifax	04/08	6.375	AA	Aa1	102.0000	6.00	+0.11	+0.23	+0.66
■ SFR									
EIB	01/08	3.750	AAA	Aaa	102.7654	3.27	–0.02	–	+0.03
Italy (REP)	07/10	3.125	AA	Aa3	96.3187	3.61	–0.01	+0.02	+0.27
JP Morgan	01/03	3.750	AA–	A1	100.6177	3.33	+0.01	+0.02	+0.30
Gen Elect.	07/09	3.125	AAA	Aaa	96.9906	3.56	–0.01	–	+0.24
■ YEN									
IBRD (World Bk)	03/03	4.500	AAA	Aaa	107.7810	0.08	–	–0.03	+0.02
Spain (Kingdom)	03/02	5.750	AA+	Aa2	104.3260	0.14	–	+0.03	+0.13
KFW Int	03/10	1.750	AAA	Aaa	107.2010	0.89	–0.02	–0.10	–0.18
Procter & Gamble	06/10	2.000	AA	Aa2	105.4580	1.35	–0.02	–0.09	+0.28
■ A$									
IBRD (World Bk)	02/08	6.000	AAA	Aaa	97.3890	6.49	–0.03	+0.37	+0.61
Queensland Trsy	06/05	6.500	AAA	Aaa	101.8678	5.97	–0.04	+0.44	+0.30
S. Aus Gov Fin	06/03	7.750	AA+	Aa2	103.5030	5.87	–0.03	+0.39	+0.57
Quebec, Provn of	10/02	9.500	A+	A2	104.5000	5.76	–	+0.27	+0.89
■ €									
UK	01/03	4.750	AAA	Aaa	100.557	4.37	+0.02	–0.04	–0.01
Denmark	09/08	4.625	AA+	Aaa	97.199	5.10	+0.02	+0.01	+0.29
Sweden	01/09	5.000	AA+	Aaa	98.869	5.18	+0.01	+0.00	+0.28
ADB	10/07	5.500	AAA	Aaa	101.582	5.20	+0.01	+0.01	+0.47
EIB	04/09	4.000	AAA	Aaa	91.971	5.28	+0.02	+0.05	+0.38
Eurofima	12/09	5.625	AAA	Aaa	101.711	5.36	+0.01	+0.00	+0.46
World Bank	04/05	7.125	AAA	Aaa	107.744	4.85	+0.02	–0.02	+0.27
EDF	10/10	5.750	AA+	Aaa	101.419	5.55	+0.02	+0.05	+0.56
TEPCO	05/09	4.375	AA–	Aa2	92.285	5.61	+0.01	–0.02	+0.71
Iberdrola	05/09	4.500	AA–	A1	91.166	5.93	+0.01	–0.01	+1.03
Powergen (UK)	07/09	5.000	BBB+	A3	94.067	5.95	+0.01	–0.03	+1.05
BNG	10/10	5.625	AAA	Aaa	101.685	5.39	+0.02	+0.00	+0.40
Fortis Fin	04/09	4.625	A+	Aa3	94.596	5.49	+0.01	–0.01	+0.59
Deutsche Finan	07/09	4.250	AA	Aa3	91.979	5.50	+0.01	–0.01	+0.60
Bayer Hypo	01/10	5.625	A+	Aa3	100.340	5.57	+0.01	–0.01	+0.58
Reseau Ferred	04/10	5.250	AAA	Aaa	99.037	5.39	+0.01	–0.01	+0.40
Statoil	06/11	5.125	AA–	A1	93.623	5.99	–0.01	+0.08	+0.91
Alcatel	02/09	4.375	A	A1	87.533	6.48	+0.01	–0.06	+1.58
Marconi	03/10	6.375	BBB+	A3	92.695	7.54	+0.01	–0.40	+2.55
Hypo In Essen	02/03	3.000	AAA	Aaa	97.840	4.39	+0.03	–0.05	+0.01
Euro Hypo	04/06	5.000	AAA	Aaa	100.348	4.91	+0.00	+0.00	+0.26
Depfa	07/08	4.750	AAA	Aaa	97.122	5.25	+0.01	+0.02	+0.44
Rhein Hypo	07/10	5.750	AAA	Aaa	102.090	5.45	+0.00	+0.02	+0.48
Jazztel	12/09	13.250	CCC+	Caa1	47.250	31.27	+0.77	+4.60	+26.37
Huntsman ICI	07/09	10.125	B	B2	101.250	9.89	–0.05	+0.40	+4.99
Kappa Beheer	07/09	10.625	B	B2	108.750	8.85	–0.27	–0.11	+3.95
NTL Comms	11/09	9.875	B	B2	69.750	16.69	+0.08	+2.24	+11.79

US $ denominated bonds NY latest; all other London closing. Yields: Local market standard.
*Standard & Poor's. Source: FT Interactive Data.

Emerging market bonds

Jun 12	Red date	Coupon	S&P* Rating	Moody's Rating	Bid price	Bid yield	Day's chge yield	Mth's chge yield	Spread vs Govts
■ EUROPE €									
Poland	03/10	6.000	BBB	Baa1	101.5842	5.76	+0.04	+0.06	+0.52
Slovenia	03/10	6.000	A	A2	101.7899	5.73	+0.01	+0.03	+0.49
Hungary	02/09	4.375	A–	A3	92.5859	5.59	+0.05	+0.09	+0.39
■ LATIN AMERICA $									
Argentina	07/03	10.250	B	B2	74.3136	13.89	–	–1.22	+8.24
Brazil	08/40	11.000	BB–	B1	77.0500	14.29	+1.10	–0.48	+8.62
Mexico	02/10	9.875	BB+	Baa3	110.4400	8.16	–	–0.55	+2.92
■ ASIA $									
China	12/08	7.300	BBB	A3	104.6850	6.50	+0.04	+0.10	+1.37
Philippines	01/19	9.875	BB+	Ba1	88.2900	11.43	–0.08	–0.93	+6.01
South Korea	04/08	8.875	BBB	Baa2	112.8225	6.52	–0.04	–0.08	+1.39
■ AFRICA/MIDDLE EAST $									
Lebanon	10/09	10.250	B+	B1	99.4758	10.34	–0.07	–0.44	+5.14
South Africa	05/09	9.125	BBB–	Baa3	108.0215	7.75	–0.07	–0.60	+2.55
Qatar	06/30	9.750	BBB+	Baa2	113.5097	8.49	–0.07	–0.59	+2.84
■ BRADY BONDS $									
Argentina	03/23	6.000	B	B2	68.2881	9.46	+0.08	–0.95	+3.96
Brazil	04/14	8.000	BB–	B1	76.2500	11.60	+0.02	–0.36	+6.28
Mexico	12/19	6.250	BB+	Baa3	93.1549	6.91	–0.08	–0.46	+1.49
Venezuela	03/20	6.750	B	B2	77.5000	9.30	–0.21	–0.39	+3.86

London closing. *Standard & Poor's. Source: FT Interactive Data.

Redemption date March 2020

Yield to maturity

Yield spread (premium) on a Viacom bond above the US government rate

Yield spread (premium) above what the US government would have to pay in the yen Eurobond market

Source: Financial Times, 15 June 2001. Reprinted with permission.

Euro medium-term notes and domestic medium-term notes

By issuing a note a company promises to pay the holders a certain sum on the maturity date, and in many cases a coupon interest in the meantime. These instruments are unsecured and may carry floating or fixed interest rates. Medium-term notes (MTN) have been sold with a maturity of as little as nine months and as great as 30 years, so the term is a little deceiving. They can be denominated in the domestic currency of the borrower (MTN) or in a foreign currency (EMTN), and are usually sold in relatively small quantities on a continuous or an intermittent basis, as the need for fresh financing arises.

Eurocommercial paper and domestic commercial paper[2]

The issue and purchase of commercial paper is one means by which the largest commercial organisations can avoid paying the bank intermediary a middleman fee for linking borrower and lender. Commercial paper promises to the holder a sum of money to be paid in a few days. The lender buys these short-term IOUs, with an average life of about 40 days (normal range 30–90 days), and effectively lends money to the issuer. Normally these instruments are issued at a discount rather than the borrower being required to pay interest – thus the face value will be higher than the amount paid for the paper at issuance. Large corporations with temporary surpluses of cash are able to put that money to use by lending it directly to other commercial firms at a higher rate of effective interest than they might have received by depositing the funds in a bank. This source of finance is usually only available to the most respected corporations with the highest credit ratings, as it is usually unsecured lending. Standard & Poors and Moody's use a different grading system for short-term instruments (e.g. A–1 or P–1 are the highest ratings). While any one issue of commercial paper is short term it is possible to use this market as a medium-term source of finance by 'rolling over' issues. That is, as one issue matures another one is launched. A commercial paper programme can be set up by a bank whereby the bank (or a syndicate of banks) underwrites a specified sum for a period of five to seven years. The borrower then draws on this by the issue of commercial paper to other lenders. If there are no bids for the paper the underwriting bank(s) buys the paper at a specified price. Eurocommercial paper is issued and placed outside the jurisdiction of the country in whose currency it is denominated.

PROJECT FINANCE

A typical project finance deal is created by an industrial corporation providing some equity capital for a separate legal entity to be formed to build and operate a project, for example an oil pipeline, an electricity power plant. The project finance loan is then provided as bank loans or through bond issues direct to the separate entity. The significant feature is that the loan returns are tied to the cash flows and fortunes of a particular project rather than being secured against the parent firm's assets. For most ordinary loans the bank looks at the credit standing of the borrower when deciding terms and conditions. For project finance, while the parent company's (or companies') credit standing is a factor, the main focus is on the financial prospects of the project itself.

To make use of project finance the project needs to be easily identifiable and separable from the rest of the company's activities so that its cash flows and assets can offer the lenders some separate security. Project finance has been used across the globe to finance power plants, roads, ports, sewage facilities and telecommunications networks. A few recent examples are given in Exhibit 11.22.

Exhibit 11.22

Project finance has funded . . .

A telephone infrastructure

In 2000 Hutchinson UK 3G raised £3bn by way of project finance to part-fund the building of the UK's fifth mobile network. This was three-year debt without recourse to shareholders (*see* below)

A power plant in Indonesia

In 1994 banks lent the developers of the $1.8bn Paiton 1 power plant project $180m with no government guarantees, repayable over eight years at a rate of 2.25 percentage points over LIBOR.

Electricity generating in Victoria

In 1996 banks agreed to lend A$2bn to PowerGen (the UK company) for the development of the coal-fired plant at Yallourn in Victoria, Australia despite the fact that there was no power purchase agreement in place – this is unusual as the lenders like to see reasonable certainty over the cash flows of the project before committing themselves. Here they are taking the risk that the price of electricity might fall.

Source: Based on *Financial Times*, 21 August 1996, p. 15 and *Financial Times*, 27 October 2000.

Project finance has grown rapidly over the last 25 years. Globally, about £50bn is lent in this form per year. A major stimulus has been the development of oil prospects. For the UK, the North Sea provided a number of project finance opportunities. Many of the small companies which developed fields and pipelines would not have been able to participate on the strength of their existing cash flow and balance sheet, but they were able to obtain project finance secured on the oil or fees they would later generate.

There is a spectrum of risk sharing in project finance deals. At one extreme the parent firm (or firms) accepts the responsibility of guaranteeing that the lenders will be paid in the event of the project producing insufficient cash flows. This is referred to as *recourse finance* because the lenders are able to seek the 'help' of the parent. At the other extreme, the lenders accept an agreement whereby, if the project is a failure, they will lose money and have no right of recourse to the parent company. If the project's cash flows are insufficient the lenders only have a claim on the assets of the project itself rather than on the sponsors or developers.

Between these two extremes there might be deals whereby the borrower takes the risk until the completion of the construction phase (for example, provides a completion guarantee) and the lender takes on the risk once the project is in the operational phase. Alternatively, the commercial firm may take some risks such as the risk of cost overruns and the lender takes others such as the risk of a government expropriating the project's assets.

The sums and size of projects are usually large and involve a high degree of complexity and this means high transaction and legal costs. Because of the additional risk to the lenders the interest rates charged tend to be higher than for conventional loans. Whereas a well-known highly creditworthy firm might pay 20 basis points (0.20 per cent) over LIBOR for a 'normal' parent company loan, the project company might have to pay 100 basis points (1 per cent) above LIBOR.

Advantages of project finance

Project finance has a number of advantages.

1 *Transfer of risk* By making the project a stand-alone investment with its own financing, the parent can gain if it is successful and is somewhat insulated if it is a failure, in that other assets and cash flows may be protected from the effects of project losses.

This may lead to a greater willingness to engage in more risky activities which may benefit both the firm and society. Of course, this benefit is of limited value if there are strong rights of recourse.

2 *Off-balance-sheet financing* The finance is raised on the project's assets and cash flows and therefore is not recorded as debt in the parent company's balance sheet. This sort of off-balance-sheet financing is seen as a useful 'wheeze' or ploy by some managers – for example, gearing limits can be bypassed. However, experienced lenders and shareholders are not so easily fooled by accounting tricks.

3 *Political risk* If the project is in a country prone to political instability, with a tendency towards an anti-transnational business attitude and acts of appropriation, a more cautious way of proceeding may be to set up an arm's length (separate company) relationship with some risk being borne by the banking community, particularly banks in the host country. An example of this sort of risk is given in Exhibit 11.23.

4 *Simplifies the banking relationship* In cases where there are a number of parent companies, it can be easier to arrange finance for a separate project entity than to have to deal with each of the parent companies separately.

Exhibit 11.23 'Regulatory risk' exists in many parts of the world . . .

Enron

In 1995 the state of Maharashtra in India suddenly revoked the contract it had with Enron for the construction of a power project, creating major problems for Enron and its bankers.

SALE AND LEASEBACK

If a firm owns buildings, land or equipment it may be possible to sell these to another firm (for example a bank, insurance company or specialised leasing firm) and simultaneously agree to lease the property back for a stated period under specific terms. The seller receives cash immediately but is still able to use the asset. However the seller has created a regular cash flow liability for itself. For example in 2000 Abbey National, the mortgage bank, sold its branch network and its Baker Street head office (221b Baker Street – the home of Sherlock Holmes) totalling 6.5m sq.ft. The 722 branches and head office will be occupied by Abbey National under leases as short as one year, and as long as 20. The objective was to obtain flexibility in accommodation so that the bank can change with its customers and with the industry. It allowed the firm to 'concentrate on banking rather than being property developers, which is not our job' (John Price, director of property, *Financial Times*, 20 October 2000, p. 27).

In 2001 Marks and Spencer planned to sell and then lease back £300m of its high street stores. This followed British Telecommunications £2bn, 7,000-property deal with Land Securities. These deals release cash tied up in assets, allowing the firms to concentrate on what they regard as their core businesses. A number of retailers have used their extensive property assets for sale and leaseback transactions so that they could plough the proceeds into further expansion.

In a number of countries the tax regime also propels sale and leaseback transactions. For example, some property owners are unable to use depreciation and other tax allowances (usually because they do not have sufficient taxable profits). The sale of the asset to an organisation looking to reduce taxable profits through the holding of depreciable assets enables both firms to benefit. Furthermore, the original owner's subsequent lease payments are tax deductible.

A sale and leaseback has the drawback that the asset is no longer owned by the firm and therefore any capital appreciation has to be forgone. Also long lease arrangements of this kind usually provide for the rental payments to increase at regular intervals, such as every three or five years. There are other factors limiting the use of sale and leaseback as a financial tool. Leasing can involve complex documentation and large legal fees, which often make it uneconomic to arrange leases for less than £20m. There is also a degree of inflexibility: for example, unwinding the transaction if, say, the borrower wanted to move out of the property can be expensive. Another disadvantage is that the property is no longer available to be offered as security for loans.

One of the attractions of sale and leaseback is the possibility of flattering the balance sheet. As Exhibit 11.24 makes clear, this practice is being curtailed.

Exhibit 11.24

Watchdog moves against off-balance sheet schemes

Listed companies face a crackdown on creative accounting after regulators yesterday signalled that they would not allow sale and leaseback transactions to flatter the performance of companies.

The Financial Reporting Review Panel, an investigative sister body of the Accounting Standards Board, yesterday agreed with Associated Nursing Services, the long-term care provider, that its accounts should be amended.

Sir Neil Macfarlane, chairman of ANS, said the panel's action had 'far reaching implications' for 'hundreds of companies in the UK which have entered into sale and leaseback transactions'.

Under such deals, companies sell fixed assets, such as buildings, to a financial institution or other purchaser, thereby removing the asset's value and any associated liabilities, such as mortgages, from their balance sheets. The purchaser then rents the asset back to the company so that it can go on using it.

In the ANS case, a nursing home was sold on this basis but the terms of the contract were such that the panel concluded that ANS retained many of the rights and risks associated with ownership.

The panel would not comment but it is known that its chairman, Mr Edwin Glasgow QC, wants the City to realise that such off-balance sheet schemes – which greatly reduce a company's gearing – can be in breach of the rules.

Merchant banks, accountants and auditors will see the panel's action as proof that it is prepared to defend the principle that a company's accounts should reflect the substance of a transaction, not just its legal form . . .

ANS entered into a complex sale and leaseback agreement involving a nursing home in which not all the rights and risks were transferred to the purchaser – Nursing Home Properties. The panel said the asset should therefore have stayed on the balance sheet.

Source: Jim Kelly, Accountancy Correspondent, *Financial Times*, 18 February 1997, p. 1. Reprinted with permission.

Hilton Group and Jarvis Hotels have negotiated interesting sale and leaseback deals – *see* Exhibit 11.25.

Exhibit 11.25

Jarvis goes for innovative style of financing
Scheherazade Daneshkhu funds the hotels group opting for a new sale and leaseback

Jarvis Hotels, the midmarket operator, is expected today to return cash to shareholders with money released from a sale and leaseback deal with Royal Bank of Scotland.

It would be the third significant sale and leaseback transaction the bank has struck in the sector this year, following a £312m deal with Hilton Group and last month's £1.25bn deal to help Nomura International fund its £1.9bn purchase of the Le Méridien chain.

Sale and leasebacks, under which the hotel owner sells the freehold to an investor in exchange for a lease and then pays rent, are nothing new.

Charles Forte – now lord Forte – used them to finance his first hotel purchase, the Waldorf in London, in 1958. But the Royal Bank of Scotland deals were the hot topic at a recent London hotels conference because of an innovative type of contract.

The transactions differ from previous deals in that the lease payment is variable and linked to sales. The minimum guaranteed payment is also comparatively low.

In the case of Hilton, Royal Bank paid paid £312m for 11 hotels with a book value of £278m and granted Hilton 20- and 30-year leases.

Hilton is to pay 25 per cent of sales to Royal Bank, expected to total £22.5m this year.

The minimum payment is almost half this amount – £12.5m, or 5 per cent of sales. 'That's a lower turnover than during the Gulf War,' said David Michels, chief executive of Hilton Group.

'I've been around long enough to remember original leasebacks set at 15 per cent and you paid that whatever [the hotels trading conditions]. This arrangement is attractive because we keep our flag on the hotels yet it releases money for overseas expansion.'

The capital raised helped fund Hilton's subsequent £612m acquisition of Scandic Hotels.

The downside is that, unlike sale and leasebacks that give the operator an option to buy back a property if it rises in value above an agreed level, the hotel operator gives away capital appreciation of the assets.

Investors can be wary too of off-balance sheet liabilities but the terms of the Hilton contracts have been well disclosed.

Source: Scheherazade Daneshku, *Financial Times*, 12 June 2001, p. 30. Reprinted with permission.

SECURITISATION

In the strange world of modern finance you sometimes need to ask yourself who ends up with your money when you pay your monthly mortgage, or your credit card bill or the instalment payment on your car. In the old days you would have found that it was the organisation you originally borrowed from and whose name is at the top of the monthly statement. Today you cannot be so sure because there is now a thriving market in repackaged debt. In this market, a mortgage lender, for example, collects together a few thousand mortgage 'claims' it has (the right of the lender to receive regular interest and capital from the borrowers); it then sells those claims in a collective package to other institutions, or participants in the market generally. This permits the replacement of long-term assets with cash (improving liquidity and gearing) which can then be used to generate more mortgages. The borrower is often unaware that the mortgage is no longer owned by the original lender and everything appears as it did before, with the mortgage company acting as a collecting agent for the buyer of the mortgages. The mortgage company usually raises this cash by selling asset-backed securities to other institutions (the 'assets' are the claim on interest and capital) and so this form of finance is often called *asset securitisation*. These asset-backed securities may be bonds sold into a market with many players.

Asset backed securitisation involves the pooling and repackaging of a relatively small, homogeneous and illiquid financial assets into liquid securities.

The sale of the financial claims can be either 'non-recourse', in which case the buyer of the securities from the mortgage firm bears the risk of non-payment by the borrowers, or with recourse to the mortgage lender.

Securitisation has even researched the world of rock. Iron Maiden issued a long-dated $30m asset-backed bond securitised on future earnings from royalties in 1999. It followed David Bowie's $55m bond securitised on the income from his earlier albums and Rod Stewart's $15.4m securitised loan from Nomura. Apparently, some artistes are said to be worried about tarnishing their images by being seen to court the financial markets.

Tussauds has securitised ticket and merchandise sales, Keele University has securitised the rental income from student accommodation and Newcastle United has securitised its future ticket sales. The new issue market in asset-backed bonds in Europe in 2000 amounted to $81bn.

This form of securitisation is regarded as beneficial to the financial system, because it permits banks and other financial institutions to focus on those aspects of the lending process where they have a competitive edge. Some, for example, have a greater competitive advantage in originating loans than in funding them. This is illustrated in the example of Barclays' €1bn securities move (*see* Exhibit 11.26).

Exhibit 11.26

Barclays to issue bond securitised on card debt

Move follows aggressive push by US providers

Barclays Bank is to break new ground in the UK by becoming the first British bank to launch a bond secured against debt owed by consumers to its credit card subsidiary.

The bond, which will total about €1bn (£643m), will also be comfortably the largest credit card securitisation to be arranged by a European bank.

It follows the aggressive move of US credit card providers, such as MBNA and Discover, into the UK and continental European market. A number of US credit card providers have also launched bonds in the European bond market this year.

A securitisation is a bond which is backed up by the collateral of future income streams such as credit card receivables, mortgages, autoloans and even film royalties. 'The Barclays deal is the first of what will probably be a large volume of UK credit card securitisations,' said Tamara Adler, a senior official at Deutsche Bank.

Under a securitisation, the bank removes assets from its balance sheet which allows it to free up regulatory capital originally set aside against those assets. The capital can then be put to more profitable uses without the bank losing its original customer base.

Source: Edward Luce, Capital Markets Editor, *Financial Times*, 12 October 1999, p. 27. Reprinted with permission.

THE TERM STRUCTURE OF INTEREST RATES

Until now we have assumed that the annual interest rate on a debt instrument remained the same regardless of the length of time of the loan. So, if the interest rate on a three-year bond is 7 per cent per year it would be 7 per cent on a five-year bond of the same risk class. However it is apparent that lenders in the financial markets demand different interest rates on loans of differing lengths of time to maturity – that is, there is a term structure of the interest rates. One of these relationships is shown in Exhibit 11.27 for lending to the UK government. This diagram, taken from a 2001 edition of the *Financial Times*, represents the rate of return that the UK government had to offer on its bonds. 'Years' means number of years to maturity. Note that default risk remains constant here; the reason for the different rates is the time to maturity of the bonds. Thus a one-year bond has to offer 5.3 per cent whereas a 20-year bond offers 5.1 per cent.

An upward-sloping yield curve occurs in most years but occasionally we have a situation where short-term interest rates (lending for, say, one year) exceed those of long-term interest rates (say, a 20-year bond). This downward-sloping term structure is shown in Exhibit 11.28(a). It is also possible to have a flat yield curve, like the one shown in Exhibit 11.28(b).

Exhibit 11.27 An approximation to the term structure of interest rates for UK government securities*

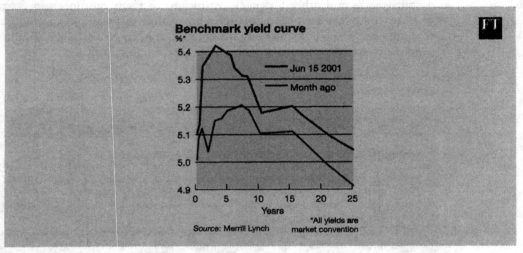

Note: *Using the benchmark yield curve as an example of term structures of interest rates may offend theoretical purity but it is a handy approximate measure and helps illustrate this section.

Source: *Financial Times*, 18 June 2001, p. 28. Reprinted with permission.

Exhibit 11.28 Downward-sloping and flat yield curves

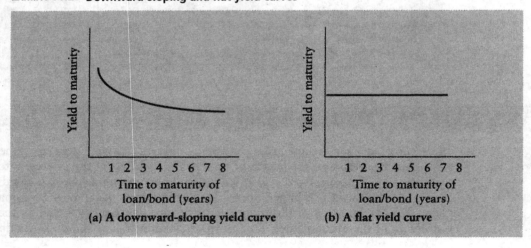

Three hypotheses have been advanced to explain the shape of the yield curve:

a the expectation hypothesis;
b the liquidity-preference hypothesis; and
c the market-segmentation hypothesis.

The expectation hypothesis

The expectation hypothesis focuses on the changes in interest rates over time. To understand the expectation hypothesis you need to know what is meant by a 'spot rate of interest'. The spot rate is an interest rate fixed today on a loan that is made today. So a corporation, Hype plc, might issue one-year bonds at a spot rate of, say, 8 per cent, two-year bonds at a spot rate of 8.995 per cent and three-year bonds at a spot rate of 9.5 per cent. This yield curve for Hype is shown in Exhibit 11.29. The interest rates payable by Hype are bound to be greater than for the UK government across the yield curve because of the additional default risk on these corporate bonds.

Exhibit 11.29 The term structure of interest rates for Hype plc at time 2001

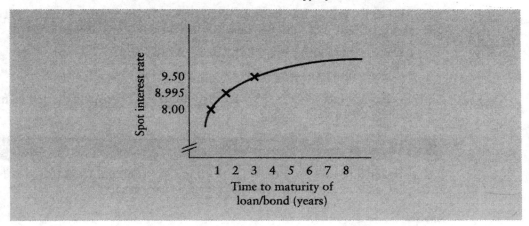

Spot rates change over time. The market may have allowed Hype to issue one-year bonds yielding 8 per cent at time 2001 but a year later (time 2002) the one-year spot rate may have changed to become 10 per cent. If investors expect that one-year spot rates will become 10 per cent at time 2002 they will have a theoretical limit on the yield that they require from a two-year bond when viewed from time 2001. Imagine that an investor (lender) wishes to lend £1,000 for a two-year period and is contemplating two alternative approaches:

1 Buy a one-year bond at a spot rate of 8 per cent; after one year has passed the bond will come to maturity. The released funds can then be invested in another one-year bond at a spot rate of 10 per cent, expected to be the going rate for bonds of this risk class at time 2002.
2 Buy a two-year bond at the spot rate at time 2001.

Under the first option the lender will have a sum of £1,188 at the end of two years:

£1,000 (1 + 0.08) = £1,080

£1,080 (1 + 0.1) = £1,188

Given the anticipated change in one-year spot rates to 10 per cent the investor will only buy the two-year bond if it gives the same average annual yield over two years as the first option of a series of one-year bonds. The annual interest required will be:

£1,000 $(1 + k)^2$ = £1,188

$k = \sqrt{(1{,}188/1{,}000)} - 1 = 0.08995$ or 8.995 per cent

Thus, it is the expectation of spot interest rates changing which determines the shape of the yield curve according to the expectation hypothesis.

Now consider a downward-sloping yield curve where the spot rate on a one-year instrument is 11 per cent and the expectation is that one-year spot rates will fall to 8 per cent the following year. An investor considering a two-year investment will obtain an annual yield of 9.49 per cent by investing in a series of one-year bonds, viz:

£1,000 (1.08) (1.11) = £1,198.80

With this expectation for movements in one-year spot rates, lenders will demand an annual rate of return of 9.49 per cent from two-year bonds of the same risk class.

$k = \sqrt{(1198.8/1000)} - 1 = 0.0949$ or 9.49% per year

or $\sqrt{(1.08)(1.11)} - 1 = 0.0949$

Thus in circumstances where short-term spot interest rates are expected to fall, the yield curve will be downward sloping.

Worked Example 11.2 SPOT RATES

If the present spot rate for a one-year bond is 5 per cent and for a two-year bond 6.5 per cent, what is the expected one-year spot rate in a year's time?*

Answer
If the two-year rate is set to equal the rate on a series of one-year spot rates then:

$$(1 + 0.05)(1 + x) = (1 + 0.065)^2$$

$$x = \frac{(1 + 0.065)^2}{1 + 0.05} - 1 = 0.0802 \text{ or } 8.02\%$$

*In the financial markets it is possible to agree now to lend money in one year's time for, say, a year (or two years or six months, etc.) at a rate of interest agreed at the outset. This is a 'forward'.

The liquidity-preference hypothesis

The expectation hypothesis does not adequately explain why the most common shape of the yield curve is upward sloping. The liquidity-preference hypothesis helps explain the upward slope by pointing out that investors require an extra return for lending on a long-term basis. Lenders demand a premium return on long-term bonds compared with short-term instruments because of the risk of misjudging future interest rates. Putting your money into a ten-year bond on the anticipation of particular levels of interest exposes you to the possibility that rates will rise above the rate offered on the bond at some point in its long life. Thus, if five years later interest rates double, say because of a rise in inflation expectations, the market price of the bond will fall substantially, leaving the holder with a large capital loss. On the other hand, by investing in a series of one-year bonds, the investor can take advantage of rising interest rates as they occur. The ten-year bond locks in a fixed rate for the full ten years if held to maturity. Investors prefer short-term bonds so that they can benefit from rising rates and so will accept a lower return on short-dated instruments. The liquidity-preference theory focuses on a different type of risk attaching to long-dated debt instruments other than default risk – a risk related to uncertainty over future interest rates. A suggested reinforcing factor to the upward slope is that borrowers usually prefer long-term debt because of the fear of having to repay short-term debt at inappropriate moments. Thus borrowers increase the supply of long-term debt instruments, adding to the tendency for long-term rates to be higher than short-term rates.

Note that the word liquidity in the title is incorrectly used – but it has stuck so we still use it. Liquidity refers to the speed and ease of the sale of an asset. In the case of long-term bonds (especially government bonds) sale in the secondary market is often as quick and easy for short-term bonds. The premium for long bonds is compensation for the extra risk of capital loss; 'term premium' might be a better title for the hypothesis.

The market-segmentation hypothesis

The market segmentation hypothesis argues that the debt market is not one homogeneous whole, that there are, in fact, a number of sub-markets defined by maturity range. The yield curve is therefore created (or at least influenced) by the supply and demand conditions in each of these sub-markets. For example, banks tend to be active in the short-term end of the market and pension funds to be buyers in the long-dated segment. If banks need to borrow large quantities quickly they will sell some of their short-term instruments, increasing the supply on the market and pushing down the price and raising the yield. On the other hand pension funds may be flush with cash and may buy large quantities of 20-year bonds, helping to temporarily move yields downward at the long end of the market. At other times banks, pension funds and the buying and selling pressures of a multitude of other financial institutions will influence the supply and demand position in the opposite direction. The point is that the players in the different parts of the yield curve tend to be different. This hypothesis helps to explain the often lumpy or humped yield curve.

A final thought on the term structure of interest rates

It is sometimes thought that in circumstances of a steeply rising yield curve it would be advantageous to borrow short term rather than long term. However this can be a dangerous strategy because long-term debt may be trading at a higher rate of interest because of the expected rise in short-term rates and so when the borrower comes to refinance in, say, a year's time, the short-term interest rate is much higher than the long-term rate and this high rate has to be paid out of the second year's cash flows, which may not be convenient.

EUROTUNNEL

The sub-set of financial knowledge known as long-term debt finance is vast and daunting, as well as complex and challenging. Yet it is important that firms face up to the challenge because if mistakes are made there can be a heavy price to pay further down the line. To get an appreciation of the role of financial expertise in this area consider the following two articles (*see* Exhibits 11.30 and 11.31) about Eurotunnel's debt crisis in the mid-1990s:

Exhibit 11.30 By September 1995 shareholders had lost a fortune and the company was chronically overburdened with debt . . .

Still digging

With characteristic bravado, Sir Alastair Morton has called his bankers' bluff; they have responded with characteristic inertia. Even though Eurotunnel suspended payments on its £8bn of junior debt yesterday, banks have not pulled the rug on the company. But Eurotunnel's problems are far from over: it is chronically overburdened with debt, and unable to trade its way out. Yesterday's drama has merely postponed the day of reckoning. The suspension of interest payments may last up to 18 months. But unpaid interest will continue to be added to Eurotunnel's pile of debt. The company is also about to draw down the second tranche of its senior debt facility.

Eurotunnel hopes that during this period the two parties will agree a restructuring plan. But the banks' do-nothing tendencies may mean that action comes later rather than sooner. There is some logic to this inertia. The banks do not want to take control of Eurotunnel since they do not believe the problem lies with the management of the company; they do not want to take possession of it because it would be hard to sell; and they do not want to force it into administration, partly because of France's unfavourable treatment of creditors – the company operates under both French and English law.

They may be hoping that a third rights issue will raise more cash from the company's long-suffering shareholders, but, given the company's admission that it cannot service existing debt, this is a long shot. Given also the company's failure to meet the targets set in the last rights issue prospectus, it might be difficult to find a bank to sign off the prospectus.

There is still only one long-term solution: a debt-for-equity swap, which would leave the company with a workable balance sheet. Eurotunnel currently has debt totalling more than £8bn and a market value of £700m. It could probably service around £4bn of debt. However, such a swap would

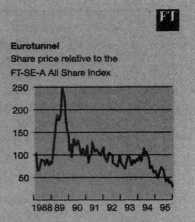

Eurotunnel
Share price relative to the
FT-SE-A All Share Index

effectively wipe out shareholders' capital.

Sir Alastair is right to point out that the company's problems originated from the delays in building the tunnel and the overshoot on costs, as well as the shortfall in revenues. But whatever the injustices heaped upon Eurotunnel in the past, compensation from governments and contractors is unlikely to make up the shortfall in Eurotunnel's capacity to service its debt.

Source: Financial Times, 15 September 1995. Reprinted with permission.

Exhibit 11.31 In October 1996 an innovative and complex agreement was worked out with the bankers, creating new forms of debt instrument . . .

Eurotunnel stable, but still in intensive care

Is Eurotunnel dead? Not quite – if nothing else, the company and its bankers this week succeeded in fending off that day by several years. Shareholders are still left needing a miracle, though.

Eurotunnel this week returned from the land of the living dead when, in a complex deal with its banks, it restructured £4.7bn of its crippling £9.1bn debts, and dangled before investors the hope of a dividend within 10 years.

Acknowledging the necessity that the pain be shared by its shareholders and its 225 banks, outgoing co-chairman Sir Alastair Morton urged both sides to accept a 'fair and robust' deal. But although his brinkmanship may have saved Eurotunnel from imminent collapse, he has still left plenty of work for his successor.

'The deal's big and long-dated enough and has enough of a cushion to ensure Eurotunnel shouldn't need a second restructuring,' said Jeff Summers, an analyst with debt trader Klesch & Co. 'But for existing shareholders to get a dividend by about 2004, the company's got to achieve a Herculean rate of growth.'

Mark McVicar, analyst at NatWest Securities, said the restructuring had bought Eurotunnel time, 'Because Eurotunnel's capital is so hard to value – there's a mish-mash of financial instruments in the middle converting into either debt or equity depending on its future performance,' he said . . .

The deal means Eurotunnel's banks initially take 45.5 per cent of the company through a £1bn debt-for-equity swap in which the shares are valued at 130p. On top, there's a raft of financial instruments designed to reduce the interest burden from a current £600m–£650m a year to £400m from now until the end of December 2003. These are:
• £1bn of debt to be exchanged for equity notes, convertible into Eurotunnel units at 155p after December 2003;
• £1.5bn of debt swapped for reset-table bonds (i.e. on which the interest rate may be subject to adjustment); and
• £1.2bn of debt exchanged for loan notes paying 1 per cent fixed interest plus 30 per cent of Eurotunnel's annual cash flow after operating costs, capital expenditure and financing costs.

For shareholders, Le Crunch comes in 2004 when the banks could convert their equity notes to give them 60.6 per cent of the company. To allow shareholders to maintain slim control, Eurotunnel is issuing them free warrants, exercisable at 150p until December 2003. If shareholders exercise these, they will redeem the bank's notes.

But the issue is complicated further because out of its present free cash flow of about £125m, Eurotunnel cannot pay even £400m a year in interest. To make up the shortfall, it has agreed £1.85bn of stabilisation notes which roll up interest-free until 2006 but can be converted into shares before then at 130p.

Sir Alastair believes the end of 'looney time' ferry pricing, thanks to the P&O/Stena-Sealink merger, and Eurotunnel's growing market share, should leave his company self-financing long before the £1.85bn runs out. But if he's wrong, the banks will end up with almost 76 per cent of Eurotunnel and it will need more-painful restructuring.

Source: Alastair Osborne, *Investors Chronicle*, 11 October 1996. Reprinted with kind permission of the *Investors Chronicle*.

CONCLUDING COMMENTS

So far this book has taken a fairly detailed look at a variety of ways of raising money by selling shares and has examined the main methods of raising funds through long-term debt. The decision to raise equity or debt finance is neither simple nor straightforward. In the next chapter we consider a wider array of financial sources and types, from leasing to factoring. Knowledge of these will enable the finance manager or other executives to select and structure the different forms of finance to maximise the firm's potential. Topics covered later in the book draw on the knowledge gained in Chapters 10, 11 and 12 to permit informed discussion of such crucial questions as: What is the appropriate mixture of debt and equity? How is the cost of various forms of finance calculated? How can the risk of certain forms of finance (for example a floating-interest-rate term loan) be reduced?

KEY POINTS AND CONCEPTS

- **Debt finance has a number of advantages:**
  - it has a lower cost than equity finance:
    - a lower transaction costs;
    - b lower rate of return;
  - debt holders generally do not have votes;
  - interest is tax deductible.

- **Drawbacks of debt:**
  - secured debt has the risk of forced liquidation;
  - the use of secured assets for borrowing may be an onerous constraint on managerial action.

- **A bond** is a long-term contract in which the bondholders lend money to a company. A straight 'vanilla' bond pays regular interest plus the capital on the redemption date.

- **Debentures** are generally more secure than **loan stock** (in the UK).

- **A trust deed** has **affirmative covenants** outlining the nature of the bond contract and **negative covenants** imposing constraints on managerial action to reduce risk for the lenders.

- **A floating rate note (FRN)** is a bond with an interest rate which varies as a benchmark interest rate changes (e.g. LIBOR).

- **Attractive features of bank borrowing:**
  - administrative and legal costs are low;
  - quick;
  - flexibility in troubled times;
  - available to small firms.

- **Factors for a firm to consider with bank borrowing:**

  Costs
  - fixed versus floating;
  - arrangement fees;
  - bargaining on the rate.

  Security
  - asymmetric information;
  - collateral;
  - covenants;
  - personal guarantees.

  Repayment arrangements:
  Some possibilities:
  - grace periods;
  - mortgage;
  - term loan.

- **A syndicated loan** occurs where a number of banks (or other financial institutions) each contribute a portion of a loan.

- **A credit rating** depends on a the likelihood of payments of interest and/or capital not being paid (i.e. default); and b the extent to which the lender is protected in the event of a default.

- **Mezzanine debt** is debt offering a high return with a high risk. It has been particularly useful in the following:
  - management buyouts (MBOs), especially leveraged management buyouts (LBOs);
  - fast-growing companies;
  - leveraged recapitalisation.

- **Convertible bonds** are issued as debt instruments but they also give the holder the right to exchange the bonds at some time in the future into ordinary shares according to some prearranged formula. They have the following advantages:
  - lower interest than on debentures;
  - interest is tax deductible;
  - self liquidating;
  - few negative covenants;
  - shares might be temporarily underpriced.

- A bond is **priced** according to general market interest rates for risk class and maturity:

Irredeemable:

$$P_D = \frac{i}{k_D}$$

Redeemable:

$$P_D = \frac{i_1}{1 + k_D} + \frac{i_2}{(1 + k_D)^2} + \frac{i_3}{(1 + k_D)^3} + ... + \frac{R_n}{(1 + k_D)^n}$$

- The **interest yield** on a bond is:

$$\frac{\text{Gross interest (coupon)}}{\text{Market price}} \times 100$$

- The **yield to maturity** includes both annual coupon returns and capital gains or losses on maturity.

- The **Eurosecurities markets** are informal (unregulated) markets in money held outside its country of origin.

- A **foreign bond** is a bond denominated in the currency of the country where it is issued when the issuer is a non-resident.

- A **Eurobond** is a bond sold outside the jurisdiction of the country of the currency in which the bond is denominated.

- A **project finance** loan is provided as a bank loan or bond finance to an entity set up separately from the parent corporation to undertake a project. The returns to the lender are tied to the fortunes and cash flows of the project.

- **Sale and leaseback** Assets are sold to financial institutions or another company which releases cash. Simultaneously, the original owner agrees to lease the assets back for a stated period under specified terms.

■ **Securitisation** Relatively small, homogeneous and illiquid financial assets are pooled and repackaged into liquid securities which are then sold on to other investors to generate cash for the original lender.

■ The **term structure of interest rates** describes the manner in which the same default risk class of debt securities provides different rates of return depending on the length of time to maturity. There are three hypotheses relating to the term structure of interest rates:
  – the expectations hypothesis;
  – the liquidity-preference hypothesis;
  – the market-segmentation hypothesis.

REFERENCES AND FURTHER READING

Altman, E.I. and Kao D.L. (1992) 'Rating drift in high-yield bonds', *Journal of Fixed Income*, 1, March, pp. 15–20. Also reproduced in S. Lofthouse (ed.), *Readings in Investments*. New York: Wiley (1994). Investigates the re-rating of bonds on US markets over time.

Arnold, G. and Smith, M. (1999) *The European High Yield Bond Market: Drivers and Impediments*. London: Financial Times Finance Management Report. A comprehensive exploration of the potential of the junk bond market in Europe – a history of the US market is also given.

Association of Corporate Treasurers. *The Treasurer's Handbook*. An annual publication with up-to-date information on credit ratings and other financial matters.

Bank for International Settlements Quarterly Review. Available online – free (www.bis.org). Terrific source of information on the international debt market (and much else besides).

Bank of England Quarterly Bulletin. Comprehensible, illustrated and up-to-date discussions of financial markets events and statistics.

Blake, D. (2000) *Financial Market Analysis*. 2nd edn. Chichester: Wiley. A technical and detailed examination of long-term debt markets.

Brett, M. (2000) *How to Read the Financial Pages*. 5th edn. London: Random House: Business Books. An easy-to-read introductory text on the debt markets.

Brigham, E.F. (1966) 'An analysis of convertible debentures: Theory and some empirical evidence', *Journal of Finance*, March, pp. 35–54. Valuation of convertibles and the major factors influencing price. Evidence that most firms issue convertibles to raise equity finance.

Buckle, M. and Thompson, J. (1995) *The UK Financial System*. 2nd edn. Manchester: Manchester University Press. The Eurosecurities markets are discussed clearly and concisely. There are useful sections on the domestic bond market and the term structure of interest rates.

Buckley, A. (2000) *Multinational Finance*. 4th edn. London: FT Prentice Hall. Some additional detail on some of the issues discussed in this chapter – easy to read.

Corporate Finance Magazine. London: Euromoney. This monthly publication has some excellent articles describing corporate activity in the bond and other financial markets targeted at senior financial personnel.

The Economist. This excellent weekly publication has a section devoted to finance. A good way of keeping up to date.

Eiteman, D.K., Stonehill, A.I. and Moffett, M.H. (2001) *Multinational Finance: International Edition*. 9th edn. Reading, Mass: Addison Wesley. Some useful, easy-to-follow, material on international debt markets.

Financial Times. Details of recent syndicated loans, Eurobonds and bank lending can be found almost every day in the *Financial Times*.

Hickman, B.G. (1958) 'Corporate bond quality and investor experience', *National Bureau of Economic Research*, Princeton, 14. Early research into the returns and default rates on bonds.

Hicks, J.R. (1946) *Value and Capital: An Inquiry into some Fundamental Principles of Economic Theory*. 2nd edn. Oxford: Oxford University Press. Liquidity-preference hypothesis to explain the term structure of interest rates.

Lutz, F.A. and Lutz, V.C. (1951) *The Theory of Investment in the Firm*. Princeton, NJ: Princeton University Press. Expectations hypothesis of the term structure of interest rates.

Maude, D. (1996) 'Eurobond primary and secondary markets', in E. Gardener and P. Molyneux (eds), *Investment Banking: Theory and Practice*. London: Euromoney. A short introduction to the Eurobond markets.

Pilbeam, K. (1998) *International Finance*. 2nd edn. London: Macmillan Business. An introductory treatment of debt markets.

Standard & Poor's (1999) *Ratings Performance 1998: Stability and Transition*, January. Evidence on returns and defaults on bonds of different ratings.

Valdez, S. (2000) *An Introduction to Global Financial Markets*. 3rd edn. London: Macmillan Business. Easy-to-read background on international bond markets.

WEBSITES

Association of Corporate Treasurers www.corporate-treasurers.co.uk

Bank of England www.bankofengland.co.uk

The Economist www.economist.com

Financial Times www.FT.com

Fitch IBCA www.fitchibca.com

International Securities Market Association www.isma.co.uk

Moody's www.moodys.com

Standard & Poor's www.standardandpoors.com

SELF-REVIEW QUESTIONS

1 What are the relative advantages and drawbacks of debt and equity finance?

2 Explain the following (related to bonds):
   a Par value.
   b Trustee.
   c Debenture.
   d Zero-coupon bond.
   e Floating-rate note.

3 The inexperienced finance trainee at Mugs-R-Us plc says that he can save the company money on its forthcoming issue of ten-year bonds. 'The rate of return required for bonds of this risk class in the financial markets is 10 per cent and yet I overheard our merchant banking adviser say, "We could issue a bond at a coupon of only 9 per cent." I reckon we could save the company a large sum on the £100m issue.' Do you agree with the trainee's logic?

4   In what circumstances would you recommend borrowing from a bank rather than a capital market bond issue?

5   What are the fundamental considerations to which you would advise a firm to give thought if it were contemplating borrowing from a bank?

6   Is securitisation something to do with anti-criminal precautions? If not, explain what it is and why firms do it.

7   In what ways does the tax regime encourage debt finance rather than equity finance?

8   Why does convertible debt carry a lower coupon than straight debt?

9   What is meant by asymmetric information in the relationship between banker and borrower?

10 What is a syndicated loan and why do banks join so many syndicates?

11 What are the differences between a domestic bond, a Eurobond and a foreign bond?

12 What is the credit rating on a bond and what factors determine it?

13 Why do bond issuers accept restrictive covenants?

14 What are high-yield bonds? What is their role in financing firms?

15 What is a bearer bond?

16 What is a debenture?

17 What is the difference between a fixed-rate and a floating-rate bond?

QUESTIONS AND PROBLEMS

1   Imagine that the market yield to maturity for three-year bonds in a particular risk class is 12 per cent. You buy a bond in that risk class which offers an annual coupon of 10 per cent for the next three years, with the first payment in one year. The bond will be redeemed at par (£100) in three years.

   a   How much would you pay for the bond?

   b   If you paid £105 what yield to maturity would you obtain?

2   A £100 bond with two years to maturity and an annual coupon of 9 per cent is available. (The next coupon is payable in one year.)

   a   If the market requires a yield to maturity of 9 per cent for a bond of this risk class what will be its market price?

   b   If the market price is £98, what yield to maturity does it offer?

   c If the required yield to maturity on this type of bond changes to 7 per cent, what will the market price change to?

3 **a** If the government sold a 10-year gilt with a par value of £100 and an (annual) coupon of 9 per cent, what price can be charged if investors require a 9.5 per cent yield to maturity on such bonds?

   b If yields to maturity on bonds of this risk class fall to 8.5 per cent, what could the bonds be sold for?

   c If it were sold for £105, what yield to maturity is the bond offering?

   d What is the flat yield on this bond?

4* The price of a bond issued by C & M plc is 85.50 per cent of par value. The bond will pay an annual 8.5 per cent coupon until maturity (the next coupon will be paid in one year). The bond matures in seven years.

   a What will be the market price of the bond if yields to maturity for this risk class fall to 7.5 per cent?

   b What will be the market price of the bond if yields to maturity for this risk class rise to 18 per cent?

5 A zero coupon bond with a par value of £100 matures in five years.

   a What is the price of the bond if the yield to maturity is 5 per cent?

   b What is the price of the bond if the yield to maturity is 10 per cent?

6 Bond 1 has an annual coupon rate of 6 per cent and Bond 2 has an annual coupon of 12 per cent. Both bonds mature in one year and have a par value of £100. If the yield to maturity on bonds of this risk class is 10 per cent at what price will the bonds sell? Assume that the next coupons are due in one year's time.

7* You are considering three alternative investments in bonds but would like to gain an impression of the extent of price volatility for each given alternative changes in future interest rates. The investments are:

   i A two-year bond with an annual coupon of 6 per cent, par value of £100 and the next coupon payment in one year. The current yield to maturity on this bond is 6.5 per cent.

   ii A ten-year bond with an annual coupon of 6 per cent, a par value of £100 and the next coupon payable in one year. The current yield to maturity on this bond is 7.2 per cent.

   iii A 20-year bond with an annual coupon of 6 per cent, a par value of £100 and the next coupon due in one year. The current yield to maturity on this bond is 7.7 per cent.

   a Draw an approximate yield curve.

   b Calculate the market price of each of the bonds.

   c Calculate the market price of the bonds on the assumption that yields to maturity rise by 200 basis points for all bonds.

   d Now calculate the market price of the bonds on the assumption that yields to maturity fall by 200 basis points.

   e Which bond price is the most volatile in circumstances of changing yields to maturity?

   f Explain the liquidity-preference theory of the term structure of yields to maturity.

8   What are the factors that explain the difference in yields to maturity between long-term and short-term bonds?

9   Find the current yield to maturity on government securities with maturities of one year, five years and ten years in the *Financial Times*. How has the yield curve changed since 2001 as shown in the chapter? What might account for this shift?

10   If the yield to maturity on a two-year zero coupon bond is 13 per cent and the yield to maturity on a one-year zero coupon bond is 10 per cent what is the expected spot rate of one-year bonds in one year's time assuming the expectations hypothesis is applicable?

11   If the yield to maturity on a one-year bond is 8 per cent and the expected spot rate on a one-year bond, beginning in one year's time, is 7 per cent what will be the yield to maturity on a two-year bond under the expectations hypothesis of the term structure of interest rates?

12   In 2001 the term structure of interest rates for UK government securities was downward sloping and in 1996 it was upward sloping. Explain how these curves come about with reference to the expectations, liquidity and market-segmentation hypotheses.

13   Iris plc borrows £50m at 9.5 per cent from Westlloyds bank for five years. What cash flows will the firm have to find if the interest and principal are paid in the following ways?

a   All interest and capital is paid at the end of the period.

b   Interest only is paid for each of the years (at the year ends); all principal is paid at the end.

c   £10m of the capital plus annual interest is paid on each anniversary date.

14   What factors should a firm consider when borrowing from a bank?

15   'Convertibles are great because they offer a lower return than straight debt and we just dish out shares rather than having to find cash to redeem the bonds' – executive at Myopic plc. Comment on this statement as though you were a shareholder in Myopic.

16   Lummer plc has issued £60m 15-year 8.5 per cent coupon bonds with a par value of £100. Each bond is convertible into 40 shares of Lummer ordinary shares, which are currently trading at £1.90.

a   What is the conversion price?

b   What is the conversion premium?

c   What is the conversion value of the bond?

17   Explain the following terms and their relevance to debt-finance decision makers:

a   Negative covenant.

b   Conversion premium.

c   Collateral.

d   Grace periods.

18   Outline the main advantages and disadvantages of fixed and floating interest rates from the borrowing company's perspective.

19 (*Examination level*) Flying High plc plans to expand rapidly over the next five years and is considering the following forms of finance to support that expansion.

    a A five-year £10m floating-rate term loan from MidBarc Bank plc at an initial annual interest of 9 per cent

    b A five-year Eurodollar bond fixed at 8 per cent with a nominal value of US$15m.

    c A £10m convertible bond offering a yield to redemption of 6 per cent and a conversion premium of 15 per cent.

    As the financial adviser to the board you have been asked to explain each of these forms of finance and point out the relative advantages and drawbacks. Do this in report form.

20 'We avoid debt finance because of the unacceptable constraint placed on managerial actions.' Explain what this executive means and suggest forms of long-term borrowing which have few constraints.

ASSIGNMENTS

1 Review the long-term debt instruments used by a company familiar to you. Consider the merits and drawbacks of these and explain alternative long-term debt strategies.

2 Write a report for the senior management of a company you know well explaining your views on the wisdom of using some of the firm's assets in a sale and leaseback transaction.

CHAPTER NOTES

1 This example is designed to show the effect of leverage. It does lack realism in a number of respects; for example it is unlikely that profits will continue to rise at 25 per cent per annum without further investment. This can be adjusted for – the time taken to pay off the debt lengthens but the principles behind the example do not alter.

2 This topic and the previous one do not sit perfectly in a chapter on long-term finance, but they help to give a more complete view of the Euromarkets.

Production and Operations Management

Chapters from:
Operations Management 4th *Edition*
Nigel Slack, Stuart Chambers
and Robert Johnston

chapter one

Operations management

Source: Corbis.

key questions

● What is operations management?

● What are the similarities between all operations?

● How are operations different from each other?

● What do operations managers do?

Introduction

Operations management is about how organizations produce goods and services. Everything you wear, eat, sit on, use, read or knock about on the sports field comes to you courtesy of the operations managers who organized its production. Every book you borrow from the library, every treatment you receive at the hospital, every service you expect in the shops and every lecture you attend at university – all have been produced. While the people who supervised their 'production' may not always be called operations managers, that is what they really are. And that is what this book is concerned with – the tasks, issues and decisions of those operations managers who have made the services and products on which we all depend. This is an introductory chapter, so we will examine what we mean by 'operations management', how operations processes can be found everywhere, how they are all similar yet different, and what it is that operations managers really do. The model which is developed to explain the subject is shown in Figure 1.1.

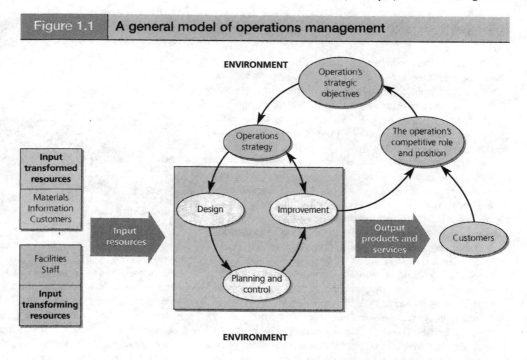

Figure 1.1 A general model of operations management

Effective operations management

If we want to understand operations management we must start by studying real operations and we will do this in every chapter except the last. So we will start with two retail operations – IKEA, the furniture and homeware retailers, and Pret A Manger, a high quality sandwich and snack food chain (see the two examples).

Both these examples seem to understand their markets and how they can serve the needs of their customers. Just as important, both rely for their success on the way they organize the delivery of their services. This is the responsibility of both companies' *operations management*, and for both companies it is a vitally important activity. Both sets of operations managers are also concerned with the same basic task – managing the processes which transform a set of 'inputs' (in these cases furniture items or sandwich ingredients together with the customers who enter their stores) into 'outputs' of satisfied customers, happy with their furniture or sandwich purchase. They do this by using their staff and facilities effectively and efficiently. Yet there are also important differences between each company's operations. The scale of their individual stores, for example, or the typical time for a customer to make a purchase. But although these differences are real and important, the operations managers in each company will be making the same *type* of decision (even if *what* they actually decide is different). They must decide on their overall operations approach built on their business strategy. They must design their processes as well as their products and services. They must run their operations processes on a day-by-day basis, ensuring the appropriate delivery of their services. Finally, and perhaps most importantly, they must constantly seek out ways of improving the way they create and deliver their products and services.

In fact these two examples demonstrate the issues that the rest of this chapter will cover.

- That operations management is *important* to all businesses.
- That all operations managers manage *processes*.
- That the processes in different operations can have *different characteristics*.
- That all operations managers have a similar set of responsibilities and *activities*.

5

IKEA[1]

With over 100 giant stores operating throughout the world, IKEA has managed to develop its own special way of selling furniture. Customers often spend around two hours in the store – far longer than in rival furniture retailers. This is because of the way it organizes its store operations. IKEA's philosophy goes back to the original business, started in the 1950s in southern Sweden by Ingvar Kamprad who was successfully selling furniture, through a catalogue operation. Because customers wanted to see some of his furniture, he built a showroom in Stockholm. Not in the centre of the city where land was expensive, but on the outskirts of town. Instead of buying expensive display stands, he simply set the furniture out as it would be in a domestic setting. Also, instead of moving the furniture from the warehouse to the showroom area, he asked customers to pick the furniture up themselves from the warehouse, an approach that is still the basis of IKEA's process today.

IKEA offers 'value for money' furniture with a wide range of choice, usually designed to be stored and sold as a 'flat pack' which the customer assembles at home. The stores are all designed around the same self-service concept – that finding the store, parking, moving through the store itself, and ordering and picking up goods should be simple, smooth and problem-free. At the entrance to each store are large noticeboards which proclaim IKEA's philosophy and provide advice to shoppers who have not used the store before. Catalogues are available at this point showing product details and illustrations. For young children, there is a supervised children's play area, a small cinema, a parent and baby room and toilets, so parents can leave their children in the supervised play area for a time. Each child is attired in a yellow numbered top while in this area and parents are recalled via the loudspeaker system if the child has any

problems. Customers may also borrow pushchairs to keep their children with them.

Parts of the showroom are set out in 'room settings', while other parts show similar products together, so that customers can make comparisons. IKEA like to allow customers to make up their minds in their own time. If advice is needed, 'information points' have staff who can help. Every piece of furniture carries a ticket with a code number which indicates the location in the warehouse from where it can be collected. (For larger items customers go to the information desks for assistance.) After the showroom, customers pass into an area where smaller items are displayed, and can be picked directly customers. Customers then pass through the self-service warehouse where they can pick up the items they viewed in the showroom. Finally, the customers pay at the checkouts, where a ramped conveyor belt moves purchases up to the checkout staff. The exit area has service points, and often a 'Swedish Shop' with Swedish foodstuffs. A large loading area allows customers to bring their cars from the car park and load their purchases. Customers may also rent or buy a roof rack. ■

Before that, it is necessary to establish some definitions.

Operations function
- The **operations function** of the organization is the arrangement of the resources which are devoted to the production and delivery of its products and services. Every organization has an operations function because every organization produces some type of products and/or services. However, not all types of organization will necessarily call the operations function by this name. (Note in addition that we also use the shorter terms 'the operation' or 'operations' and, at times, the 'operations system', or 'operations processes', interchangeably with the 'operations function'.)

Operations managers
- **Operations managers** are the staff of the organization who have particular responsibility for managing some, or all, of the resources which comprise the operations function. Again in some organizations the operations manager could be called by some other name. For example, he or she might be called the 'fleet manager' in a distribution company, the 'administrative manager' in a hospital, or the 'store manager' in a supermarket.

Operations management
- **Operations management** is the term that is used for the activities, decisions and responsibilities of operations managers.

6

Pret A Manger

Described by the press as having 'revolutionized the concept of sandwich making and eating', Pret A Manger opened their first shop in the mid-1980s, in London. Now they have over 130 shops in UK, New York, Hong Kong and Tokyo. They say that their secret is to focus continually on quality – not just of their food, but in every aspect of their operations practice. They go to extraordinary lengths to avoid the chemicals and preservatives common in most 'fast' food say the company. 'Many food retailers focus on extending the shelf life of their food, but that's of no interest to us. We maintain our edge by selling food that simply can't be beaten for freshness. At the end of the day, we give whatever we haven't sold to charity to help feed those who would otherwise go hungry. When we were just starting out, a big supplier tried to sell us coleslaw that lasted sixteen days. Can you imagine, salad that lasts sixteen days? There and then we decided Pret would stick to wholesome fresh food – natural stuff. We have not changed that policy.'

The first Pret A Manger shop had its own kitchen where fresh ingredients were delivered first thing every morning, and food was prepared throughout the day. Every Pret shop since has followed this model. The team members serving on the tills at lunchtime will have been making sandwiches in the kitchen that morning. They rejected the idea of a huge centralized sandwich factory even though it could significantly reduce costs. Pret also own and manage all their shops directly so that they can ensure consistently

high standards in all their shops. 'We are determined never to forget that our hardworking people make all the difference. They are our heart and soul. When they care, our business is sound. If they cease to care, our business goes down the drain. In a retail sector where high staff turnover is normal, we're pleased to say our people are much more likely to stay around! We work hard at building great teams. We take our reward schemes and career opportunities very seriously. We don't work nights (generally), we wear jeans, we party!' Customer feedback is regarded as being particularly important at Pret. Examining customers' comments for improvement ideas is a key part of weekly management meetings, and of the daily team briefs in each shop. ■

Operations management is important

Operations management can reduce costs

Operations management can increase revenue

Operations management can reduce the need for investment

Operations management can enhance innovation

As we have seen both in IKEA and Pret A Manger, if the operations function is to contribute to the success of the organization it must use its resources effectively, producing goods and services in a way that satisfies its customers. To do this it must be creative, innovative and energetic in improving its processes, products and services. An effective operation can give four types of advantage to the business.

- It can reduce the **costs** of producing products and services by being efficient.
- It can increase **revenue** by increasing customer satisfaction through good quality and service.
- It can reduce the amount of **investment** (sometimes called capital employed) that is necessary to produce the required type and quantity of products and services by increasing the effective capacity of the operation and by being innovative in how it uses its physical resources.
- It can provide the basis for *future* **innovation** by building a solid base of operations skills and knowledge within the business.

The new operations agenda

These four advantages from well run operations have always been important in giving any organization a competitive advantage. (Or, in a not-for-profit organization, the means to fulfil the organization's long-term strategic goals.) But, in addition, recent developments

7

Table 1.1	Changes in the business environment are shaping a new operations agenda
The business environment is changing . . .	*Prompting operations responses . . .*
For example. . . • Increased cost-based competition • Higher quality expectations • Dlemands for better service • More choice and variety • Frequent new product/service introduction • Increased ethical sensitivity • Environmental impacts are more transparent • More legal regulation • Greater security awareness	For example. . . • Globalization of operations networking • Technologies replacing manual jobs • Internet-based integration of operations activities • Supply chain management • Flexible working patterns • Mass customization • Fast time-to-market methods • Lean process design • Environmentally sensitive design • Supplier 'partnership' and development • Failure analysis • Business recovery planning

in the business environment have made them even more important and have also added some new pressures for which the operations function has needed to develop responses. Table 1.1 lists some of these business pressures and the operations responses to them. Together these operations responses now form a major part of a *new agenda* for operations. Parts of this agenda are trends which have always existed but have accelerated in recent years. This includes the increased globalization of operations networks to reduce costs, or the use of new technologies. Part of this agenda involves seeking ways to exploit new technologies, most notably internet-based technologies, whose potential is still not fully understood. Some new issues are based on changing the way operations managers think about their activities and responsibilities. 'Supply chains' (examined in Chapters 6 and 13) for example are not new, they have always existed. But thinking from a *supply chain perspective* is relatively new and brings new opportunities. Other ideas deliberately challenge what used to be conventional wisdom. 'Lean' operations (that reduce all forms of waste) and mass customization (the idea that even when operations produce in vast quantities, each product or service can be different) are examples of this. Yet other issues are specific responses to concerns which have emerged in society at large – environmentally sensitive operations practices and risk avoidance, or security practice for example. Of course, the list in Table 1.1 is not comprehensive, nor is it universal. Different companies in different industries will be subject to different pressures and therefore have a different set of operations issues But (and this is the main point) very few businesses will be unaffected by some of these concerns. Most businesses are having to cope with a more challenging environment, and are looking to their operations function to help them respond.

Operations in the organization

The operations function is central to the organization because it produces the goods and services which are its reason for existing, but it is neither the only, nor necessarily the most important, function. It is, however, one of the **three core functions** of any organization. These are:

Three core functions

• the marketing (including sales) function – which is responsible for *communicating* the organization's products and services to its markets in order to generate customer requests for service;

8

Core functional activities	Internet service provider (ISP)	Fastfood chain	International aid charity	Furniture manufacturer
Table 1.2	**The activities of core functions in some organizations**			
Marketing and sales	Promote services to users and get registrations / Sell advertising space	Advertise on TV / Devise promotional materials	Develop funding contracts / Mail out appeals for donations	Advertise in magazines / Determine pricing policy / Sell to stores
Product/service development	Devise new services and commission new information content	Design hamburgers, pizzas, etc. / Design decor for restaurants	Develop new appeals campaigns / Design new assistance programmes	Design new furniture / Coordinate with fashionable colours
Operations	Maintain hardware, solftware and content / Implement new links and services	Make burgers, pizzas, etc. / Serve customers / Clear away / Maintain equipment	Give service to the beneficiaries of the charity	Make components / Assemble furniture / Deliver furniture

- the product/service development function – which is responsible for *creating* new and modified products and services in order to generate future customer requests for service;
- the operations function – which is responsible for *fulfilling* customer requests for service throughout the production and delivery of products and services.

Support functions

In addition, there are the **support functions** which enable the core functions to operate effectively. These include, for example:

- the accounting and finance function – which provides the information to help economic decision making and manages the financial resources of the organization;
- the human resources function – which recruits and develops the organization's staff as well as looking after their welfare.

Remember that different organizations will call their various functions by different names and will have a different set of support functions. Almost all organizations, however, will have the three core functions, because all organizations have a fundamental need to sell their services, satisfy their customers, and create the means to satisfy customers in the future. Table 1.2 shows the activities of the three core functions for a sample of operations.

In practice, functional names, boundaries and responsibilities do vary significantly between organizations; nor is there a clear division either between the three core functions or between core and support functions. In fact many of the interesting problems in management (and the opportunities for improvement) lie at the overlapping boundaries between functions. This leads to some confusion over where the boundaries of the operations function should be drawn. In this book we use a relatively **broad definition of operations** (see Figure 1.2). We treat much of the product/service development, engineering/technical and IT activities and some of the personnel, marketing, and accounting and finance activities as coming within the sphere of operations management. Most significantly, we treat the core operations function as comprising all the activities necessary for the day-to-day fulfillment of customer requests. This includes sourcing products and services from suppliers and transporting products and services to customers. Therefore, what in some organizations are the separate functions of 'purchasing' and 'distribution' are, to us, a core part of operations management.

Broad definition of operations

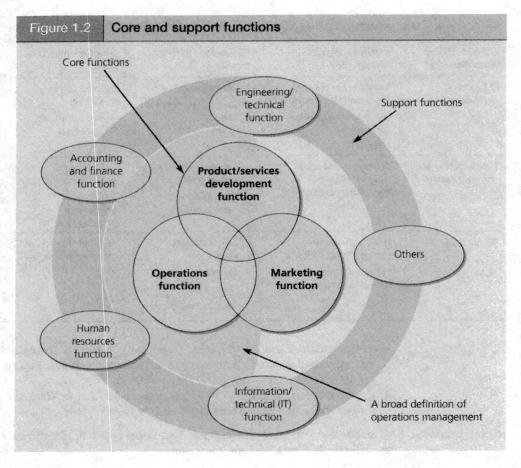

Figure 1.2   **Core and support functions**

Core functions

Engineering/
technical
function

Support functions

Accounting
and finance
function

**Product/services
development
function**

Others

**Operations
function**

**Marketing
function**

Human
resources
function

Information/
technical (IT)
function

A broad definition of
operations management

Operations management in the smaller organization

Theoretically, operations management is the same for any size of organization. However, in practice, managing operations in a small or medium-size organization has its own set of problems. Large companies may have the resources to dedicate individuals to specialized tasks but smaller companies often cannot, so people may have to do different jobs as the need arises. Such an informal structure can allow the company to respond quickly as opportunities or problems present themselves. But decision making can also become confused as individuals' roles overlap. Small companies may have exactly the same operations management issues as large ones but they can be more difficult to separate from the mass of other issues in the organization. However, small operations can also have significant advantages; the box on Acme Whistles illustrates this.

Operations management in not-for-profit organizations

Terms such as *competitive advantage*, *markets* and *business*, which are used in this book, are usually associated with companies in the for-profit sector. Yet operations management is also relevant to organizations whose purpose is not primarily to earn profits. Managing the operations in an animal welfare charity, hospital, research organization or government department is essentially the same as in commercial organizations. **Operations managers have to take the same decisions** – how to produce products and services, invest in technology, contract out some of their activities, devise performance measures, improve their operations performance and so on.

Operations
decisions are the
same in commercial
and not-for-profit
organizations

10

Acme Whistles[2]

Acme Whistles can trace its history back to 1870 when Joseph Hudson, decided he had the answer to the London Metropolitan Police's request for something to replace the wooden rattles that they used to attract attention and sound the alarm. So the world's first police whistle was born. Being the height of the British Empire many other police forces adopted the same police whistle as the London Police, so Acme Whistles grew to be the premier supplier of high class whistles for police forces around the world. Within a year Hudson had moved from having no employees to having fifty. The success of his company has continued from that point. *'In many ways'*, says Simon Topman, owner and Managing Director of the company, *'the company is very much the same as it was in Joseph's day. The machinery is more modern, of course, and we have a wider variety of products, but many of our products are very similar in design to their predecessors. For example, football referees seem to prefer the traditional snail-shaped whistle. So, although we have dramatically improved the performance of the product, our customers want it to look the same. Most importantly, we have also maintained the same manufacturing tradition from those early days. For example, the original owner insisted on personally blowing every single whistle before it left the factory. We still do the same, not by personally blowing them, but by plugging each whistle into an airline and subjecting it to the equivalent of normal lung pressure. This means that the same tradition of quality has endured.'*

The company's range of whistles has expanded to include sports whistles (they provide the whistles for the soccer world cup), distress whistles, (silent) dog whistles, novelty whistles, instrumental whistles (used by all of the world's top orchestras), and many more types. Although the whistle may seem a somewhat old fashioned object, both it and the technology behind it, are undergoing a resurgence. For example, although police use mobile radios predominantly, these can be lost, damaged or stolen. A whistle, on the other hand, is simple and robust as well as compact and therefore provides a useful back-up. Less expected perhaps is the use of whistle technology in such high-tech applications as monitoring the air flow into protective fire resistant suits. Any variation in air flow makes a whistle embedded in the air pipe sound and provides an audible warning. *'We are always trying to improve our products'*, says Simon, *'it's a business of constant innovation. Sometimes I think that after 130 years there is surely nothing more to do, but we always find some new feature to incorporate. You cannot find a single decade since the company was founded where we have not produced a novel and patentable innovation.'*

'Managing the operations in a small company is, of course, very different to working in a large one. Everyone has much broader jobs; we cannot afford the overheads of having specialist people in specialized roles. But this relative informality has a lot of advantages. It means that we can maintain our philosophy of quality amongst everybody in the company, and it means that we can react very quickly when the market demands it.' Nor is the company's relatively small size any barrier to its ability to innovate. *'On the contrary'*, says Simon, *'there is something about the culture of the company that is extremely important in fostering innovation. Because we are small we all know each other and we all want to contribute something to the company. It is not uncommon for employees to figure out new ideas for different types of whistle. If an idea looks promising, we will put a small and informal team together to look at it further. It is not unusual for people who have been with us only a few months to start wanting to make innovations. It's as though something happens to them when they walk through the door of the factory that encourages their natural inventiveness.'* ■

Question

1 What is the overlap between operations, marketing and product/service development at Acme Whistles?

11

However, the strategic objectives of not-for-profit organizations may be more complex and involve a mixture of political, economic, social or environmental objectives. Because of this there may be a greater chance of operations decisions being made under conditions of conflicting objectives. So, for example, it is the operations staff in a children's welfare department who have to face the conflict between the cost of providing extra social workers and the risk of a child not receiving adequate protection. Nevertheless the vast majority of the topics covered in this book have relevance to all types of organization, including non-profit, even if the context is different and some terms may have to be adapted.

Operations management is about managing processes

Processes

Transformation process model

Input resources

Outputs of goods and services

Operations management is concerned with managing **processes**. All operations produce goods and services by managing these processes to change the state or condition of something to produce *outputs*. Figure 1.3 shows this general **transformation process model** which is used to describe the nature of operations. Put simply, operations processes take in a set of **input resources** which are then used to transform something, or are transformed themselves, into **outputs of goods and services** which satisfy customer needs.

All operations conform to this general input–transformation–output model. Table 1.3 illustrates how a wide range of operations can be described in this way. However, there are differences between different operations. If you stand far enough away from, say, a hospital or a motor vehicle plant, they might look the same. Each is likely to be a large building into which staff enter and deliveries take place. But move closer and clear differences do start to emerge. For a start, one is a manufacturing operation producing largely physical goods, and one is a service operation which produces changes in the physiological condition, feelings and behaviour of patients. The nature of the processes which each building contains will also be different. The motor vehicle plant contains metal cutting and forming machinery and assembly processes, whereas the hospital contains diagnostic, care and therapeutic processes. Perhaps the most important difference between the two operations, however, is the nature of their inputs. Both have 'staff' and 'facilities' as inputs to the operation but they act upon very different things. The motor vehicle plant uses its staff and

| Figure 1.3 | All operations are input–transformation–output processes |

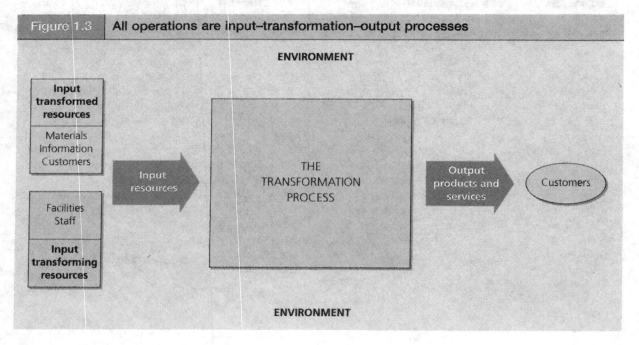

12

Table 1.3	Some operations described in terms of their processes		
Operation	What are the process inputs	What do the operation's processes do?	What are process outputs?
Airline	Aircraft Pilots and air crew Ground crew Passengers and freight	Move passengers and freight around the world	Transported passengers and freight
Department store	Goods for sale Sales staff Computerized registers Customers	Display goods Give sales advice Sell goods	Customers and goods assembled together
Police	Police officers Computer systems Information Public (law-abiding and criminals)	Prevent crime Solve crime Apprehend criminals	Lawful society Public with feeling of security
Frozen food manufacturer	Fresh food Operators Food-processing equipment Freezers	Food preparation Freeze	Frozen food

facilities to transform steel, plastic, cloth, tyres and other materials. They make them into vehicles which are eventually delivered to customers. The staff and technology in the hospital, on the other hand, transform the customers themselves. The patients form part of the input to, and the output from, the operation – it is they who are being 'processed'. This has important implications for how the operation needs to be managed.

Inputs to the process

Transformed resources

One set of inputs to any operation's processes are **transformed resources**. These are the resources that are treated, transformed or converted in the process. They are usually a mixture of the following:

- materials
- information
- customers.

Processing materials

Processing customers

Processing information

Often one of these is dominant in an operation. For example, a bank devotes part of its energies to producing printed statements of accounts for its customers. In doing so, it is **processing materials** but no one would claim that a bank is a printer. The bank also is concerned with **processing customers**. It gives them advice regarding their financial affairs, cashes their cheques, deposits their cash, and has direct contact with them. However, most of the bank's activities are concerned with **processing information** about its customers' financial affairs. As customers, we may be unhappy with badly printed statements and we may be more unhappy if we are not treated appropriately in the bank. But if the bank makes errors in our financial transactions, we suffer in a far more fundamental way. This is not to say that materials processing or customer processing is unimportant to the bank. On the contrary, it must be good at these things to keep its customers happy. Error-free, fast and efficient information processing, though, is its central objective.

Table 1.4 gives examples of operations with their dominant transformed resources.

13

Table 1.4	Dominant transformed materials of various operations	
Predominantly materials processors	Predominantly information processors	Predominantly customer processors
All manufacturing operations	Accountants	Hairdressers
Mining companies	Bank headquarters	Hotels
Retail operations	Market research company	Hospitals
Warehouses	Financial analysts	Mass rapid transports
Postal services	News service	Theatres
Container shipping line	University research unit	Theme parks
Trucking companies	Archives Telecoms company	Dentists

Transforming resources

The other set of inputs to any operations process are **transforming resources**. These are the resources which act upon the transformed resources. There are two types which form the 'building blocks' of all operations:

Facilities
Staff

- **facilities** – the buildings, equipment, plant and process technology of the operation;
- **staff** – the people who operate, maintain, plan and manage the operation. (Note we use the term 'staff' to describe all the people in the operation, at any level.)

The exact nature of both facilities and staff will differ between operations. To a five-star hotel, its facilities consist mainly of buildings, furniture and fittings. To a nuclear-powered aircraft carrier, its facilities are the nuclear generator, turbines, and sophisticated electronic detection equipment. Although one operation is relatively 'low-technology' and the other 'high-technology', their facilities are important to both operations. A five-star hotel would be ineffective with worn and broken furniture just as an aircraft carrier would be with inoperative electronics. Staff will also differ between operations. Most staff employed in a factory assembling domestic refrigerators may not need a very high level of technical skill. In contrast, most staff employed by an accounting company are, hopefully, highly skilled in their own particular 'technical' skill (accounting). Yet although skills vary, all staff have a contribution to make to the effectiveness of their operation. An assembly worker who consistently misassembles refrigerators will dissatisfy customers and increase costs just as surely as an accountant who cannot add up.

Operations will also vary in their balance between facilities and staff resources. So, for example, a computer chip manufacturing company, such as Intel, will have a considerable quantity of money invested in its physical facilities. A single chip fabrication plant generally costs in excess of $2 billion. Not surprisingly, operations managers in this industry spend a lot of their time managing the performance of their facilities. Conversely, a management consultancy firm depends largely on the quality of its staff for its success. Here operations management is largely concerned with the development and deployment of skilled consultants and the knowledge which they possess. Of course, good staff are important in chip manufacture, and good buildings and information technology are important in management consulting. But the balance is different, as are the concerns of their operations' management.

Within the process

What happens within a transformation process depends on what inputs it is transforming.

Materials processing

Operations which process materials could do so to transform their *physical properties* (shape or composition, for example). Most manufacturing operations are like this. Other operations process materials to change their *location* (parcel delivery companies, for

All these businesses seem different, but they are all operations with inputs, processes and outputs and they are all managed by operations managers, even if they are called by another title

example). Some, like retail operations, do so to change the *possession* of the materials. Finally, some operations *store* materials, such as warehouses.

Information processing

Operations which process information could do so to transform their *informational properties* (that is the purpose or form of the information); accountants do this. Some change the *possession* of the information, for example market research companies sell information. Some *store* the information, for example archives and libraries. Finally, some operations, such as telecommunication companies, change the *location* of the information.

Customer processing

Operations which process customers might change their *physical properties* in a similar way to materials processors: for example, hairdressers or cosmetic surgeons. Some *store* (or more politely *accommodate*) customers: hotels, for example. Airlines, mass rapid transport systems and bus companies transform the *location* of their customers, while hospitals transform their *physiological state*. Finally, some customer-processing operations are concerned with transforming their *psychological state*, for example most entertainment services such as music, theatre, television, radio and theme parks.

Outputs from the process

Tangibility

All processes exist to produce products and services, and although products and services are different, the distinction can be subtle. Perhaps the most obvious difference is in their respective **tangibility**. Products are usually tangible: for example, you can physically touch a television set or a newspaper. Services are usually intangible. You cannot touch consultancy advice or a haircut (although you can often see or feel the results of these services). Also, services may have a shorter stored life. Products can usually be stored for a time, some food products only for a few days, some buildings for thousands of years. The life of a service is often much shorter. For example, the service of 'accommodation in a hotel room for tonight' will perish if it is not sold before tonight – accommodation in the same room tomorrow is a different service.

Most operations produce both products and services

'Pure' goods

'Pure' service

Facilitating services

Some operations produce just goods and others just services, but most operations produce a mixture of the two. Figure 1.4 shows a number of operations positioned in a spectrum from **'pure' goods** producers to **'pure' service** producers. Crude oil producers are concerned almost exclusively with the product which comes from their oil wells. So are aluminium smelters, but they might also produce some services such as technical advice. Services produced in these circumstances are called **facilitating services**. To an even

15

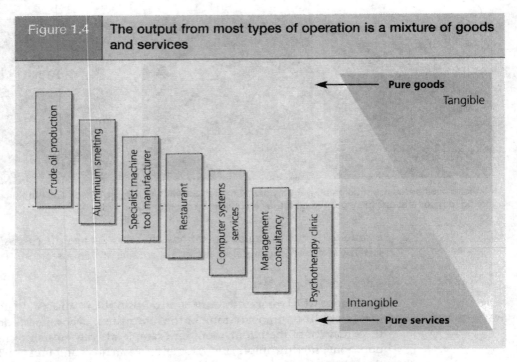

Figure 1.4   The output from most types of operation is a mixture of goods and services

greater extent, machine tool manufacturers produce facilitating services such as technical advice, applications engineering services and training. The services produced by a restaurant are an essential part of what the customer is paying for. It is both a manufacturing operation which produces food and a provider of service in the advice, ambience and service of the food. A computer systems services company may produce software 'products',

Facilitating products   but primarily it is providing a service to its customers, with **facilitating products**. Certainly, a management consultancy, although it produces reports and documents, would see itself as a service provider which uses facilitating goods. Finally, some pure services do not produce products at all. A psychotherapy clinic, for example, provides therapeutic treatment for its customers without any facilitating goods.

Services and products are merging

Increasingly the distinction between services and products is both difficult to define and not particularly useful. Information and communications technologies are even overcoming some of the consequences of the intangibility of services. Internet-based retailers, for example, are increasingly 'transporting' a larger proportion of their services into customers' homes. Even the official statistics compiled by governments have difficulty in separating products and services. Software sold on a disk is classified as a product. The same software sold over the internet is a service. Some authorities see the essential purpose of all businesses, and therefore operations processes, as being to

All operations are service providers   'service customers'. Therefore, they argue, **all operations are service providers** who may produce products as a means of serving their customers. Our approach in this book is close to this. We treat operations management as being important for all organizations. Whether they see themselves as manufacturers or service providers is very much a secondary issue.

The process hierarchy

Within operations there are other operations. Look inside most operations and they will be made up of several units or departments, which themselves act as smaller versions of the whole operation of which they form a part. For example, a television programme and video production company may have inputs of production, technical and administrative staff, cameras, lighting, sound and recording equipment, studio space, props, recording media, and so on. It transforms these into finished programmes and promotional videos, etc. Within this overall operation, however, there are many smaller operations or processes. For example, there will be, amongst others:

● workshops which manufacture the sets, scenery and props for the productions;
● marketing and sales staff who liaise with potential customers, test out programme ideas and give information and advice to programme makers;
● an engineering maintenance and repair department which cares for, modifies and designs technical equipment;
● production units which organize and shoot the programmes and videos;
● the finance and costing department which estimates the likely cost of future projects and controls operational budgets.

The whole television programme and video production operation is a *macro* operation, while its departments are micro operations (see Figure 1.5). These micro operations have inputs, some of which will come from outside the macro operation but many of

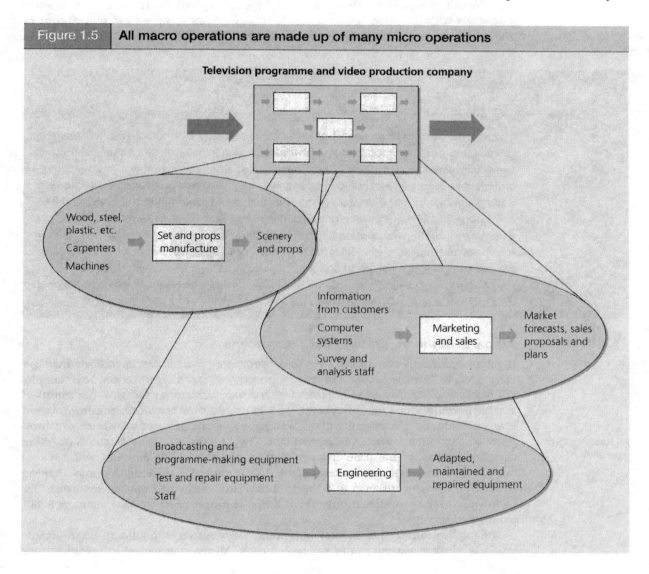

Figure 1.5 — **All macro operations are made up of many micro operations**

Television programme and video production company

Wood, steel, plastic, etc.
Carpenters
Machines
→ Set and props manufacture → Scenery and props

Information from customers
Computer systems
Survey and analysis staff
→ Marketing and sales → Market forecasts, sales proposals and plans

Broadcasting and programme-making equipment
Test and repair equipment
Staff
→ Engineering → Adapted, maintained and repaired equipment

which will be supplied from other internal micro operations. Each micro operation will also produce outputs of goods and services for the benefit of customers. Again though, some of each micro operation's customers will be other micro operations. This concept of macro and micro operations can be extended further. Within each micro operation there might be sections or groups, smaller process that can also be considered as operations in their own right. In this way any operations function can be considered as a **hierarchy of operations**.

Hierarchy of operations

Internal customers and internal suppliers

Internal customer
Internal supplier

The terms **internal customer** and **internal supplier** may often be used to describe micro operations which take outputs from, and give inputs to, other micro operations. So we could model any operation as a network of micro operations engaged in processing materials, information or customers (that is staff) for each other. Each micro operation being at the same time an internal supplier and an internal customer for other micro operations. The internal customer concept provides a model to analyse the internal activities of an operation. If the macro operation is not working as it should, we can trace the problem back along the internal network of customers and suppliers. It can also be a useful reminder to all parts of the operation that, by treating their internal customers with the same degree of care that they exercise on their external customers, the effectiveness of the whole operation can be improved.

critical commentary

The internal customer concept is seen by some as being over-simplistic. In reality the relationship between groups and individuals is significantly more complex than that between commercial entities. One cannot treat internal customers and suppliers exactly as we do external customers and suppliers. External customers and suppliers usually operate in a free market. If an organization believes that in the long run it can get a better deal by purchasing goods and services from another supplier, it will do so. But internal customers and suppliers are not in a 'free market'. They cannot usually look outside either to purchase input resources or to sell their output goods and services (although some organizations are moving this way). Rather than take the 'economic' perspective of external commercial relationships, models from organizational behaviour, it is argued, are more appropriate.

All parts of the organization are operations

If micro operations are similar to macro operations, then many operations management ideas will be useful for all units and groups within the organization. For example, the marketing function of an organization is a transformation process. It has inputs of market information, staff, computers, and so on. Its staff transform the information into such outputs as marketing plans, advertising campaigns and sales force organizations. In fact, **all functions are operations**. They are there to provide goods or (more usually) services to the other parts of the organization. Each function will have its 'technical' knowledge. In marketing, this is the expertise in designing and shaping marketing plans; in finance, it is the technical knowledge of financial reporting. Yet each will also have an operations role of using its processes to produce plans, policies, reports and services.

All functions are operations

The implications of this are very important. Every manager in all parts of an organization is to some extent an operations manager. All managers need to organize their resource inputs effectively so as to produce goods and services. It also means that we must distinguish between two meanings of 'operations':

Operations as a function

Operations as an activity

- **operations as a function**, meaning the part of the organization which produces the products and services for the organization's external customers;
- **operations as an activity**, meaning any processing of input resources in order to produce products and services, for either internal or external customers.

The first meaning of 'operations' is the most commonly used, and the one we shall use in this book, but it is always worth remembering the second usage of 'operations'.

Business processes

Breaking a whole operation down into its constituent micro operations processes helps to demonstrate that operations management applies to all parts of the organization. But stand back and think about the various ways in which the macro operation services its customers. Each micro operation will probably contribute some part to 'producing' its products and services. For example, the television programme and video production company, described previously, produces several products and services. Each of these, to different extents, involves the micro operations within the company. So, preparing

| Figure 1.6 | Example of how each micro operations process contributes to the 'end-to-end' business processes which fulfil external customer needs |

quotations (estimates of the time and cost involved in potential projects) needs the contributions of the marketing and sales micro operation and the finance and costing micro operation more than the others. Providing technical support (which involves designing systems for, and advising, other media companies) mainly involves the engineering micro operation, but does also need some contribution from the others. Figure 1.6 illustrates the contribution of each micro operations processes to each product or service. No particular sequence is implied by Figure 1.6. The contributions of each micro operations processes will not all occur in the same order. In fact the flow of information, materials or customers between micro operations might be complex, involving delays and recycling.

'End-to-end' business processes

Business process reengineering

These collections of contributions from each micro operations process that fulfil customer needs are called **'end-to-end' business processes** and often cut across conventional organizational boundaries. Reorganizing (or 'reengineering') layouts and organizational responsibilities around these business processes is the philosophy behind **business process reengineering** (BPR) which is discussed further in Chapter 18.

Operations processes have different characteristics

Although all operations processes are similar in that they all transform input resources into output products and services, they do differ in a number of ways, four of which are particularly important:

Volume
Variety
Variation
Visibility

- the **volume** of their output;
- the **variety** of their output;
- the **variation** in the demand for their output;
- the degree of **visibility** which customers have of the production of the product or service.

The volume dimension

Let us take a familiar example – the production and sale of the internationally ubiquitous hamburger. The epitome of high-volume hamburger production is McDonald's, which serves millions of burgers around the world every day. Volume has important implications for the way McDonald's operations are organized. Look behind the counter and the first thing you notice is the **repeatability** of the tasks people are doing. Because tasks are repeated frequently it makes sense to *specialize*: one person assigned to cooking the burgers, another assembling the buns, another serving, and so on. This leads to the **systemization** of the work where standard procedures are set down in a manual, with instructions on how each part of the job should be carried out. Also, because tasks are systematized and repeated, it is worthwhile developing specialized fryers and ovens. The most important implication of high volume, though, is that it gives *low unit costs*; the fixed costs of the operation, such as heating and rent, are spread over a large number of products or services.

Repeatability

Systemization

Now consider a small local cafeteria serving a few 'short order' dishes. The range of items on the menu may be similar to the larger operation, but the volume will be far lower. Therefore the degree of repetition will also be far lower. Furthermore, the number of staff will be lower (possibly only one person) and therefore individual staff are likely to perform a wider range of tasks. This may be more rewarding for the staff, but less open to systemization. Fewer burgers cooked also makes it less feasible to invest in specialized equipment. For all of these reasons it follows that the cost per burger served is likely to be higher (even if the price is comparable).

Dealing with variety – two examples example

The Bombay Tiffin Box Suppliers Association (TBSA) operates a service to transport home-cooked food from workers' homes to office locations in downtown Bombay. Workers from residential districts must ride commuter trains some 30–40 km to work. Typically, they are conservative diners, and are also constrained by strong cultural taboos on food handling by caste, which discourage eating out. TBSA arranges for food to be picked up in the morning in a regulation tin 'tiffin' box, deposited at the office at lunchtime, and returned to the home in the afternoon. TBSA takes advantage of public transport to carry the tins, usually using otherwise under-utilized capacity on commuter trains in the mid-morning and afternoon. Different colours and markings are used to indicate to the (sometimes illiterate) TBSA workers the process route for each tin.

For as long as ships have navigated the seas, ports have had to handle an infinite variety of cargoes with widely different contents, sizes and weights, and, whilst in transit or in storage, protect them from weather and pilferage. Then the transportation industries, in conjunction with the International Organization for Standardization (ISO), developed a standard shipping container design. Almost overnight the problems of security and weather protection were solved. Anyone wanting to ship goods in volume only had to seal them into a container and they could be signed over to the shipping company. Ports could standardize handling equipment and dispense with warehouses (containers could be stacked in the rain if required). Railways and

Standard tiffin boxes being transported from home to office

trucking companies could develop trailers to accommodate the new containers. Such was the success of the new design that very soon specialist containers were developed which still conformed to the ISO standard module sizes. For example, refrigerated containers provide temperature-controlled environments for perishable goods.

Questions

1 What are the common features of these two examples?

2 What other examples of standardization in transport operations can you think of?

Standardized shipping containers

The variety dimension

A taxi company offers a high-variety service. It may confine its services to the transportation of people and their luggage, but it is prepared to pick you up from almost anywhere and drop you off almost anywhere. It may even (at a price) take you by a route of your choice. In order to do this it must be relatively *flexible*. Drivers must have a good knowledge of the area, and communication between the base and the taxis must be effective. The variety on offer by the service does allow it to match its services closely to its customers' needs. However, this does come at a price. The cost per

21

kilometer travelled will be higher for a taxi than for a less customized form of transport such as a bus service. Although both serve, more or less, the same customers with the same needs by providing transport over relatively short distances (say, less than 20 km), the taxi service has, in theory, an infinite number of routes to offer its customers, while the bus service has a few well-defined routes. The buses travel these routes according to a set schedule, published well in advance and adhered to in a routine manner. If all goes to schedule, little, if any, flexibility is required from the operation. All is standardized and regular. More significantly, the lack of change and disruption in the day-to-day running of the operation results in relatively low costs compared with using a taxi for the same journey.

Standardization

One way of minimizing the costs associated with variety is to have as much **standardization** as possible in the process that produces the products or services. The two examples in the box, 'Dealing with variety – two examples' illustrate this.

The variation dimension

Consider the demand pattern for a successful summer holiday resort hotel. Not surprisingly, more customers want to stay in summer vacation times than in the middle of winter. At the height of 'the season' the hotel could possibly accommodate twice its capacity if it had the space. Off-season demand, however, could be a small fraction of its capacity; it might even consider closing down in very quiet periods. The implication of such a marked variation in demand levels is that the operation must change its capacity in some way. It might, for example, hire extra staff for the summer period only. But in flexing its activities the hotel must try to predict the level of demand it is likely to receive. If it gets this wrong and adjusts its capacity below the actual demand level, it will lose business. All of these factors have the effect of increasing the hotel's costs. Recruitment costs, overtime costs and under-utilization of its rooms all make for a relatively high cost per guest operation compared with a hotel of a similar standard with level demand.

Conversely, a hotel which is close to both a major road network and a tourist attraction might be patronized by business travellers during the week and by tourists at weekends and holiday periods. Its demand is therefore relatively level. Under these circumstances the hotel can plan its activities well in advance. Staff can be scheduled, food can be bought and rooms can be cleaned in a *routine* and *predictable* manner. This results in a high utilization of resources. Not surprisingly, the unit costs of this hotel are likely to be lower than those of the comparable hotel with a highly variable demand pattern.

The visibility dimension

Visibility is a slightly more difficult dimension of operations to envisage. It means how much of the operation's activities its customers experience, or how much the operation is **exposed** to its customers. Obviously customer-processing operations have more of their activities visible to their customers than most material-processing operations. But even customer-processing operations exercise some choice as to how visible they wish their operations to be. For example, in clothes retailing, an organization could decide to operate as a chain of conventional shops. Alternatively, it could decide not to have any shops at all but rather to run an internet-based operation.

Visibility means process exposure

The 'bricks and mortar' shop operation is a high-visibility operation insomuch as its customers experience most of its 'value-adding' activities. Customers in this type of operation have a relatively *short waiting tolerance*. They will walk out if not served in a reasonable time. They might also judge the operation by their perceptions of it rather than always by objective criteria. If they perceive that a member of the operation's staff is discourteous to them, they are likely to be dissatisfied (even if the staff member meant no discourtesy), so high-visibility operations require staff with good customer contact skills. Customers could also request goods which clearly would not be sold in such a shop, but because the customers are actually in the operation they can ask what they like! This is called **high received variety**, and will occur even if the variety of service for which the operation is designed is low. This does not make it easy for high-visibility operations to achieve high productivity of resources, with the consequence that they tend to be relatively high-cost operations.

Contrast the clothes shop with the internet-based retailer. It is not a pure low-contact operation; it still has to communicate with its customers through its website. It may even be interactive in quoting real-time availability of items. As with the 'bricks and mortar' shop, customers will react badly to slow, poorly designed or faulty sites But over-all the operation has far lower visibility. Most of the process is more 'factory-like'. The *time lag* between the order being placed and the items ordered by the customer being retrieved and dispatched does not have to be minutes as in the shop, but can be hours or even days. This allows the tasks of finding the items, packing and dispatching them to be *standardized* by organizing staff, who need no **customer contact skills**, so as to achieve *high staff utilization*. The internet-based organization can also centralize its oper-ation on one (physical) site, whereas the 'bricks and mortar' shop, because of its high-contact nature, necessarily needs many shops close to centres of demand. For all these reasons the catalogue operation will have lower costs than the shop chain.

Mixed high- and low-visibility operations

Some operations have both high- and low-visibility micro operations within the same macro operation. This serves to emphasize the difference which the degree of cus-tomer contact makes. Take an airport as an example: some of its activities are totally 'visible' to its customers (ticketing staff dealing with the queues of travellers; the infor-mation desk answering people's queries; caterers serving meals and drinks; and passport control and security staff checking documentation and baggage). These staff operate in what is termed a **front-office** environment. Other parts of the airport have relatively little, if any, customer 'visibility' (the baggage handlers; the overnight freight opera-tions staff; the ground crew putting meals on board and refreshing the aircraft; the cleaners preparing them for their next flight; the cooks and the administrators). We rarely see these staff; they perform the vital but low customer contact tasks, in what is termed the **back-office** part of the operation. Many operations have a mixture of front-office, high-visibility and back-office, low-visibility micro operations.

The implications of the four Vs of operations

All four dimensions have implications for the cost of creating the products or services. Put simply, high volume, low variety, low variation and low customer contact all help to keep processing costs down. Conversely, low volume, high variety, high variation and high customer contact generally carry some kind of cost penalty for the operation. This is why the volume dimension is drawn with its 'low' end at the left, unlike the other dimensions, to keep all the 'low cost' implications on the right. Figure 1.8 summarizes the implications of such positioning.

To some extent the position of an operation in the four dimensions is determined by the demand of the market it is serving. However, most operations have some discretion in moving themselves on the dimensions. Look at the different positions on the visibility dimension which banks have adopted. At one time, using branch tellers was the only way customers could contact a bank. The other services have been developed by banks to cre-ate different markets. For almost any type of industry one can identify operations which inhabit different parts of the four dimensions and which are therefore implicitly compet-ing for business in different ways. Figure 1.9 illustrates the different positions on the dimensions of the Formule 1 hotel chain (see the box on Formule 1) and a very different type of hotel. An island resort hotel in the Caribbean, for example, provides the same basic service as any other hotel. However, it could very well be of a small, intimate nature with

Margin notes: High received variety · Customer contact skills · Front-office · Back-office

23

Formule 1 – the most affordable hotel chain[3] | example

Hotels, by the nature of their services, are high-contact operations – they are staff-intensive and have to cope with a range of customers, each with a variety of needs and expectations. So, how can a highly successful chain of affordable hotels avoid the crippling costs of high customer contact? Formule 1, a subsidiary of the French Accor group, manage to offer outstanding value by adopting two principles not always associated with hotel operations – standardization and an innovative use of technology. Formule 1 hotels are usually located close to the roads, junctions and cities which makes them visible and accessible to prospective customers. The hotels themselves are made from state-of-the-art volumetric prefabrications. The prefabricated units are arranged in various configurations to suit the characteristics of each individual site. Figure 1.7 shows some configurations. All rooms are nine square metres in area, and are designed to be attractive, functional, comfortable and soundproof. Most important, they are designed to be easy to clean and maintain. All have the same fittings, including a double bed, an additional bunk-type bed, a wash basin, a storage area, a working table with seat, a wardrobe and a television set.

The reception of a Formule 1 hotel is staffed only from 6.30 am to 10.00 am and from 5.00 pm to 10.00 pm. Outside these times an automatic machine sells rooms to credit card users, provides access to the hotel, dispenses a security code for the room and even prints a receipt. Technology is also evident in the washrooms. Showers and toilets are automatically cleaned after each use by using nozzles and heating elements to spray the room with a disinfectant solution and dry it before it is used again.

To keep things even simpler, Formule 1 hotels do not include a restaurant as they are usually located near existing restaurants. However, a continental breakfast is available, usually between 6.30 am and 10.00 am, and of course on a 'self-service' basis!

Questions

1 What is the role of technology in allowing Formule 1 to keep its costs low?

2 How does the concept of 'standardization' help Formule 1 to keep its costs down?

| Figure 1.7 | Some configurations of Formule 1 pre-manufactured room units |

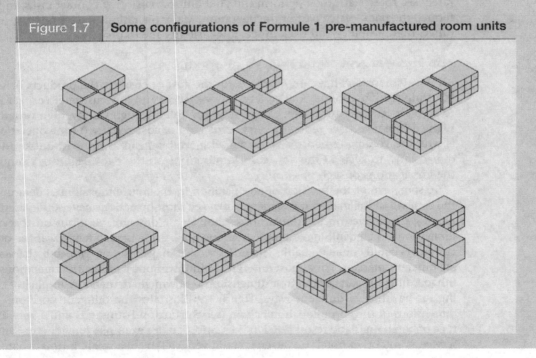

Figure 1.8 | A typology of operations

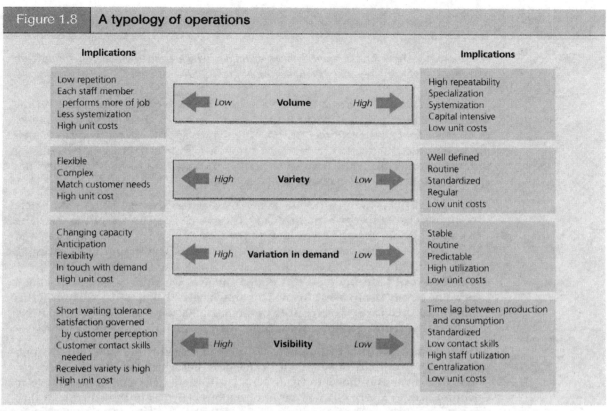

Figure 1.9 | Profiles of two operations

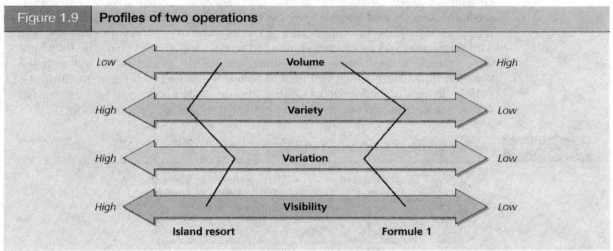

relatively few customers (some hotel resorts of this type cater for only 10 or 20 guests at a time). Its variety of services is almost infinite in the sense that customers can make individual requests in terms of food and entertainment. Variation might be very high, with the resort closing in the off-season. Finally, customer contact, and therefore visibility, in order to ascertain customers' requirements and provide for them, is likely to be very high. All of which is very different from Formule 1, where volume is high (although not as high as in a large city-centre hotel), variety of service is strictly limited, and business and holiday customers use the hotel at different times, which limits variation. Most notably, though, customer contact is kept to a minimum. The island resort hotel has very high levels of service but provides them at a high cost (and therefore a high price). Conversely, Formule 1 has arranged its operation in such a way as to minimize its costs.

25

(Most chapters have one or more worked examples which help to guide you through an operations analysis. They may be qualitative or quantitative, or both.)

Quentin Cakes make about 20,000 cakes per year in two sizes, both based on the same recipe. Sales peak at Christmas time when demand is about 50 per cent higher than in the more quiet summer period. Their customers (the stores who stock their products) order their cakes in advance through a simple internet-based ordering system. Knowing that they have some surplus capacity, one of their customers has approached them with two potential new orders.

- The *Custom Cake* Option – this would involve making cakes in different sizes where consumers could specify a message or greeting to be 'iced' on top of the cake. The consumer would give the inscription to the store who would e-mail it through to the factory. The customer thought that demand would be around 1,000 cakes per year, mostly at celebration times such as Valentine's Day and Christmas.
- The *Individual Cake* Option – this option involves Quentin Cakes introducing a new line of very small cakes intended for individual consumption. Demand for this individual sized cake was forecast to be around 4,000 per year, with demand likely to be more evenly distributed throughout the year than their existing products.

The total revenue from both options is likely to be roughly the same and the company have only capacity to adopt one of the ideas. But which one should it be?

A four Vs analysis is shown in Figure 1.10. The Custom Cake Option would involve Quentin Cakes in a very different set of operations activities to those in which they currently engage. Currently the company's production is high volume, low variety, medium variation, and low visibility. The Custom Cake Option would involve producing products in low volume, high variety, very high variation, and with some degree of 'visibility' (there will be contact required to pass on the inscriptions). The Individual Cake Option, by contrast, is high volume, low variety, low visibility and with less variation in demand (which will help to reduce the impact of the current Christmas peak in demand). The Individual Cakes Option is likely therefore to have lower costs and, given that the revenue for the two options is similar, higher profitability.

Figure 1.10	Four Vs analysis for Quentin Cakes

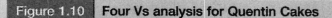

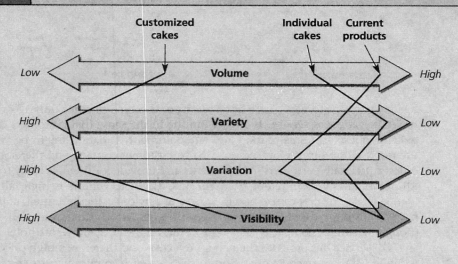

The activities of operations management

Operations managers have some responsibility for all the activities in the organization which contribute to the effective production of goods and services. Here, we divide these responsibilities into:

Direct responsibility

Indirect responsibility

Broad responsibility

- **direct responsibility** for the activities which produce and deliver products and services;
- **indirect responsibility** for the activities of other functions of the organization;
- **broad responsibility** to respond to the emerging challenges for operations management in the future.

The direct responsibilities of operations management

The exact nature of the operations function's direct responsibilities will, to some extent, depend on the way the organization has chosen to define the boundaries of its operations function. There are some general classes of activities, however, which apply to all types of operation no matter how functional boundaries have been drawn.

Understanding the operation's strategic objectives

The first responsibility of any operations management team is to understand what it is trying to achieve. This means developing a clear vision of how the operation should help the organization achieve its long-term goals. It also means translating the organization's goals into their implications for the operation's performance objectives, quality, speed, dependability, flexibility and cost. All these issues are discussed in Chapter 2.

Developing an operations strategy for the organization

Operations management involves hundreds of minute-by-minute decisions. So it is vital that operations managers have a set of general principles which can guide decision making towards the organization's longer-term goals. This is an operations strategy. It involves being able to place operations strategy within the general strategy, i.e. decision making of the organization. It also involves reconciling the often conflicting pressures of market requirements and operations resource capabilities. Chapter 3 deals with operations strategy.

Designing the operation's products, services and processes

Design is the activity of determining the physical form, shape and composition of products, services and processes. Although direct responsibility for the design of products and services might not be part of the operations function in some organizations, it is crucial to the operation's other activities. We examine the design of processes in general in Chapter 4 and the design of products and services in Chapter 5. At the most strategic level, process design means designing the whole network of operations which provide inputs to the operations function and deliver its output to customers. This is treated in Chapter 6. At a more immediate level, operations managers need to design the layout of their processes, an issue treated in Chapter 7, and the process technology and staffs' jobs which make up the processes, treated in Chapters 8 and 9, respectively.

Planning and controlling the operation

Planning and control is the activity of deciding what the operations resources should be doing, then making sure that they really are doing it. Chapter 10 explains the nature of planning and control activities, while the planning and control of capacity

27

so as to meet fluctuating demand levels is treated in Chapter 11. The planning and control of the flow of the transformed resources through the operation are treated in Chapter 12, which deals with inventory management, and Chapter 13, which deals with 'supply chain' management. Some specific approaches to planning and control have been developed for particular circumstances. For example, enterprise requirements planning (ERP) is treated as part of Chapter 14, just-in-time (JIT) or 'lean' planning and control is described in Chapter 15, while Chapter 16 treats planning and control in project operations. Finally, Chapter 17 treats the management of the quality of products and services.

Improving the performance of the operation

The continuing responsibility of all operations managers is to improve the performance of their operation, and Chapter 18 describes how the process of improvement can be organized within the operation. The other side of making operations better is stopping them going wrong in the first place. Chapter 19 deals with how failures are prevented in operations, and how the operation can recover when failure does occur. Finally, powerful improvement ideas of total quality management (TQM) are covered in Chapter 20.

The indirect responsibilities of operations management

Many decisions taken outside the operations function still can have an effect on operations activities. For example, developing advertising plans is quite clearly in the marketing domain, but it may have a significant impact on operations by affecting overall demand levels and the exact mix of products and services which customers will want. In these circumstances the responsibility of operations management is to explore the possible consequences of the advertising plans with the marketing function. It should understand their impact on the operation, make clear to marketing what the operation can and cannot do in response to any change in demand, and work together with marketing to find ways of allowing them to meet, or manage, market needs while also allowing the operation to run efficiently and effectively.

It is working together with the other parts of the organization which forms the most important indirect responsibilities of operations management. Not that 'indirect' means that these responsibilities are unimportant. On the contrary, it is a fundamental of modern organizational principles that functional boundaries should not hinder efficient internal processes. So developing and improving the relationships between operations and the other functions of the firm should be central to operations' contribution to overall performance.

Figure 1.11 illustrates some of the responsibility relationships between the operations and other functions. While the flow of information between the functions is not comprehensive, it does give an idea of the nature of each relationship. However, note that the support functions have a different relationship with operations than the other core functions. Operations management's responsibility to support functions is primarily to make sure that they understand operations' needs and help them to satisfy these needs. The operations function is clearly the internal customer. The relationship with the other two core functions is more equal – less of 'this is what we want' and more 'this is what we can do currently – how do we reconcile this with broader business needs?'

The broad responsibilities of operations management

Both the direct and indirect responsibilities of operations management are largely focused on those concerns which are of clear and immediate benefit to the organization itself. But increasingly it is recognized that all businesses, including their operations

Figure 1.11 Some interfunctional relationships between the operations function and other core and support functions

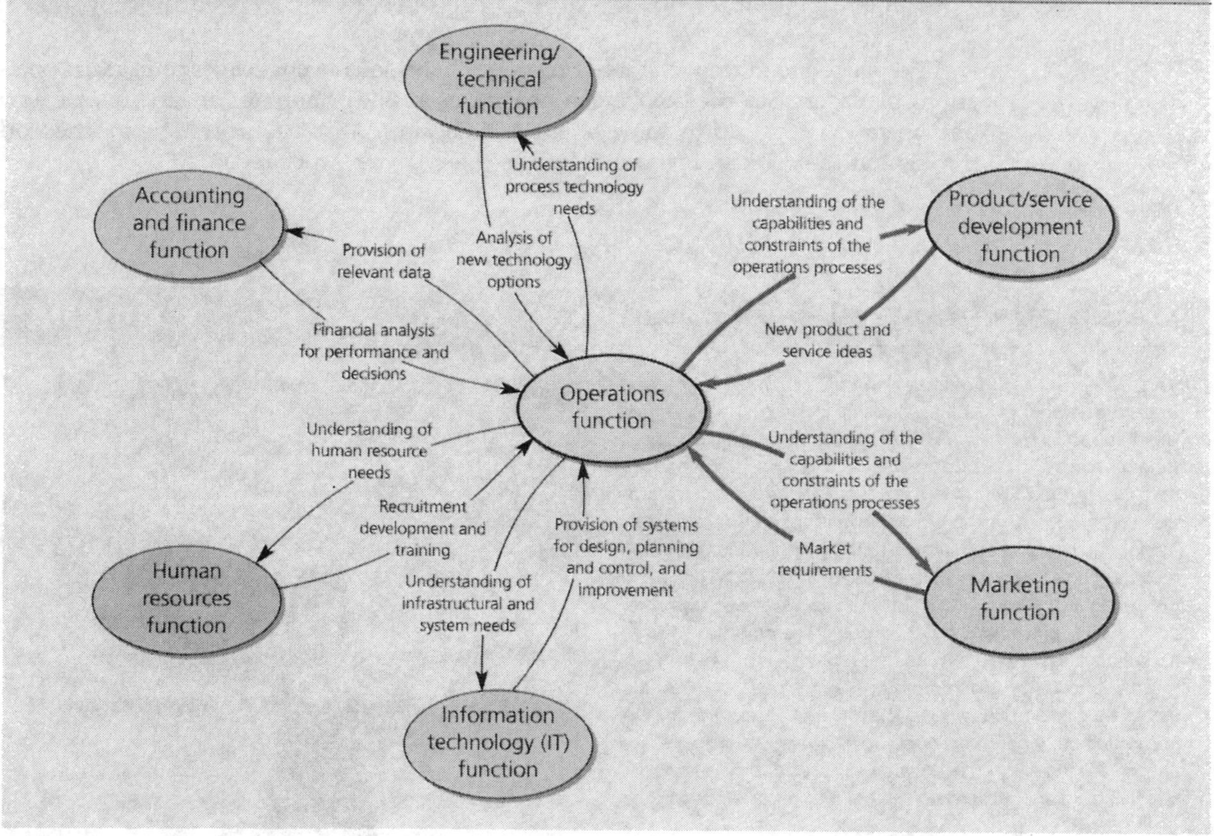

managers, have a set of broader responsibilities. Some of these are to the longer-term interests of the business, some are to the environment in which the business operates and some to the well-being of the people who the business employs. All businesses will interpret these broader responsibilities in different ways. Here we identify six that are of particular relevance to operations managers.

Globalization

- **Globalization** – the world is a smaller place; very few operations do not either source from or sell to foreign markets. How do operations managers cope with this expanded set of opportunities?

Environmental protection

- **Environmental protection** – operations managers cannot avoid responsibility for their organization's environmental performance. It is often operational failures which are at the root of pollution disasters and operations decisions (such as product design) which impact on longer-term environmental issues.

Social responsibility

- **Social responsibility** – the way in which an operation is managed has a significant impact on its customers, the individuals who work for it, the individuals who work for its suppliers and the local community in which the operation is located. How can operations be managed to be responsible employers and good neighbours?

Technology awareness

- **Technology awareness** – technology has always been a central part of operations management's concerns. But, in times of particularly fast changing technologies, operations managers have a further responsibility to understand the implications of technologies which could, in the future, become important. How many operations in 1995, for example, understood the full impact that internet technologies would have on almost all types of operation?

29

- **Knowledge management** – increasingly it is recognized that the key resource in businesses is the knowledge they contain. Knowledge is gained through experience, experience through activity, and activity (doing things) is what operations management is about.

All of these broad responsibilities represent considerable challenges to modern operations managers. See the box 'Green operations at Body Shop' for an example of how one operation faces up to some of these challenges. All of them will be touched on throughout the book and we will return to them in the last chapter.

Green operations at Body Shop[4] | example

The Body Shop formulates and manufactures skin- and hair-care products, but perhaps it is best known for its highly successful shops which brim with brightly coloured lotions, soaps, shampoos and oils. It is also renowned for its positive approach to environmentally conscious operations. The company has led the field in green operations by using only minimal and simple packaging, encouraging the recycling and refilling of containers, by not testing products on animals, by using natural materials wherever possible, and by having explicit social policies. Although not without its critics, Body Shop argues that it wanted to prove that it is possible to develop a profitable business and at the same time maintain a respect for the environment, the communities where its operations have an impact, its employees and its customers. This philosophy affects its operations management policies in a number of ways:

- *Socially responsible purchasing.* At one time wooden foot rollers were purchased from a company in Frankfurt. The company now sources them from a workshop which it set up in an Indian village to provide employment and training for the older children in an orphanage. Ignoring the lower costs, the company paid the same price to the workshop, the revenue being used to help the village to improve its education, health and nutritional standards. Six similar workshops have now been established in India.
- *Using renewable sources.* The company took a lead in encouraging a Nepalese paper factory to switch from clearing the local forest for its raw materials to using renewable sources such as banana skins.
- *Social location.* The company bought an abandoned factory in a deprived area of Glasgow and converted it into a soap factory which now makes over 25 million bars, sold throughout the world. As well as bringing much needed employment to the area, a quarter of the profit is returned for community projects.
- *Re-using.* The company provides a refill service in all its shops where empty plastic bottles can be refilled in return for a reduction on the purchase price. Over two million bottles are refilled every year in the UK alone.

- *Recycling waste.* Most synthetic polymers which can be recycled need to be sorted prior to recycling. The company has a standard labelling scheme which identifies the type of plastic used on each of its packages. This makes the sorting process, and therefore recycling, easier.

Questions

1 How do you think Body Shop's environmental policy relates to its overall business strategy?

2 What do you think are the dilemmas posed by the decisions described above for the company's operations managers?

The model of operations management

We can now combine two ideas to develop the model of operations management which will be used throughout this book. The first is the input–transformation–output model and the second is the categorization of operations management's activity areas. Figure 1.12 shows how these two ideas go together. The model now shows two interconnected loops of activities. The bottom one more or less corresponds to what is usually seen as operations management, and the top one to what is seen as operations strategy. This book concentrates on the former but tries to cover enough of the latter to allow the reader to make strategic sense of the operations manager's job.

Figure 1.12	A general model of operations management and operations strategy

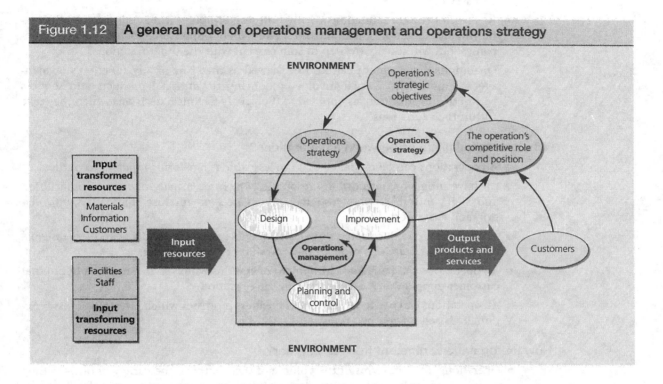

critical commentary

The central idea in this introductory chapter is that all organizations have operations processes which produce products and services and all these processes are essentially similar. However, some believe that by even trying to characterize processes in this way (perhaps even by calling them 'processes') one loses or distorts their nature, depersonalizes or takes the 'humanity' out of the way in which we think of the organization. This point is often raised in not-for-profit organizations, especially by 'professional' staff. For example, the head of one European 'Medical Association' (a Doctors' Trade Union) criticized hospital authorities for expecting a *sausage factory service based on productivity targets*.[5] No matter how similar they appear on paper, it is argued, a hospital can never be viewed in the same way as a factory. Even in commercial businesses, professionals, such as creative staff, often express discomfort at their expertise being described as a 'process'.

summary answers to key questions

 *All chapters have a summary that relates to the key questions posed at the beginning of the chapter. The companion website to the book, **www.booksites.net/slack**, also has a brief 'Study Guide' to each chapter.*

What is operations management?

- Operations management is the term used for the activities, decisions and responsibilities of operations managers who manage the production and delivery of products and services.

- It is one of the core functions of any business, although it may not be called operations management in some industries. The span of responsibility varies between companies, but will usually overlap to some extent with the other functions.

- Operations management can also be viewed as that part of any function's or manager's responsibility which involves producing the internal products and services within the organization, as opposed to the strictly technical decisions which they take within their functions.

What are the similarities between all operations?

- All operations can be modelled as a process which transforms inputs into outputs.

- All have inputs of transforming resources, which are usually divided into 'facilities' and 'staff', and transformed resources, which are some mixture of materials, information and customers.

- All operations produce some mixture of tangible goods or products and less tangible services. Few operations produce only products or only services.

- All operations can be divided into micro operations which form a network of internal customer–supplier relationships within the operation.

- All operations can be viewed as a set of business processes which often cut across functionally based micro operations.

How are operations different from each other?

- Operations differ in terms of the volume of their outputs, the variety of outputs they produce, the variation in demand with which they have to cope, and the degree of 'visibility' or customer contact they have.

- High volume, low variety, low variation and low customer 'visibility' are usually associated with low cost.

What responsibilities do operations managers have?

- Direct responsibilities include the translation of into operational action, the design of the operation (not only the products and services themselves, but the systems or processes which produce them), the planning and controlling of the activities of the operation, and the improvement of the operation over time.

- Indirect responsibilities include working closely with other functional areas of the business.

- Broad responsibilities include understanding the impact on the operation of globalization, environmental responsibility, social responsibility, new technologies and knowledge management.

32

ANLG Bank
by Alan Betts

We've grown and reorganized so much in the last five years that it has become difficult to maintain a common approach to our operations. We have to get it right, never before have we been so dependent on how we manage our service delivery in all parts of the bank. Large retail banks like us are under immense pressure from the niche companies. They will take just one part of our range of services, such as loans or insurance or home mortgages, and really concentrate their operation on providing specifically what that market wants. They can be focused and single minded on just one part of the financial services market. Compared with them we can seem slow and unresponsive. Our advantages are the recognition our brand gets in the market, our ability to 'cross-sell' (that is, use the contact with customers in one service, for example a simple current account, to sell other services, for example a credit card), and our potential to achieve economies of scale. The challenge for us is to do two things at the same time. First, we need to deliver exceptional customer service. Big banks do not have the best reputation for their quality of service, so the first to really develop a genuine reputation for quality could reap substantial benefits. Second, we need to exploit our size to keep costs down. We are several times larger than most of the specialist financial service providers, we should be able to do things substantially cheaper than them.

(Jan Krechner, Operations Director, ANLG Bank.)

The problems faced by ANLG were not unusual in the banking industry. ANLG operated largely in the Netherlands, but big retail banks all over Europe faced the same issues. They had to attempt to get the 'best of both worlds' of improving customer service while reducing the costs of providing that service. Jan knew that the only way to do this was through improving the performance of all the operations processes which produced and delivered the bank's services. Most banks, including ANLG, had moved progressively towards organizing themselves around a network of large processing centres. This was very different to how banks were organized only a few years earlier. Then each branch of a bank was far more self-contained. Managers had considerable discretion and each branch had its own back-office operation. This would record customer requests, process all financial transactions such as cheques and standing orders, issue cheque books, purchase stocks and shares for their customers and so on. Only a limited number of activities such as cheque clearing, or the physical movement of cash, was organized centrally by the bank's headquarters.

Now branches are mainly sales operations. They have managers but generally have far less individual discretion. Back-office operations are now entirely centralized. Account management centres open accounts and set up standing orders, printing departments manufacture cheque books, voucher processing centres process cheques and other documents, call centres deal with various services such as loans or credit card queries, and so on. ANLG, like most banks, had saved considerable sums from reorganizing in this way. But Jan knew that more needed to be done.

I am sure that we have barely scratched the surface in terms of exploiting the cost savings which are possible from the reorganizations, but just as important we have to overcome some of the quality issues which have arisen because of the communication problems between the back-office centres.

To help him do this Jan had organized an 'operations development programme' (ODP). Initially this was a working group which had been asked to develop some core principles for improving operations performance. One of the first problems the working party faced was that different parts of the bank regarded themselves as being different from all the other parts. To stimulate thought and debate Jan asked managers of four of the different back-office centres to attend a working group meeting and present their thoughts on 'My biggest issue'. The four people chosen were a Call Centre manager dealing with customer service enquiries, a manager in charge of Credit Control for personal customers, a manager running a Voucher Processing centre and a manager who works in a subsidiary company dealing with 'High Net Worth' (rich) clients.

Call Centre

My biggest issue is the Inbound Calls Screen. That tells me the amount of calls being handled by the operators and the amount queueing. Monday morning just after 9 am the screen is going crazy, that's when we are at our busiest. Sometimes during the night shift it's a real surprise when the phone rings. The next biggest issue is staff turnover as it takes usually four weeks to recruit and a similar time to train someone as we look to handle 15 basic banking enquiries from our customers and people need a fair amount of background knowledge.

Credit Control

Very occasionally we will speak to a customer but really we are a back-office operation. We monitor the 'Out of Control' accounts. Every day we get a list of customers who have exceeded their overdraft levels and it is our job to decide whether to bounce the cheque or send a letter. The number of lines on the printout varies a little bit but not really that much. I look after the personal team who basically work to strict rules whilst corporate credit control is monitored by a different team as there is a need for more interpretation.

33

Voucher Processing

It's really about keeping the cheque encoding machines rolling. Cheques come to us by courier from branches in a wide geographical area and we process them through four large and extremely expensive machines. They start arriving around lunchtime and carry on until around 7 pm. Monday is our busiest day as shopkeepers deposit their weekend takings. Sometimes running up to Christmas it can be manic and we really struggle to get the work finished before cut-off time. If a machine breaks down on the Monday before Christmas we are in real difficulties.

High Net Worth Banking

I guess flexibility is the key word. Our customers are extremely wealthy and extremely demanding. We never know what the next phone call will bring but we have to be able to deal with it because if we can't we know someone else will. Sometimes it is a small query but the customer will ask for their regular point of contact, sometimes it is a really big issue and one of our account executives will have to get over to the customer's workplace – or often their home – straightaway. It is the personal touch that really matters.

Jan thanked the managers for their presentations and summarized:

I am coming to see that the issue of 'similarities versus differences' is the key to our future improvement. On one hand, we must have a common set of principles which all the business can use to continuously improve its operations performance. On the other hand, we have to recognize that not all parts of the business are the same. And because they are different they will need to develop different skills and possibly even different approaches to 'fine tuning' their operations improvement activities. ■

Questions

1 What are the inputs, transformation processes and outputs from the processes described in the case?

2 Determine the similarities and differences between the four back office units using the '4Vs' approach.

3 In the light of your findings, to what extent do you believe common sets of principles apply?

4 What do you think are the different skills and different approaches to 'fine tuning' the improvement activities that Jan speaks about?

 *All chapters have case exercises. Other short cases, and worked answers, are included in the companion website to this book, **www.booksites.net/slack**.*

study activities

 *All chapters have study activities. Some of them can be answered by reading the chapter. Others will require some general knowledge of business activity and some might require an element of investigation. All have hints on how they can be answered on the companion website for this book which also contains more discussion questions, **www.booksites.net/slack**.*

1 Visit a furniture store (other than IKEA) and a sandwich or snack shop (other than Pret A Manger). Observe how each shop operates, for example, where customers go, how staff interact with them, how big it is, how the shop has chosen to use its space, what variety of products it offers, and on. Talk with the staff and managers if you can. Think about how the shops you have visited are similar to IKEA and Pret A Manger, and how they differ. Then consider the question, *'What implications do the differences between the shops you visited and the two described in the first two boxes in Chapter 1 have for their operations management?'*

2 Write down five services that you have 'consumed' in the last week. Try and make these as varied as possible. Examples could include public transport, a bank, any shop or supermarket, attendance at an education course, a cinema, a restaurant, etc. For each of these services, ask yourself the following questions.

▶

34

- Did the service meet your expectations? If so what did the management of the service have to do well in order to satisfy your expectations? If not, where did they fail? Why might they have failed?
- If you were in charge of managing the delivery of these services what would you do to improve the service?
- If they wanted to, how could the service be delivered at a lower cost so that the service could reduce its prices?
- How do you think that the service copes when something goes wrong (such as a piece of technology breaking down)?
- Which other organizations might supply the service with products and services? (In other words, they are your 'supplier', but who are *their* suppliers)?
- How do you think the service copes with fluctuation of demand over the day, week, month or year?

These questions are just some of the issues which the operations managers in these services have to deal with. Think about the other issues they will have to manage in order to deliver the service effectively.

3 Visit and observe three restaurants, cafés or somewhere that food is served. Compare them in terms of the Volume of demand that they have to cope with, the Variety of menu items they service, the Variation in demand during the day, week and year, and the Visibility you have of the preparation of the food. Think about/discuss the impact of volume, variety, variation and visibility on the day-to-day management of each of the operations and consider how each operation attempts to cope with its volume, variety, variation and visibility.

4 (Advanced) Find a copy of a financial newspaper (*Financial Times, Wall Street Journal, The Economist*, etc.) and identify one company which is described in the paper that day. Using the list of issues identified in Table 1.1, what do you think would be the *new operations agenda* for that company?

Notes on chapter

1 Sources: Thornhill, J. (1992) 'Hard Sell on the High Street', *Financial Times*, May 16. Horovitz, J. and Jurgens Panak, M. (1992) *Total Customer Satisfaction*, Pitman Publishing. Walley, P. and Hart, K. (1993) IKEA (UK) Ltd, Loughborough University Business School, company website (2000).

2 We are grateful to Simon Topman of Acme Whistles for his assistance.

3 Sources: Groupe Accor published accounts 1999, *Formule 1, The Most Affordable Hotel Chain*, company information brochure. Sharon Dannelley (1993) 'Groupe Accor', *Warwick Business School Report*.

4 Source: Discussion with company staff.

5 Quote from Chairman of the British Medical Association, speech from the Annual Conference, 2002.

Selected further reading

Chase, R.B., Aquilano, N.J. and Jacobs, F.R. (1998) *Production and Operations Management: Manufacturing and Services* (8th edn), Unwin/McGraw-Hill. There are many good general textbooks on operations management. This was one of the first and is still one of the best, though written very much for an American audience.

Hammer, M. and Stanton, S. (1999) *How Process Enterprises Really Work*, Harvard Business Review, November–December. Hammer is one of the gurus of process design. This paper is typical of his approach.

Heizer, J. and Render, B. (1999) *Operations Management* (5th edn), Prentice Hall, New Jersey. Another good US authored general text on the subject.

Johnston, R., Chambers, S., Harland, C. Harrison, A. and Slack N. (2003) *Cases in Operations Management* (3rd edn), Financial Times Prentice Hall. Many great examples of real operations management issues. Not surprisingly, based around the same structure as this book.

35

Johnston, R., and Clark, E. (2001) *Service Operations Management*, Financial Times Prentice Hall, Harlow. What can we say! A great treatment of service operations from the same stable as this textbook.

Keen, P.G.W. (1997) *The Process Edge: Creating Value where it Counts*, Harvard Business School Press. Operations management as 'process' management.

Slack, N. (ed.) (1997) *The Blackwell Encyclopedic Dictionary of Operations Management*, Blackwell Business, Oxford. For those who like technical descriptions and definitions.

Wild, R. (2002) *Operations Management* (6th edn), Continuum, London. Appeals especially to engineers, although the first few chapters are innovative enough to be of value to anyone.

Womack, J.P. and Jones, D.T. (1996) *Lean Thinking: Banish Waste and Create Wealth in your Corporation*, Simon and Schuster. An evangelical approach by two of the gurus of the 'new' approach to operations improvement. We shall deal with their ideas in Chapters 15 and 18.

chapter two

The strategic role and objectives of operations

Source: Honda Motor Co.

key questions

● What role should the operations function play in achieving strategic success?

● What are the performance objectives of operations and what are the internal and external benefits which derive from excelling in each of them?

Introduction

If any operation wants to understand its contribution to the organization of which it is a part, it must answer two questions. First, what part is it expected to play within the business – that is its *role* in the business? Second, what are the specific *performance objectives* against which the business can assess the contribution of the operation to its strategic aspirations? Both these issues are vitally important to any operation. Without an appreciation of its role within the business, the people who manage the operation can never be sure that they really are contributing to the long-term success of the business. At a more practical level, it is impossible to know whether an operation is succeeding or not if the specific performance objectives against which its success is measured are not clearly spelt out. This chapter deals with both these issues. On our general model of operations management they are represented by the areas marked on Figure 2.1.

| Figure 2.1 | This chapter covers the role and strategic objectives of operations management |

ENVIRONMENT

Covered in this chapter

Operation's strategic objectives

The operation's competitive role and position

Operations strategy

Input transformed resources

Materials
Information
Customers

Input resources

Design · Improvement

Planning and control

Output products and services

Customers

Facilities
Staff

Input transforming resources

ENVIRONMENT

Operations role and objectives

We judge operations primarily on the basis of their performance; good, bad, or indifferent. But what is more interesting is what lies behind the performance that we observe. The box on TNT Express illustrates a company whose operations processes are seen as fundamental to the delivery of excellent performance.

TNT Express[1]   example

TNT Express is the largest division of TPG (TNT Post Group) NV, a listed public company providing express, mail and logistics services across the world. The TNT Express division is the world's leading provider of on-demand business-to-business express delivery services. Established in Australia in 1946, TNT Express now operates in over 200 countries and delivers 3.6 million parcels, documents and pieces of freight a week, using its network of 1,000 depots, hubs and sortation centres. It also operates over 40 aircraft and 20,000 road vehicles. A pioneer in reliable next day door-to-door and same day deliveries, TNT has maintained its track record for innovation. Their aim, says Managing Director Alan Jones, is to *'Provide the fastest and most reliable express delivery service. We want to be recognized as the best company in the door-to-door express delivery industry. That is why we are passionate about continuous improvement and we're totally committed to providing ever-higher levels of customer care. It is also why we continue to out perform the opposition in an extremely competitive and fast-changing market'.*

Source: TNT

TNT Express sees the most important elements of the strategy as:

- providing the fastest and most reliable express delivery services;
- achieving secure outstanding levels of customer satisfaction;

- equipping employees fully to satisfy customer needs;
- saving time by adopting a 'right-first-time' approach in every part of the business;
- expanding the company-owned network of depots to offer later collection and earlier delivery times;
- developing leading-edge support technologies that provide value-added for customers.

Achieving this strategy means continually updating the TNT Express network of air, road and sortation facilities, and perfecting the seamless integration of all its

parts. This means investing in and managing some major operations projects. For example, even though the company already offered the fastest transit times by road in Europe, investment in new facilities and processes was needed at the European Express hub in Liège, Belgium and the European road hub in Arnhem in The Netherlands. The investment at Liège focused on improving 'end of sort' times to reduce door-to-door delivery times. Investments at Arnhem increased the network's capacity response to customer demand for services. ∎

TNT Express is able to maintain its reputation largely because of the performance of its operations processes. The processes that collect parcels from customers, move them around the world, deliver them on time and in good condition, and allow customers to follow their progress, all define what the company is and what it can do. So, the role and performance of the company's operations function is hugely important to TNT Express. Its operations managers must be able to *implement* the company's strategy, for example, so that the expansion at Liège and Arnhem happened smoothly and efficiently. More than this, it must actively *support* the company's strategy by providing the fast, dependable and high quality delivery on which competitiveness depends, while at the same time improving efficiency. But beyond even this the operation must provide the *drivers* of strategy, for example; the long-term capability to integrate all its processes in a way that competitors find difficult to match. How well TNT Express achieve all these objectives will be judged by its performance, and performance can be measured in many different ways. But however it is measured, it is influenced by the contribution of operations managers. These two areas of operations role and operations performance objectives are important to any organization and we deal with them in that order.

The role of the operations function

Role of the operations function

By the **role of the operations function** we mean the part it plays within the organization – the reason that the function exists. As we saw in the case of TNT Express, operations must take on three roles.

- operations should be the *implementer* of business strategy;
- operations should be a *support* to business strategy;
- operations should be the *driver* of business strategy.

Implementing business strategy

Implement strategy

The most basic role of operations is to **implement strategy.** Most companies will have some kind of strategy but it is the operation that puts it into practice. You cannot, after all, touch a strategy; you cannot even see it; all you can see is how the operation behaves in practice. For example, if an insurance company has a strategy of launching an online motor insurance service, it is the operations part of each function which has the task of 'operationalizing' the strategy. Its marketing 'operation' must organize appropriate promotions activities. The information technology 'operation' needs to supply appropriate systems. Most significantly, its operations function will have to

39

supervise the design of all the processes which allow customers to access online information, issue quotations, request further information, check credit details, send out documentation and so on. This implementation role is very significant. Without it even the most original and brilliant strategy will be rendered totally ineffective by the operations function's ineptitude.

Supporting business strategy

Support strategy

Another operations role is to **support strategy**.[2] This goes beyond simply implementing strategy. It means developing resources to provide the capabilities which allow the organization to improve and refine its strategic goals. For example, a mobile phone manufacturer wants to be the first in the market with every available new product innovation. Its operations function needs to be capable of coping with the changes which constant innovation will bring. It must develop processes flexible enough to make novel components, organize its staff to understand the new technologies, develop relationships with its suppliers which help them respond quickly when supplying new parts, and so on. The better the operation is at doing these things, the more support it is giving to the company's strategy. If the company had adopted a different business strategy, its operations function would have needed to adopt different objectives. This idea is developed further in the next chapter.

Driving business strategy

Drive strategy

The third, and most difficult, role of operations is to **drive strategy** by giving it a unique and long-term advantage. For example, a specialist food service company supplies restaurants with frozen fish and fish products. Over the years it has built up close relationships with its customers (chefs) as well as its suppliers around the world (fishing companies and fish farms). In addition it has its own small factory which develops and produces a continual stream of exciting new products. The company has a unique position in the industry because its exceptional customer relationships, supplier relationships and new product development are extremely difficult for competitors to imitate. In fact, the whole company's success is based largely on these unique operations capabilities. The operation drives the company's strategy.

Judging the operation's contribution

The ability of any operation to play these roles within the organization can be judged by considering the organizational aims or aspirations of the operations function. Professors Hayes and Wheelwright of Harvard University,[3] with later contributions from Professor Chase of the University of Southern California,[4] have developed what they call the **four-stage model** which can be used to evaluate the competitive role and contribution of the operations function of any type of company. The model traces the progression of the operations function from what is the largely negative role of stage 1 operations to it becoming the central element of competitive strategy in excellent stage 4 operations.

The four-stage model of operations contribution

Stage 1 – Internal neutrality

This is the very poorest level of contribution by the operations function. The other functions regard it as holding them back from competing effectively. The operations function is inward looking and at best reactive with very little positive to contribute towards competitive success. Its goal is to be ignored. At least then it isn't holding the company back in any way. Certainly the rest of the organization would not look to operations as the source of any originality, flair or competitive drive. Its ambition is to

Figure 2.2   Even the best operations can be let down by their operations

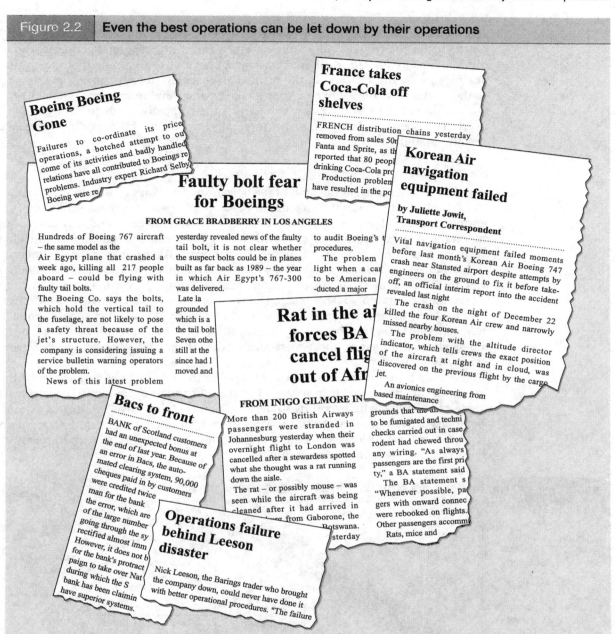

be 'internally neutral', a position it attempts to achieve not by anything positive but by avoiding the bigger mistakes.

Stage 2 – External neutrality

The first step of breaking out of stage 1 is for the operations function to begin comparing itself with similar companies or organizations in the outside market. This may not immediately take it to the 'first division' of companies in the market, but at least it is measuring itself against its competitors' performance and trying to be 'appropriate', by adopting 'best practice' from them. By taking the best ideas and norms of performance from the rest of its industry, it is trying to be 'externally neutral'.

41

Stage 3 – Internally supportive

Stage 3 operations have probably reached the 'first division' in their market. They may not be better than their competitors on every aspect of operations performance but they are broadly up with the best. Yet, stage 3 operations still aspire to be clearly and unambiguously the very best in the market. They achieve this by gaining a clear view of the company's competitive or strategic goals and developing 'appropriate' operations resources to excel in the areas in which the company needs to compete effectively. The operation is trying to be 'internally supportive' by providing a credible operations strategy.

Stage 4 – Externally supportive

Stage 3 used to be taken as the limit of the operations function's contribution. Yet Hayes and Wheelwright capture the growing importance of operations management by suggesting a further stage – stage 4. The difference between stages 3 and 4 is subtle, but important. A stage 4 company is one which sees the operations function as providing the foundation for its competitive success. Operations looks to the long term. It forecasts likely changes in markets and supply, and it develops operations-based capabilities which will be required to compete in future market conditions. The operations function is becoming central to strategy making. Stage 4 operations are creative and proactive. They are likely to be innovative and capable of adaptation as markets change. Essentially they are trying to be 'one step ahead' of competitors in the way that they create products and services and organize their operations – what Hayes and Wheelwright call being 'externally supportive'.

Figure 2.3 brings together the two concepts of the *role* and the *contribution* of the operations function. Moving from stage 1 to stage 2 requires operations to overcome its problems of implementing existing strategies. The move from stage 2 to stage 3 requires operations actively to develop its resources so that they are appropriate for long-term strategy. Moving up to stage 4 requires operations to be driving strategy through its contribution to competitive superiority.

Figure 2.3	The role and the contribution of the operations function

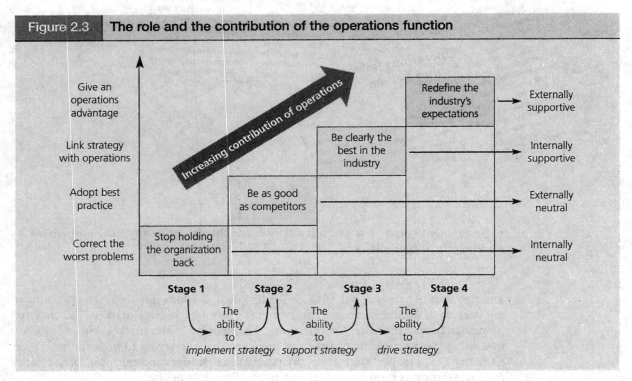

42

critical commentary

The idea that operations can have a leading role in determining a company's strategic direction is not universally supported. Both Hayes and Wheelwright's stage 4 of their four-stage model and the concept of operations 'driving' strategy do not only imply that it is possible for operations to take such a leading role, but are explicit in seeing it as a 'good thing'. A more traditional stance taken by some authorities is that the needs of the market will always be pre-eminent in shaping a company's strategy. Therefore, operations should devote all their time to understanding the requirements of the market (as defined by the marketing function within the organization) and devote themselves to their main job of ensuring that operations processes can actually deliver what the market requires. Companies can only be successful, they argue, by positioning themselves in the market (through a combination of price, promotion, product design and managing how products and services are delivered to customers) with operations very much in a 'supporting' role. In effect, they say, Hayes and Wheelwright's four-stage model should stop at stage 3. The issue of an 'operations resource' perspective on operations strategy is discussed further in Chapter 3.

Operations performance objectives

Stakeholders

A useful classification of the performance objectives which any operation might pursue can be gained from identifying the operation's **stakeholders**. Stakeholders are the people and groups of people who have an interest in the operation and who may be influenced by, or influence, the operation's activities. Some stakeholders are internal, for example the operation's employees; others are external, for example society or community groups, and a company's shareholders. Some external stakeholders have a direct commercial relationship with the organization, for example the suppliers to the operation and the customers who receive its products and services. Figure 2.4 illustrates some main stakeholder groups together with some of the aspects of operations performance in which they will be interested. Return to the TNT Express box. The company is clearly concerned to satisfy its customers' requirements for fast and dependable services at reasonable prices, as well as helping and improving its own suppliers (a whole range of organizations, from those who print packets to those who clean the offices). Similarly, it is concerned to ensure the long-term economic value delivered to those who have bought shares in the company. But the company also has a responsibility to ensure that its own employees are well treated (it has received awards for training) and that society at large is not negatively affected by the operation's activities – the company must minimize vehicle pollution, minimize wastage of materials or energy, ensure that its operations do not disrupt the life and well-being of those who live nearby, and so on.

In many not-for-profit operations, these stakeholder groups can overlap. So, a government department may be both the 'shareholder' of a public service agency and its main customer. Similarly, groups within society may also be the customers for a charitable operation, or voluntary workers in a charity may be employees, shareholders and customers all at once. However, in any kind of organization, it is a responsibility of the operations function to understand the (sometimes conflicting) objectives of its stakeholders and set its objectives accordingly.

43

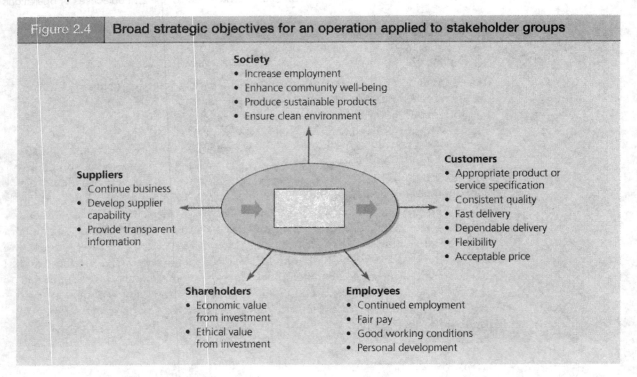

| Figure 2.4 | Broad strategic objectives for an operation applied to stakeholder groups |

Society
- Increase employment
- Enhance community well-being
- Produce sustainable products
- Ensure clean environment

Suppliers
- Continue business
- Develop supplier capability
- Provide transparent information

Customers
- Appropriate product or service specification
- Consistent quality
- Fast delivery
- Dependable delivery
- Flexibility
- Acceptable price

Shareholders
- Economic value from investment
- Ethical value from investment

Employees
- Continued employment
- Fair pay
- Good working conditions
- Personal development

The five performance objectives

Broad stakeholder objectives form the backdrop to operations decision making, but operations requires a more tightly defined set of objectives that relate specifically to its basic task of satisfying customer requirements. These are the five basic 'performance objectives' and they apply to all types of operation. Imagine that you are an operations manager in any kind of business – a hospital administrator, for example, or a production manager at a car plant, the operations manager for a city bus company or the manager of a large supermarket. What kind of things are you likely to want to do in order to satisfy customers and contribute to competitiveness?

Quality
- You would want to *do things right*; that is, you would not want to make mistakes, and would want to satisfy your customers by providing error-free goods and services which are 'fit for their purpose'. This is giving a **quality** *advantage* to your company's customers.

Speed
- You would want to *do things fast*, minimizing the time between a customer asking for goods or services and the customer receiving them in full, thus increasing the availability of your goods and services and giving your customers a **speed** *advantage*.

Dependability
- You would want to *do things on time*, so as to keep the delivery promises you have made to your customers. If the operation can do this, it is giving a **dependability** *advantage* to its customers.

- You would want to be able to *change what you do*; that is, being able to vary or adapt the operation's activities to cope with unexpected circumstances or to give customers individual treatment. Hence the range of goods and services which you produce has to be wide enough to deal with all customer possibilities. Either way, being able to change far enough and fast enough to meet customer requirements gives a **flexibility**
Flexibility
advantage to your customers.

- You would want to *do things cheaply*; that is, produce goods and services at a cost which enables them to be priced appropriately for the market while still allowing for a return to the organization; or, in a not-for-profit organization, give good value to

44

Cost

the taxpayers or whoever is funding the operation. When the organization is managing to do this, it is giving a **cost** *advantage* to its customers.

The next part of this chapter examines these five performance objectives in more detail by looking at what they mean for the four different operations previously mentioned: a general hospital, an automobile factory, a city bus company and a supermarket chain.

The quality objective

Quality means 'doing things right', but the things which the operation needs to do right will vary according to the kind of operation. In fact there are several ways of defining quality and we will deal with them in Chapter 17. Figure 2.5 illustrates how quality could be judged in the four operations mentioned previously.

All operations regard quality as a particularly important objective. In some ways quality is the most visible part of what an operation does. Furthermore, it is something that a customer finds relatively easy to judge about the operation. Is the product or service as it is supposed to be? Is it right or is it wrong? There is something fundamental about quality. Because of this, it is clearly a major influence on customer satisfaction or dissatisfaction. A customer perception of high-quality products and services means customer satisfaction and therefore the likelihood that the customer will return. The box 'Organically good quality' illustrates an operation which depends on a subtle concept of quality to ensure customer satisfaction.

Quality inside the operation

When quality means consistently producing services and products to specification it not only leads to external customer satisfaction, but makes life easier inside the operation as well. Satisfying internal customers can be as important as satisfying external customers.

Figure 2.5	Quality means different things in different operations

Quality could mean. . .

Hospital
- Patients receive the most appropriate treatment
- Treatment is carried out in the correct manner
- Patients are consulted and kept informed
- Staff are courteous, friendly and helpful

Automobile plant
- All parts are made to specification
- All assembly is to specification
- The product is reliable
- The product is attractive and blemish-free

Bus company
- The buses are clean and tidy
- The buses are quiet and fume-free
- The timetable is accurate and user-friendly
- Staff are courteous, friendly and helpful

Supermarket
- Goods are in good condition
- The store is clean and tidy
- Decor is appropriate and attractive
- Staff are courteous, friendly and helpful

(*Source:* Arup)

45

Organically good quality[4] example

Source: Photograph courtesy of Catherine Pyne, Lower Hurst Farm.

'Organic farming means taking care and getting all the details right. It is about quality from start to finish. Not only the quality of the meat we produce but also quality of life and quality of care for the countryside.' Nick Fuge is the farm manager at Lower Hurst Farm located within the Peak District National Park of the UK. He has day-to-day responsibility for the well-being of all the livestock and the operation of the farm on strict organic principles. The 85 hectare farm has been producing high quality beef for almost 20 years but changed to fully organic production in 1998. Organic farming is a tough regime. No artificial fertilizers, genetically modified feedstuff or growth promoting agents are used. All beef sold from the farm is home bred and can be traced back to the animal from which it came. 'The quality of the herd is most important,' says Nick 'as is animal care. Our customers trust us to ensure that the cattle are organically and humanely reared, and slaughtered in a manner that minimizes any distress. If you want to understand the difference between conventional and organic farming, look at the way we use veterinary help. Most conventional farmers use veterinarians like an emergency service to put things right when there is a problem with an animal. The amount we pay for veterinary assistance is lower because we try to avoid problems with the animals from the start. We use veterinaries as consultants to help us in preventing problems in the first place.'

Catherine Pyne runs the butchery and the mail order meat business. 'After butchering, the cuts of meat are individually vacuum packed, weighed and then blast frozen. We worked extensively with the Department of Food and Nutrition at Oxford Brookes University to devise the best way to encapsulate the nutritional, textural and flavoursome characteristics of the meat in its prime state. So, when you defrost and cook any of our products you will have the same tasty and succulent eating qualities associated with the best fresh meat.'

After freezing, the products are packed in boxes, designed and labelled for storage in a home freezer. Customers order by phone or through the internet for next day delivery in a special 'mini deep freeze' reusable container which maintains the meat in its frozen state. 'It isn't just the quality of our product which has made us a success,' says Catherine, 'we give a personal and inclusive level of service to our customers that makes them feel close to us and maintains trust in how we produce and prepare the meat. The team of people we have here is also an important aspect of our business. We are proud of our product and feel that it is vitally important to be personally identified with it.' ■

Questions

1 What does Lower Hurst Farm have to get right to keep the quality of its products and its services so high?

2 Why is Nick's point about veterinarian help important for all types of operation?

Quality reduces costs

The fewer mistakes made by each process in the operation, the less time will be needed to correct the mistakes and the less confusion and irritation will be spread. For example, if a supermarket's regional warehouse sends the wrong goods to the supermarket; it will mean staff time, and therefore cost, being used to sort out the problem.

Quality increases dependability

Increased costs are not the only consequence of poor quality. At the supermarket it could also mean that goods run out on the supermarket shelves with a resulting loss of revenue to the operation and irritation to the external customers. Sorting the problem out could also distract the supermarket management from giving attention to the other parts of the supermarket operation. This in turn could result in further mistakes being made. The important point here is that the performance objective of quality (like the other performance objectives, as we shall see) has both an external impact which influences customer satisfaction, and an internal impact, which leads to stable and efficient processes.

46

The speed objective

Speed means the elapsed time between customers requesting products or services and then receiving them. Figure 2.6 illustrates what speed means for the four operations. The main benefit to the operation's (external) customers of speedy delivery of goods and services lies in the way it enhances the operation's offering to the customer. Quite simply, for most goods and services, the faster customers can have the product or service, the more likely they are to buy it, or the more they will pay for it, or the greater the benefit they receive (see the box 'When speed means life or death'). So, for example, TNT Express' customers are willing to pay more for the services which deliver faster.

Speed inside the operation

Inside the operation, speed is also important. Fast response to external customers is greatly helped by speedy decision making and speedy movement of materials and information inside the operation. Internal speed can have further benefits, however.[5]

Speed reduces inventories

Take, for example, the automobile plant. The steel used to make the vehicle's door panels is first delivered to the press shop where it is pressed into shape, then transported to the painting area where it is coated for colour and protection, then moved to the assembly line where it is fitted to the automobile. This is a simple three-stage process, but in practice each door panel does not flow smoothly from one stage to the next. Following a product through the processes can take a surprisingly long time. First, the steel is delivered as part of a far larger batch, containing enough steel to make possibly several hundred products. Eventually it is taken to the press area where it is pressed into shape, and again waits until it is transported to the paint area. It then waits until it can be painted,

Figure 2.6	Speed means different things in different operations

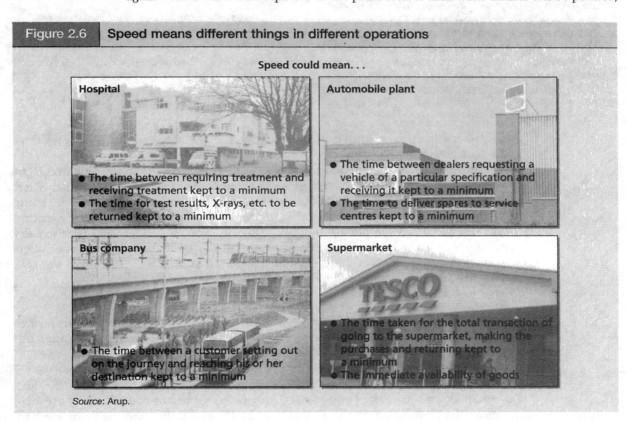

Speed could mean. . .

Hospital
- The time between requiring treatment and receiving treatment kept to a minimum
- The time for test results, X-rays, etc. to be returned kept to a minimum

Automobile plant
- The time between dealers requesting a vehicle of a particular specification and receiving it kept to a minimum
- The time to deliver spares to service centres kept to a minimum

Bus company
- The time between a customer setting out on the journey and reaching his or her destination kept to a minimum

Supermarket
- The time taken for the total transaction of going to the supermarket, making the purchases and returning kept to a minimum
- The immediate availability of goods

Source: Arup.

47

When speed means life or death[6]

example

Of all the operations which have to respond quickly to customer demand, few have more need of speed than the emergency services. In responding to road accidents especially, every second is critical. The treatment you receive during the first hour after your accident (what is called the 'golden hour') can determine whether you survive and fully recover or not. Making full use of the golden hour means speeding up three elements of the total time to treatment – the time it takes for the emergency services to find out about the accident, the time it takes them to travel to the scene of the accident, and the time it takes to get the casualty to appropriate treatment.

Alerting the emergency services immediately to an accident is the idea behind Mercedes-Benz's new TeleAid (Telematic Alarm Identification on Demand), offered initially to drivers of their S-class cars in Germany. As soon as the vehicle's air bag is triggered, an onboard micro computer reports through the mobile phone network to a control centre (drivers can also trigger the system manually if not too badly hurt). The onboard satellite facility then allows the vehicle to be precisely located, and the type of vehicle and owner identified (if special medication is needed).

Getting to the accident quickly is the next hurdle. Often the fastest method is by helicopter. When most rescues are only a couple of minutes' flying time back to the hospital speed can really saves lives. However, it is not always possible to land a helicopter safely at night (because of possible overhead wires and other hazards) so conventional ambulances will always be needed, both to get paramedics quickly to accident victims and to speed them to hospital. One increasingly common method of ensuring that ambulances arrive quickly at the accident site is to position them, not at hospitals, but close to where accidents are likely to

Speed of response in emergency services requires fast and accurate communication between the operations contributing to the service

occur. Computer analysis of previous accident data helps to select the ambulance's waiting position, and global positioning systems help controllers to mobilize the nearest unit. At all times a key requirement for fast service is effective communication between all who are involved in each stage of the emergency. Modern communications technology can play an important role in this. ■

Questions

1 Draw a chart which illustrates the stages between an accident occurring and full treatment being made available.

2 What are the key issues (both those mentioned above and any others you can think of) which determine the time taken at each stage?

---

only to wait once more until it is transported to the assembly line. Yet again it waits by the trackside until it is eventually fitted to the automobile.

The door panel's journey through the factory was far longer than the time needed to actually make and fit the product, and was also composed mainly of waiting time. When hundreds of products are moving through the plant every day, this waiting time results in large stocks (or inventories) of parts and products. If, on the other hand, the waiting can be reduced (say by moving and processing the parts in smaller batches), the parts will move faster through the plant and as a result the amount of inventories between each stage of the process will be reduced. This idea has some very important implications which will be explored in Chapter 15 on lean operations.

Speed reduces risks

Forecasting tomorrow's events is far less of a risk than forecasting next year's. The further ahead companies forecast, the more likely they are to get it wrong. The faster the throughput time of a process the later forecasting can be left. Consider the automobile plant again. If the total throughput time for the door panel is six weeks, door panels are being processed through their first operation six weeks before they reach their final destination. The quantity of door panels being processed will be determined by the forecasts for demand six weeks ahead. If instead of six weeks, they take only one week to

48

Speed and dependability are particularly important for roadside assistance services. Here a Royal Automobile Club of Victoria (RACV) patrol assists a motorist in Melbourne. RACV's communications and control systems have made it one of the most effective roadside assistance operations

move through the plant, the door panels being processed through their first stage are intended to meet demand only one week ahead. Under these circumstances it is far more likely that the number and type of door panels being processed are the number and type which eventually will be needed.

The dependability objective

Dependability means doing things in time for customers to receive their goods or services exactly when they are needed, or at least when they were promised. Figure 2.7 illustrates what dependability means in the four operations.

Customers might only judge the dependability of an operation after the product or service has been delivered. Initially this may not affect the likelihood that customers will select the service – they have already 'consumed' it. Over time, however, dependability can override all other criteria. No matter how cheap a bus service is, or how fast it is advertised as being, if the service is always late (or unpredictably early) or the buses are always full, then potential passengers will be better off calling a taxi. The box 'Taxi Stockholm' describes how one taxi company has focused on its reputation for dependability.

Dependability inside the operation

Inside the operation dependability has a similar effect. Internal customers will judge each other's performance partly by how reliable the other processes are in delivering material or information on time. Operations where internal dependability is high are more effective than those which are not, for a number of reasons.

Dependability saves time

Take, for example, the maintenance and repair centre for the city bus company. The manager will always have a plan of the centre's activities devised to keep the centre's facilities as fully utilized as possible while ensuring that the bus fleet always has enough

49

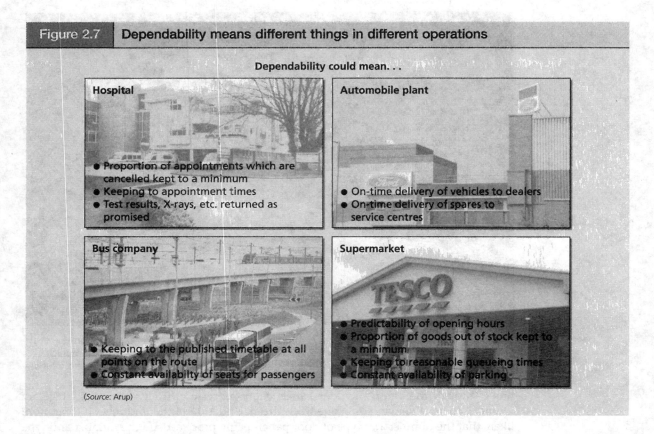

Figure 2.7 Dependability means different things in different operations

Dependability could mean...

Hospital
- Proportion of appointments which are cancelled kept to a minimum
- Keeping to appointment times
- Test results, X-rays, etc. returned as promised

Automobile plant
- On-time delivery of vehicles to dealers
- On-time delivery of spares to service centres

Bus company
- Keeping to the published timetable at all points on the route
- Constant availabilty of seats for passengers

Supermarket
- Predictability of opening hours
- Proportion of goods out of stock kept to a minimum
- Keeping to reasonable queueing times
- Constant availability of parking

(Source: Arup)

clean and serviced vehicles to match demand. But, if the centre runs out of some crucial spare parts, the manager of the centre will need to spend time trying to arrange a special delivery of the required parts and the resources allocated to service the buses will not be used as productively as they would have been without this disruption. More seriously, the fleet will be short of buses until they can be repaired and the fleet operations manager will have to spend time rescheduling services. So, entirely due to the one failure of dependability of supply, a significant part of the operation's time has been wasted coping with the disruption.

Dependability saves money
Ineffective use of time will translate into extra cost. The spare parts might cost more to be delivered at short notice and maintenance staff will expect to be paid even when there is not a bus to work on. Nor will the fixed costs of the operation, such as heating and rent, be reduced because the two buses are not being serviced. The rescheduling of buses will probably mean that some routes have inappropriately sized buses and some services could have to be cancelled. This will result in empty bus seats (if too large a bus has to be used) or a loss of revenue (if potential passengers are not transported).

Dependability gives stability
The disruption caused to operations by a lack of dependability goes beyond time and cost. It affects the 'quality' of the operation's time. If everything in an operation is perfectly dependable, and has been for some time, a level of trust will have built up between the different parts of the operation. There will be no 'surprises' and everything will be predictable. Under such circumstances, each part of the operation can concentrate on improving its own area of responsibility without having its attention continually diverted by a lack of dependable service from the other parts.

50

Taxi Stockholm[7]

Taxi Stockholm may be over 100 years old and organized as a cooperative, but it has become one of the largest and most technically advanced taxi companies in the world. *'They are absolutely trustworthy,'* according to one satisfied customer, *'I am not the only one who chooses them even when they are not first in the taxi queue.'* The company has a policy of choosing reliability over speed according to their CEO Anders Malmqvist. *'Compared to some of our rivals, productivity in our call centre is low. Our workers don't answer as many calls per hour, but that's our choice. The focus of our business is not how many calls we can answer but how many customers we can satisfy.'*

Such dependability is helped by Taxi Stockholm's automatic routing technology. Phone for a cab and a voice response system identifies your location (verified by pushing the appropriate buttons on the telephone) and the system finds and instructs the nearest available cab to your location. Plans include extending the technology to provide precise estimated times of arrival every time a cab is called and automatic callback to confirm each reservation. *'My job,'* says Malmqvist *'is to get the fleet out when customers demand it, not the other way round.'* ■

Question

1 How can Taxi Stockholm keep its dependability high during those times when demand is high and traffic is congested?

Source: Photograph courtesy of Shealagh Gaw

Source: Photograph courtesy of Shealagh Gaw

51

The flexibility objective

Flexibility means being able to change the operation in some way. This may mean changing what the operation does, how it is doing it, or when it is doing it. Specifically, customers will need the operation to change so that it can provide four types of requirement:

Product/service flexibility
- **product/service flexibility** – the operations ability to introduce new or modified products and services;

Mix flexibility
- **mix flexibility** – the operations ability to produce a wide range or mix of products and services;

Volume flexibility
- **volume flexibility** – the operations ability to change its level of output or activity to produce different quantities or volumes of products and services over time;

Delivery flexibility
- **delivery flexibility** – the operations ability to change the timing of the delivery of its services or products.

Figure 2.8 gives examples of what these different types of flexibility mean to the four different operations.

Mass customization

One of the beneficial external effects of flexibility is the increased ability of the operation to do different things for different customers. So high *flexibility* gives the ability to produce a high *variety* of products or services. Normally high variety means high cost (as we discussed in Chapter 1). Furthermore, high variety operations do not usually produce in high volume. Some companies have developed their flexibility in such a way as to achieve high variety, to the extent that products and services are *customized* for each individual customer. Yet they manage to produce them in a high volume, *mass* production manner

Mass customization which keeps costs down. This approach is called **mass customization**. Sometimes this is

---

Figure 2.8 | **Flexibility means different things in different operations**

Flexibility could mean. . .

Hospital
- Product/service flexibility – the introduction of new types of treatment
- Mix flexibility – a wide range of available treatments
- Volume flexibility – the ability to adjust the number of patients treated
- Delivery flexibility – the ability to reschedule appointments

Automobile plant
- Product/service flexibility – the introduction of new models
- Mix flexibility – a wide range of options available
- Volume flexibility – the ability to adjust the number of vehicles manufactured
- Delivery flexibility – the ability to reschedule manufacturing priorities

Bus company
- Product/service flexibility – the introduction of new routes or excursions
- Mix flexibility – a large number of locations served
- Volume flexibility – the ability to adjust the frequency of services
- Delivery flexibility – the ability to reschedule trips

Supermarket
- Product/service flexibility – the introduction of new goods or promotions
- Mix flexibility – a wide range of goods stocked
- Volume flexibility – the ability to adjust the number of customers served
- Delivery flexibility – the ability to obtain out-of-stock items (very occasionally)

(*Source*: Arup)

achieved through flexibility in design. For example, Dell is the largest volume producer of personal computers in the world, yet allows each customer to 'design' (albeit in a limited sense) their own configuration. Sometimes flexible technology is used to achieve the same effect. For example, Paris Miki, an up-market eyewear retailer which has the largest number of eyewear stores in the world, uses its own 'Mikissimes Design System' to capture a digital image of the customer and analyse facial characteristics. Together with a list of customers' personal preferences, the system then recommends a particular design and displays it on the image of the customer's face. In consultation with the optician the customer can adjust shapes and sizes until the final design is chosen. Within the store the frames are assembled from a range of pre-manufactured components and the lenses ground and fitted to the frames. The whole process takes around an hour.

Flexibility inside the operation

Developing a flexible operation can also have advantages to the internal customers within the operation.

Flexibility speeds up response

Being able to give fast service often depends on the operation being flexible. For example, if the hospital has to cope with a sudden influx of patients from a road accident, it clearly needs to deal with injuries quickly. Under such circumstances a flexible hospital which can speedily transfer extra skilled staff and equipment to the Accident and Emergency department will provide the fast service which the patients need.

Flexibility and dependability in the newsroom[8] | example

Television news is big business. Satellite and cable, as well as developments in terrestrial transmission, have all helped to boost the popularity of 24-hour news services. But news perishes fast. A daily newspaper delivered one day late is practically worthless. This is why broadcasting organizations like the BBC have to ensure that up-to-date news is delivered on time, every time. The BBC's ability to achieve high levels of dependability is made possible by the technology employed in news gathering and editing. At one time news editors would have to schedule a video-taped report to start its countdown five seconds prior to its broadcasting time. With new technology the video can be started from a freeze-frame and will broadcast the instant the command to play is given. The team has faith in the dependability of the process. In addition, technology allows them the flexibility to achieve dependability, even when news stories break just before transmission. In the hours before scheduled transmission, journalists and editors prepare an 'inventory' of news items stored electronically. The presenter will prepare his or her commentary on the autocue and each item will be timed to the second. If the team needs to make a short-term adjustment to the planned schedule, the news studio's technology allows the editors to take broadcasts live from journalists at their locations, on satellite 'takes', directly into the programme. Editors can even type news reports directly onto the autocue for the

Source: BBC Photo Library

presenter to read as they are typed – nerve-racking, but it keeps the programme on time. ■

Questions

1 What do the five performance objectives mean for an operation such as the BBC's newsroom?

2 How do these performance objectives influence each other?

Flexibility saves time

In many parts of the hospital, staff have to treat a wide variety of complaints. Fractures, cuts or drug overdoses do not come in batches. Each patient is an individual with individual needs. The hospital staff cannot take time to 'get into the routine' of treating a particular complaint; they must have the flexibility to adapt quickly. They must also have sufficiently flexible facilities and equipment so that time is not wasted waiting for equipment to be brought to the patient. The time of the hospital's resources is being saved because they are flexible in 'changing over' from one task to the next.

Flexibility maintains dependability

Internal flexibility can also help to keep the operation on schedule when unexpected events disrupt the operation's plans. For example, if the sudden influx of patients to the hospital also results in emergency surgery being performed, the emergency patients will almost certainly displace other routine operations. The patients who were expecting to undergo their routine operations will have been admitted and probably prepared for their operations. Cancelling their operations is likely to cause them distress and probably considerable inconvenience. A flexible hospital might be able to minimize the disruption by possibly having reserved operating theatres for such an emergency, and being able to bring in medical staff quickly who are 'on call'. The box 'Flexibility and dependability in the newsroom' shows how flexible technology helps to maintain the dependability of news broadcasting.

The cost objective

Cost is the last objective to be covered, although not because it is the least important. To the companies which compete directly on price, cost will clearly be their major operations objective. The lower the cost of producing their goods and services, the lower can be the price to their customers. Even those companies which compete on things other than price, however, will be interested in keeping their costs low. Every euro or dollar removed from an operation's cost base is a further euro or dollar added to its profits. Not surprisingly, low cost is a universally attractive objective. The box 'Every day low prices at Aldi' describes how one retailer keeps its costs down.

The ways in which operations management can influence cost will depend largely on where the operation costs are incurred. Put simply, the operation will spend its money on:

- *staff costs* (the money spent on employing people);
- *facilities, technology and equipment costs* (the money spent on buying, caring for, operating and replacing the operation's 'hardware');
- *material costs* (the money spent on the materials consumed or transformed in the operation).

Figure 2.9 shows typical cost breakdowns for the hospital, car plant, supermarket and bus company.

Although comparing the cost structure of different operations is not always straightforward, and depends on how costs are categorized, some general points can be made.

Many of the hospital's costs are fixed and will change little for small changes in the number of patients it treats. Its facilities such as beds, operating theatres and laboratories are expensive, as are some of its highly skilled staff. Some of the hospital's costs will be payments to outside suppliers of drugs, medical supplies and externally sourced services such as cleaning, but probably not as high a proportion as in the car factory. The car factory's payment for materials and other supplies will by far outweigh all its other costs put together. Conversely, the city bus company will pay very little for its supplies, fuel being one of its main bought-in items. At the other extreme, the supermarket's costs are

Every day low prices at Aldi[9]

example

Aldi is an international 'limited assortment' supermarket specializing in 'private label', mainly food products. It has carefully focused its service concept and delivery system to attract customers in a highly competitive market. The company believe that their unique approach to operations management make it, '... *virtually impossible for competitors to match our combination of price and quality*'.

Aldi operations challenge the norms of retailing. They are deliberately simple, using basic facilities to keep down overheads. Most stores stock only a limited range of goods (typically around 700 compared with 25,000 to 30,000 stocked by conventional supermarket chains). The private label approach means that the products have been produced according Aldi quality specifications and are only sold in Aldi stores. Without the high costs of brand marketing and advertising and with Aldi's formidable purchasing power, prices can be 30 per cent below their branded equivalents. Other cost saving practices include open carton displays which eliminate the need for special shelving, no grocery bags to encourage recycling as well as saving costs, and using a 'cart rental' system which requires customers to return the cart to the store to get their coin deposit back. ∎

Question

1 What are the main ways in which Aldi operations try to minimize their costs?

dominated by the cost of buying its supplies. In spite of its high 'material' costs, however, an individual supermarket can do little if anything to affect the cost of goods it sells. All purchasing decisions will probably be made at company headquarters. The individual supermarket will be more concerned with the utilization of its main asset, the building itself, and its staff.

Cost is affected by the other performance objectives

So far we have described the meaning and effects of quality, speed, dependability and flexibility for the operations function. In doing so, we have distinguished between the value of each performance objective to external customers and, inside the operation, to internal customers. Each of the various performance objectives has several internal effects, but all of them affect cost:

● High-quality operations do not waste time or effort having to re-do things, nor are their internal customers inconvenienced by flawed service.
● Fast operations reduce the level of in-process inventory between micro operations, as well as reducing administrative overheads.
● Dependable operations do not spring any unwelcome surprises on their internal customers. They can be relied on to deliver exactly as planned. This eliminates wasteful disruption and allows the other micro operations to operate efficiently.
● Flexible operations adapt to changing circumstances quickly and without disrupting the rest of the operation. Flexible micro operations can also change over between tasks quickly and without wasting time and capacity.

55

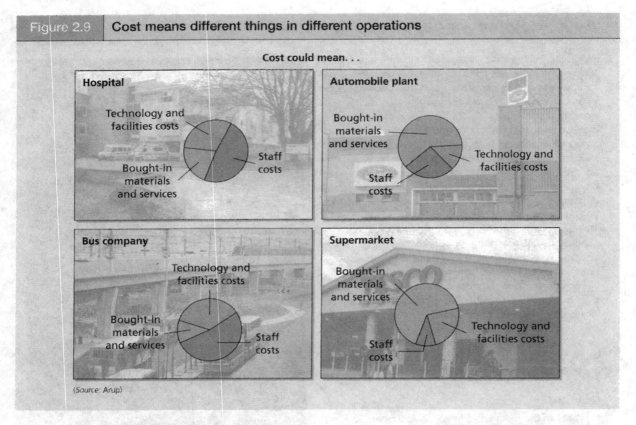

Figure 2.9   **Cost means different things in different operations**

Cost could mean. . .

Hospital
- Technology and facilities costs
- Bought-in materials and services
- Staff costs

Automobile plant
- Bought-in materials and services
- Technology and facilities costs
- Staff costs

Bus company
- Technology and facilities costs
- Bought-in materials and services
- Staff costs

Supermarket
- Bought-in materials and services
- Technology and facilities costs
- Staff costs

(Source: Arup)

Inside the operation, therefore, one important way to improve cost performance is to improve the performance of the other operations objectives (see Figure 2.10).

Other measures of operations performance

The five performance objectives used here are recognized in a wide variety of operations, but other perfectly valid measures of operations performance can be used. Some of these other measures are combinations of quality, speed, dependability, flexibility or cost. For example, judging operations in terms of their **agility** has become popular. Agility is really a combination of all the five performance objectives but particularly flexibility and speed. In addition, agility implies that an operation and the supply chain of which it is a part (supply chains are described in Chapter 6) can respond the uncertainty in the market. Agility means responding to market requirements by producing new and existing products and services fast and flexibly.

Other measures of operations performance may be very similar to one of the five performance objectives we have used. For example, **productivity** is closely related to cost, and in some definitions of productivity is almost identical to cost. In fact productivity is the ratio of what is produced by an operation to what is required to produce it.

$$\text{productivity} = \frac{\text{output from an operation}}{\text{input to the operation}}$$

Often partial measures of input or output are used so that comparisons can be made. So, for example, in the automobile industry productivity is sometimes measured in terms of the number of cars produced per year per employee. This allows different operations to be compared excluding the effects of input costs. One operation may have high total costs per car but high productivity in terms of number of cars per employee per year. The difference between the two measures is explained in terms of the distinction between

Agility

Productivity

56

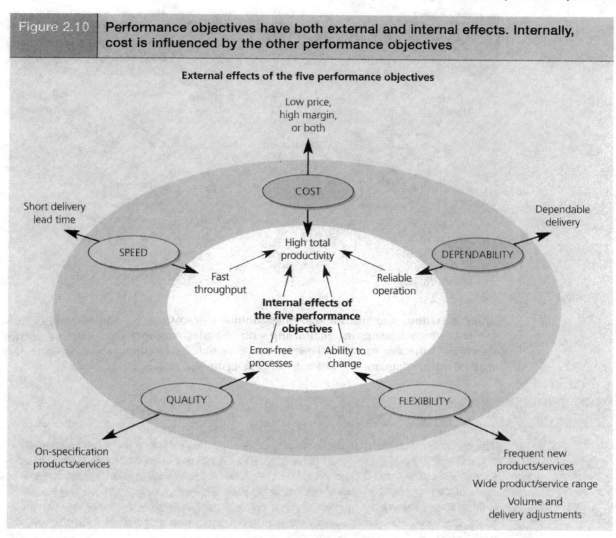

Figure 2.10 **Performance objectives have both external and internal effects. Internally, cost is influenced by the other performance objectives**

External effects of the five performance objectives

Low price,
high margin,
or both

COST

Short delivery
lead time

Dependable
delivery

SPEED

DEPENDABILITY

High total
productivity

Fast
throughput

Reliable
operation

**Internal effects of
the five performance
objectives**

Error-free
processes

Ability to
change

QUALITY

FLEXIBILITY

On-specification
products/services

Frequent new
products/services

Wide product/service range

Volume and
delivery adjustments

the cost of the inputs to the operation and the way the operation is managed to convert inputs into outputs. Input costs may be high, but the operation itself is good at converting them to goods and services.

The polar representation of performance objectives

Polar representation

A useful way of representing the relative importance of performance objectives for a product or service is shown in Figure 2.11(a). This is called the **polar representation** because the scales which represent the importance of each performance objective have the same origin. A line describes the relative importance of each performance objective. The closer the line is to the common origin, the less important is the performance objective to the operation. Two services are shown, a taxi and a bus service. Each essentially provides the same basic service, but with different objectives. The differences between the two services are clearly shown by the diagram.

Of course, the polar diagram can be adapted to accommodate any number of different performance objectives. For example, Figure 2.11(b) shows a proposal for using a polar diagram to assess the relative performance of different police forces in the UK.[10] Note that this proposal uses three measures of quality (reassurance, crime reduction and

57

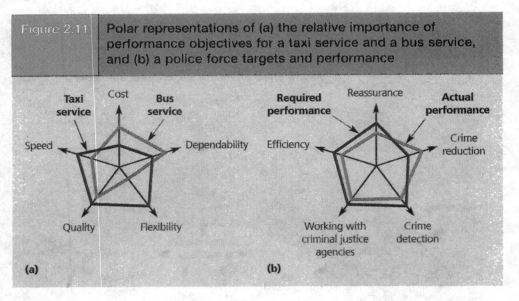

Figure 2.11 | Polar representations of (a) the relative importance of performance objectives for a taxi service and a bus service, and (b) a police force targets and performance

crime detection), one measure of cost (economic efficiency), and one measure of how the police force develops its relationship with 'internal' customers (the criminal justice agencies). Note also that actual performance as well as required performance is also marked on the diagram. We will use this idea again in Chapter 18.

worked example

The environmental services department of a city has two recycling services – newspaper collection (NC) and general recycling (GR). The NC service is a door-to-door collection service which, at a fixed time every week, collects old newspapers which householders have placed in reusable plastic bags at their gate. An empty bag is left for the householders to use for the next collection. The value of the newspapers collected is relatively small, the service is offered mainly for reasons of environmental responsibility. By contrast the GR service is more commercial. Companies and private individuals can request a collection of materials to be disposed of, either using the telephone or the internet. The GR service guarantees to collect the material within 24 hours unless the customer prefers to specify a more convenient time. Any kind of material can be collected and a charge is made depending on the volume of material. This service makes a small profit because the revenue both from customer charges and from some of the more valuable recycled materials exceeds the operation's running costs.

Draw a polar diagram which distinguishes between the performance objectives of the two services.

Analysis

Quality – is important for both services because failure to conform to what customers expect would diminish their faith in the virtue of recycling.

Speed – as such is not important for the NC service (it follows a fixed timetable) but it is important for the GR service to collect within 24 hours as promised.

Dependability – must be particularly important for the NC service otherwise newspapers would be left out causing litter in the streets, also important for the GR service though perhaps marginally less so because speed dominates.

58

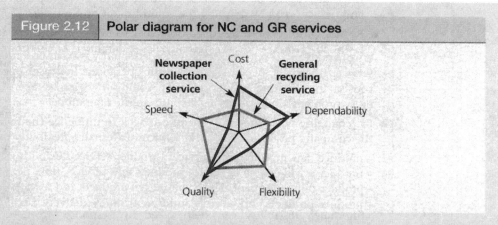

Figure 2.12 Polar diagram for NC and GR services

Flexibility – relatively little flexibility is required by the NC service, every week collections are the same with perhaps some minor variation in volume, however, the GR service has to cope with a wide range of recycling tasks at whatever volume customers' demand.

Cost – the NC service is not profitable therefore any reduction in cost in welcome because it reduces the 'loss', the GR service will have fewer cost pressures because it is naturally profitable and some customers may even pay more for an enhanced service.

Taken together the polar diagram for the two services is shown in Figure 2.12.

summary answers to key questions

*The companion website to the book, **www.booksites.net/slack**, also has a brief 'Study Guide' to each chapter.*

What role should the operations function play in achieving strategic success?

- Any operations function has three main roles to play within an organization; as an implementer of the organization's strategies, as a supporter of the organization's overall strategy, and as a leader or driver of strategy.

- The extent to which an operations function fulfils these roles, together with its aspirations, can be used to judge the operations function's contribution to the organization. Hayes and Wheelwright provide a four-stage model for doing this.

What are the performance objectives of operations and what are the internal and external benefits which derive from excelling in each of them?

- At a strategic level, performance objectives relate to the interests of the operation's stakeholders. These relate to the company's responsibility to customers, suppliers, shareholders, employees and society in general.

- By 'doing things right', operations seek to influence the quality of the company's goods and services. Externally, quality is an important aspect of customer satisfaction or dissatisfaction. Internally, quality operations both reduce costs and increase dependability.

- By 'doing things fast', operations seek to influence the speed with which goods and services are delivered. Externally, speed is an important aspect of customer service.

Internally, speed both reduces inventories by decreasing internal throughput time and reduces risks by delaying the commitment of resources.

- By 'doing things on time', operations seek to influence the dependability of the delivery of goods and services. Externally, dependability is an important aspect of customer service. Internally, dependability within operations increases operational reliability, thus saving the time and money that would otherwise be taken up in solving reliability problems and also giving stability to the operation.

- By 'changing what they do', operations seek to influence the flexibility with which the company produces goods and services. Externally, flexibility can:

  – produce new products and services (product/service flexibility);
  – produce a wide range or mix of products and services (mix flexibility);
  – produce different quantities or volumes of products and services (volume flexibility);
  – produce products and services at different times (delivery flexibility).

Internally, flexibility can help speed up response times, save time wasted in changeovers, and maintain dependability.

- By 'doing things cheaply', operations seek to influence the cost of the company's goods and services. Externally, low costs allow organizations to reduce their price in order to gain higher volumes or, alternatively, increase their profitability on existing volume levels. Internally, cost performance is helped by good performance in the other performance objectives.

Operations objectives at the Penang Mutiara[11] | case exercise

There are many luxurious hotels in the South-East Asia region but few can compare with the Penang Mutiara, a 440 room top-of-the-market hotel which nestles in the lush greenery of Malaysia's Indian Ocean Coast. Owned by Pernas–OUE of Malaysia and managed by Singapore Mandarin International Hotels, the hotel's General Manager is Wernie Eisen, a Swiss hotelier who has managed luxury hotels all over the world.

He is under no illusions about the importance of running an effective operation.

'Managing a hotel of this size is an immensely complicated task,' he says. 'Our customers have every right to be demanding. They expect first-class service and that's what we have to give them. If we have any problems with managing this operation, the customer sees them immediately and that's the biggest incentive for us to take operations performance seriously. 'Our quality of service just has to be impeccable. First of all this means dealing with the basics. For example, our staff must be courteous at all times and yet also friendly towards our guests. And, of course, they must have the knowledge to be able to answer guests' questions. The building and equipment – in fact all the hardware of the operation – must support the luxury atmosphere which we have created in the hotel. Stylish design and top-class materials not only create the right impression but, if we choose them carefully, are also

durable so the hotel still looks good over the years. Most of all, though, quality is about anticipating our guests' needs, thinking ahead so you can identify what will delight or irritate a guest.'

The hotel tries to anticipate guests' needs in a number of ways. For example, if guests have been to the hotel before, staff avoid their having to repeat the information they gave on the previous visit. Reception staff simply check to see if guests have stayed before, retrieve the information and take them straight to their room without irritating delays. Quality of service also means helping guests sort out their own problems. If the airline loses a guest's luggage en route to the hotel, for example, he or she will arrive at the hotel understandably irritated. 'The fact that it is not us who have irritated them is not really the issue. It is our job to make them feel better.'

Speed, in terms of fast response to customers' requests is something else that is important.

'A guest just should not be kept waiting. If a guest has a request, he or she has that request now so it needs to be sorted out now. This is not always easy but we do our best. For example, if every guest in the hotel tonight decided to call room service and request a meal instead of going to the restaurants, our room service department would obviously be grossly overloaded and customers would have to wait an unacceptably long time before the meals were brought up to their rooms. We cope with this by keeping a close watch on how demand for room service is building up. If we think it's going to get above the level where response time to customers would become unacceptably long, we will call in staff from other restaurants in the hotel. Of course, to do this we have to make sure that our staff are multi-skilled. In fact, we have a policy of making sure that restaurant staff can always do more than one job. It's this kind of flexibility which allows us to maintain fast response to the customer.'

Likewise, Wernie regards dependability as a fundamental principle of a well-managed hotel.

'We must always keep our promises. For example, rooms must be ready on time and accounts must be ready for presentation when a guest departs; the guests expect a dependable service and anything less than full dependability is a legitimate cause for dissatisfaction.'

It is on the grand occasions, however, when dependability is particularly important in the hotel. When staging a banquet, for example, everything has to be on time. Drinks, food, entertainment have to be available exactly as planned. Any deviation from the plan will very soon be noticed by customers.

'It is largely a matter of planning the details and anticipating what could go wrong,' says Wernie. 'Once we've done the planning we can anticipate possible problems and plan how to cope with them, or better still, prevent them from occurring in the first place.'

Flexibility means a number of things to the hotel. First of all it means that they should be able to meet a guest's requests.

'We never like to say NO!' says Wernie. 'For example, if a guest asks for some Camembert cheese and we don't have it in stock, we will make sure that someone goes to the supermarket and tries to get it. If, in spite of our best efforts, we can't get any we will negotiate an alternative solution with the guest. This has an important side-effect – it greatly helps us to maintain the motivation of our staff. We are constantly being asked to do the seemingly impossible – yet we do it, and our staff think it's great. We all like to be part of an organization which is capable of achieving the very difficult, if not the impossible.'

Flexibility in the hotel also means the ability to cope with the seasonal fluctuations in demand. They achieve this partly by using temporary part-time staff. In the back-office parts of the hotel this isn't a major problem. In the laundry, for example, it is relatively easy to put on an extra shift in busy periods by increasing staffing levels. However, this is more of a problem in the parts of the hotel that have direct contact with the customer.

'New temporary staff can't be expected to have the same customer contact skills as our more regular staff. Our solution to this is to keep the temporary staff as far in the background as we possibly can and make sure that our skilled, well-trained staff are the ones who usually interact with the customer. So, for example, a waiter who would normally take orders, service the food, and take away the dirty plates would in peak times restrict his or her activities to taking orders and serving the food. The less skilled part of the job, taking away the plates, could be left to temporary staff.'

As far as cost is concerned, around 60 per cent of the hotel's total operating expenses go on food and beverages, so one obvious way of keeping costs down is by making sure that food is not wasted. Energy costs, at 6 per cent of total operating costs, are also a potential source of saving. However, although cost savings are welcome, the hotel is very careful never to compromise the quality of its service in order to cut costs. Wernie's view is quite clear:

'It is impeccable customer service which gives us our competitive advantage, not price. Good service means that our guests return again and again. At times, around half our guests are people who have been before. The more guests we have, the higher is our utilization of rooms and restaurants, and this is what really keeps cost per guest down and profitability reasonable. So in the end we've come full circle: it's the quality of our service which keeps our volumes high and our costs low.' ■

Questions

1 Describe how you think Wernie will:

    (a) make sure that the way he manages the hotel is *appropriate* to the way it competes for business;

    (b) *implement* any change in strategy;

    (c) develop his operation so that *it drives* the long-term strategy of the hotel.

2 What questions might Wernie ask to judge whether his operation is a stage 1, stage 2, stage 3 or stage 4 operation on Hayes and Wheelwright's scale of excellence?

3 The case describes how quality, speed, dependability, flexibility and cost impact on the hotel's external customers. Explain how each of these performance objectives might have internal benefits.

 Other short cases, and worked answers, are included in the companion website to this book, www.booksites.net/slack.

61

study activities

*Some study activities can be answered by reading the chapter. Others will require some general knowledge of business activity and some might require an element of investigation. All have hints on how they can be answered on the companion website for this book which also contains more discussion questions, **www.booksites.net/slack**.*

1 At the beginning of the chapter some of the activities of TNT Express were described. In fact, this is only one of three divisions of TPG, the other two being international mail and logistics. Visit the company's websites and

(a) identify what the company sees as its stakeholders and describe how it attempts to satisfy their concerns;

(b) on the same polar diagram draw the relative required performance levels for the five generic performance objectives for each of the three divisions of the company.

2 *Step 1* – Look again at the figures in the chapter which illustrate the meaning of each performance objective for the four operations. Consider the bus company and the supermarket, and in particular consider their external customers.

Step 2 – Draw the relative required performance for both operations on a polar diagram.

Step 3 – Consider the internal effects of each performance objective. For both operations, identify how quality, speed, dependability and flexibility can help to reduce the cost of producing their services.

3 The 'forensic science' service of a European country has traditionally been organized to provide separate forensic science laboratories for each police force around the country. In order to save costs, the government has decided to centralize this service in one large central facility close to the country's capital. What do you think are the external advantages and disadvantages of this to the stakeholders of the operation? What do you think are the internal implications to the new centralized operation that will provide this service?

4 (Advanced) Visit the websites of two or three large oil companies such as Exon, Shell, Elf, etc. Examine how they describe their policies towards their customers, suppliers, shareholders, employees and society at large. Identify areas of the companies operations where there may be conflicts between the needs of these different stakeholder groups. Discuss or reflect on how (if at all) such companies try and reconcile these conflicts.

5 (Advanced) Consider the automobile plant illustrated in various figures throughout the chapter. For such a plant, think about how each performance objective can affect the others within the operation. In other words, how can quality affect speed, dependability, flexibility and cost? How can speed affect quality, dependability, flexibility and cost, and so on.

Notes on chapter

1 Source: TNT press releases.

2 This idea was first popularized by Wickham Skinner at Harvard University. *See* Skinner, W. (1985) *Manufacturing: The Formidable Competitive Weapon*, John Wiley.

3 Hayes, R.H. and Wheelwright, S.C. (1984) *Restoring our Competitive Edge*, John Wiley.

5 Source: Catherine Pyne and Nick Fuge, Lower Hurst Farm.

4 Chase, R. and Hayes, R.H. (1991) 'Beefing up Service Firms', *Sloan Management Review*, Fall.

6 Sources include: 'Smart Car will Call Police in a Crash', *The Sunday Times*, 23 February 1997.

62

7 Source: Wylie, I. (2001) 'All Hail Taxi Stockholm', *Fast Company,* May.

8 Source: Fiona Rennie, Discussions with the News Team at the BBC.

9 Source: John Hendry-Pickup.

10 Source: Miles, A. and Baldwin, T. (2002) 'Spidergram to check on police forces', *The Times,* 10 July.

11 We are grateful to the management of the Penang Mutiara for permission to use this example.

Selected further reading

Hayes, R.H. and Wheelwright, S.C. (1984) *Restoring our Competitive Edge*, John Wiley, New York, and Chase, R. and Hayes, R.H. (1991) 'Beefing up service firms', *Sloan Management Review, Fall.* Both these papers were the origins of the idea that operations role is important in determining its contribution to a business.

Pine, B.J. (1993) *Mass Customization,* Harvard Business School Press, MA. The first substantial work on the idea of mass customization.

Stalk, G. and Webber, A.M. (1993) 'Japan's Dark Side of Time', *Harvard Business Review*, Vol. 71, No. 4. Makes the point that although speed can have considerable advantages, it also has its 'dark side'.

Fine, C.H. (1998) *Clock Speed*, Little, Brown and Company, London. Another book extolling the virtue of speed. Readable.

Dale, B.G. (1999) *Managing Quality,* (3rd edn), Blackwell, Oxford. There are lots of books on quality, this one is comprehensive without getting into too much detail. Alternatively wait until we treat quality in Chapters 17 and 20.

63

chapter thirteen

Supply chain planning and control

Source: Tibbett and Britten

key questions

● What are supply chain management and other related activities such as purchasing, physical distribution, logistics and materials management?

● How can the relationship between operations in a supply chain affect the way it works?

● Are different supply chain objectives needed in different circumstances?

● What is the 'natural' pattern of behaviour in supply chains?

Introduction

Historically operations managers have been internally focused. Now, they have to look beyond an internal view if they want to manage their operations effectively. As operations outsource many of their activities and buy more of their services and materials from outside specialists, the way they manage the supply of products and services to their operations becomes increasingly important. Similarly, at the demand side of the operation, distribution and transport activities need to be integrated with other operations processes. This extended flow of products, services and information is what we described in Chapter 6 as the 'immediate' supply network or supply chain. Even beyond the immediate supply chain, there are benefits from managing the flow between customers' customers and suppliers' suppliers. This activity is now commonly termed *supply chain management*. In Chapter 6 we raised the strategic and structural issues of supply network management; this chapter considers the more 'infrastructural' issues of planning and controlling the individual chains in the supply network. Figure 13.1 illustrates the supply–demand linkage treated in this chapter.

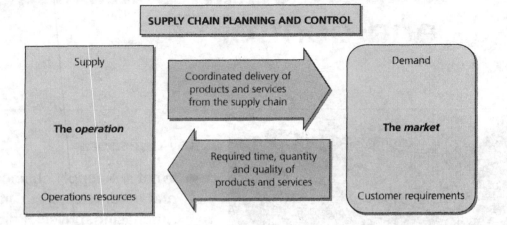

| Figure 13.1 | Supply chain management is concerned with managing the flow of materials and information between the operations which form the strands or 'chains' of a supply network |

Suppliers are vital to Lucent's success[1]   example

Lucent Technologies designs and delivers networks for the worlds' largest communications service providers. It is one of the companies that provide the infrastructure for the internet. It is a high-tech player in a high-tech industry trading on its strengths in optical, data and voice networking technologies, as well as software and services to develop the communications networks of the future. At the heart of its technology research is the world famous Bell Labs whose scientists have won six Nobel Prizes in Physics and generated more than 28,000 patents since it was founded. But even a company with the science and technology resources of Lucent cannot do everything itself. It needs close working relationships with a group of carefully chosen suppliers. 'We operate in a market that moves at light speed,' says the company, 'it is vitally important for Lucent to be able to rely upon our suppliers to provide the materials and services we need, so that we can deliver to our customers the solutions they need, when they need them, and at a price they can afford.'

Lucent's Supply Chain Networks function deals with supply chain issues throughout Lucent. One of its most significant mechanisms for managing its supply base is the Supplier Relationship Programme. 'Being a Lucent supplier is much more than being a reliable source for quality materials and services at a competitive price. We look to our suppliers to work beside us, from product design all the way through to the point of delivery to the customer and even beyond.' The Supplier Relationship Programme's objective of managing the whole supply chain from suppliers through to customers (and customers' customers) includes:

● evaluating suppliers to determine their qualification to be a supplier;

● providing suppliers with a single contact point within Lucent;

● providing a web-based Supply Chain Portal for members of the supply chain network to receive a clear view of demand, availability and the state of delivery;

● organize supplier forums to find ways of cutting costs, reducing time to market, and improving delivery.

Lucent's award winning supply chain practices have brought rewards. Profit margins have increased, in two years inventory was cut from $7bn to $2.4bn, and components costs cut by between 35 and 55 per cent. 'When we looked at our supply chain situation,' says Chief Operating Officer, Bob Holder, 'we recognized how fragmented it had become. We had decentralized manufacturing, inventory and purchasing. We had six different organizations buying the same memory chips. We said, this just doesn't make sense. So we created the supply chains networks.' Communications are also important to the company's supply chain approach. They tell suppliers of their future plans, believing that when potential changes are discussed openly, the company will have more credibility with its suppliers as well as 'more respect and a deeper and richer relationship'. Lucent's supply chain policies also include a commitment to 'supply chain diversity'. This means giving maximum opportunity to suppliers owned by ethnic minorities, women and service-disabled veterans to participate in their supply chain. As well as being ethically positive, Lucent also believe that such businesses are also often more efficient than other suppliers, so the benefits of diversity work both for suppliers and Lucent itself. ■

Even with a history of world-leading technological research behind it, Lucent understand that they still depend on suppliers to provide them with new ideas and knowledge as well as products and services. Not only that, but these suppliers have a responsibility that does not end when they deliver into Lucent's operations. Their knowledge, products and services must also contribute to Lucent's customers and Lucent's customers' customers. This 'long distance' view of supply chain responsibility, stretching beyond immediate suppliers and immediate customers is one of the features of modern supply chain management, as is Lucent's concern with the ethics of its supply chain management. Its supply chain diversity policy is an indication of how many companies are taking ethical responsibility for suppliers and customers beyond its own operational boundaries.

What is supply chain management?

In Chapter 6 we used the term 'supply network' to refer to all the operations that were linked together so as to provide goods and services through to the end customers. In this chapter we deal with the 'ongoing' flow of goods and services through this network along individual channels or strands of that network. In large organizations there can be many hundreds of strands of linked operations passing through the operation. These strands are more commonly referred to as **supply chains**.

Supply chain

Supply chains as pipelines

Supply chain management is the management of the interconnection of organizations that relate to each other through upstream and downstream linkages between the different processes that produce value in the form of products and services to the ultimate consumer. It is a holistic approach to managing across company boundaries. An analogy often used to describe supply chains is that of the 'pipeline'. Just as oil, or other liquids, flow through a pipeline, so physical goods (and services, but the metaphor is more difficult to imagine) flow down a supply chain. Long pipelines will, of course, contain more oil than short ones. So, the time taken for oil to flow all the way through a long pipeline will be longer than if the pipeline was shorter. Stocks of inventory held in the supply chain can be thought of as analogous to oil storage tanks.

Supply chain pipeline

So, on its journey through the **supply chain pipeline** products are processed by different operations in the chain and also stored at different points. Figure 13.2 illustrates this idea. In the figure the first pipeline shows the supply, manufacturing and distribution process times for a supply chain, and also the amount of finished stock kept by the supplier and the manufacturer. As oil flows down the pipeline it takes 10 days to move through the supplier's processes, spends 30 days in stock, takes a further 15 days to move through the manufacturer's processes, spends a further 45 days in the manufacturer's finished stock and finally takes 5 days to be delivered to the customer. This is a total pipeline time of 105 days. The second pipeline has been improved, both by shortening processing times and reducing the amount of inventory held. Now, a customer is receiving oil that started on its journey only 45 days ago. So, for example, if the type of oil required at the end of the pipeline changes, the longer pipelines will take 105 days to respond to this change in demand, the shorter pipeline 43 days. In fact, much of the time goods spend being processed is spent in inventories. So, reducing inventory is an important part of reducing supply chain pipeline time. This process of shortening pipeline time is called supply chain **time compression** and we deal with it further towards the end of this chapter.

Time compression

445

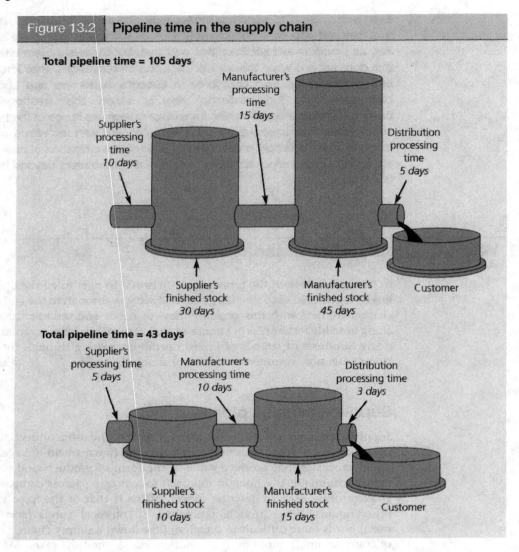

Figure 13.2 Pipeline time in the supply chain

Supply chain management objectives

It is becoming recognized that there are substantial benefits to be gained from managing a whole chain of operations so that they satisfy end customers. These benefits centre on the three key objectives of supply chain management: satisfying end customers, doing so efficiently, and responding to change in an agile manner.

A focus on satisfying end customers

Because supply chain management includes all stages in the total flow of materials and information, it must eventually include consideration of the final customer. The final customer has the only 'real' currency in the supply chain. When a customer decides to make a purchase, he or she triggers action along the whole chain. All the businesses in the supply chain pass on portions of that end-customer's money to each other, each retaining a margin for the value it has added. However, although all the operations in the chain have the immediate objective of satisfying their own immediate customer, the purpose of supply chain management is to make sure that they have a full appreciation of how, together, they can satisfy the end customer. The idea of **efficient consumer response** (ECR) has been developed to stress the importance of end customers. Although definitions of ECR vary, many stress the following interrelated factors.

Efficient consumer response

446

- Understanding customer behaviour and markets generally is vital, often through the use of information technology which can capture demand data at the point-of-sale or point-of-use. This is often referred to as 'hearing the voice of the market and responding directly to it'.
- All parts of the supply chain must be integrated to share the end customer focus. ECR is one of the many supply chain concepts that stresses the importance of achieving value for the customer by persuading all operations in the chain to work together to overcome supply problems.
- Information technology is central to sharing information along the supply chain and thereby avoid misperceptions and delays between operations. We shall return to this idea of the importance of information in supply chains later in the chapter.

critical commentary

This emphasis on understanding the end customer in a supply chain has led some authorities to object to the very term 'supply chain'. Rather, they say, they should be referred to as 'demand chains'. Their argument is based on the idea that the concept of 'supply' implies a 'push' mentality. (The difference between push and pull planning and control was discussed in Chapter 10.) Any emphasis on pushing goods through a supply chain should be avoided. It implies that customers should consume what suppliers see fit to produce. On the other hand, referring to 'demand chains' puts proper emphasis on the importance of seeing customers as pulling demand through the chain. Nevertheless, 'supply chain' is still the most commonly used term, and while not disagreeing with the importance of end customers, we continue to use it in this book.

A focus on managing the chain efficiently

Taking an holistic approach to managing an entire supply chain opens up many opportunities for analysis and improvement. For example, in a supply chain for products with low profit margins, preventing too much inventory accumulation may be critical. In these circumstances, it is important to make sure that products move down the chain quickly rather than building up as inventory. Analysing the chain as a whole to find out where most of the time delays occur allows the supply chain manager to focus attention on those 'bottleneck' businesses in order to shorten throughput time. Often, analysing the whole supply chain can increase efficiency by allowing inventory only when it is needed, identifying bottlenecks, balancing capacity and generally coordinating the smooth flow of materials. The idea of identifying waste along the whole supply chain, especially in the form unnecessary inventory, is the basis of the 'lean supply chain' concept. Again, definitions of lean supply chain approaches differ, but often include the following elements.

- An emphasis on pull planning and control to ensure that supply is initiated only when required.
- Transparency in terms of costs, quality, delivery schedules, etc. In effect this means that suppliers agree to provide customers with full information on their own operations that would normally be confidential.
- Carefully defined supply level agreements between customers and suppliers that dictate exactly what each is expected to do in terms of their relationship. We deal with supply level agreements in more detail in Chapter 17.

447

- Continuous improvement of supplier performance and the elimination of waste which allows suppliers to cut the cost of their products or services to the customer on an ongoing basis. This is sometimes formally written into the supply contract ('. . . the supplier shall reduce its prices by 5 per cent, in real terms, every year . . . ').

A focus on supply chain flexibility

Agility

All business environments contain some degree of uncertainty. Many industries, such as fashion garments or computer components, can be extremely volatile. Therefore, supply chains need to be sufficiently flexible to cope with this uncertainty and the disruption that often stems from it. In a supply chain setting, the term used to describe this type of responsive flexibility is **agility**. It is common for companies to announce that they strive for agile supply chains. The concept of agility incorporates an emphasis on market focus and leanness (where it does not interfere with flexibility) as well as fast movement of goods and services through the supply chain and shared information along the chain. What the concept of agility brings is the increased emphasis on exploring creative ways of adapting to market circumstances. *'Change and disruption is always going to be part of doing business,'* say the proponents of agility, *'accept it and move towards ways of coping with it.'* The discussion in many companies is centred around the extent to which moving towards lean supply chains is in conflict with moving towards agile supply chains. Some companies have found that, in their efforts to cut costs and become 'lean' by drastically reducing inventories and developing specialized but fast processes, they have become too rigid. This rigidity only becomes obvious when market circumstances change, for example, when a totally new product is launched on the market by a competitor.

The activities of supply chain management

Some of the terms used in supply chain management are not universally applied. Furthermore, some of the concepts behind the terminology overlap in the sense that they refer to common parts of the total supply network. This is why it is useful first of all to distinguish between the different terms we shall use in this chapter. These are illustrated in Figure 13.3.

From the perspective of a single operation in the chain (known as the focal operation), supply chain management can be seen as managing the operations that form its *supply side* and those that form its *demand side*:

- On the supply side, *purchasing and supply management* is a well-accepted term for the function that deals with the operation's interface with its supply markets.
- On the demand side, *physical distribution management* is again a well-accepted term for managing the activity of supplying immediate customers.
- *Logistics* is an extension of physical distribution management and usually refers to the management of materials and information flow from a business, down through a distribution channel. Often the end of the distribution channel is a retail store. However, with the increase of direct delivery to consumers because of such innovations and internet-based retailing, the logistics chain could extend through to the consumer, bypassing the conventional retailer. The term *third-party logistics* is sometimes used to indicate that the management of the logistics chain is outsourced to a specialist logistics company.
- *Materials management* is a more limited term than supply chain management and refers to the management of the flow of materials and information through the immediate supply chain, including purchasing, inventory management, stores management, operations planning and control and physical distribution management.[2]

448

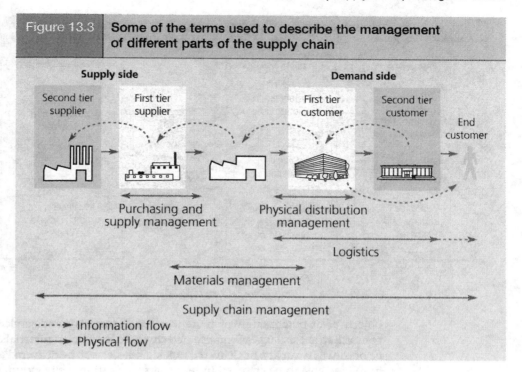

Figure 13.3 Some of the terms used to describe the management of different parts of the supply chain

Purchasing and supply management

Purchasing

At the supply end of the business, the **purchasing** function forms contracts with suppliers to buy in materials and services. Some of these materials and services are used directly in the production of the goods and services. Other materials and services are used to help run the business, for example, staff catering services or oil for machinery.

Purchasing activities

Purchasing managers provide a vital link between the operation itself and its suppliers. To be effective, they must understand the requirements of all the processes within the operation and also the capabilities of the suppliers (sometimes thousands in numbers) who could potentially provide products and services for the operation. Figure 13.4 shows a simplified sequence of events in the management of a typical supplier–operation interaction which the purchasing function must facilitate. When the operation requests products or services, the Purchasing Department uses its knowledge of suppliers and their services to identify potential suppliers and might also be able to suggest alternative materials or services for consideration. Formal requests are sent to potential suppliers so that they can prepare quotations for the business. These requests might be sent to several suppliers or a smaller group, who may be 'preferred' suppliers. The purchasing function then prepares a purchase order. This is important because it often forms the legal basis of the contractual relationship between the operation and its supplier. Again, the purchasing function needs to coordinate with the operation over the technical details of the purchase order. When the supplier receives the purchase order, it produces and delivers the products or services, usually directly to the operation, who should inform the Purchasing Department of the arrival of the products or services and their condition on delivery.

Traditional objectives of the purchasing function

Most operations buy in a wide variety of materials and services, and typically the volume and value of these purchases are increasing as organizations concentrate on their 'core tasks'. Despite the variety of purchases that a firm makes, there are some underlying

449

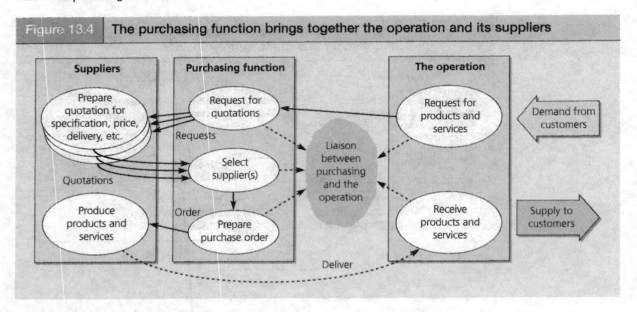

Figure 13.4 The purchasing function brings together the operation and its suppliers

objectives of purchasing which are true for all materials and services bought, and they conform to the usual performance objectives. So, purchased materials and services should be of the right quality, be delivered quickly if necessary, be delivered at the right time and in full, be able to be changed in terms of specification, delivery time or quantity (retain flexibility), and be at the right price. In addition, the activity of purchasing itself should itself be *efficient.*

Purchasing at the right quality

Traditionally, suppliers were not trusted to provide goods and services of the right quality. They were inspected to ensure that they conformed to the required specification. More recently, suppliers are being encouraged to ensure that they take responsibility themselves to provide a 'right-first-time' level of quality, and sometimes formally to certify that quality levels have been met. This self-certification is based on a level of trust and confidence which has come about partly because operations have invested time, money and effort into helping their suppliers improve quality. **Supplier quality assurance** (SQA) programmes monitor and improve levels of supplier quality, partly by assessing supplier capability in terms of their equipment, systems, procedures and training. Quality-conscious purchasing organizations such as aircraft manufacturers have always invested substantial effort in ensuring that suppliers are capable of meeting the right quality. Sometimes suppliers can self-certify their capability by having their systems and processes certified as conforming to internationally recognized standards such as ISO 9000 (discussed in Chapter 20).

Supplier quality assurance

Purchasing for fast delivery

Where competition is based on fast response or where demand is uncertain, a major purchasing objective will be to find suppliers who can themselves respond quickly. For example, clothing retailers will have some types of garment for which demand is relatively predictable. Other garments, however, will be more fashion-oriented. For these fashion products, demand will be relatively unpredictable. In choosing suppliers, therefore, it is important that they are able to supply quickly if demand is higher than expected. Speed of response is less important with the less fashionable items. Some forms of supply are difficult to organize on a quick response basis. For example, international purchasing that involves 'deep sea' transportation may mean that purchases must be made two months earlier than if they were bought locally. This allows the time

450

for the purchases to be transported to the docks, loaded, shipped over, unloaded and transported to their destination.

Purchasing for delivery at the right time and in full

Late or incomplete deliveries can cause shortage and disruption. If supply is uncertain, an operation may have to keep inventories in an effort to try and compensate for any supply failure. Remember how, in Chapter 12, safety stocks were needed when supply and/or demand were uncertain. Even early arrivals can cause problems. Bought-in services, such as cleaning services, which arrive early may not be able to provide the service if the operation is not ready for it. Similarly, materials arriving too early may not be able to be stored efficiently. Some operations use an 'expediting' function, whose responsibility is to track or 'progress' orders with suppliers. Expediters are said to 'chase' the order, an activity that adds no value to the transaction and is now seen as a failure to improve the root cause of lateness.

Purchasing to retain flexibility

Supply flexibility, whether in terms of changing specification, changing delivery time or changing quantity, will be particularly valuable to those operations which themselves are operating in fast-changing or uncertain markets. Sometimes flexible suppliers are chosen to ensure dependable supply. So, if an operation uses three suppliers to provide it with a particular product or service, it might choose two of these because they are good at cost and quality. The third supplier may not be able to match the other two in cost but, if it has high levels of flexibility, it could be used to compensate for any supply failure from the other two. Sometimes it is longer term flexibility that is required from a supplier. A supplier may be chosen, not particularly for its current performance, but because of its *potential* to develop capabilities which may be useful in the future. High technology companies (such as Lucent in the opening box of this chapter) may choose suppliers who have the capabilities to help them to develop the 'generation of products and services after next'.

Purchasing at the right price

The most obvious benefit of purchasing at the right price is that it can provide an operation with a cost advantage. Historically, this objective of purchasing has been emphasized in purchasing theory and practice. The performance of purchasing staff was even judged using cost savings as the main measure. The reason for this emphasis on 'the right cost' is understandable because purchasing can have a very significant impact on any operation's costs, and therefore profits. To illustrate the impact that price-conscious purchasing can have on profits, consider a simple manufacturing operation with the following financial details:

Total sales	10,000,000
Purchased services and materials	£7,000,000
Salaries	£2,000,000
Overheads	£500,000

Therefore, profit = £500,000. Profits could be doubled to £1 million by any of the following:

- increase sales revenue by up to 100 per cent
- decrease salaries by 25 per cent
- decrease overheads by 100 per cent
- decrease purchase costs by 7.1 per cent.

A doubling of sales revenue does sometimes occur in very fast-growing markets, but this would be regarded by most sales and marketing managers as an exceedingly ambitious target. Decreasing the salaries bill by a quarter is likely to require substantial

451

Ford Motors' team value management[3]   example

Purchasing managers are a vital link between an operation and its suppliers. But they work best when teamed up with mainstream operations managers who know what the operation really needs, especially if, between them, they take a role that challenges previous assumptions. That is the basis behind Ford Motor Company's 'team value management' (TVM) approach. Reputedly, it all started when Ford's Head of Global Purchasing, David Thursfield, discovered that a roof rack designed for one of Ford's smaller cars was made of plastic-coated aluminium and capable of bearing 100 kgs load. This prompted the questions, *'Why is this rack covered in plastic? Why would anyone want to put 100 kgs on the roof of a car that small?'* He found that no one had ever questioned the original specification. When Ford switched to using steel roof racks capable of bearing a smaller weight, they halved the cost. *'It is important,'* he says, *'to check whether the company is getting the best price for parts and raw material that provide the appropriate level of performance without being too*

expensive.' The savings in a large company such as Ford can be huge. Often in multi-nationals, each part of the business makes sourcing and design decisions independently and do not exploit opportunities for cross-usage of components. The TVM approach is designed to bring together engineering and purchasing staff and identify where cost can be taken out of purchased parts and where there is opportunity for parts commonality (see Chapter 5) between different models. When a company's global purchasing budget is $75bn like Ford's, the potential for cost savings is significant. ■

Questions

1 How do you think Ford's suppliers will react to the TVM initiative?

2 As well as obvious savings in the cost of bought-in parts, do you think the TVM initiative could result in savings for Ford's sales dealerships and service centres?

alternative investment – for example, in automation – or reflects a dramatic reduction in medium- to long-term sales. Similarly, a reduction in overheads by 100 per cent is unlikely to be possible over the short to medium term without compromising the business. However, reducing purchase costs by 7.1 per cent, although a challenging objective, is usually far more of a realistic option than the other actions.

The reason purchase price savings can have such a dramatic impact on total profitability is that purchase costs are such a large proportion of total costs (especially in some industries, see the box 'Ford Motors' team value management'). The higher purchase costs are as a proportion of total costs, the more profitability can be improved in this way. Figure 13.5 illustrates this.

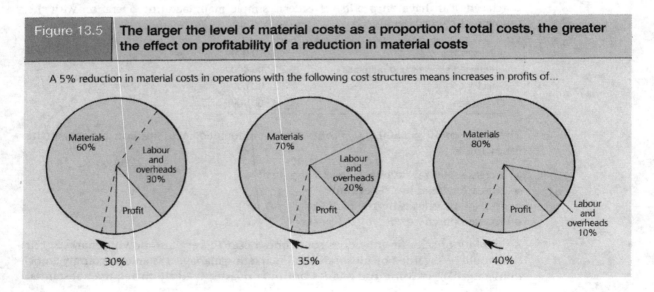

Figure 13.5 | The larger the level of material costs as a proportion of total costs, the greater the effect on profitability of a reduction in material costs

A 5% reduction in material costs in operations with the following cost structures means increases in profits of...

Materials 60% / Labour and overheads 30% / Profit — 30%

Materials 70% / Labour and overheads 20% / Profit — 35%

Materials 80% / Labour and overheads 10% / Profit — 40%

Table 13.1	Advantages and disadvantages of single- and multi-sourcing	
	Single-sourcing	*Multi-sourcing*
Advantages	• Potentially better quality because more SQA possibilities	• Purchaser can drive price down by competitive tendering
	• Strong relationships which are more durable	• Can switch sources in case of supply failure
	• Greater dependency encourages more commitment and effort	• Wide sources of knowledge and expertise to tap
	• Better communication	
	• Easier to cooperate on new product/service development	
	• More scale economies	
	• Higher confidentiality	
Disadvantages	• More vulnerable to disruption if a failure to supply occurs	• Difficult to encourage commitment by supplier
	• Individual supplier more affected by volume fluctuations	• Less easy to develop effective SQA
	• Supplier might exert upward pressure on prices if no alternative supplier is available	• More effort needed to communicate
		• Suppliers less likely to invest in new processes
		• More difficult to obtain scale economies

Single- and multi-sourcing

Single-sourcing
Multi-sourcing

An important decision facing most purchasing managers is whether to source each individual product or service from one or more than one supplier, known, respectively, as **single-sourcing** and **multi-sourcing**. Some of the advantages and disadvantages of single- and multi-sourcing are shown in Table 13.1.

It may seem as though companies who multi-source do so exclusively for their own short-term benefit. However, this is not always the case: multi-sourcing can have an altruistic motive, or at least one which brings benefits to both supplier and purchaser in the long term. For example, Robert Bosch GmbH, the German automotive components manufacturer and distributor, at one time required that subcontractors do no more than 20 per cent of their total business with them.[4] This was to prevent suppliers becoming too dependent on them. The purchasing organization could then change volumes up and down without pushing the supplier into bankruptcy. However, despite these perceived advantages, there has been a trend for purchasing functions to reduce their supplier base in terms of numbers of companies supplying any one part or service. For example, Rank Xerox, the copier and document company, reduced its supply base from 5000 suppliers to a little more than 300 over a six-year period.[5]

Purchasing, the internet and e-commerce

For some years, electronic means have been used by businesses to confirm purchased orders and ensure payment to suppliers. The rapid development of the internet, however, opened up the potential for far more fundamental changes in purchasing behaviour. Partly this was as the result of supplier information made available through the internet. Previously, a purchaser of industrial components may have been predisposed to return to

453

suppliers who had been used before. There was an inertia in the purchasing process because of the costs of seeking out new suppliers. By making it easier to search for alternative suppliers, the internet changes the economics of the search process and offers the potential for wider searches. It also changed the economics of scale in purchasing. Purchasers requiring relatively low volumes find it easier to group together in order to create orders of sufficient size to warrant lower prices.

In fact, the influence of the internet (or more accurately, the world wide web) on purchasing behaviour is not confined to *e-commerce*. Usually e-commerce is taken to mean the trade that actually takes place over the internet. This is usually assumed to be a buyer visiting the seller's website, placing an order for parts and making a payment (also through the site). But the web is also an important source of purchasing information. For every 1 per cent of business transacted directly via the internet, there may be 5 or 6 per cent of business which, at some point, involved the net, probably with potential buyers using it to compare prices or obtain technical information.

E-procurement

One increasingly common use of internet technology in purchasing (or **e-procurement** as it is sometimes known) is for large companies, or groups of companies, to link their e-commerce systems into a common 'exchange'. In their more sophisticated form, such an exchange may be linked into the purchasing companies' own information systems (*see* the explanation of ERP in Chapter 14). Many of the large automotive, engineering and petrochemical companies, for example, have adopted such an approach. Typical of these companies' motives are those put forward by Shell Services International, part of the petrochemical giant:[6]

> *Procurement is an obvious first step in e-commerce. First, buying through the web is so slick and cheap compared to doing it almost any other way. Second, it allows you to aggregate, spend and ask: Why am I spending this money, or shouldn't I be getting a bigger discount? Third, it encourages new services like credit, insurance and accreditation to be built around it.*

critical commentary

Not everyone is happy with e-procurement. Some see it as preventing the development of closer partnership-type relationships which, in the long run, could bring far greater returns. Some Japanese car makers, in particular, are wary of too much involvement in e-procurement. For example, while Toyota Motor, the world's third largest car marker, did join up with Ford, General Motors and Daimler Chrysler in a web-based trade exchange, it limits its purchases to trading in such items as bolts, nuts and basic office supplies. The main reason for its reluctance is that traditionally it has gained a competitive edge by building long-term relationships with its suppliers. This means establishing trust, getting an understanding of a trading partner's aspirations and not squeezing every last cent out of them in the short term (see the discussion on partnership relationships later). Taking this approach, e-procurement which is used primarily to drive down cost could do more harm than good.[6]

Keiretsu networks

Keiretsu

A **keiretsu** is a Japanese term which is used to describe a coalition of companies who form a 'supplier network' to a (usually large) manufacturer. Often the large manufacturer will give financial support to these suppliers through loans, or even by taking equity stakes in the companies. Keiretsu members are expected to commit to providing excellent service, technical expertise and quality improvements to the manufacturer. In return, the manufacturer assures the coalition partners of long-term continuity of

454

demand. In recent years, keiretsu have been criticized for being too cosy in their relationships. It is argued that without more open competition the coalition members become less innovative.

Global sourcing

Global sourcing

One of the major supply chain developments of recent years has been the expansion in the proportion of products and (occasionally) services which businesses are willing to source from outside their home country, this is called **global sourcing**. Traditionally, even companies who exported their goods and services all over the world (that is, they were international on their demand side) still sourced the majority of their supplies locally (that is, they were not international on their supply side). This has changed – companies are now increasingly willing to look further afield for their supplies. There are a number of reasons for this:

- The formation of trading blocks in different parts of the world has had the effect of lowering tariff barriers, at least within those blocks. For example, the single market developments within the European Union (EU), the North American Free Trade Agreement (NAFTA) and the South American Trade Group (MERCOSUR) have all made it easier to trade internationally within the regions.
- Transportation infrastructures are considerably more sophisticated and cheaper than they once were. Super-efficient port operations in Rotterdam and Singapore, for example, integrated road–rail systems, jointly developed auto route systems, and cheaper air freight have all reduced some of the cost barriers to international trade.
- Perhaps most significantly, far tougher world competition has forced companies to look to reducing their total costs. Given that in many industries bought-in items are the largest single part of operations costs, an obvious strategy is to source from wherever is cheapest. So, for example, much garment manufacture takes place where labour costs are relatively low.

There are of course problems with global sourcing. The risks of increased complexity and increased distance need managing carefully. In particular, the following issues are important:

- Suppliers who are a significant distance away need to transport their products across long distances. The risks of delays and hold-ups can be far greater than when sourcing locally.
- Negotiating with suppliers whose native language is different from one's own makes communication more difficult and can lead to misunderstandings over contract terms.
- It may not always be possible to investigate suppliers at long distance. Companies may inadvertently develop relationships with suppliers whose work practices are very much against its own ethical stance (the use of child labour, unsafe working practices, the use of bribes, etc.).

Physical distribution management

On the demand side of the organization, products and services need to be 'transmitted' or moved to the customer. In the case of manufacturing operations, this involves the physical transportation of the goods from the manufacturing operation to the customer. In the case of high customer contact services, the service is created in the presence of the customer. Here we limit ourselves to manufacturing operations that need physically to distribute their products to customers (and implicitly to those transportation operations, such as trucking companies, whose primary concern is physical distribution). Sometimes the term **logistics**, or simply **distribution**, is used as being analogous to **physical distribution management**. Generally these terms are used to describe physical

Logistics
Distribution
Physical distribution
management

455

Source: Photograph courtesy of RHM Ltd.

Managing regional warehouses and depots is a vital link in physical distribution management

distribution management beyond the immediate customer, through to the final customer in the chain. The box 'TDG serving the whole supply chain' describes a company that provides these types of services as well as broader supply chain management.

Multi-echelon inventory systems

Multi-echelon

In Chapter 12 we identified some inventory systems as **multi-echelon** systems. By this we meant that materials flowing through a system would be stored at different points, including points outside the operation, before reaching the customer. Figure 13.6 illustrates the demand-side part of the multi-echelon system we described in Chapter 12. In this case the garment manufacturer, after manufacturing the products, will store them in its own finished goods warehouse. From there they are transported to regional warehouses whose function is to serve as a distribution point for retail stores. When the retail stores require deliveries of garments, they will request them from their local warehouse who will arrange for the transportation of these garments to the retail store. The function of the warehouse is to provide an intermediate stage in the distribution system so that the manufacturer does not have to deal with every single customer. From the customers' point of view, it also means that they do not have to deal with a whole range of suppliers.

| Figure 13.6 | Multi-echelon inventory system |

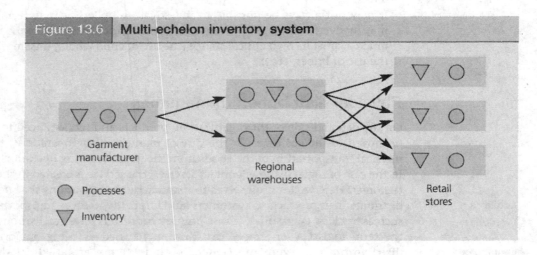

456

TDG serving the whole supply chain[7]   example

TDG are specialists in providing *third party* logistics services to the growing number of manufacturers and retailers who choose not to do their own distribution. Instead they outsource to companies like TDG, who have operations spread across 250 sites that cover the UK, Ireland, France, Spain, Poland and Holland, employ 8000 employees and use 1600 vehicles. They provided European logistics services through their own operations in the Netherlands and Ireland and, with the support of alliance partners, in several other European companies.

'There are a number of different types of company providing distribution services,' says David Garman, Chief Executive Officer of TDG, 'each with different propositions for the market. At the simplest level, there are the "haulage" and "storage" businesses. These companies either move goods around or they store them in warehouses. Clients plan what has to be done and it is done to order. One level up from the haulage or storage operations are the physical distribution companies, who bring haulage and storage together. These companies collect clients' products, put them into storage facilities and deliver them to the end customer as and when required. After that there are the companies who offer contract logistics. As a contract logistics service provider you are likely to be dealing with the more sophisticated clients who are looking for better quality facilities and management and the capability to deal with more complex operations. One level further up is the market for supply chain management services. To do this you have to be able to manage supply chains from end to end, or at least some significant part of the whole chain. Doing this requires a much greater degree of analytical and modelling capability, business process reengineering and consultancy skills.'

TDG, along with other prominent logistics companies, describes itself as a 'lead logistics provider' or LLP. This means that they can provide the consultancy-led, analytical

and strategic services integrated with a sound base of practical experience in running successful 'on-the-road' operations.

'In 1999 TDG was a UK distribution company,' says David Garman, 'now we are a European contract logistics provider with a vision to becoming a full supply chain management company. Providing such services requires sophisticated operations capability, especially in terms of information technology and management dynamism. Because our sites are physically dispersed with our vehicles at any time spread around the motorways of Europe, IT is fundamental to this industry. It gives you visibility of your operation. We need the best operations managers, supported by the best IT.' ■

Questions

1 Why do think that David Garman is moving TDG towards providing more sophisticated services to clients?

2 What are the risks in TDG's strategy?

Warehouses can simplify routes and communications

To understand how warehouses can simplify physical distribution, consider Figure 13.7. Here a manufacturing operation which has three factories is supplying six customers. In the arrangement in Figure 13.7(a), each factory supplies each customer. This means that each factory must have separate lines of communication with all six customers and each customer will need to communicate directly with each of the three factories. Now consider the arrangement in Figure 13.7(b). Two regional warehouses have been imposed between the factories and the customers. The three factories now distribute their products to the two regional warehouses from which their local customers are supplied. Significantly, each factory now has only to deal directly with two sources for its products instead of the previous six. Similarly, each customer now only has to deal with one supplier (its local warehouse) instead of six.

457

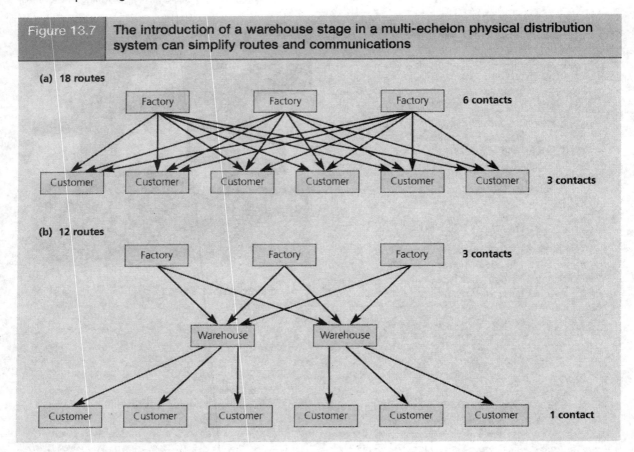

Figure 13.7 The introduction of a warehouse stage in a multi-echelon physical distribution system can simplify routes and communications

Physical distribution management and the internet

The potential offered by internet communications in physical distribution management has had two major effects. The first is to make information available more readily along the distribution chain. This means that the transport companies, warehouses, suppliers and customers who make up the chain can share a knowledge of where goods are in the chain (and sometimes where they are going next). This allows the operations within the chain to coordinate their activities more readily. It also gives the potential for some significant cost savings. For example, an important issue for transportation companies is **back-loading**. When the company is contracted to transport goods from A to B, its vehicles may have to return from B to A empty. Back-loading means finding a potential customer who wants their goods transported from B to A in the right time frame. With the increase in information availability through the internet, the possibility of finding a back-load increases. Clearly, companies which can fill their vehicles on both the outward and return journeys will have significantly lower costs per distance travelled than those whose vehicles are empty for half the total journey.

The second impact of the internet has been in the 'business to consumer' (B2C, *see* the discussion on supply chain relationships later) part of the supply chain. While the last few years have seen an increase in the number of goods bought by consumers online, most goods still have to be physically transported to the customer. Often early e-retailers (or e-tailers) ran into major problems in the **order fulfilment** task of actually supplying their customers. Partly this was because many traditional warehouse and distribution operations were not designed for e-commerce fulfilment. Supplying a 'bricks and mortar' retail operation requires relatively large vehicles to move relatively large

Back-loading

Order fulfilment

458

Source: Photographs courtesy of Corbis and Tibbett and Britten.

Distribution costs are particularly important for some products. For example, the polystyrene foam on the left is mainly composed of air. Transporting air in a truck means that transportation costs are high compared to the value of the product. The bottled water on the right is heavy but again has relatively low value. Again, this means that transportation costs are high compared to the value of the product

quantities of goods on pallets from warehouses to shops. Distributing to customers who have bought goods online requires a large number of relatively small individual orders to be delivered, all of which may be different. Some traditional retailers who had moved part of their business online were faced with the dilemma of learning new physical distribution skills or subcontracting their distribution operations.

Materials management

Materials management

The concept of **materials management** originated from purchasing functions that understood the importance of integrating materials flow and its supporting functions, both throughout the business and out to immediate customers. It includes the functions of purchasing, expediting, inventory management, stores management, production planning and control and physical distribution management. Materials management was originally seen as a means of reducing 'total costs associated with the acquisition and management of materials'.[8] Different stages in the movement of materials through a multi-echelon system are typically buffered by inventory. Where materials management is not in place to integrate these different stages, they are often managed by different people, reporting to different senior managers within the organization. These different functions are managed separately, each with its own targets, each optimizing its own small part of the total materials flow system.

Merchandising

Merchandising

In retail operations, the purchasing task is frequently combined with the sales and physical distribution task into a role termed **merchandising**. A merchandiser typically has responsibility for organizing sales to retail customers, for the layout of the shopfloor, inventory management and purchasing. This is because retail purchase operations have to be so closely linked to daily sales to ensure that the right mix of goods is available for customers to buy at any time. For example, fashion buyers have to understand what will sell and how garments will look when on display in their retail outlets. In food retailing, buyers specify in detail the packaging in terms of the printing process and materials, to ensure the product looks appealing when displayed in their stores. Daily trends of sales in some retail situations (typically food and fashion) can vary enormously. Replenishment of regularly stocked items has to be very quick to avoid empty shelves or rails. Electronic point-of-sale systems help the planning and control of fast-moving consumer goods; as items are registered as sold at the till,

459

a replenishment signal is returned to the distribution centre to deliver replacements. To facilitate this link, many retail operations use bar coding to update the inventory situation and replenish shelves and rails.

Types of relationships in supply chains

From the point of view of individual operations within a supply chain, one of the key issues is how they should manage their relationships with their immediate suppliers and customers. The behaviour of the supply chain as a whole is, after all, made up of the relationships which are formed between individual pairs of operations in the chain. It is important, therefore, to have some framework which helps us to understand the different ways in which supply chain relationships can be developed.

Business or consumer relationships?

The growth in e-commerce has established broad categorization of supply chain relationships. This happened because internet companies have tended to focus on one of four market sectors defined by who is supplying who. Figure 13.8 illustrates this categorization.

The distinction used in Figure 13.8 is whether the relationship is with the final link in the supply chain, involving the ultimate consumer, or whether it concerns one of the prior links in the supply chain, involving two commercial businesses. So, **business to business** (B2B) relationships are by far the most common in a supply chain context and include some of the e-procurement exchange networks discussed earlier. **Business to consumer** (B2C) relationships include both 'bricks and mortar' retailers and online retailers. Somewhat newer are the final two categories. **Consumer to business** (C2B) relationships involve consumers posting their needs on the web and stating the price they are willing to pay. Companies then decide whether to offer at that price. **Customer to customer** (C2C) relationships include the online exchange and auction services offered by some companies. In this chapter we deal almost exclusively with B2B relationships.

Business to business

Business to consumer

Consumer to business

Customer to customer

Figure 13.8	The business/consumer relationship matrix[9]

	Business	Consumer
Business	**B2B** *Relationship:* • Most common, all but the last link in the supply chain *E-commerce examples:* • EDI networks • Tesco information exchange	**B2C** *Relationship:* • Retail operations • Catalogue operations, etc. *E-commerce examples:* • Internet retailers • Amazon.com, etc.
Consumer	**C2B** *Relationship:* • Consumer 'offer', business responds *E-commerce examples:* • Some airline ticket operators • Priceline.com, etc.	**C2C** *Relationship:* • Trading, 'swap' and auction transactions *E-commerce examples:* • Specialist 'collector' sites • Ebay.com, etc.

460

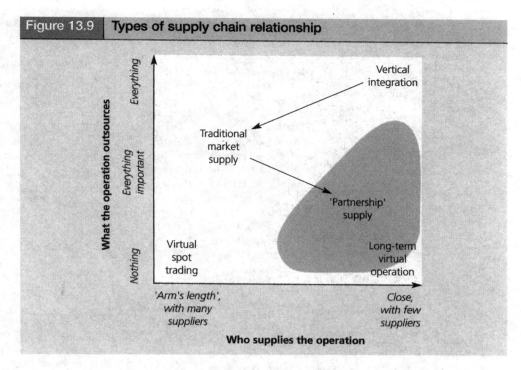

Figure 13.9 | Types of supply chain relationship

Types of business to business relationship

A convenient way of categorizing supply chain relationships is to examine the extent and nature of what a company chooses to buy in from suppliers. Two dimensions are particularly important – *what* the company chooses to outsource, and *who* it chooses to supply it.

In terms of what is outsourced, key questions are:

● How many activities are outsourced (from doing everything in-house at one extreme, to outsourcing everything at the other extreme)?
● How important are the activities outsourced (from outsourcing only trivial activities at one extreme, to outsourcing even core activities at the other extreme)?

In terms of who is chosen to supply products and services, again two questions are important:

● How many suppliers will be used by the operation (from using many suppliers to perform the same set of activities at one extreme, through to only one supplier for each activity at the other extreme)?
● How close are the relationships (from 'arm's length' relationships at one extreme, through to close and intimate relationships at the other extreme)?

Figure 13.9 illustrates this way of characterizing relationships. It also identifies some of the more common types of relationship and shows some of the trends in how supply chain relationships have moved.[10]

Traditional market supply relationships

The very opposite of performing an operation in-house is to purchase goods and services from outside in a 'pure' market fashion, often seeking the 'best' supplier every time it is necessary to purchase. Each transaction effectively becomes a separate decision. The relationship between buyer and seller, therefore, can be very short term. Once the goods or services are delivered and payment is made, there may be no further trading between

461

KLM Catering Services example

KLM Catering Services is the largest provider of aircraft catering and supply at Schiphol Airport near Amsterdam. Every day the company, which employs 1200 people, prepares around 30,000 meals and 'services' 200 flights for KLM and about 35 for other operators. It is now far more than just a food preparation operation; most of its activities involve organizing all onboard services, equipment, food and drinks, newspapers, towels, earphones, and so on.

KLM Catering Services places considerable emphasis on working in unison with cleaning staff, baggage handlers and maintenance crews to ensure that the aircraft are prepared quickly for departure (fast set-ups). Normally, no more than 40 minutes are allowed for all these activities, so complete preparation and a well-ordered sequence of working are essential. These requirements for speed and total dependability would be difficult enough to achieve in a stable environment, but there is a wide range of uncertainties to be managed. Although KLM Catering Services is advised of the likely numbers of passengers for each flight (forecasts are given 11 days, 4 days and 24 hours in advance), the actual minimum number of passengers for each class is only fixed 6 hours before take-off (although numbers can still be increased after this, due to late sales). The agreed menus are normally fixed for six-month periods, but the actual requirements for each flight depend on the destination, the type of aircraft and the mix of passengers by ticket class. Finally, flight arrivals are sometimes delayed, putting pressure on everyone to reduce the turnaround time, and upsetting work schedules.

An additional problem is that, although KLM uses standardized items (such as food trolleys, cutlery, trays and disposables), other airlines have completely different requirements. The inventory of all this equipment is moved around with the planes. Some gets damaged or lost, and it can easily accumulate at a remote airport. If an aircraft arrives without a full inventory of equipment and other items, the company is obliged to fill the gaps from its local inventory, which amounts to over 15,000 different items. ∎

Questions

1 Why would an airline use KLM Catering Services rather than organize its own onboard services?

2 What are the main operations objectives that KLM Catering Services must achieve in order to satisfy its customers?

3 Why is it important for airlines to reduce turnaround time when an aircraft lands?

Source: Virgin Atlantic Airways

Specialized companies have developed that prepare food in specialized factories, often for several airlines

462

the parties. The *advantages* of traditional market supplier relationships are usually seen as follows:

- They maintain competition between alternative suppliers. This promotes a constant drive between suppliers to provide best value.
- A supplier specializing in a small number of products or services (or perhaps just one), but supplying them to many customers, can gain natural economies of scale. This enables the supplier to offer the products and services at a lower price than would be obtained if customers performed the activities themselves on a smaller scale.
- There is inherent flexibility in outsourced supplies. If demand changes, customers can simply change the number and type of suppliers. This is a far faster and simpler alternative to having to redirect their internal activities.
- Innovations can be exploited no matter where they originate. Specialist suppliers are more likely to come up with innovative products and services which can be bought in faster and cheaper than would be the case if the company were itself trying to innovate.
- They help operations to concentrate on their core activities. One business cannot be good at everything. It is sensible therefore to concentrate on the important activities and outsource the rest.

There are, however, *disadvantages* in buying in a totally 'free market' manner:

- There may be supply uncertainties. Once an order has been placed, it is difficult to maintain control over how that order is fulfilled.
- Choosing who to buy from takes time and effort. Gathering sufficient information and making decisions continually are, in themselves, activities which need to be resourced.
- There are strategic risks in subcontracting activities to other businesses. An over-reliance on outsourcing can 'hollow out' the company, leaving it with no internal capabilities which it can exploit in its markets.

Short-term relationships may be used on a trial basis when new companies are being considered as more regular suppliers. Also, many purchases which are made by operations are one-off or very irregular. For example, the replacement of all the windows in a company's office block would typically involve this type of competitive-tendering market relationship, whereas the same firm might form a longer-term relationship with its supplier of cleaning services. In some public sector operations, purchasing is still based on short-term contracts. This is mainly because of the need to prove that public money is being spent as judiciously as possible. However, this short-term, price-oriented type of relationship can have a downside in terms of ongoing support and reliability. This may mean that a short-term 'least cost' purchase decision will lead to long-term high cost.

Virtual operations

Virtual operation

An extreme form of outsourcing operational activities is that of the **virtual operation**. Virtual operations do relatively little themselves, but rely on a network of suppliers who can provide products and services on demand. Often the network of suppliers used by virtual companies changes over time, sometimes dramatically. A network may be formed for only one project and then disbanded once that project ends. For example, some software and internet companies are virtual in the sense that they buy in all the services needed for a particular development. This may include not only the specific software development skills but also such things as project management, testing, applications prototyping, marketing, physical production, and so on. Much of the Hollywood film industry also operates in this way. A production company may buy and develop an idea for a movie, but it is created, edited and distributed by a loose network of agents, actors, technicians, studios and distribution companies.

463

The advantages of virtual operations are centred largely around the flexibility and speed with which they can operate and the fact that the risks of investing in production facilities are obviously far lower than in a conventional operation. The disadvantages come from the 'hollowing out' effect that we mentioned previously. Without any solid base of resources, a company may find it difficult to hold onto and develop a unique core of technical expertise. The resources used by virtual companies will almost certainly be available to competitors. In effect, the core competence of a virtual operation can only lie in the way it is able to manage its supply network.

'Partnership' supply relationships

Partnership

Partnership relationships in supply chains are sometimes seen as a compromise between vertical integration on the one hand (owning the resources which supply you) and pure market relationships on the other (having only a transactional relationship with those who supply you). Although to some extent this is true, partnership relationships are not only a simple mixture of vertical integration and market trading, although they do attempt to achieve some of the closeness and coordination efficiencies of vertical integration, while at the same time attempting to achieve a relationship that has a constant incentive to improve. Partnership relationships are defined as:[11]

> ... *relatively enduring inter-firm cooperative agreements, involving flows and linkages that use resources and/or governance structures from autonomous organizations, for the joint accomplishment of individual goals linked to the corporate mission of each sponsoring firm.*

What this means is that suppliers and customers are expected to cooperate, even to the extent of sharing skills and resources, to achieve joint benefits beyond those they could have achieved by acting alone. At the heart of the concept of partnership lies the issue of the *closeness* of the relationship. Partnerships are close relationships, the degree of which is influenced by a number of factors, as follows:

- *Sharing success.* An attitude of shared success means that both partners work together in order to increase the total amount of joint benefit they receive, rather than manoeuvring to maximize their own individual contribution.
- *Long-term expectations.* Partnership relationships imply relatively long-term commitments, but not necessarily permanent ones.
- *Multiple points of contact.* Communication between partners is not only through formal channels, but may take place between many individuals in both organizations.
- *Joint learning.* Partners in a relationship are committed to learn from each other's experience and perceptions of the other operations in the chain.
- *Few relationships.* Although partnership relationships do not necessarily imply single sourcing by customers, they do imply a commitment on the part of both parties to limit the number of customers or suppliers with whom they do business. It is difficult to maintain close relationships with many different trading partners.
- *Joint coordination of activities.* Because there are fewer relationships, it becomes possible jointly to coordinate activities such as the flow of materials or service, payment, and so on.
- *Information transparency.* An open and efficient information exchange is seen as a key element in partnerships because it helps to build confidence between the partners.
- *Joint problem solving.* Although partnerships do not always run smoothly, jointly approaching problems can increase closeness over time.
- *Trust.* This is probably the key element in partnership relationships. In this context, trust means the willingness of one party to relate to the other on the understanding that the relationship will be beneficial to both, even though that cannot be guaranteed. Trust is widely held to be both the key issue in successful partnerships, but also, by far, the most difficult element to develop and maintain.

464

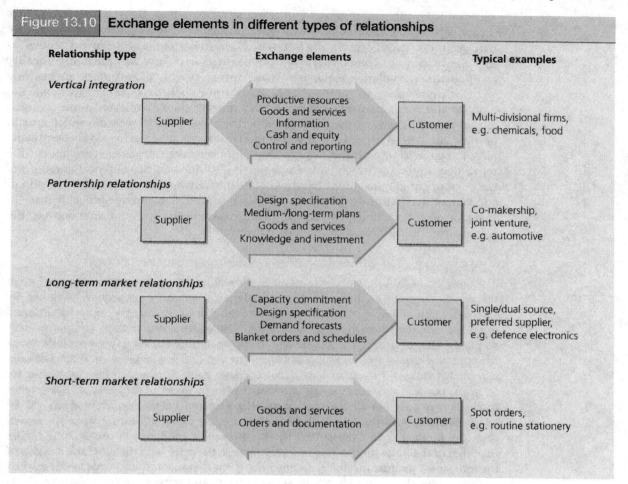

Figure 13.10 Exchange elements in different types of relationships

Relationship type	Exchange elements	Typical examples
Vertical integration	Productive resources / Goods and services / Information / Cash and equity / Control and reporting	Multi-divisional firms, e.g. chemicals, food
Partnership relationships	Design specification / Medium-/long-term plans / Goods and services / Knowledge and investment	Co-makership, joint venture, e.g. automotive
Long-term market relationships	Capacity commitment / Design specification / Demand forecasts / Blanket orders and schedules	Single/dual source, preferred supplier, e.g. defence electronics
Short-term market relationships	Goods and services / Orders and documentation	Spot orders, e.g. routine stationery

Relationships as 'exchange'

The relationships between the links of the supply chain are sometimes described in terms of the flows between the operations involved. These flows may be of transformed resources, such as materials, or of transforming resources, such as people or equipment. The term used to include all the different types of flow is *exchange*.

The different types of relationship and the main elements of exchange in the relationship are summarized in Figure 13.10.

Supply chain behaviour

In this section we deal with supply chain behaviour by examining the dynamic performance of the chain as a whole. First, we shall examine how operations can manage supply chains in different ways depending on the requirements of their customers. Second, we shall look at how the natural dynamics of supply chain behaviour affect different parts of the chain. Finally we shall look at how companies try to improve supply chain performance.

Different markets mean different supply chains

At some point, many supply chains split into two or more 'branches' that go on to serve different markets. For example, many manufacturers of automotive components serve

465

two distinctly different groups of end customers. One group (the vehicle market) buys cars which contain their components; the other group (the spares market) buys spare parts for the repair of cars already in service. The latter group of customers is known as the 'aftermarket' for components. Vehicle manufacturers want low price, high quality components. The volumes required by these customers are high and efforts are made by vehicle manufacturers to stabilize planning and control schedules so as to give some stability to the component manufacturers. By contrast, the 'aftermarket' wants a much greater variety of parts, as they have to support vehicles up to 20 years old which are still on the road. Delivery speed is also very important. Repair and service of vehicles usually have to be carried out on the same day and, in most cases, the garage carrying out the repair does not know which parts are required until the vehicle is up on the ramp. So, the component manufacturers have two quite different supply chains that value different competitive factors. However, the components for both chains are probably made in the same operation. Unless this is carefully managed, or the operation split between the two chains, this can lead to conflicting objectives.[12]

'Responsive' and 'efficient' supply chain management

The question raised by the above example is: 'How should supply chains be managed when operations compete in different ways in different markets?' One answer, proposed by Professor Marshall Fisher of Wharton Business School, is to organize the supply chains serving those individual markets in different ways.[13] He points out that many companies have seemingly similar products which, in fact, compete in different ways. Shoe manufacturers may produce classics which change little over the years, as well as fashions which last only one or two seasons. Chocolate manufacturers have stable lines which have been sold for 50 years, but also product 'specials' associated with an event or film release. These latter products may only sell for a matter of months. Demand for the former products will be relatively stable and predictable, but demand for the latter will be far more uncertain. Also, the profit margin commanded by the innovative product will probably be higher than that of the more functional product. However, the price (and therefore the margin) of the innovative product may drop rapidly once it has become unfashionable in the market.

Efficient supply chains

Responsive supply chains

The supply chain policies which are seen to be appropriate for functional products and innovative products are termed by Fisher **efficient supply chain** policies and **responsive supply chain** policies, respectively. Efficient supply chain policies include keeping inventories low, especially in the downstream parts of the network, so as to

Even heavy products such as these sports cars, may be transported by air freight if customers demand fast delivery.

466

| Figure 13.11 | Matching the operations resources in the supply chain with market requirements |

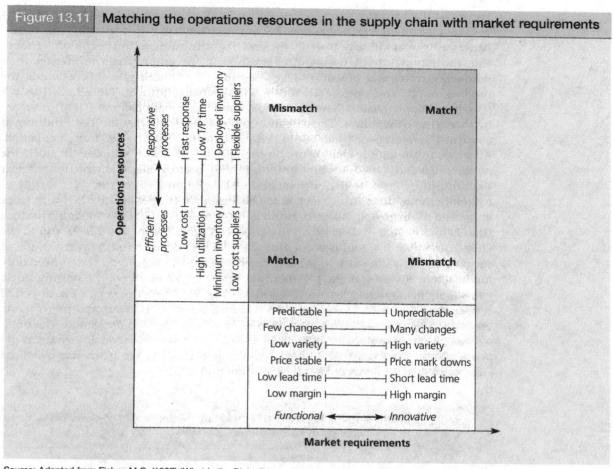

Source: Adapted from Fisher, M.C. (1997) 'What is the Right Supply Chain for Your Product?' *Harvard Business Review*, March–April, pp. 105–116.

maintain fast throughput and reduce the amount of working capital tied up in the inventory. What inventory there is in the network is concentrated mainly in the manufacturing operation, where it can keep utilization high and therefore manufacturing costs low. Information must flow quickly up and down the chain from retail outlets back up to the manufacturer so that schedules can be given the maximum amount of time to adjust efficiently. The chain is then managed to make sure that products flow as quickly as possible down the chain to replenish what few stocks are kept downstream.

By contrast, responsive supply chain policy stresses high service levels and responsive supply to the end customer. The inventory in the network will be deployed as closely as possible to the customer. In this way, the chain can still supply even when dramatic changes occur in customer demand. Fast throughput from the upstream parts of the chain will still be needed to replenish downstream stocks. But those downstream stocks are needed to ensure high levels of availability to end customers. Figure 13.11 illustrates how the different supply chain policies match the different market requirements implied by functional and innovative products.

Supply chain dynamics

It was demonstrated in the 1960s by Jay Forrester[14] that certain dynamics exist between firms in supply chains that cause errors, inaccuracies and volatility, and that these increase for operations further upstream in the supply chain. This effect is

467

known as the Forrester Effect, or the Bullwhip Effect. It is called the Bullwhip Effect because a small disturbance at one end of the chain causes increasingly large disturbances as it works its way towards the end. Its main cause is a perfectly understandable and rational desire by the different links in the supply chain to manage their production rates and inventory levels sensibly. To demonstrate this, examine the production rate and stock levels for the supply chain shown in Table 13.3. This is a four-stage supply chain where an original equipment manufacturer (OEM) is served by three tiers of suppliers. The demand from the OEM's market has been running at a rate of 100 items per period, but in period 2 demand reduces to 95 items per period. All stages in the supply chain work on the principle that they will keep in stock one period's demand. This is a simplification but not a gross one. Many operations gear their inventory levels to their demand rate. The column headed 'stock' for each level of supply shows the starting stock at the beginning of the period and the finish stock at the end of the period. At the beginning of period 2, the OEM has 100 units in stock (that being the rate of demand up to period 2). Demand in period 2 is 95 and so the OEM knows that it would need to produce sufficient items to finish up at the end of the period with 95 in stock (this being the new demand rate). To do this, it need only manufacture 90 items; these, together with five items taken out of the starting stock, will supply demand and leave a finished stock of 95 items. The beginning of period 3 finds the OEM with 95 items in stock. Demand is also 95 items and therefore its production rate to maintain a stock level of 95 will be 95 items per period. The original equipment manufacturer now operates at a steady rate of producing 95 items per period. Note, however, that a change in demand of only five items has produced a fluctuation of 10 items in the OEM's production rate.

Table 13.3 — Fluctuations of production levels along supply chain in response to small change in end-customer demand

Period	Third-tier supplier		Second-tier supplier		First-tier supplier		Original equipment mfr		Demand
	Prodion	Stock	Prodion	Stock	Prodion	Stock	Prodion	Stock	
1	100	100 / 100	100	100 / 100	100	100 / 100	100	100 / 100	100
2	20	100 / 60	60	100 / 80	80	100 / 90	90	100 / 95	95
3	180	60 / 120	120	80 / 100	100	90 / 95	95	95 / 95	95
4	60	120 / 90	90	100 / 95	95	95 / 95	95	95 / 95	95
5	100	90 / 95	95	95 / 95	95	95 / 95	95	95 / 95	95
6	95	95 / 95	95	95 / 95	95	95 / 95	95	95 / 95	95

Note: all operations keep one period's inventory.

468

Now carry this same logic through to the first-tier supplier. At the beginning of period 2, the second-tier supplier has 100 items in stock. The demand which it has to supply in period 2 is derived from the production rate of the OEM. This has dropped down to 90 in period 2. The first-tier supplier therefore has to produce sufficient to supply the demand of 90 items (or the equivalent) and leave one month's demand (now 90 items) as its finish stock. A production rate of 80 items per month will achieve this. It will therefore start period 3 with an opening stock of 90 items, but the demand from the OEM has now risen to 95 items. It therefore has to produce sufficient to fulfil this demand of 95 items and leave 95 items in stock. To do this, it must produce 100 items in period 3. After period 3 the first-tier supplier then resumes a steady state, producing 95 items per month. Note again, however, that the fluctuation has been even greater than that in the OEM's production rate, decreasing to 80 items a period, increasing to 100 items a period, and then achieving a steady rate of 95 items a period.

This logic can be extended right back to the third-tier supplier. If you do this, you will notice that the further back up the supply chain an operation is placed, the more drastic are the fluctuations caused by the relatively small change in demand from the final customer. In this simple case, the decision of how much to produce each month was governed by the following relationship:

Total available for sale in any period = total required in the same period

Starting stock + production rate   = demand × closing stock

Starting stock + production rate = 2 × demand (because closing stock

must be equal to demand)

Production rate   = 2 × demand − starting stock

This relatively simple exercise does not include any time lag between a demand occurring in one part of the supply chain and it being transmitted to its supplier. In practice there will be such a lag, and this will make the fluctuations even more marked. Furthermore, the way different parts of the supply chain batch their manufacturing quantities can cause distortions which make production volumes fluctuate in upstream suppliers. Table 13.4 shows a simple example.

In Table 13.4 there is reasonably steady end-customer demand at a rate of five items per week. The end customer orders from a local distributor at this rate, and this local distributor, perhaps because of custom and practice, places bi-weekly orders with the area distributor – for this part, this is at a rate of 10 every two weeks. The area distributor

Table 13.4	Distortion of batching in the supply chain		
Manufacturer	Area distributor	Local distributor	End customer
100	50	10	5
0	0	0	5
0	0	10	5
0	0	0	5
0	0	10	5
0	0	0	5
0	0	10	5
0	0	0	5
0	50	10	5

469

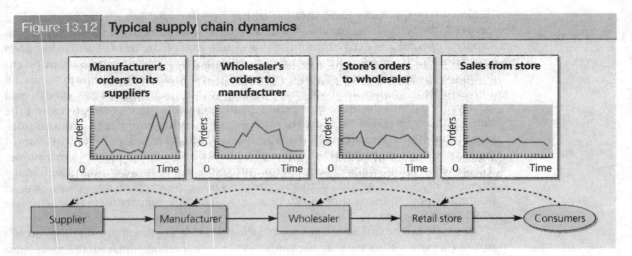

Figure 13.12 Typical supply chain dynamics

delivers at this bi-weekly rate but, to replenish its stock, places monthly orders back to the manufacturer. In Table 13.4, this involves ordering 50 in the first month, none in the second and 50 in the third. The manufacturer actually makes them in economic batches of 100, and so therefore makes them only occasionally.

Miscommunication in the supply chain

Whenever two operations in a supply chain arrange for one to provide products or services to the other, there is the potential for misunderstanding and miscommunication. This may be caused simply by not being sufficiently clear about what a customer expects or what a supplier is capable of delivering. There may also be more subtle reasons stemming from differences in perception of seemingly clear agreements. The effect is analogous to the children's game of Chinese whispers. The first child whispers a message to the next child who, whether he or she has heard it clearly or not, whispers an interpretation to the next child, and so on. The more children the message passes between, the more distorted it tends to become. When the game finishes and the last child says out loud what the message is, the first child and all the intervening children are amused by the distortion of the original message.

Figure 13.12 shows the net result of all these effects in a typical supply chain. One can see how relatively small fluctuations in the market cause increasing volatility further back in the chain.

Supply chain improvement

Given the disruptive nature of the supply chain dynamics described previously, an important aspect of supply chain planning and control is the attempt by operations managers to improve supply chain performance. While the first step in doing this is to understand the nature of supply chain dynamics, there are several more proactive actions which operations can take. Most of these are concerned with coordinating the activities of the operations in the chain.

Efforts to coordinate supply chain activity can be described as falling into three categories: information-sharing, channel alignment and operational efficiency.[15]

Information-sharing

One of the reasons for the fluctuations in output described in the example earlier was that each operation in the chain reacted to the orders placed by its immediate customer. None of the operations had an overview of what was happening throughout the chain.

470

If information had been available and shared throughout the chain, it is unlikely that such wild fluctuations would have occurred. It is sensible therefore to try to transmit information throughout the chain so that all the operations can monitor true demand, free of these distortions. So, for example, information regarding supply problems, or shortages, can be transmitted down the chain so that downstream customers can modify their schedules and sales plans accordingly.

One obvious improvement would be to make information on current demand downstream in the supply chain available to the operations upstream. Electronic point-of-sale (EPOS) systems used by many retailers attempt to do this. Sales data from checkouts or cash registers is consolidated and transmitted to the warehouses, transportation companies and supplier manufacturing operations that form its supply chain. Similarly, electronic data interchange (EDI) helps to share information (see the boxes 'Seven-Eleven Japan's agile supply chain' and 'The Tesco Information Exchange'). EDI can also affect the economic order quantities shipped between operations in the supply chain. In Chapter 12 we discussed how high ordering costs can result in large order quantities. If the effective cost of placing an order over an EDI network is small, batch sizes will reduce and therefore deliveries will become more frequent. The flow down the supply chain becomes more regular.

Channel alignment

Channel alignment means the adjustment of scheduling, material movements, stock levels, pricing and other sales strategies so as to bring all the operations in the chain into line with each other. This goes beyond the provision of information. It means that the systems and methods of planning and control decision making are harmonized through the chain. For example, even when using the same information, differences in forecasting methods or purchasing practices can lead to fluctuations in orders between operations in the chain. One way of avoiding this is to allow an upstream supplier to manage the inventories of its downstream customer. This is known as **vendor-managed inventory** (VMI). So, for example, a packaging supplier could take responsibility for the stocks of packaging materials held by a food manufacturing customer. In turn, the food manufacturer takes responsibility for the stocks of its products which are held in its customer's, the supermarket's, warehouses.

Vendor-managed inventory

One important source of misalignment between operating practices of adjacent operations in a supply chain comes from the economics of transporting whole truckloads of products. So an individual supermarket or even central warehouse may not require a full truckload of every product in every sales period. Yet its suppliers, who may only produce one or a few types of product, naturally want to deliver their product only by the truckload. In other words, there is a mismatch betweesn the volume–variety characteristics of the supplier (high volume, low variety) and those of its customer (low volume, high variety). Some customer–supplier agreements now attempt to ensure that every truckload of products delivered contains a mix of products from the supplier rather than a full truckload of the same product. Some supermarkets even use trucks with separate compartments at different temperatures so that they can transport products with different storage requirements in the same truck.

Operational efficiency

'Operational efficiency' means the efforts that each operation in the chain can make to reduce its own complexity, reduce the cost of doing business with other operations in the chain and increase throughput time. The cumulative effect of these individual activities is to simplify throughput in the whole chain. For example, imagine a chain of operations whose performance level is relatively poor: quality defects are frequent, the lead time to order products and services is long, delivery is unreliable and so on. The behaviour of the chain would be a continual sequence of errors and effort wasted in replanning to compensate for the errors. Poor quality would mean extra and unplanned orders being

471

Seven-Eleven Japan's agile supply chain[16]   example

Seven-Eleven Japan (SEJ) is that country's largest and most successful retailer with higher sales per square metre or per store than any of its competitors. Perhaps most significantly, the average amount of stock in an SEJ store is between 7 and 8.4 days of demand. This is a remarkably fast stock turnover for any retailer. Industry analysts see SEJ's agile supply chain management as being the driving force behind its success. And this agility is supported by a fully integrated information system that provides visibility of the whole supply chain and ensures fast replenishment of goods in its stores customized exactly to the needs of individual stores. This is shown in Figure 13.13.

As a customer comes to the checkout counter the assistant first keys in the customer's gender and approximate age and then scans the bar codes of the purchased goods. This sales data is transmitted to the Seven-Eleven headquarters through its own high-speed lines. Simultaneously, the store's own computer system records and analyses the information so that store managers and headquarters have immediate point-of-sale information. This allows both store managers and headquarters to, hour-by-hour, analyse sales trends, any stock-outs, types of customer buying certain products, and so on. The headquarters computer aggregates all this data by region, product and time so that all parts of the supply chain, from suppliers through to the stores, has the information by the next morning. Every Monday, the company chairman and top executives review all performance information for the previous week and develop plans for the up-coming week. These plans are presented on Tuesday morning to SEJ's 'operations field counsellors' each of which is responsible for facilitating performance improvement in around eight stores. On Tuesday afternoon the field counsellors for each region

meet to decide how they will implement the overall plans for their region. On Tuesday night the counsellors fly back to their regions and by next morning are visiting their stores to deliver the messages developed at headquarters which will help the stores implement their plans. SEJ's physical distribution is also organized on an agile basis. The distribution company maintains radio communications with all drivers and SEJ's headquarters keeps track of all delivery activities. Delivery times and routes are planned in great detail and published in the form of a delivery timetable. On average each delivery takes only one-and-half minutes at each store, and drivers are expected to make their deliveries within 10 minutes of scheduled time. If a delivery is late by more than 30 minutes the distribution company has to pay the store a fine equivalent to the gross profit on the goods being delivered. The agility of the whole supply system also allows SEJ headquarters and the distribution company to respond to disruptions. For example, on the day of the Kobe earthquake, SEJ used 7 helicopters and 125 motor cycles to rush through a delivery of 64,000 rice balls to earthquake victims. ■

Questions

1 SEJ stores typically carry around 3,000 SKUs (Stock Keeping Units, that is types of different product) compared with a large supermarket which may have over 100,000 SKUs. How do you think this affects their ability to manage their supply chain in an agile manner?

2 SEJ place a lot of emphasis on the use of their information system to achieve agility. How do you think the way in which an information system is used affects its value to a supply chain?

Figure 13.13 Seven-Eleven Japan's information system

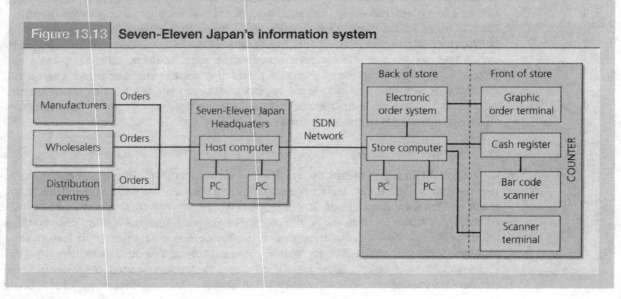

The Tesco Information Exchange[17]　　example

Tesco is one of Europe's largest supermarket chains. During 2000, in an attempt to form closer partnerships with its suppliers, as well as improve the effectiveness of supply chain coordination into its stores, Tesco launched the Tesco Information Exchange (TIE). Developed in conjunction with GE Information Services, the TIE is an 'extranet' solution (i.e. it is based on internet technology) that allows Tesco and its suppliers to communicate trading information. It is linked to a number of Tesco's internal information systems in order to give suppliers access to relevant and up-to-date information. This includes EPOS data, sales tracking and an internal directory so suppliers can quickly and easily find the right person to talk to.

Although the system was trialed initially with Tesco's larger suppliers, such as Proctor and Gamble, Nestlé and Britvic, it was designed to be used by all suppliers, including the smallest.

Security is important to the TIE. Because it uses internet technology to ensure low cost access for its small suppliers, it is important to provide security through such devices

as firewalls and passwords. Suppliers must also be confident that their own affairs are not visible to potential competitors. Suppliers only have access to data relevant to their own trading area. Figure 13.14 illustrates the TIE.

Information flows both ways in the system. Collaborative initiatives such as price discounts and other promotions can be planned jointly; tracking the progress of a sales promotion and evaluating its effectiveness can minimize stock outs and reduce production waste. It is this immediate visibility of data which helps with supply chain coordination. One experience by Proctor and Gamble, the consumer goods manufacturer, illustrates this:

During the trial we spotted that the demand for one of our lines had reached 8000 units after two days, compared with an original forecast of 10,000 units for the whole week! As a result we were able to respond and increase depot stock at short notice. This resulted in a joint business gain of around £50,000 – and more importantly, we avoided disappointing some 15,000 shoppers. ■

| Figure 13.14 | The Tesco Information Exchange |

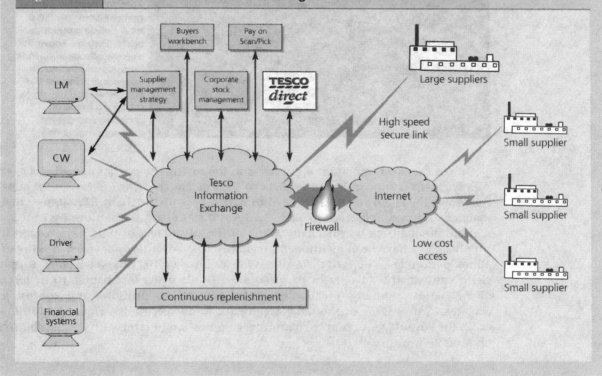

placed, and unreliable delivery and slow delivery lead times would mean high safety stocks. Just as important, most operations managers' time would be spent coping with the inefficiency. By contrast, a chain whose operations had high levels of operations performance would be more predictable and have faster throughput, both of which would help to minimize supply chain fluctuations.

473

Source: Zara Inditex.

Zara, the Spanish fashion garment company, have retail outlets around the world. They are known for their excellence in operating exceptionally fast supply chains that minimize the time between deciding to produce a batch of garments and getting them into their shops

One of the most important approaches to improving the operational efficiency of supply chains is known as *time compression*. This means speeding up the flow of materials down the chain and the flow of information back up the chain. The supply chain dynamics effect we observed in Table 13.3 was due, in part, to the slowness of information moving back up the chain. Many of the advantages of time compression in supply chains have been mentioned previously. The advantages of speed as an operations performance objective are discussed in Chapter 10, Chapter 2. In a supply chain context, the advantages of speed are also discussed in Chapter 10 in terms of *P:D* ratios. Similarly, the discussion on just-in-time planning and control in Chapter 15 uses some of the same arguments. More specifically, Figure 13.15 illustrates the advantages of supply chain time compression in terms of its overall impact on profitability.

Supply chain vulnerability

Supply chain risk

One of the consequences of the agile supply chain concept has been to take more seriously the possibility of **supply chain risk** and disruption. The concept of agility includes consideration of how supply chains have to cope with common disruptions such as late deliveries, quality problems, incorrect information and so on. Yet far more dramatic events can disrupt supply chains. For example, in early 2002 Land

474

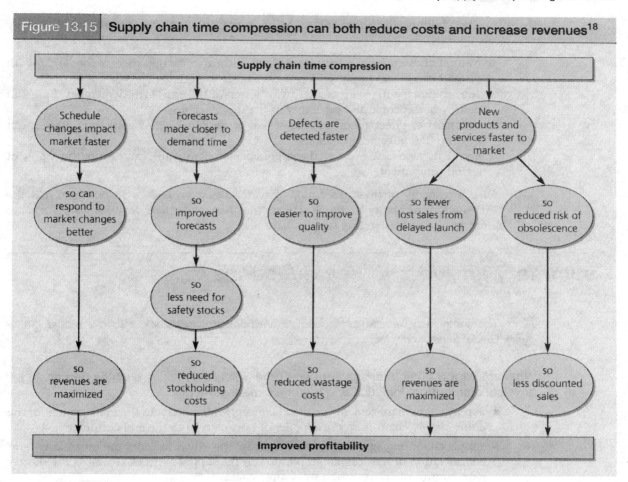

Figure 13.15 Supply chain time compression can both reduce costs and increase revenues[18]

Source: Based on Towill (1996).

Rover (a division of the Ford Motor Company) was having to cope with a threat to the supply of chassis for the Land Rover Discovery. The chassis is a major part of the vehicle but the company had some years ago subcontracted their manufacture to a single supplier, UPF Thompson. Weeks earlier this company had become insolvent and was now in the hands of the receivers who were demanding an up-front payment of around €60 million to continue supply. The receivers argued that they were legally obliged to recover as much money as possible on behalf of creditors and a single supplier agreement was a valuable asset.

In this case the outsourcing of a component had made the supply chain more vulnerable. But there are also other factors which have, in recent years, increased the vulnerability of supply. For example, global sourcing usually means that parts are shipped around the world on their journey through the supply chain. Micro chips manufactured in Taiwan could be assembled to printed circuit boards in Shanghai which are then finally assembled into a computer in Ireland. At the same time, many industries are suffering increased volatility in demand. Perhaps most significantly there tends to be far less inventory in supply chains that could buffer interruptions to supply. According to Professor Martin Christopher, an authority on supply chain management, *'Potentially the risk of disruption has increased dramatically as the result of a too-narrow focus on supply chain efficiency at the expense of effectiveness. Unless management recognizes the challenge and acts upon it, the implications for us all could be chilling.'*[19]

The 'chilling' effects that Professor Christopher speaks of can arise as a result of many disruptions.

- Natural disasters such as earthquakes and hurricanes (or outbreaks of foot and mouth disease) can block supply.
- Terrorist incidents such as the Twin Towers attack on 11th September 2001 can destroy both people and capability in the supply chain.
- Industrial or direct action such as strikes or the blockade of ports by protesters can hold up the movement of goods.
- Accidents such as fire in a vital component supplier's plant, can disrupt the supply of a vital component.

Of course many of these disruptions have always been present in business. It is the increased vulnerability of supply chains that has made many companies place more emphasis on understanding supply chain risks.

summary answers to key questions

 *The companion website to the book, **www.booksites.net/slack**, also has a brief 'Study Guide' to each chapter.*

What are supply chain management and other related activities such as purchasing, physical distribution, logistics and materials management?

- Supply chain management is a broad concept which includes the management of the entire supply chain from the supplier of raw material to the end customer.
- Supply chain management is a strategy concept which includes the broad long-term consideration of the company's position in the supply network as well as the shorter term control of flow through the supply chain.
- Purchasing is concerned with the supply-side activities of an organization. It includes the formal preparation of requests to suppliers for a quotation, valuation of suppliers, the issuing of formal purchase orders, and monitoring of delivery.
- Physical distribution management is the management of the (often multi-echelon) inventory and transportation systems which link the operation with its customers. Decisions include the number and position of warehouses in the system and the mode of physical transport which needs to be adopted.
- Logistics includes the demand-side physical distribution of goods, often beyond the immediate customers, through the supply chain to the end customer.
- Materials management is an integrated concept which includes both purchasing activities and physical distribution activities.

How can the relationship between operations in a supply chain affect the way it works?

- Supply networks are made up of individual pairs of buyer–supplier relationships. The use of internet technology in these relationships has led to a categorization based on a distinction between business and consumer partners. Business to business (B2B) relationships are of the most interest in operations management terms. They can be characterized on two dimensions – what is outsourced to a supplier, and the number and closeness of the relationships.
- Make-or-buy decisions are an operational form of vertical integration. It means doing the activity within one organizational boundary and is the closest form of relationship.

476

- Traditional market supplier relationships are where a purchaser chooses suppliers on an individual periodic basis. No long-term relationship is usually implied by such 'transactional' relationships. In the short term, this can be the cheapest way of obtaining goods and services but it makes it difficult to build internal capabilities.

- Virtual operations are an extreme form of outsourcing where an operation does relatively little itself and subcontracts almost all its activities.

- Partnership supplier relationships involve customers forming long-term relationships with suppliers. In return for the stability of demand, suppliers are expected to commit to high levels of service. True partnerships are difficult to sustain and rely heavily on the degree of trust which is allowed to build up between partners.

Are different supply chain objectives needed in different circumstances?

- Often supply chains split at some point in order to serve two or more markets. If these markets are different in their requirements, the supply chain feeding the markets may be organized in different ways.

- Marshall Fisher distinguishes between functional markets and innovative markets. He argues that functional markets, which are relatively predictable, require efficient supply chains, whereas innovative markets, which are less predictable, require 'responsive' supply chains.

What is the 'natural' pattern of behaviour in supply chains?

- Supply chains exhibit a dynamic behaviour known as the Forrester Effect. This shows how small changes at the demand end of a supply chain are progressively amplified for operations further back in the chain.

- To reduce the Forrester Effect, operations can adopt some mixture of three coordination strategies:

    - information-sharing: the efficient distribution of information throughout the chain can reduce demand fluctuations along the chain by linking all operations to the source of demand;
    - channel alignment: this means adopting the same or similar decision-making processes throughout the chain to coordinate how and when decisions are made;
    - operational efficiency: this means eliminating sources of inefficiency or ineffectiveness in the chain; of particular importance is 'time compression', which attempts to increase the throughput speed of the operations in the chain.

- Increasingly, supply risks are being managed as a countermeasure to their vulnerability.

Globalcast

case exercise

Globalcast was one of the world's largest manufacturers of metal and plastic moulded components to almost every industry, including automotive, consumer durables, telecommunications, computers, power tools, etc. With over 100 manufacturing facilities, it operated on every continent, usually in areas of established or emerging industrialization. In Europe there were large factories in the UK, Germany, France, Spain and Italy, and smaller ones in Scandinavia, Austria, Turkey and Israel. Every factory was considered to be a semi-autonomous profit centre and was headed up by a general manager. Each reported to a regional manager of one of the divisions (for example, the Plastics Division). New business was gener-

ated both by national marketing and by word-of-mouth recommendations from existing customers, but most orders were for regular repeat business or for new designs from existing customers. The role of the small technical sales team at each factory was to follow up enquiries with technical advice visits to the customer, followed by the preparation of quotations. In many cases, Globalcast provided design assistance to the customers. It was the role of the advisor to suggest ways of simplifying the overall design which would be cheaper for the customer, whilst being fast, easy and profitable to produce in the factory. Mould costs were calculated and quoted too, and in most cases the customer would pay for the moulds from the

477

outset, retaining ownership. Globalcast organized the purchase of the moulds, costing up to £50,000 each, and could make a small profit on this activity.

In the late 1990s, the market started to change rapidly. First, major customers such as Hewlett Packard, Dell, Ford, GM and Black and Decker started building new factories in developing countries. These were being established both to exploit the benefits of lower wages and overheads, and as market-entry points for these rapidly developing economies. In most cases, however, large proportions of their output would serve existing markets throughout the world. Because Globalcast was one of the most important suppliers (only about five competitors had worldwide coverage), it was often encouraged by its customers to establish supply factories in the same regions, ideally on adjacent sites. Customers explained that business was, in part, being transferred to their new sites, and since Globalcast had been selected as a preferred supplier, it had the opportunity to benefit from ongoing business development and growth. Attractive forecasts were provided, but not guaranteed. 'Partnerships' would be established where Globalcast had the benefit of sole-supplier status to the customer's local plant.

The second change was the trend for customers' products to be of globally standard designs. This allowed buyers to purchase components for their many factories around the world, from virtually any approved supplier anywhere. Therefore they were in a powerful position to restrict the number of suppliers, as well as demanding a single global, low price. For Globalcast this provided a new set of problems; its costs had varied widely around the world, depending mainly on local labour and overhead costs. Selling prices had varied according to costs and local commercial conditions, but detailed costs of production had never been disclosed to customers. However, customers would now be able to 'shop around' and find the lowest Globalcast price for themselves. At the same time, each Globalcast general manager had

tried to defend his or her business, even if that involved buying in the components from other company sites and adding a profit before selling to the customer. This was now becoming too obvious to large customers.

The third significant market trend was that customers increasingly wanted suppliers to do more assembly ('value-added') work. At its simplest, this could involve simply snapping together two parts. Alternatively, it could require complex purchasing, assembly and testing of major sub-assemblies. To do this, Globalcast would need to invest in assembly lines, testing equipment, storage, component and finished goods inventory, and systems to support purchasing and logistics. Specific approved suppliers were usually dictated by customers. Lead times from these global suppliers could be up to 12 weeks. Customers' initial delivery schedules were often stable and close to forecast levels, but could vary wildly as competitive forces affected customers' sales. But, overall, this type of work did appear commercially attractive, typically bringing in up to 10 times the revenue of a simple moulded part. The opportunity to become a 'first-tier' supplier to some of the world's leading manufacturers was hard to resist. Indeed, supplying global customers was the mainstay of the strategic plan for the new decade. ■

Questions

1 Evaluate the company's relationships with its large global customers. What does this imply about Globalcast's potential to support its customers' requirements in intensely price-sensitive global markets?

2 Would you describe Globalcast's strategic supply chain management decisions as more proactive or reactive, and why?

3 Are there other ways in which the company could organize itself to meet the challenges and market trends described in the case?

 Other short cases, and worked answers, are included in the companion website to this book, www.booksites.net/slack.

study activities

 Some study activities can be answered by reading the chapter. Others will require some general knowledge of business activity and some might require an element of investigation. All have hints on how they can be answered on the companion website for this book which also contains more discussion questions, www.booksites.net/slack.

1 If you were the owner of a small local retail shop, what criteria would you use to select suppliers for the goods which you wish to stock in your shop? Visit three shops which are local to you and ask the owners how they select their suppliers. In what way were their answers different from what you thought they might be?

478

2 What is your purchasing strategy? How do you approach buying the products and services that you need (or want)? Classify the types and products and services that you buy and record the criteria you use to purchase each category. Discuss these categories and criteria with others. Why are their views different?

3 Visit a C2C auction site (for example eBay) and analyse the function of the site in terms of the way it facilitates transactions. What does such a site have to get right to be successful?

4 The example of the bull-whip effect shown in Table 13.3 shows how a simple 5 per cent reduction in demand at the end of supply chain causes fluctuations that increase in severity the further back an operations is placed in the chain.

   (a) Using the same logic and the same rules (i.e. all operations keep one period's inventory), what would the effect on the chain be if demand fluctuated period by period between 100 and 95? That is, period 1 has a demand of 100, period 2 has a demand of 95, period 3 a demand of 100, period 4 a demand of 95, and so on?

   (b) What happens if all operations in the supply chain decided to keep only half of the periods demand as inventory?

   (c) Find examples of how supply chains try to reduce this bull-whip effect.

5 (Advanced) Revisit the example box 'TDG serving the whole supply chain' earlier in this chapter.

Step 1 – Read the description that David Garman gives of the different types of companies that offer distribution services, from 'haulage' and 'storage' companies, through to those companies that provide management of a whole supply chain.

Step 2 – Visit the websites of some distribution and logistics companies. For example, you might start with some of the following: **www.eddiestobart.co.uk, www.norbert-dentress-angle.com, www.accenture.com** (under 'services' look for supply chain management), **www.logisticsonline.com.**

Step 3 – Try and place some of the companies you have investigated on Garman's hierarchy of types of logistics service provider.

Step 4 – What do you think are:

   (a) the market promises that these companies make to their clients and potential clients?

   (b) the operations capabilities they need to carry out these promises successfully?

Notes on chapter

1 Source: Adam Grossberg and Mary Ward of Lucent Technologies and Carbone, J. (2002) 'Lucent's Supply Chain Flattens Margins', *Purchasing Magazine*, 19 September 2002.

2 Coyle, R.G. (1982) 'Assessing the Controllability of a Production Raw Material System', *IEEE Transactions*, SMC–12, Vol. 6.

3 Source: Grant, J. (2002) 'A cautionary tale of roof racks and widgets', *Financial Times*, 4 November 2002.

4 Morgan, I. (1987) 'The Purchasing Revolution', *McKinsey Quarterly*, Spring.

5 Source: Grad, C. (2000) 'A network of supplies to be woven into the web', *Financial Times*, 9 February 2002.

6 Harney, A. (2000) 'Up close but impersonal', *Financial Times*, 10 March 2000.

7 Source: Interview with David Garman, September 2002.

8 Lee, L. and Dobler, D.W. (1977) *Purchasing and Materials Management*, McGraw-Hill.

9 Source: Based on *The Economist* (2000) 'Shopping around the Web – A Survey of E-commerce', 26 February 2000.

10 From Slack, N. and Lewis, M. (2002) *Operations Strategy*, Financial Times Prentice Hall.

11 Parkhe, A. (1993) 'Strategic Alliance Structuring', *Academy of Management Journal*, Vol. 36, pp. 794–829.

12 Source: *Port of Rotterdam News*, 1994.

13 Fisher, M.L. (1997) 'What is the Right Supply Chain for Your Product', *Harvard Business Review*, March–April.

14 Forrester, J.W. (1961) *Industrial Dynamics*, MIT Press.

479

15 Lee, H.L., Padmanabhan, V., Whang, S. (1997) 'The Bull Whip Effect in Supply Chains', *Sloan Management Review*, Spring.

16 Source: Lee, H.L. and Whang, S. (2001) Demand Chain Excellent: A Tale of Two Retailers', *Supply Chain Management Review*, 3 January 2001.

17 Source: Company literature.

18 Towill, D.R. (1996) 'Time Compression and Supply Chain Management – A Guided Tour', *Supply Chain Management*, Vol. 1, No. 1.

19 Christopher, M. (2002) 'Business is Failing to Manage Supply Chain Vulnerability', *Odyssey, Issue 16, June*.

Selected further reading

Child, J. and Faulkner, D. (1998) *Strategies of Cooperation: Managing Alliances, Networks and Joint Ventures*, Oxford University Press. Very much a strategic view of supply networks, but insightful and readable.

Christopher, M. (1998) *Logistics and Supply Chain Management: Strategies for reducing cost and improving services*, (2nd edn), Financial Times Prentice Hall. A comprehensive treatment on supply chain management from a distribution perspective by one of the gurus of supply chain management.

Fisher, M.L. (1997) 'What is the Right Supply Chain for Your Product?', *Harvard Business Review*, Vol. 75, No. 2. A particularly influential article that explores the issue of how supply chains are not all the same.

Fuller, J.B., O'Connor, J. and Rawlinson, R. (1993) 'Tailored Logistics: The Next Advantage', *Harvard Business Review*, Vol. 71, No. 3. A view on how the physical distribution industry has developed.

Harland, C.M., Lamming, R.C. and Cousins, P. (1999) 'Developing the Concept of Supply Strategy', *International Journal of Operations and Production Management*, Vol. 19, No. 7. An academic paper but one that gives a broad understanding of how supply chain ideas have, and could develop.

Harrison, A. and van Hoek, R. (2002) *Logistics Management and Strategy*, Financial Times Prentice Hall. A short but readable book that explains many of the modern ideas in supply chain management including lean supply chains and agile supply chains.

Hines, P. and Rich, N. (1997) 'The Seven Value Stream Mapping Tools', *International Journal of Operations and Production Management*, Vol. 17, No. 1. Another academic paper, but one that explores some practical techniques that can be used to understand supply chains.

Macbeth, D.K. and Ferguson, N. (1994) *Partnership Sourcing: An Integrated Supply Chain Approach*, Financial Times, Pitman. A readable book that represents the arguments in favour of partnership sourcing.

Womack, J.P., Jones, D.T. and Roos, D. (1990) *The Machine that Changed the World*, Rawson Associates. One of the most influential books, not only in operations management but management in general, of the last twenty years. It deals with more than supply chains but has interesting things to say around lean supply.

480

chapter eighteen

Operations improvement

Source: Thorpe Park.

key questions

- How can operations measure their performance in terms of the five performance objectives?

- How can operations managers prioritize improvement of performance objectives?

- What are the broad approaches to managing the rate of improvement?

- Where does business process reengineering (BPR) fit into the improvement activity?

- What techniques can be used for improvement?

Introduction

Even when an operation is designed and its activities planned and controlled, the operations manager's task is not finished. All operations, no matter how well managed, are capable of improvement. In fact, in recent years the emphasis has shifted markedly towards making improvement one of the main responsibilities of operations managers. In this part of the book we choose to treat improvement activities in three stages. The first, in this chapter, looks at the approaches and techniques which can be adopted to improve the operation. The second, in Chapter 19, looks at improvement from another perspective, that is, how operations can prevent failure and how they can recover when they do suffer a failure. Finally, in Chapter 20, we look at how improvement activities can be supported through the total quality management (TQM) approach. These three stages are interrelated as shown in Figure 18.1.

Figure 18.1	Model of operations improvement showing the issues covered in this chapter

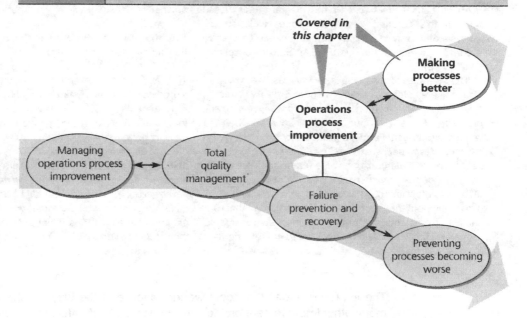

Improvement at Heineken – Part one[1]   example

Heineken International brews beer that is sold around the world. Operating in over 170 countries, it has succeeded in growing sales, especially in its Heineken and Amstel brands. However, sales growth can put pressure on any company's operations. For example, Heineken's Zoeterwoude facility, a packaging plant that fills bottles and cans in The Netherlands has had to increase its volume by between 8 and 10 per cent per year on a regular basis. In a competitive market, the company faced two challenges. First, it needed to improve its operations processes to reduce its costs. Second, because it would have taken a year to build a new packaging line, it needed to improve the efficiency of its existing lines in order to increase its capacity. Improving line efficiency therefore was vital if the plant was to cut its costs and create the extra capacity it needed to delay investment in a new packaging line.

The objective of the improvement project was to improve the plant's Operational Equipment Efficiency (OEE) (see Chapter 11 for a discussion of OEE) by 20 per cent. Setting a target of 20 per cent was seen as important because it was challenging yet achievable as well as meeting the cost and capacity objectives of the project. It was also decided to focus the improvement project around two themes: (a) obtaining accurate operational data that could be converted into useful business information on which improvement decisions could be based, and (b) changing the culture of the operation to promote

Source: Corbis

fast and effective decision making. This would help people at all levels in the plant to have access to accurate and up-to-date information as well as encouraging staff to focus on the improvement of how they do their job rather than just 'doing the job'. Before the improvement, project staff at the Zoeterwoude plant had approached problem-solving as an *ad hoc* activity, only to be done when circumstances made it unavoidable. By contrast,

▶

639

the improvement initiative taught the staff on each packaging line to use various problem-solving techniques such as cause–effect and Pareto diagrams (discussed later in this chapter). Other techniques included the analysis of improved equipment maintenance and failure mode and effective analysis (FMEA) (both discussed in Chapter 19).

'Until we started using these techniques,' says Wilbert Raaijmakers, Heineken Netherlands Brewery Director, 'there was little consent regarding what was causing any problems. There was poor communication between the various departments and job grades. For example, maintenance staff believed that production stops were caused by operating errors, while operators were of the opinion that poor maintenance was the cause.' The use of better information, analysis and improvement techniques helped the staff to identify and treat the root causes of problems. With many potential improvements to make, staff teams were encouraged to set priorities that would reflect the overall improvement target. There was also widespread use of benchmarking performance against targets periodically so that progress could be reviewed.

At the end of twelve months the improvement project had achieved its objectives of a 20 per cent improvement in OEE, not just for one packaging line but for all nine. This allowed the plant to increase the volume of its exports and cut its costs significantly. Not only that, but other aspects of the plant's performance improved. Up to that point, the plant had gained a reputation for poor delivery dependability. After the project it was seen by the other operations in its supply chain as a much more reliable partner. Yet Wilbert Raaijmakers still sees room for improvement, 'The optimization of an organization is a never-ending process. If you sit back and do the same thing tomorrow as you did today, you'll never make it. We must remain alert to the latest developments and stress the resulting information to its full potential.' ■

The improvement at the Zoeterwoude plant, and the way it achieved it, is typical of many other improvement projects in a wide variety of different types of operation. It had an emphasis on an improvement target that related directly to the operation's strategic objectives (improved capacity and reduced cost). It made an effort to collect the information from its processes that would allow it to base decisions on evidence rather than opinion, and, when there were many alternative improvements to be made, it encouraged prioritization. The project also made extensive use of simple improvement techniques that would both analyse problems and help to channel its staffs' creativity at all levels. Perhaps most importantly, the project was not a simple 'one-off' attack on process performance, rather it was the start of a never-ending cycle of continuous improvement.

Measuring and improving performance

Performance measurement

Before operations managers can devise their approach to the improvement of their operations, they need to know how good they are already. The urgency, direction and priorities of improvement will be determined partly by whether the current performance of an operation is judged to be good, bad or indifferent. All operations therefore need some kind of **Performance measurement** as a prerequisite for improvement.

Performance measurement

Performance measurement is the process of *quantifying action*, where measurement means the process of quantification and the performance of the operation is assumed to derive from actions taken by its management.[2] Performance here is defined as the degree to which an operation fulfils the five performance objectives at any point in time, in order to satisfy its customers.

Polar diagram

The **Polar diagrams** (which we introduced in Chapter 2) in Figure 18.2 illustrate this concept. The five performance objectives which we have used throughout this book can be regarded as the dimensions of overall performance that satisfy customers. The market's

640

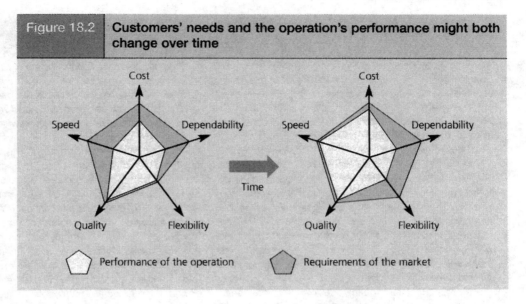

Figure 18.2 Customers' needs and the operation's performance might both change over time

needs and expectations of each performance objective will vary (as we also discussed in Chapter 3). The extent to which an operation meets its market's needs will also vary, possibly only meeting them in some dimensions. In addition, market requirements and the operation's performance could also change over time. In Figure 18.2 the operation is originally almost meeting the requirements of the market as far as quality and flexibility are concerned, but is under-performing on its speed, dependability and cost. After some time has elapsed the operation has improved its speed and cost to match market requirements but its flexibility no longer matches market requirements, not because it has deteriorated in an absolute sense but because the requirements of the market have changed.

Performance measures

Performance objectives

The five **Performance objectives** – quality, speed, dependability, flexibility and cost – are really composites of many smaller measures. For example, an operation's cost is derived from many factors which could include the purchasing efficiency of the operation, the efficiency with which it converts materials, the productivity of its staff, the ratio of direct to indirect staff, and so on. All of these factors individually give a partial view of the operation's cost performance, and many of them overlap in terms of the information they include. Each of them does give a perspective on the cost performance of an operation, however, which could be useful either to identify areas for improvement or to monitor the extent of improvement. If an organization regards its 'cost' performance as unsatisfactory, therefore, disaggregating it into 'purchasing efficiency', 'operations efficiency', 'staff productivity', etc., might explain the root cause of the poor performance. Alternatively, sometimes composite performance measures are used, see the box 'Improvement on track'.

Table 18.1 shows some of the partial measures which can be used to judge an operation's performance.

Performance standards

After an operation has measured its performance by using a 'bundle' of partial measures, it needs to make a judgement as to whether its performance is good, bad or indifferent. There are several ways it can do this, each of which involves comparing the current

641

Improvement on track³   example

Alstom Transporte SA – Systems Maintenance, the Spanish transport services company is part of the Alstom engineering and transport group. It provides a whole range of services to railway operators, mainly in Spain, Portugal and South America. Although the company's history of pioneering quality management goes back to the 1960s, it was in the late 1990s that it received Spain's highest prize, the Príncipe Felipe Award. Such a reputation for quality is a valuable asset in an increasingly competitive market, says Ms Toledo del Castillo, its director of quality and environment. *'We are continually looking for innovation in our contracts and the way we deliver our services because each of our customers wants us to give more or better service for a lower price. The continuous improvement of our processes is the only way to make our company more efficient.'*

The company uses a defined set of criteria to identify particularly critical processes within its operations. Each process is allocated a 'process owner' by the company's quality steering committee. Because the company's sites are widely spread, it is important that excellence in process management practice is identified and the lessons learnt throughout the company. This is helped by the company's 'process excellence index' (EPI) which is an indicator of the way a process performs, particularly how it is designed, controlled and improved. The EPI score, which is expressed on a scale of 1 to 100, is calculated by the process owner and registered with the quality department.

'With one figure we know the state of a process in such a way that we can measure the cost, reliability and quality of each process so that we can compare performance. If you don't measure, you can't improve. And if you don't measure in the correct way, how can you know where you are?'

Employee recognition is also an important part of the company's improvement strategy. The company's suggestion scheme is designed to encourage staff to submit several linked ideas at one time. These can be evaluated and rated as a portfolio of suggestions from each employee. No individual suggestion is finally evaluated until it has been fully implemented. Where ideas are put forward by a team of employees, the score is divided between them, either equally or according to the wishes of the team itself. These employee policies are supported by the company's training schemes, many of which are designed to ensure all employees are customer-focused.

'Not everyone has direct contact with customers, so training is a way to get them all to think as a customer and handle customer enquiries and complaints. If people assume that the customer is wrong, it becomes difficult to make sure they are helped,' says Ms Toledo del Castillo. ∎

Questions

1 What seem to be the key elements in this company's approach to improvement?

2 Do you think this approach is appropriate for all operations?

Performance standard

achieved level of performance with some kind of **performance standard**. Four kinds of standard are commonly used.

Historical standards

Historical standards would mean comparing current performance against previous performance. For example, if an organization was delivering products to its customers four weeks after the customer initially requested them, its performance would be judged to be quite good if the previous year it was taking six weeks to deliver. Historical performance standards are effective when judging whether an operation is getting better or worse over time, but they give no indication as to whether performance should be regarded as satisfactory.

Target performance standards

Target performance standards are those which are set arbitrarily to reflect some level of performance which is regarded as appropriate or reasonable. For example, if, under the circumstances, it is regarded as reasonable for the previously mentioned operation to deliver within four weeks then the performance of an operation which actually did deliver in four weeks would be regarded as acceptable. The budgets which most large organizations prepare are examples of target performance standards.

Table 18.1	Some typical partial measures of performance
Performance objective	Some typical measures
Quality	Number of defects per unit
	Level of customer complaints
	Scrap level
	Warranty claims
	Mean time between failures
	Customer satisfaction score
Speed	Customer query time
	Order lead time
	Frequency of delivery
	Actual *versus* theoretical throughput time
	Cycle time
Dependability	Percentage of orders delivered late
	Average lateness of orders
	Proportion of products in stock
	Mean deviation from promised arrival
	Schedule adherence
Flexibility	Time needed to develop new products/services
	Range of products/services
	Machine change-over time
	Average batch size
	Time to increase activity rate
	Average capacity/maximum capacity
	Time to change schedules
Cost	Minimum delivery time/average delivery time
	Variance against budget
	Utilization of resources
	Labour productivity
	Added value
	Efficiency
	Cost per operation hour

Competitor performance standards

Competitor performance standards compare the achieved performance of the operation with that which is being achieved by one or more of the organization's competitors. For example, if the operation is delivering within four weeks but most of its competitors can deliver within three weeks then its performance would not be regarded as very good. The advantage of competitor-based performance standards is that they relate an operation's performance directly to its competitive ability in the marketplace. In terms of strategic performance improvement, competitive standards are the most useful. For some operations in the not-for-profit sector, this type of performance standard needs to be modified. Comparison against competitors might not even be possible. A police department, for example, would find it difficult to identify its 'competitors' but could compare its performance with that of similar police departments elsewhere.

643

Absolute performance standards

An absolute performance standard is one which is taken to its theoretical limits. For example, the quality standard of 'zero defects' or the inventory standard of 'zero inventories' are both absolute standards. These standards are perhaps never achievable in practice but they do allow an operation to calibrate itself against a theoretical limit. In the previous example, the product which was in fact delivered in four weeks to the customer might take only four hours to be made within the factory and delivered to the customer. In practice the operation will probably never achieve a four-hour delivery time, but the standard has illustrated how much the operation could theoretically improve.

Benchmarking

One approach that some companies use to compare their operations with those of other companies, or other parts of its own company, is called **benchmarking**. Originally the term 'benchmark' derives from land surveying where a mark, cut in the rock, would act as a reference point. In 1979 the Xerox Corporation, the document company, used the term 'competitive benchmarking' to describe a process, *'used by the manufacturing function to revitalize itself by comparing the features, assemblies and components of its products with those of competitors.'*[4]

Now benchmarking is generally accepted as meaning, *the process of learning from others*, and has become common practice in many organizations. Its widespread adoption is partly the result of a growing realization amongst operations managers that (a) the problems they face in managing their processes are almost certainly shared by other operations managers somewhere, and (b) there is probably another operation somewhere that has developed a better way of doing things than they have. Put another way, unless a process is unique or the best in the world, it can learn from another process somewhere. Examples of benchmarking include a dishwasher manufacturer comparing the energy efficiency of its own products against its competitors, an online retailer of computer accessories comparing the way it organizes it warehouse and delivery processes with an online retailer of books and DVDs, a hotel chain comparing the room cleaning times in all its hotels, and a chemicals company comparing its transportation and distribution practices with a specialist logistics company.

The origins of benchmarking as now practiced go back to Xerox,[5] the document and imaging company, which created the original market for copiers. Its virtual monopoly almost became its undoing when the emerging Japanese copier companies began to threaten its market share. The company ordered an in-depth study. To understand how it should change, the company decided to evaluate itself externally (the process that became known as competitive benchmarking). The results of this study shocked the company. Its Japanese rivals were selling machines for about what it cost Xerox to make them. Nor could this be explained by differences in quality. The study found that, when compared with its Japanese rivals, the company had nine times more suppliers, was rejecting 10 times as many machines on the production line and taking twice as long to get products to market. Benchmarking also showed that productivity would need to grow 18 per cent per year over five years if it was to catch up with its rivals. Xerox saw benchmarking as helping it achieve two objectives. At a strategic level it helped set standards of performance, while at an operational level it helped the company understand those best practices and operations methods that can help it achieve its performance objectives. The benchmarking process developed by Rank Xerox has five phases (see Figure 18.3).

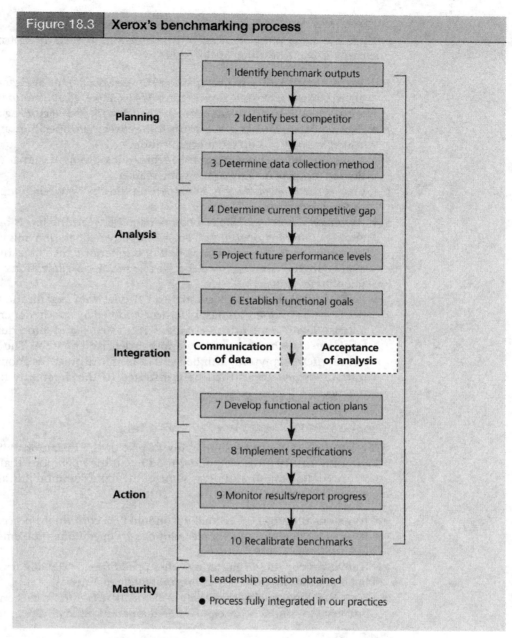

Figure 18.3 Xerox's benchmarking process

Its experience of using this approach led Xerox to a number of conclusions:

- The first phase, planning, is crucial to the success of the whole process. A good plan will identify a realistic objective for the benchmarking study, which is achievable and clearly aligned with business priorities.
- A prerequisite for benchmarking success is to understand thoroughly your own processes. Without this it is difficult to compare your processes against those of other companies.
- Look at what is already available. A lot of information is already in the public domain. Published accounts, journals, conferences and professional associations can all provide information which is useful for benchmarking purposes.
- Be sensitive in asking for information from other companies. The golden rule is: 'Don't ask any questions that we would not like to be asked ourselves.'

645

Types of benchmarking

There are many different types of benchmarking (which are not necessarily mutually exclusive), some of which are listed below:

- *Internal benchmarking* is a comparison between operations or parts of operations which are within the same total organization. For example, a large motor vehicle manufacturer with several factories might choose to benchmark each factory against the others.
- *External benchmarking* is a comparison between an operation and other operations which are part of a different organization.
- *Non-competitive benchmarking* is benchmarking against external organizations which do not compete directly in the same markets.
- *Competitive benchmarking* is a comparison directly between competitors in the same, or similar, markets.
- *Performance benchmarking* is a comparison between the levels of achieved performance in different operations. For example, an operation might compare its own performance in terms of some or all of our performance objectives – quality, speed, dependability, flexibility and cost – against other organizations' performance in the same dimensions.
- *Practice benchmarking* is a comparison between an organization's operations practices, or way of doing things, and those adopted by another operation. For example, a large retail store might compare its systems and procedures for controlling stock levels with those used by another department store. The objective is usually to see whether anything can be learned from the practices adopted by other organizations, which could then be transferred to the organization's own operational practices.

Benchmarking as an improvement tool

The widespread use of benchmarking as part of the operations improvement activity does not mean that it is well-understood by all the operations that have attempted to use it. According to one authority, some of the more common misunderstandings about benchmarking are as follows.

- It is a one-off project . . . actually it should be a continuous process of comparison.
- It provides obvious and simple solutions to operations problems . . . actually it provides information not answers.
- It involves copying or imitating other operations . . . actually it is a process of learning and adapting from others in a pragmatic manner.
- It can be done quickly and easily . . . actually it is often time consuming and labour intensive to conduct a disciplined benchmarking study.

The objectives of benchmarking

Benchmarking is partly concerned with being able to judge how well an operation is doing. It can be seen, therefore, as one approach to setting realistic performance standards. It is also concerned with searching out new ideas and practices which might be able to be copied or adapted. For example, a bank might learn some things from a supermarket about how it could cope with demand fluctuations during the day. The success of benchmarking, however, is largely due to more than its ability to set performance standards and enable organizations to copy one another. Benchmarking is essentially about stimulating creativity and providing a stimulus which enables operations better to understand how they should be serving their customers. Many organizations find that it is the process itself of looking at different parts of their own company or looking at external companies which allows them to understand the connection between the external market needs which an operation is trying to satisfy and the internal operations practices it is using to try to satisfy them. In other words, benchmarking can help to reinforce the idea of the direct contribution which an operation has to the competitiveness of its organization.

critical commentary

It can be argued that there is a fundamental flaw in the whole concept of benchmarking. Operations that rely on others to stimulate their creativity, especially those that are in search of 'best practice', are always limiting themselves to currently accepted methods of operating or currently accepted limits to performance. In other words, benchmarking leads companies only as far as others have gone. 'Best practice' is not 'best' in the sense that it cannot be bettered, it is only 'best' in the sense that it is the best one can currently find. Indeed accepting what is currently defined as 'best' may prevent operations from ever making the radical breakthrough or improvement that takes the concept of 'best' to a new and fundamentally improved level. This argument is closely related to the concept of breakthrough improvement discussed later in this chapter. Furthermore, methods or performance levels that are appropriate in one operation may not be in another. Because one operation has a set of successful practices in the way it manages its process does not mean that adopting those same practices in another context will prove equally successful. It is possible that subtle differences in the resources within a process (such as staff skills or technical capabilities) or the strategic context of an operation (for example, the relative priorities of performance objectives) will be sufficiently different to make the adoption of seemingly successful practices inappropriate.

Improvement priorities[6]

Improvement priorities

In Chapter 3, when discussing the 'market requirements' perspective, we identified two major influences on the way in which operations decide on their **improvement priorities**:

- the needs and preferences of customers;
- the performance and activities of competitors.

The consideration of customers' needs has particular significance in shaping the objectives of all operations. The fundamental purpose of operations is to create goods and services in such a way as to meet the needs of their customers. What customers find important, therefore, the operation should also regard as important. If customers for a particular product or service prefer low prices to wide range, then the operation should devote more energy to reducing its costs than to increasing the flexibility which enables it to provide a range of products or services. The needs and preferences of customers shape the *importance* of operations objectives within the operation.

The role of competitors is different from that of customers. Competitors are the points of comparison against which the operation can judge its performance. From a competitive viewpoint, as operations improve their performance, the improvement which matters most is that which takes the operation past the performance levels achieved by its competitors. The role of competitors then is in determining achieved *performance*.

Both importance and performance have to be brought together before any judgement can be made as to the relative priorities for improvement. Just because something is particularly important to its customers does not mean that an operation should necessarily

647

give it immediate priority for improvement. It may be that the operation is already considerably better than its competitors at serving customers in this respect. Similarly, just because an operation is not very good at something when compared with its competitors' performance, it does not necessarily mean that it should be immediately improved. Customers may not particularly value this aspect of performance. Both importance and performance need to be viewed together to judge the prioritization of objectives.

Judging importance to customers

Order winners
Qualifiers
Less important

In Chapter 3 we introduced the idea of **order-winning**, **qualifying** and **less important** competitive factors.

Order-winning competitive factors are those which directly win business for the operation. *Qualifying competitive factors* are those which may not win extra business if the operation improves its performance, but can certainly lose business if performance falls below a particular point, known as the qualifying level. *Less important competitive factors*, as their name implies, are those which are relatively unimportant compared with the others.

In fact, to judge the relative importance of its competitive factors, an operation will usually need to use a slightly more discriminating scale. One way to do this is to take our three broad categories of competitive factors – order winning, qualifying and less important – and to divide each category into three further points representing strong, medium and weak positions. Figure 18.4 illustrates such a scale.

Judging performance against competitors

At its simplest, a competitive performance standard would consist merely of judging whether the achieved performance of an operation is better than, the same, or worse than that of its competitors. However, in much the same way as the nine-point importance scale was derived, we can derive a more discriminating nine-point performance scale, as shown in Figure 18.5.

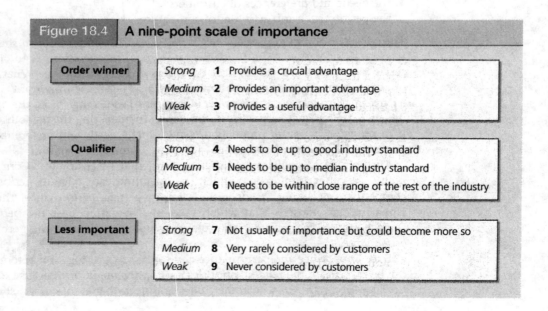

Figure 18.4	A nine-point scale of importance

Order winner		
Strong	**1**	Provides a crucial advantage
Medium	**2**	Provides an important advantage
Weak	**3**	Provides a useful advantage

Qualifier		
Strong	**4**	Needs to be up to good industry standard
Medium	**5**	Needs to be up to median industry standard
Weak	**6**	Needs to be within close range of the rest of the industry

Less important		
Strong	**7**	Not usually of importance but could become more so
Medium	**8**	Very rarely considered by customers
Weak	**9**	Never considered by customers

648

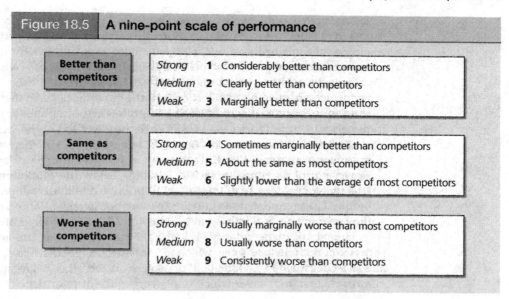

| **Figure 18.5** | **A nine-point scale of performance** |

Better than competitors	Strong	1	Considerably better than competitors
	Medium	2	Clearly better than competitors
	Weak	3	Marginally better than competitors
Same as competitors	Strong	4	Sometimes marginally better than competitors
	Medium	5	About the same as most competitors
	Weak	6	Slightly lower than the average of most competitors
Worse than competitors	Strong	7	Usually marginally worse than most competitors
	Medium	8	Usually worse than competitors
	Weak	9	Consistently worse than competitors

The importance–performance matrix

Importance–performance matrix

The priority for improvement which each competitive factor should be given can be assessed from a comparison of their importance and performance. This can be shown on an **importance–performance matrix** which, as its name implies, positions each competitive factor according to its scores or ratings on these criteria. Figure 18.6 shows an importance–performance matrix divided into zones of improvement priority. The first zone boundary is the 'lower bound of acceptability' shown as line AB in Figure 18.6. This is the boundary between acceptable and unacceptable performance. When a competitive

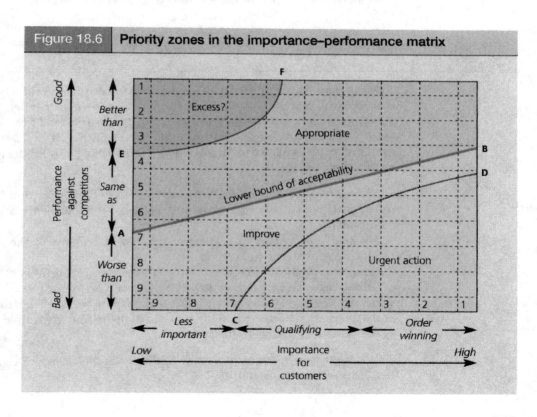

| **Figure 18.6** | **Priority zones in the importance–performance matrix** |

factor is rated as relatively unimportant (8 or 9 on the importance scale), this boundary will in practice be low. Most operations are prepared to tolerate performance levels which are 'in the same ball-park' as their competitors (even at the bottom end of the rating) for unimportant competitive factors. They only become concerned when performance levels are clearly below those of their competitors. Conversely, when judging competitive factors which are rated highly (1 or 2 on the importance scale) they will be markedly less sanguine at poor or mediocre levels of performance. Minimum levels of acceptability for these competitive factors will usually be at the lower end of the 'better than competitors' class. Below this minimum bound of acceptability (AB) there is clearly a need for improvement; above this line there is no immediate urgency for any improvement. However, not all competitive factors falling below the minimum line will be seen as having the same degree of improvement priority. A boundary approximately represented by line CD represents a distinction between an urgent priority zone and a less urgent improvement zone. Similarly, above the line AB, not all competitive factors are regarded as having the same priority. The line EF can be seen as the approximate boundary between performance levels which are regarded as 'good' or 'appropriate' on one hand and those regarded as 'too good' or 'excess' on the other. Segregating the matrix in this way results in four zones which imply very different priorities:

- The 'appropriate' zone – competitive factors in this area lie above the lower bound of acceptability and so should be considered satisfactory.
- The 'improve' zone – lying below the lower bound of acceptability, any factors in this zone must be candidates for improvement.
- The 'urgent-action' zone – these factors are important to customers but performance is below that of competitors. They must be considered as candidates for immediate improvement.
- The 'excess?' zone – factors in this area are 'high performing', but not important to customers. The question must be asked, therefore, whether the resources devoted to achieving such a performance could be used better elsewhere.

worked example

EXL Laboratories is a subsidiary of an electronics company. It carries out research and development as well as technical problem-solving work for a wide range of companies, including companies in its own group. It is particularly keen to improve the level of service which it gives to its customers. However, it needs to decide which aspect of its performance to improve first. It has devised a list of the most important aspects of its service:

- The quality of its technical solutions – the perceived appropriateness by customers.
- The quality of its communications with customers – the frequency and usefulness of information.
- The quality of post-project documentation – the usefulness of the documentation which goes with the final report.
- Delivery speed – the time between customer request and the delivery of the final report.
- Delivery dependability – the ability to deliver on the promised date.
- Delivery flexibility – the ability to deliver the report on a revised date.
- Specification flexibility – the ability to change the nature of the investigation.
- Price – the total charge to the customer.

EXL assigns a score to each of these factors using the 1–9 scale described in Figure 18.4. This is shown in Figure 18.7.

650

Figure 18.7 | Rating 'importance to customers' and 'performance against competitors' on the nine-point scales for EXL Laboratories

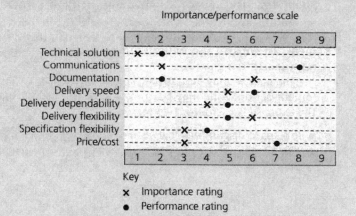

EXL then turned their attention to judging the laboratory's performance against competitor organizations. Although they have benchmarked information for some aspects of performance, they have to make estimates for the others. These are also shown in Figure 18.7.

EXL Laboratories plotted the importance and performance ratings it had given to each of its competitive factors on an importance–performance matrix. This is shown in Figure 18.8. It shows that the most important aspect of competitiveness – the ability to deliver sound technical solutions to its customers – falls comfortably within

Figure 18.8 | The importance–performance matrix for EXL Laboratories

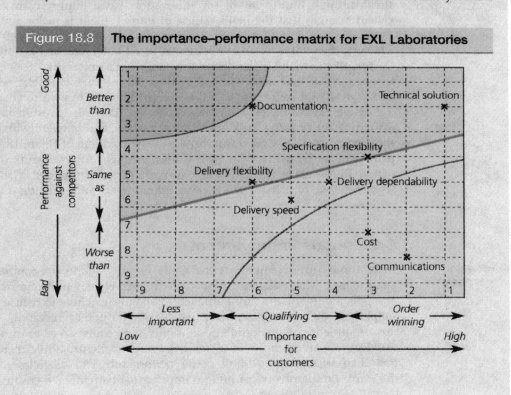

the appropriate zone. Specification flexibility and delivery flexibility are also in the appropriate zone, although only just. Both delivery speed and delivery dependability seem to be in need of improvement as each is below the minimum level of acceptability for their respective importance positions. However, two competitive factors, communications and cost/price, are clearly in need of immediate improvement. These two factors should therefore be assigned the most urgent priority for improvement. The matrix also indicates that the company's documentation could almost be regarded as 'too good'.

The matrix may not reveal any total surprises. The competitive factors in the 'urgent-action' zone may be known to be in need of improvement already. However, the exercise is useful for two reasons:

- It helps to discriminate between many factors which may be in need of improvement.
- The exercise gives purpose and structure to the debate on improvement priorities.

Approaches to improvement

Once the priority of improvement has been determined, an operation must consider the approach or strategy it wishes to take to the improvement process. Two particular strategies represent different, and to some extent opposing, philosophies. These two strategies are *breakthrough improvement* and *continuous improvement*.

Breakthrough improvement

Breakthrough improvement

Breakthrough improvement (or 'innovation'-based improvement as it is sometimes called) assumes that the main vehicle of improvement is major and dramatic change in the way the operation works. The introduction of a new, more efficient machine in a factory, the total redesign of a computer-based hotel reservation system, and the introduction of a new and better degree programme at a university are all examples of breakthrough improvement. The impact of these improvements is relatively sudden, abrupt and represents a step change in practice (and hopefully performance). Such improvements are rarely inexpensive, usually calling for high investment of capital, often disrupting the ongoing workings of the operation, and frequently involving changes in the product/service or process technology. The bold line in Figure 18.9(a) illustrates the pattern of performance with several breakthrough improvements. The improvement pattern illustrated by the dotted line in Figure 18.9(a) is regarded by some as being more representative of what really occurs when operations rely on pure breakthrough improvement.

Continuous improvement

Continuous improvement

Continuous improvement, as the name implies, adopts an approach to improving performance which assumes more and smaller incremental improvement steps. For example, modifying the way a product is fixed to a machine to reduce changeover time, simplifying the question sequence when taking a hotel reservation, and rescheduling the assignment completion dates on a university course so as to smooth the students' workload are all examples of incremental improvements. While there is no guarantee that such small steps towards better performance will be followed by other steps, the whole philosophy of continuous improvement attempts to ensure that they will be. Continuous improvement is not concerned with promoting small improvements *per se*.

652

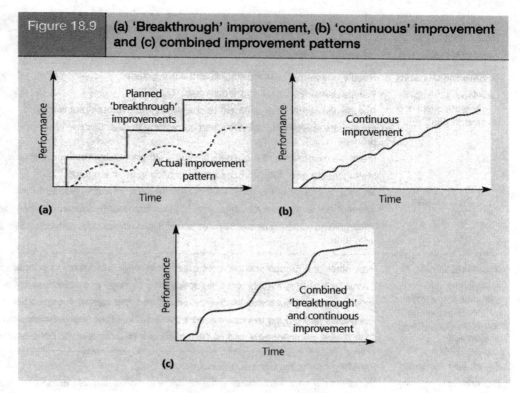

Figure 18.9 (a) 'Breakthrough' improvement, (b) 'continuous' improvement and (c) combined improvement patterns

It does see small improvements, however, as having one significant advantage over large ones – they can be followed relatively painlessly by other small improvements (see Figure 18.9(b)).

Kaizen

Continuous improvement is also known as **kaizen**. Kaizen is a Japanese word, the definition of which is given by Masaaki Imai[7] (who has been one of the main proponents of continuous improvement) as follows:

> *Kaizen means improvement. Moreover, it means improvement in personal life, home life, social life and work life. When applied to the work place, kaizen means continuing improvement involving everyone – managers and workers alike.*

In continuous improvement it is not the *rate* of improvement which is important, it is the *momentum* of improvement. It does not matter if successive improvements are small; what does matter is that every month (or week, or quarter, or whatever period is appropriate) some kind of improvement has actually taken place.

Building a continuous improvement capability

The ability to improve on a continuous basis is not something which always comes naturally to operations managers and staff. There are specific abilities, behaviours and actions which need to be consciously developed if continuous improvement is to be sustained over the long term. Bessant and Caffyn distinguish between what they call 'organizational abilities' (the capacity or aptitude to adopt a particular approach to continuous improvement), 'constituent behaviours' (the routines of behaviour which staff adopt and which reinforce the approach to continuous improvement) and 'enablers' (the procedural devices or techniques used to progress the continuous improvement effort). They identify six generic organizational abilities, each with its own set of constituent behaviours. These are identified in Table 18.2. Examples of enablers are the improvement techniques described later in this chapter.

Table 18.2	Continuous improvement (CI) abilities and some associated behaviours[8]
Organizational ability	*Constituent behaviours*
Getting the CI habit Developing the ability to generate sustained involvement in CI	People use formal problem-finding and solving cycle
	People use simple tools and techniques
	People use simple measurement to shape the improvement process
	Individuals and/or groups initiate and carry through CI activities – they participate in the process
	Ideas are responded to in a timely fashion – either implemented or otherwise dealt with
	Managers support the CI process through allocation of resources
	Managers recognize in formal ways the contribution of employees to CI
	Managers lead by example, becoming actively involved in design and implementation of CI
	Managers support experiment by not punishing mistakes, but instead encouraging learning from them
Focusing on CI Generating and sustaining the ability to link CI activities to the strategic goals of the company	Individuals and groups use the organization's strategic objectives to prioritize improvements
	Everyone is able to explain what the operation's strategy and objectives are
	Individuals and groups assess their proposed changes against the operation's objectives
	Individuals and groups monitor/measure the results of their improvement activity
	CI activities are an integral part of the individual's or group's work, not a parallel activity
Spreading the word Generating the ability to move CI activity across organizational boundaries	People cooperate in cross-functional groups
	People understand and share an holistic view (process understanding and ownership)
	People are oriented towards internal and external customers in their CI activity
	Specific CI projects with outside agencies (customers, suppliers, etc.) take place
	Relevant CI activities involve representatives from different organizational levels
CI on the CI system Generating the ability to manage strategically the development of CI	The CI system is continually monitored and developed
	There is a cyclical planning process whereby the CI system is regularly reviewed and amended
	There is periodic review of the CI system in relation to the organization as a whole
	Senior management make available sufficient resources (time, money, personnel) to support the continuing development of the CI system
	The CI system itself is designed to fit within the current structure and infrastructure
	When a major organizational change is planned, its potential impact on the CI system is assessed
Walking the talk Generating the ability to articulate and demonstrate CI's values	The 'management style' reflects commitment to CI values
	When something goes wrong, people at all levels look for reasons why, rather than blame individuals
	People at all levels demonstrate a shared belief in the value of small steps and that everyone can contribute, by themselves being actively involved in making and recognizing incremental improvements
Building the learning organization Generating the ability to learn through CI activity	Everyone learns from their experiences, both good and bad
	Individuals seeks out opportunities for learning/personal development
	Individuals and groups at all levels share their learning
	The organization captures and shares the learning of individuals and groups
	Managers accept and act on all the learning that takes place
	Organizational mechanisms are used to deploy what has been learned across the organization

654

The differences between breakthrough and continuous improvement

Breakthrough improvement places a high value on creative solutions. It encourages free thinking and individualism. It is a radical philosophy insomuch as it fosters an approach to improvement which does not accept many constraints on what is possible. 'Starting with a clean sheet of paper', 'going back to first principles' and 'completely rethinking the system' are all typical breakthrough improvement principles. Continuous improvement, on the other hand, is less ambitious, at least in the short term. It stresses adaptability, teamwork and attention to detail. It is not radical; rather it builds upon the wealth of accumulated experience within the operation itself, often relying primarily on the people who operate the system to improve it. One analogy which helps to understand the difference between breakthrough and continuous improvement is that of the sprint and the marathon. Breakthrough improvement is a series of explosive and impressive sprints. Continuous improvement, like marathon running, does not require the expertise and prowess required for sprinting; but it does require that the runner (or operations manager) keeps on going. Table 18.3 lists some of the differences between the two approaches.

Notwithstanding the fundamental differences between the two approaches, it is possible to combine the two, albeit at different times. Large and dramatic improvements can be implemented as and when they seem to promise significant improvement steps, but between such occasions the operation can continue making its quiet and less spectacular kaizen improvements (see Figure 18.9(c)).

Improvement cycle models

An important element within the concept of continuous improvement is the idea that improvement can be represented by a literally never-ending process of repeatedly questioning and requestioning the detailed working of a process or activity. This repeated

Table 18.3	Some features of breakthrough and continuous improvement	
	Breakthrough improvement	*Continuous improvement*
Effect	Short-term but dramatic	Long-term and long-lasting but undramatic
Pace	Big steps	Small steps
Time-frame	Intermittent and non-incremental	Continuous and incremental
Change	Abrupt and volatile	Gradual and constant
Involvement	Select a few 'champions'	Everybody
Approach	Individualism, individual ideas and efforts	Collectivism, group efforts, systems approach
Stimulus	Technological breakthroughs, new inventions, new theories	Conventional know-how and state of the art
Risks	Concentrated – 'all eggs in one basket'	Spread – many projects simultaneously
Practical requirements	Requires large investment but little effort to maintain it	Requires little investment but great effort to maintain it
Effort orientation	Technology	People
Evaluation criteria	Results for profit	Process and efforts for better results

Source: Based on Imai.[9]

655

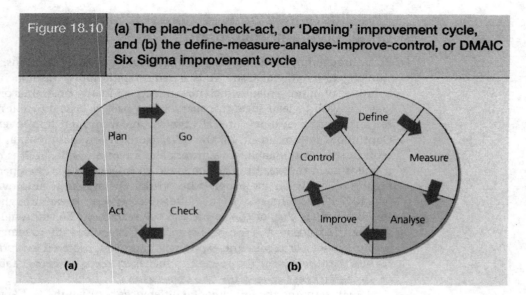

Figure 18.10 (a) The plan-do-check-act, or 'Deming' improvement cycle, and (b) the define-measure-analyse-improve-control, or DMAIC Six Sigma improvement cycle

Improvement cycles
and cyclical nature of continuous improvement is usually summarized by the idea of the improvement cycle. There are many **improvement cycles** used in practice, some of them are proprietary models owned by consultancy companies. Here we describe briefly just two of the more generally used models – the PDCA cycle (sometimes called the Deming Cycle, named after the famous quality 'guru', W.E. Deming whose work is described in Chapter 20) and the DMAIC cycle (made popular by the Six Sigma approach to improvement that is discussed in this chapter and Chapters 17 and 20).

The PDCA cycle

PDCA cycle
The **PDCA cycle** model is shown in Figure 18.10(a). It starts with the P (for plan) stage, which involves an examination of the current method or the problem area being studied. This involves collecting and analysing data so as to formulate a plan of action which is intended to improve performance. (The next section of this chapter explains some of the techniques which can be used to collect and analyse data in this stage.) Once a plan for improvement has been agreed, the next step is the D (for do) stage. This is the implementation stage during which the plan is tried out in the operation. This stage may itself involve a mini-PDCA cycle as the problems of implementation are resolved. Next comes the C (for check) stage where the new implemented solution is evaluated to see whether it has resulted in the expected performance improvement. Finally, at least for this cycle, comes the A (for act) stage. During this stage the change is consolidated or standardized if it has been successful. Alternatively, if the change has not been successful, the lessons learned from the 'trial' are formalized before the cycle starts again.

The DMAIC cycle

DMAIC cycle
In some ways this cycle is more intuitively obvious than the PDCA cycle in so much as it follows a more 'experimental' approach. The **DMAIC cycle** starts with defining the problem or problems, partly to understand the scope of what needs to be done and partly to define exactly the requirements of the process improvement. Often at this stage a formal goal or target for the improvement is set. After definition comes the measurement stage. This is an important point in the cycle, and the Six Sigma approach generally, which emphasizes the importance of working with hard evidence rather than opinion. This stage involves validating the problem to make sure that it really is a problem worth

656

Six Sigma at Xchanging – Part one[10]

'I think Six Sigma is powerful because of its definition; it is the process of comparing process outputs against customer requirements. To get processes operating at less than 3.4 defects per million opportunities means that you must strive to get closer to perfection and it is the customer that defines the goal. Measuring defects per opportunity means that you can actually compare the performance of, say, a human resources process with a billing and collection process.' Paul Ruggier head of Process at Xchanging is a powerful advocate of Six Sigma, and credits the success of the company, at least partly, to the approach.

Xchanging, created in 1998, is one of a new breed of companies, operating as an outsourcing business for 'back office' functions for a range of companies, such as Lloyd's of London, the insurance centre. Xchanging's business proposition is for the client company to transfer the running the whole, or part of their back office, to Xchanging, either for a fixed price or one determined by cost savings achieved. The challenge Xchanging face is to run that back office in a more effective and efficient manner than the client company had managed in the past. So, the more effective Xchanging is at running the processes, the greater is its profit. To achieve these efficiencies Xchanging offer larger scale, a higher level of process expertise, focus and investment in technology. But above all, they offer, a Six Sigma approach.

'Everything we do can be broken down into a process,' says Paul Ruggier, *'It maybe more straightforward in a manufacturing business, frankly they've been using a lot of*

Six Sigma tools and techniques for decades. But the concept of process improvement is relatively new in many service companies. Yet the concept is powerful. Through the implementation of this approach we have achieved 30 per cent productivity improvements in 6 months.'

'There are five stages in the improvement process,' explains Rebecca Whittaker, who is what Six Sigma practitioners call a Master Black Belt (a top practitioner) of the Sigma technique. *'First is the Define stage, this is where senior management define what it is that needs doing, the next stage is Measure this is where the team, guided by the Black Belt, will measure the process as it presently is. The third stage is Analyse, we will have obtained a lot of data in the measure stage this is where we stand back, challenge and ask questions like "why we are doing this?" The fourth stage is Improve where all the ideas, mostly generated by the team are implemented. The final stage is Control. This is where controls are put in place to ensure that the new process continues to be used. At this time the Six Sigma expert leaves the team and moves on to the next project.'* ∎

Questions

1. What are the benefits of being able to compare the amount of defects in a human resources process with those of collection or billing?

2. Why is achieving defects of less than 3.4 per million opportunity seen as important by Xchanging?

solving, using data to refine the problem and measuring exactly what is happening. Once these measurements have been established, they can be analysed. The analysis stage is sometimes seen as an opportunity to develop hypotheses as to what the root causes of the problem really are. Such hypotheses are validated (or not) by the analysis and the main root causes of the problem identified. Once the causes of the problem are identified, work can begin on improving the process. Ideas are developed to remove the root causes of problems, solutions are tested and those solutions that seem to work are implemented, formalized and results measured. The improved process needs then to be continually monitored and controlled to check that the improved level of performance is sustaining. After this point the cycle starts again and defines the problems which are preventing further improvement. (See the box 'Six Sigma at Xchanging' for a description of the DMAIC cycle.)

It is the last point about both cycles that is the most important – the cycle starts again. It is only by accepting that in a continuous improvement philosophy these cycles quite literally never stop, that improvement becomes part of every person's job.

The business process reengineering approach

Business process reengineering

Typical of the radical breakthrough way of tackling improvement is the **Business process reengineering** (BPR) approach. BPR is a blend of a number of ideas which have been current in operations management for some time. Just-in-time concepts,

657

Business process reengineering is typical of radical 'breakthrough' improvement. Here a team use process mapping to explore the redesign of a process for checking insurance claims

process flow charting, critical examination in method study, operations network management and customer-focused operations all contribute to the BPR concept. It was the potential of information technologies to enable the fundamental redesign of processes, however, which acted as the catalyst in bringing these ideas together. BPR has been defined as:[11]

> *The fundamental rethinking and radical redesign of business processes to achieve dramatic improvements in critical, contemporary measures of performance, such as cost, quality, service and speed.*

Process *versus* functions

Underlying the BPR approach is the belief that operations should be organized around the total process which adds value for customers, rather than the functions or activities which perform the various stages of the value-adding activity. We have already pointed out the difference between a conventional micro operation organized around a specialist function, and a business process (Figure 1.6 in Chapter 1 illustrated this idea). The core of BPR is a redefinition of the micro organizations within a total operation, to reflect the business processes which satisfy customer needs. Figure 18.11 illustrates this idea.

The principles of BPR

Even if BPR is not an entirely original idea, it can be seen as a useful collection of principles which embody the breakthrough approach. The main principles of BPR have been summarized as follows:[12]

- Rethink business processes in a cross-functional manner which organizes work around the natural flow of information (or materials or customers). This means organizing around outcomes of a process rather than the tasks which go into it.
- Strive for dramatic improvements in the performance by radically rethinking and redesigning the process.
- Have those who use the output from a process perform the process. Check to see if all internal customers can be their own supplier rather than depending on another function in the business to supply them (which takes longer and separates out the stages in the process).
- Put decision points where the work is performed. Do not separate those who do the work from those who control and manage the work. Control and action are just one more type of supplier–customer relationship which can be merged.

| Figure 18.11 | BPR advocates reorganizing (reengineering) micro operations to reflect the natural customer-focused business processes |

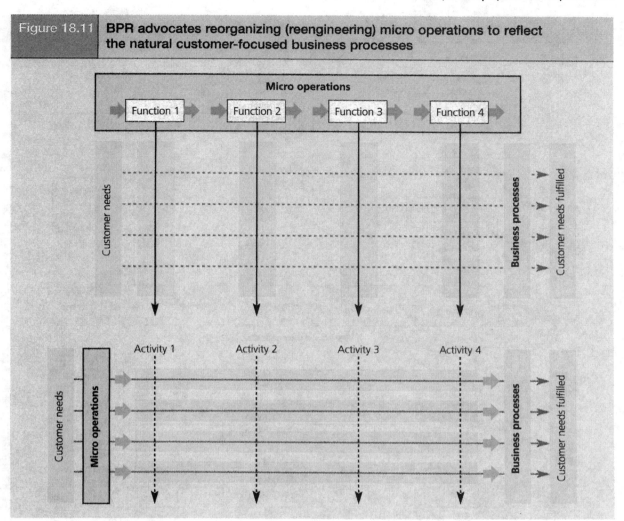

Example[13]

We can illustrate this idea of reorganizing (or reengineering) around business processes through the following simple example. Figure 18.12(a) shows the traditional organization of a trading company which purchases consumer goods from several suppliers, stores them, and sells them on to retail outlets. At the heart of the operation is the warehouse which receives the goods, stores them, and packs and dispatches them when they are required by customers. Orders for more stock are placed by the Purchasing Department which also takes charge of materials planning and stock control. Purchasing buys the goods based on a forecast which is prepared by Marketing, which takes advice from Sales which is processing customers' orders. When a customer does place an order, it is Sales' job to instruct the warehouse to pack and dispatch the order and tell, Finance to invoice the customer for the goods. So, traditionally, five departments (each a micro operation) have between them organized the flow of materials and information within the total operation. But at each interface between the departments there is the possibility of errors and miscommunication arising. Furthermore, *who is responsible for looking after the customer's needs?* Currently, three separate departments all have dealings with the customer. Similarly, *who is responsible for liaising with suppliers?* This time two departments have contact with suppliers.

Figure 18.12 **(a) Before and (b) after reengineering a consumer goods trading company**

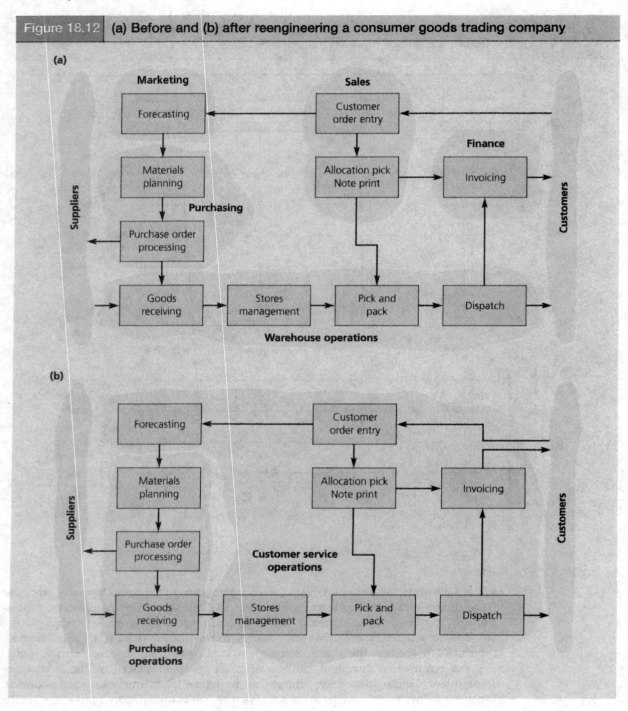

Eventually the company reorganized around two essential business processes. The first process (called purchasing operations) dealt with everything concerning relationships with suppliers. It was this process's focused and unambiguous responsibility to develop good working relationships with suppliers. The other business process (called customer service operations) had total responsibility for satisfying customers' needs. This included speaking 'with one voice' to the customer.

660

critical commentary

The whole idea of business process reengineering has aroused considerable controversy. Most of its critics are academics, but some practical objections to BPR have also been raised. At a conceptual level, criticisms of BPR include the following:

- By its nature, BPR looks only at work activities rather than at the people who perform the work. Because of this, people become 'cogs in a machine'. BPR merely 'oils the wheels' of this destructive machine.
- As an approach BPR is imprecise. Its proponents cannot agree as to whether it has to be radical or can be implemented gradually, or exactly what a process is, or whether it has to be top-down or bottom-up, or on whether it has to be supported by information technology or not.
- BPR is often treated as the latest management fad by some managers and as a cure-all for every problem. It is like, say the critics, attempting major surgery on every ailment, even those which would cure themselves naturally with some simple physiotherapy.
- BPR is merely an excuse for getting rid of staff. Companies that wish to 'downsize' (that is, reduce numbers of staff within an operation) are using BPR as an excuse. This puts the short-term interests of the shareholders of the company above either their longer-term interests or the interests of the company's employees.
- A combination of radical redesign together with downsizing can mean that the essential core of experience is lost from the operation. This leaves it vulnerable to any marked turbulence since it no longer has the knowledge and experience of how to cope with unexpected changes.

Improvement and trade-offs

One of the important questions that any operation has to answer is the relative priority of its performance objectives. To do this it must consider the possibility that one way in which it can improve its performance in one objective is to sacrifice some performance in another. Put another way, it must consider trading off one aspect of performance with another. Taken to its extreme, this implies that improvement in one aspect of an operation's performance can only be gained at the expense of performance in another. 'There is no such thing as a free lunch' could be taken as a summary of the **trade-off theory**.

Trade-off theory

Probably the best-known summary of the trade-off idea comes from Professor Wickham Skinner, the most influential of the originators of the strategic approach to operations, who said:[14]

> . . . *most managers will readily admit that there are compromises or trade-offs to be made in designing an airplane or truck. In the case of an airplane, trade-offs would involve matters such as cruising speed, take-off and landing distances, initial cost, maintenance, fuel consumption, passenger comfort and cargo or passenger capacity. For instance, no one today can design a 500-passenger plane that can land on an aircraft carrier and also break the sound barrier. Much the same thing is true in . . . [operations].*

Yet this trade-off model of performance objectives has been challenged – many companies give 'the best of both worlds' to their customers. At one time, for example, a high-quality, reliable and error-free automobile was inevitably an expensive automobile. Now, with few exceptions, we expect even budget-priced automobiles to be reliable and almost free of any defects. Auto manufacturers found that not only could they reduce

661

Not all aspects of process performance can be measured precisely. Here coffee tasters assess the characteristics of different coffees. They are able to do this only because their palates have been trained over many years to distinguish between different aspects of the taste of coffee

Source: Corbis.

the number of defects on their vehicles without necessarily incurring extra costs, but they could actually reduce costs by reducing errors in manufacture. Put in terms of the see-saw model in Figure 18.13, there are two ways to improve the position of one end of the lever. One is to depress the other end – in other words, improving one aspect of performance at the expense of another. But the other way is to raise the pivot of the see-saw. This would raise one end of the lever without depressing the other end. Alternatively, it could raise both ends. The 'pivot' in a real operation is the set of constraints which prevents both aspects of performance being improved simultaneously. Sometimes the constraints are technical, sometimes attitudinal. But the 'pivot' is stopping one aspect of performance improving without it reducing the performance of another. It should therefore be the prime target for any improvement process.

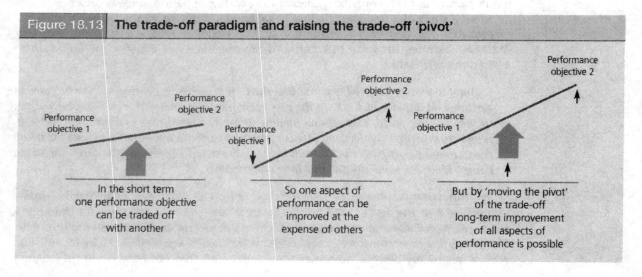

Figure 18.13 | **The trade-off paradigm and raising the trade-off 'pivot'**

In the short term one performance objective can be traded off with another

So one aspect of performance can be improved at the expense of others

But by 'moving the pivot' of the trade-off long-term improvement of all aspects of performance is possible

662

Reducing the trade-off

The approach which has been generally adopted in this book is that, although there are some situations where (especially in the short term) trade-offs between performance objectives have to be made, one of the main jobs of operations managers is to change whatever in the operation is causing one performance objective to deteriorate as another is improved. In fact, the 'pivot' of the trade-off is the main target of continuous improvement in operations.

Even trade-offs that seem to be inevitable can be reduced to some extent. For example, one of the decisions that any supermarket manager has to make is how many checkout positions to open at any time. If too many checkouts are opened then there will be times when the checkout staff do not have any customers to serve and will be idle. The customers, however, will have excellent service in terms of little or no waiting time. Conversely, if too few checkouts are opened, the staff will be working all the time but customers will have to wait in long queues. There seems to be a direct trade-off between staff utilization (and therefore cost) and customer waiting time (speed of service). Yet even the supermarket manager deciding how many checkouts to open can go some way to affecting the trade-off between customer waiting time and staff utilization. The manager might, for example, allocate a number of 'core' staff to operate the checkouts but also arrange for those other staff who are performing other jobs in the supermarket to be trained and 'on-call' should demand suddenly increase. If the manager on duty sees a build-up of customers at the checkouts, these other staff could quickly be used to staff checkouts. By devising a flexible system of staff allocation, the manager can both improve customer service and keep staff utilization high.

The techniques of improvement

All the techniques described in this book can be regarded as 'improvement' techniques insomuch as they attempt to improve some aspect of the performance of an operation. Some techniques are particularly useful for improving operations generally. For example, statistical process control (SPC) in Chapter 17 and failure mode and effect analysis (FMEA) in Chapter 19 could be used for almost any type of improvement project. In the remainder of this chapter we select some techniques which either have not been described elsewhere or need to be reintroduced in their role of helping operations improvement particularly. For example, flow charts were used in Chapter 5 as a design technique; later we will use essentially the same technique to generate improvements to existing operations.

Input–output analysis

Input–output analysis

A prerequisite for understanding any improvement opportunity is to understand the context in which the operation is set. This is the purpose of **input–output analysis**, which has three steps:

1 identifying the inputs and outputs from the process;
2 identifying the source of the inputs and the destination of the outputs;
3 clarifying the requirements of the internal customers who are served by the outputs from the process, and clarifying what requirements the process has for the internal suppliers who provide inputs to it.

Example: Kaston Pyral Services Ltd

Kaston Pyral Services Ltd (KPS) is the field service division of Kaston Pyral International, which manufactures and installs gas-fired heating systems. In the same group is KP Manufacturing, which makes the systems and spare parts, and KP Contracts, which

663

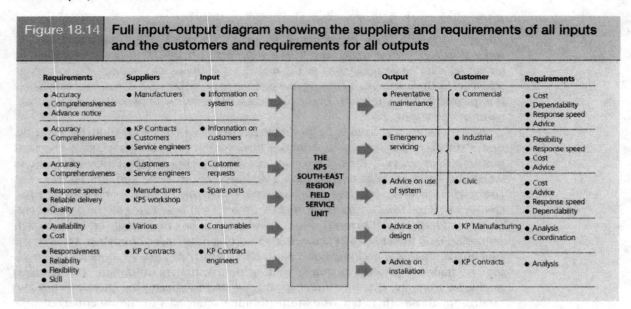

Figure 18.14 Full input–output diagram showing the suppliers and requirements of all inputs and the customers and requirements for all outputs

installs the systems. Figure 18.14 shows an input–output diagram for KPS. The purpose is to reach an agreed understanding of the operational function of whichever part of the organization the problem is set in. It is not intended that input–output diagrams give any answers as such. They do, however, provide a useful 'way in' to improvement.

Process maps (flow charts)

Process maps

Process maps (sometimes called flow charts in this context) can be used to give a detailed understanding prior to improvement. They were described in Chapter 4 and are widely used in improvement activities. The act of recording each stage in the process quickly shows up poorly organized flows. Process maps can also clarify improvement opportunities and shed further light on the internal mechanics or workings of an operation. Finally, and probably most importantly, they highlight problem areas where no procedure exists to cope with a particular set of circumstances.

Example: Kaston Pyral Services Ltd (continued)

As part of its improvement programme the team at KPS is concerned that customers are not being served well when they phone in with minor queries over the operation of their heating systems. These queries are not usually concerned with serious problems, but often concern minor irritations which can be equally damaging to the customers' perception of KPS's service. Figure 18.15 shows the process map for this type of customer query.

The team found the map illuminating. The procedure had never been formally laid out in this way before, and it showed up three areas where information was not being recorded. These are the three points marked with question marks on the process map in Figure 18.15. As a result of this investigation, it was decided to log all customer queries so that analysis could reveal further information on the nature of customer problems.

Scatter diagrams

Scatter diagrams

Scatter diagrams provide a quick and simple method of identifying whether there seems to be a connection between two sets of data: for example, the time at which you set off for work every morning and how long the journey to work takes. Plotting each journey on a graph which has departure time on one axis and journey time on the other could give an indication of whether departure time and journey time are related, and if

664

Figure 18.15 Process map for customer query

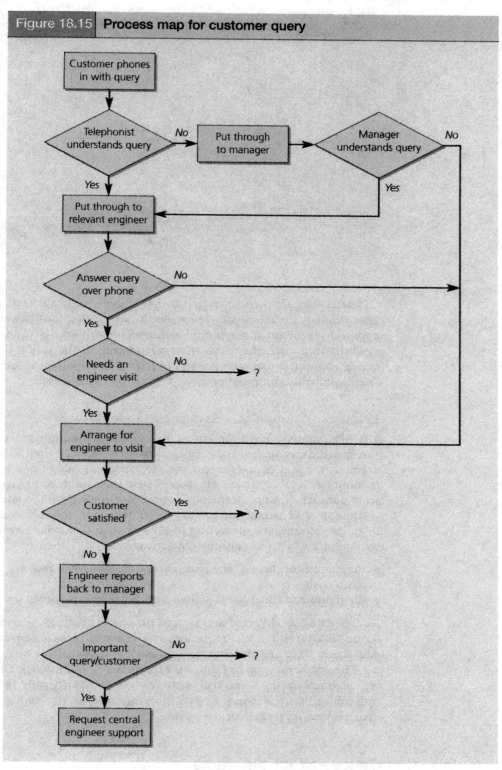

so, how. Figure 18.16 shows the graph for one person's journeys. It would seem to show:
(a) that there is a relationship between the two sets of data; (b) that the longest journeys
were when departures were between 8.15 am and 8.22 am; and (c) that the journey is
least predictable when departure is between 8.15 am and 8.30 am.

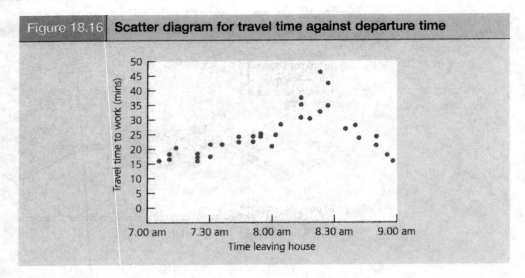

Figure 18.16 | Scatter diagram for travel time against departure time

Scatter diagrams can be treated in a far more sophisticated manner by quantifying how strong is the relationship between the sets of data. But however sophisticated the approach, this type of graph only identifies the existence of a relationship, not necessarily the existence of a cause–effect relationship. If the scatter diagram shows a very strong connection between the sets of data, it is important evidence of a cause–effect relationship, but not proof positive. It could be coincidence!

Example: Kaston Pyral Services Ltd (continued)

The KPS improvement team had completed its first customer satisfaction survey. The survey asked customers to score the service they received from KPS in several ways. For example, it asked customers to score services on a scale of one to 10 on promptness, friendliness, level of advice, etc. Scores were then summed to give a 'total satisfaction score' for each customer – the higher the score, the greater the satisfaction.

The spread of satisfaction scores puzzled the team, and they considered what factors might be causing such differences in the way their customers viewed them. Two factors were put forward to explain the differences:

● the number of times in the past year the customer had received a preventive maintenance visit;
● the number of times the customer had called for emergency service.

All this data was collected and plotted on scatter diagrams as shown in Figure 18.17. Figure 18.17(a) shows that there seems to be a clear relationship between a customer's satisfaction score and the number of times the customer was visited for regular servicing. The scatter diagram in Figure 18.17(b) is less clear. Although all customers who had very high satisfaction scores had made very few emergency calls, so had some customers with low satisfaction scores. As a result of this analysis, the team decided to survey customers' views on its emergency service.

Cause–effect diagrams

Cause–effect
diagrams

Cause–effect diagrams are a particularly effective method of helping to search for the root causes of problems. They do this by asking the what, when, where, how and why questions as before, but this time adding some possible 'answers' in an explicit way. They can also be used to identify areas where further data is needed. Cause–effect diagrams

666

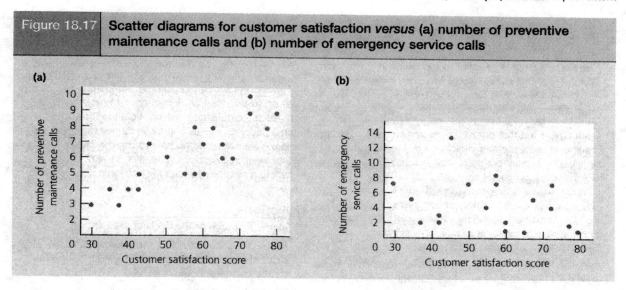

Figure 18.17 | Scatter diagrams for customer satisfaction *versus* (a) number of preventive maintenance calls and (b) number of emergency service calls

Ishikawa diagrams (which are also known as **Ishikawa diagrams**) have become extensively used in improvement programmes. Figure 18.18 shows the general form of the cause–effect diagram, and the box 'Problem identification at Hewlett-Packard' describes an application of the technique.

The procedure for drawing a cause–effect diagram is as follows:

Step 1 State the problem in the 'effect' box.
Step 2 Identify the main categories for possible causes of the problem. Although any categorization can be used for the main branches of the diagram, there are five categories which are commonly used: machinery; manpower; materials; methods and procedures; money.
Step 3 Use systematic fact-finding and group discussion to generate possible causes under these categories. Anything which may result in the effect that is being considered should be put down as a potential cause.
Step 4 Record all potential causes on the diagram under each category, and discuss each item in order to combine and clarify causes.

Some tips on using cause–effect diagrams

- Use separate diagrams for each problem. Do not confuse the issue by combining problems on a single diagram.
- Make sure diagrams are visible to everyone involved. Use large sheets of paper with plenty of space between items.

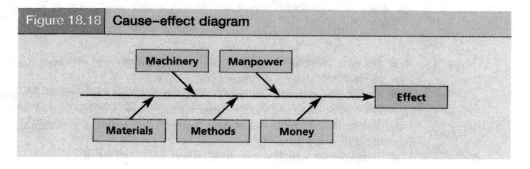

Figure 18.18 | Cause–effect diagram

Problem identification at Hewlett-Packard example

Hewlett-Packard is proud of its reputation for high-quality products and services. Because of this it was especially concerned with the problems that it was having with its customers returning defective toner cartridges. About 2000 of these were being returned every month. The UK team suspected that not all the returns were actually the result of a faulty product, which is why the team decided to investigate the problem. The cause–effect diagram which they generated is shown in Figure 18.19.

Three major problems were identified. First, some users were not as familiar as they should have been with the correct method of loading the cartridge into the printer, or in being able to solve their own minor printing problems. Second, some of the dealers were also unaware of how to sort out minor problems. Third, there was clearly some abuse of Hewlett-Packard's 'no-questions-asked' returns policy. Empty toner cartridges were being sent to unauthorized refilling companies who would sell the refilled cartridges at reduced prices. Some cartridges were

being refilled up to five times and were wearing out. Furthermore, the toner in the refilled cartridges was not up to Hewlett-Packard's high quality standards. The team went on to use the PDCA sequence of problem-solving and made suggestions which tightened up on their returns policy as well as improving the way in which customers were instructed on how to use the products. The results were impressive. Complaints in almost all areas shrank to a fraction of what they had been previously. ■

Questions

1 Take one branch of the decision tree shown in Figure 18.19 (for example, the materials branch) and expand on the possible reasons which are shown for the cartridge being returned.

2 What is your opinion of the alleged abuse of the 'no-questions-asked' returns policy adopted by Hewlett-Packard?

Figure 18.19 Cause–effect diagram for Hewlett-Packard's toner analysis

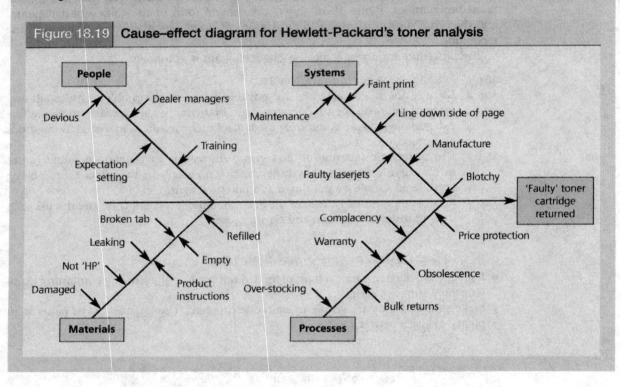

- Do not overload diagrams. Use separate diagrams for each major category on the cause–effect master diagram if necessary.
- Always be prepared to rework, take apart, refine and change categories.
- Take care not to use vague statements such as 'possible lack of'. Rather, describe what is actually happening that demonstrates the issues: for example, 'people are not filling out forms properly'.
- Circle causes which seem to be particularly significant.

668

The improvement team at KPS was working on a particular area which was proving a problem. Whenever service engineers were called out to perform emergency servicing for a customer, they took with them the spares and equipment which they thought would be necessary to repair the system. Although engineers could never be sure exactly what materials and equipment they would need for a job, they could guess what was likely to be needed and take a range of spares and equipment which would cover most eventualities. Too often, however, the engineers would find that they needed a spare or piece of equipment which they had not brought with them, and therefore they would have to return to the depot in order to collect it. Worse than that, very occasionally the required spare part would not be in stock, and so the customer would have to wait until it was brought from another part of the country. The cause–effect diagram for this particular problem, as drawn by the team, is shown in Figure 18.20.

Pareto diagrams

Pareto diagram

In any improvement process, it is worthwhile distinguishing what is important and what is less so. The purpose of the **Pareto diagram**, which was introduced in Chapter 12, is to distinguish between the 'vital few' issues and the 'trivial many'. It is a relatively straightforward technique which involves arranging items of information on the types of problem or causes of problem into their order of importance. This can then be used to highlight areas where further decision making will be useful. Pareto analysis is based on the frequently occurring phenomenon of relatively few causes explaining the majority of effects. For example, most revenue for any company is likely to come from relatively few of the company's customers. Similarly, relatively few of a doctor's patients will probably occupy most of his time. The box 'Customer service at Groupe Accor' gives an application of the technique.

The KPS improvement team which was investigating unscheduled returns from emergency servicing (the issue which was described in the cause–effect diagram in Figure 18.20) examined all occasions over the previous 12 months on which an

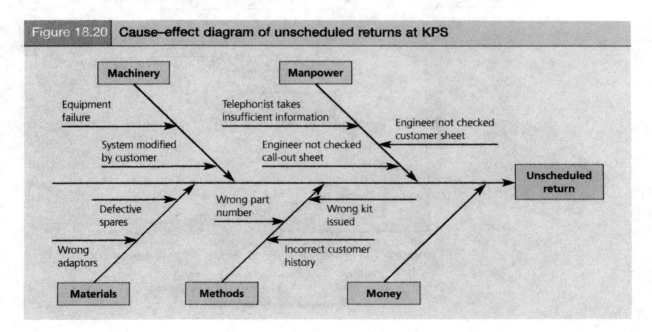

Figure 18.20 | **Cause–effect diagram of unscheduled returns at KPS**

669

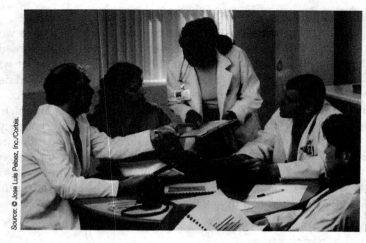

A team of nurses,
administrators and doctors
brainstorm improvements
in patient care

Source: © Jose Luis Pelaez, Inc./Corbis.

unscheduled return had been made. They categorized the reasons for unscheduled returns as follows:

1 The wrong part had been taken to a job because, although the information which the engineer received was sound, he or she had incorrectly predicted the nature of the fault.

2 The wrong part had been taken to the job because there was insufficient information given when the call was taken.

3 The wrong part had been taken to the job because the system had been modified in some way not recorded on KPS's records.

4 The wrong part had been taken to the job because the part had been incorrectly issued to the engineer by stores.

5 No part had been taken because the relevant part was out of stock.

6 The wrong equipment had been taken for whatever reason.

7 Any other reason.

| Figure 18.21 | Pareto diagram for causes of unscheduled returns |

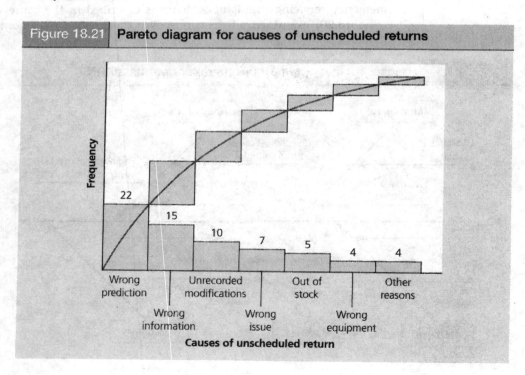

The relative frequency of occurrence of these causes is shown in Figure 18.21. About a third of all unscheduled returns were due to the first category, and more than half the returns were accounted for by the first and second categories together. It was decided that the problem could best be tackled by concentrating on how to get more information to the engineers which would enable them to predict the causes of failure accurately.

Customer service at Groupe Accor[15]　example

For over 10 years, Accor, the French hotel and restaurant group, has been developing self-managed improvement groups within its hotels. At one hotel reception desk, staff were concerned about the amount of time the desk was left unattended. To investigate this the staff began keeping track of the reasons they were spending time away from the desk and how long each absence kept them away. Everyone knew that reception desk staff often had to leave their post to help or give service to a guest. However, no one could agree what was the main cause of absence. Collecting the information was itself not easy because the staff had to keep records without affecting customer service. After three months the data was presented in the form of a Pareto diagram, which is shown in Figure 18.22. According to this, reception staff spent an average of 20 minutes away from their desk each shift. It came as a surprise to reception staff and hotel management that making photocopies for guests was the main reason for absence. Fortunately, this was easily remedied by moving the photocopier to a room adjacent to the reception area, enabling staff to keep a check on the reception desk while they were making copies. ■

Questions

1　Do you think it was wise to spend so much time on examining this particular issue? Isn't it a trivial issue?

2　Should the Pareto diagram (Figure 18.22) be used to reflect improvement priorities? In other words, was the group correct to put priority on avoiding absence through photocopying, and should its next priority be to look at absence because of the telefax service?

Figure 18.22　Pareto diagram of staff time away from the reception desk

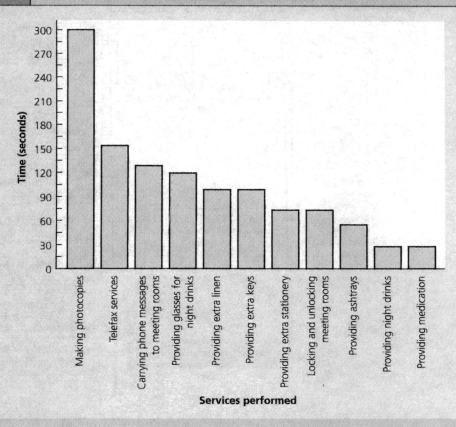

Why–why analysis

Why–why analysis

Why–why analysis starts by stating the problem and asking *why* that problem has occurred. Once the major reasons for the problem occurring have been identified, each of the major reasons is taken in turn and again the question is asked *why* those reasons have occurred, and so on. This procedure is continued until either a cause seems sufficiently self-contained to be addressed by itself or no more answers to the question 'Why?' can be generated.

Example: Kaston Pyral Services Ltd (continued)

Figure 18.23 illustrates the general structure of the why–why analysis for the KPS example discussed previously. In this example the major cause of unscheduled returns was the incorrect prediction of reasons for the customer's system failure. This is stated as the problem in the why–why analysis. The question is then asked, why was the failure wrongly predicted? Three answers are proposed: first, that the engineers were not trained correctly; second, that they had insufficient knowledge of the particular product installed in the customer's location; and third, that they had insufficient knowledge of the customer's particular system with its modifications. Each of these three reasons is taken in turn, and the questions are asked, why is there a lack of training, why is there a lack of product knowledge, and why is there a lack of customer knowledge? And so on.

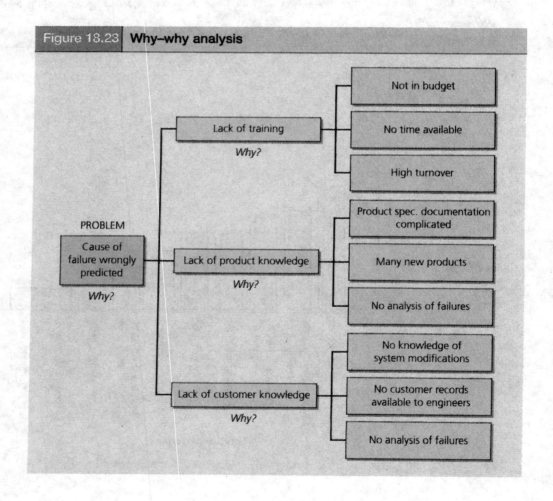

Figure 18.23   Why–why analysis

summary answers to key questions

 *The companion website to the book, **www.booksites.net/slack**, also has a brief 'Study Guide' to each chapter.*

How can operations measure their performance in terms of the five performance objectives?

- It is unlikely that for any operation a single measure of performance will adequately reflect the whole of a performance objective. Usually operations have to collect a whole bundle of partial measures of performance.

- Each partial measure then has to be compared against some performance standard. There are four types of performance standard commonly used:
  - historical standards, which compare performance now against performance sometime in the past;
  - target performance standards, which compare current performance against some desired level of performance;
  - competitor performance standards, which compare current performance against competitors' performance;
  - absolute performance standards, which compare current performance against its theoretically perfect state.

- The process of benchmarking is often used as a means of obtaining competitor performance standards.

How can operations managers prioritize improvement of performance objectives?

- Improvement priorities can be determined by bringing together the relative importance of each performance objective or competitive factor as judged by customers, with the performance which the operation achieves as compared with its competitors.

- The operation's judgement about both importance and performance can be consolidated on an 'importance–performance matrix'. Different areas on this matrix represent different relative degrees of priority.

What are the broad approaches to managing the rate of improvement?

- An organization's approach to improving its operation can be characterized as lying somewhere between the two extremes of 'pure' breakthrough improvement and 'pure' continuous improvement.

- Breakthrough improvement, which is sometimes called innovation-based improvement, sees improvement as occurring in a few, infrequent but major and dramatic changes. Although such changes can be abrupt and volatile, they often incorporate radical new concepts or technologies which can shift the performance of the operation significantly.

- Continuous improvement assumes a series of never-ending, but smaller, incremental improvement steps. This type of improvement is sometimes called kaizen improvement. It is gradual and constant, often using collective group-based problem-solving. It does not focus on radical change but rather attempts to develop a built-in momentum of improvement.

- It is claimed that compromises between these two types of improvement philosophy are possible. Organizations can improve by having occasional radical breakthroughs but utilizing a more incremental approach in between these major changes.

673

Where does business process reengineering (BPR) fit into the improvement activity?

- BPR is a typical example of the radical approach to improvement. It attempts to redesign operations along customer-focused processes rather than on the traditional functional basis.

- BPR has been responsible for some radical improvements in operations performance but it has also been criticized. The main criticisms are that it pays little attention to the rights of staff who are the victims of the 'downsizing' which often accompanies BPR, and that the radical nature of the changes can strip out valuable experience from the operation.

What techniques can be used for improvement?

- Many of the techniques described throughout this book could be considered improvement techniques, for example statistical process control (SPC).

- Techniques often seen as 'improvement techniques' are:
  - input–output analysis, which attempts to clarify the nature of transformation in processes;
  - flow charts, which attempt to describe the nature of information flow and decision making within operations;
  - scatter diagrams, which attempt to identify relationships and influences within processes;
  - cause–effect diagrams, which structure the brainstorming that can help to reveal the root causes of problems;
  - Pareto diagrams, which attempt to sort out the 'important few' causes from the 'trivial many' causes.

Lombard Direct   case exercise

One of the most significant trends in the financial services industry has been the growth in telephone access. Many financial services, such as banks, have developed a more focused approach to personal customers through 24-hour telephone access. The concept of telephone-based financial services is not new. It was first launched successfully in 1985 by Första Sparbanken in Sweden with a service called Första Direckt. This has become a blueprint for several similar services.

Typical of these 'total access' services is that described below:

You can call us 24 hours a day, 365 days a year. If you want to give us instructions to pay your gas bill on Christmas Day, that's fine. If you want to tell us to transfer money at 2.00 am, that's fine too. If you're on the other side of the world in a different time zone you can still call us . . . [we are] . . . more than just a convenient telephone banking service. Your own Personal Account Manager will offer you a highly individual approach to both your day-to-day finances and your long-term financial planning.

Financial services have developed networks of call-centre operations to support such products. Call-centre staff are linked to sophisticated telephone and computer systems where up-to-date information and customer requests are instantly available so that customers can be dealt with promptly and efficiently. Part of this sector are the companies who offer loans and related services. Typical is Lombard Direct who must have one of the best-known telephone numbers in the UK: 0800 2 15000. This is based on their slogan 'loans from 800 to 15,000 pounds'. Lombard Direct is a subsidiary of Lombard Bank, part of the National Westminster Bank group. Unsecured loans over the telephone constitute about 90 per cent of the company's business, and other products include insurance on loans, house, contents and motor insurance, savings and a credit card.

The main call centre, in Rotherham, West Yorkshire, is a 24-hour operation which operates every day of the year. The centre handles about two million calls a year. Monday is a typically busy day, when around 6000 calls are received. The call centre has around 200 'seats' or desks for their 'customer advisors' (CAs) and employs around 250 full-time equivalent staff, most of whom work part time. When potential customers call to request a loan, they are asked a number of questions to rate their creditworthiness and then allocated into a band which reflects their 'credit rating'. This risk assessment affects the size of the borrowing allowed and the rate of interest to be charged.

Control to enabling culture

Sean Guilliam is the head of the call centre and has been working with the managers and team leaders to try to move from a 'control' culture to a more 'enabling' culture. Sean explains: *'We have a great atmosphere here, people really enjoy their work and we have lots of great events to build our team spirit and also develop the business. The problem is that despite these efforts the emphasis is still too much on control.'* One problem facing Sean was how he should use 'scripts'. Scripts are the set of questions and responses which CAs follow when they talk with customers and potential customers. They are often very carefully worded so as to avoid misunderstandings.

'We need to move away from the need to follow a set script in a strict way which allows no discretion and try to work with the customer to understand his or her needs and respond to them. We would also like to put ourselves in the position of being able to offer more of our products, where appropriate. This is difficult to do when you are using a script which is devoted to loans. The script is a useful base of course. Indeed, there are several questions we are obliged to ask and information we have to provide to comply with the financial services laws. But there is a tendency to rely too heavily on the script. The problem is not people's willingness to improve but our systems which encourage them not to. For example, the CA's performance is partly assessed on tapes of their interactions with a customer. We call this "call analysis". If they are judged not to have followed the correct procedure, it is judged a "non-standard tape" and it will affect their pay, and possibly even their contract.

'We have five grades of performance, or "spot" levels, and CAs are reviewed every three months. Each level has a set of criteria based on six key measures. If someone attains a higher level for two consecutive assessments, they go up one spot level; if they perform less well over three periods they will go down. Going up a level

can mean a significant increase in pay. Also CAs need to get to level 2 before we will offer them a permanent contract, although I believe that we need to remove this barrier and put everyone on permanent contracts from the start.

'We are making progress, however. Take, for example, our call analysis measure. In the past it was just used as a means of assessing people. Now it is a developmental tool. We have identified nine different skills we expect to see, including greeting callers (what we call the verbal handshake), the general approach to the conversation, gathering information, and so on. We now have descriptors for each of these skills, defining what constitutes excellent, very good and good performance, or "an area for development". People can see exactly what we are trying to achieve. The call analysis framework tries to assess CAs but also encourages them to do the right things, such as use the caller's name, show interest in, and respect for, the customer, not ask for the same information twice, ensure that customers know all the costs involved and give customers time to make their decisions.

'Also we now refer to the script as a call guide and use about 30 cards in a simple "flip-open" type of photograph album to help the CAs. But yet when we get a new recruit, we still give them the cards and tell them to go home and learn them! The other issue is "cross-selling" other products. I compare loan conversions and insurance sales, for example. And, although we want a good ratio of insurance sales to loans, too high a ratio might mean that staff are doing too hard a sell. We don't want customers to be put off from using us again. The problem is in balancing flexibility with control, especially when a 1 per cent increase in insurance sales can contribute half a million to the bottom line.' ■

Questions

1 What do the five operations performance objectives (quality, speed, dependability, flexibility and cost) mean for call-centre operations such as Lombard's?

2 What do you think are the main operations management issues faced by call-centre managers?

3 What do you think might be the main obstacles facing Sean Guilliam in trying to improve CA performance?

 *Other short cases, and worked answers, are included in the companion website to this book, **www.booksites.net/slack**.*

675

study activities

Some study activities can be answered by reading the chapter. Others will require some general knowledge of business activity and some might require an element of investigation. All have hints on how they can be answered on the companion website for this book which also contains more discussion questions, ***www.booksites.net/slack****.*

1 Visit a library (for example, a university library) and consider how they could start a performance measurement programme which would enable it to judge the effectiveness with which it organizes its operations. Probably the library loans (if a university library) books to students on both long-term and short-term loans, keeps an extensive stock of journals, will send off for specialist publications to specialist libraries and has an extensive online database facility. What measures of performance do you think it would be appropriate to use in this kind of operation and what type of performance standards should the library adopt?

2 Find an operation and assess its overall performance using a polar diagram. You will have to devise the 'dimensions' of the polar diagram so that they are meaningful to the operation in question. Start with the five generic performance objectives (quality, speed, dependability, flexibility and cost) and change them accordingly. Overlay the operation's performance with what you perceive to be the customers' needs and discuss any differences.

3 (a) *Step 1* – Devise a benchmarking programme that will benefit the course or programme that you are currently taking (apologies to anyone who is reading this for light entertainment rather than because it is required reading on their course). In doing so, decide whether you are going to benchmark against other courses at the same institution, competitor courses at other institutions, or some other point of comparison. Also decide whether you are more interested in the performance of these other courses or the way they organize their processes, or both.

   (b) *Step 2* – Identify the institutions and courses against which you are going to benchmark your own course.

   (c) *Step 3* – Collect data on these other courses (visit them, send of for literature, or visit their internet site).

   (d) *Step 4* – Compare your own course against these others and draw up a list of implications for the way your course could be improved.

4 Think back to the last product or service failure that caused you some degree of inconvenience. Draw a cause–effect diagram that identifies all the main causes of why the failure could have occurred. Try and identify the frequency with which such causes happen. This could be done by talking with the staff of the operation that provided the service. Draw a Pareto diagram that indicates the relatively frequency of each cause of failure. Suggest ways in which the operation could reduce the chances of failure.

5 (Advanced)

   Step 1 – As a group, identify a 'high visibility' operation that you all are familiar with. This could be a type of quick service restaurant, record stores, public transport systems, libraries, etc.

   Step 2 – Once you have identified the broad class of operation, visit a number of them and use your experience as customers to identify

   ▶

676

(a) the main performance factors that are of importance to you as customers, and

(b) how each store rates against each other in terms of their performance on these same factors.

Step 3 – Draw an importance–performance diagram for one of the operations that indicates the priority they should be giving to improving their performance.

Step 4 – Discuss the ways in which such an operation might improve its performance and try to discuss your findings with the staff of the operation.

Notes on chapter

1 Source: Deaves, M. (2002) Bottoms Up! *Manufacturing Engineer*, December.

2 Based on Neely, A. (1993) *Performance Measurement System Design – Theory and Practice*, Manufacturing Engineering Group, Cambridge University, April.

3 *European Quality* (1999) 'How Alstom Transporte is Hot on Improvement', Vol. 6, No. 6.

4 Camp, C. (1989) 'Benchmarking: The Search for Best Practices Which Lead to Superior Performance – Parts 1 to 5', *Quality Progress*, January–May.

5 See Rogers, B. (1991) 'Benchmarking as a Tool in Rank Xerox's Quality Management Strategies', *Quality Link*, November–December; and Cross, R. and Leonard, P. (1994) 'Benchmarking: A Strategic and Tactical Perspective' *in* Dale, B. (ed.) *Managing Quality* (2nd edn), Prentice Hall.

6 Based on Slack, N. (1994) 'The Importance–Performance Matrix as a Determinant of Improvement Priorities', *International Journal of Operations and Production Management*, Vol. 14, No. 5, pp. 59–75.

7 Imai, M. (1986) *Kaizen – The Key to Japan's Competitive Success*, McGraw-Hill.

8 Bessant, J. and Caffyn, S. (1997) 'High Involvement Innovation', *International Journal of Technology Management*, Vol. 14, No. 1.

9 Imai, M., *op. cit.*

10 Source: Alan Betts of BF Learning Limited and discussions with company staff.

11 Hammer, M. and Champy, J. (1993) *Re-engineering the Corporation*, Nicholas Brealey Publishing.

12 Hammer, M. (1990) 'Re-engineering Work: Don't Automate, Obliterate', *Harvard Business Review*, Vol. 68, No. 4.

13 Based on an example in Kruse, G. (1995) 'Fundamental Innovation', *Manufacturing Engineer*, February.

14 Skinner, W. (1985) *Manufacturing: The Formidable Competitive Weapon*, Wiley.

15 Source: Orly, C. (1988) 'Quality Circles in France', *The Carnell HRA Quarterly*, November.

Selected further reading

Chang, R.Y. (1995) *Continuous Process Improvement: A practical guide to improving processes for measurable results*, Cogan Page.

Leibfried, K.H.J. and McNair, C.J. (1992) *Benchmarking: A Tool for Continuous Improvement*, HarperCollins. There are many books on benchmarking, this is a comprehensive and practical guide to the subject.

Pande, P.S., Neuman, R.P. and Cavanagh, R. (2002) *Six Sigma Way Team Field Book: An implementation guide for project improvement teams*, McGraw Hill. Obviously based on the Six Sigma principle and related to the book by the same author team recommended in Chapter 17, this is an unashamedly practical guide to the Six Sigma approach.

Notes

Notes

Notes

Notes

Notes